Charles A. Cooper

CHARLES A. COOPER is Minister-Counselor for Economic Affairs at the U.S. Embassy in Saigon. A graduate of Swarthmore College, Dr. Cooper participated in Harvard University's Russian Studies Program (1957-59) and received the Ph.D. in economics from Massachusetts Institute of Technology in 1960. His professional experience includes positions with the Council of Economic Advisers and The Rand Corporation, economic adviser to the President's Special Assistant for Civilian Programs in Vietnam, and associate director of USAID and economic counselor at the U.S. Embassy in Saigon. He is a member of Phi Beta Kappa, held a Ford Foundation Fellowship in 1957-59, and, in 1960, received the Superior Honor Award-USAID.

Sidney S. Alexander

SIDNEY S. ALEXANDER has been, since 1956, professor of management at Massachusetts Institute of Technology. Awarded degrees in managerial economics by Harvard University (B.S., 1936; M.A., 1938; Ph.D., 1946), he held a teaching fellowship at Harvard College (1939-40) and served as assistant professor of economics at the University from 1946 to 1949. His professional experience includes research with the National Bureau of Standards and the U.S. Treasury Department, service with the OSS, the International Monetary Fund, and the President's Materials Policy Commission, the position of economic advisor to CBS, a fellowship at the Center for Advanced Studies in the Behavioral Sciences, and the directorship of the Rand-Resources for the Future Middle East Project. Professor Alexander is a member of Phi Beta Kappa, the American Academy of Arts and Sciences, the American Economic Association, the Econometric Society, and the Royal Economic Society. He has published numerous articles on national and international economics, educational television, and the development of the Middle East.

*Economic Development
and Population Growth
in the Middle East*

THE MIDDLE EAST
Economic and Political Problems and Prospects

Studies from a research program of
The Rand Corporation
and
Resources for the Future, Inc.
Sidney S. Alexander, *Program Director*

Published

Marion Clawson, Hans H. Landsberg, *and* Lyle T. Alexander
The Agricultural Potential of the Middle East

Sam H. Schurr *and* Paul T. Homan
with Joel Darmstadter, Helmut Frank, John J. Schanz, Jr.,
Thomas R. Stauffer, *and* Henry Steele
Middle Eastern Oil and the Western World: Prospects and Problems

Charles A. Cooper *and* Sidney S. Alexander *(eds.)*
Economic Development and Population Growth in the Middle East

In Preparation

Paul Y. Hammond *and* Sidney S. Alexander *(eds.)*
Political Dynamics in the Middle East

Sidney S. Alexander
The Economics and Politics of the Middle East

Economic Development and Population Growth in the Middle East

Edited by

Charles A. Cooper

Minister-Counselor for Economic Affairs
Embassy of the United States of America
Saigon, Vietnam

Sidney S. Alexander

Massachusetts Institute of Technology
Cambridge, Massachusetts

American Elsevier
Publishing Company, Inc.

New York

AMERICAN ELSEVIER PUBLISHING COMPANY, INC.
52 Vanderbilt Avenue, New York, N.Y. 10017

ELSEVIER PUBLISHING COMPANY
335 Jan Van Galenstraat, P.O. Box 211
Amsterdam, The Netherlands

International Standard Book Number 0-444-00107-7

Library of Congress Card Number 71-158633

Manufactured in the United States of America

Contents

Chapter 9. Fertility Patterns and Their Determinants in the Arab Middle East, *T. Paul Schultz*

ix

List of Contributors

Sidney S. Alexander
   Director of Research
   The Rand-Resources for the Future Middle East Research Project

   Professor of Economics and Management
   Sloan School of Management
   Massachusetts Institute of Technology
   Cambridge, Massachusetts

Fawzi M. Al-Haj
   Associate Professor of Extension Education
   Faculty of Agricultural Sciences
   American University of Beirut
   Beirut, Lebanon

Edmond Y. Asfour
   Senior Economist
   International Bank for Reconstruction and Development
   Washington, D.C.
      (The chapter was prepared by Mr. Asfour before he joined the Bank.)

Albert Y. Badre
   Professor of Economics
   Southern Illinois University
   Carbondale, Illinois

Yoram Ben-Porath
   Senior Lecturer
   The Eliezer Kaplan School of Economics and Social Sciences
   The Hebrew University of Jerusalem
   Jerusalem, Israel

Michael Bruno
  Professor of Economics
  The Eliezer Kaplan School of Economics and Social Sciences
  The Hebrew University of Jerusalem
  Jerusalem, Israel

Charles A. Cooper
  Formerly of the Economics Department
  The Rand Corporation
  Santa Monica, California

  At present is Minister-Counselor for Economic Affairs
  American Embassy, Saigon, Vietnam

Bent Hansen
  Professor of Economics
  University of California
  Berkeley, California

Samir Khalaf
  Associate Professor of Sociology and Chairman of Department
  American University of Beirut
  Beirut, Lebanon

Michael P. Mazur
  Instructor in Economics
  University of British Columbia
  Vancouver, British Columbia, Canada

T. Paul Schultz
  Director of Population Research
  Economics Department
  The Rand Corporation
  Santa Monica, California

Salah M. Yacoub
  Assistant Professor of Rural Sociology
  Faculty of Agricultural Sciences
  American University of Beirut
  Beirut, Lebanon

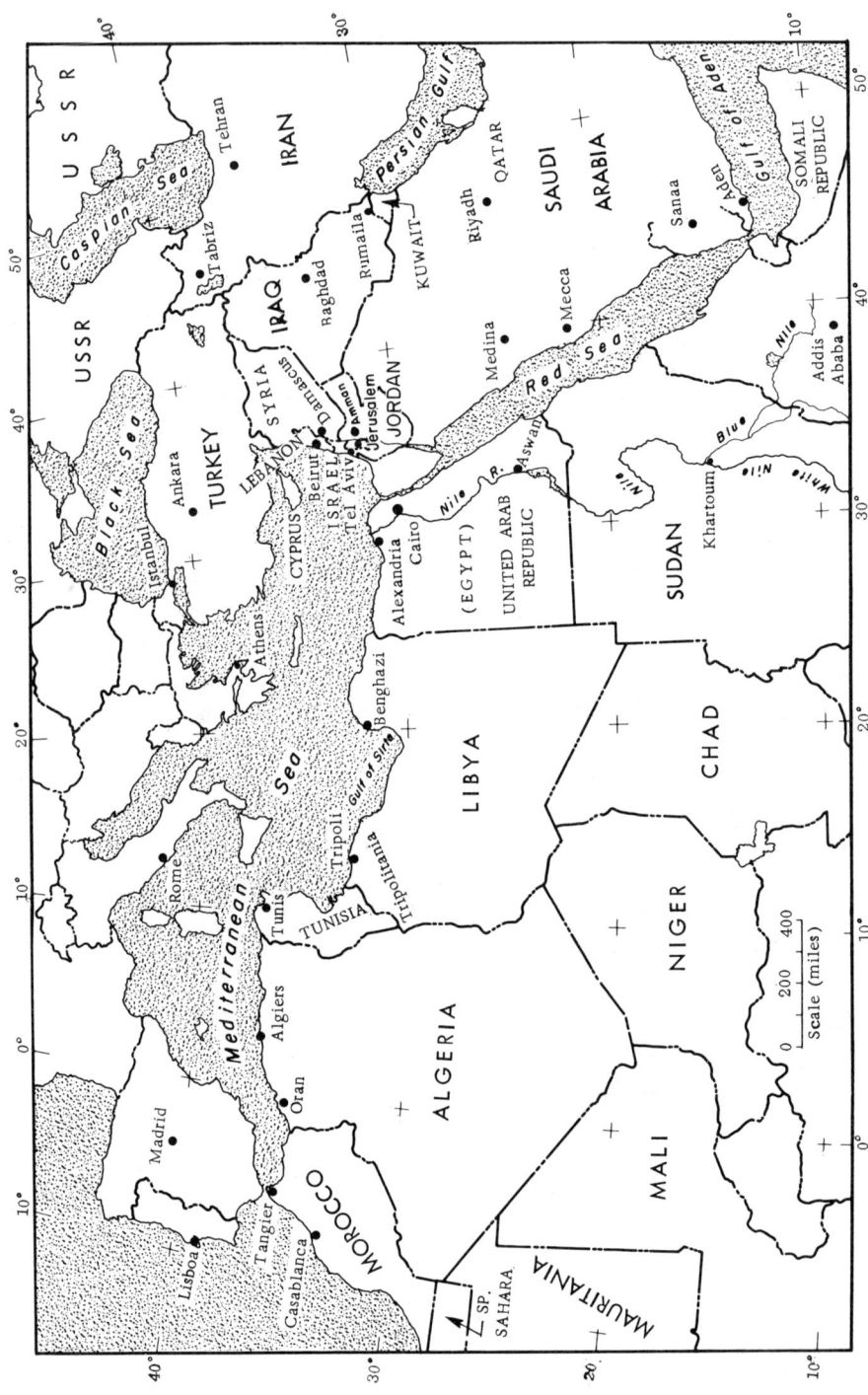

Preface

These studies of the economic and demographic problems and prospects of the Middle East form part of a broad program of research on the economics and politics of the Middle East, supported by a grant from the Ford Foundation and carried forward jointly by The Rand Corporation and Resources for the Future, Inc., under my general direction. The aim of the program is to provide such an understanding of the economic, demographic, and related political facts of life in the Middle East as is necessary for sound policy judgments on the part of all concerned.

To this end, one group of studies, published in a companion volume, was directed toward the political problems of the area.[1] Those studies, as well as the ones in this volume, were primarily the responsibility of The Rand Corporation. Two other volumes in this series, primarily the responsibility of Resources for the Future, Inc., deal with the problems related to Middle East oil and agriculture, respectively.[2] Other studies in the program have been published, or await publication, in monographic form.[3] In addition, an overview volume is now being prepared under my authorship, attempting to bring all the strands together. Following are brief observations on the relation of the economic and demographic aspects considered in this volume to the broader picture.

The Middle East and, in particular, the "core area" on which attention has been focused in this research program—Egypt and the Fertile Crescent—has been undergoing a rapid, sometimes violent, transformation under the impact of the West. This process has been triggered primarily by political developments external to the area, resulting principally from the struggles among the world

[1]Paul Y. Hammond and Sidney S. Alexander, *Political Dynamics in the Middle East,* American Elsevier, New York, 1972.

[2]Sam H. Schurr and Paul T. Homan, *Middle Eastern Oil and the Western World,* American Elsevier, New York, 1971; Marion Clawson, Hans H. Landsberg, and Lyle T. Alexander, *The Agricultural Potential of the Middle East,* American Elsevier, New York, 1971.

[3]Adel Daher, *Current Trends in Arab Intellectual Thought,* RM-5979-FF. The Rand Corporation, December 1969; William E. Hoehn, *Prospects for Desalted Water Costs,* RM-5971-FF, The Rand Corporation, October 1969; and R. E. Huschke, R. R. Rapp, and C. Schutz, *Meteorological Aspects of Middle East Water Supply,* RM-6267-FF, The Rand Corporation, March 1970.

powers. Rivalries between Britain and France from 1800 to 1945, between these two and Germany in the first half of the 20th century, between Russia and Britain up to World War I, and between Russia and the United States after World War II all have had dramatic effects on the Middle East. Under the impact of these rivalries Egypt was opened up to the West early in the 19th century, the Levant about a half century later, and what is now Iraq about a quarter century after that. With World War I the Turkish Empire, previously sustained by British support, was permitted to disintegrate, its Arab lands thereafter subject to quasi-colonial rule by Britain and France. That rule gradually gave way to the independence of the Arab states, fully achieved after World War II. Meanwhile, the state of Israel had come into existence on a basis established under the British Mandate in the inter-war period. After World War II some of the desert kingdoms adjacent to the core area, as well as Iraq within that area, joined the ranks of the world's leading oil exporters.

These events opened the way for a thoroughgoing transformation of the economies, the societies, and the politics of the area—a process that is still underway. On the economic side, the most salient aspect was a tremendous increase of production, matched through most of the period by an equally rapid growth of the population, so that for every inhabitant of the core area in 1800 there are now ten more, and at current rates of population growth there will be another 10 more before the year 2000. Aggregate output of the core area now stands over 20 times, and by 2000 it may be 80 times, that of 1800.

In this core area of the Middle East, as in other parts of the developing world, there occurred during the 1950s and 1960s a different pattern of economic development—with output growing more rapidly than the population. In some countries the difference, which constitutes the growth rate of per capita income, was small, in some moderate, and in some large. (See Table 1 of Chapter 1.) The basic question raised by the studies in this volume is whether that remarkable performance can be continued in the future and, in the case of the laggards, improved. More specifically, what are the prospects for achieving those ends and what are the problems threatening that achievement? The experts charged with investigating these questions were requested to project the future output of these countries optimistically, but still realistically, in order to set the stage for the analysis of the problems that might thwart these projections. These instructions were not always followed, however, as the impulse to predict sometimes gained the upper hand. For this their punishment need not come from us—the Middle East is hard on predictions.

In particular, the frame of reference included the assumption that a peaceful settlement of the Arab-Israel conflict was soon to be achieved. However unrealistic that assumption may be, it is required by the aim of the exercise, which is to find what the problems of economic development would be if peace *were* achieved. Absent peace, as Cooper argues in Chapter 1, and the future becomes highly speculative.

With peace however, the problems are quite clear. They are the familiar problems of aconomic development of less-developed countries. Easiest to recognize

xvi

are the tasks of stimulating exports (or of otherwise financing imports) and of mobilizing capital. Less easily characterized, but even more fundamental, are the problems, social and political as well as economic, of achieving modernization in general, and raising efficiency in particular. On the whole these economic studies pose these problems but can contribute little to their solution. On the other hand, the economic performance of some of these countries in the 1960s demonstrates that, whatever these deeper problems may be, a combination of governmental drive for development together with a favorable supply of capital in those countries can make progress in the face of them. But for other countries, particularly Iraq, the deeper problem of modernization remains as an uncrossed threshold.

The regimes of the area are committed to the achievement of modernization and economic development, not only because of their doctrinal convictions, but principally because their political life depends on it. However, this fact does not support the inference frequently based on it, that development aid can be a powerful lever on their political behavior. It is, unfortunately, overshadowed by other factors on which their political life also depends, and more immediately. The greatest of these, sometimes called pride, can be more accurately characterized as a search for dignity. American-coined slogans, such as "Water for Peace," which ring so true in our ears, are said to be insulting to an Arab. He is being offered a bribe of water for his manhood, his principles. So, although economic aid may be eagerly desired and ardently sought, it is likely to be rejected whenever its "strings" threaten the public sense of dignity.

The revolutions that have transformed the governments of many of the Arab countries have been economically determined indeed, but not in the simplistic sense that economic distress motivated rebellion. On the contrary, it was economic progress that brought the revolutions, not directly, but mediated by the process of social change, working through the dominant ethos of the military. At some critical state in each country a strategically placed group of officers joined to overthrow the established regime. Characteristically, they were motivated by the feeling that the existing government was betraying the public interest. Their slogan was typically a war on colonialism, feudalism, and corruption. Their immediate success was due not only to their control of military power, but also to the fact that there was no widespread sense of the legitimacy of the governments they overthrew. In Iraq and Libya, and to a lesser degree even in Egypt, the revolution came at a time when income per capita was growing much faster than ever before. The achievement of economic growth had no importance by itself in the absence of a general conviction in the relevant constituency that the government was working for the public welfare. Furthermore, the national dignity was placed ahead of economic considerations.

So too, in international affairs, considerations of economic progress run second to those of national dignity. Where economic aid comes in is as an attendant player. Whoever manages to achieve primary influence over Jordan must count on some development aid, or military aid, as an attendant cost. If the Soviets maintain their political positions in Egypt and Syria, they must expect to foot the bill for aid as well. The factors primarily determining the big-power orientations of the local governments are political and military rather than economic, but responsibility for economic support moves with influence.

In a more fundamental way, however, the desire for economic betterment may indeed work for peace in the area. Unless the issue is met head-on, there may well be some tendency for the pursuit of prosperity to throw some of the tensions of the area into the dim background. In particular, if a temporary relaxation of the tensions can be achieved, it is possible, although not necessary, that the diversion of attention to internal economic development will permit time to attenuate the tensions and so convert a temporary relaxation into a permanent one. If, for example, a somewhat imperfect peace settlement could be achieved between the Arabs and Israel, concern for economic development might then work to reinforce the settlement as time goes on. But there seems little possibility of a tradeoff between economic aid and symbolic objectives in achieving the settlement itself.

Whether the superpowers want to play once again the game of "positive neutrality" that Nasser played with them in the 1950s and 1960s is an open question. But the game would again become possible only if the higher order tensions were relaxed by a settlement achieved by political, or possibly military, means. Then indeed economic considerations may attain highest priority, so long as the potentially higher priority factors are in abeyance. In the final reckoning the problems and prospects dealt with in this book will have overriding importance, but for the moment they take second place to the strains of conflict.

Sidney S. Alexander

Cambridge, Massachusetts
November 5, 1970

CHAPTER 1

Introduction

Charles A. Cooper

The papers in this volume attempt to explain past progress in economic development in six Middle Eastern countries and to identify the most important determinants of their economic development in the future. For each country, the story reflects its own special circumstances in resources, experience, and policies. But the six countries have much in common as well. From the perspective of world-wide economic development, what are the main features of development problems in the Middle East?

CHAPTER 1

Introduction

I. The Recent Record

The World Bank has estimated that from 1960 to 1967 developing countries taken as a whole had annual growth rates of output of 5.0 percent and per capita rates of growth of 2.5 percent.[1] Table 1-1 indicates recent growth rates for the six countries under study. The Middle East, at least before the June War, was doing comparatively well in the growth sweepstakes, although rather less impressively in terms of per capita income in Egypt and Syria. Moreover, growth rates were high during most of the 1950s as well. Consequently, the Middle Eastern countries should, on the whole, be viewed as examples of past development success. What are the reasons for past growth? What are the prospects for continued growth?

There is no law of development guaranteeing that once a satisfactory rate of economic growth is achieved it will continue indefinitely. However, past progress is probably the best available guide to the future. A reasonable rate of economic growth in the past leads to a presumption that such a rate is repeatable in the future. With the possible exception of Syria, the past development experiences of the countries discussed in this book warrant the presumption of satisfactory future growth. For them, 6 percent growth per year is demonstrably not an impossible target. Perhaps the most important lesson in this book is that economic development in the Middle East is feasible, given sound policies and a peaceful environment. It does not require heroic sacrifice, unparalleled wisdom, nor unforeseeable good fortune.

Past growth implies not that substantial development efforts are not needed but that such efforts are likely to be rewarded. Nor is effort alone enough. What is required is enlightened effort. Heroic sacrifices can be misdirected. Each of the individual studies in this book discusses not only how much future development will cost the country but also how best to go about implementing a development strategy. Maintaining economic growth will be neither easy nor automatic. Reasonable degrees of effort and sacrifice, of wisdom, and of luck will all be needed.

[1] As reported in *Partners in Development,* Report of the Commission of International Development, Lester B. Pearson, Chairman, Frederick A. Praeger, New York, 1969, p. 28.

3

Table 1-1

Recent Growth Records of
Six Middle Eastern Countries[a]

Country	Period	Growth Rate of Output	Per Capita Growth Rate
Israel	1960-65	10.0+	8.0+
Egypt	1960/61 to 1964/65	5.5	2.9
Syria	1956-67	4.0−	1.0−
Lebanon	1956-65	7+	4.6+
Iraq	1953-65	7+	4.5+
Jordan	1954/55 to 1965/55	8.0+	5.2

[a]The numbers in this table for the various countries are based on estimates in the extended discussions of population and output growth contained in the individual chapters.

II. Three Classic Development Issues in the Middle East

Many development problems in the Middle East are similar to those in other developing nations. Three in particular stand out for their importance and their representativeness. These include the problems of determining to what extent the sources of growth are to be found in the steady accretion of capital or in the progressive transformation of old ways into new, of modernizing traditional agriculture, and of limiting population growth and adjusting to urbanization.

The Sources of Growth: Capital Accumulation and Total Factor Productivity

No issue of development theory is more clouded than the importance of capital accumulation relative to growth in what is termed "total factor productivity," changes in which are defined as the increase in output over and above what can be attributed to increased amounts of real inputs—usually capital and labor. What lies behind changes in total factor productivity is not very clearly understood, but the so-called residual factor certainly plays an important role in achieving economic growth. The papers in this volume draw very different conclusions about this issue for different countries. Bruno, for example, feels that for Israel capital accumulation is the key, whereas Hansen emphasizes the importance of increases in total factor productivity for Egypt's growth prospects, as does Mazur for Jordan. This issue is central to development policy. To the extent that capital accumulation is the engine of growth, savings and capital imports are the key policy variables. To the degree that total factor productivity is the

4

engine, intersectoral allocations, market imperfections, auxiliary industries and the infrastructure, institutions and policies, other influences on the rate of adoption and diffusion of improved technology, and many other heterogeneous factors become important.

Empirical estimates of productivity, including total factor productivity, result from combining theory and measurement. Quite apart from the often considerable theoretical controversies, there is little consensus on the validity of the resulting estimates since measurement problems are so difficult. Not only are the production functions unknown, only to be guessed at by the indirect evidence of distributive shares, but also the measures of output and inputs are themselves uncertain. If prices of outputs and inputs never changed, and if inputs and outputs differed over time only in scale and not in quality or composition, both the conceptual and the measurement problems would be far easier. But adjusting for price, compositional, and quality changes to get meaningful indexes of real output and input calls for information that is seldom available—and is particularly hard to obtain for developing countries.

It is tempting to conclude that, since the problem is inherently intractable, it should be postponed until economists are in agreement on the theory and adequate data are available for measurement. Such agreement is a long way off, judging from the current plethora of technical articles on this subject, and to give in to such temptation would be to remain silent on policy issues central to development strategy. Moreover, for developing economies there is no doubt that growth comes from sources other than increases in inputs. After all, economic development is not synonymous with economic growth. The former implies social, institutional, and policy changes over a far wider spectrum than does the latter. Simple growth models can point up important issues, but they can also obscure policy issues central to development strategy.

Output can increase in excess of the amount attributed to net increases in factor inputs either because (1) new capital equipment is more productive than old capital equipment (capital measured in "efficiency units" has increased), (2) average labor skill has increased (labor measured in "efficiency units" has increased), or (3) existing resources are combined in a more efficient manner. If all of the residual increase was attributable to the increased productivity of new capital goods, then, given the rate of growth of labor, the growth of total output would be a simple function of the rate of capital accumulation. On the further assumption that the rate of technical improvement is fixed, from the policy point of view growth would be maximized simply by maximizing the rate of capital accumulation. That a good part of this growth would really derive from new technology would be irrelevant to the policymaker, since technological change could be achieved only in proportion to gross investment. However, the assumption of complete capital embodiment of technical change seems unwarranted. It remains an open question whether slow rates of diffusion of improved technology are primarily the result of slow rates of growth of capital accumulation, of the ordinary sort of resource misallocation associated with administrative price distortions and market imperfections, of low levels of education, or of a broad set of factors that might be labeled "imperfections in the knowledge market." The present state of knowledge about the process of economic development permits no more than such uncertainty. Economists are also uncertain about the environment variables that improve efficiency and that explain why, for example, the same machine with a team to operate it will produce substantially more in one country than in another.

Although total factor productivity plays an important role in the growth perspectives of each of the country papers in this book, only Bruno and Hansen have enough empirical data to permit detailed discussion of the issue. To begin with, there is a striking paradox in their conclusions. Hansen reports a residual in Egypt of only 0.5 percent a year and sees this residual as the key to Egyptian growth. Bruno finds a residual of over 4 percent but believes that Israel's experience is a strong confirmation of the importance of capital accumulation.[2]

This paradox is even more dramatic when the past contribution of the residual relative to capital accumulation is calculated: the residual accounts for less than one-tenth of Egypt's past growth rate, for approximately one-third of Israel's, with capital accumulation accounting for about two-thirds and less than one-half for Egypt and Israel, respectively. The same relative picture holds for the future. In fact, if Bruno's projections are valid the share of future growth attributable to the residual will rise!

What appears as a disagreement about the importance of the residual turns out to be something else entirely. Hansen argues that "in the future, a given addition of capital will add less to GNP than previously" and that attaining 6 percent growth with no change in the residual would call for an increase in the investment ratio from 19 percent to 32 percent—an increase he finds infeasible. Bruno, however, accepts a substantial reduction in growth, due in part to a de-

[2] The basic aggregate model used by both authors is of the following form: $g = \alpha l^{\beta} k^{\sigma}$, where g, l, and k are the growth factors (1 plus the growth rate) of output, labor, and capital, respectively; α is 1 plus the "residual"; and β and δ are the production elasticities. Both authors find $\beta = \delta = 0.5$ as the most reasonable values to use for the recent past. These models are as follows:

	Period	*Growth Function*		
		g	α	l
Hansen:				
	1960/1–1964/5	1.055	= (1.005)	$(1.029)^{.5}$ $(1.0709)^{.5}$
	1970/1–1980	1.06	= (1.01)	$(1.026)^{.6}$ $(1.0859)^{.4}$
Bruno:				
	1953–65	1.117	= (1.044)	$(1.038)^{.5}$ $(1.108)^{.5}$
	1960–65	1.107	= (1.032)	$(1.043)^{.5}$ $(1.106)^{.5}$
	1970–75	1.096	= (1.037)	$(1.035)^{.5}$ $(1.084)^{.5}$
	1975–80	1.079	= (1.030)	$(1.027)^{.5}$ $(1.072)^{.5}$

clining rate of investment, but projects no decline in capital productivity. Apart from their different predictions over whether capital productivity will hold steady, the two authors are not in conflict because the problems they are dealing with are very different. In both cases, the residual is of major importance. But for policy purposes, the residual becomes a particularly significant factor when adequate growth is at issue. There is no doubt that rapid capital accumulation can lead to growth. What is less clear is whether, for many countries, this is feasible. If not, the residual—that catchall of efficiency and technological changes —becomes a critical factor in future growth prospects.

This issue is not simply a terminological one. There is no necessarily stable relationship between the rates of growth of capital and total factor productivity. Rapid growth based on capital accumulation can create the kind of dynamic climate where the residual factor can add an extra bonus. On the other hand, certain ways of achieving forced draft savings and industrialization can threaten the maintenance, let alone the increase, of the residual by impairing incentives and reducing efficiency. This last danger is particularly important where there is a high degree of national planning of uncertain quality. Economic development has become a major social objective in the Middle East. In trying to achieve this objective, policymakers must avoid being seduced by capital-output ratios into thinking that increasing the rate of capital accumulation will make it possible to reach any growth target desired. In fact, too much pressure on consumption and too rapid an attempt to raise investment funds can lead to serious problems of disincentives and inefficiency. Neglect of the policies and changes needed to promote the residual factor because it is an ambiguous and elusive concept, in favor of concentration on capital accumulation, could be a serious error. After all, it is hard to be sure about what causes what in development. As Denison notes, it is not at all clear that rapid growth does not cause high rates of investment rather than vice versa.[3] Much of the development process remains a black box whose impenetrability is a challenge to analyst and policymaker alike.

Modernizing Traditional Agriculture

Underlying the aggregate performance of developing economies is structural transformation. Structural change is not necessarily bounded by sector, but a major structural issue for most developing countries at an early stage of development has been the modernization of traditional agriculture. This issue can be, and has been, sectioned in many ways to make analysis more feasible: for example, the diffusion of technology in agriculture, the transfer of labor from agriculture to industry, improvements in rural markets for goods and money, the investment in social overhead capital needed for rural development, and the development of modern agro-industries. It has also been at the heart of more global concepts of economic development, such as the theory of the dual economy and

---

[3] Edward F. Denison, *Why Growth Rates Differ: Post-War Experience in Nine Western Countries,* Brookings Institution, Washington, D.C., 1967, pp. 121–122.

7

notions of balanced growth. But no simple consensus has emerged, no simple theory of structural modernization in agriculture has been found.

The problem is, of course, that there is no such thing as a typical underdeveloped economy. The concept of traditional agriculture must be applied to a highly disparate sample. It risks being so general as to be useless or to entail a high probability of being wrong in any particular case.[4] Not only is each country unique, but also within a given country regional and local differences may be so great as to vitiate the usefulness of even a national model. The alacrity with which economists generalize is a regrettable *déformation professionelle*. In their essay on technological diffusion in Lebanese agriculture, Al-Haj and Yacoub present empirical findings in support of the hypothesis of diversity within traditional agriculture. They show two areas, widely different in socioeconomic characteristics, that are farmed by peasants whose individual differences are substantial. It is not surprising that among areas, and between individuals, the responses to an array of new techniques, which themselves have many dimensions, are highly varied. Traditional agriculture is best viewed as a statistical distribution of characteristics, in which the variance is so high that it is hard to think in terms of modal concepts.

Although aspects of the issue of transforming traditional agriculture and developing modern industry are raised in the discussion of every country, the focus changes from paper to paper. Schultz highlights the importance of the dual economy; Hansen, the rural labor market in Egypt and Ricardian diminishing returns in Syria; Bruno, the absorption of labor in agriculture and import substitution in industry; Badre, agrarian reform and public investments in agriculture in Iraq and cropping patterns and labor force allocations in Lebanon; and Mazur, water control and technical change in Jordan.

The papers in this volume are noteworthy for their relative lack of emphasis on an irrational static social and economic structure as a major barrier to development. A decade ago, it was fashionable to view the rural areas of underdeveloped countries as places where villages were stable social units, isolated from the rest of the economy, whose individuals behaved according to tradition and whose chief institutions were devoted to noneconomic goals. Traditional agriculture was identified with subsistence production, disguised unemployment, unchanging technology, and hidebound peasants. Concluding that economic incentives would not work, economists began to take an interest in such matters as child-rearing practices and other allegedly basic underlying social factors. But as more evidence has been gathered, and as developing countries themselves have become more consciously devoted to speeding economic change, this caricature has been largely abandoned. The decisive change is not so much in the stereotype of the peasant, although that was certainly wrong, but in the stereotype

[4] The best available discussion of traditional agriculture in developing countries is contained in Clifton R. Wharton, Jr., ed., *Subsistence Agriculture and Economic Development*, Aldine Publishing Co., Chicago, 1969. This volume, an outgrowth of a conference held in 1965, is indispensable to serious students in this area.

of stability. Today, at least, change is the order of the day; and the placid rural backwaters where anthropologists ply their trade are increasingly hard to find. Ignorance, risk aversion, ideology, and traditional social values are important, but important as influences on an essentially rational response to new opportunities, not as absolute barriers to such a response. As Khalaf notes in his paper on the modernization process in Lebanon, social scientists are increasingly inclined to the view that attitudes and behavior are changed by opportunities and incentives; and it is questionable whether values are more basic than, say, market structure or price policies.

The one element of what has been termed the "classical" model of the role of agriculture in economic development that seems to have emerged relatively unscathed from recent empirical work is the assumption of a static technology in agricultural output itself. Even here the classical reasoning—techniques are determined culturally—is less than compelling. Al-Haj and Yacoub show in their essay that new techniques involve many dimensions, such as profitability, scale, riskiness, complexity, and the need for associated inputs; and it appears that peasant rejection of techniques that proved effective only on model farms is by no means irrational. Moreover, there is by now considerable evidence that peasants will adopt new techniques—witness the expansion of land planted to the new varieties of wheat and rye in Asia from 200 acres in 1965 to 34 million acres in 1969.[5] At issue is whether static technology remains characteristic of traditional agriculture because peasant response to better ways of farming is sluggish or because new technology is only imperfectly developed and is of dubious profitability within the institutional structures in the countries concerned. Hla Myint opts for the latter explanation: "When agricultural experts in the underdeveloped countries complain that peasants are too "conservative" to adopt modern scientific methods, it is usually the experts who are making the mistake of trying to introduce the so-called modern techniques, which are not economically advantageous to the peasants in terms of the actual extra costs and the extra money returns. . . . The real difference between the peasant from the underdeveloped countries and the American farmer is not that the former behaves less like "economic man" than the latter, but merely that the scientific and agricultural advice which the latter receives . . . is of a much superior quality. This is an argument for improving the quality of agricultural research based on the special problems of the peasants in underdeveloped countries and not for not using economic incentives."[6]

Once the previous concepts are abandoned, the development process appears more rational, more susceptible to standard policy variables. But structural change is not costless: increasing agricultural output requires agricultural distribution systems capable of transmitting favorable prices for agricultural products

[5] This example, as well as others, is cited in Lester R. Brown, *Seeds of Change,* Frederick A. Praeger, New York, 1970, p. 3.
[6] H. Myint, "Comments," in Wharton, *Subsistence Agriculture and Economic Development,* p. 102.

to the producer, increased use of costly agricultural inputs, investment in roads and infrastructure, and investment in agricultural research. Similarly, industrial growth requires capital; technical knowledge, which may not be free; and labor, which could be used elsewhere. To increase either agricultural output or industrial output, administrative and market relationships must provide appropriate incentives at all levels, and required inputs and services must be made available as and when needed. Hard economic decisions must be made about relative economic efficiency, hard political decisions about the distribution of gains. The price of a more rational world is the building of a market environment that provides incentives for rational behavior.

Recent empirical work bears out the conclusion that agriculture offers no cheap reserve army of labor. In his paper on Egypt, Hansen refers to the recent large-scale rural labor survey carried out in Egypt by the International Labor Organization and the Egyptian Institute of National Planning.[7] This survey not only fails to find empirical support for the hypothesis of disguised unemployment in a country often considered a prime example of this alleged phenomenon but also presents a picture of an "active pervasive labor market"[8] very different from previous simplistic models of rural labor markets. It shows that productive employment in rural Egypt is far higher than was previously thought, largely because of the substantial amount of nonfield and nonagricultural work. The policy implication is clear: removing labor from rural areas is costly and, other things equal, will reduce output significantly in the rural sector, though potential output gains elsewhere may make it worthwhile to do so. Moreover, Hansen notes that the objective of development should be not to mobilize child labor further, but rather to reduce sharply the amount now used.

Hla Myint warns against trying to protect peasants from exploitation "by erecting a special sociological theory around them." His conclusion deserves to be cited at some length: "The best way to protect the peasants is to emphasize that in their basic economic behavior they are not fundamentally different from anybody else, so that they should not be discriminated against. In the history of the peasants in the colonial era, special sociological theories, such as the 'backward sloping supply curve of labor,' the peasant's supposed preference for leisure as against work and material reward, the oriental peasant's supposed otherworldliness, and other such theories have been (with or without their authors' consent) used to justify the exploitation of the peasants, for the adoption of negative pressures instead of positive economic incentives, the imposition of heavy taxation and forced labor. Political independence has not lessened these dangers to the peasants, for they are now faced with governments anxious to promote economic development through rapid industrialization using peasant agriculture as the milch cow to subsidize the industrial sector. In these circumstances, it is

[7] Institute of National Planning, *Employment Problems in Rural Areas,* Cairo, 1965.
[8] B. Hansen, "Employment and Wages in Rural Egypt," *American Economic Review,* June 1969, p. 312.

10

still important to stress that the expansion of the manufacturing sector cannot be sustained for long without a 'balanced-growth' development of the agricultural output and that, to achieve this, the peasants must be given the maximum economic incentives their countries can afford, to induce them to expand output and adopt improved methods. Some of the poorer underdeveloped countries with acute population pressure may decide, after taking into account their local circumstances and their time preference for present and future consumption, that they cannot afford the resources to produce a sufficient amount of incentive consumers' goods to induce the expansion of agricultural output by relying purely on positive incentives. But this political decision not to rely purely on economic incentives should be clearly distinguished from the sociological theory that economic incentives, even if they can be given, will not work on the peasants."[9]

All that remains to be added is that there is no certainty peasants can be exploited successfully even if the attempt is made. The better alternative would seem to be to improve the social and economic institutions that influence economic behavior in rural areas and to allocate the resources needed to modernize agriculture. To the question of how much and what kind of resources, however, there is no simple answer.

Population Growth: How Big a Burden?

As the essay by Schultz in this book makes clear, not much is certain about population growth in the Middle East except that it is rapid. Data deficiencies are such that even birth and death rates have to be inferred, approximated, and even guessed at. And the deficiencies are much worse for more detailed demographic data—age-specific birth and death rates, for example. Unfortunately, assessing the present and likely future burden of population growth requires knowing more than the rough order of magnitude of the recent rate of population growth.

Data deficiencies are not surprising. What is surprising is that Schultz can say (correctly), "The social and economic consequences [of rapid population growth] are only dimly understood today." The population crisis has been a set piece for social scientists, journalists, and politicians for years. But reasonable quantitative judgments about the presumed burden of population growth in general, or for specific countries, are not easily found.

Consider first the long-run effect of population growth on the rate of growth of per capita income. For this issue, it can be assumed that the labor force and the population as a whole grow at the same rate. One way to approach this problem is to ask what proportion of current savings is needed to increase the capital stock enough to maintain average labor productivity and per capita incomes. Clearly the higher the rate of population growth, the more capital accumulation is needed just to hold labor productivity constant. But the share of capital formation that must be devoted to this purpose is influenced not only by the rate of population growth but also by the original rate of capital formation.

[9] Myint, in Wharton, *Subsistence Agriculture and Economic Development*, p. 104.

Introduction

Economies that are accumulating capital at a relatively high proportion of their income need devote a relatively smaller share of the new capital to offsetting population growth than do economies with lower rates of capital accumulation. In addition, economies where capital productivity is high have the same advantage: the share of capital accumulation they need to offset population growth is less than that required by economies where capital productivity is lower. In short, economies that are relatively successful in their development efforts can cope with population increases more easily than economies that are in trouble in this respect.

Another way to approach the problem is to ask how much faster per capita growth would be if population and labor force growth were slower but investment rates were unchanged. This is a difficult question, even if strong simplifying assumptions are made. What is being asked for is an estimate of the growth effect of deepening the capital stock more rapidly. Such estimates depend on what is known about the aggregate production functions that seemingly underlie economic growth. If it could be assumed that changes in the rate of growth of the labor force would have no effect on capital productivity, on the residual factor, or on labor productivity itself, models such as those used by Bruno and Hansen could serve to generate information about the long-run effects of population growth on economic development. But there are many pitfalls in such calculations. Economies of scale may offset population growth to a significant extent; or, if one takes a Ricardian view whereby resources are fixed in supply, population growth may be catastrophic. If there is a substantial productivity residual, especially one embodied in new investment, the extra investment needed to accommodate population growth will be smaller, the increase in output greater. This point, too, has its obverse, as Schultz points out: there may be a dual economy problem where new employment requires a higher capital investment than old, and population growth becomes more costly than in the simpler case. However, new additions to the labor force are likely to be healthier and either better educated or more easily educable than the previous workers and therefore will serve to raise labor productivity.

Such conflicting considerations suggest that the cost of population growth depends in the long run on the particular characteristics of the economy in which it is occurring. Although casual tolerance of rapid population growth is foolish, it is not enough to point with horror to the dangers of such growth in general. Careful analyses of the costs of population growth for a particular country at a particular time are needed. The one general conclusion that can be drawn with some confidence is that to an economy already in development trouble, rapid, long-run population growth will be a heavy burden. In the Middle East today, development progress is sufficiently tenuous to warrant serious concern over the negative effect of population growth in the long run. On the other hand, as Israel and Jordan (and to a lesser extent Egypt under the five-year plan) have demonstrated, a massive drive to absorb a rapidly increasing labor force in productive activity may be associated with a rapid rise in output per worker.

In the short-run view, the assumption that population and labor growth are identical is clearly inadequate. The dependency burden arising from a high ratio of children, nonworking women, and old people to the total labor force changes over time. Schultz points out that this burden is now heavy in the Middle East and is accentuated by the low participation of women in the labor force but that it is likely to fall and perhaps fall rapidly once fertility declines. The real population problem may turn out to be a transitional one, with today's apparent crisis vanishing faster than one might think. After all, it is somewhat reassuring that at various times many countries—prewar France and the Soviet Union and East European countries today—have felt their population growth was too slow. What is troublesome in the Middle East is that no decline in the birth rate is yet in sight, and in the absence of directed effort any decline may be tragically slow to arrive.

Moving from a consideration of the costs of population growth to an identification of the factors determining the rate of population growth opens up a relatively new area for research and policy. Schultz and Ben-Porath show that population policy need not be confined to reducing the number of unwanted births but can also be designed to influence the number of children desired. Indeed, if population policy is restricted to the first objective, its results may well be very limited, since changes in the preferences of parents for children may swamp feasible changes in reducing the number of unwanted children. Approaching the problem by looking at the factors influencing preferences in regard to family size not only is a better analytical approach, but also suggests that there may be more grounds for optimism than commonly thought. For example, improving women's educational opportunities has a double-barreled effect: increasing their participation in the labor force and augmenting output, while reducing the desired birth rate. And by recognizing that lower rates of infant mortality may in turn reduce birth rates, the old, infinitely sad contradiction between better health and population control is at least partly resolved.

In the Middle East today rapid population growth constitutes a major problem, but the means for dealing with it in ways consistent with humane values appear to be more extensive than is usually assumed. Population growth is not an insuperable barrier to economic growth in the Middle East. The opposite appears more nearly correct: Only if there is a major failure in development need population growth lead to human tragedy. There is one problem, not two—and that problem is soluble. The solution is not automatic; it requires a special effort. Failure to mount an effective development effort will be doubly costly in that it will not only postpone progress but also make it harder to come by.

III. Development Issues of Special Importance in the Middle East

In Section II three general development problems whose form in the Middle East is broadly characteristic of similar problems elsewhere in the developing world were discussed. There are other development issues that take on such a special character in the Middle East that they are major factors in the unique-

13

ness of the development problem in that region. Three such issues seem to me to merit special attention: the significance of the Arab-Israeli conflict for economic development, the balance of payments and trade, and social ideology and doctrine, particularly the concept of Arab socialism.

The Arab-Israeli Conflict

The duration, intensity, and outcome of the Middle East conflict may well have a greater influence on economic development in the area than any other factor. But this influence is not simple or easy to depict. More is involved than such obvious issues as the share of defense expenditures in the gross national product. The present conflict permeates all social, political, and economic developments in the region. War is not just a drain on resources—it is also a powerful influence on how resources are used and what resources are available.

It is not possible, therefore, to assess the full impact of the Middle East conflict on the future economic development of the area. It might just be possible to assess the effect of the conflict on a number of individual factors; but when it comes to adding up the result, art rather than science is called for. Consider the range of influence: the conflict affects defense budgets, employment and price levels, balance of payments deficits, sources and levels of balance of payments financing, the direction of foreign trade, physical capital stock, sectoral allocations of resources, foreign investment, transportation routes (the closure of the Suez Canal is the most dramatic but not the only example), the rate and direction of technological diffusion, the level and composition of investment in human capital, the "nationality" of labor forces, internal migration flows, the rate of population growth, domestic politics, social and economic ideology, social "power structures," regional politics and cooperation, and much else. Moreover, the effect of the conflict on such factors will be influenced by how long it goes on, how it is fought, and how it turns out. Also, the influences will vary from country to country and from time to time. In short, war is a dominant but unpredictable influence on the future history of the region.

I have avoided characterizing the impact of the conflict as being bad for future economic development. If such is the case, it is not true in any simple way. Against the clearly negative effects—high defense budgets and physical destruction, for example—must be set other effects potentially favorable: reduced underemployment, higher levels of external support, more rapid social and political change. In this connection, history offers little help, wars having stimulated some economies and impaired others. The net impact is uncertain, particularly in the long run.

Particularly significant in the Middle East is that the present state of tension dilutes political and administrative concentration on development issues. No government of any country anywhere in the world has the single objective of promoting economic development, but for many developing countries no other single objective is so important. This is not so in the Middle East today. Moreover, time lost in the Middle East, as in many areas of the developing world, is impor-

14

tant, since population growth converts standing still into going backward in all of the countries except Israel. In each of the studies that follow in this book, various influences of the present conflict are delineated. And in all of them the author's sense of urgency about economic development can be felt. Economic performance in the areas since June 1967 has not been such as to lead one to complacency about the effect of prolonged conflict. Neither does it imply, however, that continuing tension will stifle economic development. The effect is a matter of degree.

The Balance of Payments

Economists are fond of informing policymakers that the balance of payments is only the tail of the dog. Policymakers are rightly skeptical that this is the case, and reluctant to act as if it is. For most developing nations, the balance of payments is the major aggregate constraint on economic development. One reason for the central role of the balance of payments in limiting the pace of economic development is that institutional rigidities usually preclude the use of the price mechanism for equilibrating the balance of payments. As a result, the level of aggregate demand and the pace of economic growth in the economy as a whole have spillover effects on the balance of payments. Although *ad hoc* modifications through tariff changes and direct controls are a partial substitute for changes in the effective exchange rate, the limited flexibility of the latter usually imposes a real constraint on domestic economic policy.

A more fundamental linkage between domestic economic performance and the balance of payments also exists. A current account deficit, however financed, is a transfer of real resources from the rest of the world to the deficit country. For developing countries this transfer is particularly important—in part because a development effort implies a constant push against resource limitations, but also because foreign resources extend the range of goods available to a relatively far greater degree than is true for developed countries. Imports embody technology. In a highly abstract model such embodiment can be captured by relative price differentials; but as in all cases where new goods are present, price differences are an incomplete measure of value. For this reason, the ability of a developing country to finance a high level of imports—and optimally a large current account deficit—is often a major factor in its economic growth and welfare.

The Middle East has done well in this regard. From a banker's point of view, the large deficits of Egypt, Israel, and Jordan are weak spots. From a developer's point of view, however, they have been sources of strength, enlarging the range and increasing the amount of available resources. Particularly interesting is the fact that the critical factors in the balance of payments of the six countries under review are all different. For Israel, private and public transfers have been dominant; for Egypt and Jordan, foreign aid from a variety of sources. For Iraq, oil revenues have been so large as to permit a buildup in reserves and to shift the constraint from the foreign balance to internal capabilities; for Lebanon, private capital flows into the Beirut money market. Syria,

15

hitherto the least well supported of the six, may be about to move into a modest but helpful oil boom. For different reasons in the various countries the balance of payments constraint has not been as tight for the Middle East as for most developing nations.

As noted earlier, balance of payments financing has two aspects: magnitude and permissiveness. Magnitude determines how large a deficit can be supported; permissiveness, how much domestic effort is needed to increase the magnitude of financing. Permissiveness is important even if it is temporary. A whole school of economic thought has built up around the notion of the Big Push, which usually has as one of its components a temporary period of maximum balance of payments permissiveness. And, indeed, there are cases where foreign aid, or export windfalls, have been instrumental in promoting rapid economic growth. In the Middle East, Jordan and Israel and, at times, Egypt are the most dramatic examples. A permissive balance of payments position allows rapid capital expansion without a heavy load of domestic savings or taxation, increases the flow of advanced technology, and may encourage foreign direct investment. The result is higher productivity and incomes and a chance to break through the vicious circles of poverty and low savings, and of backwardness and slow diffusion of technology.

But permissiveness can be only temporary. Sooner or later, the country will have to pay more of its own way. For this reason, exports soon assume a critical importance, as do the classic development problems of import substitution and exchange regimes. In the Middle East, it appears that except for the oil producers the margin of permissiveness, on the whole, will be less generous in the future than formerly. Continuation of former levels of balance of payments financing is uncertain, let alone additional financing for growing deficits. And reducing payments deficits to levels that can be supported largely by each country's own resources and productivity is an even harder problem, and one on which the theorists of the Big Push are either silent or unconvincing. Yet, as Bent Hansen notes in his paper on Egypt, "a country with independence as a cornerstone . . . should prefer to base its economic development mainly on its own resources and efforts."[10]

With the exception of Iraq and, to a more limited extent, Syria, future balance of payments support for the Middle Eastern countries studied in this volume is a hostage to events and to attitudes and developments outside the area. Under the pressure of current stringencies Egypt has taken the lead in trying to mobilize more regional support (excluding Israel of course) and to increase financial flows from the oil-rich states to those less fortunately endowed. Asfour discusses the possibility of continuing allocations from the oil producers to Egypt and Jordan—allocations that have been running around $300 million a year since 1967. While the Arab-Israeli conflict persists, the continuation of this flow

---

[10] B. Hansen, "Economic Development of Egypt," this volume, p. 23.

is likely, but by no means certain. Settlement of the conflict would have an unpredictable effect on continued intraregional aid flows. There is some possibility that foreign support will continue at roughly present levels but at the hazard of political development. It may be that future economic development in the area, at least over the next decade, will continue to benefit from a relatively advantageous balance of payments environment. It seems unlikely that much headway will be made toward financial independence in Egypt, Israel, or Jordan, unless such progress is forced by external conditions of supply of financing import deficits. The studies in this volume sketch optimistic paths that each of these countries might pursue toward such independence.

Another aspect of the balance of payments environment is its influence on trade relations. There are many different markets in the world, and different sources of financing influence which of these markets are tapped. For example, financial support from the Communist bloc has led Egypt's foreign trade to be increasingly oriented toward the Soviet Union and Eastern Europe. United States aid in the form of PL480 grants is completely tied not only to a supplying country but also to a particular sector, and other forms of Western aid have different implications for trade. Direct investments, too, are concentrated in particular industries. In short, not only the level but also the form of balance of payments support will determine the contribution of the rest of the world to economic development in the Middle East. Although no firm conclusions can be drawn on this subject, there is a danger that continued reliance on substantial external financing will distort trade flows in the area and limit the gains from trade to an appreciable degree.

There is an impression that economic integration in the Middle East is the wave of the future. Perhaps so, but this is far from a safe bet. Formidable obstacles exist to such integration. Although regional cooperation is much in vogue, dramatic examples of cooperation among developing countries are not to be found. Even if real gains are to be had from economic cooperation, the distribution of those gains among the cooperating partners may be highly uncertain. When the problems posed in the Middle East by the existence of different political and economic systems, different levels of development, and difference balance of payments problems are taken into account, economic integration looks as if it will remain in limbo for some time to come.[11]

On the other hand, capital flows from the oil-rich countries, together with the political pressures engendered by the Arab-Israeli conflict, may spur the countries of the region toward cooperation more vigorously than in the past. What is regrettable to an outside observer is that Arab-Israeli cooperation seems an absurd notion today.

---

[11] A good discussion of the issue of economic integration in the Middle East can be found in A. G. Musrey, *An Arab Common Market*, Frederick A. Praeger, New York, 1969; and in R. El Mallakh, *Economic Development and Regional Cooperation: Kuwait*, University of Chicago Press, Chicago, 1968.

Introduction

Arab Socialism

In his paper on Egypt Hansen defines Arab socialism as "what has actually taken place in Egypt."[12] But is this adequate? Certainly the initial impetus to institutional reform after the July 1952 revolution in Egypt was pragmatism, not ideology. Over time, however, not only has a particular form of mixed economy evolved in Egypt, but a new doctrine of economic organization has also emerged. What began as pragmatism has become ideology—an ideology that "proceeded from institutional change rather than the reverse,"[13] but still an ideology. "What has actually taken place" differs among countries, but the ideology of Arab socialism extends, to varying degrees, across the Arab world. Because it is a relatively new and therefore incomplete concept, and because conditions differ from one country to another, Arab socialism is not a rigid body of dogma. In practice it will differ from country to country, since pragmatism remains an important modifying influence. For the future, though, the trend is in a particular direction toward an imperfectly defined concept but in accord with a set of values and assumptions increasingly common.

The content of Arab socialism is not precise but it is clear. The contrast with laissez faire ideology is marked. Planning, welfare, nationalization—concepts at the heart of Arab socialism—are scarcely compatible with laissez faire. This contrast may seem less than startling in a world that has long since retreated from laissez faire in its purer form, but it becomes more real when contrasted to what the Arab economies were like 10 or 15 years ago. Arab socialism is what has replaced laissez faire as an economic ideology. And it is a unique ideology: less global and rigid than that in any of the Communist countries (even including Yugoslavia) and involving more planning and a higher degree of nationalization than in the European social-democrat tradition. Although the emphasis on social welfare is not particularly heavy when compared with that in modern developed countries, it is relatively high for developing nations.

Nationalization has been the cutting edge of Arab socialism. Starting from a political decision that the leading role in development should be played by the public sector, most of Egypt's modern economy has been nationalized, with only small establishments, domestic trade, and a limited amount of export trade remaining open to private enterprise. Moreover, what remains of the private sector is subject to detailed controls. The result has been the bureaucratization of the economy. Hansen's essays on Syria and Egypt in this book raise serious questions about the way in which Arab socialism has been implemented. In theory, excessive bureaucratization is no more necessary to Arab socialism than excessive monopoly power is to laissez faire capitalism. In practice, the danger seems hard to avoid.

Agriculture has been a troublesome sector ideologically. That Arab social-

[12] B. Hansen, "Economic Development of Egypt," p. 75.
[13] Patrick O'Brien, *The Revolution in Egypt's Economic System*, Oxford University Press, London, 1966, p. 313.

18

ism has had difficulties in developing a workable concept for agriculture is not surprising. No other economic system has done much better. On one hand, private plots, cooperatives, and state farms coexist in Communist countries; on the other hand, direct controls are extensive in the agriculture sector of all modern industrial nations. De facto tolerance of seemingly antithetical institutions and policies in agriculture is characteristic of most of the world. In its agricultural cooperatives, Egypt seems to have struck a reasonable balance between collective operation and private ownership. The dilemma of finding an effective mode of agricultural organization, however, is seen clearly in Iraq. In that country, a massive land reform was undertaken in the late 1950s. The estates of the exploiting sheiks were given to the people—good socialist policy, and also good economic policy according to the ex ante prescriptions of Western observers. But it has not worked, as Badre notes in his paper. Today cooperatives and further increases in public investments are seen as the answer. If experience elsewhere is any guide, there will be no single answer to the organization of the agricultural sector in the Arab world—a frustrating conclusion for planners to accept. Continued debate and experimentation are likely to be the order of the day.

Experience with Arab socialism to date has been mixed. Certainly mistakes have been and are being made. But the same would be true under any form of economic organization. The interesting question for the future is not really whether the present forms of Arab socialism can be made to work better, but what the future forms will be. Adel Daher, in a provocative recent paper, foresees more thoroughgoing socialism. He finds that young Arab intellectuals are more radical than their immediate predecessors, in part because of the shock of the June 1967 defeat. To them, he says, "The June defeat proved the Socialist Arab Revolution was neither revolutionary enough nor socialist enough. . . . Arab revolutionaries have not adopted a scientific, secular socialism nor have they understood the deep connection between socialism and modern science."[14]

Nobody really knows what economic system is most likely to be successful in spurring the process of economic development. And in the Middle East, what system will emerge is unclear. Arab socialism is certainly the leading ideology. More conservative forces remain important, however, particularly in such financial and trade entrepôts as Beirut and Amman. In short, in thinking about the economic future of the Middle East, ideological uncertainty must be added to the uncertainties surrounding the war and the balance of payments discussed earlier. These three special factors will play important roles in shaping the future of the region, but exactly what those roles will be remains to be seen.

IV. Conclusion

Economic development in the Middle East is not a single problem, but many problems. No one factor explains the past and foretells the future. The natural

---

[14] A. Daher, *Current Trends in Arab Intellectual Thought,* The Rand Corporation, RM–5979–FF, Santa Monica, Calif., 1970, p. 23.

resource base of the area, its rate of population growth, its agricultural practices and potential, its rate of industrialization, its foreign economic relations, its forms of economic organization, its technology, or its political environment— none is decisive. Not even the present state of conflict is uniquely significant. All of these problems and their interactions are discussed in the essays that follow.

One impression does emerge clearly from this book: that the historical record lends no support to those who consider the economic future of the Middle East to be hopeless. On the contrary, all the evidence points to a potential for vigorous growth which, over not too long a period, could transform the area and the lives of its inhabitants. The conclusion of the Pearson report on this point for developing countries as a whole seems equally apposite to the Middle East in particular: "Doubt was widespread twenty years ago whether rapid progress could be achieved. Underdevelopment . . . seemed to be a vicious circle from which only a fortunate few might escape. These fears . . . proved to be exaggerated. The record of the past twenty years proves that economic development is feasible, given adequate and sound policies. It gives more ground for encouragement than is generally realized, but it also shows that growth is neither easy nor automatic."[15]

[15] *Partners in Development,* p. 26.

Economic Development of Egypt

Bent Hansen

Of the six countries analyzed in this book, the development problems of Egypt are most nearly classical. Egypt is a large country with a population of over 30 million, a large traditional agriculture sector, and a large and persistent balance of payments deficit. For many years, Egypt was assumed to represent a typical less developed country, with substantial disguised unemployment as the outstanding symptom of its lack of development. In the following essay, Bent Hansen demonstrates that this assumption is misplaced and that the unique features of Egypt's economy are so important as to make it difficult to characterize its development problems in any simple way.

Hansen finds that 6 percent growth is a reasonable target for the future but leaves the reader without any undue confidence that it will be achieved. There is nothing esoteric about the development requirements Hansen cites: limiting private consumption, raising the residual growth factor, and increasing exports. These are indeed the classic problems of development. But Hansen also finds obstacles to their solution in problems unique to Egypt: the demands of protracted war, the inefficiency of the present organizational setup, and uncertainties about future balance of payments support and trade relations. Nothing inherent is an obstacle to Egyptian development, not even Arab socialism per se. But will the external situation permit the kind of concentrated attention to economic problems needed to solve them, and will economic and social policy be pragmatic enough to break through bureaucratic and ideological barriers preventing the optimal use of resources? As Hansen concludes, "whether actual developments will provide all the favorable external and internal conditions for the projected growth rate remains to be seen." All that needs to be added is that, in the face of rapid population growth, time lost is costly indeed.

Economic Development of Egypt

I. Introduction

In 1963 it looked as if Egypt had entered on the road of sustained growth. For about 6 years its national product per capita had increased steadily by over 3 percent, and aggregate output had increased by about 6 percent per year. The level of investments and the expansion of education and health services gave good promise that the economy should be able to continue at this rate of growth. Inflationary pressures and large balance of payments deficits had arisen, however, and the shortage of foreign exchange was becoming a serious problem. Only piecemeal measures and palliatives were undertaken to meet the foreign exchange problem, which might have led to stagnation. Firm demand management and wage policies and better investment planning, however, could probably have gradually redressed the balance of payments without retarding growth. Indeed, most observers of the Egyptian economy agree that such measures could even have accelerated growth.

Two serious political miscalculations, two wars, put an end, a temporary one, it is hoped, to this promising development. Egypt's involvement from 1963 in the Yemen War, originally expected to be both limited and brief, led to soaring defense expenditures, which threw the economy more and more out of balance and caused a gradual slowdown of growth. The war of June 1967, apart from resulting in the destruction and occupation of parts of the country, brought a further increase in defense expenditures, and development came to a standstill.

This Chapter discusses the problems of whether Egypt will be able to return to a path of sustained growth, what efforts will have to be taken for that purpose, how much growth can be expected, and what factors will govern and limit the rate of growth. The issue is surrounded by many political uncertainties, and any attempt to answer these questions must be conditioned by assumptions that may never come true. The ideal policy must be comprehended as the best policy that an Egyptian government could possibly pursue under the given basic institutional setup and the known natural and human resources. It is natural to assume that a country with independence as a cornerstone of its national credo (and nations that have recently gained independence are usually very rigid in their conceptions of it) and with neutralism and nonalignment as the basis of its foreign policy should prefer to base its economic development mainly on its own resources and efforts.

This attitude should not preclude reliance on foreign advisors or some technical cooperation with foreign businesses and governments. Some foreign finance might be obtained to cover future balance of payments deficits. But it would in my opinion be entirely unrealistic—politically as well as financially, domestically as well as internationally—to assume that this could take place on a larger scale than occurred during the decade of development before the war of June 1967. Egypt relied heavily on technical assistance and cooperation in connection with certain special projects, such as the Aswan High Dam and oil prospecting; yet her development program was basically dependent on domestic personal resources. Huge balance of payments deficits, for some years running as high as 7 to 8 percent of GNP and partly induced by the development program, were covered by PL 480 aid, Russian High Dam and other loans, and other sources of foreign finance. It is difficult to imagine that in the future such finance will be available on this scale. The assumption that Egypt cannot be expected to rely more heavily on foreign technical and financial aid in the future than in the past will enable us to discuss the upper limits of future growth possibilites in the light of past performance. Whether the country will actually reach these limits will further depend on its economic policy and other domestic or international matters, which will be discussed later.

Section II briefly surveys the level of income and production expected in 1980 and in the year 2000 under reasonably optimistic assumptions. Section III discusses the growth potential of the country against the background of past developments. In Sections IV and V the problems encountered in realizing that potential are considered.

II. Production and Expected Income in 1980 and 2000

Table 2-1 presents the level of total production, the population, and the per capita production for 1964/65, the base year, and the implications for 1980 and

Table 2-1

Gross Domestic Product and Population,
1964/65, 1980, and 2000

Year	GDP at Factor Cost (million E£ at 1964/65 prices)	Population (million persons)	GDP Per Capita (1964/65 prices)	
			E£	U.S. $
1964/65	1,884[a]	29.2[b]	64.5	145.1
1980	4,663	40.9	114.1	256.7
2000	14,957	67.0	223.3	502.4

[a]*Statistical Handbook, U.A.R., 1952-1966,* Central Agency for Mobilisation and Statistics, Cairo, 1967, p. 215.
[b]*Ibid.,* p. 7.

2000 of the 6 percent growth rate in the gross domestic product (GDP) and the 2.5 percent growth rate of population, which have been chosen as reasonably optimistic projections, given the general assumptions outlined in the Introduction and specified in Section III.

Production and income per capita in 1964/65 were considerably higher in Egypt than in such countries as India and Pakistan but somewhat lower than in Turkey, for instance.[1] Under the assumptions chosen, production per capita would increase by almost 80 percent from 1964/65 to 1980. Compared with the level in 1960, at the beginning of Egypt's first five-year plan, a doubling would be achieved by 1980. Production would double again between 1980 and 2000, resulting in a per capita level comparable to that of Italy in the mid-1950s and Greece in the mid-1960s.

Real income per capita may develop differently, depending on Egypt's terms of foreign trade and net interest payments to other countries. To project the terms of trade over such a long period is not feasible, but I see no reason for the pessimism of those who believe that the terms of trade necessarily must move against underdeveloped countries in the long run. It does seem reasonable, however, to expect the interest burden on foreign debts to be substantially higher in 1980 than it was in 1964/65. By 1965 the total foreign debt amounted to almost U.S. $1,400 million, or about E£600 million. The interest payments visible in the balance of payments estimates of the Central Bank amounted to only about E£15 million in 1965/66, that is, about 2.5 percent of the net debt and 0.75 percent of the GDP. The actual interest charges, however, may have been higher.[2] Even before the war of June 1967 the total foreign debt was about E£925 million; with the replacement of military equipment it must have reached a substantially higher level.[3] Even in the absence of further borrowing, the interest burden may thus increase more rapidly than per capita production, but this factor does not essentially modify the picture shown in Table 2-1.[4] Although debt service is a heavy burden on the balance of payments, it means less in terms of national income.

[1] National domestic product and national income per capita may have been about E£60 and U.S.$135 in 1964/65.

[2] Interest rates vary from nothing on PL 480 counterpart funds to 2.5 percent on Russian High Dam loans and more than 10 percent on short-term loans with continental European banks. It is known that from around 1965/66 Egypt has not fulfilled her debt service obligations.

[3] The value of the military equipment to be replaced after June 1967 has been estimated at E£400–600 million. Part of it is supposed to have been delivered as grants, but nothing is known about the size of such grants and the payment conditions for the rest.

[4] With a foreign debt of E£1.5 billion in 1980 (assuming balance in current foreign payments from 1969 to 1980) at 4 percent, the interest burden per capita would increase from E£.5 in 1965/66 to E£ 1.5 in 1980. Per capita (gross) income would thus increase from E£64 in 1964/65 to E£112.6 in 1980, compared with per capita production of E£65.6 and E£114.1, respectively.

III. The Growth Potential of the Egyptian Economy

Population and Labor Force

The Egyptian population has been assumed to grow by 2.5 percent per annum until the year 2000. Earlier official forecasts were generally more optimistic in projecting a lower rate of population growth. Recent developments, however, do not justify assumptions of a lower rate of population increase, at least until 1980. And even 2.5 percent is rather optimistic.

Before World War II, population grew by about 1.0 percent per year, but in the 1950s the annual rate had increased to 2.4 percent, mainly because of a falling death rate. Some signs of increasing marriage age and decreasing fertility were discernible,[5] but they have not materialized, judging from available statistics. From 1960 to 1966 the rate of population growth, according to official census figures, increased further to almost 2.6 percent.[6] Unofficial adjusted census figures point even higher (2.8 percent; see below). Official population forecasts made at the beginning of the 1960s worked with alternative assumptions about fertility and projected annual rates of increase ranging from 2.0 to 2.8 percent for 1960–1970 and from 1.4 to 2.8 percent for 1970–1980.[7] A rate of increase for 1964/65–1980 of less than 2.5 percent now seems very unlikely, and some demographers expect substantially higher rates of increase.[8] For the period 1980–2000 the outlook is, of course, much more uncertain. Almost anything can happen. If the family planning policies begun in recent years succeed, fertility may fall substantially. The 2.5 percent applied in Table 2-1 for 1980–2000 may look unduly pessimistic, but I believe it is the most optimistic forecast that can reasonably be made. Family planning has met with little direct resistance in Egypt (apart, of course, from the politically unimportant Catholic Church), but a much more determined and energetic effort must be made if a radical change in the population trend is to be achieved. So far, urbanization itself does not seem to have had any effect on fertility.

The labor force is estimated to have increased by 2.9 percent per annum from 1960 to 1965, a rate of increase slightly greater than that of total population, 2.8 percent according to this estimate, during the same period.[9] The participation ratios are estimated to have fallen slightly for males and increased slightly for females.[10] Participation, however, is difficult to define precisely in

---

[5] B. Hansen and G. A. Marzouk, *Development and Economic Policy in the U.A.R. (Egypt)*, North Holland Publishing Co., Amsterdam, 1965, Chap. 2.

[6] *Statistical Handbook, U.A.R., 1952–1966*, Central Agency for Mobilization and Statistics, Cairo, 1967, p. 7.

[7] *Population Trends in the U.A.R.*, Central Statistics Committee, Cairo, 1962.

[8] Rafael Salib et al., "Prospected Employment Growth by Occupational Categories in the U.A.R., 1970–1985," *Seminar on Manpower Planning*, Cairo, 20–24 February 1968, OECD and INP, Cairo, 1968, p. 11.

[9] *Ibid.*

[10] *Ibid.*, p. 10.

agriculture [11] and certain other activities, especially for women and children, and is even more difficult to forecast. As a result of improved educational opportunities and a related fall in child labor, the tendency from 1960–1965 is expected to continue, with a slight net increase in the overall participation ratio,[12] although there are some doubts about the relevance of this sort of mechanical extrapolation. Participation ratios may be functions of demand and employment opportunities. Such relationships are known to exist as short-term phenomena in highly developed countries. They may also exist as long-term phenomena in underdeveloped countries, with female participation an important element of elasticity in the labor supply. I shall adopt the assumption of a slightly larger rate of increase of the labor force than of total population from 1965/66 to 1980, namely, 2.6 against 2.5 percent per year, with the possibility of a somewhat larger increase should employment opportunities prove more abundant. Habits and traditions, however, will most probably continue to prevent participation of married women to any large extent outside family enterprises. Elasticity of supply for married women is therefore important mainly in agriculture.

Elasticity of labor through the participation ratios, especially for married women, is thus a very different thing from the "unlimited supply" of labor from "disguised unemployment," which has long been fashionable in academic literature on development and usually is taken as an undisputed fact by planners, both on the national level and in international organizations. There is now sufficient empirical evidence to substantiate that, at least in agriculture in Egypt, disguised unemployment, apart from some seasonal unemployment and underemployment, is a red herring. To plan for economic development on the assumption that not only the natural increase in the total labor force but also a substantial part of the present agricultural labor force should immediately be shifted to urban employment, notably manufacturing industry, and that the supply of labor is practically unlimited, would therefore be disastrous. Since this point is of crucial importance, I shall elaborate on the evidence available.

The notion of surplus labor in Egyptian agriculture has been subject to long discussion, going back to the 1930s. In view of the nature of the issue and the available data, it should be no surprise that decisive evidence in either direction has been hard to produce. Recently, however, a large-scale rural employment survey undertaken jointly by the International Labour Organization, Geneva, and the Institute of National Planning, Cairo, has rather definitely tipped the balance against the labor surplus hypothesis.[13] According to this survey, adult

[11] A large-scale sample survey of rural employment shows much higher participation ratios for women in rural districts than figures of the population censuses. See Bent Hansen, "Employment and Wages in Rural Egypt," *American Economic Review,* June 1969.

[12] Salib et al. "Prospected Employment Growth by Occupational Categories in the U.A.R., 1970–1985."

[13] For a summary and discussion of the most important findings of this survey, see Hansen, "Employment and Wages in Rural Egypt," which includes a brief summary of earlier contributions to the debate on surplus labor in Egypt.

males (15 years and older) in rural areas are fully occupied during the busy summer half of the year, working an average of about 50 hours per week from March to October, with some underemployment and unemployment during the slacker winter months. Even on very small farms of less than 2 acres, adult males are fully occupied most of the year, thanks to the abundant opportunities for employment as hired laborers outside their own farms, on bigger farms, and outside agriculture. On average, it appears, women could work somewhat more outside the household, although in this respect there are large differences, such as between regions with perennial and basin irrigation. But if the agricultural work now done by children (aged 6–15 years) were added to the present work load of adults—as will be necessary to some extent once school attendance in rural areas becomes complete—both adult men and women would be overemployed, at least during the summer half of the year. With the present educational plans, the expected increase in the area made possible by the Aswan High Dam, and the still rather remote possibility of large-scale mechanization of agriculture, it seems very likely that agriculture will need an increase in the adult labor force, at least until about 1980. This is not to deny, of course, that part of the future natural increase of population in rural areas will have to find employment outside agriculture, but the supply of unskilled labor from rural areas will be limited to part of the natural increase in the labor force.

Egyptian authorities have been curiously inconsistent in their views on the problem of employment in agriculture. They have always paid lip-service to the surplus labor hypothesis and have indicated that a 20 percent surplus of labor in agriculture exists.[14] Nevertheless, they have planned for increased employment in agriculture.[15] The practical policy of government has in this respect been better than theory.

Unskilled rural labor probably does not to any large extent move directly from the fields to industry in urban areas. An important route is via construction activities. Present techniques in canal and road work, and even urban building activities, require large amounts of unskilled labor. Construction will always constitute a substantial part of investment activities and is a field where highly labor-intensive and import-saving techniques are available.[16] Indeed, construction

---

[14] *General Frame of the 5-Year Plan for Economic and Social Development,* July 1960–June 1965, Cairo, 1960, p. 118, Table 49. A footnote states that the employment "necessary" in agriculture 1959/60 is 3.245 million persons, whereas actual employment is estimated at 4.22 million. This implies a 23 percent surplus.

[15] *Ibid.,* pp. 13–14, Tables (K) and (M).

[16] On the figures of the *Statistical Handbook, U.A.R., 1952–1966,* pp. 213–214, the total value of output in construction in 1964/65 amounted to 49.7 percent of total gross investment. Some of the output from construction must, however, have been used for repair and maintenance and should not be included in gross investment. The share of construction in gross investment is thus probably somewhat below 49 percent. In 1965, the figures for this share varied among the OECD countries from 48 percent for Spain to 68 percent for Greece. The average for 14 OECD countries was 59 percent, with no clear tendency for the percentage to be related to the level of

accounted for the largest relative increase of employment in Egypt during the first half of the 1960s, and in absolute terms it was second only to industry (including extraction).[17] It was significant for the labor market situation, however, that the increase in employment in construction could take place only with a strong increase in wages for unskilled laborers not only in construction but also in agriculture.

Modern Egyptian development has had no difficulty in absorbing the supply of unskilled labor, and the substantial unemployment found in the labor force surveys of the Ministry of Labour at the end of the 1950s—amounting to about 7 percent of the labor force in cities, 4 percent in towns, and 3 percent in villages[18]—fell during the 1960s. Even after completion of the Aswan High Dam, construction will have to expand alongside other investments and will thus continue to absorb unskilled labor from rural areas.

It is more doubtful to what extent disguised unemployment exists in service industries. Little evidence is available, and casual observations of "sleeping shop-keepers" and the like should not be accepted as indicating anything except that even shopkeepers need to sleep now and then.[19] The government has often been pointed out as the main reserve of disguised unemployment. The bureaucracy has grown enormously during the last decennium (see below), partly in connection with increasing government interference in economics and other fields of life, and partly as a result of the government's employment policies (all university graduates are guaranteed employment). In addition there has been a large increase in the armed forces. Personally, I believe that government civil employment could be cut down substantially with no negative effects on production, and probably even with positive effects. There is little possibility, however, of substantiating this view statistically. By conventional national accounting, it is impossible to dismiss a government employee without a fall in GDP corresponding to his salary; his contribution to GDP is by definition equal to his salary. National accounting in terms of shadow prices would solve this problem, but the practical difficulty is, of course, to know which government employees have shadow prices below their salaries, thus representing disguised unemployment. It would be a great mistake to think that just any civil servant could be removed from the administration without negative effects. Highly efficient, overemployed civil servants can be found everywhere, but disguised unemployment also exists

---

per capita income. The share of construction in gross investment in Egypt thus seems remarkably low, a fact which may be related to the relatively low share of residential building in gross investment.

[17] *Statistical Handbook U.A.R., 1952–1966*, p. 211. See, however, footnote 25.

[18] Abdel Moneim El Shafei, "The Current Labour Force Sample Survey in Egypt," *International Labour Review*, Vol. 33, No. 5 (November 1960); *The Labour Force Sample Survey of Egypt*, Central Statistics Committee, Cairo, 1961.

[19] What is usually overlooked is how many hours shops stay open and people employed in service industries work. If retail trade concentrated on an 8-hour day, it would appear much more busy.

in government at all levels and to remedy it would require a highly selective process. These remarks apply a fortiori to defense, which, under favorable conditions, can be cut down substantially. Thus, even if there should be disguised unemployment in government, it is difficult to account for the gains in transferring such labor to other activities. Only the differential between the wages and salaries (in kind and cash) of these workers in the government sectors and their marginal value product in the sector to which they are transferred will appear as a gain in a conventional national accounting system; even the transfer of a soldier from the army to agriculture would not necessarily imply a transfer gain statistically.[20]

Thus, although there may be some labor reserves in Egypt that future development can draw upon, the actual development during the last decade, together with the employment situation in agriculture, make it clear that the supply of labor for development outside agriculture is limited, and that economic planning will go very wrong if it assumes unlimited supplies of unskilled labor, even in the short run. The reserves in agriculture are mainly seasonal and are partly (married women) available only for agriculture itself. It is important, therefore, to economize on the use of labor at all levels, and efficiency in production and increase of labor productivity become imperative for future development. It is generally recognized that development requires improved quality of labor in the sense that a larger proportion of skilled workers, foremen, technicians, managers, and the like is needed. In this respect, Egypt has an advantage over many other underdeveloped countries in having an ample supply of engineers and other academically trained people necessary for production and administration. Both the base and the top of the labor force pyramid thus exist, although the exodus of skilled, energetic people, which has accelerated during the last few years, is eroding the top somewhat. Hence an urgent problem in Egypt is to overcome the shortage of skilled workers, foremen, and lower technicians, and any successful development program must establish facilities for creating such cadres. With a limited supply of unskilled labor also, the efficiency problem becomes much more general and can be recognized as a basic one in Egyptian development.

Natural Conditions for Growth

I have chosen to work with a 6 percent GDP growth rate as a reasonably optimistic basis for the projections. To justify this choice, I shall look at natural conditions, past developments in GDP, sectoral developments, and investment requirements.

The first problem is the "physical growth capacity" or potential of the country. This notion has some affinity with the "absorption capacity" sometimes

[20] Wages in cash and kind (food, clothes, lodging) for a simple conscript amount to about E£60 per year, calculated on the basis of the 1968 expenditure norms of the armed forces. Employed 300 days per year as a laborer in agriculture, such a person would, before 1967, have earned about the same annual income; with wages equal to marginal value productivity, this would be the amount of agricultural value added.

discussed in connection with foreign loans to underdeveloped countries. It is related to the country's possibility of increasing employment, improving the quality of labor, expanding the stock of real capital, and employing better and more suitable technologies. Almost by definition, a country cannot grow faster than its physical capacity permits.[21] But it certainly may grow more slowly, depending partly on its ability to take advantage of its physical possibilities and partly on its ability to finance growth expenditures such as real investments, education, and health expenditures. It is not easy to say what is the upper limit of a particular country's growth rate, and perhaps, strictly speaking, no rigid upper limit can be determined. Yet it is obvious that the physical conditions for growth vary between countries and that differences in actual growth rates can be explained to some extent by differences in physical endowments, national peculiarities, and fundamental institutions.

A survey of a country's unused resources may give a rough idea of the growth potential, unused resources being interpreted broadly to include unused technical knowledge. Egypt has very few known natural resources that are not already utilized. With the completion of the Aswan High Dam, the practical possibilities of expanding the cultivated area at reasonable cost will almost be exhausted. Certain minerals (limestone, phosphate rock) are available in sufficient quantities to serve as the basis for further expansion of modern industry (cement, fertilizer, glass). Although iron ore deposits are being exploited by the steel works at Helwan, the quality of the ore is low, and exploitation, even of the best deposits in the western desert, is hardly economical. Otherwise, oil is the only mineral resource of real importance. The oil industry has expanded rapidly since the 1950s, and the country is self-sufficient in most oil products. New oil finds along the Libyan frontier and in the Red Sea and gas finds in the Delta give good promise for further expansion of crude oil production and the petrochemical industry and of net exports on a modest scale; but so far there is nothing to indicate that the oil will be an economic miracle similar to that in Libya, although the possibility must be kept in mind. Thus nature has not given Egypt any short cuts to development; the country will have to follow the long, narrow road of building up the productive capacity of the people through increasing their skills and equipment.

Egypt has the same "advantage" of all other underdeveloped countries in lagging behind the highly developed countries, thus having the opportunity to achieve rapid growth through simple imitation. It might be argued that the relative abundance of engineers and other educated workers in production and administration would help Egypt to catch up relatively quickly. As mentioned pre-

---

[21] A qualification is needed unless growth is measured in terms of GDP. If it is measured in terms of GNP or national income, the terms of trade and net factor payments abroad may modify the growth rate. And even when growth is measured in terms of GDP, we encounter the problem of the weights (prices) used in making constant price estimates. This problem is far from trivial in Egypt, where price relations are highly distorted through government intervention.

viously, however, the exodus of skilled, energetic people, which is beginning to take on serious proportions, may wipe out this advantage. Moreover, rapid catch-up is probably conditioned also by the existence of relevant skills in the lower echelons, and here Egypt has no particular advantage over many other underdeveloped countries. Similar arguments apply to the existence of unused capacity in industry; unused capacity may be a symptom of underdevelopment itself and is not necessarily a source of easy progress, even temporarily. In summary, it is difficult to point to any particular physical circumstances that should make it easy for Egypt to obtain and keep a high rate of growth as compared with other underdeveloped countries.

The Growth Rate in Retrospect

In order to gauge more precisely the physical growth capacity of Egypt and its ability to take advantage of given physical possibilities, a look at past performance will be helpful. The highest average growth rate actually sustained for a prolonged period may be taken as a lower limit for physical growth possibilities, unless particularly favorable conditions that no longer exist then prevailed. If special obstacles in the past can be removed, the actual limit for growth would be correspondingly higher.

The period chosen for finding limits to growth in this way is somewhat arbitrary. It seems natural to relate it to the phases of modern economic development in Egypt. However, development phases may be defined in many different ways. The revolution of 1952, although politically important, had few immediate consequences for economic development; the land reform had impact mainly on the distribution of wealth and income and was more a social than an economic reform. The withdrawal of the British had limited immediate economic implications.

A more relevant interpretation of the modern economic history of Egypt is to divide it into a preindustrialization phase extending from the middle of the last century to 1930, concentrating on agriculture (cotton); a second phase from 1930 to 1956,[22] with industrialization beginning on private initiative but with substantial government support through the erection of tariff barriers, import controls, subsidies, and so on; and a third phase from 1957 (after the Suez War), with active and growing government participation, control, and initiative in both investments and current production. In terms of growth rates, there was little difference between the first two phases. Total GDP increased somewhat faster between 1930 and 1956 than earlier, but so did population and labor force, and production per capita was probably only about 10 percent higher in 1956 than in 1930. From 1957 until 1965, on the other hand, per capita production increased steadily by about 3 percent per year. It is to this period, therefore, that

---

[22] The year 1930 is selected as the line of demarcation between these two phases not only because it was the first year of the great agricultural world crisis but also because it was the year when Egypt obtained tariff autonomy.

32

we direct attention to find limits for the growth rate; relatively high growth rates were obtained also at the end of the 1940s, but they were clearly related to the postwar recovery and the Korean boom, from which Egypt profited greatly.

We have good reason for selecting the years 1960/61–1964/65 for finding limits to the physical growth capacity of the country.[23] These were the years of the first five-year plan, when the government concentrated harder and more systematically on development and growth. The average rate of growth of total GDP for these years may have been about 5.5 percent.[24] During the 3 years preceding the first five-year plan, 1957–1959/60, the growth rate was a little higher, but here recovery from both the post-Korean boom slack and the Suez War played a role. Against this background, it does not seem unreasonable to assume that the economy should be able to grow by 6 percent per year over a prolonged period. During the last 2 years of the first five-year plan period, growth may already have been somewhat hampered by the Yemen War and the mounting foreign exchange difficulties. Crop conditions were relatively normal at the beginning and the end of the period, and the serious cotton crop failure in 1961 was followed by bumper crops the next year.

In one respect the assumption of 6 percent growth in the future is even stronger than appears from the simple comparison with the 5.5 percent rate from 1960 to 1965. The 5.5 percent rate was based on an almost 3 percent increase of labor input[25] and a 2.5 percent annual increase in labor productivity.

[23] Throughout this paper, the notation 1960/61, etc., indicates the fiscal year 1 July 1960 to 30 June 1961, etc.

[24] The official estimates, as published in *Statistical Indicators for the U.A.R. 1952–1965,* Cairo, 1966, show an average growth rate of 6.7 percent. The official fixed price estimates of GDP suffer, however, from certain deficiencies. After correction of these deficiencies a figure of 5.5–6 percent appears. See Hansen, "Planning and Economic Growth in the U.A.R. (Egypt) 1960–1965," in P. J. Vatikiotis, ed., *Egypt since the Revolution,* Studies on Modern Asia and Africa, No. 7, Allen and Unwin, London, 1968. One of the deficiencies (for the construction sector) was later corrected by the Ministry of Planning itself, and this correction alone brings the growth rate down to 6.0 percent. A reweighting of GDP at shadow prices would probably pull down the average growth rate further, because the rapidly growing industry sector is overpriced and the slow-growth housing sector is underpriced. The estimate of 5.5 percent therefore seems fair for these years.

[25] The official employment estimate *(Statistical Handbook, U.A.R., 1952–1966,* p. 221) shows an increase of total employment by 4.1 percent per annum, from 1959/60 to 1964/65. This estimate grossly exaggerates the employment increase in agriculture around 1960 (Hansen, "Planning and Economic Growth in the U.A.R."). Moreover, deductions have to be made for shorter working hours in larger enterprises. It underestimates, on the other hand, the absolute level of employment because "disguised" unemployment has been deducted in agriculture, industry, and certain services (not government). It is not clear how disguised unemployment has been estimated, nor is it known whether a constant percentage deduction has been applied (otherwise the rates of increase will be affected). In identifying the

If, as mentioned, an increase in the labor force of 2.6 percent per year is assumed for the period 1965/66–1980, the rate of increase of labor productivity has to reach almost 3.5 percent in order to make the 6 percent growth rate of GDP possible. By comparison with the actual development during the first five-year plan period, I thus assume that it will be possible to speed up the productivity increase by about one-third.

My 6 percent assumption thus appears quite optimistic. An argument against it might be that it was exactly in productivity increase that the first five-year plan failed. It had called for 7 percent growth of GDP at 3.2 percent annual increase of employment and, implicitly, almost 4 percent increase in labor productivity.[26] The actual productivity increase, however, was about 2.5 percent. The assumption that 3.5 percent annual increase in labor productivity—more modest than that of the first five-year plan but exceeding actual achievement—should be possible rests mainly on the fact that economic planning and policy were far from perfect during this period and in certain respects had detrimental effects on efficiency and labor productivity. It does not seem feasible to accomplish the necessary productivity increase simply by pouring more capital into production (this would require unrealistically high investment ratios in the future), but I shall argue in Section V that more nearly ideal, but still fully realistic, policies would lead to the necessary improvements in efficiency and labor productivity.

Sectoral Developments

Egypt is no longer a predominantly agricultural economy. It is true that in 1964/65, the base year for this projection, agriculture still employed somewhat more than half of the gainfully employed working force, and was responsible for more than half the foreign exchange earnings of the country. But its importance in both of these respects has been declining over the last decades; and, in terms of value added, agriculture is now only slightly larger than industry. (The distribution of value added in 1964/65 is shown in Table 2-2, column 2.) Twenty-eight percent of GDP was then produced in agriculture, against 24 percent in industry (including extraction, electricity, and public utilities). Industry includes, however, handicraft and small-scale industries; what might be called modern industry produced hardly more than 15 percent of GDP. Transport and communications constitutes a relatively large sector (9 percent of GDP); it includes the Suez Canal, which accounted for more than one-third of the value added in this sector. Housing appears remarkably unimportant, partly because only houses in

---

increase in labor input with the increase in labor force (as estimated by Salib et al., "Prospected Employment Growth by Occupational Categories in the U.A.R., 1970–1985"), we assume that shortening working hours has been offset by a fall in open unemployment. This assumption is debatable, of course.

[26] *General Frame of the 5-Year Plan for Economic and Social Development;* Hansen, "Planning and Economic Growth in the U.A.R.," p. 31.

cities and towns are included, and partly because rents are controlled and have for a long time been kept at a low level. In general, the value-added distribution is distorted by the government's price policies; they tend to exaggerate the importance of industry and keep down the contribution of housing. Otherwise it is the large size of other services, including the government sector (administration and defense), that dominates the picture; government accounts for a substantial part of the value added in the other services.

The distribution of value added in 1964/65 within the industry sector is not known.[27] In 1959/60 no less than 28 percent of total industrial value added was produced by the food, beverage, and tobacco industries (including such things as butchers and bakers); 17 percent by the textile industry (spinning and weaving); 13 percent by the oil and petroleum industries (including extraction); and 5 percent by the chemical industry (including cement and fertilizer), just to mention the four largest industries. The remaining 37 percent was produced by miscellaneous industries, particularly electricity, clothing and shoes, printing and publishing, and metals and machinery.

The expansion by about 50 percent of industrial value added (at constant prices) from 1959/60 to 1964/65 has probably somewhat reduced the dominance of food and textiles industries. Oil production and electricity output more than doubled, and old industries such as fertilizer and paper increased markedly. A number of new industries were created (rubber and plastics and pharmaceutical industries, for instance), and the production of consumer durable goods was initiated. The production of iron and steel increased until 1964, when a peak of about 400,000 tons was reached; since then, production has declined somewhat.

Until the end of the 1950s, industry was begun mainly in fields where the country had some natural advantage (because of high transport costs elsewhere or the availability of cheap raw materials in Egypt). With the Industrialization Plan of 1957 and the first five-year plan of 1960, however, the government also started many new industries for which the country had no special advantages apart from the existence of a domestic market. Some of these have been successful. Others (car production, shipbuilding) have been failures, however, wasting large amounts of capital; the steel industry must also be considered a wasteful undertaking. A special role in industrial development is played by the military factories attached to the Ministry of Defence, which produce mainly for the armed forces. Relatively little is known about them. Contrary to many of the civil industries, they have aimed at producing high-quality products; technically they are relatively advanced and employ comparatively skilled people. Some of them have complementary civil production programs (submachine guns are counterbalanced by sewing machines, for instance).

Even disregarding electricity, with a growth rate of 18 percent, industry was not the most rapidly expanding sector during the years of the first five-year

---

[27] Official publications show only current price data for the breakdown of industrial output, excluding so-called government and military factories, etc. See *Statistical Handbook, U.A.R., 1952–1966*, p. 14.

plan. The next highest growth rate, 11.1 percent, occurred in transport and communication, partly because of the vigorous expansion of Suez Canal traffic. Construction followed closely at 10.4 percent, and industry came next with 8.5 percent.[28] In general, what could be called the modern sectors show the highest growth rates. Compared with that of most other underdeveloped countries, Egypt's growth rate in agriculture, 3.3 percent, was quite high, particularly in view of the difficulties in expanding the crop area in Egypt. But the most remarkable feature is the relatively high rate of expansion in the "other services" sector. Here government activities were responsible for all the growth. The government sector not only is large, but also has expanded rapidly. This was entirely contrary to the original expectations of the first five-year plan and constitutes probably the most serious problem in the development of the Egyptian economy. Many of the problems that the Egyptian economy has encountered since the beginning of the 1960s can be related to the overexpansion of government administration and defense.

Mechanical Projections

Projections of future sectoral developments require additional assumptions. One method would be to assume that the sectoral growth rates actually achieved during the first five-year plan period will prevail from 1964/65 to 1980. These growth rates have been discussed, and the figures are shown in Table 2-2, column 1. Another method is to apply to our projected income and population the elasticities of production per capita income and total population.[29] In this way the projections of Table 2-2 are estimated.[30]

[28] The growth figures in Table 2-2, column 1, are from Hansen, "Planning and Economic Growth in the U.A.R.," p. 31. They do not correspond to the official figures for all sectors. The growth rates of the construction and "other services" sectors had to be estimated by various indirect evidence, the official figures for these sectors being entirely unacceptable; see also footnote 39.

[29] This method of mechanical long-term sectoral projection was suggested by H. B. Chenery, "Patterns of Industrial Growth," *American Economic Review*, Vol. 50, No. 4 (September 1960), and has been applied by the United Nations in *A Study of Industrial Growth*, United Nations Division of Industrial Development, New York, 1962. The basic relationship postulated by this method is

$$v_i = \alpha_i y^{\beta_i} N^{\gamma_i} ,$$

where v denotes value added per capita, y income per capita, and N total population, and i indicates the sector.

[30] With some slight modification I have used the elasticities suggested by Hans Linnemann in a similar study, *The Long-run Development of Different Sectors of the U.A.R. Economy*, Institute of National Planning, Memo. No. 285, Cairo, April 1963. Linnemann's elasticities were based on international intercountry studies, modified in various respects to apply to Egypt. For finance and trade, housing, and other services the same elasticities have been applied. This is not very satisfactory, but separate elasticities were not available.

Table 2-2

Sectoral Developments

Sector	Actual Annual Growth Rates, 1959/60-1964/65[a] (percent) (1)	Value Added at Constant 1964/65 Prices				Projected Annual Growth Rates, 1964/65-1980 (percent) (6)
		Actual 1964/65[b]		Projected 1980		
		(million E£) (2)	(percent) (3)	(million E£) (4)	(percent) (5)	
Agriculture	3.3	528	28.0	913	19.6	3.7
Industry	8.5	423	22.5	1451	31.1	8.5
Electricity and public utilities	18.0	31	1.6	100	2.2	8.0
Construction	10.4	92	4.9	273	5.9	7.4
Transport and communications	11.1	174	9.2	476	10.2	6.9
Finance and trade	3.3	169	9.0	385	8.3	5.6
Housing	1.9	79	4.2	180	3.9	5.6
Other services	4.1	388	20.6	885	19.0	5.6
Total	5.5	1884	100.0	4663	100.0	6.0

[a]Bent Hansen, "Planning and Economic Growth in the U.A.R. (Egypt) 1960-1965," p. 31, Table 8.
[b]Statistical Handbook, U.A.R. 1952-1966, p. 215.

The projections in columns 4 and 6 thus show the sectoral distribution for 1980 and the sectoral growth rates for 1964/65–1980 that will be achieved if Egypt generally follows the world pattern, given the assumed rates of population and per capita income growth.

For the two largest sectors, agriculture and industry, the projected growth rates almost coincide with the growth rates actually obtained in 1959/60–1964/65, which does not imply that either is optimal. The projected rates in the other sectors deviate significantly from those attained in 1959/60–1964/65. This is not necessarily an optimal pattern for Egypt. Nevertheless, these projections, together with the actual growth rates for the first five-year plan period, may be useful for the discussion of the optimal sectoral developments. I shall discuss first some specific factors that *predetermine* the sector developments to some degree. We are left then with the problem of *optimal* sectoral distribution, which will be discussed in some detail. For national sectors, that is, sectors with no direct competition through foreign trade, where exports and imports for all practical purposes are impossible, the mechanical projections will presumably lead to reasonable results, since demand elasticities for broad classes of goods seem to be similar in various countries on the same income level. But special conditions (in both demand and supply) may make a country deviate from the world average, even for these sectors. The greatest problem is with the international sectors, that is, those whose products may be exported and imported: agriculture, industry, and the Suez Canal. To the extent that its basic conditions and potentials differ from the world average, Egypt will have an opportunity to choose a sectoral development pattern different from the world average. It may not be possible to quantify the optimal sector developments, but it may be possible to indicate the optimal direction of deviation from the world average.

Predetermined Developments

Actual sectoral growth rates for 1964/65–1980 (whether optimal or not) may to some extent be predetermined by earlier decisions and investment projects in process, the High Dam at Aswan being the most important example. The High Dam will influence both agricultural and industrial developments, the latter through increased supply of electricity. Almost all the benefits from this project will appear after 1964/65, although about half the investment costs were made before 1965/66. The generators at the High Dam are planned to produce about 10 billion kilowatt-hours per year (the first generator was started in 1967, and maximum production may be obtained in 1970), compared with an output of 5.2 billion kilowatt-hours in 1964/65.[31] Evaluated at 1964/65 prices, this would imply an increase in the value of electricity production from E£ 39.1 million in

---

[31] Another problem is whether the country will be able to increase the use of electricity to such an extent so suddenly. There are also misgivings about the quality of the equipment delivered from the Soviet Union; too frequent breakdowns may lead to a lower level of production.

1964/65 to about E£115 million in 1980. It is difficult to estimate value added in the future electricity output from the High Dam (partly because of joint costs), but the value added per Egyptian pound of output will be much greater than in the existing thermal power plants. It would seem, therefore, that the High Dam electricity alone will be able to increase the electricity and public utilities sector as projected in Table 2-2.[32] Although some old power plants are likely to be closed as the output from the High Dam increases, public utility production must expand somewhat, and other electricity projects are contemplated (at the Nile barrages and elsewhere). It is already clear that electricity and public utilities will grow by the rate projected in Table 2-2, whether optimal or not. It seems unlikely, however, that they will grow much faster.

Available estimates of the agricultural benefits of the High Dam vary somewhat. Recent official estimates state that 1.3 million feddan will be reclaimed so as to increase the cultivated area by about 20 percent, while 0.7 million feddan will be converted from basin to perennial irrigation with at least two crops per year instead of one.[33] The number of crops per year on the reclaimed areas is not known, and the fertility of these areas remains to be seen. If they yield only one crop per year, the total crop area would increase by about 20 percent.[34] Since a shift to more profitable crops (rice in particular) will be possible, it does not seem overoptimistic to expect an increase of agricultural output by some 20 percent, that is, about E£150 million, with a similar percentage increase of value added, namely, about E£100 million (at 1964/65 prices), as a result of the High Dam.[35] This would by itself contribute 1.2 percentage points to the annual growth rate of agriculture to 1980, and thus make probable a higher growth rate in this sector than was actually obtained from 1959/60 to 1964/65.

The transport and communications sector includes the Suez Canal, which in 1964/65 accounted for more than one-third of the sector's value added. The high growth rate obtained from 1959/60 to 1964/65, 11.2 percent, was due equally to Suez Canal and to other traffic. Prospects for the canal traffic are rather bleak, even on the assumption that the canal will be opened soon. Apart from the present closure and its effects, the tendency toward shipping oil in supertankers that

[32] Value added for 1980 is here evaluated at 1964/65 prices. This is not to deny that in 1980 electricity may have become relatively cheaper (in terms of shadow prices, at least) and that the contribution of electricity to growth estimated at 1980 prices thus may become much lower. However, this is a general index problem, which in principle applies to all sectors. I shall not deal with it here.

[33] *Statistical Handbook, U.A.R., 1952–1966*, pp. 247f.

[34] Surveys by the FAO point to a smaller increase in the reclamation possibilities. On the other hand, it seems unlikely that none of the reclaimed areas would give more than one crop per year.

[35] The decrease in the silt content of the irrigation water will necessitate a relatively strong increase in the input of fertilizers. The costs of this may not exceed E£10 million, but there are considerable differences of opinion as to the size of this cost factor.

cannot pass through the canal without a deepening of the present draught of 38 feet will certainly slow down the growth of canal revenues. What is more uncertain is whether Middle East oil will decline in importance for Europe.

Several alternatives are open, depending on the investments made to deepen the canal.[36] By deepening it to 60 feet, even larger supertankers could pass through loaded. In this case it would perhaps not be unduly optimistic to expect a 7–8 percent growth per year of canal revenues. But this alternative would probably require an investment of E£400–500 million. By deepening the canal to 42 feet, supertankers in ballast would be able to pass through on the way from Europe to the Persian Gulf.

In 1960 the canal authorities presented a five-year plan for deepening the canal to 48 feet. As an extreme case, one might imagine that all oil is shipped around the Cape of Good Hope in supertankers, all of which return unloaded through the canal. The nonoil traffic would continue as usual through the Canal. The share of nonoil traffic in 1964/65 was about 20 percent in terms of annual income. Since the toll rates are lower for ships in ballast than for loaded ships, the income from oil tankers would fall by about two-thirds. Total canal revenue would thus fall to about 45 percent of the actual revenue in 1964/65. If the continuation of this proportion in the future and a growth rate of the traffic by 10 percent are assumed, canal revenues would rise (after an initial fall) to E£162 million in 1980 from the actual E£82 million in 1964/65. The canal would still be a substantial factor in the Egyptian economy, although with a smaller relative importance. The investment costs in this alternative are estimated at about E£100 million, which would seem a sound economic proposition. An additional benefit would accrue from the planned pipeline from Suez to the Mediterranean; this would involve further investments, however, and the net profits are rather uncertain, depending on negotiations with the oil companies.[37] The problem is whether one can rely on the continuation of past growth rates. With a declining proportional dependence of Western Europe on Middle East oil, caused not so much by competition from North African oil as by a possible shift away from consumption of "dirty," sulphur-rich oil like that of the Middle East, the growth rates of oil traffic from the Persian Gulf to Europe may become smaller. Even with stagnating canal revenues between 1964/65 and 1980,[38] the transport and communications sector would still show an annual increase of 7.5 percent, assuming domestic transport to keep the same very

[36] See *Maritime Transport 1967,* OECD, Paris, 1968; *The Times (London),* Business Review, July 31, 1968, p. 21. See also Ragaei El Malakh, *Economic Development and Regional Cooperation: Kuwait,* University of Chicago Press, Chicago, 1968, pp. 174 ff., 199.

[37] Some contracts seem already to have been made with oil companies. The Israeli pipeline is not thought to be serious competition for purely political reasons. Oil companies will presumably prefer to be on good terms with the oil-producing Arabs rather than to please Israel.

[38] Assuming an initial fall followed by a slow increase.

high growth rate of 11.0 percent as in 1959/60–1964/65. This is perhaps less likely, but if some increase in canal revenues is assumed, the projected growth rate of 6.9 percent for transport and communications does not seem unrealistic. It is out of the question that a growth rate similar to that of 1960/61–1964/65 can be attained.

Within the industry sector also, certain developments seem predetermined. It might be thought that the use of electricity from the High Dam had been planned carefully and that this would have become decisive for the industrial development pattern. Such does not seem to be the case, however. The planning for the use of the High Dam electricity should presumably have been integrated into the second five-year plan, which (for political reasons) was never made; the so-called Accomplishment Plan covering the years 1967/68 and 1969/70 mainly includes projects already decided on. It would seem, however, that some very capital-intensive industries (fertilizers, aluminum) will be expanded, partly on this basis.

Two other developments exert opposing influences. Oil finds in the western desert and the Red Sea and gas finds in the Delta promise a substantial expansion of the oil and petrochemical industries. Though capital-intensive, the extraction industry has a low capital-output ratio. If successful, this industry will give much value added "for nothing." Some of what will be gained by this industry may, however, be wasted on the steel project announced in 1968, which is a large extension of the existing steel industry at Helwan. Production is to be based on ore deposits in oases in the western desert. Although this ore is better than the Aswan ore currently used, production costs are expected to be substantially above present international steel prices. The project, to be financed and constructed by the Soviet Union, will take place in two stages, the first of which should make Egypt self-sufficient in steel by about 1975. Total investments, for both stages, are estimated to be about E £ 400 million.

Optimal Sector Development

As already pointed out, neither the actual sectoral growth rates during the first five-year plan period, 1960/61–1964/65, nor those projected or predetermined are necessarily optimal for the future. It is difficult to discuss optimal patterns on aggregates as large as the sectors considered in Table 2-2. But I shall make an attempt that distinguishes between "national" sectors, where (practically speaking) exports and imports cannot take place, and "international" sectors, where competitiveness in foreign trade is the basic problem.

An optimal sectoral development plan for the national sectors should, in principle, plan for satisfying domestic demand at the expected growth of population and disposable income (in the case of consumer goods), or production (in the case of intermediary goods), or investment (in the case of capital goods), and at the expected price developments. The prices, in turn, are dependent on demand and supply conditions. In this way we may appraise the sectoral growth rates of Table 2-2, columns 2 and 6, for at least the construction, domestic

41

transport, trade and finance, and housing sectors. Government is a somewhat different case.

Construction activities are closely related to the volume of gross investment. Later I shall argue that the ratio of gross investment to GDP probably will have to increase substantially from below 20 to about 26 percent during the period 1965/66–1980. If value added were a fixed proportion of the value of output of construction, and output of construction were a fixed percentage of gross invest-nent, a 6 percent growth of GDP would imply a growth rate of 8.5–9 percent for value added in construction. The projected rate of 7.4 percent is somewhat lower; the actual rate for 1960/61–1964/65 was correspondingly above.[39] The need for construction output depends also on the government's policy toward residential building activity. The higher the share of residential building in gross investment, the larger will be the share of construction in gross investment. I shall argue later that the optimal growth of housing is somewhat higher than the actual rate achieved from 1960/61 to 1964/65. It follows that the share of con-struction in gross investments will have to increase, and this points to an even higher growth rate of construction than the 8.5–9 percent mentioned above. For this sector, the projections in Table 2-2, column 6, are too low.

I have already discussed the communications and transport sector, whose growth rate is highly dependent on the future of the Suez Canal; domestic traffic is closely related to production and consumption, and a considerably lower growth rate for the sector than that occurring during the years 1960/61–1964/65 seems likely. Finance and trade can be assumed to change in proportion to the general growth rate; the Egyptian economy is already highly monetized and commercialized. The projected rate of 5.6 percent for trade and finance is close to the general rate of growth of 6 percent, and the rate obtained for 1960/61–1964/65 may have been underestimated.[40]

For housing we find a large discrepancy between projected rate, 5.6 per-cent, and actual rate for 1960/61–1964/65, 1.9 percent, which is worth some de-tailed comments. In terms of demand, we should expect housing to increase by at least 2.5 percent per year; population is assumed to rise by 2.5 percent, and

[39] Construction is probably the weakest point in the value-added estimates for Egypt. The actual growth rate figure of 10.4 percent for 1960/61–1964/65 was estimated on the basis of rather shaky employment figures (Hansen, "Planning and Economic Growth in the U.A.R.") and may exaggerate the rate of growth in consruction. Estimates of the consumption of cement and other materials by Naiem El Sherbini, "A Study of the Foreign Exchange Restraint in Development Planning: The Case of Egypt," unpublished Ph.D. thesis, University of California, Berkeley, 1969, indicate a somewhat lower actual rate of growth of 7–8 percent. However, the High Dam itself and related canal works may have lowered the average cement content in construction output; the High Dam is a rock-fill dam which has required little cement in relation to its size.

[40] Value-added increase in trade and finance is estimated on the basis of employment statistics and is therefore probably downward biased.

the number of families may be assumed to increase at about the same rate. In addition, personal disposable income per family will increase somewhat, perhaps about 3.5 percent per year (see Section IV), and continued urbanization may itself raise the demand for housing.[41] Against this background, an annual increase of about 5 percent does not seem exaggerated. The actual low rate of increase for 1960/61–1964/65 was the outcome of deliberate government policies to keep residential building activity below demand through both licensing and credit restrictions. The argument for doing so was the high capital-output ratio in housing, which promised little value added per unit of investments. This argument—well known from other underdeveloped countries—is not convincing. It is true that demand has been kept at a level substantially above the existing supply of housing, thanks to the government's rent controls and subsequent low level of rents.[42] Rents for old apartments have remained almost unchanged since 1939, and rents on apartments in new houses have been calculated and fixed on the basis of costs, including interest on capital, which has been much lower than what would correspond to the social scarcity price of capital. The planners were right in maintaining that they should not try to catch up with demand at this artificially low level of rents. If rents were fixed at a level that would wipe out the present excess demand for housing, and in the future rents for new houses were fixed in line with costs at the scarcity price of capital, the present excess demand would disappear. In this sense, the need for an increase in the supply of housing would be diminished once and for all. But henceforth the annual percentage increase in demand for housing would presumably be about the same.[43] The projected 5.6 percent growth of housing seems much closer to the optimum than the 1.0 percent achieved during the years 1960/61–1964/65.

If the consumers of housing are charged the full scarcity price of capital,[44]

[41] The mud-brick dwellings of villagers are kept outside both official value-added and investment statistics.

[42] A cut in the building taxes in the 1960s worked in the same direction.

[43] It may be argued that the rate of urbanization would be hampered by the higher level of rents in the cities and that this might help to keep down the future rate of growth of demand for housing.

[44] By the "full scarcity price" of capital I mean the social opportunity costs of using capital, which may differ from existing market loan rates. In underdeveloped countries with private credit institutions (incidentally, the same usually holds true where credit institutions are nationalized), loan rates to housing are usually much lower than those to industrial investments. This interest differential is related to the higher risks in industrial activities in such countries. However, if the government plans for industrial expansion, and the plan is sound, industrial investments undertaken within the plan should not necessarily be more risky than investments in housing. There would thus be no "social risk" differential, although private lenders and credit institutions might continue to believe that there was. The problem is complicated, however, by the possibility that the government may attach special social importance to housing, which may result in loans to housing at lower rates than to other investment activities. The differential in the market loan rates may

and supply is adjusted to demand on that basis, the high capital-output ratio (which, incidentally, will no longer be as high) is irrelevant for determining the optimum rate of residential building. Let it be added that the necessary rent increase for existing apartments can be accomplished through raising the tax on rents (the so-called buildings tax), and need not lead to an increase of income for owners of buildings. With the nationalized credit institutions in the hands of the public, the higher interest charges for housing loans need not lead to an increase in private income from capital either. I shall return to this point in Section IV, because taxation on rent of both land and buildings seems to be a feasible method of increasing government revenue and bringing demand and supply into equilibrium in the economy.

The output of the electricity and public utilities is used partly for industrial purposes, partly for private consumption. The first problem here is how the predetermined increase from the High Dam should be used. As already pointed out, this has not been planned in detail, but the big issue—whether the accent should be on electricity-intensive new industries (such as fertilizer and aluminum) or on electrification of the villages—has already been settled in favor of heavy industry, although the case for village electrification is quite strong. From a social point of view, village electrification would be most valuable and could create the basis for small-scale village industry that would help to utilize rural labor during the slack seasons and to create local mechanical activities, which are a necessary prerequisite for later mechanization in agriculture. The problem is whether, for this or other reasons, an expansion of electricity and public utilities greater than the 8 percent projected in Table 2-2, column 6, and consistent with the given output from the High Dam would be justified. Any answer to this question should take into account that after completion of the High Dam, Egypt has very few remaining natural advantages in electricity production. Further expansion will have to be based mainly on thermal power plants using local supplies of fuel (from the oil industry), and producing at much higher costs than the High Dam plant. It would take a detailed discussion of future industrial development to settle this question; but, given the probably inoptimal decision of using High Dam electricity mainly for large-scale industry, village electrification may itself motivate a stronger expansion than 8 percent per year.

Of the national sectors, we are left with the other services sector. What interests us here is government, for which optimal size and growth rate, literally speaking, are a matter of taste. The actual growth rate for other services in 1960/61–1964/65 was a little lower, 4.1 percent, than the rate projected, 5.6 percent. This looks a bit odd. It points against a more rapid growth of the government sector, which all observers agree has expanded excessively in the past. We do not have a breakdown of the other services sector for government and the

---

thus (albeit for the wrong reasons) point in the right direction. But in that case the government should, of course, aim at satisfying the demand at the low rents, irrespective of the capital-output ratio.

rest, but available employment figures indicate that in 1960 government accounted for about 80 percent of the total employment in the sector.[45] Since the average government employee salary probably is somewhat lower than the average for professionals and others in other services, the government's share of value added for the sector may be between one-half and two-thirds.[46] Government must thus have grown considerably more than the average 4.1 percent for the sector; if the rest of the sector has been stagnant, government must actually have grown by 8 percent per year. The sector does contain some stagnant or even declining services (such as household services), although the services of professionals must have shown some increase. It should also be recalled that in 1960 the contribution of the government sector to GDP was rather high as measured by international standards. A more adequate indicator of the excessive growth of government employment is that of a total increase in employment in the country from 1959/60 to 1964/65 of close to one million persons, about one-quarter was in other services, presumably mainly in government.[47]

The future size and development of the government sector are related to two basic policy issues. The first one is the question of the role of the government in the economy in general. Section IV argues that, given the present institutional setup with respect to ownership, great economies can be obtained in civil government employment (and general efficiency outside government) through a better overall and partial balance between demand and supply in the economy, and through greater decentralization in both production and investment decisions, quite apart from the possibility of the existence and reduction of disguised unemployment in the government sector.

Even more basic and intricate is the second issue; the question of the future of the country's defense expenditures. Here everything depends on the future political relations in the Middle East. In several countries of this region defense expenditures have been running at exorbitant levels. In Egypt they seem to have reached a pre-June 1967 maximum of 10–11 percent of GNP in 1965/66 during the third year of the Yemen War. Under optimistic assumptions, defense expenditures can probably return to the 5 percent level of GNP, where they were from the beginning of the 1950s until the start of the Yemen War. This happens also to be the approximate level of defense expenditures in certain other neutral-

[45] See Don Mead, *Growth and Structural Change in the Egyptian Economy,* Richard D. Irwin, Homewood, Ill., 1967, p. 134; *Statistical Handbook, U.A.R., 1952–1966,* p. 215.
[46] Public consumption is estimated to have been about 17 percent of GNP in 1960/61; see Table 2-4, column 7. By the mid-1950s the share of wages and salaries in public consumption was about two-thirds. The share of government value added in total GDP should thus be about 11–12 percent in 1960/61. The share in GDP of value added in other services in 1960/61 was 21 percent.
[47] *Statistical Handbook, U.A.R., 1952–1966,* p. 221, shows an increase of employment by 1.327 thousand persons. However, the estimate for employment in agriculture between 1959/60 and 1960/61 is clearly exaggerated. For details see Hansen, "Planning and Economic Growth in the U.A.R."

ist countries that are not confronted with any direct threats or conflicts. What this reduction would mean in value added and manpower transfer from the government sector is uncertain. In 1960, defense employed 226,000 persons, and this number must have increased substantially since then.[48] Perhaps some 150,000 persons (mainly young males), corresponding to about 2 percent of the total labor force, could be transferred to other sectors from defense alone. To this number we have to add what could be carried over from civil administration through the above-mentioned rationalizations of economic policy. Thereafter, even if it would be optimal for the government sector to grow by the same 6 percent as GDP, the annual absorption of manpower by the government would diminish somewhat (as compared with the previous period) and would allow more growth in other sectors. Whether the transfer of labor would imply gains in value added (as conventionally measured) is more uncertain.[49]

Our discussion of *national* sector developments thus leads to the conclusion that the projected growth rates in Table 2-2, column 6, come closer to what may be considered optimal than the actual growth rates obtained during the first five-year plan period. In relation to the projected rates, however, I found reason to expect faster increase of construction and a probably slower increase of government.[50] In relation to the actual growth rates obtained in the past, the optimal pattern implies a faster increase of housing and a slower increase of government. In terms of employment, the down-scaling of government employment, particularly defense, could easily provide construction with manpower for its faster expansion.

In regard to the international sectors, we have already discussed the Suez Canal in some detail. Under favorable international conditions it is clear that substantial investments are motivated and are even needed in order to prevent the canal revenues from declining. From an employment point of view, the canal is not very important.

The biggest international sector is agriculture. Its actual growth rate in 1960/61–1964/65 was 3.3 percent. The projected rate is 3.7 percent. The *Indicative World Plan* of the FAO works with an increase of only 3.0 percent for the period 1965–1975, which seems unduly pessimistic.[51] In addition to benefits from the High Dam, substantial gains can be realized through improved drainage and (to a smaller extent) more efficient irrigation, increased use of chemicals (fertilizers, pesticides, etc.), improved cereal seed varieties, and a change in the composition of crops toward more profitable crops (particularly vegetables and fruits in case the European markets will be available for Egyptian agricultural products). Thus it seems to be more reasonable for Egypt to aim at an an-

[48] Mead, *Growth and Structural Change in the Egyptian Economy*, p. 134.
[49] See footnote 20.
[50] Considering both the immediate reduction of the government sector and its future growth.
[51] FAO, *Indicative World Plan for Agricultural Development, 1965–85, Near East*, Subregional Study No. 1, CCP 67/16, Vols. I and II, 3 January 1966, Vol. II, p. 8.

nual increase of at least 4 percent of agricultural production. This would imply an increase of value added by about 3.5 percent annually (see below). Some capital investment will be needed for this purpose, but in order to reach such a high rate of growth the stress must obviously be on efficiency and productivity of available resources and improved technology, rather than on massive injections of capital. The solution of the balance of payments problem is closely related to the growth rate in agriculture; for this reason, the government should aim for agricultural growth more than for anything else.

Industry is so heterogeneous that it is difficult to discuss its future growth rate on an aggregate basis. Two extreme cases can be disposed of quickly. A few branches of industry are for all practical purposes "national"; they include certain traditional food industries and repair shops. Such industries should not be expected to develop at a very high rate, and they are not unimportant. At the other extreme, the growth of industry depends entirely on new oil finds and thus does not lend itself easily to prediction. Oil production is a "natural advantage" industry which, of course, should expand as fast as possible, but what is "possible" is not quite clear. An expansion in the production of crude oil of about 30 million tons per year is expected within the next few years. For the period until 1980 this might amount to a 1–2 percent growth of industry as a whole.

It is remarkable that certain other "natural advantage" industries—after 35 years of industrialization, one industrialization plan, and one comprehensive five-year plan—still have not been expanded to the limit of the natural advantage. Specifically, these are the cement and fertilizer industries, where domestic availability of raw materials, in combination with high transport costs, makes Egypt competitive not only within the country, but also relative to neighboring countries.[52] At the beginning of the 1960s, Egypt developed a cement export industry, particularly to other Arab countries. A rapid increase in the domestic consumption of cement, not foreseen by the five-year plan and caused partially by an acceleration of the construction of the High Dam, wiped out most of these exports. A more rapid expansion of the production capacity of the cement industry would have been appropriate even though cement exports might not be possible in the long run. The other Middle East countries have the raw materials and the fuel necessary to build competitive cement industries and have actually embarked on this undertaking. But for some time Egypt might here have had a profitable export industry; even if the exports had later shrunk, domestic demands would have caught up with the capacity created.

For the fertilizer industry, similar remarks apply; here the planners did not expand the industry sufficiently for domestic consumption to reach its optimal size; even less did they plan for exports, although the industry might have been able to compete effectively in the Middle East and Sudan, Somali, and Ethiopia (at least at more realistic exchange rates than the prevailing ones). Had these

[52] The following paragraphs are based mainly on Naiem El Sherbini, "A Study of the Foreign Exchange Restraint in Development Planning."

two industries been expanded more vigorously during the years of the first five-year plan, Egypt could have considerably improved its foreign trade position, not only because of direct export from these industries, but also because certain fertilizer imports would have been unnecessary, and a better fertilizer supply would have led to a more rapid increase of agricultural production and made some of the food imports of this period unnecessary.

Another industry has obtained a "natural" advantage through recent technological developments. Methods have been developed that permit pulp and paper production from bagasse, a by-product of domestic sugar production. Before 1960 the small Egyptian paper industry was based on imported pulp together with rice straw and other domestic raw materials. A substantial expansion in this field, sufficient even to provide a certain level of export, will be possible before this new natural advantage is exhausted.[53]

For the textile industry, everything depends on which markets are available for Egypt in the future. With the European and American markets open and unprotected, Egypt might have a good chance of supplying high-quality fabrics based on raw cotton from the famous Egyptian long-staple varieties. Although limited in comparison with the demand before synthetics appeared, there is still a market for such products in the West, from which Egypt has been virtually cut off since the Suez War. This development would require, of course, a radical change in the present textile policies of Western Europe and North America (based on the World Textiles Agreement).

Setting aside, then, the natural advantage industries, it would seem that Egypt has reached a stage in industrial development where advantages have to be created, where the country will become competitive only through self-built skill and efficiency. There is always, however, a certain advantage, in terms of transport, marketing, and other costs, in producing for the domestic market. Other things being equal, a country should therefore first develop the industries for which the domestic market is big enough to permit optimal production scales, and for which the necessary skills and efficiency are easiest to acquire. Egyptian industrial planning has sinned grossly against both of these elementary rules. Modern durable consumer goods—from TV sets to automobiles—are difficult to produce efficiently, and they need long production lines to become competitive. Nevertheless, the production of these goods was begun at a time when the country still was importing pins, nails, paper clips, and other simple products in domestic demand. Simple mass-produced consumer goods and intermediary products used as inputs by industry itself and by other sectors, particularly agriculture, will form the basis for industrialization for a long time to come, while industrial exports on a significant scale presumably will be limited to the natural advantage industries mentioned above. Even these industries may have missed

---

[53] Although pulp and paper production from bagasse seems to be competitive at a bagasse price equal to its fuel equivalent (previously bagasse was used as fuel only in the sugar industry), it is an open question whether it would also be competitive at a price calculated to make the sugar industry break even at international prices.

their chance because similar ones are rapidly developing in the Arab Middle East countries: cement everywhere, and fertilizers in particular in the Persian Gulf.

These circumstances by themselves limit the possible rate of growth of industry. Until cadres of skilled labor have been created, the country should not dream of producing machinery and equipment on any significant scale, apart, perhaps, from certain simple things, such as pumps for irrigation purposes. Since the production of intermediary goods for domestic industry cannot grow faster in the long run than industry itself (in the beginning there may, of course, still be some import substitution to take care of), the growth rate of industry will depend mainly on the growth of consumer demand for manufactured industrial products and on agricultural growth. At a rate of growth (private and public) of consumption of some 5 percent, and a strong shift of demand from food to other consumer goods (for balance of payments reasons I advocate such an economic policy in Section IV), it seems likely that consumer demands for industrial products may grow at an annual rate above the 8.5 percent projected in Table 2-2. If agricultural output increases by about 4 percent annually, inputs bought from other industries will increase at a somewhat higher rate. It is something of a "development law" that, whereas inputs of intermediary products in industry increase in proportion to output, in agriculture such inputs increase at a greater proportional rate than output.[54] This has actually happened in Egypt during this century,[55] and there is good reason to expect this tendency to prevail.[56] Unfortunately, agricultural output has fluctuated so heavily during this century (mainly in connection with the two big wars) that it is difficult to establish the long-term relationship between the rates of output growth and input growth. But it would not seem unlikely that a 4 percent increase of agricultural output will be accompanied by at least a 6 percent increase of its inputs from other industries, particularly from manufacturing industry. Finally, since some industrial output may be delivered as input to sectors with a higher growth rate (transportation, construction), the 8.5 percent growth rate projected for industry in Table 2-2, column 6, seems very reasonable indeed.

Sectoral Developments and Productivity Gains

Sector developments have a bearing on productivity developments. Even at constant labor productivity within each sector, a change in the sector distribution

[54] T. W. Schultz, *The Economic Organization of Agriculture*, McGraw-Hill, New York, 1953; S. Kuznets, "Economic Growth and the Contribution of Agriculture: Notes on Measurement," *International Journal of Agrarian Affairs*, Vol. 3 (1967); also J. W. Kendrick, *Productivity Trends in the United States*, NBER, No. 71, Princeton, N.J., 1961.

[55] See Bent Hansen, "The Distributional Shares in Egyptian Agriculture, 1895–1960," *International Economic Review*, Vol. 9, No. 2 (June 1968).

[56] See FAO, *Indicative World Plan for Agricultural Development, 1905–85, Near East*, Vol. II, p. 188.

implies a change in average productivity per employed person. Estimates show that during the first five-year plan period, 1960/61–1964/65, the productivity gain related to the change in sector distribution amounted to 1.0 percent of GDP per year. With a similar sector development for 1965/66–1980, the gains would be the same. On the basis of the projections in Table 2-2, columns 4 and 6, for 1965/66–1980, with the modifications mentioned above, the corresponding gain would be slightly lower, 0.8 percent per year. This would mean that the average sectoral productivity per worker, which in 1960/61–1964/65 rose by 1.5 percent per year (2.5 minus 1), would have to increase from 1964/65 to 1980 by 2.6 (3.4 minus 0.8). In this calculation I have not included possible transfers from other services. Part of the reason is the difficulties connected with appraising the value added by those transferred from other services (compared with Table 2-2). But in addition, as already pointed out, a transfer from government (even of simple conscripts) would not necessarily imply a transfer gain, other things being equal, in conventional national bookkeeping terms. The possibility of lower transfer gains in productivity strengthens our earlier conclusions that the critical point in future development is to increase labor productivity rapidly enough.

Transfer gains may be obtained only at some expense of capital. Higher output per worker is often conditioned by a higher capital intensity per worker and perhaps a high capital-output ratio. Unfortunately, little is known about capital intensities by sector in Egypt, and it is difficult to gauge the implication of the change in sector growth for total capital requirements. The two most conspicuous factors tend to neutralize each other. In capital-intensive electricity production, increase of production will be obtained at a relatively low additional amount of capital (because a substantial part of the investments were made before 1964/66). On the other hand, the Suez Canal may require large investments simply to prevent a fall in revenues, whereas hitherto canal revenues automatically increased with little need for investments. What a shift from other services (particularly defense) to, say, agriculture will imply for capital requirements is difficult to say. In ordinary national accounting, defense requires hardly any capital (military equipment being counted as current expenditure). In many respects, however, the acquisition of military equipment is similar to the purchase of capital goods; moreover, some of the increase in agricultural production will be attained at low capital costs (again, because substantial investments were made before 1965/66). The increased expansion of housing points clearly, however, toward increased capital requirements.

Investment Requirements

My final concern in this section is the level of investments required to bring about a 6 percent GDP growth rate. For a 6 percent growth rate to be feasible, the corresponding investments must be feasible too, both financially and physically. For the moment, I shall assume that the financial problem will be solved somehow, no matter what the level of investment, and shall concentrate on the purely physical side of the matter.

During the decade between the Suez War and the June 1967 War, Egypt succeeded in markedly increasing its investments. Measured in percentage of GNP at market prices, gross investments increased from an average level of about 14 percent in 1957/58 to almost 20 percent in 1965/66.[57] In real terms, the increase may have been somewhat less; prices for investment goods may have risen more on average than the implicit GNP deflator; but an increase by 5 percentage units during 8 years can be safely assumed. Shortages occurred during this process, not only in foreign exchange, but also in the supply of competent engineers and other skilled labor. In increasing the investment ratio so fast, Egypt strained her domestic resources to the utmost, and both investment planning and execution suffered. After 1965/66, the investment ratio fell, largely because the government started cutting back the investment appropriations in an attempt to ease the balance of payment crisis and to diminish domestic inflationary pressures. The investment ratio probably fell to about 15 percent the last year before the June 1967 War. It is interesting to note—and this has a bearing not only on the situation in Egypt, but also on the more general question of inflation and development—that the government at that time firmly believed that a smaller volume of investments in terms of costs laid down on investment projects might imply an unchanged or even larger volume of effective investments in terms of physical capital goods actually created, simply because the elimination of bottlenecks and disorganization would increase productivity in making investments.[58] Be this as it may, development during the 1960s proved that there are limits to the speed at which the ratio of investments can be increased on the basis of domestic personnel resources and that Egypt had reached this limit.

The implication of this experience is not that an investment ratio of 20 percent cannot be surpassed, but that there is a limit to how much it can be surpassed until 1980. A straightforward extrapolation from 1964/66 would lead to an upper limit of nearly 29 percent for 1980; but when the present hostilities are settled the country will have to start again from a much lower investment ratio than 20 percent (for 1967/68 it seems to have been as low as 12–13 percent), and this may make it impossible for the country to reach the 29 percent level. If in addition we take for granted that the economy should not be overstrained the

[57] In discussing the rate of gross investment, it seems adequate to start from 1957, which was the year of the first agricultural and industrialization plans, when the investment push really started. The investment ratio fluctuated somewhat during the second half of the 1950s and happened to be particularly low in the base year 1959/60 for the first five-year plan. The 14 percent used in the text is an average for the years 1956/57–1959/60. With 1959/60 included, the average is 13.8 percent; with 1959/60 excluded, it becomes 14.3 percent.

[58] Minister of the Treasury, Dr. N. Deif, in conversation with me.

way it was in 1965/66 and that foreign personnel should not be used to any larger extent than before, an investment ratio of 27–28 percent in 1980 seems the most that we can hope for.

On the basis of usual capital-output ratio analysis, everything might then be in order, and our 6 percent rate of growth might even seem low. Even at a capital-output ratio of 4.0, a growth rate of 6 percent might require only a 24 percent investment ratio if we follow a usual way of calculating; compared with the capital-output ratios ordinarily assumed, a ratio of 4.0 looks quite high. Analysis of this primitive kind is entirely unsatisfactory for our purpose, however. It does not allow explicitly for the increasing reinvestments ratio that accompanies a rise in the average capital-output ratio; it does not take into consideration limitations of labor supply and the interaction in production between labor and capital; and it does not permit a direct analysis of productivity changes. In addition, our knowledge of capital-output ratios in Egypt, particularly at the sectoral level, is so poor that there is nothing to gain from simple capital-output analysis;[59] since assumptions have to be made in any case, they can just as well be made in connection with a more adequate analytical apparatus.

I have chosen to analyze the capital and investment requirements along the same lines as used by Denison and others for the growth rates in developed countries. Capital and labor were assumed to have contributed to production during 1960/61–1964/65 in such a way that a 1.0 percent increase in the stock of capital or labor input would lead to a production increase of 0.5 percent. These elasticities of production inputs were chosen on the basis of what is known about the distribution of national income in Egypt between wage and nonwage income.[60] In addition, it was assumed that, even at constant capital and labor input, production would tend to grow automatically by 0.5 percent per year as a consequence of technical progress, education, and the like. This "residual factor" is somewhat lower than that found in most developed countries, but this is only what we should expect for a country whose policies have been far from perfect and in some ways actually detrimental to efficiency in production.[61] Given the actual growth rates of production and labor input, this relationship aids in estimating the rate of growth of capital from 1959/60 to 1964/65, which, in connection with information on gross investments and an assumption of a 5 percent rate of depreciation, leads to an indirect estimate of the stock of capital at the beginning of 1965/66. This forms the starting point for

---

[59] No fixed price estimates of investments, either in total or sectoral, are available. Marginal capital-output ratios estimated on the basis of current price figures of investments and GDP changes will suffer from a serious downward bias implied by the increase in prices.

[60] *Statistical Handbook, U.A.R., 1952–1966*, pp. 215, 222. The share of wages in total gross value added is shown at 46 percent in 1964/65.

[61] Robert Mabro of the London School of Oriental and African Studies has informed me that estimates made there actually point to a "residual factor" of about 0.5 percent for Egypt during the 1950s and 1960s.

the estimate of the capital and investment requirements for 6 percent annual growth of GDP from 1965/66 to 1980.[62]

[62] Briefly the calculations run as follows. We start from a growth function

$$g = \alpha l^{\beta} k^{\delta}$$

where g, l, and k are the growth factors (1 plus the growth rates) of GDP, labor, and capital, respectively, while α is the "residual factor" and β and δ are the production elasticities. For the years 1960/61–1964/65 we have $g = 1.055$, $l = 1.029$, $\alpha = 1.005$, and $\beta = \delta = 0.5$. It follows that $k = 1.0709$ for these years. Total cumulated gross investments at current prices for 1960/61–1964/65 amounted to E£1.513 million. Deducting E£200 million High Dam investments (which did not result in output during this period) and allowing for about 10 percent price increase on average, total non-High Dam investments at constant 1959/60 prices may have been about E£1.200 million. I assume the rate of depreciation of capital to be 5 percent per annum. Letting K_{60} denote the capital value at 1959/60 prices at July 1, 1960, we have

$$K_{60} \times 1.0709^5 - K_{60} = 1.200 - K_{60} \times 0.05 \times \frac{1.0709^5 - 1}{0.0709}$$

from which $K_{60} = $ E£1.723 million. Then K_{65} becomes E£2.427 million at 1959/60 prices, and approximately E£2.700 million (excluding High Dam investments) at 1964/65 prices.

For 1965/66–1980 we first calculate mechanically with $g = 1.06$, $\alpha = 1.005$, $l = 1.026$, $\beta = 0.6$, and $\delta = 0.4$. We find then $k = 1.0993$. K_{80} becomes E£10.765. Gross investments required in 1965/66 become $(0.0993 + 0.05) \times 2,700 = $ E£403 million, that is, 18.7 percent of GNP, and in 1980 no less than $(0.0993 + 0.05) \times 10,765 = $ E£1,610 million or about 32 percent of GNP.

Allowance has to be made explicitly for the High Dam investments, capital, and value-added contribution; in addition we shall assume that, as from 1970/71, $\alpha = 1.01$.

For 1965/66–1969/70 assume $\alpha = 1.005$, $\beta = 0.6$, $\delta = 0.4$, $l = 1.026$, and $g = 1.06$. As above, k becomes 1.0993. Then K_{69} (excluding High Dam investments) becomes E£3.948 million, and GDP for 1969/70 becomes E£2.521 million. Including High Dam investments (about E£50 million annually), the required investment ratio over GNP is 20 percent for 1965/66 and almost 24 percent for 1969/70. For 1970/71 we obtain, incorporating the High Dam and allowing for some shortfall of other investments and GDP during the previous years, $K_{70} = 3.948 \times 1.0993 + 400 - 700 = $ E£3.940 million, 400 being the High Dam capital and 700 the assumed shortfall of other investments (the latter figure is probably very optimistic). Then GDP in 1970/71 becomes $2.521 \times 1.06 + 200 - 200 = $ E£2.672 million, the High Dam being assumed to contribute to value added with E£200 million annually, equal to the income loss from the shortfall of other investments. For the years 1965/66–1969/70 the average investment ratio is thus assumed to be about 17 percent, which may not be entirely unrealistic.

From 1970/71 to 1980 we put $g = 1.06$, $\alpha = 1.01$, $l = 1.026$, $\beta = 0.6$, and $\delta = 0.4$. This reduces k to 1.0859 and K_{80} to E£9,600 million.

This model implies a 1-year lag between gross investment and production increase (disregarding the High Dam investments). This is presumably a rather short average lag.

53

Our discussion of the necessity of a higher increase in labor productivity in order to reach 6 percent growth points to a relative increase in capital requirements. In accordance with the discussion of the sectoral projections, I shall assume that in the future a given addition of capital will add less to GDP than previously. Indeed, it has been assumed that the elasticity of production with respect to capital will fall to 0.4, while that for labor will increase to 0.6. This is also in line with the expected development of the share of labor. Developed countries have a considerably higher share of labor in GDP than 0.5. Some additional assumption was necessary to allow for the effects of the High Dam (which led to a flow of investments from 1959 to 1970, but with no increase of output until around 1968–70), and for the shortfall of investments and production from 1967 to the end of the current hostilities and the normalization of the economy. On these assumptions, a strong increase of the investment ratio from about 19 percent in 1965/66 to about 32 percent in 1980 would be required. This is clearly beyond the capacities of the economy; under these assumptions even 6 percent growth would seem out of the question.

The only hope, then, for a 6 percent growth rate is through increase of the "residual factor." Partly because of imperfect government policies, this growth factor was probably relatively low in the past. Ideal economic policies should be

Table 2-3
Capital, GDP, and Gross Investment Ratios

	Actual[a]		Required to Maintain 6 Percent Growth	
	1960/61	1965/66	1970/71	1980
Average capital–GDP ratio	1.4	1.4[b]	1.5	1.1
Incremental capital–GDP ratio[c]	1.7[d]	2.3[b]	2.6	4.0
Gross investment–ΔGDP ratio	3.4[e,f]	3.6[b]	3.6	5.0
Gross investment–GDP ratio	0.17[g]	0.20[g]	0.20	0.26

[a]For the first two rows, assuming GDP and gross investments to have increased exponentially from 1959/60 to 1964/65.
[b]Excluding previous High Dam investments.
[c]The incremental capital–NDP ratio would be 1-2 decimal points bigger.
[d]Excluding High Dam investments; with them, the figure would be 2.3.
[e]Including High Dam investments; without them, the figure is 3.1.
[f]Measured on undeflated values of gross investments (including High Dam investments) and GDP increase for the period 1960/61-1964/65 as a whole, this ratio becomes only 2.5 (E£1.513 over (E£ 99). Thus, the downward bias involved in ignoring deflation is very strong.
[g]Measured on undeflated actual values of gross investments and GDP, including High Dam investments.

able to increase it substantially for some time, say from 0.5 percent to about 1.0 percent, which is a high residual factor compared with the levels in developed countries, but the gains realized from improved policies and institutional arrangements seem so substantial that this increase should be possible. On this assumption, the investment requirements take on more human proportions. The investment ratio has to increase from about 20 percent in 1965/66 to about 26 percent in 1980, and this is just below the upper limit to which earlier experience pointed.

For those who like to think in terms of capital-output ratios, Table 2-3 shows the average capital-GDP ratio (defined as total capital over total GDP), the incremental capital-GDP ratio (defined as increase of capital stock—*net* investment—over increase of GDP), and the ratio of gross investment to GDP increase (the latter ratio is sometimes inadequately called the incremental capital-output ratio), together with the gross investment over GDP ratio for four different periods.

The High Dam investments, for which the lag between investment costs and output is so great, are difficult to account for; they make the instantaneous capital-output ratios rather uninteresting for the 1960s. At any rate, Table 2-3 reveals the very substantial increase in the capital and investment requirements from 1970. These requirements are based on the assumption of doubling the residual factor. If economic policy cannot accomplish this, the country should not dream of a rate of growth of 6 percent in the future.

IV. Problems of Financing Growth

The Basic Obstacles

My projections of a 6 percent annual increase in GDP and a 2.5 percent population increase are based on fragile assumptions. There is little chance, unfortunately, that things will turn out to be more favorable to Egypt than I have assumed. Major oil finds, and perhaps also a complete pacification of the Middle East necessitating only token defenses, are the only circumstances that might brighten the outlook significantly. A number of factors could tip the scale in the other direction and, at the worst, make the picture very gloomy indeed.

In the first place, the rate of population increase might become higher instead of lower, as assumed here. Specifically, it might rise during the 1970s and not decline until later. This would make it more difficult to reach the projected 3.5 percent increase in per capita income. The labor force would grow more slowly than the total population, and the more rapidly increasing scarcity of land and natural resources would be increasingly difficult to overcome through capital investments.

Second, it has tacitly been assumed that the current hostilities will be terminated soon, that the Egyptian economy will rapidly recover from its present difficulties, and that peaceful conditions will prevail in the future. These assumptions may break down in several ways. There is the problem of future frontiers.

Their exact location is not too important from our point of view; the major part of Sinai is economically worthless. Their relation to economic growth is mainly a question of whether and when the Suez Canal zone, including the canal itself and the west coast of Sinai, will become economically available to Egypt again. This part of the country contributed significantly to production and national income, perhaps by about 7–8 percent, of which approximately half has been compensated for through contributions from Kuwait, Saudi Arabia, Libya, and other Arab countries; the canal was a major and rapidly expanding source of foreign exchange. Our discussion has tacitly assumed that the future frontiers between Egypt and Israel will be identical to those before June 1967, and that the canal will be reopened soon so as to minimize the damages of its closure to future revenues from this source. Prolonged Israeli occupation of Sinai would certainly cripple the future growth possibilities of Egypt unless the loss of foreign exchange from the canal continues to be covered by the other Arab countries. The level of production and income would be correspondingly lower, and growth would become more difficult. A related problem concerns the future level of defense expenditures, which, I have assumed, can be cut down to 5 percent of GNP. Even after withdrawal of the Israeli occupation forces, however, political relations might continue to be so strained that defense forces would have to be kept at their present size and state of alertness. With continued Israeli occupation, reduction of defense expenditures is presumably out of the question. This would have serious consequences in regard to the manpower available for civil purposes, the balance of payments, and the level of investments.

A third factor of possible concern involves foreign aid. In the attempt to find an upper limit to the growth capacity, I assumed that in the future Egypt will not rely on financial or technical aid to any greater extent than during the years of the first five-year plan. This is probably a very realistic assumption. But there may be less aid available. Technical aid will probably be adequate, but financial aid will surely become more limited and the conditions of loans less advantageous. The availability of grants and loans will presumably depend on power politics and may be related to resolution of the present hostilities. But even if unlimited availability of foreign loans is assumed, Egypt might do well not to rely upon foreign finance for its future development. This decision would depend partly on the government's preferences and the possibilities of self-financing, and partly on loan conditions (interest rates, amortization periods, and political strings).

Even if Egypt is prevented from increasing foreign debts further, or chooses not to increase them, this will not necessarily imply a decline in the future growth rate. On the assumptions that defense expenditures will decline to 5 percent of GNP and that the country will be able to consolidate present debts on reasonable conditions, Egypt will be able to finance the investments necessary to achieve a 6 percent rate of growth. This will require a good economic policy, tough demand management and wage policies, and success in tackling the problem of efficiency; but it should be within the administrative capability of the country. And although such a program would severely limit the scope for expansion of private consumption, it would by no means impose inhuman suffering upon the population. Indeed, a certain increase in private consumption per capita would still be possible.

Section III pointed to the necessity of increased efficiency and productivity of labor. In order to keep investment requirements at a manageable level, the "residual factor," that is, the "automatic" component of the increase of production, has to be increased from 0.5 to about 1 percent per annum. Lack of success will show up in a correspondingly lower growth rate. Section V argues that even without changing the basic features of the present institutional framework there should be sufficient scope for improvements in economic policy, decision-making, and implementation.

The Scope for Private Consumption

"Financing development" means making domestic savings, private and public, sufficiently large to cover the investments required, with due regard to the possibility of borrowing from abroad. It is a question of keeping down private consumption and such public consumption as does not bear on the growth of production sufficiently to make room for investments and current public growth expenditures (especially for education and health), within the limits set by the national product plus the permissible balance of payments deficit. From a pure financing point of view there is little point in distinguishing between public growth and nongrowth expenditures; and since more than 90 percent of the investment expenditures in Egypt are undertaken by the government, the financing problem is really one of keeping private consumption down sufficiently to make room for public consumption and investments. The scope for private consumption is important not only because raising the standard of living is a major object of economic policy, but also because the political feasibility of a particular economic policy depends much on consumers' reactions to it.

In line with my discussion on investment requirements, I assume that gross investments will have to increase from 19 to 26 percent of GDP from the time of the solution of current hostilities, say 1970 to 1980. In 1965/66 (the last year for which statistics are available) public consumption had reached between 25 and 26 percent of GDP, and defense accounted for 10–11 percent. With defense cut down to 5 percent of GDP, public consumption should run at a level of 20 percent of GDP. The share of GDP for educational and health expenditures should probably be increased beyond the level reached in 1965/66. On the other hand, there is, quite apart from defense, substantial possibility for a relative reduction of non-growth government expenditures (see below). I therefore presume that public consumption need not exceed 20 percent of GDP. Finally, I allow for net interest payments abroad because I work with shares of GDP rather than GNP. Assume that such payments will amount to about 3 percent around 1970, and fall to 1.5 percent in 1980.[63] With the share of investments increasing from 19 to 26 percent, public consumption running at 20 percent, and interest payments to other countries falling from 3 to 1.5 percent, the total share of these items will be about 42 percent in 1970 and will increase to 47 percent in 1980. The share of private consumption in GNP seems to have been about 60–61 percent in 1965/66. It would thus have to be lowered from 58 percent of GDP in 1970 to 53 percent in 1980 *plus* whatever net loans are obtained abroad.

With sufficient foreign borrowing, a fall in the share of private consumption can be avoided, but at the cost of an increase in the total foreign debt and interest payments abroad. In order to keep the share of private consumption constant, foreign borrowing would have to be accelerated. To keep the share of 1965/66, foreign borrowing would need to total 3–4 percent of GNP in 1970 and (considering the acceleration of interest payments) almost 10 percent in 1980. This development cannot go on indefinitely; with foreign interest payments increasing more rapidly than GDP, the share of interest payments would continually increase and the balance of payments would become more and more strained. Moreover, loans of this size would presumably not be available at reasonable interest rates. Thus, in the long run, the share of private consumption must be reduced, depending on what size and growth of the net debt are considered tolerable. In the short run, the government might prefer a certain increase in the foreign debt rather than a reduction of the share of consumption. However, the possibilities of borrowing will be limited, particularly for a country whose first problem is to consolidate an already substantial debt. Indeed, there is a very real possibility that once the short-term debts have been converted to long-term ones, little room will remain for borrowing beyond the necessary renewal of expiring, longer-term loans.[64]

[63] If, at the end of hostilities, total foreign debt has reached E£1.5 billion, and the average rate of interest (after consolidation of debts) is about 4 percent, then total interest payments will amount to E£60 million per year. At an unchanged debt (i.e., balance of payments in equilibrium) over the period, the share of interest payments will then fall from about 3 to 1.5 percent at growing GDP. With an increasing debt, interest payments will rise correspondingly. It is difficult to forecast interest payments, even if the size of the debt is known. Conditions for loans to underdeveloped countries show large variations. Most probably, however, loan conditions will be tighter in the future, particularly for a country that has large, older debts to consolidate.

[64] The present debt structure is most disadvantageous and cannot be continued in the future. Some of the loans are extremely expensive, either because interest rates are exorbitant (like the short-term loans from continental Europe banks) or because they weaken the country's bargaining position (debit balances on bilateral clearing accounts). Other loans are expiring automatically. The Russian High Dam loans should be paid back over 12 years, and the American PL 480 counterpart funds are slowly being used by the U.S. government. Replacements for these cheap loans must be found relatively soon.

Table 2-4

Expenditure Pattern of the United Arab Republic, 1959/60-1966/67

(percent of GDP)

| Year | GDP at Current Market Prices (million E£)[a] (1) | Growth Expenditures, (3) + (4) (2) | Gross Investments, Public and Private (mainly fixed)[a] (3) | Public Consumption[b] | | | | Private Consumption[c] (8) | Total Expenditures (9) | Balance of Payments Deficit[d] (10) |
				Education and Health (4)	Defense (5)	Civil Nongrowth Expenditures (6)	Total (7)			
1959/60	1376	16.3	12.4	3.9	5.5	4.6	14.0	73.3	99.7	-0.3
1960/61	1459	n.a.	15.5	n.a.	n.a.	n.a.	16.9	68.8	101.2	1.2
1961/62	1513	21.3	16.6	4.7	5.8	6.8	17.3	71.7	105.6	5.6
1962/63	1685	n.a.	17.8	n.a.	5.6	n.a.	18.9	69.5	106.2	6.2
1963/64	1888	25.2	19.8	5.4	9.4	7.2	22.0	65.5	107.3	7.2
1964/65	2099	23.7	18.2	5.5	10.2	9.2	24.9	60.4	103.5	3.5
1965/66	2266	24.9	19.9	5.0[e]	10.4-11.0[e]	9.8[e]	25.2-25.8[e]	61.1-60.5[e]	106.2[e]	6.2
1966/67	(2500)[f]	(20.0)	(14.9)[g]	5.1	n.a.	n.a.	n.a.	n.a.	103.2[e]	(3.2)[e]
1967/68	...	n.a.	(12)[h]	...	...	...	n.a.	n.a.	...	...

[a]Ministry of Planning.
[b]Department of Treasury.
[c]Residual item including some stock changes.
[d]International Monetary Fund statistics.
[e]Provisional (lower limits based on provisional treasury estimates; upper limits, my estimate)
[f]My guess.
[g]My estimate.
[h]Based on budget estimate.

Therefore, I assume that until 1980 no further net borrowing will take place and that the current foreign payments have to be kept in balance. Thus, to cut the share of private consumption to 58 percent of GNP in 1970 and to 53 percent by 1980 is the real financial problem involved. Is it realistic to assume that the share of private consumption can be cut to that level, which is rather low even in comparison with that in highly developed welfare countries? To answer this question it is useful to look at past performance. Table 2-4 and Figure 2-1 give the relevant data.[65]

Both growth expenditures proper (investments, education, and health) and public nongrowth expenditures (defense and civil) have increased sharply. From 1959/60 to 1965/66, the share of growth expenditures in GDP rose from 16 to 25 percent and public nongrowth expenditures from 10 to 21 percent of GDP. Although the share of private consumption fell sharply from 73 to 60 percent, a 6 percent balance of payments deficit appeared. The increase in public nongrowth expenditures was equally divided between defense, which rose from 5 or 6 percent to 10 or 11 percent, and civil nongrowth expenditure (from 4.5 to 10 percent). The increase in defense expenditure took place in 1963/65 and 1964/65 in connection with the Yemen War. This increase in defense expenditure led to stagnation of the share of growth expenditures and a heavy fall in the share of private consumption and did not erode the balance of payments further. It was the increase in growth expenditures until 1962/63 that was basically responsible for creating the balance of payments deficit. Civil nongrowth expenditures, however, grew rapidly during the whole period, even after 1963/64, when growth expenditures began to stagnate.

Apart from the defense expenditures, which have their own philosophy and logic, there are two remarkable features of Table 2-4. First, while growth expenditures have been increased to an adequate level, civil nongrowth government

[65] The figures for shares of GDP presented in Table 2-4 are calculated on the basis of current price estimates, which may be adequate for discussions of financial matters. There is an interesting and somewhat puzzling discrepancy between the public employment figures available and the figures for public consumption. Government employment in 1959/60 may have been about 13–14 percent of total employment, and it may have increased to about 17 percent in 1964/65. Public consumption at the same time increased from 14 to 25 percent of GDP. If the figures are accepted at face value (the estimates of both public employment and consumption are very uncertain), there are two possible explanations of this difference. One is that government salaries and wages have increased substantially more than the GDP deflator. This should have taken place mainly through upgrading, bonuses, extra payments, etc., because there has been no general salary increase. The other possible explanation is that purchases of goods and services produced outside government administration have increased more rapidly than government employment. This could be due to the great expansion of defense, its increasing mechanization, and the operations in Yemen. Personally, I doubt whether this is sufficient to explain the difference completely. The figures for the increase in government employment are probably on the low side.

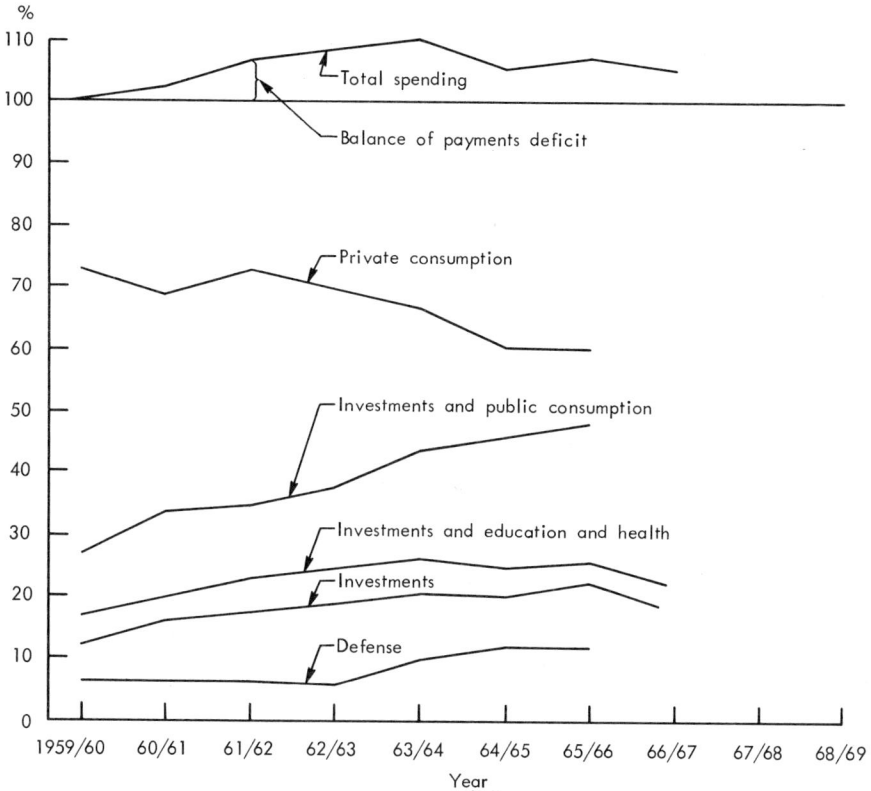

Fig. 2-1. Egypt: Shares of GDP at current market price

expenditures have grown faster than anything else (including defense). Such expenditures cover the costs of ordinary administration; their growth is probably pure waste. This is one of the weak points in the government's policy. Second, there is the fall in the share of private consumption, most of which took place after 1962/63. Part of the fall may be fictitious. Private consumption is estimated as a residual and thus includes most stock changes, which on the average presumably were negative during the 1960s. Even so, the fall in the share of private consumption from above 70 percent in 1959/60 to 60–61 percent in 1964/65 is impressive.[66] The question is whether a further decrease to 58 percent in 1970/71 and to 53 percent in 1980 can be accomplished. This is partly an administrative, partly a political, issue.

The administrative problem is basically one of raising sufficient tax and other revenues. Before discussing how this could be done, it is necessary to con-

[66] The figure 73.3 percent was rather high in comparison with previous years. See the earlier remarks on the ratio of investments in 1959/60.

61

sider the balance of payments problem, the solution of which depends to a considerable extent on how exactly consumption is held back.

The political problem is closely related to the implications of per capita consumption. It may be politically feasible to retard an increase but impossible to reduce per capita consumption directly.

As per capita consumption may have increased by 2 or 3 percent per annum from the Suez War until 1963/64. But from 1963/64 to 1965/66, a reduction took place that may have lowered per capita consumption below the level of 1960. (This, by the way, shows that even an outright reduction may be politically possible.) I have optimistically assumed that by 1970/71 the growth trend corresponding to an annual continuous increase of 6 percent of GDP will have been reached again, thanks partly to the benefits of the Aswan High Dam and partly to "postwar" recovery. A fall of the share of private consumption from 60–60.5 percent in 1965/66 to 58 percent of GDP in 1970/71 permits an increase of 5.2 percent per annum in total private consumption, that is, an increase per capita of 2.7 percent per annum from 1965/66 to 1970/71. This relatively strong increase is made possible by the assumptions of a full recovery of the economy and a full cut in defense to 5 percent of GNP, together with the fact that the required ratio of investments at that time will still be relatively low. This increase will slightly more than restore the peak level of per capita consumption reached in 1963/64. A further rise in total consumption by 4.4 percent and in per capita consumption by 1.9 percent per annum will then bring the share of private consumption in GDP down to 53 percent by 1980. This should be politically feasible, although the increase in per capita consumption is rather modest. What matters from a political point of view is probably the return to the old per capita consumption level, followed by *some* increase. In this sense, self-financing without foreign borrowing appears perfectly realistic.

The Balance of Payments

So far I have assumed that the balance of payments is in equilibrium, with no deficit or surplus on current account. Our discussion has shown only the crude macro conditions for a domestic demand-supply equilibrium. It has not dealt with the size and direction of foreign trade, which may be crucial for domestic productivity and per capita income.

Before discussing exports and imports and the balance of trade, we have to consider three important predetermined changes on the services balance—the relative reduction of Suez Canal revenues, the reduction of military purchases (which appear on the service balance under "Government expenditures"),[67] and the increase of interest payments. The reduction of canal revenues and military purchases may cancel out around 1970. Military foreign purchases (or, rather, payments) seem to have reached a level of E £ 25–30 million in 1965/66. If no heavy military equipment is purchased from the end of current hostilities

---

[67] Central Bank classification; see *Economic Review*, Central Bank of Egypt.

to 1980, this item (which would otherwise increase by 6 percent per annum according to my basic assumption of defense expenditures) could disappear from the expenditure side. Outstanding debts (if any) for all earlier deliveries of military equipment are assumed to be consolidated with the remaining debts. The initial fall in canal revenues may (on the optimistic assumption of deepening the canal to 42 feet plus pipelines) amount to a similar sum.[68] We are left then with the increase in debt service, that is, interest payments (since debt consolidation with unchanged net debt is assumed). At an interest rate of 4 percent (an optimistic figure), annual payments may run to E£60 million, compared with E£15 million in 1965/66. This would be the net deterioration of the service balance around 1970. It will lose in relative importance as GDP increases, and the increase in Suez Canal revenues following the initial fall may sooner or later compensate for the rise in interest payments, so that about 1980 there may be no serious deterioration of the service balance.

In terms of commodity exports and imports, my assumption of balance in the current payments requires a large increase in exports or a substantial fall in imports. It may be useful first to look at the problem at the 1965/66 level of exports and imports. With exports in 1965/66 at about E£250 million, and imports about E£415 million, the trade deficit was E£165 million, the service surplus was about E£65 million, and the total deficit on current accounts was about E£100 million. My assumptions about the service balance surplus (by 1970) imply an increase in the total deficit to E£145 million. To wipe out this deficit would require a 60 percent increase in exports or a 35 percent decrease in imports, or a combination of both. By 1980, Suez Canal revenues may have outgrown the increase in interest payment. Measured at the 1965/66 level, the deficit then would be only 100 million, corresponding to 40 percent of exports or 25 percent of imports. Still, these are dramatic changes. Can they be accomplished?

With complete control of foreign trade, imports can, of course, be cut to any level. But if the supplies of raw materials and capital goods are to be left untouched—otherwise my assumptions about the level of current production and investments and of greater labor productivity would break down—the whole burden will have to fall on the import of consumer goods, particularly cereal foods. Food accounted for about 30 percent of imports in 1964/65, so elimination of food imports should be sufficient to solve the problem. Is this possible? We have already shown that the domestic balance of demand and supply—at balanced current foreign payments—permits an increase of total private consumption and even a modest increase of per capita consumption. The possibilities of increasing exports are equally questionable because the most important exportables are food (such as rice) and cotton, which in production competes with food.

This is the well-known dilemma of the Egyptian balance of payments problem (one shared with many other underdeveloped countries). Fortunately, the

[68] Assuming, of course, that the compensation payments from the other Arab countries are terminated.

High Dam at Aswan should create the basis for a solution. One of the benefits from the High Dam should be an increase of agricultural gross production by about 20 percent. At 1964/65 prices this may amount to about E£150 million, virtually all exportables (cotton and rice) or import substitutes (wheat and barley). This increase in the production of exportables and import substitutes should appear around the time when it is needed to equalize the balance of payments, that is, in 1970. And the amount is just sufficient to wipe out a deficit of the size actually experienced in 1965/66, including the initial deterioration of the service balance. High Dam agricultural benefits should thus suffice for the initial rectification of the balance of payments, as long as the domestic consumption of agricultural products does not increase in connection with the rise in agricultural production. If, in addition to the High Dam benefits, agricultural production can be increased by at least 2.5 percent per year (that is, by the same rate as population), it will be possible to keep per capita food consumption constant without any need of food imports in the future. Unchanged consumption of food per capita is a feasible target, considering the relatively satisfactory average intake of calories and protein. The FAO estimates the average caloric intake to have been 2,390 in 1960–1962, compared with a "requirement" of 2,380; the intake of protein was 69.7 grams per day, while the "requirement" was only 64 grams.[69] This is not to say that the nutritional standards are in all respects satisfactory. The intake of animal protein is low, and part of the population suffers from a deficit of proteins and certain minerals and vitamins. A shift to less expensive though also less tasty cereals (from rice and wheat to barley and corn) would permit an increase in the consumption of more valuable nutrients without decreasing the calories or raising the total food bill.

From a domestic policy point of view, the foregoing measures would obviously require tough demand management, not only with respect to disposable income. A change in relative prices sufficient to shift demand somewhat from agricultural products to other goods and services would also be necessary.

So far I have dealt with the balance of payments problem on the basis of the actual situation in 1965/66, without considering the growth in imports that will naturally follow the increase in production and income. With food imports eliminated, consumer demand for manufactured goods, producer need for raw materials and intermediary products to be used as inputs, and the requirement of capital goods for investment purposes will exert pressure for increased imports.

The demand for manufactured consumer goods can be diverted toward domestic industrial products through taxation and, if necessary, continued import controls for these kinds of commodities. Efforts to accomplish a more equal income distribution will work in the same direction. The people in the lowest income brackets do not demand sophisticated, high-quality products. Demonstration effects and the need of living up to the Western Joneses are typically middle- and upper-class phenomena. The poor classes have simpler needs to think

[69] FAO, *Indicative World Plan for Agricultural Development, 1965–85, Near East,* Vol. II, p. 54.

upon. The fellahin do not buy cars and television sets; when they expand their purchase of manufactured consumer goods, it will be to simple commodities—lamps and kerosene stoves, pots and pans, better clothes, shoes, and, perhaps, a bicycle. There are good reasons for believing that simple, unsophisticated, low-quality consumer goods constitute a field where underdeveloped countries may have an advantage and be competitive.

The demand for imported raw materials and intermediary products for current production will depend on the ability of the government to plan for and establish industries wherever linkages require complementary production. The increasing need for inputs in agriculture (fertilizers and other chemicals, oil for pumps, and so on) should not necessitate direct imports if sufficient capacity is created in industry. The same holds true for transport and electricity, where at least the fuel, tires and tubes, and certain other spare parts can be produced locally. Industry, too, can to some extent be supplied domestically. Certainly, imports to be used as inputs need not grow as fast as production. The increasing ratio of investments, of course, points in the other direction. However, construction's increasing share in gross investments—and I have already given some reasons for expecting this—would help to keep down the demand for imported capital goods. Apart from a few minor items, there is little point in attempting to establish domestic production of machinery and heavy equipment in the few decades ahead; such products are generally too sophisticated.

Thus it is hardly overoptimistic to predict a slower growth of imports than of GDP, once food imports have been eliminated. Let us assume that a 6 percent increase in GDP will imply a 6 percent increase in imports. At the starting point, with food imports eliminated and a deterioration of the service balance, imports (measured at the 1965/66 level)[70] would be about E£265 million, with exports approximately E£250 million. At a rate of 6 percent per annum, imports would have grown to about E£540 million by 1980. We thus need an increase in foreign exchange earnings of about E£275 million in order to keep the balance of payments in equilibrium. Of this, more than E£100 million may come from increasing Suez Canal revenues (after the initial fall already accounted for). Agricultural exports (perhaps about E£170 million in 1965/66) would, at a 2.7 percent annual increase in agricultural production (about 4 percent minus 1.3 percent due to the High Dam benefits already accounted for), reach about E£250 million in 1980. This leaves a gap of only E£95 million in 1980, which would have to be earned through increased industrial exports (in-

---

[70] In that year imports were unusually high, not only because food imports were large, but also because capital goods imports were very high. Yet it may be argued that the level of imports (except food) was below optimum. Certain industries suffered from a shortage of raw materials. Since investments that year actually exceeded the requirements for continued 6 percent growth (according to my calculations), it may also be argued that capital imports were above the requirements, and that thus total imports (apart from food) may not have been suboptimal, whereas the composition was inoptimal.

cluding oil) or greater tourist revenues. Egypt has great possibilities for tourism; but even disregarding any increase in tourist revenues, an annual increase in industrial exports of only about 5.5 percent would be enough to make up the balance.

The assumptions behind this calculation are cautious with respect to industrial exports, tourist revenues, Suez Canal revenues, and import requirements. Section III pointed out the industries that could produce the necessary increase in industrial exports; oil alone may do the trick. Tourist revenues can hardly fail to increase substantially once peaceful relations are established in the Middle East, even if the present Western hostility toward Egypt lingers. Suez Canal revenues have already been discussed (Section III), and the elasticity of imports with respect to production and income was deliberately estimated conservatively. The key to the solution of the balance of payments problem is thus to be found in securing a high growth rate of agricultural output (4 percent) and curbing the domestic consumption of agricultural products. Although these are feasible targets and are much more realistic than dreams of solving the balance of payments problem through accelerated industrialization, they require determined and rational policies.

A final question is the future of foreign exchange rates, specifically, the value of the Egyptian pound. The Egyptian pound depreciated by about 20 percent in 1962 (most of this depreciation had actually taken place earlier); until then, it had formally followed the pound sterling. In 1967 it followed the U.S. dollar and thus almost re-established its old parity with the pound sterling. Domestic inflation during the 1960s increased money wages so much that in spite of the 1962 depreciation the currency at the outbreak of the June 1967 war was clearly overvalued.[71] Money wages in agriculture increased some 40 percent from 1960 to 1965;[72] including social security contributions from employers, industrial wage costs per unit of labor input may have risen almost at the same rate.[73] In order to make both agricultural and industrial exports profitable at present wage levels, it would seem natural to accept a new depreciation (to some extent this has already taken taken place de facto through the introduction of various kinds of fees on foreign trade); otherwise, the government will have to work with elaborate subsidy schemes.

[71] Opinions are somewhat divided on whether the Egyptian pound was overvalued also during the 1950s. I have argued (see Hansen and Marzouk, *Development and Economic Policy in the U.A.R. (Egypt)*, Chap. 8.4) that the balance of payments deficit at that time was mainly the result of excessive demands at an essentially adequate cost level and that thus the balance of payments could be permanently rectified without a depreciation through domestic demand management measures. I have some doubts now whether this view was correct.

[72] Hansen, "Employment and Wages in the U.A.R."

[73] *Statistical Handbook U.A.R., 1952–1966,* pp. 221–222, with allowance for shorter working hours.

Demand Management

In the two preceding subsections I defined the task of domestic demand management. Demand and supply of goods and services must be in equilibrium at balanced current foreign payments. To this end, the share of private consumption has to be cut down to 58 percent of GNP in 1970 and to 53 percent in 1980, with the implication that total private consumption can be allowed to increase by about 4.5 percent per annum and per capita consumption by about 2 percent. Per capita consumption of food and other agricultural products should be kept constant at the level reached in 1965/66, in spite of the increase in total per capita consumption. Thus, a substantial shift in the composition of private consumption is required. If commodity rationing, which would hardly work, is discounted, this calls for strong changes in relative prices, which could be accomplished through taxation.

The quantitative dimensions of the task of overall demand management depend primarily on (1) the development of the share of private income in total national income, (2) the automatic increase in tax revenues and the rise in private disposable income, and (3) the development of the rate of private savings. Other factors, such as private income distribution, may be added.

It seems likely that private income will increase more slowly than national income. The discussion of sectoral developments in Section III showed that the largest increases will occur in sectors where public enterprises predominate: industry (including extraction electricity), construction, and transport and communication. With public investments accounting for 90–95 percent of total investments, the government's share of production for sale should increase. It is more difficult to say what will happen to profit margins in public enterprises. It seems reasonable to assume that in the longer run wage ·rates ·in public enterprises will follow productivity in the private sector, where wages are determined, by and large, by demand and supply, and where, disregarding central administration, by far the largest part of the labor force is employed. If, as seems likely, productivity increases more in public than in private enterprises (dominated by agriculture and retail trade), the profit margin in public enterprises will, other things being equal, tend to increase. The price structure—which I shall discuss later—will presumably change in the same direction.

On the other hand, it is doubtful whether tax revenues will increase automatically in proportion to private income without important changes in the tax system.[74] Land taxes are based on assessments of rental value in 1949 (land reform areas are not taxed at all), and the revenue increases only to the extent that rates are increased or taxable acreage is expanded. Taxable acreage will be expanded during the period, but land tax revenues (at the existing rates) will increase much less than total agricultural income. The same holds true for the

---

[74] For an outline of the tax system, see Hansen and Marzouk, *Development and Economic Policy in the U.A.R.* (Egypt), Chap. 9.5.

"building tax," imposed on the rental value of a building. Payroll taxes for social security will increase in proportion to wages and to salaries in larger (mainly public) enterprises, and may therefore tend to rise more than in proportion to national income. The same probably holds true for the progressive income tax, which is levied mainly on civil servants and employees in public enterprises and on persons in the professions. Indirect taxes, which consist largely of customs duties, tend to follow the value of imports given their composition. To judge from earlier developments (which are very difficult to appraise because there have been numerous discretionary changes in tax rates and norms and because tax payments are delayed) and the nature of existing taxes, it seems likely that the elasticity of tax revenues with respect to total private income is low, perhaps even below unity.[75]

Concerning the rate of private savings, the marginal rate may be expected to equal the average rate in the longer run. This is a well-established long-term pattern in high-income countries, and I am aware of no evidence to the contrary for low-income countries. The limited information about Egypt in this respect for the postwar period points to a stable average rate of private savings of some 5–7 percent of disposable income.[76] A strong, permanent shift in income distribution in favor of entrepreneurs (cultivators, retail dealers, and the like) might lead to an increase in the savings ratio, but it is questionable whether such a shift in income distribution should and would be allowed (see below).

The evidence suggests that, without special measures, private consumption may tend to increase roughly in proportion to national income. Since monetary policies presumably have little effect on private consumption patterns (housing being the most important exception), the main burden of overall demand management must be borne by discretionary tax increases. The quantitative task of the tax policy will be to reduce the rate of increase of real disposable income from 6 to 4.5 percent per annum. In principle this can be done equally well by direct (income) or indirect (commodity) taxes. We know that a substantial relative price increase for food and other agricultural consumer goods is necessary, which may be accomplished by gradually eliminating the present substantial food subsidies, and thereafter levying taxes on food at rates that increase each year. The size of this annual increase will depend on the income and price elasticities of food demand. Its effect on total consumption will depend on the income and cross elasticities of nonfood consumption in relation to food prices. The annual increase in food taxes will have to be high, assuming the price elasticity for food to be relatively low. It is even conceivable that the food taxes alone may suffice to prevent total per capita consumption from increasing by more than 2 percent per annum and thus total consumption in the country by

---

[75] In developed countries the tax revenue elasticity varies between 1.0 and 1.3; see Bent Hansen, *Fiscal Policy in Seven Countries, 1955–1965,* OECD, Paris, 1969, Chap. 2.

[76] This is exactly the same rate as in the United States!

more than the permitted 4.5 percent.[77] Otherwise, additional general taxes will have to be imposed in order to reduce disposable income sufficiently. The obvious candidates here are the income taxes, particularly the schedular taxes on land and buildings, and the payroll taxes.

This however, oversimplifies the problem. It is not possible to tax the peasants' consumption of their own products directly. In order to prevent food consumption from increasing in rural areas, food taxes should be supplemented by an increase in the land tax. As a consequence the land tax would have to be imposed on the cultivator rather than on the owner, but this is no problem, since the land tax is already collected from the cultivator, and the current legal maximum in rent paid to the owner is far below the hypothetical market rent. The

---

[77] Assume that, on a per capita basis, the consumption function is

$$c = k \, (y/P)$$

where c is the volume of consumption per capita, y is disposable money income per capita, and P is the consumer goods price index. Let the demand function for food be

$$f = h \left(\frac{y}{P} \right)^{E} \left(\frac{p}{\pi} \right)^{e}$$

where f is the volume of food consumption per capita, p is the price of food, π is the price of nonfood consumer goods, E is the income elasticity, and e is price and numerical cross elasticity at given real income. Let $E = 0.5$, $e = -0.3$, and $f = 0.5c$. Balance in the economy requires now $\dot{c}/c = 0.02$, $\dot{f}/f = 0$. Keeping π constant, we obtain $\dot{p}/p = 0.033$, $\dot{P}/P = 0.016$, and $\dot{y}/y = 0.036$. In other words, disposable money income per capita can be allowed to increase by 3.6 percent per year while food taxes have to be increased by 3.3 percent each year. But I have already argued that, at given tax laws, disposable money income per capita will increase by about 3.5 percent per year. It follows that, apart from the increasing food taxes, no other discretionary tax changes should be necessary, given the consumption and demand functions in this example. Also, for food consumption per capita the volume is unchanged and both the price and the value will increase by 3.3 percent per year; for nonfood consumption, the price remains unchanged, and the value as well as the quantity will increase by 3.7 percent per year. The total demand for nonfood consumer goods will thus increase by 6.3 percent per year. With the supply of housing services increasing only about 4.5 percent (see Section III, p. 43) and prices for personal services rising at the rate of productivity increase in the private sector, the annual increase in the demand for products from the domestic manufacturing industry will be rather high. I have already used this assumption in discussing the optimal growth rate for industry.

The FAO *Indicative World Plan for Agriculture Development, 1965–85, Near East*, Vol. II, p. 51, works with an income elasticity in Egypt for calories of 0.21, and for proteins of 0.25. With a food income elasticity of 0.25 $\dot{p}/p$ becomes 0.05 and $\dot{y}/y$ 0.045. Food taxes would thus have to increase more rapidly, while a certain increase of disposable income through direct subsidies or lower direct taxes would be possible.

only problem is that, in order to keep the peasants' per capita consumption constant, their disposable income per capita has to be kept constant too. This could be achieved through a sufficient increase in the land tax, but this solution would involve a continuous shift in income distribution from the peasants to the rest of the population, who would experience an annual increase of real disposable income per capita. Considerations of social equity might argue against such a policy.

On the other hand, it is difficult to visualize another policy that would increase the peasants' per capita income without leading to increased food consumption. One possibility would be to lower food consumption per capita slightly in the urban areas, in which case food consumption could be allowed to increase somewhat in rural areas. There are some population groups (middle and higher income brackets) who would only benefit if their excessive food consumption was forced down. How much this could contribute quantitatively is not clear, but it points toward the need for a firm, income-equalizing policy of taxation. Another possibility would be to compensate the peasants through expanding nonpecuniary benefits, such as health services, a potable water supply, and educational and religious services. The products of manufacturing industries could perhaps be sold at subsidized prices in the villages.

Finally, the constant per capita income of peasants might be made more palatable if land reforms were carried through so as to give all land to the actual cultivators. Whether this would mean that income would be transferred from absentee owners to cultivators depends entirely on the expropriation compensations paid (or not paid) to the owners. Apart from this consideration, the cultivators would regard such extension of the land reforms as a great benefit, which might compensate them for an unfavorable income distribution.

This is not the only social and income distributional problem that the policies suggested here will engender. There will undoubtedly be a need to subsidize groups in the lower-income brackets directly; they will be hit particularly hard or may even now be living under such conditions that their level of consumption should be increased. As already pointed out, this is not the general case, but there are always some groups who need special treatment. In order to handle such social problems, the government will need revenues in addition to those already discussed. Although I cannot enter upon a general discussion of the Egyptian tax system and possible reforms here, it should be stressed that administratively there should be no difficulty in increasing government revenues substantially. A few remarks about some of the existing taxes may clarify this point.

Quite apart from the problem of keeping down the peasants' food consumption, there is much to be said in favor of taxing land rents heavily. Most land improvements are made through government investments, and the costs of upkeep and operation of the irrigation and drainage system are paid largely from the budget. There is no reason why agriculture itself should not pay for these. Indeed, the social profitability of agriculture cannot be correctly assessed unless these costs are deducted from agricultural income. It would seem entirely appropriate, for instance, that the land rents on the areas that the High Dam will bring under cultivation be taxed at 100 percent. In order to obtain the best incentive effects, the land tax should not be assessed according to actual rents but should be fixed at a level proportional to the average rent for land of specified fertility. This would be completely in line with existing practices.[78] The tax could then be increased every year, say in proportion to the total value of expected agricultural output or average income per feddan (in order to avoid making annual assessments superfluous). In relation to the individual farmer's efforts, the tax would thus be constant, although it would follow the average income over time. This might preserve the incentives to improvements while automatically increasing the revenues from the land taxes. Unfortunately, it is difficult to make land taxes progressive. To do so would first require great improvement in the present system of land registration,[79] and it might create an undesired tendency to diminish the size of farms. On the other hand, there is no doubt that equity considerations call for progressive taxation of agricultural incomes more than anything else.

It has already been mentioned that in order to clear the housing market a sizable increase of the existing tax on rents (the so-called building tax) would be appropriate. This tax would mainly hit (although unevenly) the middle and higher income brackets and would thus be favorable from an equity point of view. Since it can also be made progressive, it might fulfill some of the functions of a general progressive income tax, which is not administratively feasible at present. Actually, such a tax does exist (as a surtax on higher incomes); but it is very ineffective, and with a majority of the population illiterate, a unified income tax dependent on tax declarations is out of the question. If we add the possibility of taxing durable consumer goods, gasoline, and other items of high-income consumption, it seems clear that there are many possibilities for taxing the higher-income groups in favor of the poor.

V. The Efficiency Problem

The second big policy issue concerns the efficiency and productivity of the existing factors of production, the question of increasing the "residual factor." Making progress and raising the standard of living automatically via the residual factor is an old dream of politicians. Progress is supposed to cost nothing, impose hardships upon no one, and come like manna from heaven. To the extent that this is true, the residual factor is unfortunately not amenable to policy manipulations. Many are the politicians who have had to learn this lesson. And to the extent that this factor is amenable, it usually costs something to increase it, though the rate of return may be large. Educational efforts, scientific research, vocational training, and the acquisition of know-how, including the purchase of patent rights, are well-known examples of the kind of investment required.

[78] At the time of the Byzantine Empire land in the Nile Valley was taxed this way.
[79] Which in any case is badly in need of reform.

71

Although there is certainly much to be done in these fields, I have little concrete to suggest. My concern is rather a series of institutional obstacles that probably have helped to keep down the residual factor in the past 10 years and whose removal might increase it again over the coming decade. I shall discuss some specific Egyptian institutional features, but the basic problems are much more general. They are closely related to the question of socialism in underdeveloped countries. The problem of economic efficiency in Communist countries has received wide attention in recent years, but there has been little discussion of similar problems in the many underdeveloped countries that have chosen a mixed system, with large public and private sectors existing side by side. I believe that to such countries the ideas of market socialism, with an appropriate blend of Lange and Lerner, have real application. Let it suffice to call attention to this general problem. Egypt may not be typical in all respects of underdeveloped countries that have chosen a socialist way, but most of her problems will be familiar to students of such countries.

The Present Institutional Setup

Since 1956 (some would say 1952)[80] a metamorphosis has taken place in the Egyptian economy, transforming it from a private enterprise society into what is now officially labeled "Arab socialism." It is a mixed economy with state ownership of all larger enterprises and extensive direct control over the remaining private sector. Some observers believe that these deep institutional changes, through some sort of historical necessity, grew out of the economic policy problems encountered during this period.[81] They should thus be conceived of as the logical, optimum (or at least second-best) solutions to concrete problems imposed upon the economy from outside or required by the government's own targets for economic development. Were this view correct, we should not need to ask whether the present institutional setup is conducive to growth.

This view not only postrationalizes events; it also overlooks important, probably at times decisive, sources of inspiration for institutional change. To be sure, Egypt encountered more problems during this period than many other countries, and some of the institutional changes were related to these problems. But reforms have often followed upon rash decisions from the top based on intu-

---

[80] The main impact of the land reforms of 1952 was on the distribution of income and wealth; the cooperative system, introduced in the land reform areas, albeit quantitatively not very important, did signify a beginning transformation of the agricultural production and marketing system. There is no reason, however, for calling the cooperative system of the land reform areas socialist. It was copied directly from the British Gezira project in Sudan and was adopted as a clever way of combining large-scale advantages in irrigation, crop rotation, and marketing with small-scale production and private initiative.

[81] Patrick O'Brien, *The Revolution in Egypt's Economic System,* Oxford University Press, London, 1965, tends to rationalize developments in this way.

BENT HANSEN

ition rather than on cool and careful expert advice.[82] Too often they have just been expedient palliatives and piecemeal measures chosen along the line of least popular dissatisfaction. With increasing state ownership and interference and alleged socialism in many of the new third-world countries, it stands to reason that imitation and international persuasion were important driving forces behind the institutional transformation in Egypt. It is not just by chance that Egypt embarked upon the road to socialism after the Suez War and during the Algerian War. This was the time when the Communist countries emerged, to some Arab leaders, as the true friends of the third world against Western imperialism. It was also the heyday of third-world conferences, when the cautious and conservative Nasser suddenly found himself in the company of such figures as Chou En-lai, Nehru, Sukarno, Tito, and Nkruma, for whom socialism (of greatly diverging definitions, to be sure) was the answer to all the problems of underdeveloped countries. Add the very impressive growth rates of the Communist countries during the second half of the 1950s and the beginning of the 1960s, when the West was troubled by recessions and slow growth in some leading countries, and the major sources of inspiration for the "revolution in Egypt's economic system" have probably been listed.

If these views on the institutional reforms are correct, we must also ask whether the present setup is conducive to growth, and especially whether the system is capable of living up to the increased demands of the future with respect to productivity, foreign trade, and domestic public savings. But before I discuss the virtues and shortcomings of the system, I shall briefly survey what the system actually is.[83]

Through nationalization, Egyptianization,[84] and sequestration, mainly from 1956 to 1961, the state became the owner of all large-scale business. The sectors in which private ownership still predominates are agriculture, retail trade, small-scale industry and handicrafts, housing, and the professions. Even these sectors, however, are subject in various ways to direct government control. In agriculture, the irrigation system has always been administered by the public sector, which gives the government great influence over agricultural production. The land reforms of 1952 and later imposed area limitations on ownership and tenure, fixed maximum rents on land, and regulated conditions of tenure in various ways. Agricultural cooperatives were first introduced in land reform areas and

[82] A civil servant who took part in the formulation of the nationalization decrees of 1961 once told me that he and his collaborators were brought into the project without warning and preparation less than 3 days before the publication of the decrees.
[83] For more detailed descriptions, see Charles Issawi, *Egypt in Revolution,* Oxford University Press, London, 1963; O'Brien, *The Revolution in Egypt's Economic System;* and Hansen and Marzouk, *Development and Economic Policy in the U.A R. (Egypt),* Chaps. 10 and 11.
[84] Egyptianization meant that foreign ownership in Egyptian joint stock companies was replaced by Egyptian interests, in effect, the Egyptian government.

73

now extend over most of the country. Created and largely controlled from above, they have assumed important functions in the trading of major crops and inputs (seeds and fertilizers). Crop rotation, production itself, is subject to increasing direct intervention. For all major crops and inputs, prices are fixed by the government. Retail trade, small-scale industry, and handicrafts are also subject to some extent to price control and are often dependent on commodity and raw material allocations. In retail trade, government shops ("cooperatives") play a certain role. Housing, finally, is subject to rent control and is dependent on building licenses.

Apart from the traditional public utilities (railways, gas, electricity, etc.), which are administered directly by government bodies, state-owned enterprises are mostly organized as joint stock companies with the state as the major or only shareholder. Each public enterprise is attached to one of a large number of organizations, which in turn are subordinate to the various ministries. The largest organizations and enterprises belong to the Ministries of Industry and Economics. The system was designed to permit a large degree of decentralization in current production decisions; however, it gives ministers who want to interfere good opportunities to do so. Investment decisions are subordinated to the national plans and thus are basically centralized. Exactly how the system works in practice is not clear, but it varies greatly from industry to industry and from ministry to ministry. The tendency seems to be toward increasing direct intervention in current production decisions by the supervising ministries. The lack of a comprehensive plan since 1964 makes it difficult to know how investment decisions are actually taken. Apart from special projects of national importance, such as the Aswan High Dam, each ministry (or organization) usually decides independently about individual investment projects within the framework of the total investment expenditures approved for it. Even under the first five-year plan, the coordination of investment decisions has been deficient, and there have been no clear criteria for the choice of investments.

Perhaps even more important is government's pervasive influence on production and investment through its tight controls of foreign trade and allocation of import goods. These controls affect both public and private enterprises. Foreign trade control has several dimensions. It originated in the 1950s because of the increasing foreign exchange shortage. Its main purpose then was simply to keep down the demand for foreign exchange. Since 1961, however, foreign trade has become almost completely nationalized and thus is subject to control by the Ministry of Economy. Moreover, exports and imports are largely determined by bilateral trade and aid agreements between the governments of Egypt and other countries (with some details perhaps left to administrative discretion). For these reasons, both imported capital goods and raw materials are now distributed through a complicated, centralized allocation system that often is decisive for the investment and production possibilities of individual enterprises. Although the basic system of nationalized enterprises was designed to permit a high degree of decentralization, the foreign trade situation has in fact led to a partial centralization of decisions whereby the decisionmaking administrations have little responsibility for the consequences of their decisions with respect to production. Thus it is very difficult to specify to what extent the system is dependent on centralized decisions with respect to production conditions. Generally speaking, both private and public enterprises are free to produce for the market—to the extent that they do not get direct orders from the government and to the extent that raw materials and other inputs are allocated for the purpose. Which of course does not say very much. It is clear, however, that the influences exerted on production by the supervising ministry, the foreign trade and exchange authorities, and the market are badly coordinated and often conflicting.

Socialism and Bureaucracy

Arab socialism, the term used simply as a label applied to what has actually taken place in Egypt, differs from both Eastern and Western socialism. With about half the national income produced in the private sector and, for the present at least, no intentions to interfere with private ownership of land, residential buildings, and small-scale trade and industry, the system bears little resemblance to those of Communist countries. Interference with income distribution (beyond that implied by land reform, nationalization, and sequestrations), directed mainly at the highest income brackets, has been rather moderate. Such interference and the stress on social security with social insurance arrangements and some labor participation in the management of enterprises are much in line with Western European income redistribution- and social-democratic thinking, although it is of course a far cry from the social security and income redistribution systems of Western European welfare states to those of a poor, backward country like Egypt. And state ownership hardly goes beyond what old-fashioned European social-democrats (British trade unionists, for instance) might easily agree to.

Yet in one important respect developments in Egypt more nearly resemble those of the Communist countries: the increasing size and power of the bureaucracy, and the tendency—if not in theory, certainly in practice—to identify socialism with government control of any kind and to rely on discretionary administrative decisions rather than on automatic responses in the system. The extraordinary increase in expenditures for civil administrative (nongrowth) purposes—from 5 percent of GDP in 1959/60 to 10 percent in 1965/66—indicates that expansion of the bureaucracy may be the most important institutional change to have taken place in the Egyptian economy. Egypt has always had relatively large, centralized administrations at the service of an autocratic ruler. Arab socialism has changed nothing in this respect, but it has led the bureaucracy into fields in which, at least from the middle of the last century, it had no functions, and has entangled the country in "red tape" to an extent never seen before. Any attempt to increase efficiency in the country must tackle this problem.

Why did bureaucracy grow so excessively? Both historical tradition in Egypt and the military background of the regime made it natural for the government to look for administrative solutions to whatever problem cropped up. The political setting, with little public debate and criticism, and the initiative in all matters taken by the government, often advised by the civil service, has no built-in checks and balances that could put a brake on the expansion of administration. Moreover, the dual character of the governmental system (with a presidency on top of the traditional government) results in duplication of many functions.

The basic political decision (apparently made after the Suez War) to let the public sector take the lead in development would itself have caused an expansion of administration. Planning must be done by some authority, and none of the old ministries could take over this function. All countries that have introduced planning have set up a new authority for this purpose; Egypt should not be criticized for having done the same. The Ministry of Planning has never done any planning worth the name, however, but has served mainly as a statistical bureau, duplicating some of the functions of the statistical department, while most investment planning has been carried out in the planning departments of the other ministries. Modern welfare policies require extensive public services, and a social insurance system must be administered. Egypt's attempts to modernize welfare policy, even if her achievements have been modest, also explain some of the expansion of the central administration. Nationalization, finally, should not necessarily have required a big addition to the existing administrations if the government was in favor of decentralized production decisions. Nevertheless, a huge superstructure of organizations was created over the nationalized industries, Even where there was good cause to enlarge the administrative machinery, the tendency has always been to overexpand.

A special factor in overstaffing is the government's employment policy toward university graduates. As mentioned previously, all graduates of universities and similar institutions, irrespective of their field of study and their competence, are guaranteed government employment if they want it. Combined with educated Egyptians' traditional preference for working for the government, this has contributed not only to overstaffing but also to inadequate staffing.

Most important may have been the reluctance of the government to initiate sufficient demand management measures to keep the economy in balance. Government expenditures for investment and public consumption increased, and a domestic inflationary pressure slowly emerged. To increase current government revenues correspondingly was presumably ruled out by political considerations. Since the government also considered a stable price level a political necessity, the only solution was to increase the direct controls over prices and to introduce some commodity allocation and rationing. The simultaneous balance of payments strains worked in the same direction, as already mentioned. This point is crucial. To the extent that controls and red tape are the consequences of attempts to repress inflation in spite of excess demand, the controls will become superfluous as soon as the inflationary pressures are removed by general and selective demand management measures. The government began to realize this around 1964 and to act accordingly when it became increasingly clear that the situation could not be managed administratively without harmful effects on allocation and income distribution, effects that in the long run might be more unpopular than a straightforward mopping up of purchasing power.

The traditional arguments for inflation in underdeveloped countries pertain to open inflation, wherein prices are allowed to run away; but in Egypt it has been a question of repressed inflation, which probably has even more harmful effects in underdeveloped countries than elsewhere. The parallel to Western Europe during the first postwar years is striking: mopping up purchasing power and creating better balance greatly benefit productivity by permitting a relaxation of controls. Some socialists in Egypt, like some of their Western European colleagues, will probably resist such policies, objecting to any relaxation of government controls. What were palliatives and half-measures at the time they were introduced have grown into the system and become sacred cows for the ideologists. The administrators themselves will tend to oppose any reduction of the machinery, not only because it would reduce their own employment and advancement possibilities, but also because they benefit from the system: they have always been first in line for scarce, price-controlled goods and services and have got them at the low official prices.

An important consequence of the nationalization and similar policies has been the tendency for the nationalized enterprises themselves to function like government departments and for their employees to be transformed into quasi civil servants. Even without direct commands from the ministries, this would have been sufficient for the inefficiency of the central administration to contaminate the enterprises. Among the factors responsible for this development, two are particularly important. Mainly for reasons of income equalization and social justice, a grading system for wages and salaries in public enterprises, similar to the one applied for central administration, was introduced in 1963. This pay system, which in effect guarantees the employee a fixed income no matter what he is doing and makes grading and advancement dependent on highly mechanical procedures, has had marked disincentive effects from top to bottom in the enterprises.[85] At the same time, for social security reasons reforms were instituted that made it virtually impossible to dismiss employees and difficult to enforce discipline on the shop floor. The result has in many cases been detrimental to productivity.[86] The introduction of free medical service in factories has had similar consequences. In addition, the government's employment drive in

---

[85] The introduction of the system seems to have implied a pronounced wage increase and contributed to inflation, from the demand side to the extent that prices did not follow costs, and from the cost side to the extent that prices were raised as a consequence. Many of the price increases since 1964 are an adjustment to the higher cost level.

[86] As a probably extreme example, after the nationalization of the cotton pressing industry at Alexandria, productivity (measured by number of bales pressed per hour per steampress) fell by 39 percent. Management ascribed this decline entirely to disciplinary difficulties and claimed that it had nothing to do with interference from the ministry.

1961/62 led to widespread overstaffing and "disguised" unemployment in the enterprises, with corruptive effects on discipline. Nationalized enterprises thus face many of the efficiency problems from which the central administration suffers.

In spite of the increasing field of activity of government and the new role of the public sector as a vehicle of development, remarkably little has been done to reform and reshape the administrative system. Some new, imaginative ministries have been created, among them the Ministries of Planning and Scientific Research. Each could fulfill a real function, but neither seems to do so. Otherwise, the expansion of the central administration has occurred mainly in the old ministries, in some cases by dividing them up, in other cases by adding offices to the existing setup; this is true also of the organizations that supervise the nationalized enterprises. Two important activities, however, have been kept entirely outside the traditional machinery, namely, the Suez Canal and the construction of the High Dam at Aswan. Both are independent enterprises headed by competent specialist engineers who have been given exceptionally wide powers and are responsible directly to the President. Their conspicuous success proves that governmental undertakings in Egypt not need be inefficient if cast in the appropriate organizational form.

This does not mean that there have been no attempts to reform administration. Observers will find the ministries boiling with reform activities. Any new minister—and since 1964 there has been a rapid turnover—will announce great reforms to improve his administration, but the continuous stream of decrees seems to cause more confusion than real reform. Moreover, the reforms always begin (and very often end) by creating new offices and new positions. None of them really goes to the root of the matter, the basic imbalance in the economy, and no reform ever gets sufficient time to prove itself useful.

Thus, much of what is labeled socialism in Egypt is little more than increased bureaucracy, most of which was introduced as a palliative and persists because the political system contains no checks and balances against the inherent tendency for any administration to expand. Sadly enough, some genuine social reforms have contributed to make nationalized enterprises work more like government offices than productive units.

Some Biases in Economic Thinking

Various ideas in economic planning and policymaking in Egypt have led to inefficiency in the economic system. Egypt probably shares these biases with many other developing countries, but this does not make them any better. In discussing the bias toward administrative solutions and increased bureaucracy, the preceding section dealt with these problems in a general way. Here we are concerned with more specific and concrete ideas.

Principles of Planning

It may seem strange to discuss the planning principles of a country that has had no comprehensive plan in the last few years. However, the effects of these years may not have been much different from those under the first five-year plan of 1960/65. Apart from the projects of national importance (including those that are aid-financed and come up for government negotiation), concrete investment decisions seem to have been made in the ministries within government budgetary frameworks. This kind of "planning in stages" can work well only if the lower stages are provided with adequate criteria for choosing among investment projects. But no such general investment criteria seem to have been laid down. Ministries choose investment projects that seem important to them. Considerations of backward/forward linking (within the sphere of a particular ministry, that is —between ministries the contacts are weak and sometimes even nonexistent), self-sufficiency, diversification, and import substitution seem to play an important role. Even according to these criteria, investment planning has been inefficient.

Studies of the fertilizer industry show, for instance, that important causes of unutilized capacity and low production in the Suez plant have been the lack of adequate storage facilities and packing material (paper bags).[87] Trivial though these things are, they cause bottlenecks and severely slow down production. Here, forward and backward linking has failed. The missing storage facilities can only be traced back to deficient investment planning, but the insufficient packing material involves foreign trade controls also. Those who designed the Suez factory may have taken for granted that inputs could be imported. The example teaches a very general lesson. For production to function smoothly, the system of foreign trade has to be so flexible that it will always permit the import of inputs in short supply. Economic planning generally is imperfect and needs such complementary safety valves. In addition to foreign exchange shortage and inflexible foreign trade controls, bad linkage planning has done much to create inefficiency. It is exactly in this respect that a better balance in foreign trade and the foreign exchange situation would be highly productive.

Ideas of import substitution and self-sufficiency have led to grotesque planning mistakes in the past and seem likely to continue to do so. There is nothing wrong with concentrating more on replacing imports than on building up export industries. The existence of transport and sales costs abroad means that a country should, in general, begin with import substitution rather than exports. The mistake lies rather in taking import substitution (and thus foreign exchange saving) as a sufficient criterion for investments. What has been almost completely lacking in Egyptian planning is profitability calculations based on international commodity prices and reasonable shadow prices for capital and foreign exchange in particular. (Value-added estimates have always been based on domestic market prices, which differ greatly from international prices; see below.) Through such calculations, planners could appraise import substitution and other projects according to efficiency and could choose projects more rationally. Even

[87] Naiem El Sherbini, "A Study of the Foreign Exchange Restraint in Development Planning."

if only crude calculations were made, such fancy projects as the ill-fated Nasr Motor Car Company would never have seen daylight.[88]

As in so many other countries, the heavy industry syndrome also has led Egyptian planners astray. The outstanding example is the steel industry. Here military considerations may have played a role, although it should have been plain at the outset that Egypt could not expect to produce steel of high enough quality for modern weapons. More likely, the decision to achieve self-sufficiency in steel was made on the basis of naive ideas of self-sufficiency and the need to have a heavy industry basis for light and medium-heavy industries. It is probably significant that the Soviet Union is going to finance the extension of this industry; for Soviet planners, steel production is always worth its price. But even with the new ore deposits in the western oases, the steel industry can hardly be defended on purely economic grounds. Cost calculations for the extended production have not been published, if they have been made at all; but critical articles in the press have hinted at a very high cost per unit of steel.[89]

Planners seem also to have been much more interested in building new large-scale enterprises than in improving efficiency and quality in existing ones. The preoccupation of agricultural planning with "horizontal" expansion (reclamation) rather than "vertical" expansion (drainage, fertilizers, new plant varities) exemplifies this bias. It is said that there has been a change in attitude about this problem in recent years, but I do not know what the practical consequences have been. On the other hand, a general tendency to choose excessively capital-intensive techniques has not been apparent in the investments actually made. Of course, examples of projects with extremely elaborate techniques can easily be given (Heikal's new printing office, for instance), but it is perhaps more significant that the choice of technique has tended increasingly to be determined by the nature and capacity of the deliverers. With the shift in the composition of foreign trade and aid toward the Communist countries, Egypt has suffered in having to accept the technologies used in these countries; the West could offer a wider choice of more advanced techniques.

Before World War II, Egypt was a typical one-commodity exporter, raw cotton accounting for about three-quarters of the total export value. For this reason the country has suffered exceptionally wide fluctuations in its terms of trade. At the time of the agricultural world depression in the early 1930s, deteriorating terms of trade inflicted a loss of about 10 percent of the national income. In the years leading up to the Korean boom, the terms-of-trade gain may have amounted to as much as 20 percent of the national income, a gain that soon was largely lost. It is not surprising, therefore, that the authorities have been anxious

---

[88] This company, which assembled Fiat cars at about double the cost of an imported car, seems to have been inefficient by any standard. It was not even foreign-exchange saving. It used more foreign exchange per assembled car than was needed to import a finished car.

[89] *Ahram El Iqtisadi,* Cairo, August 1968.

to accomplish diversification of production and exports. There has been some success: by 1964/65 the share of raw cotton in total export value had fallen to almost one-half. Unfortunately, diversification is often taken to exclude specialization and thus to imply an extreme degree of self-sufficiency. For this reason there has been a tendency in Egyptian planning to try to diminish dependence on foreign trade in general. But this does not follow logically. Through specializing in a limited number of products, the country may obtain a sufficient hedge against terms-of-trade fluctuations without losing the advantages of specialization. It is impossible to say whether optimal planning leads a priori to a relative increase or decrease in foreign trade. At least in Europe, diversification and specialization have gone hand in hand and have led to increasing foreign trade relative to GNP.

The planning of some countries has suffered from a bias in favor of industry as opposed to agriculture, which has led to gross neglect of the latter. This can hardly be said about Egypt. The High Dam was conceived as an agricultural expansion project (although subsequently stress has been placed on the production of electricity), and Egyptian planners have never lost sight of the country's natural advantages in agriculture. If there has been a sectoral bias in Egyptian planning, it has mainly been against housing, as pointed out above.

Principles of Pricing

A decentralized decision system will work only if it is combined with an adequate pricing system. These are two sides of the same coin. This lesson, which has sent the Communist world into spasms, has been reluctantly and incompletely apprehended in Egypt, although the government has never been opposed to decentralization, market forces, and price mechanisms as such. Reluctance in using prices for efficiency purposes has little in common with Communist prejudice; it is much more akin to the Western socialist preoccupation with income distributional aspects of pricing, together with a lack of understanding of the allocative aspects.

Price controls in Egypt date back to World War II, when they were introduced for much the same reasons as in wartime Europe and the United States. When the controls continued during the 1950s, they were always defended by reference to the need for keeping down excessive profits and the cost of living. Agricultural price support schemes aimed mainly at giving the peasants a fair income without jeopardizing the cost of living. Allocative considerations entered in connection with the protection of industry through high tariffs, import licensing, and the like, but here the government found itself facing the dilemma of keeping prices high to promote private industrial development while keeping profits and cost of living low. With the nationalization of a major part of industry this dilemma should have disappeared. High profits in industry have ceased to be a source of income for private capitalists and are now just another form of government revenue; from an income distributional point of view they can now be regarded as indirect taxes and are thus an alternative to other means of keeping total demand in the economy at an appropriate level. This should make it easier for the government to let individual commodity prices be determined by allocation considerations. There seems now to be an increasing understanding of this change in the role of profits, and from 1964 price adjustments made primarily to clear the markets have become more frequent. But, of course, without simultaneously creating overall balance in the economy a complete rationalization of the price structure is impossible.

There is no reason for believing that price mechanisms would not work in Egypt. Nothing is more competitive than the Middle Eastern bazaar, and its spirit still pervades all economic activities, wherever permitted. Moslem fatalism —which probably belongs more to Western notions of the Middle East than to reality—certainly does not extend to the field of economics. If *homo oeconomicus* exists at all, it must be here. Even the responsiveness of agriculture to prices is well documented and is of special importance to future foreign trade. Should European agricultural protectionism ever give way, Egypt would—to take an important example—have a bright future as the fruit and vegetable garden of Europe, provided that the country can solve the problem of standardizing qualities. The history of Egyptian cotton proves that with sufficient price incentive even illiterate peasants can be brought to produce and deliver quality agricultural products that compare well with those of any developed country. But price incentives are obviously required all the way through, from the salesman abroad to the fellah in the village; the production and export of high-quality fruit and vegetables are not compatible with red tape.

The government's concern with income distribution has led to interference not only with commodity prices but also with factor prices: rents on land, interest rates, and wages. In all cases the result has been unintended misallocation of resources, the consequences of which are less conspicuous but probably more serious than those related to commodity pricing. Factor pricing is a field in which there does not seem to be much understanding of the needs of change.

Rents on land (but not land prices) were fixed by the land reform of 1952 on the basis of tax assessments from 1949, and have not been changed since. Immediately after the breakdown of the Korean boom, the official maximum rents were probably in line with what free market rents would have been, but since then a large gap has grown between official rents and hypothetical "market rents." If rents were free, their general level would probably more than double.[90] Moreover, the relative rents on different lots of land are becoming increasingly out of line with relative marginal-value productivities because of changes in water supply, patterns of production, land improvements, and the like. As a result, absentee landowners (who still own substantial areas, albeit in

---

[90] The value of agricultural production has more than doubled since 1949, and the size of the (black market) *bon-de-sorties* paid for tenure contracts points in the same direction.

smaller plots) have become increasingly uninterested in making land improvements; this may have been offset, however, by government efforts and a greater interest in improvements by tenants who have obtained more secure and longer-lasting terms of tenure. Probably the most serious allocation effect of the fixed rents is that there is no longer any mechanism (aside from the black market) to ensure that the most competent people cultivate the land. In this respect the upper limit for tenure (50 feddan) has probably also had important negative effects.

The government's policy with respect to interest rates and the price of capital generally has been to keep interests and profits down. Since more than 90 percent of the investment decisions have been in the hands of the government and hardly have been influenced by profitability considerations, this policy has had little effect on the actual choice of investments. But investment planning might look very different if scarcity prices of capital had been applied. A case in point is housing, as mentioned earlier. For the wrong reasons, planners rightly felt that they should not try to match investments in housing with demand at the present low, controlled rents for houses; on the other hand, they have kept the increase in the supply of housing below the increase in demand, even at rents that would cover the scarcity price of capital.

Wage controls and their disincentive effects have already been mentioned. The controls are based on the statutory minimum wages (effective mainly in public enterprises and public works), the grading system for public enterprises, and the grading system for public administration. Outside the public sector, wages are largely market-determined and follow changes in demand and supply closely.

An issue that has gained importance during recent years is the relationship between industrial and agricultural prices. There has been a clear tendency to let the terms of trade of agriculture deteriorate as a means of financing industrialization.[91] In other (particularly Communist) countries, this policy has had detrimental effects on agricultural development and has led to compulsory deliveries of certain minimum quantities at official prices. In Egypt the results seem to be much the same. If agriculture is to expand more rapidly than in the past, price policies have to be more favorable to agricultural production. Devaluation (see Section IV, p. 66) would clearly have this effect if allowed to influence agricultural producer prices. The result would be an increase of income in agriculture with consequences for food consumption in rural districts and the balance of payments. As mentioned previously, these incomes could easily be siphoned off through an increase of the land tax without detrimental effects on production, but the government does not seem to understand this crucial role of the land tax.

[91] Before World War II, fertilizers were imported duty free. Although this policy was dictated mainly by the wishes of the landlords, it obviously had positive allocation effects. Since the 1950s the government has sold fertilizers to the peasants at prices generally above import prices, probably as a device to tax agriculture

Foreign Trade and Aid

Since the mid-1950s, Egyptian foreign trade has been increasingly oriented toward the Communist countries, especially Eastern Europe. Up to a point, this was probably economically advantageous.[92] The concept of neutralism adopted by Egypt (and many other third-world countries) made it only natural that the Communist countries' share of Egyptian foreign trade should increase. Economic and political considerations pointed in the same direction. Behind these developments we find French colonial and British power policies, American discrimination against neutralist countries, and the one-sided attitude of Western countries toward the Palestine problem. Although difficult to quantify, the distribution of trade between East and West is important. In principle, the Communist countries trade at world market prices, but for many commodities world market prices are difficult to define. It seems likely that, if the quality of the imported goods is taken into consideration, part of the present volume of imports from the Communist countries implies a loss in terms of trade.[93]

With the exception of American PL 480 aid, which assumed very large proportions during the Kennedy administration's attempt to reshape American policies toward the Middle East, Egypt has tended to become more and more dependent on Russian aid (quite apart from military deliveries). Russian aid (loans) is always bilateral and tied to specified projects, meaning that the recipient has to accept the projects that the donor is able or willing to finance. These are not always the projects that are most urgent from the recipient's point of view. The apparently sound High Dam project and the obviously unsound extension of the Helwan steel works represent the extremes. This is not to say that Western aid is necessarily preferable. Much Western aid is also bilateral and project bound; PL 480 aid has its own special drawbacks. Quite apart from the political implications, however, it stands to reason that, at least from a technological point of view, Western aid is superior to Russian aid. Otherwise, the main conclusion to be drawn from the Egyptian experience is that underdeveloped countries should avoid positions in which they are completely dependent on the donors and forced to take whatever they can get. Aid and independence are difficult to reconcile.

A special problem is that of trade in the Middle East among the Arab countries themselves, and with Israel. There has been much discussion and some agreements on Arab custom unions and free trade areas, but practically nothing

[92] George K. Kardouche, *The Flow of Financial Resources,* United Arab Republic: case study of aid through trade and repayments of debts in goods and local currencies, UNCTAD, TD/B/C, 3/63, 13 December 1968.

[93] Kardouche actually found that for comparable commodities Egypt seems on average to have had slightly better terms of trade with Communist countries than with the rest of the world in 1962 and 1963. Machinery and equipment, for instance, were not included in this comparison, however, and it seems likely that here the terms of trade may have been unfavorable, considering quality, service, and supply of spare parts. *(Ibid.)*

has been accomplished. The Arab countries have relatively little to offer each other at the present stage of development, and fluctuating political relations among these countries have led to repeated ruptures in their foreign trade. In textiles, for instance, Egypt has traditionally enjoyed a good market in some of the other Arab countries and would gain from more stable relations with them. With Israel there have been no economic relations at all, but the Arab countries have probably lost little on this account. Although Israel is technically, commercially, and administratively superior to the Arab countries, there is little Israel can offer them that they cannot procure just as economically from other developed countries. In this sense the question of economic relations between the Arab countries and Israel—so crucial for Israel—is a marginal one for the Arab countries and will always rank low in their deliberations. Disregarding the basic political problem of the recognition of Israel, Arab resistance to economic relations with Israel is, rightly or wrongly, related mainly to fears of Israeli (and thus, allegedly, American) economic penetration of the Arab world and the creation of a new foreign economic and technical hegemony. The issue parallels that of direct American investments in Western Europe. Notions of imperialism are mixed with more concrete arguments concerning possible economic effects. The whole issue is rather vague, and it is fortunate that we do not need to consider it more closely. The Arab countries have lost little, in any case, in not having economic relations with Israel.

Measures to Increase Efficiency

A Balanced Economy

Before anything else, demand and supply must be balanced and inflationary conditions ended if increased efficiency is to be achieved.[94] The balance should be established within the limits of possibilities of net borrowing in the future. Egypt should even aim at building up and maintaining sufficient working balances of foreign exchange to circumvent temporary domestic bottlenecks in production through imports without difficulty or delay.

Investment Planning

Profitability comparisons based on efficiency prices, not only within but also among ministries and organizations, are a prime need in this sphere. Nobody expects such profitability calculations to be very sophisticated; it is not easy to determine efficiency prices with great accuracy. But even the crudest calculations, used as a basis for choosing investments, will be a basic improvement. Externalities, learning by doing, and similar effects—much too often used as a pretext for

---

[94] It has been argued in the development literature that in order to induce business to expand there must be excess demands in the economy. Whatever the merits of this argument for a private enterprise economy, it does not apply to an economy whose expansion the government is leading. The government planners do not need excess demand in order to plan for expansion.

doing something that in any case would be done for other reasons—should be allowed to influence the investment choice only if there is positive evidence for their existence. If demand and supply are balanced, unforeseen gaps between the demand and supply of domestic inputs can be filled through foreign trade, and problems related to forward and backward linkage will lose importance because production bottlenecks will have been prevented. In investment planning it will still be important to trace linkages because foreign transport costs tend to make investments profitable wherever linkages exist. With foreign borrowing at a minimum, dependence on aid for take-it-or-leave-it projects should disappear. In this way, Egypt would be free to plan investments rationally; at the same time, the inevitable mistakes in planning would have much smaller consequences for current production. These changes would require that the Ministry of Planning play a much more important role, and that something of a revolution in the thinking of the planners take place.

Centralization and Decentralization in Production

The present organization of public enterprises permits a high degree of decentralization in current production. Indeed, being joint stock companies, all the nationalized enterprises could be run exactly as independent corporate businesses, with interference by the government, mainly as the majority shareholder, only in investments, appointments of management, and other long-term activities of the enterprise. The problem of combining decentralization in current production with centralization in investment decisions is therefore no greater than that of allocating decisionmaking in a privately owned joint stock company. There is, however, at least one point of overlap between current production and investment decisions: repair and maintenance. Centralized decision systems, particularly in underdeveloped countries, tend to ignore repair and maintenance, and Egypt is no exception. Decisions in this respect should be decentralized so that at least the nationalized enterprises could purchase spare parts and the like abroad, if necessary, without licenses or other controls. The argument extends logically to the import of raw materials and other inputs. (Here we limit ourselves to nationalized enterprises in order to avoid or at least minimize the problem of illegal capital flight via double invoicing and similar subterfuges; this was one of the motives for nationalizing foreign trade.)

All this is not to deny that in some production processes certain decisions about current production can be made better by a central authority than by individual enterprises. Irrigation in agriculture is probably one of these; the large-scale advantages in agriculture can probably be best taken care of by direct central decisions.

Employment and Wages

The decentralization of production should be extended to employment. Public enterprises should not be compelled to employ superfluous workers, as has been done since the employment drive of 1961/62. Moreover, enterprises should be

86

given sufficient powers to enforce discipline on the shop floor. Here we run into the difficult problem of reconciling social security and productive efficiency. This problem is well known in advanced countries (the United Kingdom, for instance) but is much more complex in underdeveloped countries. To rely solely on the "socialist spirit" of the employees would be inexcusable romanticism; such a spirit does not exist. However, much could probably be gained through a change in the wage and salary system. If the position of management itself was made dependent on showing good results, that is, good profits, and if piece-rate work were introduced wherever possible, reconciliation of social security with efficiency would probably turn out to be a minor problem.

Price Policy

I have recommended the use of efficiency prices in investment planning. Things would be greatly facilitated if efficiency prices and producers' actual buying and selling prices could be brought to coincide. This would mean a complete overhaul of the price system and would involve important changes in relative prices at both the producer and the consumer level. The greatest problem would be how to handle the resulting changes in income distribution. There is nothing wrong with income distribution targets, and we cannot ignore them; the question is whether the government can handle income distribution problems through appropriate taxes and transfers without interfering with producer prices. It should prove no great problem to collect the necessary revenues. The main question is, therefore, whether the direct or indirect subsidies can be administered equitably.

East versus West Trade

In the discussion of defense expenditures, it was assumed that the solution of the present conflict would imply that Egypt's dependence on deliveries of military equipment from Communist countries, as well as Western discrimination against Egypt, would disappear and that Egypt would be able to choose the most economical pattern of trade. This would lead to a relative expansion of trade with the West, although it is difficult to judge how large a shift would be advantageous. It is not clear how good a market Egypt would have for her cotton products in the West after having been excluded from these markets for so long. And Egypt's future as a supplier of fruit and vegetables to Europe depends greatly on the agricultural policies of the European Economic Community and the European Free Trade Association. Another problem is to what extent East and West trade would have to be balanced separately or how surpluses in one could be used to cover deficits in the other.

The Bureaucracy

Except for investment planning, perhaps, all the measures proposed here would involve a smaller or at least a less rapidly growing bureaucracy. Reduction of the armed forces, part of our general assumptions, would work in the same direction. This would meet with natural resistance from the bureaucracy itself and would create the long-run problem of finding employment for the large number of university graduates. The educational system might need to be over-hauled, reducing the annual influx into the universities in order to prevent a growing army of unemployed graduates. A general reform of the administrative system is also needed for better adaptation to the increased functions of government. The more general problem of creating efficiency and initiative in adminis-tration, whatever the actual system is, remains basic. Egypt has no shortage of competent administrators. If higher civil servants could exercise freedom in making decisions without the fear of severe punishment in case of mistakes and the prospect of no reward in case of success, there should not be great problems at the higher levels of administration. The most challenging problem is to in-crease efficiency at the lower levels and to wipe out nepotism and similar phe-nomena.

VI. Summarizing Remarks

It has been argued in this paper that under favorable external conditions and with good domestic policies Egypt should be able to keep per capita income growing at about 3.5 percent per year in the long run. This is not a very high rate of growth. But it is respectable, and it will suffice for raising the country's economy to a level by the end of the century which is comparable to that of a country like Greece today. There is no need to inquire as what level Greece may have reached by that time. What matters for the Egyptian people is that their country will begin to approach the status of what we today call an economically developed state, where extreme poverty need no longer be tolerated and a decent standard of life can be secured for everybody.

"Favorable external conditions" is here taken to mean, above all, conditions that permit Egypt to reduce her armed forces to less than half their size before the June 1967 War; that return to her the territories, including the Suez Canal, now occupied by Israeli forces; and that permit her to choose the most favorable pattern of trade. It presumes, furthermore, that Egypt will be able to consolidate her very large and partially very expensive foreign debt. It would be natural if a solution of the present conflict—together with so many other issues—also settled this one, perhaps by encouraging the rich Arab oil countries to take over Egypt's total foreign debt at reasonable interest and amortization conditions and with the debt service guaranteed by a big power consortium.

"Favorable external conditions" is not taken to mean, however, that further foreign aid or loans should necessarily be made available to Egypt. Among the underdeveloped countries Egypt does not belong to the really poor ones, after all. Starvation and hunger are virtually unknown. The crumbs that fall from the table of the rich countries ought to be reserved for those at the bottom of the ladder; Egypt is quite a number of steps higher up. Under favorable external conditions, as defined above, Egypt is fully capable of financing future develop-ment exclusively by private and public domestic savings. This course would not impose inhuman hardships on the population, and it would give the country a freer hand to choose an optimal trade pattern. Only financially independent countries, it might be added, should dream about neutralism, economic as well as political.

Good domestic policies mean tough demand management and wage policies, and far reaching reforms to remove red tape and promote efficiency. These two sides of economic policy are closely related. The demand management and wage policies should aim at removing inflationary demand pressures and cost increases. In order to provide sufficient exports and reduce imports, food consumption per capita should be kept constant through heavy, increasing taxation on food consumption, and only the broad population's nonfood consumption of services and simple, unsophisticated industrial products should be allowed to increase. This would necessitate important changes in the tax system, and it is important to stress that such demand management policies would be entirely consistent with income-equalizing policies.

Good demand management is a necessary, but certainly not a sufficient, condition for the removal of red tape and the improvement of efficiency. More is needed. Appropriate organizational forms to promote efficiency must be instituted. Inefficiency should not be accepted as an inherited national characteristic about which nothing can be done. Some very fine examples of efficiency can be found in the economic history of Egypt. Under the present system we can point to the administration of the Suez Canal, the construction of the Aswan High Dam, and the cooperative system of the land reform areas. Under the old system the spectacular success of Egyptian cotton proved that even illiterate peasants may be turned into efficient producers of high-quality export commodities. These examples not only show that a high degree of efficiency can be reached in Egypt but also indicate that what matters is not capitalism or socialism, in the sense of ownership to big enterprises, but rather the concrete organizational forms under which the economy works. Both capitalism and socialism can be made to perform badly if cast in the wrong institutional forms. On the other hand, both can be made to perform well. The basic problem for Egypt is not to choose between more or less socialism (this it may do also, of course), but to stamp out the traditional civil servant spirit and practices that now pervade the economy at all important points and replace them by profit and price incentives at all possible levels, not least in relation to foreign trade.

Whether actual developments will provide all the favorable external and internal conditions for the projected growth rate remains to be seen. It is outside the scope of this paper, fortunately, to discuss what may happen under the most unfavorable conditions.

CHAPTER 3

Economic Development Problems of Israel, 1970-1980

Michael Bruno*

*For very helpful comments on an earlier draft I am indebted to Mordecai Fraenkel, Aryeh L. Gaathon, and Eliezer Sheffer of the Bank of Israel; to Eytan Berglas, Tel-Aviv University; to Reuven Gronau, Hebrew University; and last but not least, to Sidney Alexander and Charles Wolf, Jr., of The Rand Corporation.

Bruno is certainly right in the following essay that Israel's growth performance is "remarkable and almost unique." A tiny country, having scant natural resources and beset by the demands of war, Israel has nevertheless achieved a growth rate since 1948 of over 10 percent per year. But the secret of this performance lies as much in the enormous capital inflows from abroad as in anything else. Israel, in short, has found it possible to live well beyond its means. No statement in Bruno's essay is so revealing as the following: "The massive accumulation of capital since 1948 was achieved mostly through government and public institution fund raising abroad with almost no net domestic savings."

The whole story of Israeli development is not captured, however, by looking at her large capital imports. No reader of Bruno's essay can fail to escape the impression of good economic management, with the exception of the demand squeeze that overshot in 1966/67. The successful absorption of large numbers of poor and poorly educated immigrants, the rapid growth of exports, the extensive increase in education, the development of an efficient armaments industry, the application of technology to the agricultural resource base and agriculture practices —all testify to informed and effective economic policy.

Past success notwithstanding, Israel's economic future remains uncertain. As is true for all the countries involved, the continued state of warfare in the Middle East poses a major problem for Israel in the cost of maintaining a modern military establishment on a scale far out of proportion to the country's size. The Israeli balance of payments problem looks no closer to solution than ever as imports continue to grow rapidly, never permitting exports to close the gap. Little scope remains for more efficient import substitution, and whether past rates of export growth can be maintained remains the central problem in closing the export gap. Still, although Bruno asserts that "the Israeli experience re-emphasizes the importance of capital," Israel's past success in applying modern technology and in managing economic policy seem to offer the best reasons for optimism about the future.

Economic Development Problems of Israel, 1970-1980

I. Introduction and General Perspective

At the end of 1965, a 15-year period of sustained, uninterrupted, and very rapid growth in Israel, during which real GNP grew at over 10 percent a year, came to a sudden, though temporary, end. Immigration dropped to a trickle, the growth of GNP halted, and unemployment rose from its previous level of 3 percent to about 12 percent. By the time the government came to recognize the depth of the depression and took a number of strong counter-cyclical measures, the sudden, unexpected political and military upheavals of June 1967 completely changed the scene. Quite apart from the effects of the major changes in the territory and population under effective political and economic control by Israel since the war, the downturn in economic activity also came to an abrupt end.

By mid-1969 the economy had gone through a very rapid upswing. In 1968, GNP rose over 13 percent, investments by 44 percent, exports by 21 percent. Unemployment fell to about 5 percent, and immigration into Israel was rapidly increasing. But even in victory the war brought new problems—primarily a very high and sustained level of defense expenditures, while the balance of payments gap widened very rapidly and foreign exchange reserves began to fall.

Looking ahead to 1980 reveals many problems. The political future is uncertain, and so might seem the chances of another prolonged period of rapid growth. Yet there is room for optimism, even if it must be qualified.

Israel is a tiny country, about 21 thousand square kilometers.[1] It is rather poor in natural resources. With the exception of the rich Dead Sea deposits (mainly of potash) and some minor deposits of phosphate and copper, there are no mineral sources of substance. Its soil, though in places quite fertile, has to be irrigated for most modern agricultural use, and water resources are limited and costly. Although Israel is quite well located in terms of potential land and sea trade with neighboring countries, for political reasons its trade is confined to much more distant partners, which puts it at a natural disadvantage relative to competitors. In spite of all these factors, Israel stands out as one of the few countries outside Europe, North America, and Oceania to have successfully de-

---

[1] This does not include the territories administered after the Six-Day War.

veloped. Per capita income of around $300 in 1950 grew to reach an average of approximately $1,000 in 1969.[2]

Israel's remarkable and almost unique growth performance in the few years of its existence cannot be explained in terms of any one factor. A few of the important elements that have singled it out from among the broader group of developing economies include the growth and composition of its immigrant population, its particular sources of investment finance, and the motivation of its people. No serious assessment of future prospects and problems can be made without an analysis of the present and future role of these factors, as well as a number of additional elements that will be discussed later in this study.

Free immigration of Jews into Israel had been one of the ideological cornerstones of the long political campaign for Israel's independence and has formed one of the main social and economic policy objectives ever since independence was achieved in 1948. As a result, the population of Israel has grown extremely rapidly, but at a very uneven rate.

From a total figure of 915,000 (of which 759,000 were Jews and 156,000 were non-Jews) at the end of 1948, population rose to 2,841,000 at the end of 1968 (of which 2,435,000 were Jews and 406,000 were non-Jews).[3] The average annual rate of population growth for the period 1948–1965, at which time immigration virtually stopped, was 6.3 percent.[4] This average was derived from a 28 percent increase in 1949, 15–17 percent per year in the subsequent two years, and rates fluctuating between 3 and 5 percent thereafter. Net Jewish immigration into Israel accounts for about 60 percent of this total increase in population and the total natural increase for around 40 percent.

Not only the size but also the sources of this immigration are important. During the period 1949–1965, over 55 percent of the immigrants came from Asian and African countries and less than 45 percent from Europe and the Americas. This fact had a marked effect on the characteristics of the labor force in Israel and on some of the educational and social problems that the country still faces; it also has important implications in terms of the remaining potential future sources of immigration. In the past most of the immigration has been in the nature of "rescue" immigration. Unless the Soviet Union opens its doors, however, most of future immigration will be immigration by choice, for which economic conditions in Israel, job opportunities, and the like will be of increasing relative importance. Of about 14 million Jews living in the world today, 2.4 mil-

[2] If the official exchange rate is used, the figure is even higher—$1,200.

[3] These include about 66,000 in Eastern Jerusalem since June 1967. See Central Bureau of Statistics (CBS), *Monthly Bulletin of Statistics,* Vol. XX, No. 3 (March 1969), Table 1.

[4] For detailed figures see CBS, *Statistical Abstract 1968,* Table B/1; and for an analysis thereof see N. Halevi and R. Klinov-Malul, *The Economic Development of Israel,* Frederick A. Praeger, New York, 1968, Chap. 4, on which part of the discussion is based.

lion live in Israel, only about 0.7 million remain in Asia and Africa, about 2.5 million are in the U.S.S.R., and almost all the remaining, over 8 million, live in the United States (about 5.7 million) and other western countries.

In 1966/67, net immigration came almost to a standstill and the population growth rate fell to 2 percent. Since the June 1967 War, however, there has been a new upsurge of net immigration into Israel—12,000 in 1968, and a further increase in 1969.

The main challenge to the economy, especially in the early post-independence period, has been to achieve the economic and social absorption of this massive immigration and at the same time to raise income and product per capita. One measure of success is indicated by the fact that unemployment fell steadily from 8.9 percent in 1954 to 3.3 percent in 1964. The immigrants into Israel in the 1930s and 1940s in a sense supplied their own means of absorption. Most tangible capital was supplied through immigrant transfers from abroad. Moreover, these immigrants were, on the whole, well endowed with the education and skills obtained in their countries of origin. In contrast, the immigrants since 1948 have largely lacked financial resources and have had a much lower level of education and skills.

The massive accumulation of capital since 1948 was achieved mostly through government and public institution fund raising abroad with almost no net domestic savings. The public channels of investment finance in turn meant a substantial government control over resource allocation and economic activity in general.

The Israeli experience re-emphasizes the importance of capital accumulation to rapid development. This relationship often tends to be obscured by studies of economies where growth has been slower, such as the United States and several European countries. But even by comparison with rapid growers (for example, Western Germany and Japan), capital accumulation is much more important as a source of growth to Israel. This can be seen by analyzing the components of GNP growth in terms of factor inputs and productivity change along the lines of Solow-Kendrick-Denison.[5] If one considers the total private economy of Israel (after exclusion of government services, for which no productivity measure exists, and dwellings) during the period 1953–1965, there is an average annual rate of growth of 10.8 percent for the capital input, 3.8 percent for the labor input, and a GDP growth rate of 11.7 percent. Depending on the weights

---

[5] See John W. Kendrick, *Productivity Trends in the United States,* National Bureau of Economic Research, Princeton University Press, Princeton, N.J., 1961; Robert M. Solow, "Technical Change and the Aggregate Production Function," *The Review of Economics and Statistics,* Vol. 39, No. 3 (August 1957), pp. 312–320; and Edward F. Denison, *Why Growth Rates Differ: Post-War Experience in Nine Western Countries,* The Brookings Institution, Washington, D.C., 1967. The major Israeli study in this field is A. L. Gaathon, *Economic Productivity in Israel 1950-65,* Frederick A. Praeger, New York, 1969.

used for the two major inputs of capital and labor,[6] capital explains between 30 and 45 percent of the total growth of GNP, and total factor productivity only between 35 and 25 percent, with labor accounting for the rest. This is in contrast, for example, to 20–25 percent for capital and over 60 percent for total productivity in Western European countries during the 1950s. If a later subperiod, 1960–1965, is considered for Israel, these shares turn even more markedly in favor of capital.

Even after one makes corrections for the increased degree of utilization of capital and labor, and for the reduction and later increase in the average level of education of the labor force, there remains a "hard core" of about 4 percent per annum of total factor productivity increase that cannot be explained by any other known factor.[7] This residual, resembling that found for more developed countries and higher than the residuals for some less developed economies such as in Latin America,[8] is evidence of other factors that must have been at play in Israel, such as increasing returns to scale and the capacity to adopt new techniques, issues to which I shall return subsequently.

Development and productivity growth have certainly not affected all major sectors equally over time. Agriculture has been the sector to which attention was already focused in pre-State years and was accelerated in the early years after 1948. This was partly the concomitant of the immigrant absorption process, which took the form of settling and reclamation of largely virgin land and of large-scale water resource development. Production for home consumption, import substitution, and exports (mainly citrus) resulted in a growth rate of 11.2 percent for real GDP in agriculture during 1953–1965, 8.9 percent on a per worker basis(!), and 5.9 percent in total factor productivity (on Gaathon's

[6] The observed market shares are approximately 30 percent and 70 percent, respectively, but there are good reasons to believe that the more correct weights are 50 : 50 (see below).

[7] If we consider Gaathon's basic figure of 5.5 percent per annum for the private economy during 1953–1965, we can use various partial studies for tentative corrections as follows:

Basic productivity estimate:		5.5 percent
Corrections:	1. Different index procedure	−0.2
	2. Increasing utilization of capital	−0.4
	3. Increasing utilization of labor	−0.1
	4. Net lowering of average labor skills	+0.4
	5. Disequilibrium in factor markets	−1.4
Resulting modified estimate:		3.8 percent

Corrections 1–4 are based on an unpublished M.A. thesis of Y. Manzali at Hebrew University, and correction 5 is based on M. Bruno, "Estimation of Factor Contribution to Growth under Structural Disequilibrium," *International Economic Review,* February 1968.

[8] See H. J. Bruton, "Productivity Growth in Latin America," *American Economic Review,* December 1967.

basis). There is evidence of a slight deceleration in the more recent subperiod, 1960–1965, the figures being 7.5 percent for total GDP, 8.0 percent per worker, and 4.3 percent for total productivity. In recent years there has thus been a net outflow of labor from agriculture. The superior quality of the early settlers, plus a high degree of mechanization from the start (labor was almost always quite costly) and a long learning process all have had their marked effect.

Manufacturing, on the other hand, was a later starter. Large-scale investment in manufacturing did not begin until reparation money from Germany started flowing in by 1954/55. The government allocated these funds to investment in the form of massive cheap development loans, partly to the public sector but mainly to the private sector. Output performance in manufacturing, though quite impressive for the period 1953–1965 as a whole, really picked up momentum in the more recent period, 1960–1965, when real annual GDP growth rate was 13.8 percent, or 6.8 percent on a per capita basis,[9] and 4.9 percent in terms of total factor productivity. Israel's future, as we shall see, depends to a considerable extent on whether this industrialization process can be continued. Overall industrial output and productivity performance is clearly not a sufficient measure of success. No less important are the composition of this output and the suitability of the present industrial structure for the kind of challenge that lies ahead. Much of industry has developed behind a highly protective tariff wall whose gradual elimination, together with much greater orientation toward exports, is the main problem lying ahead.

The large-scale development effort was made possible with only a small participation of domestic savings. Large-scale capital imports imply large deficits in the current balance of payments account. On one hand, this has brought about the growth of a considerable external debt (now approaching $2 billion) and at the same time has focused attention on the need to divert an increasing share of resources to the closing of this gap. Here the smallness of the country and its lack of almost all basic raw materials are again relevant. Israel is highly dependent on imports for almost all raw materials as well as for most of its equipment. Raw materials and other intermediate goods constitute over 60 percent of imports; the rest is divided among finished consumer goods, equipment, and defense products. Israel's import-GNP ratio, about 40 percent, is of the order of magnitude of that of Holland or Belgium, and imports have grown approximately at the rate of GNP growth. During 1953–1965, imports grew 3.5-fold, from $365 million in 1953 to $1,271 million in 1965.

Import substitution was nonetheless a factor of considerable importance in the industrial (and earlier agricultural) growth of the 1950s, when the food, textile, fertilizer, and paper industries were the main ones developed. Much of government policy from the beginning was focused on means to foster import sub-

[9] There was a clear process of acceleration or "learning" in the growth rate of gross output per worker. This rose from 3.5 percent in 1961 through 5.9 (1962), 6.0 (1963), 7.4 (1964), to 9.3 percent in 1965. See Bank of Israel, *Annual Report, 1967*, Table XII-1.

stitution, at first chiefly through quantitative restrictions and various related administrative measures, and by direct allocation of development loans. After the last large official devaluation (1962) the quantitative restrictions were largely replaced by tariffs, whose effect can be more easily calculated, but these are still highly protective and rather arbitrary. Recently a conscious effort has been made to bring down and standardize tariff rates across commodities, but the situation is still far from consistent with what seems desirable from the long-run point of view (see also Section III).

The potential for further import substitution decreased considerably during the 1960s, and the only real remaining candidates for import substitution are certain kinds of equipment and defense items. All in all, import substitution and tariff policy are more likely to affect the composition of imports and the efficiency of domestic production than the overall level of imports.

The main attention, from the balance of payment deficit point of view, has thus had to be shifted to the development of exports. Here, too, the government gave active support in the form of subsidies on value added and various allocative measures. During the period 1953–1965 exports indeed grew 7.5-fold (from $102 million to $750 million) with manufacturing exports taking much of the lead. Exports of citrus, of much greater importance in the past, have diminished in relative terms. Obviously growth was not even over the period, and exports, on the whole, encountered much greater difficulties toward the latter part of the period, because of problems in world markets and soaring inflation on the home front (see also Section III).

The ratio of exports to imports thus increased from about 28 percent in 1953 to approximately 60 percent in 1965, a feat which in itself is quite impressive. Even so, the current deficit doubled over the period in absolute terms, and reached a level of $521 million in 1965. Although the means to finance this deficit were there at the time and reserves were even accumulating, it was generally felt that developments could not continue in that direction for a long time.

The period 1953–1965 was not a homogeneous one in terms of general developments, and it is 1960–1965 to which I shall refer most often in my projections. This was a period of full employment growth and general prosperity, which was achieved at the cost of a considerable increase in the import gap. A devaluation of the Israeli pound from 1.80 to 3.00 I£ per dollar at the beginning of 1962 failed to curb the import gap for a number of reasons. In terms of the exchange rate for exports, the devaluation was only a legalization of an already existing effective subsidy rate of close to 3.00 I£ per dollar before devaluation. As far as imports were concerned there was some shift from administrative to fiscal protection, and excessive rates were brought somewhat closer to the average. The main hindrance, however, was the complete absence of domestic absorptive measures, both fiscal and monetary, to curb the extra inflationary pressures brought about by the devaluation at a time of full employment. Capital imports continued to flow into the country in increased amounts, partly for speculative reasons, as the government guaranteed the rate of exchange at which investments could be repatriated. The period 1963–1964 was one of repressed demand inflation, which turned into open wage inflation in 1965.

As mentioned previously, by the end of 1965 this sustained and very rapid growth came to a sudden end. The ensuing slump resulted from a combination of a number of factors, a fall in immigration with a concomitant drop in construction activity and a decrease in foreign investments, and on top of this was superimposed a planned government squeeze that overshot rather miserably. The Hebrew term *Mitun,* meaning a planned light recession, often applied to 1966/67, is clearly a misnomer. But on the face of it there was one measure of success—the current deficit fell from $520–530 million in 1964/65 to $445 million in 1966. The new upsurge in economic activity that followed after June 1967 was also accompanied by an extremely rapid increase in the current deficit, which by 1969 reached a record of almost $900 million.

Although a considerable part of the present and expected future increase in foreign exchange expenditures is no doubt directly connected with defense, one major reason for this rapid rise in the import surplus is connected with an underlying structural weakness whose symptoms the slump period helped to mitigate temporarily, but could by no means cure. The drop in the deficit during 1966/67 is wholly explained by the sudden cessation in imports, together with the halting GNP growth rate, exports growing more or less at their previous rate. Similarly, the sudden upsurge in 1968 is more than wholly[10] explained by the renewed rise in imports, although a large part of the latter is due, no doubt, to defense.

These developments are very important for the analysis of Israel's long-run problems because they bring out very clearly the dilemma of the trade-off between rapid growth and the reduction in the balance of payments deficit. Section III will have more on this topic and will also indicate the costs and benefits of alternative ways of solving this problem.

The main theme of this study will be a more detailed discussion of some of the problems already indicated here, as well as a few others, as viewed against the background of a projection of the economy into the future. This projection will be based on favorable, though realistic, assumptions and, like any other projection, may be sensitive to them. Section III of this study will indicate how, if at all, changes in these assumptions might affect the figures and qualitative assessments. Moreover, I shall discuss the implications for economic policy of the solution of problems that this projection will bring out.

In my basic projection I assume that there will be no major changes in the political and military situation—neither an outbreak of another major war nor a general peace settlement between Israel and its neighbors. Defense expenditure is assumed to continue to be high and growing; but its relative *share* in total resources, if rapid overall growth continues, will decline gradually from its recent record level. The analysis will refer mainly to the economy of what is, as of

[10] Indeed, exports, as already indicated, rose more than average in 1968.

1968, officially defined as Israel, including Eastern Jerusalem. On the other hand, the current tendency for workers from outside these boundaries to enter the Israel labor force is assumed to continue. Also, the analysis will be conducted under the assumption that Israel will, at least for some time, continue to administer the areas left in its hands after the Six-Day War (Sinai, the Gaza Strip, Judea, and Samaria). Since the economics of the administered areas is the subject of another study, I shall mention its aspects only to the extent that there are any direct implications for the present topic.

Jewish immigration into Israel is assumed to continue at a rate of 30,000 (gross) a year; this implies that for the time being there will be no immigration from Soviet Russia. Israel will also continue to receive financial support from outside, which for part of the time may still be high in absolute amounts but will continue to fall in relative importance. As my analysis will show, there are good chances that Israel may soon be able to go on growing without further external financial support. Such "economic independence" can be reached by 1980.

The evaluation of possible future developments is my concern in Section II of this study, with a projection through 1980 of population, labor force, and productivity per head, thus determining potential GDP. The sectoral composition of GDP is then estimated through 1980. I then turn to the capital required by the projected output and the corresponding investment needed to build up that capital. Next I forecast public consumption and analyze the expected foreign trade flows of exports and imports. Section II ends with a summary forecast of uses and resources during 1970–1980.

It is always very difficult to be specific about the timing of various developments. In the present context I nonetheless deemed it useful to analyze the 1968–1980 period by using 1970 and 1975 as intermediate time-posts. In my opinion, 1969/70 is likely to witness a continued rapid emergence from the slump into full employment, and I forecast an 11 percent growth rate in GNP for this brief period.[11] From 1970 to 1975, the economy will continue to grow quite rapidly (over 8 percent per annum), but a major effort will have to be undertaken with respect to both balance of payments and domestic policies. The 1975–1980 figures represent a settling down to a long-run, somewhat lower, steady growth, about 7 percent, also representative of the years after 1980. These time divisions are somewhat arbitrary and should be taken as illustrative rather than concrete in detail; nevertheless, they seem more useful than looking at 1970–1980 as a single homogeneous period.

The main discussion in Section III starts with the analysis of problems of balance of payments, foreign capital inflow, export marketing, and the exchange rate policies implied by the projection. Next I turn to investment promotion and finance and the increased role of domestic savings. The third general topic in this section revolves around population, production and productivity, manpower and education, problems and policies. Then comes a discussion of prices, income, and wages, ending with a few general comments on economic planning.

---

[11] Judging from developments in the first half of 1969, this rate seems to be valid.

II. Projections

Population—Immigration and the Natural Increase

As already stated in the Introduction, there has been a new upsurge of immigration into Israel since the June 1967 War. However, it is hard as yet to give a good numerical estimate of the present rate of net immigration. In the case of new residents from the Western Hemisphere it is difficult to distinguish between immigrants and temporary residents. There is clear evidence, however, that immigration has increased considerably, and the gross immigration figure for 1968 may very well have reached 25,000, of which about half were of Western origin. It also seems that the number of residents emigrating from Israel, which has been around 10,000 a year throughout and reached over 12,000 in the two depression years, has decreased considerably; moreover, there has been a considerable increase in the number of returning residents. Official Jewish Agency estimates put the future expected gross immigration at 35–40,000 a year. The estimate to which I shall keep is an average annual gross immigration figure of 30,000.[12] This question will be discussed further in Section III.

The average rate of natural increase is higher in Israel than in a typical country of the same per capita income level, but it has been going down steadily over time. The rate now has declined to approximately 1.8 percent, from 2.5 percent in 1951–1955, 2.1 percent in 1956–1960, and 1.9 percent in 1961–1965.[13] This rate is an average over very heterogeneous ethnic groups.

The drop in the overall rate reflects mainly the reduction in the birth rate of the Jewish population; the death rate has been fairly constant. This reduction mainly comes from the decline in the proportion of women of child-bearing age in the Jewish population.[14] The natural increase among Jews is now down to 1.5 percent, having been 2.4 percent in the early 1950s. Among non-Jews, on the other hand, there has been an increase in the rate, until very recently, because of a declining death rate and a rising birth rate; the net rate of natural increase reached 4.3–4.4 percent in 1961–1966, probably the highest in the world.[15] The birth rate among non-Jews has also been declining in the last few years, however, and their net rate of increase is now about 3.9 percent.

My population projection takes into account the various elements and

[12] This I shall assume to be divided roughly equally between Asia-Africa and Europe-America. This division is important for purposes of assumptions about fertility rates, labor force participation rates, and net emigration rates, which differ.
[13] See footnote 4.
[14] The total fertility of child-bearing Jewish women has been constant on the average. Families that have immigrated from Asia-Africa usually have a high fertility rate, but they also tend to reduce family size after staying in the country for some time. On the other hand, there has been some increase in family size among Jews of European origin. (See Halevi and Klinov, *The Economic Development of Israel.*)
[15] The death rate is down to 0.66 percent, only very slightly higher than in the Jewish population; the decline reflects the considerable improvement in health conditions.

trends mentioned here. It is based on a forecast for 1985 prepared by the Central Bureau of Statistics in 1966 and modified to take into account changes since 1966 and a more optimistic immigration estimate.[16]

By 1980 the total population of Israel is thus estimated to reach an average of 3.8 million (of which 650,000 will be non-Jews), compared with 2.8 million in 1968, an average rate of growth of 2.5 percent, compared with an average rate of 3.8 percent for 1960–1965 and rates of 2.6 percent in 1966 and 2.0 in 1967. Details are given in Table 3-1. Assuming a rate of 2.2 percent, say, for the period 1980–2000, I obtain a population forecast of 5.9 million for the year 2000.

The most important feature of this projection is the diminishing role of immigration even with a reasonably optimistic immigration forecast. Of the projected population increase during 1968–1980 *only about 20–25 percent at most is expected to come from immigration* as compared with over 60 percent in the past.[17] This has important implications for comparisons of future development prospects with past developments.

It might be useful to note also the expected order of magnitude of the population in the areas currently administered by Israel: the West Bank, the Gaza Strip, and Sinai. The figure for 1968 is about 1 million, which may be estimated to increase to 1.2 or 1.6 million by 1980, depending on the birth rate and migration.[18]

Labor Force and Potential Employment

Israel has a high proportion of children and a low proportion of working-age people, making for a comparatively low proportion of labor force in the population. To this must be added a relatively high rate of school attendance and a comparatively low participation rate for women, especially those from Asia-Africa, whose working habits for a time resemble the customs in their countries of origin. However, this latter effect tends to weaken with length of residence in Israel. All in all, the ratio of the labor force to total population is almost 10 percentage points lower than in Europe.[19]

[16] The CBS forecast assumes a constant birth rate among Jews of European-American origin, a slight reduction among Jews of Asian-African origin, and a very slight decline among non-Jews. Alternative immigration estimates (gross) were 15,000 and 25,000 per annum, of which in each case 5,000 are from Asia-Africa. I have corrected the forecast for the inclusion of Eastern Jerusalem (66,000 in 1967), the decline in immigration in 1966/67, and a higher projected immigration figure (30,000 gross, divided equally between the two main groups).

[17] Two issues to be discussed further below are (1) the eventuality of a larger immigration wave, and (2) the important contribution of the "new" immigration in terms of skills and human capital content.

[18] This assumes a rate of 3.7 percent for the natural increase. The lower figure assumes an emigration out of these areas at the same rate as for the years before June 1967, that is, about 2.5 percent per annum.

[19] See Halevi and Klinov, *The Economic Development of Israel,* Table 25, p. 85.

Table 3-1
Actual and Forecast Population, Labor Force, and "Potential" Employment, 1965-1980

	Actual			Projected	
	1965	1968	1970	1975	1980
Population (thousands)[a]	2563	2806	2942	3357	3793
Civilian labor force[a]					
Participation rate (percent)	35.6	34.6	35.7	36.1	35.8
Numbers (thousands)	912	970	1050	1211	1358
Employment of Israeli nationals					
Percentage of labor force	96.4	93.9	96.5	97.0	97.0
Numbers (thousands)	879	911	1013	1175	1317
"Outside" workers	. . .	5	15	46	79
Total domestic employment	879	916	1028	1221	1396

Average annual growth rates (percent)	1960-65	1968-70	1970-75	1975-80	1968-75	1968-80
Population	3.8	2.4	2.7	2.5	2.6	2.5
Employment of Israeli nationals	4.7	5.4	3.0	2.3	3.8	3.2
Total domestic employment	4.7	5.9	3.5	2.7	4.2	3.6

[a]These estimates are based in part on the Central Bureau of Statistics population forecast for 1985 and also on some revised estimates prepared by M. Hershkowitz of the Bank of Israel.

Source: Bank of Israel, Annual Report, 1968, Chap. IX.

During the high employment years 1960–1965 the participation rate went up steadily from 34.8 percent in 1960 to 35.6 percent of total population in 1965. However, in the depression years 1966/67 it fell to 34.4 percent (1967),[20] but began to rise again in 1968.

My estimates for the future are based on a combined extrapolation of the specific participation rates by sex and age group during the years 1960–1965 and an assumed overall rise in the near future due to the upsurge in economic activity. The resulting overall participation rates are given in Table 3-1. I obtain a rise to 35.7 by 1970, another slight increase to 36.1 by 1975, and the setting in of a long-term falling trend thereafter (35.8 in 1980).

My projection of the unemployment rate for the future assumes a continued reduction from 5 percent at the beginning of 1969 to 3.5 percent by 1970 and 3.0 percent in 1975 and thereafter. In an immigration country there is bound to remain a hard core of frictional or structural unemployment even during a boom period. In Israel this is estimated at about 40,000.

Table 3-1 summarizes the resulting "potential employment" forecast. For the twelve-year period 1968–1980 as a whole, the estimate is a *3.2 percent annual growth rate in employment,* compared with 2.5 percent for population during the same period and a 4.4 percent employment growth rate during 1960–1965. The average, however, conceals markedly different growth rates for the three subperiods, mainly because of my "cyclical" assumptions. The rates are an annual average of 5.6 percent for 1968–1970, and then 3.0 percent and 2.3 percent, respectively, for the subsequent two five-year periods (1970–1975 and 1975–1980).

The estimate of potential employment would not be complete without taking into account a very recent phenomenon: a growing influx of workers from the administered areas. They are concentrated mainly in Jerusalem and in several areas along the previous border. The official government policy started with a complete prohibition of such influx in the early postwar months, then partly eased the restrictions. The influx is now subject to control dependent on conditions in the Israeli labor market and specific shortages in the various sectors of the economy. The chief lines of employment are construction work and seasonal employment in agriculture, primarily unskilled labor. There are no reliable statistics on the extent of influx so far. Semiofficial estimates place the figure for 1968 at 5,000, and the planned increase for 1969 was 5,000–10,000.

It is hard to make any estimates of this influx for the future. The new liberal policy has recently come under attack by several influential political and labor leaders. Nevertheless, to the extent that there is a continued demand for such workers, I have no doubt that this development will continue. It is reasonable to assume, however, that it will be controlled and gradual, to prevent the upsetting of a very unstable equilibrium in the labor market. I shall therefore as-

[20] Actually the comparable figure, excluding Eastern Jerusalem, is 34.7 percent in 1967. See Bank of Israel, *Annual Report,* 1967, Chap. IX.

sume a gradual increase of about 5,000 workers per annum from this source. This would imply a component of about 80,000 workers from these areas,[21] employed inside Israel by 1980, out of a total Israeli labor force of 1,400,000.

A similar phenomenon took place in the early 1960s, when an easing of restrictions inside the Israeli labor market brought about a considerable influx of temporary Arab workers from villages into the Jewish sector. It is estimated that at the height of the boom, in 1965, some 54 percent (33,000) of the total Israeli Arab male work force were employed outside their area of normal residence.[22]

The implication of this assumption is to increase the overall rate of growth of potential employment by almost 0.5 percentage point, and this I take as the basis for my projection. The detailed forecasts are given in Table 3-1.

Overall Labor Productivity

To pass from a potential employment forecast to a forecast of potential GNP we need an estimate of the overall rate of growth of labor productivity. For the whole economy real gross domestic product per worker increased 6.3 percent annually during 1953–1965.[23] The figures for the two more recent subperiods are as follows: 1955–1960, 5.4 percent; 1960–1965, 5.1 percent per annum. During the subsequent recession and turning point, 1965–1968, the annual average was 4.3 percent, which can certainly not be considered the long-run potential.

Since in 1969 there was still some unutilized capacity, I believe an average 5.0 percent growth rate for aggregate labor productivity during 1968–1970 is perfectly feasible. This I assume to be followed by a 4.8 percent annual growth rate during 1970–1975, and for the last part of my forecast horizon, 1975–1980, I assume a lower productivity growth rate, 4.5 percent, consistent with a general slowing down of the growth rate in the economy. This way of looking at things implicitly makes the "Verdoorn Law" assumption that labor productivity growth is itself a function of the overall product growth rate.[24] I shall later check back on my overall estimates after looking at the implied growth rates for the "private" economy, the disaggregated productivity growth assumptions by major

[21] Such an assumption is dependent principally on internal Israeli considerations and less on any particular political solution for the "administered areas," since it is reasonable to assume that the old border will never be completely sealed again.

[22] An analysis of developments until 1961 is given in Y. Ben-Porath, *The Arab Labour Force in Israel,* Falk Institute, Jerusalem (also Frederick A. Praeger, New York), 1966. For data on later periods see CBS, *1968 Abstract,* Table K/9-11, pp. 259–262.

[23] See Gaathon, *Economic Productivity in Israel 1950–65,* Appendix V-1.

[24] See P. J. Verdoorn, "Complementarity and Long Run Projections," *Econometrica,* Vol. 24, No. 4 (October 1956), pp. 429–450. An alternative interpretation could be the deceleration of productivity growth that comes as the country approaches "best practice" technology. The incremental ratio between the rate of growth of average labor productivity and that of the total product is taken to be 0.27.

Table 3-2
Forecast of the Gross National Product

Rates of Growth (percent)	Actual				Projected		
	1960-65	1965-68	1968-70	1970-75	1975-80	1968-75	1968-80
Total employment	4.7	1.1	5.9	3.5	2.7	4.2	3.6
Labor productivity	5.1	4.3	5.0	4.8	4.5	4.9	4.7
Total GDP	10.0	5.4	11.2	8.5	7.3	9.3	8.4
Absolute levels	1968		1970	1975	1980		(2000)[b]
GNP[a] (million I£, 1968 prices)	14,045		17,364	25,994	36,808		(129,800)
GNP (million $ at 3.50 I£/$)	4,012		4,961	7,426	10,516		(37,100)
GNP (million $ at 5.00 I£/$)	2,809		3,473	5,199	7,362		(25,960)
GNP per capita (at 3.50 I£/$)	1,430				2,770		(6,290)
GNP per capita (at 5.00 I£/$)	1,000				1,940		(4,400)

aThe difference between GNP (gross national product) and GDP (gross domestic product) consists of net payments to factors abroad, that is, interest payments and wages paid to "foreign" workers. The growth rate of GNP is expected to be approximately 0.1 percent per annum less than that of GDP.

bAssuming a 6.5 percent GNP growth rate for 1980-2000.

Sources: 1960-1965, A. L. Gaathon, *Economic Productivity in Israel, 1950-65,* 1968, Bank of Israel, *Annual Report,* 1968, Chap. II.

106

economic sector, and alternative "total" productivity estimates that incorporate the separate contribution of the capital stock. Other considerations are the quality of the labor force and everything that comes under education and human capital, as well as "technology." For these considerations see Section III. Table 3-2 summarizes the ingredients and the results of such GNP projection.[25]

Gross national product is to rise from a level of I£ 14 billion in 1968 to almost 37 billion in 1980 (in 1968 prices), that is, by a factor of 2.6.[26] In per capita terms the economy is expected to almost double during this period and to reach at least the level of Germany and France today, if not that of Canada and Sweden.[27] Table 3-2 gives all the relevant figures, including a conversion to U.S. dollar terms by means of two alternative exchange rates: the present official rate, 3.50 I£ per dollar, and a higher "equilibrium" rate of 5.00 I£ per dollar. If we want to reckon in national income rather than in gross product terms, the figures in the table must be reduced by about 20 percent to take account of net indirect taxes and depreciation of capital.

If we assume a 6.5 percent GNP growth rate for 1980–2000, GNP per capita by 2000 will reach approximately the present U.S. level (reckoned at 5.00 I£ per dollar).

Sectoral Output and Employment Levels

Tables 3-3 and 3-4 give a GDP and employment projection by major sector consistent with the overall projection given above. In working out the disaggregated figures I have used a number of factors:

1. The different long-run elasticities of sectoral output with respect to the economy's total output. These I have worked out on the basis of schedules of solutions obtained from a long-run interindustry programming model for Israel.[28]

2. I have considered the different patterns of growth expected for the three subperiods 1968–1970, 1970–1975, and 1975–1980. For example, during 1968–1970 a particularly large growth rate is expected for the construction industry, which is still emerging from the slump.

3. In making the disaggregated employment projection I have used Gaathon's sectoral labor productivity growth estimates for the period 1953–1965 and, in particular, for the subperiod 1960–1965, plus Verdoorn considerations. Here,

---

[25] I have ignored the problem of the difference between the input of workers and of working hours. Since I am consistent with the base-period definitions, however, labor productivity growth may be assumed to incorporate whatever changes there may be in working hours, providing their *rate* of change in the future will not be different than in the past.

[26] During the 12-year period 1953–1965 it grew by a factor of 3.4.

[27] Depending on what exchange rate is being used for conversion into dollars.

[28] See M. Bruno, "A Programming Model for Israel," in Adelman and Thorbecke, eds., *The Theory and Design of Economic Development*, The Johns Hopkins Press, Baltimore, 1967.

Table 3-3

Forecast of Gross Domestic Product by Major Sector, 1968-1980

(1967 prices)

Sector	Actual				Projected			
	Rate of GDP Growth, 1960-65 (percent)	GDP, 1968 (million I£)	GDP Growth Rate, 1968-70 (percent)	GDP, 1970 (million I£)	GDP Growth Rate, 1970-75 (percent)	GDP, 1975 (million I£)	GDP Growth Rate, 1975-80 (percent)	GDP, 1980 (million I£)
Agriculture	7.5	834	8.5	982	6.5	1,346	5.5	1,759
Manufacturing and mining	13.8	3,752	15	4,964	12	8,742	10	14,075
Construction		978	20	1,408	7	1,975	5	2,522
Transportation	12.3	1,486	13	1,898	10	3,056	9	4,703
Public sector and nonprofit institutions	7.4	2,621	7	3,001	5	3,832	5	4,893
Dwellings	6.8	1,271	7	1,455	6	1,947	5	2,486
Services and trade[a]	8.9[b]	2,648	8.2	3,103	7.2	4,386	4.7	5,516
Total economy[c]	10.0	13,590	11.2	16,811	8.5	25,284	7.3	35,954
Private nondwelling economy[d]	10.7	9,698	12.9	12,355	9.6	19,505	7.9	28,575

[a]Includes public utilities.
[b]Includes construction.
[c]The total does not include import taxes (I£410 million in 1967).
[d]Defined as the total economy less dwelling, public sector, and nonprofit institutions.
Sources: 1960-1965, Gaathon, *Economic Productivity in Israel, 1950-65*, Appendix I-1. 1968, Bank of Israel, *Annual Report*, 1968, Chap. II.

Table 3-4

Employment by Major Sector, 1955-1980

Sector	Rate of Change, 1960-65	1968 (thousands)	Rate 68-70	1970 (thousands)	Rate 70-75	1975 (thousands)	Rate 75-80	1980 (thousands)
Agriculture	-0.4	103	-1.0	98	-1.0	93	-1.0	89
Manufacturing and mining	6.6	238	7.0	273	4.9	347	4.0	422
Construction	5.8	76a	11.1	94	1.9	103	1.0	108
Transportation	4.7	66	5.1	73	2.8	84	2.8	96
Government and public services	5.2	217	5.0	239	4.5	284	2.7	324
Other services and trade	4.1	216	7.8	251	4.3	310	2.9	357
Total	4.6	916	5.9	1028	3.5	1221	2.7	1396

Percentage breakdown	1955	1960	1965	1968	1970	1975	1980
Agriculture	17.6	17.3	13.0	11.2	9.5	7.6	6.4
Manufacturing and mining	21.9	23.2	25.4	26.0	26.6	28.4	30.2
Construction	9.3	9.3	10.5	8.1	9.1	8.4	7.7
Transportation	6.2	6.2	6.9	7.3	7.1	6.9	6.9
Government and public services	21.2	22.0	22.6	23.8	23.3	23.3	23.2
Other services and trade	23.8	22.0	21.6	23.6	24.4	25.4	25.6
Total	100.0	100.0	100.0	100.0	100.0	100.0	100.0

aThe figures for the 3 years 1965-1967 were 92.0, 76.3, 63.0, a marked symptom of the depression.

Sources: 1960-1965, Gaathon, Economic Productivity in Israel 1950-65, Appendix V-1, and Central Bureau of Statistics, 1968 Abstract, Table K/11. 1968, Bank of Israel, Annual Report, 1968, Chap. IX.

109

too, I assume labor productivity to grow faster during periods of rapid growth (1968–1970 and, to a somewhat lesser extent, 1970–1975) than during slower growth years (1975–1980). Clearly, it is quite probable that the estimates for the period 1968–1980 as a whole carry a larger measure of credence than those for the subperiods.

Agriculture, manufacturing, and transportation are expected to be the fastest productivity growth sectors (the orders of magnitude being 7–7.5 percent annually during 1968–1975, and about 6 percent thereafter). For both agriculture and transportation this is consistent with past performance. For manufacturing I base my optimism on the evidence of a "learning" process during the period 1960–1965, which showed a marked acceleration in the rates of growth.[29]

My projections for the annual labor productivity growth rates in manufacturing are 7.5 percent (1968–1970); 6.8 percent (1970–1975); and 5.8 percent (1975–1980).[30] Maintenance of a high rate in the future depends, of course, on suitable capital accumulation performance.

Three most marked changes are to be expected in the product and employment breakdown:

1. The share of manufacturing product will probably increase from 27.6 percent in 1968 to 39.1 percent in 1980 (see Table 3-3). Because of expected rapid productivity growth, the change in the employment share is much smaller (from 26.0 percent to 30.2 percent of total employment).

2. As in the past, total employment in agriculture is expected to fall slightly in absolute terms over the period as a whole, with its relative share declining from its present 11.2 percent to 6.4 percent by 1980, orders of magnitude reminiscent of those in the United States. This has been a high-productivity and highly mechanized sector all along. Manufacturing has been going through its breakthrough only very recently.

3. The construction sector, which reached a record 10.5 percent of employment at the height of the boom (1965) and dropped sharply during the slump, is now picking up again (to reach 9.1 percent by 1970) but is, on the whole, expected to settle to a share of no more than about 8 percent in the long run. This reflects a relative reduction in the importance of construction for new immigrants.

Capital Input Requirements and Total Factor Productivity

The single most important prerequisite for continued rapid growth in Israel is a sustained high level of investment. The Introduction stressed the singular role of physical capital in the remarkable past performance. Later discussion takes up the question as to how, if at all, such investment is likely to be financed in the

[29] See footnote 9.
[30] Here the incremental ratio between the annual rate of growth of labor productivity and that of total product is taken to be 0.5.

MICHAEL BRUNO

future, and for the moment I confine myself to the estimate of capital *requirements*.

Two alternative approaches suggest themselves here. One, more naive but nonetheless quite realistic, is to assume that labor and capital are complementary factors, so that the relevant production function would be something like

$$Y = \text{Minimum } (AK^a, BL^b)$$
$$\text{or} = \text{Minimum } (AKC^t, BLD^t), \text{ say,}$$

where K = capital stock, L = labor, Y = product, t = time, and all other letters denote fixed parameters. This approach would be consistent with the way in which I tried to estimate labor requirements from the GDP forecast by sector. It implies that capital requirements are estimated by projecting from past relations between capital and output by sector.

The alternative approach, somewhat more consistent with conventional analytical finesse, is to take a Kendrick-Solow-Gaathon line and to consider output as emerging from a so-called neoclassical production function of the kind in which substitution between capital and labor is assumed and growth of total output can be broken down into its separate capital, labor, and "technical progress" contributions. (Or, in the case of a Cobb-Douglas function, $Y = AK^gL^{1-g}H^t$.)

The approach I shall take here is to use the first method for estimation and, once having product, employment, and capital input projections, apply the second "method" only to check whether the implied total productivity ("technical progress") factor looks about right when viewed against past performance. Clearly this is no independent check, only a qualitative assurance that we have probably not gone too far astray.

All this does not, of course, apply to the capital stock invested in residential housing, where an independent projection is made. The results of the first (complementary-factor) approach are given in Table 3-5.[31] Capital is defined as the "gross" stock. For 1968–1970 I take into consideration that capital in the base year (1968) was still partly underutilized, at least in industry. A related underlying assumption is that in services, transportation, and irrigation part of past investment has been in the nature of long-lived infrastructure and that investments of this type will not be repeated at the same level during the coming decade.

If the resulting estimates for the growth rates of capital, labor, and product are put side by side, we obtain the figures for all industries combined (excluding dwellings on the capital side, as well as government and nonprofit institutions on the product and employment side), as shown in Table 3-6.

On the basis of past performance the estimates for total productivity growth rates during 1970–1975 and 1975–1980 seem reasonable: 3.7 percent–3.0 percent (with 50:50 weights) or 4.6 percent–3.9 percent (with 30:70 weights). Whether the economy is likely to achieve such rates in the future and what education and technology problems and policies are implied will be discussed in Section III.

[31] The method follows the "perpetual inventory" method as used by Gaathon.

111

Table 3-5
Forecast of Capital Stock 1968-1980[a]
(beginning of year figures, million I£, 1968 prices)

	Annual Rate,[b] 1960-65	1968[c]	Annual Rate, 1968-70	1970	Annual Rate, 1970-75	1975	Annual Rate, 1975-80	1980
Agriculture	6.0	3,564	2.5	3,746	4	4,560	4	5,549
Irrigation	9.6	1,722	3.4	1,842	4	2,241	4	2,728
Manufacturing, mining, and construction	11.7	4,951	8.9	5,871	10	9,452	9	14,547
Electricity	7.5	1,401	6.7	1,593	8	2,341	7	3,284
Transportation	15.2	4,850	12.8	6,172	10	9,937	8	14,597
Services and trade	14.0	5,302	10.8	6,510	9	10,018	7	14,055
Total industries	10.6	21,790	8.7	25,734	8.4	38,549	7.3	54,760
Dwellings	9.6	12,973	5.4	14,412	7	20,220	6	27,054
Grand total		34,763		40,146		58,679		81,814

[a]Based on a complementary factor approach. See p. 00.
[b]See Gaathon, *Economic Productivity in Israel, 1950-65*, Appendix II-3.
[c]See Bank of Israel, *Annual Report*, 1968, Table V-8.

Table 3-6
Actual and Projected Growth of Total Productivity

	Average Annual Rates of Growth[a]			Estimated Total Productivity Growth Rate[b] (percentage annual rate of growth)	
	Capital	Labor	GDP	Using 50:50 Weights	Using 30:70 Weights
Actual					
53-65	10.8	3.8	11.7	4.4	5.8
60-65	10.6	4.5	10.7	3.2	4.4
Projected					
68-70	8.6	6.2	12.9		
70-75	8.4	3.5	9.6	3.7	4.6
75-80	7.2	2.7	7.9	3.0	3.9

[a]Excluding government, non-profit institutions, and dwellings.
[b]The measure given here is only very rough, using the formula

Growth of   Total productivity $= G_y - [mG_k + (1 - m)G_l]$

where G refers to *average* annual rate of growth, m and $(1 - m)$ are the two respective weights, and the subscripts y, k, and l refer to GDP, capital, and labor, respectively. Gaathon measures these rates year by year and then obtains a geometric average (his figure for 1953-1965 is 5.5 percent instead of 5.8 percent as above).

For the problem of the proper weights (m) see footnote 7 and Bruno (cited therein). In the latter it is shown that the marginal product of capital in the past was higher, and that of labor lower, than their observed average market prices. Factor weights should thus be corrected accordingly.

Investment Requirements

Having estimated the required capital stock, we can obtain an annual investment estimate based on the projected rates of growth of the capital stock by sector plus an estimate of replacements of worn out or obsolescent capital.[32] Table 3-7 gives such an estimate by major sector. At the bottom of the table I have computed the required share of total gross investment in GNP. This is estimated to run around 19–21 percent, compared with 27 percent in 1965 (and even higher in earlier years). The main reason for this fall is to be found in the reduction in the overall investment activity in housing, which was almost halved during the slump. The last row of Table 3-7 shows a much smaller drop between 1965 and 1968, when housing is excluded. Even though this sector is now expected to re-

[32] The details of the replacement estimate are not given here; the method followed is consistent with that of Gaathon.

Table 3-7

Forecast of Gross Investment by Sector, 1968-1980

(million I£, 1968 prices)

	Actual			Projected	
	1965	1968	1970	1975	1980
Agriculture	156	163	227	266	304
Irrigation	81	61	79	89	108
Manufacturing and mining	505	528	840	1,202	1,658
Power	124	99	177	255	320
Transportation	503	659	955	1,126	1,360
Services and trade	747	649	737	1,115	1,376
Subtotal for industries	2,116	2,159	3,078	4,053	5,126
Housing	1,035	612	990	1,212	1,624
Inventory increase	90	174	174	260	368
Total gross investment	3,241	2,945	4,242	5,525[a]	7,118[b]
Percentage of housing	31.9	20.8	23.3	21.9	22.8
Total gross investment as percent of GNP	26.9	21.0	24.4	21.3	19.3
Same as above, excluding housing	18.3	16.6	18.7	16.6	14.9

[a]Of this, I£770 million is replacements.
[b]Of this, I£1,130 is replacements.

Source: 1965, 1968, Bank of Israel, *Annual Report*, 1968, Chap. V.

cover very rapidly, I do not believe the economy will return to the record levels reached during the height of construction for immigrants and recipients of restitution payments in the 1960s, until at least 1970. The most marked growth in investment activity is, of course, required in manufacturing, which has suffered from lack of investment during the slump. Even though manufacturing investment almost doubled in 1968 (compared with 1967), it was barely past its 1965 absolute level.

In spite of the tremendous increase in investments that is required in manufacturing and mining (if growth is to take place along the lines drawn out here), the overall picture is optimistic in the sense that the economy is expected to be able to grow quite fast with a somewhat lower investment ratio in the future. One reason is the shift of emphasis from housing, with the reduction in the relative importance of the immigration factor. The other contributing factor is a slightly smaller emphasis (already mentioned above) on investment in infrastructure such as large-scale irrigation schemes[33] and new urban centers of the scope that has marked the developments of the previous decade. The expected reduction in the long-run growth of GDP itself implies an adjustment downward in the overall investment ratio.

Public Consumption

In Israel, public consumption is defined to include not only the central government and local authorities but also the so-called national institutions, such as the Jewish Agency, whose functions, for example, absorption and settlement of immigrants, could be performed by a central government. The national institutions are financed primarily by unilateral transfers from abroad. However, their share in the total resources at the disposal of the economy (GNP + imports) is only about 1 percent.[34]

In the years 1960–1965 total public consumption amounted to about 16–18 percent of total resources, with the central government taking 13–14 percent and the local authorities taking the remaining 2–3 percent. Although this is a very high figure compared with many other countries (but approximately equal to the public consumption share of the United States, Sweden, and the United Kingdom), two further points magnify the size of the problem even more. The first relates to the so-called nonprofit institutions, which have the unusually high share of an additional 5–6 percent of resources. These include the Histadruth (the Trade Union Organization with all its health and other services), Hadassah (Health Service), and the institutions of higher education. Here again part of

---

[33] Even though large-scale desalination projects are being considered, I believe these will enter the picture only toward the second half of the 1970s and in any case may be stretched in expenditure over a longer period.

[34] For this figure and others up to 1965 see Halevi and Klinov, *The Economic Development of Israel,* Table 64, p. 190.

the finance comes from abroad,[35] and the functions are of the kind that in many countries are supplied by the public sector. National accounting tradition, however, classifies these institutions in the private sector (and their expenditure to be included in private consumption). I shall follow tradition and adhere to the narrower and more conventional definition of public consumption.[36]

Public consumption has rapidly increased in 1967 and 1968, quite out of proportion with the general development of the economy. The share of public consumption (not including nonprofit institutions) in total resources has grown from 15 percent in 1965 to 22 percent in 1967, and was approximately 20 percent in 1968. Most of this increase, though not all of it (high wage increases in 1966 pushed up the figure by about 2 percentage points), is, of course, due to a very rapid increase in defense expenditure from the June 1967 War and its aftermath. Estimates that have been quoted in the newspapers would now place defense expenditure at about 14–15 percent (or more) of total resources. Why this is so hardly needs an explanation. Israel is a tiny country in terms of geographical and population size, yet its defense needs are like those of a much larger nation. There has always been a very high threshold of defense expenditure below which the country would run the risk of being exterminated.[37]

The other 8 percent of resources included under public consumption services (in itself not a low figure)[38] comes from a high demand for certain services —health, education, and general welfare—arising in large part from mass immigration and its special demographic characteristics. This 8 percent, as is often pointed out, is also the reflection of a relatively large import surplus, as capital imports have been channeled through the government sector. This is changing gradually.

During the 1956 Sinai campaign public consumption shot up, but in 1957 it very quickly declined again to "normal" levels. After 1967, this pattern is not likely to be repeated. Egypt has rearmed very quickly, and the whole postwar scene does not justify a reduction in defense expenditure but points rather to a continued increase. At the same time, however, I assume that another major all-out war is not in near sight. It thus seems reasonable that defense expenditure

[35] This constitutes a problem when we look at foreign capital inflow as financing investment rather than consumption. See Halevi and Klinov, *The Economic Development of Israel*, pp. 96–99; and D. Patinkin, *The Israel Economy: The First Decade*, Falk Institute, Jerusalem, 1959.

[36] The problem will be mentioned again in the context of savings behavior and policies (Section III).

[37] There are good reasons to suggest that the gross real cost of defense is even higher, since some of the expenditures on roads, settlements, etc., now recorded under various economic activities are in the nature of defense expenditures. This point, however, could be balanced by the side benefits accruing from defense activities, such as education, labor training, and the development of certain modern industries.

[38] If we add the 5–6 percent of nonprofit institutions here, we get 13–14 percent, which is one of the highest in the world (like that of Sweden, approximately).

116

will continue to go up but at a lower rate. For other components of public expenditure I assume a continued rate of increase. All in all public consumption is assumed to grow at an annual rate slightly lower than that of GNP and total resources after 1970: 15 percent during 1968–1970, 8 percent during 1970–1975, and 6 percent henceforth. This is the basis for the projections incorporated in Table 3-10 below.

Exports of Goods and Services

Israel's present dependence on imports, which I believe will remain at least as high in the future (assuming the country is to behave rationally), puts a special emphasis on the question of import finance and in particular on the future development of exports. I now turn to a projection of exports, on favorable assumptions, and leave the deficit finance problem and policy implications, as well as the required exchange policies, to the subsequent discussion.

As mentioned earlier, one of the marked features of the considerable export drive in the past has been a substantial shift of emphasis from the traditional predominance of citrus exports to a rapid development of manufacturing exports. In 1950 citrus was half of merchandise and 30 percent of total gross export revenue,[39] but its share has gone down consistently, reaching a figure of 15 percent only for its share of merchandise exports in 1968 (and less than 8 percent of total export revenue). The absolute figures appear in Table 3-8. During the same period the exports of miscellaneous manufacturing goods (excluding polished diamonds) rose to a level of *about half* of merchandise exports in 1968.

These trends are expected to continue in the future. With competition in the European markets and the depletion of fertile land and water resources, the long-run rate of growth of citrus exports is expected to be only about 5 percent. Recently there has been a new development of specialized agricultural exports other than citrus, such as flowers and tropical fruits and vegetables. In a short time this export category has grown very rapidly from virtually nothing to a level of almost one third of that of citrus exports. Here transportation is partly by air, and the natural climatic and know-how advantages of Israel are assumed to make for a sustained and rapid growth of these items in the future. Another item that has had a recent spurt is tourism, and this, too, I believe will go on growing very rapidly in the future.

The main question mark is Israel's ability to turn from its "traditional" manufacturing exports, such as polished diamonds, textiles, plywood, cement, and tires, to the "growth" industries—electronic equipment, scientific instruments, fine chemicals, and the like—for which transportation costs are of less importance, skill and know-how could be developed, and potential markets exist. I assume a future rate of growth in the total manufactures group of the order of

[39] The share is even higher if we reckon the *net* export share (i.e., after deduction of the import content in exports) since the component of value added in citrus is much higher than the average.

117

Table 3-8
Forecast of Exports, 1968-1980
(million $)

	Actual (current prices)					Projected (1968 prices)			Annual Rate of Growth (percent)			
	1950	1955	1960	1965	1968	1970	1975	1980	1960-68	1968-70	1970-75	1975-80
Citrus	17	32	47	71	88	105	134	171	8.1	9.2	5	5
Other agricultural goods	...	2	16	15	24	32	64	113	5.2[a]	15	15	12
Polished diamonds	9	20	61	132	194	236	332	444	15.6	10.3	7	6
Miscellaneous manufactures[b]	9	35	92	186	290	384	879	1,768	15.4	15	18	15
Total merchandise exports f.o.b.	35	89	216	404	596	757	1,409	2,496	13.5	12.7	13.2	12.1
Transport services	4	27	71	148	198	263	515	907	13.7	13.7	14.5	12
Tourism	5	7	27	55	96	100	201	404	17.2	2.1	15	15
Other services	13	21	51	142	231	250	503	886	20.8	15	15	12
Total goods and services[c]	57	144	365	749	1,121	1,370	2,628	4,693	15.1	10.6	13.9	12.3

[a]The corresponding figure for the more recent period, 1965-1968, is 16.4 percent.

[b]In 1967/68 this includes receipts from sale of ships and aircraft (19 in 1967 and 4 in 1968).

[c]Excludes exports to the administered areas (estimated at $59 million in 1968, of which $52 million was merchandise exports, $1 million was tourism, and $5 million was other services).

Source: 1950-1968, Bank of Israel, *Annual Reports,* 1955-1968, Chap. III.

magnitude of past performance. Because of foreseen difficulties in the European market an average rate of only 15 percent for this group is assumed during the first period 1968–1970 (compared with 15.4 percent during 1960–1968 and a record 27 percent in 1968 itself), and an export spurt of 18 percent during 1970–1975. However, this projection is optimistic and will, in fact, be justified only if the government undertakes the appropriate policies. (See Section III.) The annual rate of growth of total export receipts on both commodities and services is projected to be 10.6 percent during 1968–1970 and 13.9 percent for 1970–1975, slowing down to 12.3 percent thereafter. The breakdown by major category is given in Table 3-8. Miscellaneous manufactures (excluding polished diamonds, in which the projected rate is lower than in the past), are expected to include over one-third of total export revenue by 1980 (and some two-thirds of merchandise exports).

Imports of Goods and Services

Table 3-9 gives the ingredients of an import projection taken to be consistent with the projection of GDP and the various components of final demand. The increase in the rate of growth of consumption goods is a reflection of import liberalization policies, to be discussed further below. The imports of uncut diamonds are a function of exports of polished diamonds. Raw material imports should increase at a rate that is slightly higher than that of output, except that the 1968–1970 rate is assumed to be somewhat lower because of a large accumulation of inventories in 1968. Investment goods imports follow the initial spurt in investments assumed for the beginning of the period (which still reflects recovery from the slump). Implicit also is a certain amount of import substitution (see Section III). Invisible imports are, on the whole, assumed to follow a slightly lower rate of growth after 1970, especially for capital servicing and government n.e.s. (not elsewhere specified). The latter's very rapid growth up to 1970 reflects the extremely high defense expenditure.

The overall projected rate of growth of imports comes out very close to the growth rate of GDP from 1970 onward (see the bottom of Table 3-9) and slightly higher for goods alone. In the past total imports grew at least as fast as output, so this forecast might be considered conservative. However, one can check it using an alternative method by applying import coefficients to the final uses.[40]

I have ignored a component of Israel's exports and imports that has emerged since the 1967 War: the country's trade with the administered areas.

---

[40] The import components per unit of final use at 1968 prices in 1968 are roughly estimated as follows:

Private consumption	0.20 (of which 0.06 is direct imports)
Public consumption	0.36 (of which 0.30 is direct imports)
Gross investments	0.37 (of which 0.24 is direct imports)
Exports	0.44 (all indirect)

These are based on rough input-output calculations done at the Bank of Israel.

Table 3-9
Imports Actual and Projected
(million $)

	Actual (current prices)			Projected (1968 prices)			Annual Rate of Growth (percent)			
	1960	1965	1968	1970	1975	1980	1960-65	1968-70	1970-75	1975-80
Consumption goods	48	83	110	146	257	414	11.6	15	12	10
Fuel	35	53	63	73	102	136	8.6	8	7	6
Uncut diamonds		97	162	200	267	357		6	6	6
Other raw materials	284	407	530	635	1,022	1,537	12.2	9.5	10	8.5
Ships and aircraft	37	32	38	55	85	109		20	9	5
Other investment goods	86	147	168	260	348	444	11.3	24	6	5
Less: returns and adjustments		−24	−44	−53	−85	−137				
Total merchandise imports c.i.f.	491	795	1,027	1,316	1,996	2,860	10.1	13.2	8.7	7.5
Transport services	44	94	129	162	261	383	15.7	12	10	8
Tourism	11	44	52	65	110	169	32	12	11	9
Insurance	22	50	73	90	145	213	15.4	11	10	8
Capital servicing	51	94	135	170	275	440	15.8	12	10	10
Government n.e.s. (not elsewhere specified)	58	147	347	580	740	945	17.7	27	5	5
Other services	19	47	68	82	132	194	24.5	10	10	8
Total goods and services[a]	696	1,267	1,831	2,465	3,659	5,204	12.8	16	8.2	7.3
Rate of growth of GDP							10.2	11.2	8.5	7.3

[a]Excludes imports from administered areas (estimated at $45 million in 1968, of which $15 million were merchandise imports, $22 million were tourism, and $8 million were other services).

Source: 1965-1968, Bank of Israel, *Annual Report*, 1968, Chap. III.

The net magnitudes involved are small, and Israel is most probably going to have a surplus in its trade of goods with the areas but a deficit on payments to workers. It seems not too unrealistic to assume that the two flows will approximately balance each other, and I accordingly ignore this ambiguity in the trade accounts after 1968.

In the absence of any information to the contrary, world export and import prices are assumed to remain constant over the period concerned.[41]

A Summary of National Accounts for 1968–1980

Table 3-10 presents a complete set of aggregate national accounts for the years 1970, 1975, and 1980, based on the various magnitudes described in the previous sections. Private consumption, here estimated as a residual, is allowed a rate of growth of 10.3 percent during 1968–1970, 6.9 percent during 1970–1975, and 5.2 percent during 1975–1980. This implies an annual per capita rate of growth in private consumption of about 4 percent over the period 1968–1980 as a whole, but a higher than average rate during the beginning of the period, which in part is still the result of an upswing from a recession (plus an election year). The degree of realism of this result and the implied savings problems and policies will be analyzed in Section III. For comparison, during 1960–1965 per capita private consumption grew at a rate of over 6 percent but fell to virtually zero or was even slightly negative during the slump.

III. Problems and Policies

A considerable part of what has been said so far could in some sense also be classified as "problems and policies." In particular it is hard to distinguish the projection and the assumptions about policies that underlie it from a "plan." This section attempts to throw additional light on what are believed to be the critical factors on which the realization of the projection depends, on the sensitivity of Israel's economic development to deviations in some of these factors from the conditions assumed, and on the implied policy framework within which a sensible government is expected to act during the coming decade.

The Balance of Payments—The Import Gap and its Finance

The forecasts of exports and import requirements (Tables 3-8 and 3-9) imply a certain time profile of the balance of payments deficit on current account, and two questions come to mind. First of all, what is the implied time profile of the gap and how does it relate to whatever estimate one can make of the means of finance, unilateral transfers, and other capital movements from abroad? Second, there is the question of the export potential itself. Is the projection of Table 3-8 a realistic one, what are the implied problems and policies, and if such

---

[41] In recent years (excluding 1968) there has been a parallel but small increase in prices on both items.

Table 3-10
National Accounts, 1968-1980
(million I£, 1968 prices)

	Annual Rate of Growth[b] 1960-65	1968[f]	Annual Rate of Growth, 1968-70[g]	1970[g]	Annual Rate of Growth, 1970-75[g]	1975[g]	Annual Rate of Growth, 1975-80[g]	1980[g]
Private consumption	10.3	9,289	10.3	11,308	6.9	15,801	5.2	20,413
Public consumption	10.1[c]	4,109	15	5,436	8	7,985	6	10,684
Gross investment	10.8[d]	2,945	20	4,242	5.4	5,525	5.2	7,118
Exports[a]	13.3	4,027	8.6	4,746	13.9	9,093	12.3	16,240
Total uses	10.8	20,370	12.4	25,732	8.3	38,404	7.2	54,455
Imports[a]	12.4	6,325	15	8,368	8.2	12,410	7.3	17,647
GNP	10.3[e]	14,045	11.2	17,364	8.4	25,994	7.2	36,808

[a]The figures here differ slightly from those in Tables 3-8 and 3-9 (converted at a rate of exchange of 3.50 I£/$), as they include imports and exports to administered areas (assumed to balance after 1968) and exclude government payments and receipts of interest abroad.

[b]Bank of Israel, *Annual Report*, 1967, Appendix to Chap. II.

[c]The average growth rate of public consumption during the subsequent period, 1965-1968, however, was 16.5 percent.

[d]Investments in 1965-1968 fell by 3.1 percent per annum, on the average.

[e]The average annual growth rate of GNP during 1965-1968 was only 5.1 percent.

[f]Bank of Israel, *Annual Report*, 1968, Chap. II.

[g]Projected as of 1969.

122

projection is not going to materialize what is the implication for the rate of growth and the rest of the economy?

In 1969 the deficit on current account rose to an unprecedented record of almost $900 million, more than twice its level in 1966. According to my projection, with an assumed continued rapid rate of growth and given the export prospects foreseen, this deficit is going to continue to rise, reaching about $1,100 million in 1970. If exports from 1970 on grow at the rate specified in Table 3-8 (the special conditions for this will be discussed in Section IV), and if the rate of growth of imports decelerates, with the settling down to a "normal" GNP growth rate, the implied deficit will be falling slowly to about $1,030 million in 1975. If trends follow the lines indicated, it may from then on fall much more rapidly to reach approximately $500 million by 1980 and then become a surplus a few years later. The summary figures are given in rows 1–4 of Table 3–11.

One major reason for the very rapid rise in the deficit in 1968 and 1970, in addition to the effect of the upsurge in economic activity, is the *very substantial rise in defense expenditure.* Consider the balance of payments item termed "government n.e.s." Although this is not identical with total defense expenditure in foreign exchange, it gives a fair measure of the orders of magnitude involved. Between 1965 and 1968 this item grew from $147 million to $347 million (see Table 3-9) and, according to my projection, will go on growing to $580 million in 1970. Consider a hypothetical case in which the rate of growth from 1965 onward would have been only 5 percent (which I take to be the future rate of growth only after 1970). In that case the figure for this item would have been only $170 million in 1968 and $190 million in 1970. Other things being equal, this would in turn bring the estimated total deficit on current account down to $520 million in 1968 and $700 million in 1970. In other words, there would still be an upward trend in the absolute deficit over time, but it would be a more moderate trend. Defense expenditure thus does affect the deficit figures quite substantially.

Throughout the decade preceding 1968 the total capital inflow into Israel was consistently higher than the growing current deficit, and as a result the economy accumulated foreign exchange reserves. The biggest single increase came during 1967 (mainly donations and loans from world Jewry), and at the end of that year gross reserves stood at a record level of $968 million. If we net out foreign deposits in Israeli banks, this is a *net* level of reserves of $777 million. Reserves started falling only in 1968, by almost $100 million, to reach a net level of $679 million at the end of that year. A further very rapid fall was experienced in 1969.

Table 3–11 sets out the projection of the capital inflow during 1968–1980. Unilateral transfers, which reached a peak of $521 million in 1967, declined to $425 million in 1968. These are now expected to rise from about $500 million in 1969 to approximately $550 million in 1970–1975 and from then on gradually to taper off to $450 million in 1980 and some $350 million by 1985 and thereafter. These transfers in 1969 included about $150 million in German restitution

Table 3-11

Balance of Payments, Foreign Debt, and Capital Movements, 1955-1980, Actual and Projected[a]
(million $)

	Actual (at current prices)						Projected (at 1968 prices)		
	1955	1960	1965	1967	1968	1970	1975	1980	(1985)
1. Imports of goods and services	427	696	1,269	1,456	1,831	2,465	3,659	5,204	(7,296)
2. Exports of goods and services	144	365	749	929 (−5)[b]	1,121 (+14)[b]	1,370	2,628	4,693	(7,556)
3. Current deficit (−) or surplus (+)	−283	−331	−520	−532	−696	−1,095	−1,031	−511	(+260)
4. Deficit as percentage of total imports	66.3	47.6	40.9	36.5	38.0	44.4	28.2	9.8	
5. Unilateral transfers from abroad	210	311	341	521	425	540	550	450	(350)
6. Independence and Development Bonds (net)	32	28	33	171	79	100	150	100	
7. Net private investment	8	44	98	8	−15	70	100	50	
8. Other medium- and long-term capital	36	29	116	124	155	300	300	0	
9. Total capital inflow	286	412	588	824	644	1,010	1,100	600	
10. End-year total foreign debt[c]	410[d]	709[e]	1,226	1,608	1,860				
11. Net end-year foreign exchange reserves[f]	80[g]	270[g]	592	777	679				
12. Net outstanding debt	330	440	734	831	1,181	2,021	4,695	5,675	(4,180)

[a]This is a projection under favorable assumptions. See also Table 3-12 and discussion of alternatives in text.

[b]Correction due to the account with the administered areas. This is assumed to balance out after 1968.

[c]Does not include foreign private investments.

[d]1954.   [e]1961.

[f]Does not include International Monetary Fund drawing rights and is net of foreign deposits in Israel ($237 million in 1968).

[g]Approximate figures.

Source: Bank of Israel, *Annual Reports,* various years, Chap. III.

payments (which are expected to start falling in about four years) and $175 million in private transfers by individuals, partly connected with the increased immigration into Israel; the rest, some $180 million, represents funds received by government and nonprofit institutions (mainly through the United Jewish Appeal). The latter reached a record of $314 million in 1967, came down in 1968, but are expected to rise again in the near future.[42] To this source of capital is added a net sale of another $100–150 million a year of Israel Independence and Development Bonds (row 6, Table 3-11),[43] which are assumed to start falling after 1975. I also assume that net private investments from abroad will begin rising again to the approximate levels of the early 1960s.[44]

Finally, to cover the remaining finance gap other "normal" medium- and long-term loans are required to flow at greatly increased net levels, reaching $300 million in 1970–1975, compared with $100-150 million in recent years. These could be allowed to go down to zero by 1980, with new loans to be taken only for the repayment of old ones as they become due.[45] The total capital inflow is thus required to reach a record $1-1.1 billion in the first half of the 1970s and to start falling only after 1975.

The large increases in the public unilateral transfers and the Independence and Development Bonds are in large part a reflection of a present drive by the government to obtain finance for both the exceptional new defense outlays and the newly started immigration wave. In this sense one can say that the figures for the deficit on current account and the estimated finance of it are not entirely independent. Similarly, it can be assumed that a substantial share of the much increased foreign exchange expenditure on defense (projected to be around $750 million, on the average, during 1970–1980) may be financed on credit from the main suppliers. Even so, however, we have to keep in mind that the estimates given for the capital inflow, especially in the general loan category, are of a very arbitrary nature.

The most telling result of the above projection is the implied need to increase the *net outstanding debt* of the country to a record of *$4.7 billion in 1975 and $5.7 billion in 1980*. From then on, however, if these projections are taken literally, there may ensue a very rapid reduction in the net debt. For the sake of illustration I have estimated the figures after 1980, assuming an annual rate of growth of 10 percent in exports and 7 percent in imports (and $350 million a year of unilateral transfers). I find that by 1985 the country will have reduced

---

[42] This information is based on unofficial estimates appearing in the press.

[43] Approximately one-half of the outstanding debt is in the form of these types of long-run securities, which are continually being floated and repaid.

[44] Signs of an improvement in this respect were beginning to show in 1968. The negative figure in Table 3-11 comes from a one-time purchase by the Israeli government of the pipeline to Eilath, at $26 million, from its foreign owners. The figure for 1969 is estimated at $30 million (net inflow).

[45] Or else, if a large gap emerges between the total capital inflow and the deficit on current account.

its net debt to $4.2 billion and that by the early 1990s it could reach the stage of a net creditor in its total foreign asset holdings.

Obviously these calculations are meant primarily for illustration. They do, however, point to a *serious financing problem over the next five years,* which will only be aggravated if for some reason one of the sources of capital inflow does not materialize, or if the export and import projections turn out to have been overoptimistic. The latter cases will be discussed below. As for the first possibility, past forecasts of unilateral transfers have usually turned out to be pessimistic rather than optimistic. A more questionable estimate is that of private investments. These depend to a great extent on the economic and political climate in Israel in the coming years. With the new Investment Promotion Law and the appeal in recent conferences to major Jewish financiers and industrialists to invest directly in both money and know-how in Israel, however, unless the security situation worsens, there are good chances that such investment will in fact take place. Finally, there is the open question of the general availability of loans, already mentioned.

Let us now turn back to the problem of alternative time paths of the deficit itself. We start with a general, almost trivial (but often overlooked), observation about the time pattern of the *difference* between two exponentially growing variables. If the smaller of two variables (here, exports) is growing faster than the other, larger quantity (here, imports), the difference between the two (the current deficit) will usually at first grow steadily in absolute amount (though fall in *relative* terms), then reach a maximum, and thereafter drop quite rapidly to reach zero. Until 1967 Israel was on the upward part of such a time path; the deficit had almost consistently fallen in *relative* terms,[46] but its *absolute* size had been increasing all along. During 1968–69, however, the deficit rose also in *relative* terms because of the enormous increase in defense expenditure.

Is Israel necessarily close to the maximum? The answer depends, of course, on our starting point and on the projected relative rates of growth of imports and exports. Both the time taken to reach the maximum, and afterward the level zero, under various alternatives, as well as the absolute size of the maximum, are very important to know, when it comes to judging the capacity to finance alternative time schedules and sizes of deficit.

Table 3-12 summarizes the result of a number of alternative hypothetical experiments, taking 1970 as the starting point, on the assumption that developments projected for that year can no longer be changed. It enumerates the implications of six alternative sets of assumptions as to projected average growth rates of imports and exports, in terms of the following key parameters: the year in which the deficit will reach its maximum (*t,* row 3 in Table 3-12), the value of this maximum (row 4), the year at which the deficit vanishes (*T,* row 5), the

[46] See row 4 of Table 3-11 for the ratio of the deficit to total imports; this has changed from 66 percent in 1955 to 36.5 percent in 1967. A similar trend can be observed for the ratio of the deficit to GNP.

Table 3-12

The Projected Deficit under Alternative Growth Rates of Exports and Imports[a]

	A	A'	B	C	D[b]	E
1. Annual growth rate of exports (percent)	13	10	12	12	13	12
2. Annual growth rate of imports (percent)	11	8	9	8	8	6
3. Year of maximum deficit[c] (t)	1,996	1,992	1,982	1,975	1,972	1,970
4. Value of maximum deficit (billions of dollars)	4.2	2.3	1.6	1.2	1.1	1.1
5. Year of zero deficit[d] (T)	2,003	2,002	1,992	1,986	1,983	1,980
6. Accumulated (undiscounted) deficit from 1970 until T (billions of dollars)	93.2	55.9	28.4	16.4	11.9	8.6
7. Average deficit[e] (1970 to T) (billions of dollars)	2.82	1.75	1.29	1.02	0.92	0.86

[a]The figures assumed for 1970 are as follows:

Imports $2,465 million
Exports 1,370 million
$1,095 million

$$F = M_0(1+m)^t - X_0(1+x)^t$$

Then t for F_{max} ($\bar{t}$) is obtained from $dF/dt = 0$, which gives as a rough approximation

$$\bar{t} = \left(\frac{mM_0}{xX_0} - 1\right)\frac{1}{(x-m)}$$

This is the formula used here.

d_T is obtained from $F = 0$, that is,

$$T = \frac{\log(M_0/X_0)}{\log[(1+x)/(1+m)]}$$

[b]Case D corresponds most closely to the reference projection of Part I and Table 3-11 (see also discussion in the text).

[c]If we denote the initial (1969) value of imports by M_0 and its rate of growth by m, and similarly for exports X_0 and x, respectively, we have for the deficit (F)

[e]Row 6 divided by ($T - 68$).

127

implied accumulated total deficit over the period 1969 to the year T (row 6). The last is an undiscounted summation of the deficit over time. Row 7 gives the implied *average* deficit over the same period. The latter figures must be viewed against any projected level of unilateral transfers (an average of $500 million per annum, say, for the next decade or so), as only the difference between the two flows represents an addition to the net liabilities of the economy.[47]

It is interesting to note one general feature of all of the alternatives represented in Table 3-12. Once the maximum deficit is reached, and if the same rates of growth are extrapolated beyond that point, the time to the point of complete balance (i.e., the time $T - \bar{t}$) will in almost all cases be about 10 years, with only 1–2 years' difference one way or the other. This is the case whether the difference between the two growth rates $(x - m)$ is 2 percent (case A') or 6 percent (case E).

Case A in Table 3-12 represents, in an extreme form, the implication of a continuation of the nondefense imports trend of 1960–1970 into the future. The deficit would in that case go on rising for a very long time (26 years), and at this rate a complete balance on current account could be achieved only by the end of the century. Case A' represents a similar situation, only for a lower rate of growth of the economy (taking the projected annual growth rate for the 1970s, 8 percent for GNP and imports, as a base, and only a 2 percent higher annual growth rate for exports). The timing *($\bar{t}$ and T)* will be almost the same as before, only the magnitudes involved are, naturally, much smaller.

Case D comes closest to the projection given in Section II. The average annual projected growth rates underlying Table 3-11 are, in fact, 13.1 percent for exports and 7.8 percent for imports. Alternative D is flanked on both sides by cases that seem to be of particular relevance for illustrating the kind of dilemma Israel now faces. Case C differs from case D (the "norm") in that exports are to grow at 1 percent less per annum, on the average. The impact on the timing of the maximum *($\bar{t}$)* and the zero *(T)* balance, as well as the size of the maximum, is relatively small, but in terms of additional foreign debt the effect is quite sizable. The total debt is, in this case, going to increase by about $4.5 billion dollars (over the next 15 years), and the annual average deficit by $100 million per year. This points to the importance of the export growth rate in the balance of payments. Alternative B is one step more pessimistic than C, as it assumes a 1 percent higher growth rate in imports in addition to a lower export growth rate. I shall have more to say on these possibilities in the forthcoming discussion.

Case E represents the kind of alternative "solution" on which the economy embarked during the severe depression of 1966: a very rapid reduction in the deficit by simply lowering the GNP rate and with it the rate of growth of

---

[47] Thus, in Table 3-12, if we want to calculate the net additions to liabilities represented by each alternative, we must subtract from row 6 the approximate value $0.5 (T-68)$, say.

imports.[48] This type of alternative solution is, paradoxically enough, again being mentioned by some people as a way out of the economy's present problem. If exports are not rising sufficiently rapidly and if there is a reluctance to take the required measures of export promotion (see below), a way out might be to grow at a rate of 6 percent (in GNP and imports) instead of over 8 percent. The effect in terms of the illustrative figures is a reduction of additional liabilities by $3.3 billion, or some $60 million in the annual average, as compared with case D (but $160 million less than case C), with a complete balance on current account to be reached by 1980. The cost for the economy, in such a case, is going to be very substantial indeed—a return to severe unemployment (if we assume the same productivity growth as before) or else internal policies of the kind that will reduce the rate of growth of productivity and of per capita incomes (for example, misallocative protective measures or restrictions on labor mobility).

In addition to the question of the feasibility of financing one deficit schedule or the other, there is a related question as to what kind of scheduling seems *optimal* from the economy's overall point of view, assuming that there are alternatives to choose from. A lower rate of growth implies fewer imports and therefore a smaller import gap and less foreign borrowing. One alternative is a more serious export drive and correspondingly more stringent exchange rate policies. The trade-offs between the rate of growth and the current deficit, as well as the "real" exchange rate implied, have recently been studied systematically in the Israeli context by Dougherty, Fraenkel, and myself.[49] These studies show two things. (1) With reasonable assumptions about the marginal foreign borrowing rates Israel faces and the domestic rates of return on investment it can expect to have, it pays to follow a more expansionist path of the kind outlined here and to try to avoid case E, that is, keep to a full employment and rapid growth path, continue borrowing in the near future, and repay debts toward the second half of the 1970s. (2) Even a seemingly moderate export program of the kind assumed here (case D) requires a *much higher rate of export promotion than has been given hitherto.*

If the required policy measures are not adopted and if additional foreign loans at reasonable cost will not be forthcoming, circumstances may in fact force alternative E on the economy, even though it does not seem the optimal choice.

The Problem of Exports

At first sight it might appear on the basis of past performance that exports would not constitute a problem and that case D (Table 3-12) or my basic

[48] As a rough rule of thumb, we can assume the rate of growth of imports and GNP to remain approximately the same.

[49] See M. Bruno, "A Programming Model for Israel"; and M. Bruno, C. Dougherty, and M. Fraenkel, "Dynamic Input-Output, Development and Trade," in A. P. Carter and A. Brodie, *Applications of Input–Output Analysis,* North Holland Publishing Co., Amsterdam, 1969.

Table 3-13

Breakdown of Manufacturing Exports, 1963 and 1968,
and Hypothetical Growth to 1975

	1963		1968		Average Annual Rate of Growth, 1963-68 (percent)	Hypothetical Annual Rate of Growth, 1968-75 (percent)	Hypothetical Level, 1975 (million $)
	(percent)	(million $)	(percent)	(million $)			
1. Textile products	(24.7)	32.1	(25.2)	63.7	14.7	15	169
2. Citrus products	(9.8)	12.8	(10.1)	25.4	14.7	15	68
3. Miscellaneous chemicals	(5.8)	7.6	(7.1)	17.9	18.7	17	54
4. Miscellaneous metal products	(12.7)	16.5	(10.4)	26.2	9.7	15	70
5. Aircraft industry	(1.5)	2.0	(3.2)	8.1	32.3	25	39
6. Oil products	(4.3)	5.6	(2.3)	5.8	0.7	0	6
7. Other "growth" products of which:	(10.9)	14.2	(18.2)	46.1	26.6	27.9	258[a]
8. Precision instruments		0.1		1.9			
9. Communication equipment		0.0		1.4			
10. Radio and television		0.5		1.5			
11. Industrial machinery		0.8		3.6			
12. Electrical equipment		0.2		1.0			

Table 3-13 (cont'd)

	1963		1968		Average Annual Rate of Growth, 1963-68 (percent)	Hypothetical Annual Rate of Growth, 1968-75 (percent)	Hypothetical Level, 1975 (million $)
	(percent)	(million $)	(percent)	(million $)			
13. Meat and fish products		0.3		1.1			
14. Pharmaceuticals and insecticides		2.6		11.8			
15. Tools		0.6		2.6			
16. Plastic products		1.7		4.0			
17. Bakery products		0.4		1.2			
18. Basic chemicals		4.5		11.3			
19. Printing and publishing		2.0		3.5			
20. Tanning products		0.5		1.3			
21. Other products n.e.s. (including cement, plywood, tires, paper)	(30.2)	39.3	(23.5)	59.3	8.6	8	102
Total	(100.0)	130.1	(100.0)	252.8	14.2	17.2	766

[a]33 percent of the total in 1975.
Source: 1963, 1968, Bank of Israel, *Annual Report*, 1968, Chap. III.

projection of Table 3-8 could easily be achieved. During the 12 years from 1953 to 1965, while imports grew at an average annual rate of 11 percent, total export revenue increased at an average annual rate of 18 percent. Even the more recent past history, 1960–1968, showed an annual growth rate for exports of about 15 percent. However, once we look at the breakdown by major export category, some of the problems emerge. As mentioned previously, citrus exports, which for quite a long time were a major export, are gradually diminishing in relative importance, as Table 3-8 shows, and in the future the rate of growth is expected to decline further. Israeli polished diamonds, another major export commodity, have now become a dominant factor on the world market, and in the future their rate of growth is expected to diminish also. If we can assume that with reasonable promotion policies exports of the various invisible items will go on increasing at rates similar to their past performance, the main burden of supplying the gap between "required" exports and those that could be projected under "no change" assumptions falls on the "miscellaneous manufactures" group. A further breakdown of this group may elucidate the problem of achieving a continuation of the same or even higher rates of growth for these items in the future.

Table 3-13 gives a breakdown of manufacturing exports, excluding both polished diamonds and mining products,[50] whose problems are different from those of most other manufacturing exports. In this general group of commodities, Israel's share of the world market for any commodity is bound to remain small. The main question concerns the best use of Israel's comparative advantage in developing the right export mix on the supply side in terms of both quantity and quality of products.

The first six commodity groups listed in Table 3-13 are all relatively sizable exports that have grown more or less steadily over the years.[51] Rows 8–20 list commodities that were, on the whole, small in 1963 but showed consistent and exceptionally high growth rates over the period 1963–1968. The group as a whole (see row 7) grew from a mere $14 million in 1963 to $46 million in 1968, an average annual rate of growth of almost 27 percent.[52] We can term these (along with the aircraft industry) the group of "growth" industries. Some of the commodities included in this group may be there only temporarily, and it is hard to make any predictions of their future behavior. Also, no doubt others will enter with time. But whatever the specific composition of the group, if there is anything that almost all of these products have in common, it is that they are mostly "skill" commodities.

The remaining residual group (other products n.e.s.), which as a whole

[50] These amounted to $12.3 million in 1963 and $33.7 in 1968 and consist of potash, phosphates, and copper ore, Israel's only natural resources.
[51] The classification and breakdown is that of the Bank of Israel, *Annual Report* (for example, 1968, Table III-16).
[52] They are listed by the order of highest-growing to lowest-growing product in 1967 (see Bank of Israel, *Annual Report*, 1967, Table III-22).

grew at only 8.6 percent during 1963–1968, includes some of Israel's most important manufacturing exports in the past, namely, cement, tires, plywood, and paper. These four products constituted about 60 percent of the "n.e.s." item in 1963 and 50 percent in 1968. They grew hardly at all in recent years. Very similar in behavior was the export of cotton yarn.[53] In all of these cases competition on the world market has been very fierce, partly with other developing economies, and production is of a relatively low level of sophistication. The most important factor in the past growth of these exports was the fact that they were promoted by artificial means such as bilateral trade agreements, very high effective exchange rates (for example, in the case of cotton yarn, over 7 I£ per dollar), and protective market-sharing agreements on the domestic market. With time this protection was mitigated and export promotion measures became more unified across the various export groups.

Although there has not been much systematic or detailed analysis of Israel's past successful export performance, there are partial indicators of the most important determining factors. In a recent detailed econometric model for the Israel economy, Evans found that manufacturing export performance (excluding diamonds) during 1952–1964 can be best explained by a combination of a number of factors, of which two major ones were unit value-added remuneration on the export market (including export subsidies) relative to the corresponding remuneration on the domestic market, and the rate of expansion of the relevant world market.[54] The latter factor is, of course, exogenously given to Israel, and all one can do is speculate on the continuation of similar trends in the future. The former factor, on the other hand, depends greatly on internal conditions in Israel as well as relevant government policies.

The relative foreign-domestic unit remuneration is influenced by a number of factors. Since foreign f.o.b. prices can be considered given for all of the above commodities, the first important variable is the unit cost of production. This in turn depends on productivity growth and the domestic rate of price-wage inflation. A second important element is the government exchange rate policy, including both the official exchange rate and the extra export subsidy based on value added. The latter measure was one of the main means of export promotion in the years before the large devaluation of 1962, which only "cleaned the table" so far as manufacturing exports were concerned, since the effective exchange rate (including subsidies) had already reached almost that level on the eve of devaluation. On the other hand, during the inflation years 1962–1965, the do-

[53] Included under Item 1, Table 3-13, but constituting a rapidly diminishing share of it—from two-thirds to less than one-third of "total textile products."

[54] Michael K. Evans, "An Econometric Model of Part of the Israel Economy," Discussion Paper No. 86, Department of Economics, University of Pennsylvania, 1968. The two other factors were productive capacity in the export industries and past export behavior. The elasticity of export revenue with respect to the relative price is 1.1 (with 0.6 standard error).

mestic price and wage level by far outstripped productivity growth, and the rise in unit costs greatly exceeded that in the competing industrial countries.[55]

During 1967–68 the competitive position of Israel improved again as wages stopped rising during the recession, a subsidy was reallocated to exports in 1966, and a small devaluation in December 1967 (to 3.50 I£ per dollar), following the British example, helped to increase the incentive for Israeli industry to export.[56] If we consider the period 1961–1968 as a whole, all of these developments would have netted out, more or less. The domestic price level of manufactures increased about 31 percent during this period, whereas the foreign f.o.b. price index rose only 2 percent. On the other hand, the effective exchange rate increased from close to 3.00 at the beginning of the period to about 4.00 I£ per dollar (3.50 + approximately 0.50 subsidy) per unit value added in 1968. The relative position of manufacturing exports thus stood in 1968 more or less the way it did at the end of 1961.

It would seem that an increase of the range projected here would require a considerable further boost to exports. This follows from an analysis of the resource cost per dollar value added of alternative export baskets and from the fact that as export requirements rise there is a higher marginal trade-off between exports and competing domestic uses of the same resources. At the total rate of growth specified for manufacturing exports here, the implied rate of exchange would probably have to run about 5.00–5.50 I£ per dollar.[57] An additional consideration pointing in the same direction is the fact that, with the present protection of import competing industries at an implied protective rate of at least 6.00 I£ per dollar in most relevant industries, exports are clearly discriminated against.[58]

My emphasis of the importance of price competitiveness of exports should not serve to minimize the significance of a host of other measures that the government used successfully over past years in order to promote exports. These are the fostering of trade organizations (as for various agricultural products and dia-

---

[55] For example, during 1963–1966 the hourly industrial wage in Israel rose almost 50 percent, whereas the weighted average rise in 11 large representative industrial countries rose by only about 20 percent (see Bank of Israel, *Annual Report*, 1968, Table III-19).

[56] The very substantial increase of exports in 1968 is explained partly by this development and partly by the other factor that looms large in the Evans model, namely, the very favorable conditions on the world markets.

[57] See Bruno, "A Programming Model for Israel." In that analysis a schedule is drawn specifying the relationship between the level of consumption (in 1970 and 1975), the optimal composition of exports, and the implied marginal productivity of foreign exchange (i.e., the "shadow" exchange rate) under an optimal allocation situation.

[58] A devaluation could be one step but would not solve the problem alone, since a subsequent inflation, if not properly handled, could wash out the effects very quickly, as the post-1962 experience has clearly shown.

134

monds), the provision of miscellaneous services such as setting quality standards, export risk insurance, the organization of fairs, and, generally, attempts to reduce or eliminate the initial setup costs of penetration into new markets.

Can anything more be said regarding the directions in which Israel's comparative advantage lies? It would seem that a sustained 15–18 percent rate of increase in manufacturing exports can be achieved only if Israel's exports shift further from the "traditional" emphasis on basic textiles, cement, plywood, and tires, toward more sophisticated goods in which there is a relatively large element of skill and know-how. Being comparatively well endowed with skilled manpower and relatively low-salaried and highly productive engineers, scientists, and technical personnel, Israel's comparative advantage would seem to lie in skill-intensive goods and those for which transportation costs are of relatively small importance. From Table 3-13, we can see that in recent years there have been modest but promising signs of growth in a list of goods that could be classified in these categories: books and translations, tanning, pharmaceuticals and insecticides, basic chemicals, industrial and communication equipment, optical and precision instruments, tools and electrical equipment.[59]

A further glance at Table 3-13 indicates the great dependence on the latter group of goods for the realization of export growth. In the last two columns of this table I have projected the hypothetical growth of all other exports more or less on the basis of their 1958–1963 performance. If total manufacturing exports (excluding diamonds) are to grow as projected in Table 3-8 (by 17.2 percent per annum between 1968–1975), the implication is that the group of "growth" products will have to increase at a rate of almost 28 percent per annum, slightly more than their already high rate of growth in the recent past, and will reach $258 million (or one-third of the total) by 1975. Since all of these commodities are still relatively small in scope, such continued rates of growth are not impossible but will constitute quite a feat if they are realized. Apart from the problem of competitive pricing, success will depend mainly on market penetra-

---

[59] M. Herschkovitz of the Bank of Israel, in an unpublished study, worked out the growth of direct and indirect labor input by skill level in the export of Israeli manufactures (excluding diamonds) from 1958 to 1965, using base-year input-output coefficients and taking into account only the change in *composition* of exports (not including the upgrading of skills within each industry).

The following input growth indexes for 1965 over 1958 were obtained:

Total labor (unweighted)	2.36
Unskilled	2.33
Semiskilled	2.35
Skilled	2.37
Academic and technical	2.53

This shows a small but consistent shift toward export industries using higher grades of skilled labor. An extension of this calculation to 1968 would most probably reveal an even stronger trend of this kind in recent years.

tion, on the right kind of market research, and on a suitable industrial climate. The development of more "sophisticated" products depends also on industrial research and on the transfer of the right kind of modern technology from more advanced countries.

If my projection does not materialize, and total manufacturing exports grow at a rate of only 10 percent per annum during 1969–1980, say, the implication for the total export growth rate will be a reduction of approximately 2 percent per annum, which, other things being equal,[60] corresponds to an experiment lying in the middle between case A' and case C in Table 3-12. Either the foreign debt will have to be increased substantially, or the rate of growth will have to be contracted (so as to compensate through a lower growth in imports), or both.[61]

The discussion would not be complete without mention of Israel's market for exports. Most of Israel's trade is with the industrialized world; some 80 percent of its imports and 70 percent of its exports are with Western Europe and North America (the average breakdown of merchandise exports in 1963–1966 was as follows: Common Market (EEC), 28.8 percent; EFTA countries, 25.0 percent; Council for Mutual Economic Assistance (COMECON) countries, 3.8 percent; other European countries, 5.2 percent; United States and Canada, 15.9 percent; Latin America, 1.3 percent; Asia and Africa, 16.7 percent; other countries, 3.4 percent).[62] The most natural markets for Israel would be the Arab countries, but these are closed to Israeli trade. There has been some increase in recent years in the trade with African and some Asian countries, but their share is bound to remain relatively small also in the future. In the absence of a revolutionary change in the political relations with the Arab world, most of the future expansion of Israeli exports must therefore come from trade with Europe and North America.

Several attempts to obtain some kind of association with the Common Market have failed so far, and it seems unlikely that any major change will occur in the EEC policy in the near future.[63] Nevertheless, Israel has managed to increase its exports to the Common Market of some key products; 30 percent of Israel's polished diamonds went into the Common Market in 1966, compared with

[60] Not quite equal—private consumption, say, will grow faster, assuming for the sake of illustration that the import component on the two margins of exports and consumption is the same.

[61] If the 10 percent growth rate in manufacturing exports from 1969 onward could be considered normal under "no change" in the competitive position, a rise to 17.2 percent during the 1969–1975 period would indeed require a boost of about 25–30 percent to the relative export remuneration, if the Evans-estimated elasticity can be taken as a basis. (See footnote 54.) This would corroborate my previous argument.

[62] This discussion is partly based on State of Israel, Prime Minister's Office, *Israel's Economic Development*, Economic Planning Authority, Jerusalem, March 1968, Chap. 4.

[63] But without De Gaulle there is at least some hope for a mitigation of the hard French political line on this issue.

27 percent in 1962. The corresponding figures for citrus were 52 percent and 30 percent. On the other hand, exports of food products and chemicals decreased in relative terms.

It seems quite clear that an association with the Common Market would enhance Israel's export prospects very substantially. The EEC is a natural outlet for the types of articles Israel exports—citrus products and high-quality industrial merchandise.[64] The adjustment of the tariff rates of member countries to the common external tariff of the EEC, however, will no doubt hamper these exports, although it is hard to assess the effects at this stage.

Association with the EEC could help Israel in other, more general ways, by giving it a considerable push toward greater rationalization and competitiveness of its highly protected domestic industry. The abolition of the tariff wall and the use of relevant exchange rate policies are steps that Israel has been taking and may be taking more seriously even unilaterally, but there is no doubt that an association with the EEC would help to counter firmly entrenched domestic vested interests. Finally, such an association would help to promote the flow of foreign investments mentioned above and also subcontracting arrangements with foreign firms.

Israel has been a member of the General Agreement on Tariffs and Trade (GATT) since 1962. In the "Kennedy Round" Israel is included among the developing nations and stands a chance of obtaining a reduction of duties for some of its manufacturing exports to the industrialized world. Israel could potentially further increase its share in the U.S. and Canadian markets. Recently exports to these markets have been increasing in relative terms, to 18 percent of total exports in 1967 and an even higher share in 1968.

Import Liberalization and Import Substitution

Most of what is relevant to the determination of imports has already been mentioned in previous discussions. Perhaps the most important point from the long-run view is to distinguish between the factors affecting the total level of imports and the more limited question of the right *composition* of imports. The Evans econometric study mentioned above confirms that the overall level of imports (other than defense products) is mainly sensitive to the overall level of economic activity and hardly sensitive at all to the foreign-domestic price ratio. The bulk of Israel's imports consists of raw materials and intermediate goods whose substitution by domestic production is virtually impossible at all relevant price ratios. This is not to say that no scope is left for import substitution in some goods, such as investment goods and defense items, or that tariff and exchange rate policy does not affect the *composition* of imports (and the efficiency of domestic production). However, these measures would have only a small effect on the overall rate of growth of imports at any given GNP growth rate.

As mentioned in Section I, beginning in 1962 the administrative protection system of import licensing, quotas, and complete prohibition of some imports

[64] For a more detailed discussion of this question see M. E. Kreinin, "Israel and the EEC," *Quarterly Journal of Economics,* May 1968.

was gradually replaced by a complicated system of tariffs with varying effective protective rates. Michaeli has measured in great detail the various effective exchange rates for the period 1949–1962.[65] For the period 1962–1965 there is a study by Flora Davidov, prepared at the Bank of Israel.[66] Some results of this study are shown in Table 3-14, which lists the average rate of nominal protection by branch of industry and the percentage of output still under administrative protection in 1965. There was considerable variation in the rate of protection of different industries, which also reflected different levels of efficiency and of comparative advantage.[67]

By the end of 1966 the system of administrative protection was virtually eliminated, and a new phase of import liberalization began in which tariffs were gradually reduced, especially for goods on which tariffs had been very high. Even so, however, the degree of variation among goods is quite considerable. It should also be noted that the data in Table 3-14, which are given in terms of domestic production of the goods in question, do not show those items of import for which there was hardly any tariff at all and no domestic production existed at that point—for example, certain classes of capital goods.

The above study also gives estimates of tariff rates of imports by destination. Whereas the average tariff for all of industry is 121 percent, the figure for consumer goods is 163 percent, that for investment goods is only 57 percent, and that for intermediate goods is even less—43 percent.[68]

Recently, in negotiations between industry and the government, a six-year program was agreed upon by which a gradual annual reduction in the effective protective rate will be carried out on January 1 of each year until a uniform rate of 5.50 I£ per dollar is established by January 1, 1975. This came as a compromise between two conflicting views as to the level of the final rate and the length of the transition period.[69]

Although nothing has been said in this program about the exchange rates for imports that can now be purchased at rates below 5.50 I£ per dollar, it seems quite clear that a sensible policy that would increase the subsidy rate on exports (or a corresponding devaluation) to a similar level would also have to see to it

[65] M. Michaeli, *The System of Effective Exchange Rates in Israel,* Falk Institute, Jerusalem, 1968.

[66] F. Davidov, "Input Liberalization February 1962 to May 1965," Bank of Israel, Bulletin No. 26, Jerusalem, 1966.

[67] These results agree reasonably well with estimates I prepared of the domestic resource cost per dollar earned (DRC) in exports in the years 1958–1960. For example, clothing, textiles, and food had a high DRC, whereas metal products and machinery had a low DRC and were also protected at a relatively low rate in 1965. See M. Bruno, *Interdependence, Resource Use and Structural Change in Israel,* Bank of Israel, Jerusalem, 1962, Chap. IV.

[68] This finding also helps one to suggest, as F. Davidov does, that if *effective* rather than *nominal* tariff rates had been worked out, the rates in Table 3-14 would generally come out even higher. Also the figures do not include purchase tax, which usually comes out higher on imports than on the corresponding domestic products.

[69] Certain exceptions will be worked out for the case of dumping.

Table 3-14

Nominal Tariff Rate by Branch and within Industry, 1965[a]

(percent of 3.00 1£/$)

Branch	Share of Branch in Total Manufacturing Output	Average Nominal Tariff Rate[b] (percent)	Percentage Distribution within Industry: Rates (percent)				
			0-39	40-69	70+	Quotas	Total
Food and tobacco	19.5	79	...	19	33	48	100
Textiles	8.5	231	2	14	78	6	100
Clothing	10.3	178	...	1	98	1	100
Wood products	8.3	60	19	81	...	...	100
Paper and products	5.3	50	17	12	11	60	100
Leather and products	2.9	130	8	19	73	...	100
Rubber and plastics	3.0	55	10	44	2	44	100
Chemicals	6.8	40	38	6	9	47	100
Oil refining	3.6	40	...	94	...	6	100
Nonmetallic minerals	5.1	35	61	21	5	13	100
Basic metals	2.8	37	69	19	11	1	100
Metal products	6.8	46	28	56	6	10	100
Machinery and electrical equipment	4.4	48	24	58	4	14	100
Household equipment	4.3	69	1	68	25	6	100
Vehicles	5.9	201	...	3	64	33	100
Total	100.0	121	17	29	40	14	100

... indicates insignificant. [a]Excluding diamonds. [b]Excluding the past administrative protection, for which no "rate" can be estimated.
Source: Bank of Israel, Bulletin No. 26, 1966.

that the rate on relatively cheap imports was raised to the same.[70] Once these rate unification policies have been fully carried out, it is reasonable to expect that the composition of imports will be affected and so will be the structure of domestic production. The fact that these policies are announced in advance may help producers to adjust to the competitive situation gradually. It is hard to say whether the net effect is likely to be positive saving or dissaving of foreign exchange on imports. Given the high measure of protection on many goods, it could happen that imports, on balance, might be higher than so far projected. On the other hand, the beneficial effects on domestic efficiency of production should be quite considerable. This, in turn, would also enhance the capacity to increase exports.

Supply of Capital and Demand for Investment

The first question to be discussed here relates to the way in which investment has been financed and will be financed in the future between foreign capital inflow and private and public domestic savings. Most of the investments that Israel has made in the past were financed by means of a very high level of capital inflow from abroad. This is the other side of the balance of payments picture. As Table 3-15 (rows 12–15) shows, even in 1965 (and the same was true for the period 1960–1965) only about half of gross investment was financed by domestic savings.[71] During the slump (1966/67) the savings-investment ratio went down, and even though it increased between 1967 and 1968, it still stood at only 22 percent (gross) in 1968 (see Table 3-15, row 15). Part of the enormous effort implied in high future investments with a high and then declining balance of payments current deficit can be seen by noting that this ratio is required to go up to 40 percent by 1975 and reach 80 percent by 1980, the end of the period.

An alternative way of looking at the total domestic savings effort is to examine the overall savings-GNP ratio (see Table 3-15, row 16). This fell from 14.2 percent in 1965 to 3.2 percent in 1967, then rose again to 4.6 percent in 1968, and is required to reach above its previous high level by 1980 (15.5 percent).[72]

---

[70] This has recently been done (and should have been done long ago) in regard to a number of defense items that apparently can be produced domestically at competitive costs. In this case the "right" adjustment was finally made largely for political reasons.

[71] If one looks at the figures net of depreciation (depreciation was about I£990 million in 1965), this ratio would go down to 27 percent. By using the official exchange rate one may be giving a downward bias to the role of the foreign capital inflow, which was evaluated at a rate of 3.00–3.50 I£ per dollar instead of a more realistic rate of, say, 5.00 I£ per dollar. On the other hand, there is a factor working in the opposite direction—much of the expenditure on education is really in the nature of investment and not consumption.

[72] The incremental savings-GNP ratio for 1970–1975 is required to be 18.4 percent, and for 1975–1980 32.4 percent. (If we had converted to an exchange rate of 450 I£ per dollar, the respective rates would be estimated at 19.4 and 37.4.)

The breakdown of total domestic savings into the two components of public and private savings reveals the major change that has taken place during 1965–1968. The most marked development of recent years is the fact that the public sector has turned from being a positive saver until 1964 to a large *negative* saver by 1967, with negative savings of around I£1,500 million in both 1967 and 1968 (see Table 3-15, row 7). If all taxes (net of subsidies and including net transfers from the private sector) are lumped together, the ratio of net tax receipts to GNP was 20 percent in 1965, naturally came down during the slump, but almost regained its previous level by 1968 (see Table 3-15, rows 2–5). However, total tax *receipts* (net) rose by only about 20 percent during 1965–1968, whereas public consumption almost doubled.

The total net tax figure (Table 3-15, row 4) is composed of indirect taxes net of subsidies (mainly export subsidies) and of direct taxes. Without a change in tax rates the direct tax element would by itself show a progressive rise with future GNP growth. Indirect taxes, on the other hand, might rise more or less with GNP, while subsidies would rise at a faster rate. It seems reasonable to assume that under "no change" in *rates,* the overall ratio will return to the 20 percent level by 1970 and probably stay on that level thereafter. This is the basis for the projection of columns 4–6 in Table 3-15, where by implication the onus of adjustment would have to fall on private savings. The gross private savings rate (row 11) would have to rise to 24 percent in 1975 and to 31 percent in 1980. Is this reasonable?

The private savings ratio (as a percentage of private disposable income) has shown a more or less consistent rise during the years 1964–1968, with the exception of the 1966 slump, the figures for the 5 years being 15.6, 17.7, 16.2, 18.9, and 18.6 (see Table 3-15, row 11 and footnote d). There are two major reasons for which a continued increase in the private savings rate might be expected. One derives from the fact that private disposable income and private savings include all undistributed profits along with household savings,[73] and as the corporate sector is expected to go on growing in relative terms so, it is hoped, will this savings element. Much in this respect depends on future government fiscal and incomes policy in general.[74] This argument can be applied, in a certain sense, to the whole of nonwage income, as the savings propensity out of this source is higher than that out of wage income. Ever since 1953, except in 1964

---

[73] There are no separate estimates of undistributed profit, but one gets an idea of the direction of change by looking at total nonwage income. Private savings also include the savings of nonprofit institutions, which, by the nature of their finance from abroad, are "negative savers" (see also footnote 35). Nonprofit institutions had negative savings of I£75 million in 1967 and I£51 million in 1968 (see Bank of Israel, *Annual Report,* 1968, Table VIII-9).

[74] In the past the existence of cheap untied development credit (see below) and the lack of fiscal incentives were not particularly conducive to a retaining of business earnings.

141

Table 3-15
The Finance of Gross Investment, 1965-1980
(million I£, current prices)[a]

	1965 (1)	1967 (2)	1968 (3)	1970 (4)	Projection under No Change in Taxes[b] 1975 (5)	1980 (6)	Projection under Tax Change[c] 1975 (7)	1980 (8)
1. GNP	10,845	12,098	14,045	17,364	25,994	36,808	25,994	36,808
2. Indirect taxes (net of subsidies)	1,341	1,300	1,578					
3. Direct taxes and transfers (net)	834	796	1,049					
4. Total taxes and transfers (net) [(2) + (3)]	2,175	2,096	2,627	3,473	5,199	7,362	5,606	9,591
5. Net tax as percentage of GNP [(4) ÷ (1)]	(20.0)	(17.4)	(18.7)	(20.0)	(20.0)	(20.0)	(21.6)	(26.1)
6. Public consumption	2,173	3,599	4,109	5,436	7,985	10,684	7,985	10,684
7. Gross public savings [(4) − (6)]	2	−1,482	−1,503	−1,963	−2,786	−3,322	−2,379	−1,093
8. Gross disposable private income [(1) − (4)]	8,670	10,002	11,418	13,891	20,795	29,446	20,388	27,217
9. Private consumption	7,136	8,113	9,289	11,308	15,801	20,413	15,801	20,413
10. Gross private savings [(8) − (9)]	1,334	1,889	2,129	2,583	4,994	9,033	4,587	6,804

Table 3-15 (cont'd)

	1965 (1)	1967 (2)	1968 (3)	1970 (4)	Projection under No Change in Taxes[b]		Projection under Tax Change[c]	
					1975 (5)	1980 (6)	1975 (7)	1980 (8)
11. Private savings ratio [(10):(8)]	(17.7)[d]	(18.9)	(18.6)	(18.6)	(24.0)	(30.7)	(22.5)	(25.0)
12. Total gross domestic saving [(10)+(7)]	1,536	386	647	620	2,208	5,711	2,208	5,711
13. Foreign capital inflow [= import gap]	1,484	1,538	2,298	3,622	3,317	1,407	3,317	1,407
14. Total finance of gross investment [(12)+(13)]	3,020	1,924	2,945	4,242	5,525	7,118	5,525	7,118
15. Savings-investment ratio [(12):(14)]	(50.9)	(20.1)	(22.0)	(14.6)	(40.0)	(80.2)	(40.0)	(80.2)
16. Average savings-GNP ratio [(12):(1)]	(14.2)	(3.2)	(4.6)	(3.6)	(8.5)	(15.5)	(8.5)	(15.5)

[a] 1968 prices are used for 1968-1980.

[b] Net taxes as percentage of GNP assumed 20 percent (row 5); implied private savings worked out as residual.

[c] 22.5 percent (1970); 25 percent (1975) assumed for private savings ratio (row 11). Net taxes worked out as residual.

[d] The corresponding figure in 1964 was 15.6 percent and in 1966 16.2 percent.

Source: 1965-1968, Bank of Israel, Annual Report, 1968, Chap. II.

143

and 1966, the share of wages in national income has gone consistently down,[75] and 1964 and 1966, as mentioned above, were precisely years with relatively low average savings ratios. Another possible reason for a further increase in the savings ratio is found in the fact that part of past consumption was financed from private transfers, such as private restitution money, from abroad (this is not included under disposable income in Table 3-15, whereas consumption is). As the ratio of these transfers to national income is expected to fall with time, the effect will be to reduce the measured average propensity to consume.

Studies at the Bank of Israel[76] have pointed out that household savings behavior in Israel is not markedly different from that in countries of similar income level and distribution. However, much of savings is directly tied to investment in the form of housing. A highly egalitarian income distribution[77] may make for a slightly lower average savings rate, but apparently the effect is not significant. Another problem is the Interest Law, which puts an 11 percent ceiling on the nominal interest rate. If and when this measure is abolished (and there has been serious talk of it recently), this may, among other things, also help to allow an increase in the rate of return to savings.[78] Of no lesser importance is the lack of a serious capital market. At present the market is dominated by trade in government securities, and whatever corporate paper is traded takes the form of occasional speculative waves. There is hardly any relationship between the actual rate of return on shares and the real economic forces acting on the rate of return to physical investment.

In spite of all that can be said about a potential increase in private savings, it is hard to believe that the required extra investment finance is going to come from private savings alone. In fact, a fairly sizable increase, say by about 0.5 percentage point a year, would yield an expected private savings rate (gross) of 22.5 percent in 1975 and 25.0 percent in 1980 (see row 11, Table 3-15). This turns out to be considerably less than would be required under a "no tax change" assumption. It follows that taxes would have to be increased. The required net tax rate (as percentage of GNP) would have to go up 21.6 percent in 1975 (from 18.7 percent in 1968 and 20 percent in 1970) and 26.1 percent in 1980 (see cols. 7 and 8, Table 3-15). In other words, if the private savings estimates projected above are correct, and if the import gap is to be reduced as projected, the required gross investment can be financed only by increasing the average *net tax burden by about 0.6 percentage point per year*, throughout the period 1970–1980.

[75] See M. Bruno, "Estimation of Factor Contribution to Growth under Structural Disequilibrium," and Bank of Israel, *Annual Report,* 1968, Table II-6.
[76] See E. Lisle, "Household Savings in Israel, 1954 to 1957/58," Bank of Israel, Bulletin No. 21, Jerusalem, 1964.
[77] Israel's is still one of the most egalitarian in the world, even though it has become less equal over time.
[78] The marginal productivity of capital in Israel is above the actual rate of return (see below).

Table 3-16

Share of Government Finance in Gross Investment[a]

(percent)

	Average, 1961-1964	1965	1966	1967	1968
Agriculture and irrigation	84	92	89	91	94
Manufacturing and construction	24	7	11	52	34
Mining	14	24	55	100	100
Power	22	38	23	19	29
Transportation and communication	45	54	70	79	62
Services and trade	45	43	53	60	63
Total nonhousing investment	45	44	54	70	60
Housing	33	33	36	61	47
Grand total	41	40	48	67	57

[a]The figures relate to gross credit, that is, repayment of old debt is not subtracted.

It is widely agreed among economists that some such tax increase is needed but that it can be achieved only through a substantial reform in the tax system. One major possibility is the introduction of a value-added tax. Increased taxation should reduce the negative public savings to less than one-half of its present level by 1980.

The private (and the public) savings projection is very sensitive to future developments in public consumption. If, say, defense expenditure will have to grow by more than has been suggested here in the years after 1970, my tax estimates will have to be revised upward accordingly. Needless to say, another war breaking out during the period would affect both fiscal policy and the foreign debt estimates even more adversely.

On the demand side of investments, the major factor is the overriding direct and indirect role of the government in the investment process throughout the 1960s. The large foreign capital inflow in the past has come mainly through public institutions, in particular the government Development Budget. As Table 3-16 shows, in 1967–1968 around 60–70 percent (gross) of total nonhousing investment was government financed, and the figures are even higher for agriculture and irrigation, mining, and transportation. The fact that the figures during the next 2–3 years were particularly high (as compared with the average for 1961–1964, say) reflects in part active anticyclical government policy. On the other hand, these percentages do not give a full measure of government influence, as the government also largely influences the policies of the financial intermediaries that provide additional investment finance. Finally, there are other indirect means, such as investment licensing, import protection, and export promotion schemes, that affect the allocation of investment.

Throughout most of the time in question the interest rate played only a very small role in the allocation of investment, and with the exception of the slump period excess demand for investment funds existed at given interest rate levels. A study of productivity and factor returns in the total private economy and in manufacturing during the period 1953–1965[79] showed that the marginal productivity of capital was of the order of magnitude of 30 percent (gross) from 1953 to 1964, whereas the rate of return to capital was only around 15 percent during the first part of this period. The rate of return, however, increased over the period, so that the gap has been closing gradually. This trend was reversed during the 1966/67 slump but began again with the large increase in profits in 1968.[80] To say that capital got less than its marginal product (and labor more) is not to imply that private owners of capital received less than the marginal product of their own capital. For example, if at least half of the capital stock is government financed at an effective rate of interest of no more than 3–5 percent,[81] and the average rate of return for all capital is 15 percent, the effective rate of return on own capital may reach 30 percent. These figures should be handled with great caution, of course, and they should be used only as a qualitative illustration of the problem.

During 1964–1966, before the slump set in, government financing of investment in industry declined to about 7–11 percent.[82] There was a large influx of private investment from abroad and also, in all probability, an increase in domestic own finance of investment. This was both a reflection of the underlying profitability at that time and an indication of the present potential for a renewed influx of private capital. Whether or not the government is overdoing it by renewed efforts to subsidize investment in manufacturing is unclear. The recent version of the Law for the Encouragement of Capital Investments (1968) provides a considerable boost to private investments, mainly those from abroad. It provides science-based industries, for example, with a 20 percent grant of the construction costs, a recommendation for a soft loan from the Industrial Devel-

[79] See M. Bruno, "Estimation of Factor Contribution to Growth under Structural Disequilibrium."
[80] By 1968 the rate of profit was back to its 1964–1965 level. Profits rose further in 1969.
[81] See H. Ben-Shahar, *Interest Rates and the Cost of Capital in Israel, 1950–52*, Kyklos Verlag, Basel, 1962.
[82] The figure for 1964, 11 percent, is not shown separately in Table 3-16. (The average for 1960–1963 was over 30 percent.)

opment Bank, and accelerated depreciation schemes, in addition to the previous exception from property tax, customs on imported machinery, and so on, that accrue to all "approved investments." Finally, the corporate tax is now down to 42.5 percent compared with the previous 49 percent.

It would seem that with the "right" kind of export promotion rates and fiscal incentives (for example, a differential tax on distributed versus undistributed profits) an increased flow of investment in the desired directions could be obtained without recourse to costly and drastic direct measures. Last but not least, the development during the downturn and the renewed upsurge in economic activity has amply shown that in manufacturing, at least, the private demand for investment is very definitely sensitive to changes in profits.

Manpower and Education Policy

Population growth is the basis of my GNP figures; the size of future GNP depends heavily on immigration estimates. I would consider the 30,000 annual figure as optimistic but reasonable. One possibility for which there has been much hope, but without basis so far, is a liberalization on the part of the Soviet authorities that would allow Russian Jews to leave the Soviet Union. It is hardly likely that they would all emigrate (the total figure is about 2.5 million), let alone all go to Israel, but it is reasonable to expect that a sizable portion would make use of Israel's Law of Return, which allows all Jews to settle and become Israeli citizens. Even a few hundred thousands over the present forecast horizon would, of course, alter my estimates completely. The implication would in many ways be a return to developments in the 1950s—an even higher growth rate, a larger share of investment going to housing, and a higher and much more prolonged balance of payments deficit on current account, which would have to be financed by higher transfers, loans, and investments from abroad.[83]

Another possible source of a higher population increase is the natural birth rate. There has been serious talk in Israel recently about the adoption of measures to increase the birth rate. This is partly the result of worry about the "demographic balance," that is, the forecast that by the end of the century the total number of non-Jews in Israel and what are now the administered areas will become a majority, unless there is large-scale immigration of Jews into Israel. Partly this talk is also a reaction to the loss of lives in a war. It is too early to say what kind of policy measures, if any, will be adopted. However, even if the birth rate rises (after all, some countries, such as France, have had a measure of success in this direction), this is not going to affect the employment figures until 1980.[84] It might, nonetheless, affect consumption and investment levels.

[83] Very roughly, an annual immigration of 50,000 (instead of 30,000) might shift the GNP annual growth rate by about 1 percent, and similarly for imports. In terms of the deficit, the effect might be like the shift from case C to case B in Table 3-12.

[84] This statement is not entirely accurate, as the participation rate of women might be affected.

A more important consideration from the present point of view, and one that I have not tackled so far, is the question of the composition and *quality* of the labor force. In the early years of its existence Israel had the benefit of a highly educated immigrant group. It is estimated that 55 percent of the pre-1948 veterans from Western and Central Europe and 35 percent of those from Eastern Europe had received secondary and higher education in their countries of origin.[85] With the relatively low income level of that time, no resources could be devoted to maintain comparable standards in the education system of the new state. Also, many of the immigrants could not make use of their qualifications because the country's poor technology was not adapted to such utilization.

The immigration of the early 1950s brought about a considerable decline in the average level of education. By 1954 the proportion of Jewish males with secondary and higher education had dropped from 34 to 25 percent, while the proportion of men with less than 5 years of primary schooling had risen from 22 to 33 percent. Until 1961 the average educational level remained more or less the same, but during the early 1960s the educational system began to grow quite rapidly, together with the rapid growth in the economy and the increase in demand for educated manpower. Among other things the higher demand for educated workers showed itself in a consistent reduction in the equality of the income distribution.

School attendance at age 14–17 rose from 43 percent in 1952 to 57 percent in 1964 and reached 62 percent in 1967 (compulsory free education for ages 5–13 has been provided since 1951). The percentage of the 20–24 age group attending institutions of higher learning rose from 3 percent in 1952 to 11 percent in 1964. In the employed labor force the percentage of those who have had 13 or more years of study has risen from 12.2 percent in 1963 to 15.0 percent in 1967.

Looking at the average educational level conceals one major problem Israel has been facing—the difference in both education and income levels by country of origin. The main task the educational system has had and is going to have in the future is the reduction of this inequality. This policy has already shown some measure of success, as the school attendance rate of children aged 14–17 of Asia-Africa parentage rose faster than that of children of Europe-America parentage. By 1966/67, however, there was still a considerable gap, the figures being 51 percent and 73 percent, respectively.

Recently the government passed a law making the first two years of secondary education (ages 14–15) also compulsory and free, and there is a good chance that this law will sooner or later be extended to all of secondary education. Clearly, much of the projected rise in public consumption is also a reflection of the increased expenditure on "investment" in education.

[85] This and the subsequent discussion is based in large part on Halevi and Klinov, *The Economic Development of Israel,* pp. 72–75. The specific figures mentioned above are quoted from R. A. Easterlin, "Israel's Development: Past Accomplishments and Future Problems," *Quarterly Journal of Economics,* February 1961.

The rapid changes that have taken place in the educational quality of the labor force also reflect themselves in the occupational distribution. The percentage of the labor force in the "professional and technical" class, including engineers, architects, medical and scientific personnel, and teachers, rose from 10.4 percent in 1955 to 14.2 percent of the labor force in 1967. A similar increase has taken place in the "administrative-managerial" class, now 16.4 percent. In spite of these increases, it is generally felt that with the resumption of rapid growth there will be a shortage of certain classes of professional and skilled manpower. In particular, the system is not geared to the very rapid recent growth in demand for certain classes of scientists and engineers.

Not only is the gestation period in the output of this type of highly skilled manpower very long, but also the corresponding departments in the institutions of higher learning have hardly been expanding to meet the growth in demand. For example, the number of annual graduates of the Technion, Israel's only institute of technology, has grown only from 591 in 1960/61 to 815 in 1967/68, an annual rate of increase of less than 5 percent.[86]

One factor that is likely to mitigate these foreseen shortages is Israel's ability to rely on a certain influx of professional manpower from abroad, whether returning Israeli students or the recently more numerous immigrants. An example in point is the recent emergence of a modern electronics industry (see below), which was practically nonexistent only a very few years ago but is now growing at an annual rate of some 20 percent. In the past there was no employment for an electronics engineer in Israel in most modern fields of specialization, and many Israeli electronics students chose to remain in the United States at the end of their studies. At present, however, there is a severe shortage in the domestic industry, and managers have been making considerable efforts to hire either Israeli citizens or non-Israeli Jews working abroad who may use this as an opportunity to settle in Israel. Such efforts have been crowned with a considerable measure of success, even though the salary incentive would not by itself constitute adequate inducement.

Productivity and Technological Progress

A number of additional issues relate to the ability of the economy to increase its output out of given manpower and capital resources. An increase in efficiency does, of course, come about as a result of individual effort on a firm level. In a study dealing primarily with aggregates it is impossible to go into micro detail, although a few observations can be made on the borderline between the micro and the macro levels. Some of the general factors that promote growth of efficiency throughout the economy will be mentioned in addition to those already discussed in Sections I and II.

Part of the increase in overall productivity consists of a shift from less productive to more productive lines of activity, that is, in a structural change. One

[86] Another, probably worse, problem is the lack of manager-entrepreneurs. No formal educational system can solve that problem.

way of promoting a more efficient allocation of resources in this way is to subject industries to international competition. For a long time Israel exercised an excessively autarchic policy in protecting some of its key industries against competing imports at very high effective rates of exchange. Under the protective umbrella of a very high effective tariff the country did, of course, have an extremely rapid rate of industrialization. But in many cases, such as in the textile spinning and weaving industry, the price paid was indeed quite high.

Although it is hard to assess the quantitative effects of the import liberalization policy to date, it seems to have already given a considerable incentive to some of the industries concerned to increase productivity, improve quality, and mitigate price increases. Part of my projected increase in overall productivity no doubt hinges on a further strengthening of this policy in the future. There is nothing as conducive to the promotion of productivity in a small economy, where there is often only one firm or two in an industry, as the potential or actual competition of imports.[87]

Related to this set of questions is the whole problem of the transfer of technological know-how and skill from abroad. No systematic analysis of the role of the transfer of technology in Israel has yet been made. Early industrialization efforts in specific industries were usually due to accidentally available skills or to what sometimes were believed to be available skills. Diamond cutting is a good example; here a highly profitable industry was set up by immigrants who had practiced the skill in their countries of origin. In the case of textiles, on the other hand, the potential role of immigrant skill was probably overestimated by the government authorities. Textiles were considered a traditional Jewish activity, and this no doubt was true for certain lines of clothing and finishing. It is not clear, however, what technological or skill advantage there was in the mass-production industries of spinning and weaving, where Israel could never hope to compete with the cheap-labor goods of some of its Asian competitors.

An example in which political necessity brought about the successful development of the required modern technology, partly with the aid of purchased know-how from abroad, is the armament industry, which began to be developed at the end of World War II. This is also an example of a highly successful industry that started rather modestly and has with time branched off into many articulated lines of modern industry. Although it is hard to generalize in this case, it seems that success was due to a particular blend of skillful imitation, accompanied by a learning process which led with time to the development of original and sophisticated new products.

In many other parts of Israeli industry the transfer of technology took another form: private entrepreneurs, often with government support or even initia-

---

[87] The "infant industry" argument for protection can, of course, be valid while the industry is in the learning stage, but in most relevant cases in Israel this stage has long since been passed. The interesting thing is that some of the modern industries, such as electronics, armaments, and aircraft, seem to be doing quite well without effective protection (see Table 3-14 and related text).

150

tion, either purchased know-how from foreign firms or started production as local subsidiaries of foreign firms. The suspicion and animosity with which such ties were viewed in the early years of statehood (because of fear of foreign domination and for similar reasons) soon gave way to open (and sometimes even excessive) encouragement of such relationships by what was from the beginning a socialist Israeli government. A recent conference for foreign Jewish investors organized by the Israeli government put the stress not so much on the problem of obtaining investment funds as on the need to obtain links both to foreign markets and to know-how and technological expertise from abroad in all lines of industrial activity.

Israel's future industrial growth is expected to come more and more from industries in which the skill and know-how content is relatively high. Some of these are industries in which considerable sums of money must be spent on research and development. In this respect, performance so far has been relatively poor. By 1965 Israel is estimated to have spent only about 1 percent of its GNP on research and development, compared with some 3 percent in the United States and the United Kingdom. But what is even more marked is the fact that of total R&D money only 11 percent was spent on industrial research, compared with some 50 percent in other industrialized countries. Even though Israel has some of the world's best-known basic research establishments, it cannot boast any substantial industry-oriented applied research. In part, this is so because of the nature of its industry, which is still concentrated in traditional fields: food products, textiles, wood, paper, and construction materials cover 60 percent of manufacturing output. But the main reason probably is that the small size of most establishments makes any individual R&D effort prohibitively expensive.

It is interesting to contrast the situation in industry, in this respect, with that in agriculture, where apparently the size obstacle was overcome at a very early stage. Organized research efforts, in close cooperation with producers, as well as systematic diffusion of the information from government research activities (and even before the State was formed, from the Jewish Agency), were of key importance. Of no less importance, however, was the fact that the farmers, especially in the kibbutzim (collective farms), were from the start a highly skilled and motivated group of producers who were ready and eager to adopt new techniques. The startling fact remains that, of a total of I£126 million spent on R&D (excluding defense) in Israel in the fiscal year 1966/67, only I£6.5 million was spent on industry, whereas agricultural research had a budget of I£20 million.[88] Similarly, although industry as a whole employs 25 percent of Israel's working population, it absorbs only 18 percent of the engineers and scientists, and only 10 percent of the latter group are actually employed in R&D.

There is evidence, however, that this situation is going to change very rapidly in the near future. For the first time there is a serious beginning of what might be termed a science-based industry. A number of industrial complexes,

[88] These and other figures on R&D were obtained from data collected by the National Council for Research and Development, Prime Minister's Office.

some of which are already in full production and others in the planning stage, are directly connected with the country's institutes of higher learning (at the Weizmann Institute, the Haifa Technion, and the Hebrew University). Moreover, some foreign firms have recently expressed interest in opening branches or setting up research laboratories adjacent to these centers (an example is Miles Chemicals from the United States, which has recently established three such centers).

In electronics there are now a number of plants in which output is based on local know-how developed originally at the Defense Ministry or the Technion. An outstanding recent example is one firm that was founded only in 1963 with an initial output of I£150,000. Four years later it had an output of I£5.3 million (of which $600,000 was exported), and was expected to reach over I£10 million (of which $1.5 million would be exported) in 1968. This firm exports mainly scientific and medical equipment, and its subsidiary exports a small, new, locally developed computer. In both cases exports are to highly developed countries, including the United States. The electronics industry is now growing extremely rapidly (at 20–30 percent a year).

A somewhat older industry, and also an offshoot of the defense establishment, is the aircraft industry, whose output now totals some I£100 million. In both aircraft and electronics, R&D constitutes some 8–10 percent of the annual turnover, which is quite unusual compared with the rest of Israel's industry. Also, a considerable part of the know-how in these fields is obtained abroad through agreements with foreign firms. In both cases the size of the existing industry in relation to similar industries in the United States or Western Europe is still miniature, but an extremely rapid growth is foreseen for the future. Israel seems to have a sufficiently promising reservoir of untapped scientific and technological expertise, and in recent years this type of industrial development has also had a very sympathetic climate both in the government and among private investors. Moreover, the fact that for some of these industries the defense establishment is an important large-scale market outlet with highly exacting demands also constitutes a considerable push. The future growth of these industries will no doubt depend on a further development of export markets.

From such a small technological base, it is hard to make any projections of this type of development for the future, let alone assess its effects on overall productivity. However, one thing might be said. Although in *absolute* terms Israel seems to be lagging in technological level behind countries of a similar income range, it is showing a remarkably *fast* rate of change. One more example involves the use of computers. In 1962 there were only 6 computers in the whole of Israel, and only 2 of these were using magnetic tape. By 1968 the figure had increased over *17 times*—105 computers in 70 different establishments, of which half were using magnetic tape.[89] This is evidence of a rapid adaptability and diffusion rate of new technology, even if allowance is made for the fact that a computer may in some cases be a status symbol.

[89] CBS figures, May 1969.

All in all, it seems that one prerequisite for rapid progress—the right social climate and the readiness to change—is not lacking, but there are bottlenecks that have to be overcome. The last point under this category might perhaps be classified as the "ethics of failure." Here is one field in which a lot remains to be learned from other countries. Unlike the Israeli army, or large parts of the academic and scientific establishment, in which individual progress is usually attained by merit and failure involves a price, such a general characterization cannot, as yet, be made for the existing economic-managerial class in Israel. For example, the economic failure of a public enterprise need not lead to the resignation of its management, even if it has been responsible for huge losses of public money. Management may sometimes change, but past failures do not prevent the individuals concerned from obtaining correspondingly responsible positions in other public or, for that matter, private economic enterprises. In part this is a reflection of an old-time camaraderie coupled with some measure of disdain for the profit motive, which could have fitted a small pioneering community but not a modern industrial state. In some part this is a reflection of the restrictive bureaucratic system itself, which often breeds a talent that is oriented toward finding ways of beating or joining the system rather than toward "innovation" in the true sense of the word. But more than anything else, this is probably a reflection of the shortage of Israel's scarcest resource—good modern entrepreneurs and managers of large-scale enterprise. The particular blend of formal education, acquired skill, and above all long practical experience in modern industry that characterizes such individuals is in short supply.

It is not immediately clear how, if at all, these kinds of considerations can help us to assess whether the estimates for future productivity growth are realistic. If for some reason productivity does not increase according to my estimates, and as a result potential GNP grows more slowly, the main effect is likely to be a lower rate of growth of per capita consumption. On the balance of payments side, lower import requirements would by themselves reduce the estimated current deficit. However, lower productivity growth will also hamper the growth of manufacturing exports, and the net effect is therefore unknown. All the points made above imply that there is still a sufficient "reservoir of inefficiencies" in the system, but there are also enough promising signs of their change to indicate that continued rapid technological progress *can* be made.

Prices, Wages, and Incomes[90]

During 1955–1965 the price level increased on the average by 6 percent per annum.[91] As mentioned earlier, there was a higher than average increase in

[90] For a good analysis of changes in income distribution see Halevi and Klinov, *The Economic Development of Israel,* pp. 115–123; and G. Hanoch, *Income Differentials in Israel,"* Falk Institute, Jerusalem, 1961. Inflation and wage policy is analyzed in Chap. 11 of Halevi and Klinov; see, in particular, pp. 269–281. My analysis of the past mainly draws on these sources.

[91] This refers to the price of domestic resource use (see Halevi and Klinov, *The Economic Development of Israel,* Table 76).

prices, both with the 1962 devaluation and in the years following devaluation. During 1962–1965 prices rose by 20 percent, largely as a result of excess demand, large-scale conversions of foreign exchange inflows, and inability on the parts of the fiscal and monetary authorities to carry out an anti-inflationary policy. Individual ministries within the government often succeeded in expanding activities (for example, housing construction) in spite of government budget constraints. Also, there was a largely misplaced attempt to curb inflation by regulating individual prices and freezing wages. The attempted wage freeze only accentuated the flood of wage increases that took place in 1965/66, when they could no longer be stopped.

Is inflation really such a bad thing? Whatever evidence exists in the Israeli context would no doubt point to the fact that this was a necessary concomitant of rapid growth and a reduction in unemployment. Also there is no clear evidence that without inflation Israel would, for example, have had a larger savings rate. With time the economy learned to live with inflation and adopted all the necessary price-linkage inventions for which it is famous (for example, all long-term loans were tied either to the price index or to the exchange rate). If there is one major respect in which inflation was certainly harmful, it is in the fact that it made the fixed exchange rate system plus large devaluation jumps useless from the point of view of the balance of payments objectives. Short of moving over to a flexible exchange rate system, the economy had to use partial quasi-flexible-rate measures, and inflation thus played a major role in the early development of the complex multiple rate system which still exists, in part at least, to this very day.

The realization on the part of the government that the 1962 devaluation turned out to be a failure because of its inflationary consequences had far-reaching implications for subsequent policy decisionmaking, and it probably was the major reason for the belief that the economy's ills could be cured through a recession without an accompanying foreign exchange policy. The truth, of course, is that both are needed. Having failed in 1962 in a devaluation without a domestic squeeze, and then in a recession without devaluation (1966), the government, it is to be hoped, will take none of the extreme policies by themselves again. The year 1968 witnessed a successful small devaluation (by 17 percent, in December 1967, following the British), which was absorbed with only a 2 percent once-and-for-all price increase, because there was substantial unemployment at the time. By mid-1969 the economy was on the verge of full employment, prices were virtually stable, and there was an official wage freeze policy. There is always the danger that the fear of inflation and the bad memories of 1962 may make the government sacrifice growth for price stability, and at the same time prevent it from taking the "right" exchange rate policies. Also, there is the question as to how far wage increases in the past have caused, or rather have been caused by, underlying inflationary pressures.

Figures cited earlier in this study point to the fact that during the period 1952–1964 there was a small but consistent reduction in the share of wages in national income. This was mentioned as evidence of a discrepancy between marginal productivities and relative remunerations of the factors of production, labor, and capital, and of a movement toward equilibrium. Halevi and Klinov cite the same evidence to make the additional argument that the sustained inflationary price rise during most of the period was due mainly to demand-pull and not cost-push.[92] During 1965/66 the share of wages rose again substantially, but by 1968 the share and the rate of profit were back more or less to their preslump levels. It is too early to say whether or not this trend will continue. An increase in the exchange rate in real terms would have to be reflected in a trend of this kind. In any case, a continued rapid growth with a smaller rate of inflation[93] than in the preslump past depends primarily on proper demand management and less on the holding back of individual wage claims.

One major factor in the wage structure in the past has been the cost of living allowance, often mentioned as the villain of the piece, preventing price rises (as, for example, after devaluation) not accompanied by corresponding wage increases. Whether this argument is correct or not, during the last few years various agreements between the Histadruth (the strong overall Trade Union organization) and the Manufacturers' Association have virtually deprived the COL allowance system of all its previous significance. Another important development is the general collaboration between government, Histadruth, and employers to tie wage policy to overall productivity performance and to have wage agreements for 2-year periods.

A much more problematic issue concerns income and wage *differentials*. Israel has always had one of the most (if not *the* most) egalitarian income distributions in the world. Partly this is because of the national ownership of land, which has prevented the formation of a rich, private landholding class, and the lack of large private capital holdings of any other kind. More than anything else, however, it is probably caused by a deeply rooted egalitarian socialist philosophy among the pioneers of modern Israel. Here again there is a marked difference between the picture in the absolute and its *rate* of change. Contrary to the findings for many developed countries, income distribution in Israel tends to become *less* equal over time,[94] perhaps because of a modification of the underlying philosophy or a reflection of the dominance of real economic forces, and probably reflecting both.

That the old underlying philosophy is still strong in some circles can be seen from the way in which wage agreements have always been negotiated in this country. This is done by collective bargaining among the Histadruth, the government, and the relevant producers' associations; the Histadruth has always attempted to keep wage differentials fixed between different occupations and sec-

[92] *Ibid.*, p. 275.

[93] I do not believe in sustained rapid growth without inflation but would place the optimal rate of inflation at something closer to 2–3 percent per year.

[94] See Halevi and Klinov, *The Economic Development of Israel*, Table 42, p. 120. In 10 years the Lorenz Index more or less doubled.

tors. In the course of the years, however, various professional associations (doctors, engineers, and teachers) have managed to operate more independently of the Histadruth's central authority. Although the system is still far from flexible, the evidence of increasing salary differentials points to a continued change in this direction. In many cases this change takes the form of wage payments in disguised forms, unofficial fringe benefits, and the like. Economic forces have their own way of making themselves felt, but the fact that these phenomena have to be concealed (and sometimes be ashamed of) does not contribute to a healthy modern wage incentive system.[95]

Related to these issues, although on a different level, is the need for a reform of the personal tax system, the main problem being the disincentive for work provided by the excessively high marginal tax rates in the general professional and managerial classes (the statutory marginal rate reaching 70–75 percent in what could be considered medium-high salary levels). Several suggestions for reform have been made, the main one being the introduction of the value-added tax instead of the present heavy reliance on income tax.[96] This is also superior for purposes of export promotion and GATT agreements. The company tax, which does not favor undistributed over distributed profits, should also undergo revision.

Planning and the Market

Is Israel a "planned" economy? Do all the policy measures analyzed here add up to one consistent, long-run plan that future governments are likely to follow? How much government intervention will there be in the future, or how much of it is needed in order to make these projections come true? These are some of the questions for which a fuller answer is desirable than can be given by the present study.

Israel's government has certainly had a dominating influence over economic developments in the past and still exercises a high degree of intervention, yet rarely has there been anything that resembles a central, long-run planning mechanism. The Ministry of Finance, and especially its Budget Division, is responsible for actual budget allocation in a way that in theory, at least, gives it a lot of power. At the same time, its decisions and recommendations have rarely been dictated by considerations extending beyond the next one or two fiscal years.[97] The Central Planning Authority, now in the Prime Minister's Office, works on three-year plans, but its recommendations are hardly reflected in the annual budgetary process.

[95] Another respect in which the present system is outdated and various attempts at reform are now being discussed is the lack of flexibility in transferring fringe benefits (such as pension rights) from one job to another. This greatly hampers labor mobility.

[96] The primary objective of an income tax, namely, its progressivity, could also be achieved through other channels, such as the educational system.

[97] I have shown how such questions as the approach to economic independence can be analyzed only in the context of a much longer time horizon.

Although there seems to be a substantial amount of sophisticated long-run planning on the individual ministry level (a good example is the Ministry of Agriculture), it is hard to describe exactly how the general system manages to make for consistency (let alone for optimal decisionmaking) among conflicting demands on scarce resources. The key issues are decided in the Council of Economic Ministers (headed by the Minister of Finance), and this is where by hook or by crook some coordination is forced, but again more on short-term (1–2 year) decisions. Apparently the small size of the country and the relative compactness of the higher civil service group are conducive to a great deal of informal planning. Nonetheless, even though government intervention is probably still excessive, the country could do with more long-term planning.

Have economic policy decisions shown an improvement, in some sense, over time? The answer to the question, I believe, is clearly in the affirmative. There have been serious policy mistakes (such as deficit budget financing at full employment, or excessively protectionist policies), whose lessons have been learned and will probably not be repeated. There is also a much better understanding now of the important role that market forces should play even in a system that is guided by a firm government.

CHAPTER 4

Economic Development of Lebanon

Albert Y. Badre

Planners who are fascinated by the physical production of tons of steel and yards of concrete would do well to read the following essay on Lebanon. Badre shows that Lebanese economic growth is dominated by services and that a relatively high and improving standard of living is based on economic activities that would not even be counted by Adam Smith or today's Soviet leaders, let alone counted on. Lebanon is an unusual model: growth through bookkeeping and shopkeeping. But although this model may seem fragile as a base for development, American economists who have observed the rapid growth of the service sector in their own economy should find it less surprising. Providing commercial and financial services is both an appropriate and an effective way to capitalize on natural advantages of location and talent.

Badre is well aware that the Lebanese model of development is risky and is likely to be subjected to great strains in the future. After a careful analysis of the prospects for continuous growth along the same lines as in the past, he turns in the last section to the problems of the future. Lebanon is peculiarly dependent on events in other countries over which it has little control. Providing financial services to the region can be rewarding only when the region needs or permits such services. So too with commercial services. Lebanon is an open economy; it cannot prosper in a region where all other countries are closed. Yet today prolonged war and increasing state economic controls threaten the basis of Lebanon's past prosperity. Simultaneously, domestic religious and class strains are intensifying, and Lebanon's laissez-faire approach to its own economy is becoming harder to maintain politically.

Badre's concluding section is a model of informed concern. Yet the reader is left with residual faith that "the Lebanese people, with their energy and resourcefulness" will find the solution the future demands, just as they found the one warranted by history.

CHAPTER 4

Economic Development of Lebanon

I. Introduction

On a visit to Lebanon, a United Nations expert once said, "God created the world, but Lebanon was made by the Lebanese." Much of the structure and performance of the Lebanese economy is explained by what is implied in this statement. Nature has endowed Lebanon with little physical wealth apart from a pleasant climate and a favorable location. But the Lebanese people, with their energy and resourcefulness, have created a relatively prosperous economy that has been sustaining a healthy rate of growth for over two decades. Because of the paucity of its natural resources, its special location, and its historical relations with Europe, both commercial and cultural, in recent history the country developed an economy dominated by trade and other services. In fact, it is estimated that two-thirds of the national output derives from services, which is perhaps the highest ratio of services output in the world.[1]

The growth and development of the Lebanese economy are dependent to a large extent on the innovative responses and actions of wide segments of the population. Gauging its future prospects, a task always attended with a certain amount of vagueness and uncertainty, therefore becomes much more difficult to discharge satisfactorily. There is no prominent mineral resource, as in Iraq and Saudi Arabia, on the basis of which future income and economic activity could be projected. Nor is there any dominant stable sector whose growth could be projected on the basis of alternative domestic policies, as in primarily agricultural countries. Trade and services, the prevailing sectors of the Lebanese economy, are much less stable than agriculture and industry and are influenced much more by outside forces over which the Lebanese have little control. In projecting Lebanese economic growth it is necessary to make assumptions about the highly uncertain development of external economic and political conditions and attempt under such uncertainty to predict the responses of the Lebanese people to these changes. The results can have a wide range of error.

[1] The exceptionally high services component in the national output has been a persistent phenomenon of the Lebanese economy. National income figures of 1950 and 1964 show about the same proportion. For 1950, see A. Y. Badre, "The National Income of Lebanon," *Middle East Economic Papers,* 1956, p. 34; for the 1964 figures, see République Libanaise, Ministère du Plan, Direction de la Statistique, *Les Comptes Economiques,* Vol. 1, *Résultats,* 1964, p. 108.

161

Predictions of the growth of the Lebanese economy undertaken in the early 1920s would have been very gloomy. At that time the Lebanese economy was almost wholly based on the production of natural silk. The industry had received a lethal blow from artificial silk, and the mulberry-coated Lebanese slopes were being left to wither. Who could have foretold then that in less than three decades the whole countryside would come alive with fruit trees and generate income exceeding the greatest expectations of the silk days? Or in the early 1950s, when the customs union with Syria was broken up and the government of Syria decided to develop the port of Latakia and to restrict the activity of Lebanese merchants in Syria, who could have foretold that Lebanese import trade was going to find other channels and prosper as it never did before? Or again when emigrant remittances had become a declining and uncertain source of income in the early postwar years, who would have predicted that within a decade Beirut would develop into an international financial center with earnings that would completely dwarf the inflow of emigrant remittances?

Projections into the future are made even more difficult by the lack of quantitative data relating to Lebanese economic activity. The country has had no population census since 1932. Proposals for population censuses have been consistently resisted for fear that the results may disturb the distribution of political and administrative public offices, based conventionally on supposed proportions of people adhering to various religious sects. There has been no census of occupation, no agricultural census, no housing census, and only spotty censuses of industry. Statistics of national accounts are only partial, and they leave wide gaps. Under such conditions the assessment of the future performance of the economy cannot be based so much on a projection of a quantitatively determined past performance as on a subjective judgment deriving from an intimate, but somewhat intuitive, knowledge and appreciation of the total situation.

Such a projection will be attempted in Section III. However, it will first be useful to describe and evaluate the performance of the economy in the recent past. This perspective on past development is undertaken in Section II, which describes very briefly the pattern that characterized the country's economic development since the departure of the last foreign troops in 1946 and examines the forces that helped determine such a pattern. The purpose behind this historical analysis is not only to explain how the economy reached its present levels but also to identify with greater clarity the problems of development policy that are likely to face the country in the future. The discussion of these policy problems will be undertaken in Section IV.

II. Perspectives

Contrary to the situation in many a less developed country, the initiative for economic development in Lebanon has not come primarily from the government, nor has it been the result of planned and deliberate action. The Lebanese economy is market-oriented. Its growth cannot be gauged by tracing the activity of a single agency, such as a planning board, as might be possible in countries that work out central blueprints for their development covering several years at a time and reaching into many sectors. Although private business activity undertaken for profit accounts for the major part of the country's development, government policy and action has had a significant influence on the course of this development. Forces in both the private and the public domains have helped to shape the structure of the economy and have contributed to the determination of the directions and levels of its performance.

General Sectoral Transformation

Like most countries of the region that formed part of the Ottoman Empire, Lebanon[2] was predominantly agricultural. But perhaps to a larger extent than any of the other southern parts of the empire, it carried on cultural and commercial relations with Mediterranean Europe. These relations became much stronger after 1860 when Lebanon was made the political ward of seven European nations. During the period 1860–1920 the silk industry prospered and made possible the formation of a comparatively large agricultural capital in terraces and in mulberry trees. Although agriculture remained dominant, it was precisely in this period that the foundation was being laid for trade, which was destined later to become the leading sector. Throughout the nineteenth century, Ottoman trade, especially foreign trade, tended to be captured predominantly by Christians in the empire. The leading trade groups were the Greeks and the Armenians in the north. Following this general trend, the Lebanese and other Arab Christians became the leading traders in the south but on a smaller scale. This general tendency was strengthened further by the relative freedom enjoyed by Lebanon under the multination trusteeship.

During this period Lebanese emigration to the Western Hemisphere, to Egypt, and to other parts of Africa took place on a comparatively large scale. Emigrants not only sent money back to relatives still living in Lebanon but also channeled in new ideas, contributed to the propagation and financing of education back home, and in many instances established trade connections between residents and emigrants and among immigrant groups abroad. Trade horizons were widened further as a result of Armenian immigration into Lebanon after World War I.

During the French mandate, considerable change occurred in the structure of the economy. The silk industry declined sharply as a result of competition with artificial silk, which was rapidly capturing international markets. Agricultural capital, output, and income declined. As the agricultural sector shrank, the

[2] "Lebanon" in this context refers to all the parts that constitute the present Republic of Lebanon, although before the establishment of the French Mandate in 1921, the term referred to the central part of the present state, which is known as Mount Lebanon.

163

trade and services sectors expanded. The area under French mandate comprised both Lebanon and Syria, with a combined population of more than five million by the eve of the World War II. Because of the historical advantage the Lebanese had in education, in commercial techniques, and in the liberal professions, Lebanese merchants became the leading traders in the whole mandated area. Lebanese schools multiplied and expanded with students from neighboring countries, particularly Syria, Palestine, and Iraq. Lebanese banking, insurance, and transport facilities serviced the whole mandated area and beyond. And Lebanese mountains were turned into summer resorts receiving several thousand visitors every year from the surrounding region.

As a consequence of these developments, trade outstripped agriculture and became the dominant sector. By the end of the mandate it was generating almost 30 percent of the national income, as opposed to only 20 percent generated by the agricultural sector.[3] World War II served to strengthen this tendency. The expenditures of the Allied armies during the war led to a large accumulation of foreign balances by the countries of the region. When international lanes were reopened to commerce after the war, much of this pent-up demand was met through the intermediacy of Lebanese merchants. Trade may also have received a further impetus when the port of Haifa was closed to Jordanian shipping in 1948, although this factor, in my opinion, tends to be overrated even by leading economists.[4] Lebanese figures for transit trade show a continuous growth in the use of Lebanese facilities by Jordan and Syria even after the promotion of Aqaba and Latakia as leading ports in these two countries. For instance, in the period 1962–1967, transit trade to Syria grew from L£62 million to L£68 million, and that to Jordan grew from L£10 million in 1962 to L£17 million in 1966.[5] Trade is dependent not only on the existence of port facilities but also, and to an even greater degree, on the competence and efficiency of the traders. Lebanese merchants have been able to capture a large portion of the Levant trade, despite the growth of rival port facilities, in competition not only with Syrians and Jordanians but European merchants as well.

Agriculture

The postwar period in Lebanon was characterized by significant transformations in important sectors of the economy. In the agricultural sector, the most prominent development was the wide expansion of fruit growing. Banana and citrus fruits grew on the coast; new and better varieties of grapes replaced the old

[3] Badre, "The National Income of Lebanon," p. 13.
[4] See Yusuf Sayigh and Mohammed Atallah, *A Second Look at the Lebanese Economy* (in Arabic), Dar-el Talia'a, Beirut, 1966, p. 30; also see Charles Issawi, "Economic Development and Liberalism in Lebanon," *Middle East Journal,* Vol. 18 (Summer 1964), p. 285.
[5] Ministère du Plan, Direction Génerale de la Statistique, *Recueil de Statistiques Libanaises, 1967,* Beirut, 1968, pp. 250–251.

grape cultivation in the lower heights; and in the middle and upper heights fresh and elaborate terracing proceeded vigorously for raising such hitherto nontraditional fruits as apples, peaches, pears, and cherries. Mulberry trees were replaced by these new fruit trees, which now cover wide expanses of the mountain slopes and have spread into the Bekaa Valley. This spectacular ttransformation in agriculture, entirely an undertaking of the private sector, is reflected clearly in the figures for fruit production and export. The leading fruit products are citrus fruits and apples. The production of citrus fruits more than doubled in a little over a decade, rising from 108,500 tons in 1956 to 228,000 in 1967. Apple production increased almost five and a half times during the same period, rising from 29,000 tons in 1956 to 157,000 tons in 1967.[6] Large quantities of fruits are exported every year to other countries in the region, and small quantities go to Europe. Fruits constitute a large portion of the country's exports: in 1967 they accounted for almost 30 percent of the total value of merchandise exports excluding species. The value of exported fruits rose from L£38 million in 1960 to L£72 million in 1967.

Despite this vigorous expansion of fruit cultivation, however, the agricultural sector as a whole did not keep pace with the growth of other sectors in the economy. The gross domestic product arising in the agricultural sector almost doubled in the 15-year period from 1950 to 1966.[7] This, however, represents a growth of less than 5 percent a year, which is substantially less than the average growth of the national product. As a consequence, gross domestic product arising in the agricultural sector declined from a ratio of 20 percent of total product in 1950 to almost 12 percent in 1965.

Industry

Industry in Lebanon received a strong impetus during World War II because of the extraordinary protection it derived from the shrinkage of European exportable products and the constriction of Mediterranean trade routes. But with the return of foreign competition after the war, and with Lebanese nonprotective low-tariff policy, many newly established industrial firms faced great hardship. Industrial difficulties were compounded by the rupture in 1950 of the customs union with Syria. Nevertheless, many firms were able to hang on during the early postwar years and to become more firmly established as market conditions later improved. The postwar boom in trade, services, and construction, together with the flow into the country of oil money and the spectacular growth in tourism, widened the domestic market sufficiently to ensure the survival of many industries. Furthermore, the expansion of domestic markets in the oil-producing countries opened new and important channels for the export of Lebanese industrial products. It is estimated that industrial products currently constitute

[6] *Ibid.*, 1965, pp. 82–83; 1967, pp. 88–89.
[7] Compare Badre, "The National Income of Lebanon," with *Recueil de Statistiques Libanaises, 1967*, p. 345.

20–25 percent of the total exports of Lebanon, going mostly to other Arab countries.[8]

The two biggest industries in Lebanon are petroleum refining and cement, consisting of two refineries and three cement factories. Apart from these, Lebanese industry is composed mainly of light industries producing consumer goods. Food processing is the biggest group, constituting 23 percent of all establishments employing 5 or more persons and 14 percent of all labor engaged by these establishments.[9] More than 90 percent of Lebanese factories are owned by individuals or family partnerships, and the vast majority of these operate on a small scale. Of the 2,099 establishments employing at least 5 persons in 1964, less than 3 percent were of corporate form, and only 7 percent had 50 workers or more, although altogether they employed more than half of the total labor force.[10] This means that 93 percent of the establishments included in the census employed less than half the labor force. The establishments not included in the census because they employed fewer than 5 persons are estimated to be 2–3 times as many as those that were surveyed, indicating that Lebanese industry as a whole is not very far beyond the handicraft stage.

This pattern, however, should not obscure the considerable progress experienced by the industrial sector in the last 10 or 15 years. The expansion of the gross domestic product arising in the industrial sector has more or less kept pace with the growth of the total domestic product. From 1950 to 1965 industrial products continued to form about 13 percent of the rapidly growing total product.[11] The growth was chiefly in textiles, weaving, clothing, shoes, paper products, petroleum refining, cement, and metallic products.

There have been only two industrial censuses, conducted 9 years apart, in 1955 and 1964.[12] Some comparisons from these censuses indicate the nature and extent of change occurring in the industrial sector during this period. The total number of establishments employing 5 or more persons increased from 1,861 in 1955 to 2,099 in 1964, a total growth of 12.8 percent in 9 years. The number of workers engaged by these establishments, however, grew at the faster rate of 17.3 percent, rising from 35,013 in 1955 to 41,093 in 1964. The expansion in scale indicated above is demonstrated further by the still higher rate of growth in the number of establishments employing at least 50 persons, which in-

[8] Mustapha Al-Nusuli, *Toward a Better Future for Lebanese Industry* (Arabic: Nahwa Ghadin Afdal Lissina'a Al-Lubnania), Department of Statistics Press, Beirut, 1968, p. 4.

[9] Direction Centrale de la Statistique, *Recensement de L'Industrie au Liban: Resultats Pour 1964*, Department of Statistics Press, Beirut, 1967, pp. 24, 25, 28, 29.

[10] *Ibid.*, pp. 28, 29.

[11] Compare Badre, "The National Income of Lebanon," p. 13, with *Les Comptes Economiques, 1965*, p. 14.

[12] Republic of Lebanon, Ministry of National Economy, *Industrial Census 1955*, Beirut, 1957; and Direction Centrale de la Statistique au Ministère du Plan, *Recensement de L'Industrie au Liban: Resultats Pour 1964*, Beirut, 1967.

creased by 41 percent from 100 in 1955 to 141 in 1964. These relatively large establishments constituted 5 percent of the total and employed 43 percent of the working force in 1955, but had risen to 7 percent of the total and employed 51 percent of the labor force in 1964. Furthermore, the corporate form of industrial enterprise, a rough index of the pooling and expansion of capital, rose by over 60 percent from 38 corporations in 1955 to 61 in 1964. This substantial expansion in scale has been accompanied by a greater expansion in productive efficiency, as is indicated by the spectacular rise of value added in industry from L£155 million in 1955 to L£312 million in 1964, a growth of over 100 percent in 9 years.

Trade and Finance

Although both agriculture and industry experienced healthy growth during the postwar period, it was not in these sectors but in real estate, trade, transport, finance, and tourism that the economy really boomed. Perhaps the most potent force contributing to the flourishing of these activities has been the edge that the Lebanese enjoyed over other Arabs in education, business sophistication, and external contacts and connections. Because of this advantage, the Lebanese were able to capitalize on the postwar oil boom in the region and the upsurge of tourism in the world. Oil prosperity proved a strong impetus for the development of an important financial center in Beirut. Following a policy of minimum restriction on the movement of goods, capital, and persons and minimum government interference in business, Lebanon succeeded early in establishing confidence in its currency and in the competence of its financial institutions.

Since Lebanon assumed responsibility for its own currency in 1948, the Lebanese pound has shown remarkable stability with a tendency of a slight rise over a twenty-year period. The average annual free exchange market value of the dollar was L£3.5 in 1948; with relatively mild fluctuation, the Lebanese pound rose in twenty years to an average rate of L£3.2 in 1967.[13] The law requires that the note issue in circulation possess a full cover as follows: at least 50 percent should consist of gold and foreign currencies, provided the value of the gold cover does not fall below 30 percent of the notes in circulation; the remaining maximum of 50 percent can be composed of loans to or guaranteed by the government and of commercial bills, provided the latter never exceed 15 percent of the total cover. The monetary authorities pursued a very conservative policy within the rather flexible bounds of the law. When Lebanon took over from France in 1948, the gold cover was only 2 percent. It was raised to 25 percent the following year and by 1955 had reached 95 percent.[14] In ensuing years it was brought down from this exceptionally high level but kept at a level of 80–90 percent, where it continues currently.[15] This policy was possible because

---

[13] *Recueil de Statistiques Libanaises, 1967*, p. 274.

[14] Ministry of National Economy, *Bulletin Statistique Trimestriel*, 3ème Trimestre, 1958, p. 27.

[15] *Recueil de Statistiques Libanaises, 1967*, p. 274.

receipts in the foreign sector have exceeded payments almost every year, resulting in a continuous growth of foreign assets and a rise in the gold stock.

Confidence in the Lebanese pound, open borders, and the competence of Lebanese and foreign financiers operating in the country attracted enormous amounts of capital from oil-producing and other neighboring countries. The inflow of capital was further invigorated by capital flight from neighboring countries that had embarked on policies of nationalization and of restricting capital movements. In the meantime Lebanon had enacted a banking secrecy law permitting bankers to withhold from the government or any other agency the identity of clients owning numbered accounts and the amounts lodged in such accounts. Although some of the capital flowing into the country sought refuge in these secret accounts, other capital came in search of investment opportunities either in Lebanon or elsewhere in the world through the intermediacy of Lebanese bankers. Figures of capital inflow are not accurate, yet, when taken over a long period, they give a fairly good notion of the tremendous growth in this activity. The total net inflow in 1951 is estimated at L£15 million.[16] Of this, at least L£2 million must have been government receipts, leaving not more than L£13 million in short and long-term net private capital inflows. In 1965, the net private inflow amounted to L£220 million,[17] rising almost 17 times in 14 years. This tremendous inflow of capital, which does not seem to have abated despite the financial shake-up of 1966 and the June War of 1967, is placing the country in an increasingly precarious financial situation. In all other countries total bank deposits of all kinds outstanding at any moment of time amount only to a fraction of national income, but in Lebanon they sometimes exceed national income.[18] What makes the situation still less stable is that the greater portion of the inflows—about two-thirds in 1964 and 1965—constitutes short-term capital in the form of deposits, which can be withdrawn on demand.[19]

It is estimated that some 60 percent of the long-term transfers[20] have gone into real estate, with most of the rest going into trade and industry. This external participation in the domestic real estate market has had some positive influence on the sustained boom in that sector. Although there are no figures of the actual value of construction, we can gain a fairly accurate notion of the extent of change in real estate activity over time by comparing the licensed construction area in the metropolitan regions of Beirut and Tripoli, where the bulk of

[16] Edward Fei and Paul J. Klat, *The Balance of Payments of Lebanon of 1951 and 1952*, Economic Research Institute, Beirut, 1954, p. 5.

[17] George S. Medawwar, *Lebanese Balance of Payments for 1964 and 1965* (in Arabic), Ministry of Planning and Economic Research Institute, Beirut, 1967, p. 16.

[18] Sayigh and Atallah, *A Second Look at the Lebanese Economy*, p. 22.

[19] Medawwar, *Lebanese Balance of Payments for 1964 and 1965*, p. 16.

[20] Elias Saba, "Private Foreign Capital and Development in Lebanon" (in Arabic); *Financial Sources and Development in Lebanon* (in Arabic), Development Studies Association, Beirut, 1967, p. 367.

construction has occurred. In 1952, 381,412 square meters were licensed in these two localities. In 1966, more than three times this area, or a total of 1,243,000 square meters of construction, was licensed.[21] There have been considerable fluctuations in the intervening years, but with an unmistakable upward trend. As reflected in this index and in the transfer of titles, real estate activity has tended to be influenced perceptibly by the general conditions of the economy. For instance, the years 1956 to 1958, from the Suez crisis to the end of the internal civil strife, showed a continuous decline in licensed area and in the transfer of titles. Then both indexes moved upward to a record high in 1966. However, with the failure of Intra Bank toward the end of that year, and the Six-Day War a few months later, the licensed area fell in 1967 by 45 percent, and title transfers by 26 percent.[22]

The oil boom in the region has had great repercussions on the Lebanese economy, extending beyond the invigoration of the financial and real estate markets. Transit trade, transport, and insurance owe much of their spectacular upsurge to oil-based demand. The value of the returns for services by residents in connection with transit and triangular trades as estimated for balance of payments purposes almost doubled in fifteen years, rising from L£113 million in 1951 to L£208 million in 1965.[23] After the breach of the customs union with Syria and the development of Latakia as the chief Syrian port, it was feared that Lebanese transit trade would be seriously injured. In fact, trade with Syria as destination declined from an all-time high of L£275 million in 1955 to L£68 million in 1967. Also transit trade issuing from Syria declined from L£8 million to a mere L£696,000 in the same period.[24] Despite this sharp decline in the trade for which Syria was a source or destination, other channels were cultivated and the loss was more than compensated for. The biggest single item of transit trade today is oil flowing from Iraq and Saudi Arabia through Lebanon to the Mediterranean. But trade flowing in the opposite direction and destined to these two countries has also grown considerably over the past several years, so that the value of commodities in transit to Iraq, for instance, has become in recent years more than one and a half times that of goods destined to Syria. Transit trade originating in Middle East countries (including oil) constitutes about half the total transit trade. In 1967 it amounted to 55 percent, whereas transit trade destined for Middle East countries constituted 38 percent during the same year.[25] Since the closure of the Suez Canal in 1967 the volume of transit trade handled by the port of Beirut has almost doubled.[26]

[21] *Recueil de Statistiques Libanaises, 1967,* p. 138.

[22] *Ibid.,* p. 277.

[23] Fei and Klat, *The Balance of Payments of Lebanon of 1951 and 1952,* p. 5; and Medawwar, *Lebanese Balance of Payments for 1964 and 1965,* p. 16.

[24] *Recueil de Statistiques Libanaises, 1963,* p. 180, and *1967,* p. 181.

[25] *Ibid.,* pp. 248–251.

[26] *Mid East Commerce,* Vol. XII, No. 3 (March 1969), p. 33.

Transportation

Transportation and insurance are two more activities that grew rapidly in the postwar period. The facilities of the Beirut port were expanded and modernized in the late 1940s and early 1950s. At about the same time the International Airport in Beirut was constructed and opened to commercial traffic. The road network, already developed under the mandate, was expanded and improved in the 1950s. With the great expansion of trade and tourism, transportation experienced a tremendous growth. The number of passengers going through the port of Beirut in both directions rose from 57,391 in 1954 to 122,279 in 1966; and merchandise handled by the port rose from 1,451,000 tons in 1954 to 2,193,000 in 1966.[27] The growth of air traffic was far greater. The total number of travelers going through Beirut Airport amounted to 261,678 in 1953. In 1967, the number rose to 1,254,237.[28] Motor vehicles in use similarly rose several-fold between 1954 and 1967: cars, from 18,687 to 114,242; buses, from 1,013 to 2,168; and trucks, from 3,536 to 12,763.[29] This very substantial growth in transport facilities came less as a response to internal demand than as a consequence of the extension of Lebanese services to foreigners. The net receipts from transport and insurance, appearing in statements of the Lebanese balance of payments, show a spectacular growth in a decade and a half, rising from L£7 million in 1951 to L£178 million in 1965.[30]

Tourism

Tourism has flourished considerably since World War II. During the mandate Lebanon could hardly be considered as a tourist attraction. At that time a few summer resorts in the hills attracted a small number of visitors, mainly from Syria, Palestine, and Egypt. It was not until after the war that the Lebanese began to be conscious of the great potential of the country for tourism. Great public and private effort was successfully exerted in building up tourist facilities and in promoting tourist attractions. Modern hotels conforming to the highest international standards grew rapidly, restaurants and night clubs multiplied in number and improved in quality, places of historical interest or natural beauty, as well as archaeological sites, were widely publicized, and summer and winter sports were vigorously promoted. These efforts were bolstered further by a free exchange policy, an easygoing customs procedure, and a well-regulated tourist traffic to neighboring countries, particularly to the cities of Damascus and Jerusalem.

The number of foreign visitors coming into the country, for tourism and other purposes, is a fairly good barometer of the general condition of the econ-

[27] *Recueil de Statistiques Libanaises, 1967*, pp. 290–291.
[28] *Ibid.*, pp. 297–299.
[29] *Ibid.*, pp. 294–295.
[30] Fei and Klat, *The Balance of Payments of Lebanon of 1951 and 1952*, p. 5; and Medawwar, *Lebanese Balance of Payments for 1964 and 1965*, p. 16.

omy. From a low of 38,000 in 1951 after the breach of the customs union with Syria, the number of foreign visitors jumped to 213,000 in 1952, progressing upward every succeeding year to reach a level of 901,000 in 1955. In the period 1956–1959, marked by the Suez conflict and internal unrest, foreign visitors declined continuously, reaching a trough of 305,000 in 1960.[31] In the period of relative stability between 1960 and 1966, the number of foreign visitors again rose steadily from 536,000 in 1961 to 1,515,000 in 1966. Although the events of 1967 brought about a dip to 1,218,000,[32] it is estimated that in 1968 the number reached a new peak.

By far the greater number of foreign visitors come from Arab countries. In the 1960s, about one-half of all foreign visitors came from Syria, one-quarter from other Arab countries, and one-quarter from the rest of the world. The objects of attraction of these visitors to Lebanon vary considerably, as do their levels of expenditure. In general, it is believed that a large proportion of the visitors from Arab countries come for business, education, or medical care or else they pass through in transit to or from other countries. A good many come to summer resorts, and some are attracted by night life and other holiday pleasures. On the other hand, visitors from outside the region are either businessmen or tourists chiefly visiting historical sights in Lebanon and surrounding countries. Disturbances in the country and the region do not affect these two groups in the same way. Arab visitors seem to be influenced more by troubles in Lebanon than elsewhere in the region. The opposite appears to be true of the other classes of visitors. For instance, the total number of visitors declined almost by 60 percent in the years of domestic trouble between 1956 and 1959. This sharp decline was due chiefly to the drastic shrinkage (by 66 percent) of Arab visitors; the non-Arab visitors decreased by less than 1 percent. On the other hand, the decline in total visitors occurring in the wake of the June War in 1967 amounted to about 20 percent; the decline in Arab visitors was only 17 percent, however, whereas the decrease in other visitors was almost 28 percent.[33]

Lebanese income from tourism and from services rendered to foreign visitors is a substantial part of total national income. Because expenditures by visitors permeate several sectors and are not distinguishable from expenditures by residents, it is difficult to assess their contribution to national income. According to one estimate, Lebanese services, including trade services, purchased by foreigners amount to 24 percent of national income.[34] The departure of Lebanese services on the outside world and the high proportion of services in the composition of the Lebanese national product make Lebanon highly vulnerable to domestic and regional political and social instability, which could interrupt continued growth of the flow of foreign expenditures. Although there are no fig-

[31] *Recueil de Statistiques Libanaises, 1963,* p. 46.
[32] *Ibid., 1967,* p. 66.
[33] *Ibid.*
[34] Sayigh and Atallah, *A Second Look at the Lebanese Economy,* p. 25.

ures showing income from tourism and the sale of services to nonresidents, the expansion of the hotel industry and balance of payments estimates of net receipts from travel and tourism will give a fair notion of the extent of growth of the income in question.

Beirut hotels are perhaps the best index of the total industry, since they receive the largest number and the wealthiest visitors. In 1960, there were 45 hotels in Beirut; by the end of 1967 the number had grown to 79, a rise of 75 percent in seven years. Even more indicative of the extent of growth of tourism is the increase in luxury hotels conforming to the international classification of four stars. There were 6 of these in 1960 in Beirut; their number was almost tripled by the end of 1967, reaching 17. The number of beds in these hotels increased in more or less the same proportion, rising from 1,130 in 1960 to 3,252 in 1967. Although capacity was rapidly expanding, the utilization rate varied from year to year. Only 55 percent of available beds in luxury hotels were used in 1960. The percentage fell to 50.8 in 1962, mainly because of a faster growth in capacity rather than a shrinkage in absolute utilization, which in fact rose substantially. In 1967, however, utilized capacity dropped from 58.4 to 38.7 percent. The drop was partly due to fast increase of capacity in the earlier part of the year; nevertheless, the number of passenger-nights spent in these hotels dropped sharply from 553,000 in 1966 to 464,000 in 1967.[35]

One more index that might be quoted as an indication of the spectacular upsurge of Lebanese tourist activity in the postwar period is the annual number of visitors to the famous Roman temples at Ba'albek. In 1951, there were 17,000 visitors; the number rose to a peak of 48,000 in 1955, which was a banner year in practically all economic activities. With the Suez Canal conflict and the domestic unrest in the following three years, the number of visitors declined to 40,000, 33,000, and 15,000 in 1956, 1957, and 1958, respectively.[36] It picked up again in 1959, reaching 37,000, and increased steadily every year to a peak of 154,000 in 1966. But again in 1967 it dropped sharply to 86,000, as a consequence of the Six-Day War.[37]

Income from all tourist activities and from the sale of goods and services to foreign visitors must have followed the same pattern of ups and downs manifested by the indicators mentioned above. It must have risen from 1951 to a peak in 1955, declined in the following three years to a trough in 1958, picked up again in 1959 and moved steadily upward to a peak in 1966, dropped sharply in 1967, and picked up dramatically in 1968, remaining high until the Israeli attack on the Beirut Airport at the end of the year. Despite these fluctuations the general trend has been unmistakably upward. This long-term trend can be seen very clearly from the balance of payments estimate of net receipts from travel and tourism, which were calculated at L£20 million in 1951 and at L£177

[35] *Recueil de Statistiques Libanaises, 1967*, p. 398.
[36] *Ibid., 1963*, p. 254.
[37] *Ibid., 1967*, p. 396.

million in 1965.[38] The change in net receipts may reflect the extent of growth of income from tourism and allied activities, but it does not show the magnitude of such income. Moreover, there are no official calculations of this income. My own rough estimate is that expenditures of foreign visitors in the Lebanese market of goods and services are responsible for some 10 percent of national income. This would place tourist income at about L£315 million for 1965, the last year for which national income figures are available. Another estimate places the 1966 figure at about L£320 million and that of 1968 at L£360 million.[39] These are all very rough estimates, but they indicate that tourism has grown spectacularly in the postwar period and has now become an important source of national income.

The Public Sector

As stated earlier, the initiative for the growth in the Lebanese economy came chiefly from the private sector. However, the public sector did contribute to general prosperity, restricted as its role may have been. It is difficult to define government economic policy in Lebanon. Until 1965, the government had never adopted a development program covering a period of several years. Ad hoc projects and annual appropriations have been the prevailing pattern of public participation in economic development. Even the five-year plan formally accepted by the Council of Ministers in 1965 was neither properly funded nor rigorously administered but served more or less as a general guideline for government expenditures of a developmental character. Yet from occasional official declarations, from the pattern of public expenditures over the years, from monetary and fiscal policy, and from the tenor of legislation, it could be construed that the dominant policy in action during most of the postwar period was one of favoring the promotion of trade and services, leaning heavily toward restricting the role of government in economic affairs and toward assuring the greatest degree of individual freedom in internal and external economic relations.[40]

Some economists maintain that the freedom characterizing the post-war period in Lebanon was achieved by default, partly because of the inertia of those in power, who continued along the paths they had trodden under the mandate, partly because of their inability to institute competent administration for proper direction and control, and partly because of subservience to private business interests or complicity in the gains therefrom.[41] There is some truth in this observation, but the restriction of government economic intervention and the reliance on private initiative arose basically, and in a very great measure, from a

[38] The 1951 figure is taken from Fei and Klat, *The Balance of Payments of Lebanon of 1951 and 1952*, p. 5; and the 1965 figure from Medawwar, *The Lebanese Balance of Payments for 1964 and 1965*, p. 16.

[39] *Mid East Commerce*, March 1969, p. 33.

[40] A. Y. Badre, "Lebanese Economic Policy" (in Arabic), *Les Conferences du Cénacle*, Beirut, 1956, p. 357 passim.

[41] Sayigh and Atallah, *A Second Look at the Lebanese Economy*, p. 102.

conscious conception on the part of policymakers of what they believed to be the best interest of the country. In the special regional circumstances arising after the war, businessmen did discover Lebanese opportunity for expansion in trade, tourism, and financial and other services. Those in high office, in both the executive and the legislative branches—many of them businessmen, or lawyers with business orientation—shaped public policy to accommodate this private thrust into trade, finance, and services. As a consequence, the movement of goods, capital, and persons was subjected to the least amount of restrictions. Similarly, the government pursued a policy of freedom in dealing with gold and foreign exchange. It has also favored a preponderantly conservative fiscal policy whereby taxes were kept low and, until recently, expenditures always fell short of revenues. Government administration was kept on a relatively small scale and suffered perenially from inefficiency and corruption.

In addition, the government has kept out of many spheres that have elsewhere become legitimate public domain, even in advanced market-oriented countries in Western Europe. Many public utilities are still privately owned and run. The country has only two television stations, both private. Until 1964, money issue and control was run as a concession by a private bank which acted as the country's central bank. This public policy, which favored the free exercise of private entrepreneurship, together with special postwar developments in the region and elsewhere, led to the inordinate growth of trade, tourism, and services.

Apart from this general policy of ensuring freedom for private enterprise, the government contributed directly to economic development through public expenditures, legislation, and the establishment of public agencies and departments designed to serve some economic and social developmental purposes. This government activity came essentially in the form of ad hoc projects that did not constitute a part of any long-term plan. In fact, development planning in Lebanon has not been rigorous or systematic, nor has it even been binding.

As early as 1953 the government established a Board of Economic Planning and Development under the chairmanship of the Minister of National Economy. The Board was charged with the task of assessing the country's resources, laying down a comprehensive long-term plan for development, and suggesting sources of finance. But not given the means to employ a full-time professional staff, it became a small study and advisory group. In 1954 the planning administration was reorganized; a new Ministry of Planning was created, and the Board, with the Director of Agriculture and Public Works removed from it, became a part of that Ministry, but continued to be composed of part-time employees. Its activity was mainly one of evaluating projects referred to it, and advising the Council of Ministers on courses of action relating thereto. Occasionally, it initiated and recommended projects to the Council of Ministers. It also put together, after four years of operation, a collection of proposed projects, termed it a five-year plan covering the years 1958–1962, and submitted it to the Council of Ministers early in 1958.[42] The program was comprehensive in coverage, ranging from projects designed for the development of the infrastructure to geological surveys, education, social welfare, and administrative reforms. The cost over the five-year period was estimated at L£800 million. The development of roads and water resources accounted for 73 percent of the total cost; projects of social welfare amounted to another 13 percent; and the remaining 14 percent was distributed among agriculture, industry, tourism, and other fields.[43] The projects were merely skeletal indications of objectives; there was no detailed analysis of requirements, availability of resources, modes of execution, or other details usually associated with the readying of projects for implementation. The program was neither adopted formally nor pursued further by the government, although a few projects became implemented in the normal cause of operation of some government departments.

This effort by the Planning Board, however, pointed out the general pattern of priorities, whereby roads and other transport facilities, irrigation, and utilities —in particular, the expansion of the network of water and electricity to outlying villages—received the greatest portion of public attention and funds. Furthermore, it laid the groundwork for the next period of planning. In 1959, a French research group, Institut de Recherche et de Formation en Vue de Développement Harmonisé (IRFED), was charged with the task of studying the conditions of the country and proposing a long-term development plan, which it concluded and submitted to the government in 1964, covering the five years 1965–1969. The plan, after some modifications, was adopted by the Council of Ministers in April 1965[44] and declared the government official policy of development. As in the previous plan, transportation, irrigation, and utilities remained the claimants to the largest portion of expenditures, and social welfare projects were in second place. Their shares of the total, however, varied from the previous plan, being 52 and 21 percent, respectively, as opposed to 73 and 13 percent. The total program was estimated to cost L£1,080 million, L£200 million more than the previous plan. The fate of this plan was not basically different from that of its predecessor. It was not adhered to, funds were inadequate, and the administration of projects was poor.

Since 1959, government attitudes toward planning have been undergoing some change. The Ministry of Planning has been given a larger budget and a better cadre of technical personnel, and other government departments have gradually begun to cooperate with it to a greater degree. Furthermore, since 1959, there has been a greater public consciousness of government responsibility in the economic and social spheres, particularly a greater urgency for treating social weaknesses. As a consequence, the 1960s witnessed the creation of a num-

[42] Ministry of Planning, *Five-Year Program for Economic Development in Lebanon* (in Arabic), Sader Press, Beirut, 1958.

[43] *Ibid.*, p. 12 passim.

[44] Ministry of Planning, *Five-Year Development Plan, 1965, 1969*, Beirut, 1965.

ber of new government agencies having some administrative autonomy and not subject to the procedural regulations of ordinary government departments. Among these were the Department of Social Welfare, covering social service, promotion of rural cottage industry, urban slum clearance, social security, labor training, employment offices, and so on; the "Green Project" for soil conservation, reclamation of waste land, and rural community development; the National Council for Scientific Research; and the Development Institute for training government officials. Also in this same period the Central Bank was established, and new legislation was enacted for regulating banking operations. Budgetary provisions were made for all these agencies, and some of them have done very well. In summary, development planning in the 1960s, although leaving much to be desired, became much more of a serious undertaking than it had been in the previous decade.

The financing of government development projects relied mostly on tax revenues. Until the end of 1958, development funds came from surpluses in the ordinary budget and were included in what was referred to officially as "the extraordinary budget." In those years the government never issued a consolidated statement of all public revenues and expenditures, nor was it mandatory that all budgets be passed by parliament simultaneously. There were in fact four budgets: ordinary, special, municipal, and extraordinary. The special budgets pertained to public enterprises that defrayed expenses from the sale of such services as telephone, water, electricity, and the national lottery. The over 600 municipal budgets in 1966[45] got their revenue from special municipal taxes, from taxes levied by the central government with a portion earmarked for municipalities, and from loans or grants extended by the Treasury or the Central Bank; in the case of Beirut there was even a foreign loan from the Kuwait Fund. Extraordinary budgets were financed by special annual legislation, mainly from the surpluses of ordinary budgets. Their funds were tied either to specific projects or to specific semiautonomous agencies that were not immediately selling a product or service to the public. These expenditures were undertaken for development purposes and consisted predominantly of capital expenditures.

In regard to ordinary budgets, it was the practice in that early period to present to Parliament a supposedly balanced budget, but one that overstated expenditures and understated income, so that a surplus was generated year after year. It was from these surpluses, which went automatically into the Treasury reserves, that the extraordinary budget was funded every year by a special law. In one decade, 1948–1958, the total surpluses were close to L£300 million, or about 23 percent of the total expenditures of the period.[46] Some L£250 million

---

[45] Ministry of Planning, *Local Municipal Administration in Lebanon* (in Arabic), Beirut, 1967, p. 6.

[46] The figures of revenue and expenditures for the years 1948–1951 were obtained from the records of the Ministry of Finance; those for 1952–1963, from *Recueil de Statistiques Libanaises, 1963,* p. 244; and those for 1964–1967, from *Recueil de Statistiques Libanaises, 1967,* p. 340.

of this surplus was rechanneled into development, making development expenditures average about 19 percent of total expenditures of the ordinary budget during the period. In the next 3 years, 1959–1961, surpluses continued to accumulate, but development expenses were not stepped up proportionately. In fact they dropped slightly as a ratio of total expenditures of the ordinary budget. These were the initial years of a new regime, and were devoted mainly to study and preparation for expanded dimensions in development. It was in this period that the IRFED mission conducted its studies and made its preliminary recommendations.

In 1962 there was a radical change in development spending. Development expenditures during that year rose to 35 percent of total expenditures, and it was the first year that showed a substantial deficit. In 1959, the accounting procedure had been altered to have the ordinary budget include in it development expenditures expiring in the budgetary year. A supplementary budget was voted for projects extending beyond a year. In 1962 the ordinary budget accounts, which included L£ 67.2 million of development expenditures, showed a slight surplus of L£ 2.6 million, but an additional expenditure of L£ 57.8 million in the supplementary account indicated a dip into the reserves of L£ 55.2 million.[47] Since then, deficits of this kind, arising through supplementary spending on development projects, have occurred every year. As a consequence, the reserves have been exhausted and the government has gone into debt.

The debt admittedly is not of an alarming proportion, but today Lebanon does face a finance problem that it has not faced since achieving its independence in 1943. Development in the early years was spread over a longer time and executed only within the financial capabilities of the ordinary budget and its surpluses. Expenditures for roads, expansion of the ports of Beirut and Tripoli, the International Airport, the national stadium, a certain expansion of the network of water and electricity, some irrigation schemes, and the construction of some government buildings all came out of these funds. The development of the Litani River for hydroelectric power and irrigation water also received some financing from the same source but relied additionally on a loan from the International Bank for Reconstruction and Development. In the 1960s, however, the government adopted a new approach to development, expanding its scope and increasing its pace, which brought about the deficit financing noted above. By the end of 1966 the government had an outstanding debt with the Central Bank of L£ 175 million, and according to some estimates the figure is likely to reach L£ 500 million by the end of 1971.[48]

There is currently a controversy over whether to slow down the pace of development or to seek an increase in financial resources. The attitude in the legis-

---

[47] *Recueil de Statistiques Libanaises, 1967*, p. 340.
[48] Khattar Shibly, "The Policy of Financing Development in Lebanon" (in Arabic), *Financial Sources and Development in Lebanon* (in Arabic), Proceedings of the Second National Conference on Development Sponsored by the Development Studies Association, Beirut, 1967, p. 115.

lature toward public debt is still predominantly conservative, despite some leniency shown toward a restricted internal debt for long-term capital-forming projects and toward very small external debts such as those from the Kuwait Fund. If development is not to be slowed down, tax revenues must be increased. Total government revenues have risen between seven- and eight-fold since 1948, representing an annual increase between 10 and 12 percent a year.[49] Despite this rapid increase in total revenue, tax revenue, which constituted some 85 percent of total revenue and amounted to about 9 percent of national income in the early 1950s, had risen to only 12 percent of national income in the mid-1960s and now accounts for 80 percent of total revenue. This low ratio of tax revenue to national income is due partly to deficiencies in the tax structure, partly to low tax rates, and in good measure to evasion. It is believed that with greater determination, and barring any serious setbacks to general economic prosperity, tax revenues could be increased sufficiently to resolve a major portion of the growing financial problem without reducing the scale of development or slowing down its pace.

III. Prospects

In attempting to assess the prospects of the future growth of national output, two important variables, the labor force and the capital stock, must be examined and analyzed. The purpose of such analysis is to arrive at a reasonable estimate of the likely rates of growth for these variables and the effect that such growth will have on the aggregate output, recognizing that the behavior of the aggregate output can be explained only partially by the behavior of labor and capital.

Aggregate Output

There is no continuous series of national accounts for Lebanon. The first official figures were issued by the Ministry of Planning in 1967 and covered only the year 1964.[50] This account was followed in 1969 by another estimate, on the same basis, for the year 1965.[51] Previously, there had been two series of partial accounts showing net product at factor cost. The first covered the years from 1948 to 1956, with 1951 missing.[52] This series was revised in the light of the findings of the census of industry conducted in 1956/57 and covering the year 1955. The revised figures, reproduced in Table 4-1, included an extrapolation for the year 1951 and rough estimates for 1957 and 1958.[53] The other series, cover-

[40] See footnote 46.

[50] *Les Comptes Economiques,* 1965.

[51] *Ibid.*

[52] Calculated by the author and quoted in United Nations, *Economic Developments in the Middle East,* 1953–1954, p. 153 (for the years 1948–1950), and 1956–1957, p. 69 (for the years 1952–1956).

[53] United Nations, Food and Agricultural Organization, *Mediterranean Development Project, Lebanon Country Report,* Document FAO 59/10/7238, Rome, 1959, p. II-13.

Table 4-1

Net National Product at Factor Cost, Current and Constant Prices

(million L£)

Year	Current Prices	Constant Prices (1956 = 100)
1950	1,042	1,052
1951	1,086	885
1952	1,115	949
1953	1,168	1,146
1954	1,256	1,335
1955	1,374	1,445
1956	1,467	1,467
1957	1,503	1,474
1958	1,325	1,287
1961	1,789	1,737
1962	1,877	1,877
1963	1,951	1,895
1964 (UN)	(2,038)	(1,984)
1964 (Revised)	2,861	2,726
1965	3,154	2,983

Source: The sources from which this table is extracted are included in footnotes 51-54. The Beirut wholesale price index *(Recueil de Statistiques Libanaises, 1967,* p. 253) has been used for deflating current prices.

ing the four years from 1961 to 1964, was prepared by the United Nations Statistical Office.[54]

If one were to seek what might be termed an average normal rate of growth as reflected by the first series, covering the period 1950–1958, it would be necessary to eliminate 1958 because of internal civil strife, which led to a decline in the national product. Furthermore, the figures for 1957 and 1958 were only rough estimates. Hence it may be more reflective of normal growth to take the period 1950–1956. During this period the net national product at factor cost and

[54] International Monetary Fund, *International Financial Statistics,* February 1969, p. 198 (for the years 1961–1964).

179

current prices grew at the annual rate of 5.87 percent, and at constant prices at the rate of 5.74 percent. The year 1950 was a year of relatively high economic activity; by comparing it with 1956, higher growth rates during the same period are masked, as is seen below:

Period	Current Prices (annual growth rate, percent)	Constant Prices (annual growth rate, percent)
1950–56	5.87	5.74
1952–56	7.11	11.52
1953–56	7.89	8.58

The exceptionally high rate of 11.52 percent for the period 1952–1956 in constant prices results in large measure from the use of the Beirut wholesale index for deflating the series. The index made an abrupt leap to a peak in 1951 after the Korean War. Although it declined the following year, the 1952 level remained considerably higher than the level of both 1950 and 1953. A general wholesale index of 90 items is perhaps not the best deflator of national product figures, particularly when, as in this case, it pertains to a sectoral market that is much more sensitive to international price movements than the rest of the country and that has a higher proportion of products moving in international trade than is found in the composition of the aggregate output. The real growth rate, therefore, is likely to be much lower than is shown above for 1952–1956, and perhaps to be closer to the growth rate of the period 1953–1956, 8.58 percent.

In the light of the figures presented by the first series of national accounts, it is possible to state that annual rates of growth ranging between 6 and 8 percent are indicative of Lebanese experience in the 1950s. Furthermore, comparison of the first series with government official figures for the years 1964 and 1965 reflects similar rates of growth over a longer period. The annual growth rate over the 15-year period from 1950 to 1965 is 7.20 percent, and for the period of 1956–1965 it is 8.21 percent. These rates may be slightly exaggerated because there are some differences in the methods of calculation between the two series, suggesting that the earlier figures may have a comparatively downward bias. Any reasonable synchronization of the two series, however, will still leave the rates of growth within the range of 6–8 percent.

On the other hand, the series emanating from the United Nations for the period 1961–1964 is out of keeping with either of the other two series and seems to yield an unduly low estimate. According to this series, the annual rate of growth of the net product for 1961–1964 was only 4.54 percent. In addition, the 1961 figure of L£1,737 million seems too low. This figure would reflect an annual growth rate for 1956–1961 of only 3.44 percent, and such a low rate of growth for this particular period is highly improbable.

Those who are closely acquainted with the Lebanese economy recognize certain indexes as roughly reflecting the degree of vigor of economic activity and

Table 4-2
Economic Indicators, 1957-1959

Indicator	Unit	1957	1958	1959	Percentage Change of 1959 over 1957
Foreigners entering Lebanon from non-Arab countries	thousands	77	n.a.	94	22.1
Imports	million L£	626	518	699	11.7
Demand deposits	million L£	551	559	778	41.2
Passengers embarking at Beirut Airport	thousands	189	162	231	22.2
Direct taxes	million L£	63	53	71	12.7
Indirect taxes	million L£	118	105	135	14.4
Full-rate tourists at Ba'albek	thousands	33	15	37	12.1
Value of real estate transfer of titles	million L£	72	56	135	87.5
Construction licenses	1,000 square meters	430	389	606	40.9
Generation of electricity	million kilo-watt-hours	286	290	367	28.3

Source: Recueils de Statistiques Libanaises, 1963.

hence indicating upper and lower limits for the growth of aggregate output. Some of these indicators are listed in Table 4-2 for the 3 years 1957–1959. An inspection of this table clearly suggests the occurrence of a decline in economic activity for the year 1958, a year of civil unrest. Practically every indicator is lower than in 1957. The year 1959, on the other hand, shows a considerable rise in each indicator over the levels not only of 1958 but of 1957 as well. These indicators reflect activity in the most important sectors of the economy and, indeed, in the sectors that are likely to fluctuate, such as trade, tourism, transportation, finance, and real estate. Agricultural and industrial outputs are not likely to fluctuate as much, nor do they constitute anywhere as big a share of total output as do the outputs of these other sectors.

Since we have no estimates of the national product for 1959 and 1960, and only rough estimates for 1957 and 1958, I have had to make guesses for the missing years on the basis of indicators in various sectors, including the ones listed above. It appears that the total product for 1959 was at least some 15 percent higher than that for 1957. The years 1960 and 1961 showed considerable growth over 1959 in all sectors, but particularly in tourism and trade, where the year 1961 was outstanding. Hence, as stated above, I believe the United Nations estimate of total product for that year as L£1,737 million (1956 prices) to be grossly understated. According to my gauging of Lebanese economic activity from a variety of indicators, the net national product for 1961 could not be less than L£2,000 million in 1956 prices, and closer perhaps to L£2,100 million. The latter figure would reflect an annual rate of growth of 7.55 percent over 1956, the last relatively properly estimated year of the first series, and a rate of 9.08 percent from 1961–1964, the first year of the third, official series. These rates of growth appear to be much less unrealistic than the corresponding rates of 3.44 percent and 16.20 percent that would result if the United Nations figure for 1961 was used in the calculations. I am inclined, therefore, to disregard the series of 1961–1964, particularly as the United Nations Statistical Office has recently revised its series and adopted the official figures for 1964 and 1965.[55] However, I have left unaltered the figures for 1961–1963, with a resulting growth rate from 1963 to 1964 of 44 percent, which is absurd.

The growth rates obtained from relating the first series to the official figures of 1964 and 1965 range from a little over 7 percent to slightly over 8 percent. The net national product in 1956 prices shows an annual growth of 7.20 percent from 1950 to 1965, and 8.21 percent from 1956 to 1965. Since the two series do not have exactly the same basis of calculation, these rates may reflect a bias. The bias is upward if, as I believe, the first series is somewhat more conservative than the current official series. The average rate of growth is probably closer to 7 than to 8 percent. In the light of these findings and other indicators of past performance, under normal conditions the average rate of growth is not likely to drop below 6 percent per annum, and more probably it will be in the neighborhood of 7 percent—in any case, below 8 percent. Consequently, I am basing my analysis on an expectation of a growth rate lying between 6 and 7 percent per annum from 1970 to 1980.

Figures for aggregate product covering the years 1966–1969 are not available. Various indicators suggest, however, that the national product rose considerably in 1966, possibly by more than 7 percent. There was a recession in 1967; such indicators as the consumption of electric current, government revenue from the income tax, and basic agricultural and industrial output continued to rise, though at a slower rate; but imports, tourists, construction permits, real estate transfers, and other indicators showed some decline. Another year of booming activity was 1968, with all the important indicators showing large increases over the previous year. In the absence of national product figures covering the period 1965–1970, I have had to be guided by these rough indicators in estimating, or rather trying to ascertain, a possible rate of growth. Output at constant prices must have grown during this period at about 6 percent. This is the rate I use for calculating the 1970 national product.

[55] *Ibid.,* Vol. XXIII, February 1970, p. 198.

Using past rates for projecting future growth is admittedly not a very satisfactory method, although it may be a fair approximation if underlying conditions do not alter appreciably in the future. Projection would be much more credible if it were possible to make an accurate assessment of the contribution to past growth of each factor of a whole battery of production factors. This, of course, cannot be done. Instead I group factors of some similarity into labor and capital and try to foresee the course of change in these two grouped factors and the effects of such change upon the growth of output. But labor and capital do not account for all the growth of output. There is always a substantial unexplained residual, attributable to a whole variety of causes, such as technical progress, improvement in skills, management, institutions, and other elements. This residual can be referred to simply as "unexplained progress or productivity." The growth of output, therefore, will depend on the growth of the quantities of labor and capital (starting from a given magnitude) and the unexplained productivity. The greater the increase in the latter, the less will be the needed increase in labor or capital to yield a given increase in output.

The Labor Force

The task here is twofold: to determine, first, the current size of the labor force and, second, the rate at which it grew in the recent past in the expectation that such knowledge will be useful in attempting to forecast the future magnitude and growth of this important production factor. But again there are data deficiencies. No official figures show the size of the labor force in Lebanon at any time, and unofficial estimates vary widely. I have used a sample population study conducted by the Ministry of Planning[56] as a base for my estimate of the labor force. The breakdown of this study by appropriate age groups relating to small administrative subdistricts permits differentiation of the estimates of the subdistricts on the basis of general knowledge of employment differences among various Lebanese groups, especially with reference to woman and child labor and also to differences in health conditions. The population figures in question related to the year 1964, and my estimate of the labor force for that year came to 35 percent of the total population, or some 770,000 persons. This percentage seems reasonable, considering that those aged 14 years and below, plus those aged 60 years and above, together constituted 52.75 percent of the total population. Although this estimated percentage of the labor force lies a little above the figures for some Asiatic countries, such as Iran and Pakistan (32 and 33.5 percent, respectively), it falls short of ratios obtaining in some Mediterranean countries, for example, Spain, Yugoslavia, and Greece (38.4, 45.2, and 43.7 percent, respectively).[57]

In the absence of proper labor statistics I have used the population growth rate as an approximation of the rate of growth of the labor force. But here again

[56] Ministère du Plan, *La Population de Liban,* Beirut, 1967.
[57] Benjamin Higgins, *Economic Development—Principles, Problems, and Policies,* Rev. ed., W. W. Norton and Co., New York, 1968, pp. 888–889.

population figures in Lebanon are very unreliable. The last proper census was conducted in 1932. A later census, conducted in 1942 primarily for the purpose of organizing the administration of rationed supplies, is not considered very accurate. The official population figures reflect the registration since 1932 of births, deaths, naturalization, and lapse of citizenship. This process suffers from considerable inaccuracy partly because the reporting of births and deaths is deficient, but even more because migration is not accounted for. Every year a good number of Lebanese emigrate and varying numbers of foreigners come to settle in Lebanon. Official figures, therefore, may not give an accurate idea of the resident population. In periods of substantial immigration, such as in the years 1948–1950, characterized by a large influx of Palestinians, official population figures fall below the real number of residents. In normal years, on the other hand, they tend to lie somewhat above the real number, since Lebanese citizens who leave the country continue to be included in the official figures unless they formally renounce Lebanese citizenship, which very few do even after acquiring foreign nationalities. This discrepancy widens further in periods marked by a high rate of naturalization, as in the 1950s and early 1960s.

Any statement of the size and the rate of growth of the Lebanese population can only be guesswork. A sample survey conducted by the Ministry of Planning published in 1967 shows actual resident population in 1964 to be 2,179,700, excluding some 67,000 Palestinian refugees in camps.[58] The official figures of the Ministry of Interior, based on the registers, stand at 2,367,000 for 1965. Obviously there is a discrepancy between the two figures, for the population could not have grown by the 8.5 percent reflected in these two figures. Since the figures of the Ministry of Interior are biased upward, I accept the figure of the Ministry of Planning as the base, rounding it to 2,200,000 for 1964. Of these, it is estimated that some 390,000 are not Lebanese citizens but are mainly Syrians and Palestinians.[59]

If determining the number of Lebanese residents is a matter of open estimation, determining the population rate of growth is even more prone to possible error. One estimate that gained currency in official circles is an annual growth rate of 2.7 percent.[60] The Department of Statistics considers this rate too low.[61] Investigations with various government officials and others concerned with population lead me to believe that, on the contrary, a rate of 2.7 percent is perhaps a little too high. It would also appear so from an examination of some previous estimates. A comparison of the two censuses of 1932 and 1942 (adjusted to 1944) show an average rate of growth over the 12-year period of 2.48 percent. To be sure, the figures of the Ministry of Interior taken from the official

[58] *La Population de Liban,* p. 14.

[59] *Recueil de Statistiques Libanaises, 1965,* Vol. 2, p. 40.

[60] Ministère du Plan, Mission IRFED-LIBAN, 1960–1961, *Besoins et Possibilités de Développement du Liban,* Beirut, 1961, p. 78.

[61] *Recueil de Statistiques Libanaises, 1965,* p. 41.

registers show a higher annual growth rate of 4.4 percent for 1953–1965. But this is an exaggerated rate. We know that the period from 1953 to 1961 was marked by an exceptionally high rate of registration of new citizenship granted to Palestinians, Syrians, and Egyptians of Lebanese origin. The official registers, therefore, are bound to show a rate well above the real rate of growth. In a period where new citizenships were a less dominant factor, as in the years 1961–1965, the annual rate of growth indicated by the same official registers was only 2.41 percent. The actual rate of natural growth for this period may be even less, since there is a continuing tendency to report births more accurately than deaths.

In the light of the foregoing information the rate of population growth in recent years has averaged about 2.4 percent a year. This is the rate adopted in projecting population growth for the purposes of the present study and also the one I use as a basis for estimating the growth of the labor force.

Capital

No assessment has been made of the value of the national capital stock at any time. Thus there are no figures of average capital-output ratio or of the rate of growth of the capital stock. All that is available in this connection are some estimates of capital formation covering the years 1950–1957 and the two years 1964 and 1965. These are reproduced in Table 4-3. From these figures alone it is obviously not possible to tell the growth rate of total capital stock, although some notion can be derived with regard to capital-output relationships over time. Annual gross capital formation has increased at a higher rate than the gross national product. For the 15-year period from 1950 to 1965 GNP increased at an annual rate of 7.68, whereas gross capital formation increased at the higher rate of 8.52 percent. This suggests that the capital-output ratio rose during the period in question. Although this may be so, it would not necessarily represent a continuing trend leading to the deduction that capital-output ratio is likely to rise in the coming decade.

On the contrary, there are reasons to believe that capital-output ratios were relatively high in the 1950s on account of the surge of capitalization in apples and other fruits, which did not lead to increased output until the 1960s. Furthermore, prices of apples declined in the 1950s but were more stable in the 1960s, accentuating the tendency for a comparatively higher capital-output ratio in the 1950s. In fact, if we define incremental capital-output ratio as the ratio of net capital formation every year to the increment of the net national product over the previous year, the figures in Table 4-3 yield a ratio of 3.4 as the average of the incremental capital-output ratios for the years 1950–1956, whereas for the year 1965 the resulting ratio is only 2.0. These ratios do not seem unreasonable considering that, in addition to the large agricultural capitalization mentioned above, capital formation in the 1950s was heavily weighted with the development of the infrastructure, including such major projects as the Beirut Interna-

Table 4-3

Capital Formation, 1950-1957 and 1964-1965

(million L£)

Year	Net National Product	Net Capital Formation	Percentage of Net National Product	Gross National Product	Gross Capital Formation	Percentage of Gross National Product
1950	1,042	160	15.4	1,114	232	20.8
1951	1,086	131	12.1	1,162	207	17.8
1952	1,115	150	13.5	1,192	227	19.0
1953	1,168	155	13.3	1,249	236	19.0
1954	1,256	165	13.1	1,343	252	18.8
1955	1,374	206	15.0	1,459	291	19.9
1956	1,417	225	15.9	1,516	324	21.4
1957	1,503	233	15.5	1,608	338	21.0
1964	2,861	511	17.9	3,055	705	23.1
1965	3,154	580	18.4	3,368	793	23.6

Source: The figures for net capital formation are taken from Food and Agricultural Organization, *Mediterranean Development Project: Lebanon Country Report,* FAO 59/10/7238, Rome, 1959, p. II-25, for the years 1950-1957. The figures for 1964 and 1965 are taken from *Rapport sur les Comptes Economiques.* The gross figures for 1950-1957 are extrapolated.

tional Airport, the ports of Beirut and Tripoli, major road networks, and most of the large hotels. Capital formation in the 1960s was associated more heavily with trade, finance, and other services that are characterized by lower capital-output ratios.

From the data presented in Table 4-3, the average incremental ratio for the period 1950–1965, calculated on the basis of the years with available data, amounts to 3.2. If this is a true average of the period despite the data gaps, that is, if supplying the missing data will not alter it, then it would be a ratio in harmony with my previous assessment of the growth rate of GNP. As can be seen from the table, gross capital formation ranged between 17.8 and 23.6 percent of gross national product. The average for the whole period 1950–1965 is 21.4 percent. At an incremental capital-output ratio of 3.2, this rate of gross investment should represent a rise in GNP at the annual rate of 6.6 percent, which is identical to the rate independently determined earlier on the basis of the figures for GNP.

Does this imply that in order to maintain the same growth rate for the future the economy must continue to have an annual rate of gross investment amounting to 21 percent of GNP? There is no definite answer to this question. Much depends on the nature of future growth and the extent to which that growth is not attributable to the mere quantitative augmentation of labor and capital. The maintenance throughout the 1970s of the same rate of annual gross investment, together with the same growth rate of GNP, implies a constant incremental capital-output ratio. But this is precisely what we cannot take for granted. In fact, even from the incomplete data at our disposal, there are indications that the incremental capital-output ratio fluctuated considerably but was probably higher in the 1950s than in the 1960s. There are also indications that the average capital-output ratio might have experienced a slight rise during the 15 years in question. This would suggest that the average ratio was lower than the incremental ratio. In fact, considering the nature of the Lebanese national product, it may have been considerably lower.

It will be seen from Table 4-3 that the annual net capital formation for the period 1950–1965 averaged about 15 percent of the net national product and that the latter had grown at the annual rate of 7.68 percent. If in the light of the statistical discrepancies between the two series mentioned earlier we accept a lower growth rate of the net national product, namely, the 6.6 percent indicated before, then, in order for capital to grow at the same rate as output, we need to have an average capital-output ratio of 2.4. As mentioned earlier, however, there are strong indications that average capital-output ratio rose slightly. Under such conditions the average ratio should be lower than 2.4. If this is true, and if the marginal ratio should precipitate in the 1970s toward the average ratio after the past period of spurtive investment in projects of high capital-output ratio, then the projected rate of growth could be achieved in the 1970s at net investment rates lower than 15 percent of national income, or gross investment rates lower than 21 percent of GNP. Conversely, a higher growth rate could be achieved in the future than in the past while maintaining gross investment at 21 percent of GNP. What should be examined next is the ability of the country to maintain and finance such a high rate of gross investment. Before doing that, however, it may be useful to show the magnitude of growth that might be expected during the next decade on the basis of the growth rates of product and population considered in the foregoing analysis.

Growth Projection

The most recent year for which an estimate of the net national product at factor cost is available is 1965. National accounts covering that year are prepared by the Department of Statistics at the Ministry of Planning.[62] These figures are taken here as the base for my projection. According to the previous analysis, the long-term annual growth rate of the national product at constant prices seemed to lie between 6 and 7 percent and closer to 7 percent. For the years 1965–1970, however, 6 percent is considered more representative of the real growth rate,

---

[62] *Les Comptes Economiques,* 1965.

Table 4-4

Projections of the Net National Product

	1965	1970	1980
Net national product (million L£ in 1965 prices)	3,154	4,221	7,922
Population (thousands)	2,253	2,537	3,226
Net national product per capita (L£)	1,400	1,610	2,146
Net national project per capita (U.S.$ at $1 = 3.15 L£)	444	511	681

since the period was marked by some setbacks experienced in the wake of the failure of Intra Bank in 1966 and the Arab-Israeli military engagements in 1967. With expectations of reasonably good conditions in the 1970s, real product is projected to grow at 6.5 percent, which is closer to the long-term growth rate observed for an earlier 15-year period. Furthermore, the resident population seems to have been increasing in the recent past at the rate of 2.4 percent per annum.

The resulting total and per capita net products are shown in Table 4-4, from which it can be seen that the net national product per capita will have risen by the end of the decade to some $680 or perhaps $700. For whatever international comparisons are worth, Lebanon in 1970 will be comparable in per capita income with such countries as Spain and Greece five years ago; and after a decade it will be comparable to Japan, Argentina, and Ireland in 1965. If its progress continues at the same pace, by the end of the century Lebanon will reach a per capita income level similar to the 1965 level of West European countries such as Britain and France.[63]

Financing Growth

The rate of aggregate growth used in the above projection is based on the analysis of past growth rates. Will Lebanon be able to sustain and finance such growth in the coming decade? An examination of the country's productive resources reveals a high degree of uncertainty, and an inordinate dependence of future economic development on peace and stability in the region and on the maintenance of cordial relations with neighboring countries that would facilitate the movement of goods and factors.

The growth of Lebanon's capital resources over the last 20 years has been remarkable. Average gross capital formation is estimated to be about 21 percent

[63] See United Nations, *Yearbook of National Accounts,* 1967 (UN-ST/Stat-Y3), New York, 1968, pp. 824–827.

of GNP. Of course, future growth of product at the projected rate may be effected with a smaller proportion of capital formation if the areas of future expansion in output require proportionately less capital, or if there is an upward shift in the production function attributable in a higher proportion than in the past to noncapital cooperant factors. There is no way of determining this matter with any degree of certainty. It may be more sensible, while keeping this possibility in mind, to reckon on a gross capital flow amounting to 21 percent of the gross product and to examine the possibilities of financing such a rate.

The prospects of gross capital formation continuing to grow at such a high rate cannot be considered as certain. More than four-fifths of the capital formation of the country is undertaken by the private sector. Private capital formation amounted to 17.24 percent of the gross national product in 1964, and to 18.20 percent in 1965; public capital formation was only 4.04 and 3.60 percent, respectively,[64] for the two years. The uncertainty of the future can best be appreciated by examining some of the sources of the private capital formation. Gross domestic savings, calculated from the 1964 figures, come to L£270.7 million. If to this amount is added the net factor income from abroad, calculated at L£141.8 million, the result is a national savings figure of L£412.5 million, considerably short of the gross investment figure of L£704.5 million.[65] Perhaps it is in the explanation of this gap of L£292 million between national saving and national investment in 1964, and similar discrepancies in other years, that the risks involved in the future growth of the economy can best be appreciated. Since this gap is identical to the net exports of goods and services plus net factor payments from abroad, one should look for the explanation, not in receipts incorporated in the movement of goods and services, but rather in non quid pro quo items in the foreign sector. Every year the Lebanese balance of payments shows items in this category of substantial magnitude.

A statement of the balance of payments for five years is shown in Table 4-5. For the year 1964, for instance, net gifts and remittances amounted to L£108.5 million, and the net inflow of capital totaled L£190.6 million. Although the sum of these two items happens to be almost equal to the gap between national saving and investment, there is no intention to imply a direct transformation of these financial items into national capital. It is a fact of national accounting procedures, however, that gifts and capital transfers do not constitute a part of national income and cannot, therefore, figure in the calculation of national savings. On the other hand, we know that many Lebanese emigrants remit money to their relatives in Lebanon. In recent years, an increasing portion of these remittances has been made by Lebanese who emigrate to other parts of the Arab world but who intend to return to their native country. Large parts of these remittances are intended for investment in Lebanon. Emigrant remittances for 1964 were estimated at some L£85 million.[66] Likewise, a sub-

[64] *Les Comptes Economiques,* 1965, pp. 11, 12.
[65] *Ibid.,* 1964, p. 107.
[66] *Lebanese Balance of Payments,* Vol. 3, p. 16.

Table 4-5

Balance of Payments, 1961-1965

(million L£)

	1961	1962	1963	1964	1965
Current account					
Exports-imports	− 812.9	− 737.9	− 855.9	− 899.7	− 1,064.5
Nonmonetary gold	− 7.4	− 7.0	− 7.0	− 9.3	− 9.4
Travel and tourism	117.6	126.0	148.6	135.5	176.7
Transport and insurance	122.0	166.0	160.2	161.5	178.3
Investment income	72.2	67.5	68.1	74.4	77.7
Government services	67.7	65.9	68.0	83.4	79.1
Other services	188.4	189.7	198.8	198.0	208.2
Total goods and services	− 252.4	− 129.8	− 219.2	− 256.2	− 353.9
Transfers	120.2	98.0	108.8	108.5	108.2
Total	− 132.2	− 31.8	− 110.4	− 147.7	− 245.7
Errors and omissions	52.9	9.9	42.1	75.3	46.6
Capital movements					
Long-term private capital	44.0	52.4	50.1	63.1	74.3
Short-term private capital	103.7	67.0	58.0	107.0	146.6
Long-term government capital	18.3	11.0	7.2	20.5	4.8
Total	166.0	130.4	115.3	190.6	225.7
Surplus (+) or deficit (−)	+ 86.7	+ 108.5	+ 47.0	+ 118.2	+ 26.0

Source: The table is compiled from the three volumes on the Lebanese balance of payments (in Arabic) prepared under the joint auspices of the Ministry of Planning and the Economic Research Institute. The first volume, covering 1961, and the second, covering 1962 and 1963, prepared by Khalil Salem; the third volume, covering 1964 and 1965, is prepared by George Medawwar.

stantial portion of the continuous stream of capital transfers to banks in Lebanon from other Arab countries gets locked up in domestic investment.

It is clear that the high rate of capital formation prevailing in the last 10 or 15 years could not be financed from domestic savings alone. The future maintenance of such a rate of capital formation will depend on the continuance of substantial capital transfers. Unlike countries whose income derives in large measure from a lucrative natural resource, from a natural advantage in the raising of staple crops, or from a vigorous and dynamic industry, Lebanon depends on sources of income that can be very unstable. Trade, tourism, emigrant remittances, and middlemanship in capital movements are all activities that require a high degree of internal and regional political stability and a relatively free movement across political boundaries of goods, capital, and persons. I estimate that in the 5 years from 1961 to 1965 almost one-third of total personal income could be attributed to the following activities: local expenditure of tourists, transport of goods and persons across boundaries (excluding purely internal transport), transit, entrepôt and triangular trade, emigrant remittances, and capital transfers. These activities can be seriously hurt by such events as the internal strife of 1958, the failure of Intra Bank in 1966, and the Six-Day War of 1967. They can also be hurt by restrictions on the regional and international movement of goods and factors. The maintenance of conditions favorable to the future growth of these sectors depends on circumstances that, for the most part, lie beyond the scope of Lebanon's public policy and over which the country has little control.

The rates of growth postulated in this study are based on the assumption that future conditions will not be overrestrictive to the regional and international movements of goods, capital, and persons. If this assumption proves to be faulty, it may not be possible to attain the rate of capital formation projected above, unless the decrease in foreign remittances and transfers reduces consumption rather than investment expenditures, that is, unless it results in an increase of domestic savings rather than a reduction in domestic investment. This possibility, however, would have been more likely with the pattern of remittances prevailing in the 1920s and 1930s, when the major part was composed of help to relatives in maintaining a certain level of consumption. In the current pattern, remittances and transfers are linked more to investment, and their reduction is more likely to result in a decline of investment than of consumption. If such shrinkage in the foreign sector occurs, it may not be possible to attain the growth targets projected in this study by 1980, unless, as pointed out earlier, shifts in the production function arising from noncapital cooperant factors reduce the capital-output ratio.

On the other hand, the possibility of increasing domestic savings must not be summarily dismissed. Rather, it must be examined in the light of the expected pattern of national expenditure. Table 4-6 may shed some light on the question. The projections shown in the table for the years 1970 and 1980 reflect my assumptions about the future structure of the economy and my expectations of its future growth. It is clear from the small ratio of public to total expenditures

Table 4-6
Lebanese National Expenditure Projections
to the Year 2000
(million L£)

	1964	1965	1970	1980
Private consumption expenditures	2,636	2,935	3,870	7,095
Public consumption	261	323	400	800
Private fixed capital formation (including increase in stocks)	571	663	880	1,630
Public capital formation	134	130	210	400
Net exports of goods and services	− 434	− 528	− 560	− 835
Total expenditures on gross domestic product	3,168	3,523	4,800	9,090
Net factor income from abroad	142	117	154	205
Total expenditures on gross national product	3,310	3,640	4,954	9,295
Provision for capital consumption	194	213	290	545
Net national product at market prices	3,116	3,427	4,664	8,750
Indirect taxes less subsidies	254	273	443	828
Net national product at factor cost (national income)	2,862	3,154	4,221	7,922

Source: Ministère du Plan, Direction Centrale de la Statistique, *Rapport sur les Comptes Economiques,* 1964, Vol. 1; *Résultats,* Beirut, 1968, p. 107; (for 1965) *Les Comptes Economiques,* 1965 (with interpolations), Beirut, 1969, pp. 12, 18, 20, 23.

shown in Table 4-6 that I assume the continuation of the private sector as the dominant source of economic activity. Furthermore, the price level in Lebanon has been relatively very stable; the wholesale price index has risen by less than 1 percent a year for the last ten years.[67] I assume the continuation of this relative price stability, which will enable us to disregard the effects of the price level on the development of employment and output. This assumption may not be unrealistic in view of the deeply ingrained policy of balancing the public budget, on one hand, and a persistent import gap which is continuously more than covered

[67] *International Financial Statistics,* September 1966, p. 194, and February 1969, p. 198.

by capital inflows, on the other hand. However, the foreign sector is not expected to grow at a uniform but rather at a decreasing rate because of some anticipated slowing down in capital inflows.

This expectation is embodied in Table 4-6. If we add the exports of goods and services to the net factor income from abroad and deduct the imports of goods and services, the resulting figure, representing the net gap in the foreign sector, amounts to 8.8 percent of GNP in 1964. It will presumably decline to something like 8.2 and 6.8 percent in 1970 and 1980, respectively. If such decline does occur, the pattern of national expenditures will be affected appreciably. In 1964, for instance, total consumption, both private and public, amounted to 87.5 percent of the gross national product. If the Lebanese economy had been a closed one, investment could not have been more than 12.5 percent of gross product. Yet actual investment amounted to 21.3 percent; the difference of 8.8 percent is accounted for by the foreign gap discussed above. If my predictions come true, however, and the gap narrows in relation to GNP, then a compensating decline becomes necessary in the percentage of either consumption or investment or both. Where the squeeze would occur is a question of policy based on national priorities and administrative capabilities.

The present study has stipulated an annual growth rate of 6.5 percent. This rate is predicated upon annual investment in the neighborhood of 21 percent of GNP. Since this is about equal to the current rate of investment, the squeeze necessitated by a slowing growth in the foreign sector will have to fall on consumption. It may not fall equally, however, on public and private consumption. In fact, I foresee the necessity of considerable expansion in public consumption, particularly in the realms of health, education, and social services. In 1965 expenditure on these public functions, a large proportion of which have been performed by church and other private organizations, constituted less than 5 percent of total public expenditures.[68] There is an increasing pressure for the expansion of public responsibility in the field of education in particular, but also in health care and social services, and I envision a more than proportionate expansion of public responsibility in these fields.

I also expect a total growth in public expenditure at a higher rate than the growth rate of the national product. Public expenditures rose from a level of L£111 million in 1954 to L£526 million in 1965.[69] This represents an expansion rate of over 11 percent a year. Although, as a matter of policy, the public sector should not be permitted to expand at this high rate in the future, it will nevertheless expand at a rate higher than the 6.5 percent postulated for the growth of national output. It follows from these expectations that the ratio of public consumption to the gross national product will also rise. The extent of this increase can be calculated from Table 4-6, yielding the following percentages: 7.9, 8.0, and 8.6 for the years 1964, 1970, and 1980, respectively.

[68] *Les Comptes Economiques,* 1965, p. 19.
[69] *Recueil de Statistiques Libanaises, 1965,* pp. 420 and 421.

The squeeze will then have to be applied entirely to private consumption. This is shown in the ratios that can be calculated from the table. Private consumption amounted to about 80 percent of GNP in 1964. In 1970 and 1980 it is expected to decline to 78 and 76 percent, respectively. Despite this proportionate decline, per capita consumption will increase at an annual rate of 3.6 percent during the coming decade.

This squeeze on private consumption should not be inordinately difficult to achieve through an increase in tax rates or a tightening up of tax administration. Total government revenue in 1964 amounted to only about 14.65 percent of GNP. The tax part of this revenue was only 11.80 percent of the national product, and of this only 4.35 percent represented direct taxes. On the basis of the low tax figures of 1964, which are fairly representative of other years, it is reasonable to expect successful results in formulating and implementing a policy of reducing private consumption through a rising tax burden. According to this analysis the long-term target would then be the reduction of total consumption from the level of 87.5 percent of GNP prevailing in 1964 to 84.9 percent by 1980. In this way it will still be possible to maintain an investment level of 21 percent of GNP, despite the expected decline in the growth of the foreign sector.

Sectoral Distribution of Growth

Changes are also expected in the composition of the national output. These changes are shown in Table 4-7. All along, trade has been the leading sector of the Lebanese economy. In 1950, it generated over 30 percent of the total domestic product. By 1964, it had declined to 27 percent of total output. It is expected to continue as the largest sector but with a declining lead, so that by 1980, although the volume will have grown to more than two and a half times that of 1964, trade will be generating only 24.8 percent of the domestic product. Agriculture is another sector expected to grow in volume but decline in relative importance, coming down from 13 percent in 1964 to 11 percent in 1980. Present trends show that industry is likely to grow at a faster rate than total domestic product. At present industry generates between 13 and 14 percent of total output. I expect it to reach a level between 15 and 16 percent by 1980. The public sector is also likely to grow somewhat in relative importance, mainly by expansion of public consumption. According to my estimates, public investment will maintain the same proportion, about one-fourth of private investment or one-fifth of total investment. However, the public sector as a whole will rise in importance from generating about 7 percent of the domestic product in 1964 to almost 9 percent in 1980. Services, including financial activities, will continue growing faster than total domestic product but perhaps considerably less than the gain registered in the past two decades.

The foregoing discussion reflects more or less what I foresee for the Lebanese economy in the decade ahead. In many instances the image is admittedly blurred. Several of the projections are highly uncertain because some of my expectations about the relevant variables may not materialize. These expectations

194

Table 4-7

Gross Domestic Product at Factor Cost by Industrial Origin

(million I£ and percent)

	1964		1970		1980	
	Amount	Percent of GDP	Amount	Percent of GDP	Amount	Percent of GDP
Agriculture	382.1	13.1	540	12.4	917	11.1
Industry (including mining)	389.9	13.4	614	14.1	1,272	15.4
Construction	169.6	5.8	248	5.7	463	5.6
Electricity and water	53.7	1.8	83	1.9	165	2.0
Transportation and communication	251.9	8.7	362	8.3	694	8.4
Trade (wholesale and retail)	790.1	27.1	1,160	26.6	2,050	24.8
Ownership of dwellings	243.0	8.3	348	8.0	644	7.8
Public administration	212.5	7.3	348	8.0	719	8.7
Services (including banks, insurance, etc.)	421.8	14.5	654	15.0	1,338	16.2
Gross domestic product at factor cost	2,913.6	100.0	4,357	100.0	8,262	100.0

Source: The 1964 figures are taken from *Rapport sur les Comptes Economiques*, 1964, p. 108. The figures for 1970 and 1980 are projected at 1965 prices.

195

are based partly on my interpretation of the history of Lebanese economic performance to date and partly on a subjective appreciation of current problems and of policy measures evolved or contemplated for dealing with these problems.

IV. Problems and Policy

The problems dealt with in this section are primarily those relating to the future prosperity of the country. In particular, attention will be focused on what might turn into impediments to economic progress. Sometimes obstacles to economic development arise chiefly in the economic sphere and pertain directly to economic factors or to institutions connected with such factors. In other instances obstacles to progress arise chiefly in noneconomic spheres. In the case of Lebanon, the major threats to continued growth and prosperity probably lie in the political and social spheres. Although politics and social relations fall outside the scope of this study, and consequently will not be treated here in any great detail, their effect on economic growth is an integral part of this analysis. Economic problems and policies, which are the central object of inquiry in this section, can be analyzed and understood better, particularly in the case of Lebanon, when projected against an illuminated sociopolitical screen.

Conflict of Loyalties

In the political sphere the basic problem of Lebanon is one of loyalties. The Lebanese people are not unified with respect to their ultimate loyalties and aspirations. There is no strong consensus on the destiny of the country and the future pattern of its internal and external relations. Its schismatic political ethos derives from a history of cultural conflict steeped in differences of religious experience and outlook. Religion not only is the basis of contemporary Lebanese politics but also has been for a long time the raison d'être of the country's distinguishable identity. Its political status undulated through the centuries; boundaries waxed and waned, sharpened and dimmed; but the essence of the Lebanese question has remained the same throughout: the existence in the Lebanese hills of a compact Christian community. Without understanding the characteristics of this community, the vision of Lebanese realities can at best be hazy, and political assumptions necessary for economic projections can be widely off base.

The Christians of Lebanon have had very strong cultural ties with Europe. The Maronites and other Roman Catholic groups had close relations for centuries with Mediterranean Latin countries, and the Greek Orthodox with Russia. As far back as the middle of the seventeenth century official pronouncements declared France to be the protector of the Maronites of Lebanon.[70]

[70] On April 28, 1659, Louis XIV of France issued a declaration which contained in part the following excerpts: "Let it be known: that we, by the advice of the Queen Regent, our very honored lady and mother, having taken and placed, as by these signs of our hand we do take and place in our protection and special safeguard the Most Reverend Patriarch and all the prelates, ecclesiastics and Maronite Christian

ALBERT Y. BADRE

For most of the Ottoman period the Christians of Lebanon had a special status enabling them, unlike Christians in other parts of the empire, to partake of a fully Christian culture without unease or self-consciousness. When this special status was challenged in the nineteenth century, the struggle opened up the community and perhaps the whole empire to international intrigue, culminating in the massacres of 1860 and the landing of French troops in Lebanon. In the wake of this crisis the conflict was resolved by Lebanon's reasserting unequivocally the unique status of the Lebanese Christians and accepting without challenge their special ties with the European community. The solution of 1860, which lasted over half a century, was to make an autonomous unit of the mountain section populated predominantly by Christians and to place it under a Christian governor, with a seven-nation guarantee of this status.

During World War I the Ottoman government revoked this status, and the inhabitants of Mount Lebanon were placed under forced isolation which precipitated famine and widespread death. Under the postwar French mandate, the boundaries of Lebanon were enlarged and new districts with non-Christian majorities were added. The philosophy of the new order was to make the country economically viable in size but with a Christian majority and a dominance of Christian culture. Prominent positions in the civil service, the army, and the political structure were occupied overwhelmingly by Christians. Even before the end of the mandate Moslem resentment began to be felt, and a move toward greater economic and political sharing was underway. At the termination of the mandate a sort of understanding, known as the "national pact," was reached with hesitation and with a certain amount of mutual equivocation between the Christian and Moslem communities. The Christians wanted a Lebanese identity totally apart from other Arabic-speaking countries and belonging culturally to Mediterranean Europe. The Moslems, on the other hand, regarded Lebanon as a fully Arab country destined ultimately to become part of a pan-Arab union.[71] These two outlooks were liable to conflict, particularly when the goals of Western Europe and the Arab world diverged, as occurred earlier with respect to colonial relations and most recently in relation to Zionism.

At the time of the liquidation of the mandate, the conflict was sharp. The Lebanese were faced with the alternatives of seeking to continue some attachment to France or other Western nations, splitting the country, merging with

---

laics, who dwell particularly in Mount Lebanon: . . . so that there will not be accorded to them any ill treatment, but on the contrary, that they may continue freely their spiritual exercises and functions." J. C. Hurewitz, *Diplomacy in the Near and Middle East,* Vol. I, Van Nostrand, Princeton, N. J., 1956, p. 24.

[71] The terms Christian and Moslem in this context are used rather loosely to express cultural affiliations with Western Europe on the one hand, and with Arab and Islamic countries on the other. The first group, made up largely of Christians, does include Moslems, and the second group, made up largely of Moslems, does include Christians.

Syria, or establishing an independent republic with the same boundaries as existed under the mandate. The last alternative prevailed. It was possible to attain it only by a compromise whereby the Christians would support independence from France while the Moslems would accept independence from any future Arab union.

Reaching a political compromise, however, does not alter basic loyalties or instantly remove suspicions. Whatever the truth about the loyalties of these two communities, each suspected, and still suspects, the motives of the other. The Christians believe that the Moslems wish to liquidate Lebanon and merge it into an Arab bloc; the Moslems believe that the Christians, deliberately or unwittingly, aid Western imperialistic designs on the Arab world. The "national pact" formula, enshrouded with such suspicions, has lasted now for a quarter of a century. The political situation has been continuously uneasy, however, erupting occasionally in widespread national crises which threaten the continuation of the present setup, as happened in 1958 with reference to posture toward Egypt, and is happening currently with reference to posture toward Israel.

Not only does controversy continue regarding relations with the outside, but also differences in the interpretation of the "national pact" and in attitudes toward it have given rise to much internal controversy. The Christians seek in the pact the continuation of the political dominance they enjoyed under the mandate; the Moslems resist Christian dominance and seek to establish their own. Political, administrative, and elective offices have been apportioned by sects, presumably on the basis of the comparative numbers constituting the various sects. The Christians cling to a number basis established before independence. The Moslems deny the validity of this basis and ask for a population census, which no administration coming to power since independence was achieved has agreed to conduct. Moreover, the Maronites cling to the tradition of having the presidency of the republic confined to their group, since they are the largest single sect in the country.

In summary, the sectarian basis, which gave the country a modicum of political stability in the past, is now becoming a source of internal instability. There is increasing dissatisfaction with the system, a denial of the validity of the population figures on which it is purportedly based, and a growing impatience with the fraudulent practices and hypocritical comportment of governments trying to keep together groups that have no overriding common loyalty. With the increasing tensions in the Middle East and the widening rift between the Western powers and the Arab world, the internal tensions in Lebanon have intensified, giving rise, in important quarters, to second thoughts about the "national pact" itself and the present structure of the country. Ideas relating to partitioning, border alterations, and transfer of populations are being entertained.

The conclusion to be drawn from this analysis is that the political future of the country cannot at this juncture be considered firm. Changes in political structure or in the degree of internal stability will evidently have drastic effects on economic projections such as those made in Section III. In undertaking these projections I have assumed that the Lebanese will succeed in keeping the country united and in containing political instability, although the political hazards facing the country render irrelevant the entire economic analysis.

Class Conflict

But even if the assumption regarding national unity and political stability holds for the future, the country may still have to face a serious domestic problem of a sociopolitical nature that is likely to have considerable influence on its economic growth. In the past, except for brief moments of intense crisis, the basic political schisms in the country did not affect its economic growth. Sectarian rivalry found its arena in the public sector. But the public sector was kept relatively small and limited in responsibility and power. Business grew in an atmosphere of freedom approaching abandon, and as a result the country advanced in the economic sphere much more rapidly than in the social sphere. In fact, the social institutions and services of Lebanon fell below those of some other countries having a similar income level. Nor did business leaders manifest strong social consciousness or concern for the low-income groups.

It was not until the early 1960s that popular pressure upon the government to assume greater social responsibilities began to be felt effectively. Government consequently assumed greater responsibility in education, training, housing, social security, and other social services. But coupled with this expansion in government responsibility has been a growing acceptance by the public of a government role as regulator and controller. This can be an extremely significant development. On the face of it, it sounds a desirable goal that government should be better organized to cope with social problems; in the case of Lebanon, however, such expansion of the public sector in size and power, unless properly harnessed, can have undesirable repercussions on the economy.

It has been generally felt that the economic progress achieved in the postwar period has mainly benefited a small group of merchants, bankers, contractors, and real estate dealers, leaving the poorer classes of society with very little gain. Consciousness of this imbalance has been increasing, and more people now talk and write about the politics of the country being controlled by the rich few. Labor organization is too weak and ineffective to be a political force. Hence the political system of democratic representation seems always to send to parliament a majority of representatives who either support legislation generally favoring the richer groups or at best are insufficiently attuned to the problems of the poor. At any rate, regardless of the reality of the situation, there seems to be growing articulation of the belief that the system does not favor the poor. Although similar class tensions are encountered in other democratic societies at various levels of development, these tensions take on special significance in Lebanon because the poorer classes have larger proportions of Moslems and the richer classes have larger proportions of Christians. What might be simply a conflict of interests among social classes elsewhere can take on a sectarian aspect in Lebanon.

The significance of a sectarian conflict in this sphere is that what is essentially social and economic would turn political. Many of the spokesmen for the poor classes in Lebanon are admirers of the approaches to the problems of poverty adopted by such countries as Egypt, Syria, and Iraq. They believe that the basic tenets of Arab socialism would be beneficial for the poverty-stricken classes of Lebanon. To such leaders the condition of the poor can best be ameliorated by a radical alteration in the system, involving reduction of the political power of financial capital, nationalization of key enterprises, increase of public investment, expansion of the government budget by placing a far greater burden on the rich, drastic alteration of the pattern of public expenditures, regulation of business, control of the exchanges, restriction of the movement of capital, and various other measures of restriction and control. Many of those who advocate such an approach are sincere in their beliefs and are genuinely concerned about the fate of the poorer classes. They argue on patriotic grounds that unless such radical changes are effected the country will inevitably run into social disorder, which will destroy its prosperity. Few among them seriously accept the counter argument that freedom from undue restrictions on business, low taxes, weakness of the labor organization, open exchanges, and other similar market policies have been the chief driving power behind Lebanese prosperity and that a resort to restrictions and government control would subject business to the chaotic influences of local politics and eventually reduce the chances of continued prosperity in the future.

However, those who hold this latter point of view, and who are usually entrenched in the establishment, do not seem to have much to offer for improving the lot of the low-income groups. This is a basic dilemma facing the country: how can a pattern of more equitable distribution be attained without impairing growth and prosperity? With the political structure as it is, with the growing awareness of a social class cleavage that runs somewhat parallel to political schisms, with the social approaches adopted by important Arab countries, and with a deepening rift between the Western powers and the leading nations of the Arab world, a safe course requires policy skills that may elude even the Lebanese.

Unemployment

In the economic sphere proper there are two major problems: unemployment and the excessive reliance of the economy on the foreign sector. There seems to be a general agreement that the economy is faced with chronic unemployment, but there is no agreement on the dimensions of the problem. In the absence of systematic quantitative information on the extent of unemployment one encounters a whole variety of guesses ranging from zero unemployment on up to some fantastic ratios. A recent figure places the number of unemployed in 1964 at 165,000 persons.[72] If this were true, it would mean that the country has over 20

---

[72] *Etude Mensuelle sur L'Economie et les Finance des Pays Arabes,* Vol. XII, March 1969, p. 5.

percent unemployment. I have a very strong feeling that the percentage of unemployment is substantially less than this figure. If those who cannot be employed under any circumstances, the unemployed in refugee camps, and any
frictional unemployment or underemployment are omitted from unemployment
figures, then I believe that, except in a national crisis, involuntary unemployment
has not at any time in the recent past exceeded 6 percent of the total labor force
and in fact may have been, most of the time, considerably less.

In order to gauge the dimensions of this problem and make fairly valid pronouncements on its future course, it is necessary to know not only the current
extent of unemployment but also the size and growth of the labor force, the rate
of increase in labor productivity, and the future growth rate of the national
product. Quantitative information on the labor force, employment, and labor
productivity is not available. In the absence of such information we cannot determine past behavior and invoke it as a guide for the future.

I have already estimated the labor force for 1964, at 770,000, 35 percent of
the total population.[73] With expected changes in the population structure and an
increased participation in the labor market by women and by senior citizens, the
ratio of the labor force to total population should rise slightly in the future:

	1964	1970	1980
Labor (thousands)	770	913	1,220
Percentage of total population	35	36	38

A second ratio that needs to be determined and forecast is labor productivity. Again, as indicated above, there are no figures reflecting the growth of labor
productivity in the past that we could use as guidance for future projections. Estimates here can only be highly conjectural. Nevertheless, by partial inference
drawn from the evolution of some manufacturing industries and some services,
by observation of the general pace of economic growth, and by comparison with
other countries, the growth in labor productivity over the years could not have
been less than 3 percent per annum and indeed may have been considerably
more. In consequence, I have based my analysis on 3 percent as the lower limit
of growth in total labor productivity and have postulated 3.5 percent as the
likely rate, recognizing the possibility of a higher rate.

It will be recalled that the rate adopted for projecting the growth of GNP
from 1970 to 1980 was 6.5 percent (Section III). It was pointed out, however,
that the growth of the aggregate product was dependent on so many unpredictable forces that the rate chosen for projecting growth did not have a high degree
of certainty, and that predictions are surer if based on a band rather than a single rate. The band I proposed was 5–7 percent. Whether the actual rate would
fall closer to 6 or to 7 percent is rather crucial to the problem of unemployment.
To demonstrate the importance of this variable, let us start with a rate of 6 percent. At this rate of growth in product, and if labor productivity grows at the ex-

[73] See p. 183.

201

pected rate of 3.5 percent per annum, and if we start in 1970 from a level of employment estimated to be 94 percent of the labor force, then the economy will not be able to absorb the full increase in labor resources and unemployment will in fact grow from the estimated level of 6 percent in 1970 to 10 percent in 1980, unless some external outlet for labor is found. According to these calculations, the labor force will grow from 913,000 in 1970 to 1,220,000 in 1980. But if only 858,000 are employed in 1970, then the total labor to be absorbed during the decade in question will be 362,000, or an average of 36,000 persons a year. Under the stipulated conditions only 232,000 will be absorbed, an average of 23,000 a year. Unless emigration absorbs the surplus, some 13,000 persons a year will be added to the ranks of the unemployed.

Of course if labor productivity does not grow at the rate of 3.5 percent but at some lower rate, say 3 percent, then the employment imbalance will be reduced somewhat. If the same amount of national product is attained at this lower rate of increase in productivity, more labor will be absorbed and unemployment in 1980 will stay at about the same 6 percent level of 1970. Under these conditions the augmentation of unemployment over the 10 years would be reduced from 130,000 in the previous case to 77,000. A similar reduction in unemployment will result if the 6 percent estimate of unemployment in 1970 proves too high. If there is no unemployment other than frictional in 1970, and if productivity grows at 3.5 percent per annum, the surplus labor by 1980 will be only 61,000, or about 6,000 persons a year. If net emigration should continue at the current rate of over 5,000 persons per year, there would be hardly any unemployment problems in 1980.[74] Only if net emigration is reduced or completely halted will unemployment rise and by 1980 reach a maximum of 5 percent. This would be the case with a 3.5 percent rate of increase in productivity. If productivity increases at only 3 percent, the surplus labor over the decade of the seventies will amount to some 4,000 persons, which is less than the net emigration of one year. Under these conditions there will be no unemployment problem, even if emigration dwindles to the unlikely low figure of 400 persons a year. Indeed, in this situation the problem may become one of slight labor shortage, which calls for a policy of discouraging emigration and raising labor productivity.

In the foregoing discussion I have assumed 6 percent annual growth in GNP. If the GNP grows at the rate of 5 percent instead, there will be an acute unemployment problem. Even with the most favorable conditions for employment, as with full employment in 1970 and productivity increases at only 3 percent per annum, the surplus labor during the 10 years will reach 113,000. With no net emigration, this will mean an unemployment rate of 9 percent in 1980. If emigration continues at current rates, unemployment in 1980 will still be at the

[74] The net emigration figures for 1967 and 1968 were 5,158 and 5,493, respectively. See Ministère du Plan, Direction Centrale de la Statistique, *Bulletin Statistique Mensuel,* Vol. 6, No. 9 (September 1968), p. 12, for the 1967 figures, and Vol. 6, No. 12 (December 1968), p. 14, for the 1968 figures.

level of 5 percent. For the elimination of unemployment under these conditions, emigration will have to double. If we assume what appears to be more likely conditions, namely, that in 1970 there is 6 percent unemployment and that productivity increases at 3.5 percent, the unemployment problem in 1980 will become gigantic. Surplus labor during the 10 years will be about 230,000, or almost 20 percent of the labor force. If emigration continues at current rates, unemployment will still be as high as 15 percent in 1980.

On the other hand, if GNP increases at 7 instead of 5 percent, there will be no employment problem in 1980 even if we start with 6 percent unemployment in 1970 and productivity grows at 3.5 percent. Under these conditions surplus labor will amount to only some 23,000, which is less than half the net emigration calculated at current rates. Equilibrium in the labor market could be attained even if net emigration were to be reduced by one-half.

With such a wide range of possibilities it is extremely difficult to visualize the extent of the unemployment problem in the next decade. The best we can do is to assess the problem on the basis of intuitive expectations, namely, growth of labor productivity at 3.5 percent a year, a level of unemployment of 6 percent at the end of 1970, and a decline of some 20 percent in the rate of emigration. Under these conditions there will be no unemployment problem of any consequence by 1980, provided aggregate output grows at the projected annual rate of 6.5 percent. In fact unemployment will be reduced from the 1970 level of 6 percent to less than 3 percent in 1980. On the other hand, if aggregate output grows at a lower rate, say 6 percent, then the level of unemployment in 1980 will rise to 7.5 percent. Of course, if the level of unemployment in 1970 is higher than my guess of 6 percent, the level of unemployment in 1980 will be more than 7.5 percent, at an output growth rate of only 6 percent. Likewise, if productivity grows at more than 3.5 percent, the unemployment problem will be aggravated further. It is clear that for coping adequately with the problem of unemployment it is almost necessary that the national product grow at an annual rate of not less than 6.5 percent. Such a high rate is not easy to achieve.

The Foreign Sector

Perhaps the most serious problem facing Lebanon in the economic sphere is the excessive reliance of the economy on the foreign sector. Some two-thirds of the national income of the country is attributable to the production and sale of services, and unduly large proportions of these services are sold to nonresidents. Most prominent in this sphere are tourist and financial services. The market for these services is highly volatile and is likely to be greatly affected by domestic and regional political tensions. The financial sphere is becoming increasingly dependent on international financial and monetary conditions. Because of the inordinately large magnitudes of foreign liabilities involved in this sector, it constitutes a growing threat to the economy.

According to some estimates the net entry of private capital into Lebanon in recent years have averaged between L£150 million and L£200 million a year, or something on the order of 7 percent of national income.[75] Roughly, about two-thirds of these capital items are short-term items, chiefly in the form of interest-bearing demand deposits or time deposits on short notice. Bank loans form the larger part of the portfolios and are commercial loans of short currency, but they would still produce a liquidity gap of several months between assets and liabilities. Besides, several banks were lured into lax practice in the past by holding long-term claims in unsafe proportions in their portfolios. The failure of Intra Bank in 1966 was caused in part by this practice. Although the Central Bank has been trying since 1967 to promulgate sounder banking practices, the presence of "hot" international obligations in such large quantities is a continuous threat and can at any moment precipitate a crisis that would force the monetary authorities to resort to restrictions on capital movements. In such an eventuality the damage to the economy could be very great, arising not only from a shaken confidence in the Lebanese financial market on the part of foreigners but also, and ever more seriously, from a possible flight of Lebanese capital.

The solution to this problem lies not in discouraging the inflow of capital but rather in luring large parts of it into direct long-term investments. Such a policy target would call for the promotion of an institutional structure for dealing with long-term investments. It would also call for the expansion of domestic investment opportunities well beyond what is currently available in real estate and stocks in trade. Vigorous promotion of the industrial sector would then become a necessity, not only for reducing the financial hazard in question but also for providing a greater balance between the production of goods and services. The extent to which the expansion of the industrial sector would reduce Lebanese dependence on the outside world is not easy to gauge. It is almost certain that the industrial sector cannot, on the force of the domestic market alone, grow in the proportions needed for affecting a significant difference in the disposition of the inflowing capital; expansion of the export market is necessary. How much substitution of goods for services in the foreign market will be brought about by this process and to what extent dependence on the outside world may be reduced are matters not easily determinable. It is clear, however, that the needed export markets are likely to be predominantly Arab, and perhaps to a large extent in the countries from which the investment capital originated. Such expectation is borne out by the recent evolution of the direction of Lebanese trade. The value of Lebanese goods exported to Arab countries amounted to 53 percent of the total value of Lebanese exports in 1960. The proportion rose to 59 percent in 1962 and to 67 percent in 1967.[76]

---

[75] Mohammed Atallah, "Private Arab Capital," *Financial Sources and Development in Lebanon* (in Arabic), Proceedings of the Second National Conference, Development Studies Association, Beirut, 1967, p. 254. Also in the same publication, Elias Saba, "Private Capital" (in Arabic), p. 365.

[76] *Recueil de Statistiques Libanaises;* for the 1960 figure see the 1965 issue, p. 326; for the 1967 figures see the 1967 issue, p. 238.

Here again we encounter the basic Lebanese problem. Economically the country is increasingly dependent on other Arab countries. Spiritually and culturally large groups of Lebanese, notably the Christians, are attached to Western Europe. But other Lebanese, notably the Moslems, are culturally concordant with other Arab Moslems in the region. The Lebanese problem is easily containable when there is no strong conflict between the Western powers and the Arab world. But when such conflict sharpens, the Lebanese problem becomes acute. The tension has not yet reached the point of rupture because the Arab countries are divided among themselves regarding their relationships with the Western powers. The expansion of Lebanese exports to Arab countries has somewhat reflected this division. If Algeria, Egypt, Iraq, Sudan, Syria, and Yemen are considered to be in one group and all the other Arab countries in another, Lebanese-Arab trade will appear in a different light. In 1960, exports to the first group constituted 42 percent of Lebanese exports to all Arab countries, and exports to the second group amounted to 58 percent. By 1967 the picture had changed drastically; only 18 percent went to the first group and 82 percent went to the second.[77] Should the political situation in the region alter radically so that several more countries move out of the second group and join the first, as Libya did in 1969, then Lebanon is bound to face a serious crisis indeed. The economic interests of all the citizens will then point in one direction, but cultural attachments will continue to be split. The problem of Lebanon will once again be the problem of the Christians, who will have to make a choice between economic and cultural interests in deep conflict.

V. Conclusion

The Lebanese economy is primarily an economy of trade and services. Its development in this direction over the last half century was the result of an efficient exploitation of its comparative advantages. Inhabiting a country not endowed with rich mineral resources or vast agricultural lands, but possessing a higher level of skills than their neighbors, and having better business connections with the more developed parts of the world, the Lebanese people promoted trade, tourism, finance, and other services. Their success in these pursuits owes much to the utilization of their services by their Arab neighbors. Also favorable was the persistent policy of business freedom pursued at home. Low taxes, restricted government, strong money, conservative public finance policies, low tariffs, minimum restrictions on foreign trade, and similar measures turned Lebanon into a regional trade entrepôt and made it an attractive place for the inflow of tourists and foreign capital. The success of this policy was bolstered further by a growing autarchy and burdensome business restrictions in some countries of the region, leading to a flight of capital and talent from these countries into Lebanon. The influx of Palestinian skill after the establishment of the State of Israel and

[77] *Ibid.*

the closing of the Palestinian ports to Arab trade contributed further to Lebanese growth. But above all it was the spectacular growth of oil wealth in the region that gave the Lebanese economy its greatest boost.

In the next decade, no radical transformations are expected in the economy. Growth is likely to follow very much the same broad directions of the recent past. The road ahead, however, is likely to become harder. Lebanese middlemanship may decline and be partially replaced by direct contact with ultimate markets on the part of business men in Arab countries who now use Lebanese intermediacy. Combating this tendency will place a heavier burden on Lebanese firms, particularly financial firms, to manifest even greater efficiency in order to continue attracting foreign capital. In addition, new investment outlets must be created within the country. In particular, foreign capital must be increasingly channeled into industry. Although the promotion of industry may somewhat redress the imbalance between the output of goods and services, it will probably not help very much in reducing the dependence of the economy on the foreign sector, except insofar as the industrial output may face a less elastic foreign demand than the output of services. Industrial expansion, however, cannot be supported by the domestic market alone but will require the expansion of export markets. It is more likely than not that these will have to be Arab markets. The Lebanese economy will thus continue to depend on Arab countries, not only as sources of foreign capital but increasingly also as instruments to assure the conditions for the continuing inflow of such capital, which is vital for Lebanese economic growth.

Any drastic reduction in the inflow of foreign capital is likely to have strongly deleterious effects on the growth and stability of the economy. It is clear that the high level of investment enjoyed by the economy in the recent past would not have been possible without the large inflow of foreign capital. It is not possible to finance the desired high level of capital formation from domestic savings alone. A decline in the rate of capital formation is almost certain to aggravate the problem of unemployment and to lead to internal social and political instability unless Lebanese emigration continues high and even accelerates. But the direction of emigration in the recent past has been increasingly toward Arab countries, especially the oil-rich countries. It is also from these same countries that the bulk of foreign capital has flowed into Lebanon. Any developments that impede the free flow of capital from these countries, particularly if such developments are the outcome of political forces, are likely also to impede the flow of Lebanese emigrants and thus result in a double squeeze on the Lebanese economy.

Recent changes in the direction of Lebanese foreign trade may be significant indicators of possible future dangers. Lebanese trade in recent years, while expanding substantially with "Arab capitalist" countries, declined drastically with "Arab socialist" countries. The economic and social outlook of Arab socialism seems to be gaining ground in the Arab world. Should the spread of Arab socialism be associated with further alienation of Arab socialist countries from the Western world—an eventuality that is not necessary but possible—Lebanese economic problems will worsen. Internally the country faces a subtle class conflict between the rich and the poor, which threatens to develop into a sectarian and cultural conflict between upper-income Christians and lower-income Moslems. With a worsening economic situation domestically, the pressure will increase to move Lebanon closer to the program and approach of Arab socialism. This will create an economic dilemma for the country. Moving toward Arab socialism would call for greater restrictions on business, greater government controls, and an undermining of the traditional forces that contributed significantly to prosperity in the past. On the other hand, refusing to join, should the Arab world move predominantly toward socialism, would mean for Lebanon the loss of vitally needed sources of foreign capital and markets for the outflow of goods, services, and persons.

In addition to this economic dilemma, such overriding political changes in the Arab world are likely to precipitate a political-cultural dilemma in Lebanon that could have far-reaching effects on the economic future of the country. The Lebanese are split in their cultural affinities. The alienation of more Arab countries from the Western world is almost certain to force the Christians of Lebanon to face up to a hard choice between their deep-rooted cultural interests and their economic interests and desire for national solidarity. These national and regional sociopolitical currents are basic to the Lebanese economic problem. The directions that they take will determine the economic future of the country.

CHAPTER 5

Economic Development of Jordan

Michael P. Mazur*

*The author is indebted to Dr. Richard J. Ward, of Peat, Marwick & Mitchell, whose valuable paper on the prospects for the Jordan economy, prepared for the RAND-RFF Research Program, was used in the preparation of this study.

The continued rapid growth of the Jordanian economy since the early 1950s has been contrary to all earlier expectations. Mazur finds the explanation to lie in the large inflow of foreign aid and the remarkably efficient use of capital. His view is that aid provided the fuel, but the engine of growth operated far more powerfully than in most countries. Foreign aid made it possible to generate substantial investment even though gross domestic savings were essentially zero. Another view is that aid was the means by which Jordan's large defense expenditures were financed.

As to what explains Jordan's remarkably efficient use of capital, Mazur is less clear. Jordan's economic structure is unusual, with the service sector uncommonly important, as in Lebanon. But this is no explanation of her low capital-output ratio. Nor does the allocation of capital offer any explanation. On the contrary, large allocations to transport and housing would normally lead to higher than average capital-output ratios. Mazur stresses the importance of the growth of education since the early 1950s. But this appears highly conjectural as an explanation of how Jordan has managed to grow so rapidly. Certainly Mazur is correct that the apparently large "residual" factor in Jordan's growth contains the key to "what is unique about the Jordanian growth experience." However, the reason for the large residual remains elusive.

If Jordan's past is hard to account for, her future must also be hard to predict. Mazur foresees increasing foreign exchange stringency and increasing domestic savings rates as essential to maintain past growth. Structurally, he feels that industrial development will have to operate over a wide range and become more complex. The greatest uncertainties certainly concern the effects of the present conflict. The transitional problem of moving from a wartime economy supported by aid to a peacetime economy with more normal levels of aid support will pose a great challenge to Jordan, particularly since even with the stimulus of war overall unemployment has remained high.

On the whole, the foreseeable problems are no greater in the future than they were in the past. The problems that appeared intractable two decades ago have been solved. Still, economics is not known as the Dismal Science for nothing, and Jordan's future rate of development is likely to be significantly less rapid than it has been, past high residuals and low capital-output ratios notwithstanding.

Economic Development of Jordan

I. The Base for Development

The formation of the Hashemite Kingdom of Jordan in 1950 joined the backward economy of Transjordan to a West Bank economy disoriented by separation from the remainder of Palestine and burdened by a large influx of refugees from the part of Palestine that became the country of Israel. The citizens of the new Jordanian state numbered about 1.3 million: 400,000 Transjordanians, 500,000 West Bank Palestinians, and 400,000 refugees.

Before the 1948 War that resulted in the establishment of Israel, Transjordan's economy was based on a primitive, largely self-sufficient agriculture. Nomadism was extensive, and many farmers were recently settled nomads. Industry was almost nonexistent, being limited to such activities as flour milling, olive pressing, and weaving. In its limited economic relations with the outside world, Transjordan was largely a satellite of the more developed Palestine economy, where a number of its citizens found casual or seasonal employment. Over 80 percent of Transjordan's exports were either sold to Palestine or exported through the Palestinian port of Haifa. The government of Transjordan governed but little, and it relied for its finances upon British grants.

Although the West Bank was the less developed part of Palestine, it was considerably more developed than Transjordan, both in its economy and in the education and outlook of its people. The reasons for this superiority included a more settled population; the possession of Jerusalem, not only an economic but also an intellectual and cultural asset, drawing pilgrims and missionaries to the area; extensive contact with European Jewish settlers in Palestine, mainly since the late nineteenth century; and more active and extensive British activity in the area under the Mandate.

The West and East Banks were not so much economically complementary to each other as they were both complementary to that part of Palestine which became Israel, in which were located the region's major commercial and industrial centers and which provided a key market for the agricultural output of the two banks. The transport network of the East and West Banks was directed to the West, particularly toward the Mediterranean port of Haifa. When the establishment of Israel closed off this traffic, Jordan was faced with high transport costs and the necessity of developing a new transport system along north-south lines.

Economic Development of Jordan

Jordan's natural resource endowment was meager, limited principally to substantial high-grade phosphate deposits in Transjordan and to mineral salts in the Dead Sea. Of the small area of land suitable for cultivation (about 10 percent of the total land area) much the greater part was eroded and of low quality. There was very little opportunity for expansion of the sown area, except by the costly method of irrigation—and even here the possibilities were limited.

Water resources were poor. Only in the northern hills of the East and West Banks did average annual rainfall exceed 24 inches. In a sizable part of the cultivated area the average was below 16 inches, making the area unsuitable for regular rotation of winter and summer crops or for the cultivation of fruit trees and vineyards. Where average rainfall is so close to minimum requirements, irregularity of rainfall can be especially damaging. Jordan's agricultural production, almost completely rainfed in the early 1950s, was subject to this extreme instability, which was especially costly because of the lack of storage facilities to carry crops over from one season to the next.

In the early 1950s prospects for irrigation in Jordan seemed limited. There were no perennial surface water sources other than the Jordan River and its tributaries. The Jordan River, despite its prominence in religious literature and folklore, is actually quite small. Since most cultivable land in Jordan is on hills or plateaus, the potential for irrigation with water from low-lying rivers is further limited by the cost of pumping. Ground water resources are also quite scanty. Village growth was inhibited by dependence on springs and reservoirs, and these were often clogged and silted. Even the principal cities, Amman and Jerusalem, were without adequate water supplies and suffered seasonal shortages.

The percentage of the Jordanian population that was employed in the early 1950s was substantially lower than in many other countries because the influx of refugees resulted in high unemployment, a high population growth rate caused a large percentage of children in the population, and the prevailing attitude discouraged female employment in most occupations. A small number of workers accordingly had to support a large consuming population. The unemployed labor, however, represented a potential asset that could be utilized if Jordan mobilized cooperating factors of production.

The continuing state of tension between Israel and the neighboring Arab states, the volatility of intra-Arab politics since the Arab setback in 1948, and internal tensions in Jordan all required the maintenance of security forces that were large in relation to Jordan's small size and low per capita income. This reduced resources available for capital formation. These tensions and recurrent crises may also have hindered potential entrepreneurs from otherwise profitable investments—a factor of particular importance in a country relying on private enterprise as much as Jordan does.

Jordan, with its small population and low per capita income, offered only a limited market for domestically produced goods, thus handicapping the establishment of industries operating under economies of scale. Industrialization was also hindered by the high cost of power, Jordan having limited hydroelectric potential and being unable to take full advantage of economies of scale in thermal electric generation. Furthermore, Jordan lacked industrial raw materials, other than olive oil, tobacco, and hides.

In this situation Jordan had to rely heavily on imports for consumers' goods, investment goods, and inputs into domestic industries. But the country was penalized—both as importer and as exporter—by the high costs of transport. In its early years almost all Jordan's trade passed by way of Beirut and Damascus, a costly trip. The port of Aqaba became progressively more important, but this trip too was expensive.

Jordan possessed the rather negative advantage of beginning from a low level of development. Per capita net national product in 1953 was probably not much more than $100,[1] just a little less than that of Egypt at the time (about $120), but above that of India ($60) and Pakistan ($70). With domestic industry in its infancy, it was possible to achieve rapid industrial growth via import substitution in such industries as food processing, building materials, household furnishings, textiles, clothing, and footwear.

Jordan possessed an undeniable economic asset in the tourist potential entailed by its sovereignty over the principal shrines of the Holy Land. In addition, Jordan had added significantly to its educated merchant, civil service, and professional groups as a result of the flight of educated Palestinians from Israel-occupied territory and from the annexation of the West Bank. This cadre provided a fairly high level of sophisticated leadership in government, banking, and general commercial and farm development activity.

Land tenure in Jordan was more satisfactory than in many other developing countries. Most land was in small and medium-size holdings, mainly owner-operated. However, many owners had extremely small holdings, and most holdings were divided into a number of scattered plots. Registration of land claims was essentially completed during the period between the two world wars. Also during this period lands held under a particularly inefficient form of communal tenure were divided and registered as individually owned parcels. Rural indebtedness was a problem in Jordan, as elsewhere among the less developed countries of the world.

[1] Throughout this paper economic statistics in Jordan dinars are expressed in U.S. dollars by conversion at the rate of 1 Jordan dinar = $2.80. Generally, the use of official exchange rates for conversion of currencies overstates differences in per capita income because goods and services not traded internationally are, on balance, relatively inexpensive in poorer countries. However, this does not so much change the *rankings* of different countries in terms of per capita income. In Jordan's case there may be an additional distortion, since relatively large foreign aid inflows (see below) permit the maintenance of a higher exchange rate than would otherwise be the case. Thus, numerical estimates of Jordan's per capita income should not be given too much credence. In the most important cross-country comparisons utilized further on in this paper, the general conclusions would not be much affected by even large percentage changes (e.g., a 50 percent reduction) in the measure of Jordan's per capita income.

Table 5-1

Industrial Origin of Gross National Product,
Averages for 1954/55, 1959/60, and 1965/66[a]

(million \$U.S., current prices)

	1954/55[b]	1959/60	1965/66
Agriculture	34.40	41.58	86.46
Crops and forestry	25.30	27.10	54.64
Livestock	9.10	14.48	31.82
Mining, manufacturing, and electricity	12.32	20.26	52.40
Construction	4.76	12.82	24.01
Transport	14.84	30.55	37.83
Trade and banking	30.52	54.95	91.32
Ownership of dwellings	9.80	18.80	30.65
Public administration and defense	24.50	43.04	60.82
Services	12.18	22.46	37.48
Gross domestic product at factor cost	143.32	244.46	420.97
Indirect taxes	12.46	24.41	52.57
Gross domestic product at market prices	155.78	268.57	473.54
Factor income from abroad	11.48	18.19	39.31
Gross national product at market prices	167.26	286.76	512.85

[a]All items are arithmetic averages of the two pertinent years, converted from current price figures in Jordan dinars to U.S. dollars at the exchange rate of 1 Jordan dinar = \$2.80. Figures for 1959/60 and 1965/66 are taken from statistics in Jordan dinars in Jordan Department of Statistics, *The National Accounts 1959-1967*, p. 10.

[b]For 1954/55 the paper of R.S. Porter, *Economic Trends in Jordan 1954-1959*, Beirut, 1961 (mimeographed), supplied the underlying data, to which I have made a number of adjustments to reconcile it with the Department of Statistics estimates for the later years. In the main this consisted of comparing for each industrial sector the estimates of 1959 value added presented in the Porter paper and those presented in *The National Accounts*. If, say, the Statistics Department estimate of 1959 value added in a sector exceeded the Porter estimate by *X* percent, then the 1954 and 1955 Porter estimates in that sector were raised by *X* percent. Somewhat more refined approaches were used in the sectors of livestock, manufacturing, transport, services, and factor income from abroad.

II. Economic Growth Before 1967

The Growth of Output: Aggregate and Sectoral Developments

In the 1950s Jordan's economic prospects were regarded almost universally as dismal. The World Bank mission that visited Jordan in 1955 estimated that gross domestic product in current prices had grown at an average annual rate of about 10 percent from 1952 to 1954, but it did not believe that such a high rate could be sustained in the future. The mission set 4 percent as an attainable annual growth rate for GNP, but suggested that the achievement of such a rate would not be easy. It would require a capital-output ratio of 4, which the mission suggested might also be difficult to attain.[2]

The performance of the Jordanian economy has run completely counter to such pessimistic expectations. The growth rate of gross domestic product at current market prices from 1954 to 1966 continued to average over 10 percent per year.[3] The momentum of growth was sustained pretty much throughout the 1954–1966 period, although there may have been a slight slowdown after 1960. Tables 5-1 and 5-2 present the basic statistics that summarize this growth.

The growth rates in Table 5-2 have been derived from national income estimates at current prices, except that smoothed constant-price estimates are used for the value of agricultural production of grains, vegetables, and fruits. Although there exists no satisfactory index for deflating the national accounts, there is substantial evidence that the rate of inflation in these accounts is low, most probably less than 2 percent per year. (See notes to Table 5-2.) Even allowing for a 2 percent rate of inflation, the Jordanian growth rate would remain one of the highest in the world.

As shown in Tables 5-1 and 5-2, economic growth over the 1954–1966 period proceeded along a broad front and was not dominated by developments in any one sector. Output in mining and manufacturing grew rapidly from a very small base, as did construction, whose growth is attributable mainly to the increased demand for housing that followed the influx of the Palestine refugees and large government investment in the development of transportation. There seems to have been some change in the sectoral pattern of growth over the period. In the earlier years the fastest-growing sectors were construction and transport, as deficiencies in the transport system were remedied. In the later years the growth of these sectors slowed markedly, and that of the mining, manufacturing, and electricity sector accelerated sharply.

Jordan's industrial structure is not at all typical of a "normal" less developed country with comparable population and per capita GNP (see Table 5-3). In 1961/62 only about 36 percent of the employed labor force and 21 percent of value added were in the agricultural sector, compared with "normal" ratios of 56 percent and 37 percent, respectively. This deficit is not made up by the mining, manufacturing, and construction sector, whose share of the 1961/62 GNP was also below average. The services sector is predominant in the economy, contributing 66 percent of 1961/62 total value added—a remarkably high share when compared with an average share of 42 percent for less developed coun-

[2] The International Bank for Reconstruction and Development, *The Economic Development of Jordan,* Baltimore, 1957, pp. 10, 66–68. A similarly pessimistic view was expressed by James Baster in "The Economic Problems of Jordan," *International Affairs,* January 1955.

[3] See Table 5-2.

Table 5-2
Annual Growth Rates by Sectors[a]
(percent)

	1954/55- 1965/66	1954/55- 1959/60	1959/60- 1965/66
Agriculture, value added	7	7.5	7
Value added in crops and forestry	5	7	3.5
Value of crops and forestry output	5	6.5	4
Intermediate costs	6.5	6	7
Value added in livestock	12	10	14
Value of livestock output	11.5	8.5	15
Intermediate costs	11	3	18
Nonagricultural value added	11	13	9
Mining, manufacturing, and electricity	14	10.5	17
Construction	16	22	11
Transport	9	15.5	3.5
Trade and banking	10.5	12.5	9
Ownership of dwellings	11	14	8.5
Public administration and defense	8.5	12	6
Services	11	13	9
GDP at factor cost	10	12	8.5
Indirect taxes	14	14	14
GDP at market prices	10.5	12	9
Factor income from abroad	12	10	14
GNP at market prices	10.5	12	9

[a]Crop production at constant prices; other items at current prices.

All growth rates are annual rates compounded annually. The growth rates for all sectors except crops and forestry were calculated from Table 5-1. Crop output is expressed in current prices in Table 5-1 and is unadjusted for rainfall variations. The growth rates for crops and forestry output given here are derived from crop data expressed in constant 1964 prices and adjusted for rainfall fluctuations. The division at 1959/60 is purely arbitrary, taken simply to represent an earlier and a later period and to suggest changes in trends.

In deriving the estimates from which these growth rates were taken, the effects of fluctuations in rainfall on crop output were removed by the use of logarithmic regressions, generally on rainfall and time, for the crops most affected by rainfall fluctuations. Since this does not eliminate all random fluctuations in the national accounts, I have used the arithmetic averages of the years (1) 1954 and 1955, (2) 1959 and 1960, and (3) 1965 and 1966.

Although Jordanian national income estimates are of fairly recent origin, they have been improving rapidly and are now reasonably good, considering Jordan's level of economic development and small size. However, the statistics of agricultural production are based on tries. Almost 40 percent of the employed labor force (excluding family workers) was employed in the services sector in 1961.

A number of factors are responsible for Jordan's unusual industrial structure, with its high concentration on services.

1. Jordan is relatively poorly endowed with agricultural resources, a circumstance which contributes to the low share of agriculture in GDP.

2. With the development of irrigation in the Jordan Valley added to fruit cultivation on the Palestine hills, Jordan is particularly well suited to the production of fruits and vegetables, which have high trade margins relative to grains and legumes.

---

subjective estimates by agricultural district officers; although their accuracy is probably poor, there is no clear evidence of a systematic bias in the growth rates. In addition, a large share of GNP in Jordan derives from sectors whose statistical estimation is inevitably difficult, for example, commerce, transport, construction, services, and factor income from abroad.

The estimates used in deriving the growth rates of this table are in current prices, except for crop output, which has been put in 1964 prices. However, there are a number of reasons for thinking that the inflation reflected in the national accounts has been small. The years 1954-1959 are widely believed to have been years of low inflation, but we do not have much concrete evidence on this point. For the years 1959-1966, however, there is a considerable amount of partial evidence that the growth rate of GNP has not been significantly inflated by price rises:

1. The Jordan Department of Statistics has calculated a cost of living index for civil servants for the two years 1958 and 1968 *(Family Expenditures and Cost of Living Index for Civil Servants 1968,* Amman, 1968). Inflation varied between 1 and 2 percent per year, depending on the income class of the civil servants.

2. The value-added estimates of several sectors in the national accounts are based, either explicitly or implicitly, on constant or near-constant prices. These sectors are livestock, construction, and transport.

3. Prices of cement and petroleum products, two key industrial products, both fell between 1954/55 and 1965/66. A liberal exchange system and low tariffs have permitted substantial imports, which tend to keep down the prices of competing domestically produced goods, and the relative ease of smuggling into Jordan has the same effect. A 3 percent across-the-board tariff increase in 1965 was the only major tariff increase during the period. This all suggests, but does not prove, a low level of inflation in the industrial sector.

4. Value added in commerce is derived from the application of constant percentage markups (varying with different goods) to the value of traded goods. Hence inflation in goods should be reflected in similar inflation in the commerce sector. In Jordan the greater part of value added in commerce derives from trade in agricultural products. I have calculated an implicit deflator for crop output that roughly indicates a 2 percent per year price rise for 1954/55-1965/66.

5. Although rents in cities, particularly Amman, have risen markedly, much of this increase is not recorded in the national accounts estimates of value added in ownership of dwellings. In Jordan a tenant has the legal right to continue renting at the same rent indefinitely; in a period of rapidly rising rents few tenants move. Thus rental inflation is reflected mainly in newly constructed housing and to some degree in owner-occupied homes.

6. In the government sector civil service pay scales have not been changed since 1958.

Table 5-3
Share of Industrial Sectors, Jordan and "Normal" Country
(percent)

	Value Added[a]		Labor Force[b]	
	Jordan, 1961/62	Normal Country	Jordan, 1961	Normal Country
1. Primary production	22.2	36.6	38.5	
A. Agriculture	21.0	36.2	35.7	56.4
B. Mining	1.1	1.4	2.8 ⎫ 25.0	17.6
2. Industry	11.4	17.2	22.2 ⎭	
A. Manufacturing	6.6	12.4	9.8	
B. Construction	4.9	4.8	12.4	
3. Services	66.4	42.3	39.3	26.1
A. Transport	11.5	5.8	3.7	3.4
B. Commerce	21.1	12.6	9.2	6.5
C. Other services	32.8	22.2	26.4	16.1

[a]All ratios are calculated in current prices.

Data for Jordan from *The National Accounts 1959-1967*. The "normal country" ratio for transport includes value added in communications; for Jordan this item is included in "other services." In both cases commerce comprises trade, banking, and insurance.

Items 1, 2, and 3 of the normal country ratios are calculated from the B equations for small countries given in Hollis B. Chenery and Lance Taylor, "Development Patterns: Among Countries and Over Time," *Review of Economics and Statistics*, November 1968. Kuznets derives average ratios for seven groups of countries ranked from I to VII in descending order of average GNP per capita. He also presents ratios for combinations of these seven groups. I used the ratios for the combined group V-VI-VII, whose median value of GNP per capita is close to Jordan's 1961-1962 GNP per capita.

Ratios 1.A, 1.B, 2.A, 2.B, and 3.A for the normal country were estimated from equations in Hollis B. Chenery, "Patterns of Industrial Growth," *American Economic Review*, September 1960. Again the 1961-1962 Jordan population and GNP per capita were used; there is only one equation, for countries of all sizes.

Ratios 3.B and 3.C are from Simon Kuznets, "Quantitative Aspects of the Economic Growth of Nations: II," *Economic Development and Cultural Change*, July 1957 supplement, pp. 10, 13. The ratios are derived by group averages according to per capita GNP.

[b]The normal country ratios are from Kuznets, "Quantiative Aspects of the Economic Growth of Nations: II," pp. 23, 27. The ratios are derived by group averages according to per capita GNP. The ratios here are for the combined group V-VI-VII.

The ratios for Jordan are derived from data in Jordan Department of Statistics, *First Census of Population and Housing, 18th November 1961*, Amman, April 1964, Vol. 3, p. 10. From total active population in Jordan I subtracted unpaid family workers, those seeking work, those of unclassified economic status and those in "activities not adequately described." Kuznets classifies those in the armed forces as part of the services sector, whereas

3. Because there was very little unutilized land in Jordan at the time of the great refugee influx in 1948/49, most of the refugees who found work must have been employed outside agriculture.

4. The mining and manufacturing sector was extremely underdeveloped in the early years of the kingdom, nor was the growth of this sector particularly rapid during the 1950s. The inadequacy of transport facilities limited industrial development during this period, and government effort was concentrated on transport investments, mainly in roads and the development of the port of Aqaba. Not until about 1960 did the growth rate of this sector become really high, averaging 17 percent per year over the 1959/60–1965/66 period (Table 5-2). Accordingly, the share of mining and manufacturing value added in GDP rose from 7.5 percent in 1959/60 to 11.2 percent in 1965/66.

5. Jordan's relatively large defense establishment results in a large share of GDP and of the labor force being concentrated in the service sector.

6. The importance of tourism in the economy probably also causes some increase in the share of the services sector.

7. Jordan has maintained a large import surplus because of heavy inflows of foreign aid and remittances from Jordanians abroad. The import surplus consists largely of goods because of the infeasibility of trading most services internationally. The economy adjusts to this by producing a larger share of services.

Despite a rate of growth in agricultural output that is enviable by the standards of most developing countries, domestic food production was able to do little more than keep up with the growth in the domestic demand for food. Domestic output of food in current prices grew at an annual rate of 10 percent from 1954/55 to 1965/66. This was only slightly faster than the 9 percent annual growth of food consumption. This high rate of growth in the demand for food is due to a population growth rate of about 3 percent per year and a growth in food consumption per capita of 6 percent per year, the latter naturally being attributable to the rapid growth in disposable incomes over the period. Thus agricultural development did not play an important part in improving Jordan's foreign trade balance. (Of course, if food output had grown more slowly, more food imports would have been required and the trade balance thereby worsened.)

The manufacturing sector, in spite of extremely rapid growth in value added since 1959 (averaging 16 percent per year), remained quite underdeveloped in 1966, even for a country at Jordan's low level of per capita income. In

the Jordan census puts them under "activities not adequately described." There were roughly 30,000 persons in the Jordanian armed forces in 1961. Accordingly, I added 30,000 persons to the number employed in the services sector.

The transport sector comprises transport and communications both in the figures for Jordan and in the normal country figures.

Unpaid family workers are omitted, since statistics on them are generally highly unreliable.

1966 only 9.5 percent of national income originated in the manufacturing sector, compared with the 15.1 percent that is normal for a country with Jordan's 1966 population and per capita income.

Although most manufacturing firms were very small (over 90 percent of the total number of establishments in 1966 employed fewer than 10 persons), a few firms, mainly of recent origin, dominated the sector in terms of production and value added. In 1966 two firms producing almost solely for the domestic market—the petroleum refinery and the cement plant—jointly accounted for 26 percent of value added in manufacturing. Another 10 percent originated in a vegetable oil firm, four cigarette plants, a tannery, and a firm producing batteries. Only in the last was production for export important relative to production for domestic consumption.

Neither production for investment nor production for export was important in Jordanian manufacturing. In 1966 only 0.9 percent of manufacturing output went directly into investment uses and 3.6 percent into exports. Most manufacturing output (64.4 percent in 1966) was for final consumption. Only 31.1 percent went into intermediate uses, mostly outside the manufacturing sector. Jordan's interindustrial relationships were few and were of the most elementary kind, such as the sale of leather to the shoe industry.

Manufacturing growth over the 1959–1966 period was characterized by rapid expansion from an underdeveloped base. The East Bank was almost completely devoid of industry at the time of its union with the West Bank in 1950. Although Palestine was highly developed in relation to most other areas of the Middle East at that time, most of its industry was located in the area that became the state of Israel. During the 1950s much investment went into housing construction, and development efforts were concentrated on the transportation network. Manufacturing value added was only 6.6 percent of national income in 1961/62 (see Table 5-3). Labor productivity in manufacturing was low: relative sectoral product per worker in Jordan manufacturing was significantly below that of other low-income countries.[4] However, labor productivity in manufacturing has grown rapidly since then, averaging 8.5 percent per year over the 1959–1966 period.

[4] The relative sectoral product per worker in sector i is defined as the share of sector i in GDP divided by the share of sector i in the labor force. This is equivalent to average productivity of labor in sector i divided by average productivity of labor in the economy as a whole.

I have calculated relative sectoral product per worker for Jordan and compared the results with averages for countries at Jordan's level of development as given in Simon Kuznets, "Quantitative Aspects of the Economic Growth of Nations: II. Industrial Distribution of National Product and Labor Force," *Economic Development and Cultural Change,* supplement to Vol. V, No. 4 (July 1957), pp. 36, 41, 44. To summarize the results, transport and communications are above normal in Jordan, and agriculture; mining, manufacturing, and construction; and other services are below average. Since the groups used are large, there is the possibility of substantial deviations for subsectors of these groups.

In no sector of manufacturing, with the minor exception of machinery (that is, batteries), was export growth a significant factor in the increase of output since 1959. Jordan's industrial development since 1959 was associated with substantial import substitution, particularly in textiles, clothing and footwear, petroleum products, chemical products, basic metal products, and machinery. Yet the original level of industrial development in Jordan was so low that in 1966 substantial possibilities for import substitution remained, even in final consumption goods. Major exceptions were the tobacco, leather products, and petroleum products sectors, in which most of domestic consumption was being supplied out of domestic production. The 1964–1970 plan called for investment in a large number of import-substituting products, including processed foods, refined sugar, textiles, woolen clothes, ceramics, glass products, cosmetics, pharmaceuticals, cleaning products, paint, and plywood.

Foreign Aid, Savings and Investment

Jordan's per capita receipts of foreign aid have been far above average.[5] Only a few countries (including Israel, if German reparations are counted as aid) have received more aid per capita. Since 1958 most of Jordan's foreign aid receipts have come from the United States in the form of "budget support," simply an outright grant not associated with any specific projects. Before 1958, most aid came from the United Kingdom under similar arrangements. Thus, after years of large aid inflows, Jordan's anticipated debt burden remains low. Except for United Nations Relief and Works Agency (UNRWA) and U.S. Food for Peace aid in kind (and for a brief, unsuccessful attempt by the United States from February 1961 to January 1962), aid has not been tied to particular commodities or suppliers.

Realized foreign aid averaged around 17 percent of GNP during 1959–1962 and 13 percent during 1963–1966 (Table 5-3). For the 1959–1966 period as a whole, foreign aid equaled gross domestic investment, implying that gross domestic savings were zero (see Table 5-4). From 1959–1962 to 1963–1966, domestic savings rose and foreign aid fell in relative importance. Both an increase in private saving and a relative decline in the government deficit contributed to this result, the latter contribution being more important.[6]

---

[5] For 1962 and 1963 Jordan averaged $37.50 in annual grants per capita from the United States and OECD member countries and multilateral organizations. Total of such aid to all developing countries amounted to $4.10 per capita. This relationship would not be greatly changed if other aid, mainly that from the Communist bloc, were included, or if we looked at other years. See I. M. D. Little and J. M. Clifford, *International Aid,* Allen & Unwin, London, 1965, p. 66.

[6] Savings and investment statistics are invariably among the less reliable data in the national accounts of less developed countries. Furthermore, in Jordan and elsewhere, savings statistics are subject to substantial year-to-year variations, which make the detection of underlying trends very hazardous, particularly when acceptable statistics are available for only a very short time series.

Table 5-4
Ratios to Gross Domestic Investment[a]

	Foreign Aid	Gross Domestic Savings	Gross Private Savings	Gross Government Savings
1959-62	1.17	−0.17	0.49	−0.65
1963-66	0.87	0.11	0.53	−0.41
1959-66	1.00	0.00	0.51	−0.51

[a]Derived from current-price data in *The National Accounts 1959-1967*. The definition of government savings used in Table 5-3 and elsewhere in this paper differs from the definition used by the Jordan Department of Statistics (JDS) in the national accounts. To get government savings, the JDS subtracts government expenditures from the sum of (1) government domestic revenues and (2) current account loans and grants to government from abroad. The distinction between foreign transfers on current account and those on capital account is not, I believe, based on meaningful economic differences. I therefore do not include foreign transfers on current account as part of government income in calculating government savings but instead consider them part of foreign aid. In short, the JDS national accounts treat foreign transfers to government on current account as income, whereas I treat them as financing a deficit. As a result, my estimate of government saving is much less than the corresponding figure in the national accounts.

As shown in Table 5-4, gross private saving was sufficient to cover half of gross domestic investment, but it was offset by an equally large government deficit. Although Jordan's low level of domestic saving is due mainly to a deficit on current government account, in part occasioned by its heavy defense burden, net private savings have also been rather low for a country of Jordan's level of disposable private income per capita. For the 1959–1966 period as a whole, net private saving was about 60 percent of that to be expected from an average country of the same level of net private disposable income per capita.[7]

There was a substantial decline in the relative importance of the government deficit from 1959–1962 to 1963–1966 (Table 5-4). A fall in relative size of defense expenditures (Table 5-13) accounted for about half of the decline in the relative size of the government deficit shown in Table 5-4.[8] Despite the de-

[7] Determined by use of a regression equation from H. S. Houthakker, "On Some Determinants of Saving in Developed and Under-Developed Countries," in E. A. G. Robinson, ed., *Problems in Economic Development,* St. Martin's Press, London, 1965. Since Houthakker's relationship involves net figures, some assumption about private sector depreciation was necessary. I assumed that private sector depreciation was the same share of total depreciation as private investment was of total investment.

[8] By "relative" size, I mean relative either to investment (as in Table 5-4) or to GNP (as in Table 5-14). Since the ratio of investment to GNP has been constant

cline in the defense burden over the 1959–1966 period, the share of defense expenditures in GNP was still large at the end of the period (10.7 percent for 1965/66). If the Middle East had not experienced continuous tension after the establishment of Israel, Jordan probably need not have devoted more than 5 percent of its GNP to defense expenditures.[9]

The Capital-Output Ratio and Sources of Growth

The receipt of large amounts of foreign aid was not the sole cause of Jordan's high GNP growth rate, for the country has made particularly effective use of the capital available to it. The gross incremental capital-output ratio (ICOR) can serve as an approximate indicator of this effectiveness, a low value suggesting an effective use of capital. Jordan's ICOR averaged 1.5 for the 1954–1966 period, compared with a figure of 3 for the average country at Jordan's level of development.[10] The ICOR appears to have risen somewhat over time, from 1.2 for the 1954–1959 period to 1.8 for the 1960–1966 period.[11]

---

over the 1959–1966 period, the two alternative meanings of the term relative can be used interchangeably in this discussion.

[9] If this 5 percent ratio had prevailed in 1965/66, and if all the savings on defense had been successfully devoted to reducing foreign aid, then foreign aid, as defined here, could have been reduced from 9.4 percent to 3.7 percent without reducing the growth rate of GNP. However, this conclusion rests on the unrealistic assumption that domestic resources devoted to defense could have been used in exchange-saving activities with a productivity equal to their earnings in defense. In view of the unemployment and underemployment that has prevailed through Jordan's history, this assumption is unjustifiable for the roughly two-thirds of defense expenditures paid as wages and salaries of military personnel.

[10] The average ICOR for other countries is given in Simon Kuznets, "Quantitative Aspects of the Economic Growth of Nations: V," *Economic Development and Cultural Change*, Vol. VIII, No. 4, Part II (July 1960), pp. 43–54. The same methodology was used for the calculation of Jordan's ICOR as was used in Kuznets' article. Gross domestic capital formation is taken from R. S. Porter, *Economic Trends in Jordan 1954–1959*, Beirut, 1961 (mimeographed), and from Jordan Department of Statistics, *The National Accounts 1959–1967*. The data for 1954–1958 in the Porter paper were revised in proportion to the ratio of the national accounts estimate for 1959 to the Porter estimate for 1959 of capital formation in construction, machinery and equipment, and transport equipment. No corrections were attempted for changes in stocks, which must be considered very unreliable.

[11] The low ICOR is not accounted for by discovery of natural resources or exploitation of additional land. The margin of cultivation has long been on land of very poor quality and sparse rainfall; in fact, total cropped area declined slightly from 1954–1966 to 1964–1966. The only noteworthy natural resource in Jordan is phosphates; but if all the growth of value added in phosphates were eliminated, the effect would not be large enough to alter the long-term growth of GDP by more than a fraction of a percentage point.

Thus Jordan seems to have used the available capital resources very productively as compared with other countries at a similar level of development. This is rather surprising, for particularly in the early years much investment had to go into "social overhead capital," in sectors such as transport and housing, which have high capital-output ratios. (Note the rapid growth of the transport and construction sectors shown in Table 5-2.) A relatively high percentage of investment in Jordan has gone into the construction of dwellings. If Jordan had had a "normal" allocation of investment between dwellings and other investment, its ICOR would have been lower, possibly about 1.5 for the 1960–1966 period, instead of 1.8.[12]

An increase in the price level will bias an undeflated ICOR downward. If we assume 2 percent per annum price increase for all components of GDP and investment—a maximum plausible figure—the gross aggregate ICOR for 1954–1966 is raised from 1.5 to 2.0. The ratio for 1954–1959 is raised from 1.2 to 1.6, and for 1960–1966 from 1.8 to 2.4. These figures are still quite low for a country at Jordan's level of development, in fact, for any country.[13]

From the theoretical viewpoint, the ICOR is a crude surrogate for an aggregate production function. However, the ICOR possesses two practical advantages. First, the greater availability of ICOR estimates permits cross-country comparisons with a fairly large sample of less developed countries. In addition, sources-of-growth analysis based upon an aggregate production function requires information that is either not available or is unreliable in most less developed countries. Jordanian statistics are inadequate for a really respectable sources-of-growth analysis. Nevertheless, I present my best estimates of the sources of growth over the 1960–1966 period, with the caveat that the numerical estimates should be taken as only rough approximations.

[12] From 1959 to 1966, 31 percent of gross domestic capital formation was investment in dwellings. A "normal" figure for a country at Jordan's level of development would be 17 percent (cf. Kuznets, "Quantitative Aspects of the Economic Growth of Nations: V," p. 33). If 31 percent of investment is in dwellings with an ICOR of 10, then to get an overall ICOR of 1.8 the ICOR for nondwelling investment must be 1.3. Applying the figures of 10 and 1.3 to a 17–83 percent split between dwelling and nondwelling investment gives 1.5.

[13] If depreciation estimates were generally available and accurate, we could compare Jordan's *net* ICOR with those of other countries, for this is the more relevant concept. It is possible that a comparison of net ICORs would reveal less difference between Jordan and the average, because depreciation as a share of gross domestic investment seems to be relatively low in Jordan—25 percent for 1959–1966, compared with an average figure of 30–40 percent. If true—and all figures for depreciation in developing countries are highly uncertain—this would reflect a sharp rise in the rate of investment, particularly in long-lived assets, after 1948 and presumably could not be expected to continue. Simply as an illustration, a gross ICOR of 2.5 with depreciation at 25 percent of gross domestic investment would be raised to 3.1 by a 35 percent figure. Because of the uncertainty of depreciation statistics in general this discussion is highly speculative.

Sources-of-growth analysis requires information on the growth rate of net domestic product at factor cost (NDP), the growth rate of employment, the growth rate of the capital stock, and the relative shares of capital and labor in NDP. An estimate of the growth of NDP is readily available.[14] For employment I have used the annual growth rate between 1961 and 1966 estimated in Table 5-7. An estimate of capital stock is possible if we know the value of annual investment over the relevant period and the value of the economy's capital stock in some base year, but the latter is not available for Jordan or indeed for any but a few countries. Alternatively, capital stock may be estimated if we know the rate of return on capital in the economy.[15] I have accordingly estimated it by assuming a net (of depreciation) rate of return on net investment of 15 percent and 20 percent, two figures that are plausible enough in the light of the experience of other countries but that admittedly rest on no information derived from the Jordanian economy itself. With several adjustments, available data are adequate to estimate the relative shares of capital and labor in NDP, although with a sizable margin of error. My estimates suggest that NDP is divided between labor and nonlabor income in the proportion 60 : 40, a reasonable ratio in the light of results from other countries.[16]

The results of the sources-of-growth analysis are presented in Table 5-5.[17] The residual contribution to growth, or the growth of "total productivity," appears to have caused 30–40 percent of growth over the 1960–1966 period—quite a high percentage. By itself, it accounts for 2.5–3.5 percentage points of the 8.5 percent annual growth of net domestic product. The analysis in Table 5-5 makes no allowance for price rise, except in the value of output of crops. If there has been a significant price rise, adjustment for such price changes would reduce the importance of the growth of total productivity. Allowance for a price rise of 2 percent a year in sectors other than crops might, as a rough guess, re-

---

[14] I have used current-price figures for NDP derived from *The National Accounts 1959–1967*, except that the value of crop production has been smoothed to remove the influence of year-to-year rainfall fluctuations and has been expressed in constant 1964 prices.

[15] If b = the share of nonlabor income in NDP, r = the net rate of return on capital, Y = NDP, and K = the value of the stock of capital, then

$$b = rK/Y$$

Given estimates of b, r, and Y, we can solve for K, the value of the capital stock. With statistics of annual net investment from the national accounts, we can then derive the growth rate of the capital stock.

[16] For details see notes to Table 5-5. I have carried out sources-of-growth analysis for factor shares other than 60–40, which are not presented here. Although changes in distributive shares affect the relative contributions of labor and capital to growth, they have a quite small effect on the size of the residual contribution.

[17] The growth rates in Table 5-5 are annual exponential rates, rather than the annually compounded rates used elsewhere in this paper.

Table 5-5

Growth Rate of Net Domestic Product
at Factor Cost and Sources of Growth, 1960-1966[a]

(percent)

	Net Rate of Return on Capital = 15 Percent	Net Rate of Return on Capital = 20 Percent
1. Annual exponential growth rate of NDP	8.53	8.53
Labor		
2. Annual exponential growth rate	3.92	3.92
3. Contribution to NDP growth rate (row 2 X 0.6)	2.35	2.35
4. Relative contribution to NDP growth rate (row 3 ÷ row 1)	27.6	27.6
Capital (including land)		
5. Annual exponential growth rate	7.15	8.99
6. Contribution to NDP growth rate (row 5 X 0.4)	2.86	3.60
7. Relative contribution to NDP growth rate (row 6 ÷ row 1)	33.5	42.2
Residual		
8. Contribution to NDP growth rate (row 1 − row 3 − row 6)	3.32	2.58
9. Relative contribution to NDP growth rate (row 8 ÷ row 1)	38.9	30.2

[a]Row 3, the contribution of labor to the growth rate of net domestic product at factor cost, is arrived at by multiplying the exponential growth rate of labor by the share of labor in net domestic product (0.6). Row 6, capital's contribution to NDP growth, is similarly derived from the exponential growth rate of capital and the share of nonlabor incomes in NDP (0.4). The method requires the customary assumption of perfect competition.

The shares of labor and nonlabor earnings in NDP (60 percent and 40 percent, respectively) were derived as follows. For 1965 and 1966 the national accounts give a breakdown of gross domestic product at factor cost into (a) compensation of employees, (b) income from property and (c) income from farms, professions, and own-account workers, for each of the 10 industrial sectors of GDP. There are no estimates for earlier years, so we must assume constancy of the distributive shares over time. I divided category (c) between labor and property incomes by using two assumptions: (1) the share of family workers and own-account workers on the one hand, and employees on the other, in the work force of each duce the share of the residual from 30–40 percent to 20–30 percent, which is still quite high.[18]

Balance of Payments

Before 1967 Jordan was making steady progress toward balance in the foreign accounts, but there remained a long way to go (see Tables 5-6 and 5-11). Although exports of goods grew rapidly up to 1967, this development proceeded from a very small base. In no year did total exports (including re-exports) of goods exceed one-fifth of goods imports. Over 90 percent of earnings from goods exports were in primary products, mainly fruits and vegetables (particularly tomatoes) and phosphates.[19]

Before the 1967 War, exports and re-exports of goods provided less than one-fourth of Jordan's foreign exchange earnings, the remainder coming from services and factor income from abroad. Some indication of the orders of magnitude for 1965/66 is given by column 1 of Table 5-11, which brings out the relative importance of earnings from tourism and remittances from Jordanians temporarily resident abroad. A relatively large share of foreign exchange earnings is derived from "other services." The greater part of this comes from payments by UNRWA, other UN agencies, and charitable agencies to Jordanians, particularly Jordanians employed as teachers in UNRWA schools. This form of

[18] In estimating the effect of a 2 percent annual price rise in noncrop value added, I have assumed that all expenditure categories experienced the same rate of price increase. Allowance for a 2 percent annual price rise in investment reduces the contribution of capital stock growth to the rate of NDP.

[19] The most important goods exported and their average annual values in 1965 and 1966 were (millions):

Phosphates	$7.78
Vegetables	7.04
Fruits and nuts	2.68
Cigarettes	1.03
Batteries	.47
Miscellaneous	4.10
Total	$23.10

As in Jordanian official publications, these export values are presented gross (i.e., imports in the same categories are not netted out). In Table 5-11, however, agricultural imports and exports are presented net. In both cases the figures do not include the value of re-exports.

industrial sector was unchanged between the 1961 census and 1965/66; (2) the imputed wage of family workers and own-account workers was the same as the average wage earnings of employees within the same sector. With these assumptions I simply multiplied the average 1965/66 wage bill for an industrial sector by the ratio of family and own-account workers to employees to get the wage component of income from farms, professions, and own-account workers. The property income component was obtained as a residual.

A 1-year lag has been assumed between investment and output. Although this is arbitrary, other plausible assumptions would not significantly change the results.

Table 5-6

Growth Rates and Share in Total Resources of Domestic and Foreign Sources and Uses

(current prices)

	Domestic Use of Resources [a] (1)	Goods and Services Exports (2)	Factor Income from Abroad (3)	Total Resources (4)	Gross National Product (5)	Goods and Services Imports (6)
Growth rate (percent), 1959/60-65/66 [b]	8.5	16.5	13.5	9.5	10	7.5
Share in total resources, 1959-62 [c]	85.8	9.3	4.9	100	71.0	29.0
1963-66	83.3	11.4	5.2	100	72.0	28.0

[a] Domestic use of resources is defined as the sum of expenditures on private and government consumption and gross domestic capital formation.
[b] Growth rates are annual rates annually compounded, rounded to the nearest half percentage point.
[c] For each year or group of years the following relation holds: column 1 + column 2 + column 3 = column 5 + column 6 = 100. Any deviation from this relationship is attributable to rounding error.

Source: Jordan Department of Statistics, *The National Accounts 1959-1967*, p. 9. All underlying data in current prices.

services export would largely vanish with economic development and solution of the refugee problem. Two other noteworthy exchange earners were oil company payments for pipeline transit rights and earnings on the Central Bank's substantial foreign asset holdings.

The two most important exchange earners were tourism and remittances from Jordanians abroad.[20] Both of these sectors, and particularly tourism, exhibited rapid growth up to the June War, and the prospects for continued growth seemed good. However, although tourism earnings offered the best and possibly the only substantial hope for future economic self-sufficiency at a reasonably high and growing level of income, they were not large enough during the 1950s and 1960s to be a dominant factor in Jordan's economic growth. The growth of tourism earnings, in fact, accounted directly for less than 1 percentage point of Jordan's 10 percent annual growth of GDP. That the foreign exchange earned by tourism was not absolutely critical to Jordan's growth may be seen from the fact that the country added to its reserves over the 1963–1966 period an amount equal to 75 percent of its earnings from tourism over the same period.[21]

Sometimes growth is "export-led," in that a rapid growth in a country's exports of some commodity is the primary cause of growth throughout the economy. Given heavy reliance upon foreign goods, particularly intermediate and capital goods, and given certain practical limits to the rate at which import substitution can economically take place, the overall growth of an economy may be largely dictated by the development of its exports. In Jordan this was clearly not the case; if there is any candidate for "growth-leader," it is foreign aid, which financed over 50 percent of imports until the immediate prewar years. Because of the level of foreign aid, foreign exchange was generally not very scarce. Jordan was able to maintain a liberal exchange system and generally low tariffs and still build up substantial foreign exchange assets.

In view of the small contribution of agriculture to Jordan's economy, it is not surprising that some 25 percent of the country's imports were in foodstuffs. Food imports included a number of products in which import substitution is possible, such as cereals and meat, as well as others whose production is not economical, such as coffee, tea, and sugar. Not unexpectedly, the most rapidly growing import categories have been, first, capital goods and, second, intermediate products, each constituting about one-quarter of imports.

[20] Although the statistical reliability of the estimates of these items is low, there is no doubt about their importance. The figures for remittances, in particular, are likely to be underestimates.

[21] Looking at it in another way, tourism covered only 10 percent of imports over the 1959–1966 period. From the point of view of value added, tourism accounted for less than 5 percent of GDP during the immediate prewar years, using the seven-year plan's assumption of a 32 percent direct and indirect import component of tourism. Data are from *The National Accounts 1959–1967*. Tourism earnings used here are as presented in that source; they are not net of the expenditures of Jordanians on tourism abroad.

Although most of the Arab Middle Eastern countries have not achieved a high degree of economic interdependence with the others, prewar Jordan was an exception in its dependence on the region for much of its foreign exchange earnings. Jordan's exports of goods to the region consisting of Iraq, Kuwait, Lebanon, Saudi Arabia, Syria, and the United Arab Republic constituted 67 percent of its total goods exports during the 1961–1965 period, a markedly higher ratio than for other countries of the region. Although phosphate exports went largely outside the region to such countries as Yugoslavia and India, exports of agricultural products were almost entirely concentrated in the region. Jordan's limited exports of manufactures were also concentrated in the Arab Middle East.[22] In addition, Jordanian merchants have profited from a modest transit trade involving nearby Arab countries. With the development of good road communications to northern Saudi Arabia, currently in progress, both this transit trade and exports of Jordanian products should be enlarged.

The regional economy is even more important to Jordan's earnings from remittances. Jordanians employed abroad (mainly Palestinians) are concentrated in the Arab oil-producing states of Saudi Arabia, Libya, Kuwait, and the other small states of the Persian Gulf, all of which have a severe shortage of native trained manpower. To a small degree, the Jordanians abroad have further stimulated Jordanian exports by their demand for certain products, such as olive oil, from their native land.

Although Europeans were the most important source of Jordan's pre-1967 tourism earnings, earnings from Arab visitors were not inconsiderable and were growing rapidly. Jordan, particularly in the area around Ramallah on the West Bank, had been developing as a summer vacation area for Arabs fleeing the hot summer climates of Saudi Arabia and the Persian Gulf—the sort of enterprise that has been very profitable for nearby Lebanon.

The development of Jordan's foreign exchange earnings has been greatly helped, both directly and indirectly, by the continued rapid growth of the oil industry in Arab countries of the region—for example, Lebanon, which is one of Jordan's more important export markets and has itself benefited from regional oil development. Probably at least half of Jordan's foreign exchange earnings in the 1960s are directly attributable to the countries of the Arab Middle East. Although Jordan has a trade deficit on goods account with these countries, this is undoubtedly converted to a sizable surplus when travel, remittances, and pipeline transit payments are taken into account (even allowing for substantial expenditures by Jordanians on travel and education in Arab countries).

Population, Labor Force, and Employment

The 1961 census enumerated 1.76 million Jordanians, of whom about 60,000 were resident abroad.[23] By 1967 there were about 2.0 million Jordanian citizens

[22] "International Co-operation and Trade Expansion in Various Countries in the Middle East," in United Nations Economic and Social Office in Beirut, *Studies on Selected Development Problems in Various Countries in the Middle East,* New York, 1967.

[23] *First Census of Population and Housing,* Vol. 1, p. 3.

in Jordan and other countries. The number abroad had undoubtedly risen since 1961, possibly to as many as 100,000.

The Jordanian birth rate for the 1959–1963 period has been estimated at 4.7 percent per year—a high figure. Combined with a death rate of 1.6 percent for the same period, this gives a natural growth rate of population (defined as the birth rate minus the death rate) of 3.1 percent per year during 1959–1963.[24] This natural growth rate probably remained pretty much constant throughout the 1950s and early 1960s. Because of emigration, the resident Jordanian population grew at a rate lower than the rate of natural increase. Between the 1952 and 1961 censuses the number of persons living in Jordan grew at an average annual rate of 2.8 percent.[25] If, as we might expect, economic development and concomitant medical improvements further reduce the death rate,[26] the rate of natural increase of population will rise to an unusually high level, unless the birth rate declines. There is no sign, however, of an imminent fall in the birth rate; birth control activities in Jordan have been rather limited and have never been given formal official backing. The natural growth rate of population might rise to a rate above 3.5 percent. Such a rapid population increase does not seem impossible in view of the very high rates of natural increase that have prevailed among the Arab inhabitants of Israel (averaging 4.3 percent per year over the 1960–1962 period,[27] said to be the highest in the world).

According to the 1961 census, only 22.9 percent of the total population of Jordan was economically active, a very low rate.[28] Among males 15–64 years of

[24] Jordan Department of Statistics, *Analysis of the Population Statistics of Jordan,* prepared by the Demographic Section under the supervision of Dr. Hilde Wander, Vol. I, Amman, 1966, First Report.

[25] Data from *First Census of Population and Housing,* Vol. 1, pp. 3, 29. We do not have reliable information on emigration, temporary or permanent, from Jordan. The 1961 census does give us a figure for the number of Jordanians abroad in that year. This is only approximately accurate, however, as it was arrived at from information given by relatives or neighbors in Jordan. If we assumed that there were no Jordanians abroad in 1952 and that the 1961 figure includes all emigrants since 1952, this would imply average annual emigration of 0.4 percent of the population and a 3.2 percent natural rate of population growth between 1952 and 1961. In fact, there must have been a substantial number of Jordanians abroad in 1952, but the effect of this on our estimate of the rate of emigration is partly offset by the likelihood that some emigrants were not recorded in the 1961 census, particularly permanent emigrants who had taken foreign citizenship. On balance, these considerations may reduce the emigration rate, but probably only slightly, perhaps to 0.2–0.3 percent of the population per year.

[26] As Jordan's per capita income rises to the $300–$400 range, the death rate may be expected to fall to near 1.0 percent. For comparative figures see Simon Kuznets, *Modern Economic Growth: Rate, Structure and Spread,* Yale University Press, New Haven, 1966, p. 438.

[27] Yoram Ben-Porath, *The Arab Labor Force in Israel,* Maurice Falk Institute, Jerusalem, October 1966, p. 5.

[28] *Analysis of the Population Statistics of Jordan,* Third Report, p. 33. Several factors seem to be responsible for this: the methods of the 1961 census appear to have un-

age, the figure was 81.4 percent, still rather low for that population group.[29] The 1961 census gives an unemployment rate of 7 percent, but the true figure was probably closer to 15 percent.[30] The widespread existence of part-time and seasonal employment greatly reduces the significance of any quantitative employment estimates. Nevertheless it seems likely that the continued high rate of GNP growth since 1961 reduced unemployment further, so that by early 1967 most of the labor force may have had at least part-time employment.

The most serious unemployment in 1966 was among recent secondary school graduates. Skilled workers have generally not lacked employment opportunities, and the opportunities for unskilled workers have improved, as indicated by substantial rises in the wage rate for unskilled and seasonal labor. Many in-camp refugees found part-time or seasonal employment harvesting fruits and vegetables in the area of the East Ghor irrigation project or in housing construction, which continued at a high level of activity throughout the period.

Total employment in all sectors except agriculture, construction, and commerce may have increased at an annual rate of about 4½ percent between 1961 and 1966. Although manufacturing value added grew rapidly (14 percent per year), employment in that sector increased by only 5 percent per year, because of the dominant role in manufacturing growth played by capital-intensive indus-

---

derstated the rural female labor force substantially; there is a large percentage of children in the population; there is substantially lower employment of children and the aged in Jordan than in many other Arab countries. See *ibid.*, pp. 31–43.

[29] Comparable figures for other Arab countries are as follows: Iraq (1957), 91.6 percent; Syria (1960), 87.9 percent; United Arab Republic (1960), 90.5 percent, and Tunisia (1956), 85.3 percent (International Labour Office, *Yearbook of Labour Statistics, 1966*, Geneva, Table I). The Jordanian figure probably reflects disguised employment, involving men who were not seeking jobs because they knew jobs were unavailable. It may also reflect some seasonal workers who were neither employed nor seeking work in the period immediately preceding the census, but who were employed at other times of the year. The census defined persons economically active as those who were currently employed, who were currently seeking work, or who had been employed during the previous 6 months. Since the census was taken in November, and since the first half of the year provides the greatest seasonal employment, a number of seasonal workers may have been omitted. Furthermore, there were indications that a number of people interpreted the questions to refer only to their status at the time of the census.

[30] If Jordan had had a participation rate equal to the average of the four countries mentioned in footnote 29 (88.8 percent), the labor force would be increased by about 31,000 and the unemployment rate would be raised from 7 to 13.8 percent. This should probably be considered a minimum figure. The unemployment rate would probably be raised further by other factors, such as the possibility that the participation rate among women aged 15–64 also hides some unemployment, the possibility that employment was overstated in the 1961 census, and the possibility that the 88.8 percent participation rate taken as "normal" itself includes some hidden unemployment.

tries such as the petroleum refinery. The number of classified civil servants grew at 6 percent per year, which particularly reflects the rapid extension of education in Jordan. However, the annual growth rate of military employment was probably below 4 percent.

There is some information suggesting an increase in employment in the trade sector, but in view of the relatively slow rise in value added from 1961 to 1966 (averaging 4.4 percent per year), it is difficult to conceive of rapid employment growth except as a form of disguised unemployment, since it would involve a marked decline in labor productivity at a time of rapidly rising per capita incomes. Value added in construction increased at an annual rate of 15½ percent from 1961 to 1966. It is widely believed that there has been very little technological change in Jordanian construction, particularly in dwelling construction, which constitutes almost half of total construction. Even allowing for a substantial increase of labor productivity in construction as a whole, say 6–9 percent per year, this would imply a rapid rate of employment growth in the construction sector of about 6–10 percent per year over the 1961–1966 period.[31]

If then we make the highly conjectural estimate of a 3 percent annual growth of employment in commerce and 8 percent in construction, it appears that nonagricultural employment grew at about 5 percent per year from 1961 to 1966. In absolute figures this would involve an increase over the period of about 62,000—almost enough by itself to absorb the increase in the labor force of about 66,000.[32]

The usefulness of the small amount of information available on agricultural employment is largely vitiated by differences in the timing and definition of the studies. Even if we take account of the possibility of disguised unemployment among men of working age recorded as not participating in the labor force, agricultural unemployment in 1961 was most probably less than 5 percent (as compared with a possible 15 percent for the economy as a whole, using comparable methods of estimation). Presumably, developments since then have further reduced unemployment and have also lowered underemployment, in the sense of increasing the average number of days worked per year. Given high rural-urban migration and consequent low rate of growth of the agricultural labor force (about 1½ to 2 percent per year), this suggests a growth rate for agricultural employment of 2-3 percent per year and full employment in the agriculture sec-

[31] This should be qualified by the realization that construction employment in Jordan, particularly in dwelling construction, is frequently casual and part-time. It is possible that most of this increase in employment simply involved those already employed working more days in the year. There is, however, no way in which we can adjust for this uncertainty.

[32] The presumed increase in the domestic labor force is obtained from Projection III/1-2 of *Analysis of the Population Statistics of Jordan,* Fourth Report, p. 15. See the source for details of assumptions about mortality, emigration, and changing participation rates.

tor by 1966.[33] Had there been no such increase in agricultural employment, the growth of labor productivity in agriculture would have had to be very high, in view of the 7 percent average annual increase in agricultural value added. This would be rather implausible, since there has not been much technological change in Jordan's agriculture, nor has cultivated acreage expanded significantly. The rapid growth in livestock, fruit, and vegetables—relatively labor-intensive activities—probably accounts for much of the increase in employment.

On the basis of the foregoing considerations, I have prepared the estimates of the changes in sectoral employment and in unemployment from 1961 to 1966 presented in Table 5-7. These are highly conjectural and are offered only as suggestive of orders of magnitude. They are geared to the results of the 1961 census; no attempt has been made to correct for presumed errors in the census such as understatement of unpaid farm labor by women and children. The table suggests an overall employment growth of 4 percent per year over the 1961–1966 period, which implies a productivity growth on the order of 6 percent per year (but this is as much an assumption as a conclusion, since for cer-

[33] Estimates of agricultural employment are given for 1959 by Jordan Department of Statistics, *The National Income for Jordan in 1959,* Amman (no date); for 1961 in the 1961 census; and for the first quarter of 1967 by Jordan Department of Statistics, *Population and Labor Force in the Agriculture Sector 1967,* Amman, 1968. The last study made clear what had earlier been suspected: that the employment of women and children in unpaid work on family farms had been understated in the 1961 census. The number of men employed as own-account workers, employers, and family workers grew moderately between 1961 and 1967, but the number of employees doubled over the period, presumably reflecting seasonal differences (the 1961 census was taken in November, a fairly slack time, whereas the 1967 study covered the first 3 months of 1967, during which hired labor is needed for the harvest in the Jordan Valley) and the increase in paid labor available in the Jordan Valley as a result of the East Ghor project. The average farm worker worked about one-third of the available days in 1967. There exists no way to compare this with earlier periods. Therefore, the possibility of substantial changes in the amount of work performed by each employed worker necessarily limits the significance of the estimates.

Recorded agricultural unemployment was less than 0.5 percent in 1961, but some persons recorded as voluntarily inactive were probably in fact unemployed. Still, when account is taken of those still in school, probably about 88–89 percent of the males 15–64 in farm areas were economically active, and some recorded as inactive must have been employed seasonally. Therefore, 5 percent unemployment constitutes a clear upper limit.

Between 1952 and 1961 the rural and Bedouin populations grew at an average annual rate of 1.4 percent. The rural labor force probably grew even more slowly, since the migrants were disproportionately from the male population of working age. Internal migration to the cities since 1961 has continued high, although the annual rate of growth of the agricultural labor force may have risen slightly in comparison with the 1952–1961 period.

234

tain sectors I made some a priori guesses about productivity change to arrive at figures for employment change).

If we take 1961 unemployment to have been 7 percent, the 4 percent per year growth in employment, as against the 3.3 percent annual increase in the labor force, would have cut the unemployment rate in half by 1966. If we use the 15 percent rate for 1961, we may infer that the unemployment rate was reduced by about one-quarter. In any case employment growth between 1961 and 1966 reduced unemployment substantially, but did not eliminate it. It seems likely that the annual shift of 0.7 percent of the labor force from unemployment to employment has contributed only about four-tenths of 1 percentage point to Jordan's 8.5 percent annual exponential growth rate of net domestic product over the 1960–1966 period.[34]

The 1961 census indicated that the average level of education of the population was not especially high, but this reflects low school attendance in the years before 1950. Since then, growth in enrollments has been rapid, particularly for girls.[35]

At the time of the June War the number of university students was about 15 percent of the number of Jordanians in the age range 18–22. About 90 percent were studying outside Jordan, financed largely by themselves or their families. The number of university-trained Jordanians is very large when compared with the requirements of an economy in which industry is still quite unimportant.[36] Although the annual number of graduates, particularly university graduates, has exceeded the ability of Jordan to provide suitable employment,[37] widespread white collar unemployment has been forestalled by the availability of employment outside Jordan in such countries as Kuwait and Saudi Arabia. In 1961 about 8 percent of all economically active Jordanians

[34] Calculated according to the method of Table 5-5, using the figures given there for distributive shares and the exponential growth rate of net domestic product.

[35] At the time of the June War over 75 percent of the children of eligible age were attending elementary and secondary schools (the first 9 years). At the twelfth grade the percentage had fallen to 25 percent—still rather high for a less developed country.

[36] In 1961 there were only 18,316 persons in the occupational groups of "professional, technical, and related workers" and "administrative, executive, and managerial workers." At the same time 9,130 Jordanians were studying abroad, almost all of whom were in higher education. Compare *First Census of Population and Housing*, Vol. 1, p. 329; and Vol. 2, p. 68. Since then, the number of university students has increased rapidly, to perhaps 30,000 by 1967, while domestic employment opportunities for university graduates have nowhere near kept pace.

[37] This conclusion is not contradicted by the fact that the civil service has suffered from temporary shortages and high turnover in certain categories of educated employment (particularly teachers). Civil service salaries have remained essentially unchanged since 1958, over a period when average per capita money incomes have about doubled. This situation, combined with the availability of high-paid employment opportunities abroad, has resulted in high turnover rates.

Table 5-7

Labor Force and Sectoral Employment, 1961-1966[a]

	1961 Employment (thousands)	1966 Employment (thousands)	Average Annual Percentage Change, 1961-66	Absolute Change, 1961-66 (thousands)
1. Agriculture	137.2	155.2	2.5	18.0
2. Mining	9.2	10.1	1.8	.9
3. Manufacturing and utilities	34.2	43.4	5.0	9.2
4. Construction	39.9	58.7	8.0	18.8
5. Commerce	31.4	36.3	3.0	4.9
6. Transport	11.9	13.8	3.0	1.9
7. Services	53.5	70.7	5.7	17.2
8. Not adequately described	45.4	54.4	3.7	9.0
9. Total employed	362.7	442.6	4.0	79.9
10. Labor force	390.0	458.7[b]	3.3	68.7
11. Seeking work	27.3	16.1		−11.2
12. Seeking work as percent of labor force	7.0	3.5		

[a]Figures for 1961 are from the 1961 census. The 1966 figures are my own estimates, largely conjectural. See the text for discussion of rows 1, 4, 5. Rows 2, 3, 7, 8 have been estimated by using employment growth rates for major components. For activities "not adequately described" I used the average annual growth rate of the armed forces between 1955 and 1966. For services I used a weighted average of the average annual 1961-1966 growth rate of the number of classified civil servants and the average annual 1963-1966 growth rate of employment in selected services as given by the national accounts. For transport I took the increase in the number of public buses, trucks, and taxis and multiplied by 1.2 persons per vehicle. This gives reasonable results, since road transport predominates to a great extent over other transport in Jordan.

[b]The 1966 labor force is from Jordan Department of Statistics, *Analysis of the Population Statistics of Jordan,* Fourth Report, p. 15. It may be a slight overestimate because the assumptions about emigration seem rather conservative. Correction for this would somewhat reduce the rate of unemployment.

were in foreign countries. Workers abroad were, on average, better educated and were concentrated in more skilled occupations than domestically employed workers.[38]

[38] Compare percentage distributions of persons by highest level of schooling completed and by employment category from *First Census of Population and Housing,* Vol. 1, pp. 178–179, 327, 338–339; and Vol. 2, p. 68.

Although the employment of educated persons abroad does represent a "brain drain," it seems likely that in the Jordanian case the balance of effects is highly advantageous, particularly in view of the scarcity of suitable domestic employment. Most of the emigrants are believed to be only temporarily abroad. When they return, they bring skills, experience, and capital; some returnees have established their own enterprises. Furthermore, those employed abroad remit very substantial sums to their families in Jordan. Remittances in 1961 were estimated at $450 per employed person abroad—a very large sum in Jordanian circumstances.[39]

Because a large number of Jordanian nationals are temporarily employed in nearby countries, shortages of educated manpower are likely to present a much less serious problem than would otherwise be the case. If shortages develop in particular skill areas, these may often be filled by recruitment among nationals abroad or by raising salaries and attracting workers from abroad. The employment abroad of Jordanians with a wide variety of skills thus gives considerable elasticity to the domestic labor supply in various categories of skill.

There appears to be no shortage of middle-level manpower overall, as for some time unemployment has been fairly high among recent secondary school graduates. A 1966 survey of employment in private establishments in the sectors of mining, manufacturing, trade, electricity, finance, and services, which employed a total of 41,510 (excluding own-account and family workers), reported only 922 vacancies. Many were for positions requiring little technical training, such as salesmen, porters, waiters, stone cutters, tailors, and janitors. There were few vacancies for technically skilled workers.[40]

Although the growth in school enrollments has been rather high in percentage terms, particularly in the upper grades and at the university level, this is not likely to have had a great effect on the average educational level of the employed labor force or (consequently) on the growth rate of gross domestic product. The most rapid growth in enrollments has been among women, only a small percentage of whom enter the labor force. In addition, a disproportionately large number of emigrants are educated males of working age. Finally, rapid economic growth has brought into the employed labor force previously unemployed workers, among whom the unskilled and uneducated presumably predominate.

III. Postwar Economic Developments

Immediately after the June 1967 War the East Bank economy fell into a sharp recession. Excess capacity developed in industry, although certain industries,

---

[39] *Ibid.*, Vol. 1, p. 329, for the number of Jordanians employed abroad in 1961. Remittance figures are from *The National Accounts 1959–1967*, p. 19. The estimates of remittances are subject to great uncertainty, but they are probably conservative.

[40] Jordan Department of Statistics, *Labor Force Study, 1966, in the Sectors of Mining, Manufacturing, Wholesale and Retail Trade, Electricity, Finance and Services* (in Arabic), Amman, July 1968, pp. 95–98.

such as cement and cigarettes, found some relief in increased exports. Investment in all areas fell off drastically. The only favorable factors were good rainfall and a consequently abundant harvest in 1967 and the continued growth of phosphate exports. With a rise in foreign aid, principally the Khartoum payments (see below), the government was able to be lenient in collecting taxes in 1967; moreover, it pumped money into the economy by public works projects and subsidies to firms in trouble. In addition, the Jordan government supports the refugees from the West Bank who were not refugees from the 1948 conflict and so are not eligible for UNRWA support. Thus the money supply exhibited a remarkable increase, which largely took the form of hoarded currency in the hands of individuals.

In 1968 and 1969, however, the East Bank economy moved into a very pronounced, if somewhat artificial, prosperity, one of whose signs has been a sharp rise in prices. By far the most important factor in this development is the large grants from Kuwait, Libya, and Saudi Arabia. Aid from Arab countries was about $105 million in 1967 and $130 million in 1968. In per capita terms these are remarkably large figures, implying some $100 per capita aid in 1968 for an economy whose gross national product per capita was only about $270 in 1966.[41]

The grants from the oil-rich Arab countries, agreed upon at Khartoum in 1967, are said to be intended for financing military activities only; but since substantial domestic resources would otherwise have been directed to defense, they have the effect of releasing funds for more directly productive activities. The funds are used not only to import military equipment but also to meet domestic military requirements, thus financing nonmilitary imports and the accumulation of foreign exchange reserves.

The post-1967 accumulation of foreign exchange reserves and the strength of the Jordan dinar on the free market have accordingly been the result largely of the huge aid payments, plus sizable payments to the Arab commando groups in Jordan, local expenditures by Iraqi and Saudi Arabian troops stationed in Jordan, and a reduction in the imports of capital goods caused by the continuing stagnation of industrial investment. These have more than offset such negative factors in the balance of payments as the decline in tourist earnings and remittances, increased purchases of military equipment, and possibly some capital flight. Jordan's gold and foreign exchange reserves increased from $195.3 million in December 1966 to $306.4 million in December 1968.[42] Such a buildup now seems necessary, for at present Jordan is highly vulnerable to sudden reductions in aid, whose continuation is highly subject to political changes and hence is uncertain.

[41] If, in addition, we include U.S., U.K., and UN aid, the total aid figure for 1967 and 1968 is raised to an annual rate of over $140 million. The Arab aid figures also omit substantial amounts of unrecorded aid in kind.
[42] Central Bank of Jordan, *Fifth Annual Report 1968,* Table 4.

Industry has largely recovered from the serious slump of the immediate postwar period, although industrial investment remains stagnant. Favorable tariff reductions in neighboring Arab states have permitted the expansion of manufactures, particularly cigarettes. The loss of the petroleum refinery's market in the West Bank has been compensated for by increased demand from an expanded Jordanian army, from commando groups, and from the Saudi Arabian and Iraqi troops stationed in the country. The cement plant is now fully occupied in supplying the domestic market, which is undergoing a boom in housing construction, a persistent phenomenon in Jordan's economic history now further stimulated by a new wave of refugees.

The tourism and agriculture sectors continue somewhat depressed. The Jordan Valley and the Ghor Safi area south of the Dead Sea, two important areas of irrigated fruit and vegetable cultivation, have suffered seriously from continuing conflict, but some cultivation continues.

Although there are no complete figures on employment, it appears that by 1969 unemployment was even lower than before the June 1967 War despite the influx of some 300,000 refugees to the East Bank. The main factors in this decline have been expansion of the army and of civilian government employment, recruitment of commandos, and the boom in housing construction.[43]

Contacts between the East Bank and the West Bank continue. The West Bank exports mainly fresh produce and olive oil, partly destined for markets beyond Jordan, such as Kuwait. West Bank imports from the East Bank have been very small, but travel by West Bankers on the East Bank is a significant source of exchange. The Jordanian government continues to pay salaries to civil servants on the West Bank, whether they actually work or not, and in addition distributes funds to West Bank municipalities accruing as the latter's share of taxes on imports.

If the flow of very large amounts of aid continues, there is little reason to think that Jordan cannot maintain its current aid- and war-based prosperity, despite the level of physical attrition that can be expected from continued conflict. The present conditions, with swollen employment in the armed forces, the public security forces, and the commandos, pose serious, but certainly not insurmountable, problems of readjustment in the event of a peace settlement.

It is important for our further discussion to realize that as of the beginning of 1970 the war damage to Jordan's physical capital has not been extensive enough significantly to affect forecasts. The greatest damage has probably occurred in the Jordan Valley, where the canal system has been damaged and a number of fruit trees destroyed. In the event of a settlement, restoration of the canal system should not be particularly costly either in time or in money. The

---

[43] Between July 1967 and July 1968 the armed forces expanded by 23,000, an increase which by itself accounts for about a third of the employable 1967 refugees; compare The Institute for Strategic Studies, *The Military Balance 1967–1968*, London, 1967, p. 45, and *1968–1969*, p. 45.

most serious damage to the economy has been that of lost opportunities, of passing through a period of standstill interrupting a period of very rapid growth. This is largely reflected in the continued stagnation of nonresidential investment.

My later projections will be based on the assumption of restoration of the West Bank to Jordan, consistent with the terms of reference of the study. I present here a discussion in qualitative terms of the economic relationship between the two banks. This, combined with my forecasts for a reunited Jordan, may shed some light on the implications for the East Bank if it were not to be reunited with the West Bank. The conclusions will be approximate and tenuous, but that is the unavoidable nature of the problem with which we are dealing.

A wide variety of alternative future possibilities can affect the development prospects of Jordan if the West Bank is not returned. In addition, available economic data pertaining to the two banks separately suffer from various limitations. Without attempting to be quantitatively precise, let us bring out the salient features in the relationship between the East and West Banks.

At the outbreak of the June War the populations of the two banks were close to equal, with that of the East Bank slightly larger. There had been large and regular migration from the West to the East Bank over the preceding years, largely because of the faster development and greater economic opportunity on the East Bank. A large proportion of the migrants seem to have been refugees from the 1948 partition of Palestine.

The West Bank produced considerably less than half of countrywide GDP, possibly about 40 percent. Industry was especially concentrated on the East Bank; only about 30 percent of industrial value added originated on the West Bank, and most West Bank industries were small-scale. About 40 percent of agricultural value added was on the West Bank, concentrated mainly in fruits and vegetables, grain output being concentrated on the East Bank. Some 50 percent of nongovernment services originated on the West Bank. The share of the West Bank in GNP was presumably somewhat larger than its share in GDP, since a disproportionate share of factor income from abroad accrued to the West Bank.

Per capita income on the West Bank was roughly 75 percent of that on the East Bank in the period immediately preceding the June War.

Past investment and growth were concentrated on the East Bank. It has been suggested that this unbalance represented a policy of discrimination against the West Bank, of East Bank Transjordanians against West Bank Palestinians. It is not possible to establish the truth or falsity of this allegation in any rigorous way, but we can cite a number of economic reasons for greater development of the East Bank.

Whether by way of Lebanon and Syria or by way of Aqaba, virtually all of Jordan's foreign trade must pass through the East Bank. The large amount of investment in transport was then quite logically concentrated on the East Bank, particularly the development of the Port of Aqaba and the access routes to it. Furthermore, the geography of the East Bank requires much more extended lines of communication, particularly with Aqaba, than does the West Bank, where small distances are involved. Finally, the transportation system in the East Bank was the most underdeveloped in the 1960s; in particular, good roads were needed south of Amman to Aqaba and to Karak and Madaba.

Some of Jordan's major industries, particularly cement and phosphates, use resources found in the East Bank. In addition, many industries use mainly imported raw materials and thus are most economically located on the East Bank closer to the port of entry.

The location of Amman, the capital and by far the largest city in Jordan, on the East Bank provides a natural attraction for industry. Just before the June War one-quarter of Jordan's population was in the Amman-Zarqa urban area, and this represented an even larger share of the Jordan domestic market for manufactured goods.

As recent events have demonstrated, the West Bank is more vulnerable to Israeli attack. Some activities may accordingly have been located on the East Bank because of defense considerations.

Jordan's largest single investment project, the East Ghor irrigation project, is nominally located on the East Bank. But the Jordan Valley is a geographic area distinct from the highlands of the East and West Banks. The fact that the first stage of the Jordan Valley irrigation project happened to be located on the Eastern side of the Jordan River certainly cannot represent discrimination against Palestinians, particularly since the Jordan Valley has a very large proportion of Palestinians and many beneficiaries of the East Ghor project were Palestinian refugees.

When the two banks were joined to form the state of Jordan in 1950, the East Bank was much more backward than the West Bank. In certain spheres, such as education, expenditures had to be concentrated on the East Bank to raise it to a level comparable to that of the West Bank.

In considering the effect of the loss of the West Bank on Jordan we must keep in mind that the migration of some 300,000 refugees from the West to the East Bank after the June 1967 War has caused a significant fall in average per capita GNP on the East Bank. This is simply a case of many more people being thrown onto very limited resources (both natural and capital). Under current conditions of stagnating investment, there is little prospect of this loss being redressed by aid-financed investment. Current high levels of aid per capita are maintaining average per capita income and consumption at close to prewar levels, but this represents essentially a holding operation.

The Israel Economist (October-November 1967) suggested that the West Bank represented a deficit area and that Jordan was consequently better off without it. Besides assuming that the welfare of West Bankers is of no concern to East Bank residents, this viewpoint overlooks the fact that Jordan as a whole was a deficit area, the deficit being covered by foreign aid inflows. On *The Israel Economist's* reasoning, any aid-receiving country could be made better off by partition. Moreover, the West Bank deficit calculated by *The Israel Economist* was substantially smaller per capita than that for Jordan as a whole, so that in a certain restricted sense the West Bank might even be considered a surplus area.[44] This means that separation from the West Bank could improve average per capita incomes on the East Bank only if it elicited increased per capita aid. Voluntary partition for this purpose implies a certain lack of self-respect on the part of the recipient of such aid, rather like a beggar who disfigures himself to elicit sympathy from potential benefactors.

In light of the economic resources of the country itself, is it true that the development prospects for the East Bank are much better than those for the West Bank, so that the East Bank would be better off "going it alone"? Jordan's most valuable mineral resource, phosphate, is located on the East Bank, but this resource is mined for export, and the loss of the West Bank market is unimportant. Against this must be put the loss of the tourist trade. Most tourist expenditures were on the West Bank; travelers on the East Bank were either pilgrims to Mecca (whose expenditures in Jordan were generally low) or visitors primarily to the West Bank who had added East Bank tourist sights to their itinerary and would not have made these stops had they not been visiting the West Bank. Since the future "economic independence" of Jordan will depend heavily on whether the relatively large potential tourist earnings can be realized, it is in this sector that failure to regain the West Bank would most seriously impair Jordan's prospects.

The past rate of economic growth has been higher on the East Bank than the West. But the East Bank has received a disproportionately large share of investment, and this may account for all the difference. It is difficult to see why the intrinsic growth potential or the productivity of investment should be significantly greater for the East than for the West Bank.

The fact that we cannot predict the effect of the loss of the West Bank market on Jordan's economic development should not obscure its possible importance. Because Jordan's economy is not now highly interdependent, the consequences of the loss of the West Bank may appear small, but the long-run effect may well be significant.

IV. Prospects and Perspectives

Jordan's long-run economic future is highly uncertain. At the time of writing there exists a wide range of possible events impinging upon the economic development, covering numerous possible peace solutions and various forms of prolonged conflict. My approach is to take one optimistic but plausible political so-

---

[44] In particular, the West Bank would represent a surplus area if aid donors made contributions on a per capita basis and, other things equal, reduced them in proportion to any population loss. If aid were given for economic development purposes alone, this would be quite rational policy. I doubt, however, that this policy accurately characterizes the behavior of aid donors, who on average probably give more aid per capita to small countries than to large ones.

lution, the conclusion in 1971 of a peace that returns Jordan to its pre-1967 boundaries, and to make projections on that assumption. The result is a broad outline of long-range potentialities, rather than a detailed picture of all the various possibilities.

Tourism and employment abroad are particularly important elements in Jordan's economy. Both are highly dependent on uncertain political and economic developments elsewhere. In manufacturing, particularly manufactured exports, the economy is so little developed at present that the existing situation offers only slight guidance to the future pattern. The development of new manufacturing activities will be very important compared with the expansion of existing operations, and this is inherently less certain.

A sizable share of Jordan's past high growth rate is not explainable by growth in the conventional inputs of capital and labor. The unusually large residual or "total productivity" growth rate may in part represent chance or transitory factors; it may also represent elements deeply embedded in the culture. Although there is reason to believe that some part of the total productivity growth is temporary, my projections assume the persistence of a substantial part of this residual growth factor. To reduce the residual growth rate down to some average level on the grounds of "conservatism" would completely deny what is unique about the Jordanian development experience. Nonetheless, whenever one projects a performance that is markedly above average, some extra uncertainty must be attached.

Because of the uncertainty associated with my projections, they should be taken as suggestive only. The average annual GNP growth rates of 5.5 percent projected for 1966–1975 and the 8.0 percent rate for 1975–1980 might best be considered optimistic assumptions. The rest of the projections can then be viewed as the likely pattern of growth, contingent on the realization of these rather conjectural aggregate growth rates. In particular, my projections assume, not as a prediction but as an analytic device, the conclusion of a Middle Eastern peace in 1971, to be followed by a period of rapid recovery and growth; this later period of growth is responsible for the achievement of respectable average growth rates over the 1966–1975 period as a whole. The average 1966–1975 growth rates that will actually be attained are highly dependent on the exact date when in fact a settlement takes place. Even ignoring the possibility of no settlement at all, it is quite unlikely that I have guessed correctly the date of a settlement; certainly, I could be off by many years.

A mutually acceptable settlement is likely to involve some resettlement of Palestinian refugees in Israel and the payment of compensation to others. Here it is so difficult to make an estimate of the magnitudes involved that I have omitted consideration of these factors from my forecasts. The projections should provide a framework within which the reader may consider the implications of the situation he considers most likely. I shall here review the projections and survey the reasoning behind them. More detailed analysis of critical areas is presented in the next section.

Table 5-8 is a projection of GNP and population to 1980. The 1966–1975 sectoral projections in Table 5-9 relate the fairly rapid GNP growth rate, projected at 5.5 percent per annum (5.2 percent for GDP), to a rapid growth in the sectors of construction and ownership of dwellings, which is currently underway

Table 5-8

Projections of Gross National Product and Population, 1975 and 1980

	Actual		Projected			
	1954-1966	1966	1966-1975	1975	1975-1980	1980
Gross national product[a] (million $U.S. in constant 1966 prices)		532.4		863.6		1,268.6
Percent growth per annum	10.0		5.5		8.0	
Population[b] (thousands)		1968		2545		2964
Percent growth per annum	2.9		2.9		3.1	
GNP per capita ($U.S. in constant 1966 prices)		271		339		428
Percent growth per annum	7.0		2.5		4.8	

[a]For 1966 from *The National Accounts 1959-1967*. This shows $520 million GNP for 1966, but I have averaged 1965 and 1966 agricultural value added to take account of year-to-year fluctuations.

The 1954-1966 growth rate is approximate, reflecting a rough adjustment for price change of the figure given in Table 5-1.

[b]The 2.9 percent growth rate for 1954-1966 represents the 3.1 percent natural growth rate for 1959-1963 from *Analysis of the Population Statistics of Jordan*, less net emigration of 0.2 percent of the population per year. The latter figure is approximate, but it seems very likely that the true figure lies somewhere in the range of 0.2-0.3 percent, leaving a range of domestic population growth between 2.9 and 3.0 percent. For 1966-1975 I assume a population growth rate of 2.9 percent, which is the result of a rise in the natural rate to 3.2 percent due to declining death rates and a rise in emigration to 0.3 percent because of current tensions. For 1975-1980 I assume a natural rate of 3.3 percent and emigration at 0.2 percent.

Table 5-9

Projection of Value Added by Sector, 1975 and 1980

	Actual Growth, 1954/55-65/66[a] (1)	Actual, 1966[b] (2)	Projected Growth, 1966-75[a] (3)	Projected, 1975[b] (4)	Projected Growth, 1975-80[a] (5)	Projected, 1980[b] (6)
Value added at factor cost						
Agriculture	7.0	89.5	3.0	116.6	6.0	156.0
Manufacturing and mining	14.0	48.4	5.0	75.1	16.0	157.7
Electricity and water		6.3	7.0	11.6	14.0	22.3
Construction	16.0	26.0	9.0	56.5	10.0	91.0
Transport	9.0	40.4	3.0	52.7	6.0	70.5
Trade	10.5	81.0	5.5	131.1	7.0	184.7
Banking		7.8	7.0	14.7	15.0	29.6
Ownership of dwellings	11.0	31.4	10.0	74.0	8.0	108.7
Public administration and defense	8.5	61.7	4.0	87.8	3.0	101.8
Services	11.0	39.0	4.0	55.5	9.0	85.4
Indirect taxes	14.0	58.5	5.5	94.7	7.5	136.0
Net foreign income	12.0	42.4	9.0	93.3	6.0	124.9
GNP at market prices	10.5	532.4	5.5	863.6	8.0	1,268.6

[a]Figures in columns 1, 3, and 5 are average annual percentage rates of change, rounded to the nearest one-half percentage point. Column 1 is taken from Table 5-2, based on current-price data, except for crop output in constant prices.

[b]Figures in columns 2, 4, and 6 are in million $U.S. in constant 1966 prices. Data in column 2 are derived from statistics in *The National Accounts 1959-1967*. Figures here for value added in agriculture and for total GNP in 1966 differ somewhat from the same figures in official statistical publications, because I have used an average of 1965 and 1966 value added in agriculture to take account of fluctuations in crop production.

on the East Bank and is likely to continue in the event of a settlement, and in net foreign income, resulting from increased emigration since 1967 and higher earnings from Jordan's much larger foreign exchange reserves. Tourism is not expected to recover sufficiently by 1975 to permit rapid growth in the services sector. With the assumed peace settlement, a sizable reduction in the defense burden would be possible, but the expansion of military activity has been so great since 1967 that value added in the public sector will still have to be considerably larger in 1975 than in 1966. The growth of the commerce sector is expected to be in proportion to that of GNP. Although the growth rate for agriculture is projected below the pre-1967 rates, it is nonetheless optimistic in view of the damage to the Jordan Valley agricultural areas. The projected growth of agriculture is based on ongoing public investment in the sector since 1967 and on the restoration and reactivation of the East Ghor project area, which had not achieved its full potential in the years immediately before the June War. Growth in the mining and manufacturing sector is also projected at a rate lower than that of 1959–1966. Growth expectations of this sector over the 1966–1975 period are based on continuing expansion of phosphate mining and expansion of production in existing activities as the market expands. Relatively little import substitution is expected over the 1966–1975 period.

For 1975–1980 I project the resumption of an aggregate GNP growth rate almost as high as in the prewar period. The critical determinants of the high growth rate are a rapid expansion in the industrial sector, continued growth in construction as industrial investment rises, and growth in services as tourism recovers. The forecast of rapid growth in industry is based on making up the ground lost during 1966–1975 and on the underdevelopment of industry in Jordan in 1966, with substantial import substitution possibilities still remaining.

The projected 6 percent rate of growth of agricultural value added is optimistic but, I believe, attainable. It is based partly on the existence of further irrigation opportunities, which will permit increased cultivation of crops with high value per acre. In addition, there is substantial possibility for technological improvement in agriculture, which is still underdeveloped, particularly in cereals, fodder, and livestock.

Value added in commerce is expected to fall somewhat in proportion to GNP as a result of import substitution and a fall in the size of the import surplus relative to GNP. (When domestic production is substituted for imported goods, the total value of goods consumed is unchanged, and hence earnings from trade margins on goods will be little changed, even though GNP has risen.) The slow growth in public administration and defense derives from gradual reduction in the relative importance of the armed forces, which would be made possible by a mutually acceptable peace settlement.

I have not made quantitative projections of the post-1980 period, but the long-run post-1980 growth rate should be somewhat lower than the 1975–1980 rate because of the exhaustion of opportunities for investment in irrigation and for "easy" import substitution in industry. Fairly rapid growth in agriculture is possible in the early post-1980 years, say to 1985, from increased production in the area of the proposed Yarmuk project. In view of Jordan's outstanding growth achievements before the June 1967 War, a long-run post-1980 GNP growth of about 7 percent per year may reasonably be hoped for. Although industrial growth is not likely to continue at the rate projected for 1975–1980, industry will remain one of the faster-growing sectors, along with services, which will be carried along by growing tourism.

In the immediate prewar period average labor productivity increased at a rate of about 5 percent per year. If this average rate of change were to persist throughout the 1966–1980 period, the 1966–1980 GNP increase projected in Tables 5-8 and 5-9 would imply a growth of employment under 2 percent per year. Although this is well below the expected growth rate of the labor force, 5 percent is a very high rate of productivity increase, and it does not seem reasonable to expect such a high rate to prevail in the future. Nevertheless, in view of the fact that a growth rate of 9 percent in GNP seems to have been associated with a 4 percent growth of employment between 1961 and 1966 (Table 5-7), even the rather optimistic aggregate economic growth projected to 1980 should at best reduce unemployment only very gradually and may possibly not be sufficient to absorb the increase of the labor force.[45]

My projections of investment requirements (Table 5-10) are based on an assumed gross incremental capital-output ratio of 2.4—rather higher than prevailed in the past, but still lower than for the average less developed country. The ICOR for the years 1966–1975 is increased to take account of the need to repair war-incurred damage, whereas the equally high ICOR for 1975–1980 reflects reduction in certain "easy" growth opportunities, particularly in irrigated crop production, livestock, and manufacturing. The investment figures for 1975, taken with the projected 1966–1975 average growth rate of gross domestic product, seem to suggest a higher ICOR, because the greater part of investment and growth takes place during the years 1971–1975; that is, investment and output do not grow smoothly between 1966 and 1975, but growth is concentrated in the later years. For 1975–1980, however, a steady growth of output and investment is projected.

Table 5-10 presents my projections of savings and its major determinants and of investment. In making the projections I used what I considered achievable ratios of government spending and revenue to GNP and of private savings to private disposable income to derive 1980 values. My projections imply a very large increase in the importance of domestic savings relative to foreign aid. Gross domestic saving is expected to finance 80 percent of gross domestic investment in 1980, compared with only 20 percent in 1966. However, in absolute terms only a modest reduction in foreign-supplied resources is anticipated. Not all of this need be met by foreign aid, as it should be possible for Jordan to meet some of its foreign payments needs by drawing on foreign reserves.

[45] Labor productivity can change as a result of a "compositional effect," when rapid output growth is concentrated in high-productivity sectors, and low-productivity sectors predominate among the slow-growing sectors, or vice versa. I have made calculations that show there was no large compositional effect for the 1961–1966 period. Furthermore, my projections for 1975 and 1980 do not imply a significant compositional effect.

Table 5-10

Projections of Investment and Savings, 1975 and 1980

	Actual, 1966[a] (1)	Projected Growth, 1966-75[b] (2)	Pro- jected, 1975[a] (3)	Projected Growth, 1975-80[b] (4)	Pro- jected, 1980[a] (5)
1. Gross national product[c]	532.4	5.5	863.6	8.0	1,268.6
2. Private disposable income	457.8	5.0	703.8	7.5	1,014.9
3. Private consumption	418.2	4.5	629.9	7.5	893.1
4. Gross private savings = (row 2 − row 3)	39.6	7.0	73.9	11.0	121.8
5. Government domestic revenues	87.0	7.0	159.8	10.0	253.7
6. Government current defense expenditures	57.0	3.0	75.0	−3.0	63.4
7. Government current nondefense expenditures	53.5	5.5	86.6	8.0	126.9
8. Government current expenditures = (row 6 + row 7)	110.5	4.5	161.6	3.5	190.3
9. Government savings = (row 5 − row 6)	−23.5	. . .	−1.8	. . .	63.4
10. Gross domestic capital formation	78.6	6.5	138.2	11.0	228.3
11. Gross domestic savings = (row 4 + row 9)	16.1	18.0	72.1	21.0	185.2
12. Foreign transfers and change in foreign assets = (row 10 − row 11)	62.5	0.5	66.1	−8.0	43.1

Some Important Ratios

Row ÷ Row				
2	1	86.0	81.5	80.0
4	2	8.6	10.5	12.0
5	1	16.3	18.5	20.0
6	1	10.7	8.7	5.0
7	1	10.0	10.0	10.0
8	1	20.8	18.7	15.0
10	1	14.8	16.0	18.0
11	1	3.0	8.3	14.6
11	10	20.5	52.2	81.1

One of my most critical and uncertain assumptions is that there will be no growth in defense expenditures over the 1966–1980 period as a whole, resulting from the conclusion of a mutually acceptable peace settlement. This involves a reduction in the share of defense expenditures in GNP from 10.7 to 5.0 percent. If, instead, the 1966 ratio were maintained in 1980, the foreign resources required in that year would be considerably more than doubled.

In Table 5-11 I present projections of nonaid current account payments and receipts for 1975 and 1980. Largely because of the different treatments in the two tables of payments to individuals by UNRWA, other UN, and other charitable institutions,[46] the definition of the savings-investment gap in Table 5-10 (line 12) differs from that of the foreign exchange deficit in Table 5-11, so that there is a difference even in the 1965/66 *ex post* gaps given in the two tables.

The projections for 1975 and 1980 are ex ante, and there is therefore no reason for equality in the projections for those years of the savings-investment and balance-of-payments gaps defined on a comparable basis. Accordingly, we may draw some conclusion about which problem is likely to be more serious in the future: the scarcity of savings or the scarcity of foreign exchange. My projections suggest that foreign exchange will be the more serious constraint on economic growth, particularly during the later years, when a high GNP growth rate is projected. Other studies have arrived at a similar conclusion.[47]

Table 5-11 projects substantial increase in the deficit during the years of rapid GNP growth from 1975 to 1980. This is the result of rapid rise in imports, rather than any slowdown in the growth of receipts. In this respect there are two key developments. (1) Rapid growth in industry, based largely on import substitution by processing imported materials, will produce rapid growth in raw materials imports. (2) I have assumed a rapid growth rate of GNP of 8 percent per

---

[46] In Table 5-11 these are taken as financing part of the deficit. In Table 5-10 they are part of private income and thus contribute to domestic rather than foreign-supplied savings.

[47] See the studies by Kanaan and the United Nations Economic and Social Office in Beirut, cited in the notes to Table 5-11.

---

[a]Figures in columns 1, 3, and 5 of rows 1-12 are in million $U.S. at constant 1966 prices.

[b]Figures in columns 2 and 4 of rows 1-12 are average annual percentage rates of change, rounded to the nearest half percentage point.

[c]Gross national product for 1966 is derived as described in the notes to Tables 5-7 and 5-8. The remaining items for 1966 are derived by averaging 1965 and 1966 estimates from *The National Accounts 1959-1967*. Since average GNP for 1965 and 1966 is less than my figure, I increased all items proportionately, so that each item's share in GNP was the same as its share in average GNP for 1965 and 1966. The use of average 1965/66 figures is necessary because of the large year-to-year variations in the historical statistics of savings.

As elsewhere in this paper, my definition of government saving differs from that of the national accounts, because I exclude budget support grants and loans from government income.

Table 5-11

Balance of Payments Projections, 1975, 1980

	Actual Average, 1965/66[a]	Projected Growth, 1965/75[b]	Projected, 1975[a]	Projected Growth, 1975-80[b]	Projected, 1980[a]
	(1)	(2)	(3)	(4)	(5)
Payments[c]	188.16	5.5	302.09	9.0	457.93
Goods imports (net of re-exports)	162.65	5.5	259.35	9.0	395.63
Agricultural goods (net of exports)[d]	22.20	6.5	39.35	8.0	57.18
Rice	3.56		5.10		7.03
Wheat	8.90		10.53		10.08
Vegetables	e		.50		4.14
Fruits	2.83		8.26		13.75
Olives	e		.90		2.13
Livestock	6.92		14.06		20.05
Other consumption goods[f]	71.68	4.5	108.45	6.0	145.72
Intermediate goods[f]	53.14	5.5	84.39	12.0	148.73
Capital goods[f]	15.62	6.5	27.16	10.5	44.60
Services imports	25.51	6.0	42.74	8.0	62.30
Travel	13.33	6.0	22.06	9.0	33.71
Other services	12.18	6.0	20.68	6.5	28.59

Nonaid receipts	101.62	8.0	205.15	9.5	323.50
Goods exports (excluding re-exports)	17.15	10.5	41.60	11.0	70.00
Agricultural goods (net of imports)[d]	4.45		g		g
Vegetables	4.20		g		g
Olives	.25		g		g
Phosphates[h]	7.78	16.0	30.00	8.0	45.00
Others[j]	4.92	10.0	11.60	16.0	25.00
Services exports	41.27	6.0	69.75	13.0	129.70
Tourism[k]	29.50	4.0	42.00	15.0	85.00
Other[m]	11.77	10.0	27.75	10.0	44.70
Factor income[n]	40.71	9.0	88.40	6.0	116.60
Remittances	27.59	9.0	59.90	6.0	80.20
Investment income and oil transit dues	13.12	9.0	28.50	5.0	36.40
Nonaid transfers to households[p]	2.49	9.0	5.40	9.0	7.20
Deficit	86.54	1.5	96.94	6.5	134.43

[a]Columns 1, 3, and 5 are in million $U.S.

[b]Columns 2 and 4 are average annual growth rates rounded to the nearest half percentage point.

[c]Imports of goods and services have been projected on the basis of equations in Taher H. Kanaan, "Projections of Jordan's Foreign Trade 1970, 1975," United Nations Conference on Trade and Development, Projections Section (no date, unpublished). A revised and abbreviated version of the same paper is presented in "Plan Formulation and Development Perspectives in Jordan," in United Nations Economic and Social Office in Beirut, *Studies on Selected Development Problems in the Middle East 1969*, New York, 1969. In using the equations I have, of course, utilized my own projections of the independent variables. Certain minor adjustments have been made on the basis of my own qualitative judgments.

[d]Imports and exports of wheat, vegetables, fruits, and livestock have been combined, reflecting the assumption that any surpluses of these crops can be exported without difficulty. The UN studies use the same approach.

[e]Net exports. By themselves, goods exports and imports have no real significance, although their difference represents the excess of total agricultural imports over exports.

[f]My breakdown of imports into other consumption goods, intermediate goods, and capital goods is made on the basis of the 1965 and 1966 input-output tables. The UN studies apparently made the breakdown on the basis of commodity groupings. The growth *rates* of each category, however, are arrived at by using the UN equations. Note that "other consumption goods" includes a few agricultural goods, such as maize and barley. Unlike agricultural imports, they are not net of exports.

[g]Net imports. My projections of agricultural imports and exports make use of consumption elasticities used in the UN studies but involve somewhat more optimistic projections of production. I assumed that 1980 production would have increased over 1965/66 by 150 percent for wheat, 100 percent for livestock, and 50 percent for fruit and vegetables.

[h]The *Seven Year Program for Economic Development of Jordan 1964-1970* (p. 39) estimates phosphate exports of $20 million per year by 1970. I use a somewhat lower growth rate for 1970-1975 and 1975-1980 than the plan's projected rate for 1965-1970. Current hostilities are not expected to interrupt progress in this sector.

[j]Exports of goods other than agricultural products grew at an average annual rate of 21 percent between 1958/59 and 1965/66, but this was from a very small base. Manufactured exports have continued to grow since 1966, and I have accordingly used the optimistic growth rate of 10 percent per annum for the 1965/66-1975 period, in spite of the slow growth projected for manufacturing output as a whole. In accordance with my projections of rapid industrialization during 1975-1980 I have used a high growth rate for industrial exports in that period.

[k]Even with a peace settlement in 1971, it is unlikely that 1975 tourist earnings will be much greater than those of 1965/66 for two reasons: (1) it will take time for some tourists to recover confidence in the peacefulness and stability of the region; and (2) because of the low level of investment in tourist facilities in Jordan since 1967, accommodations for travelers will have increased only a little between 1965/66 and 1975, even if tourism investment is large between 1971 and 1975. Resumption of rapid growth in tourism earnings after 1975, however, is anticipated. The growth rates used here should be taken as highly approximate.

[m]The definition of other services exports here is that of the Central Bank's annual reports, rather than that of the national accounts. The latter includes payments by UNRWA, other UN, and other charitable agencies for services by Jordanians. The Central Bank counts this item as a transfer payment. I also omit it from services exports because I wish my estimate of the balance of payments deficit to show capital inflow required from all sources, including UNRWA, other UN, and other charitable agencies. Projections for 1975 and 1980 are based on simple extrapolation of past trends.

[n]In view of past trends and a presumed increase in emigration during the post-1967 years of tension, I assume a rather high rate of growth of remittances from Jordanians temporarily abroad for 1965/66-1975 and a lower rate for 1975-1980.

year and an ICOR of 2.4—higher than in the past. As a result, rapid growth in investment is required, with a concomitant rise in capital goods imports.

According to the projections in Table 5-11 Jordan will continue as a net importer of agricultural products. In fact, net agricultural imports are expected to grow as fast as GNP. Although Jordan was a net exporter of vegetables and olives in the immediate prewar years, the country is expected to be a net importer of these products by 1975. Because of the early growing season in the Jordan Valley, exports of fruits and vegetables will undoubtedly continue, even though the balance will be in favor of imports.

The conclusion that Jordan cannot rely on net agricultural exports for foreign exchange seems inescapable. With rapid population growth, a high growth rate of per capita income requires rapidly increasing supplies for a country at Jordan's low level of per capita income. I have forecast annual growth rates in agricultural value added of 3 percent for 1966–1975 and 6 percent for 1975–1980. I believe that in view of Jordan's severely limited agricultural resources it will be exceedingly difficult to surpass these rates; therefore increased net imports of foodstuffs will certainly be required if the projected growth rates are attained.

To help finance its large and growing import requirements, Jordan will accordingly have to rely mainly on earnings from mineral exports, manufactured exports, tourism, and remittances from Jordanians abroad. I have projected a fairly rapid growth in exports of phosphates. The world market is expected to grow rapidly, and anticipated Jordanian exports are small enough in relation to total world supply that there should not be insurmountable marketing difficulties. Recovery and export of potash from the Dead Sea has long been contemplated in Jordan, but low-cost world supplies of potash make this an unprofitable investment at present and probably in the future. I assume no production or export of potash throughout the period of projection.

The Jordan seven-year plan anticipated a 13 percent annual growth rate of manufactured exports between 1965 and 1970.[48] Exports of cigarettes, cement,

[48] Jordan Development Board, *The Seven Year Program for Economic Development of Jordan 1964–1970*, Amman (no date), p. 39.

There may be some drawing down of foreign reserves after a peace settlement, but the growth since June 1967 has been so large that the 1975 figure will still represent a rapid-growth nonremittance factor in income from abroad to 1975. Reserves will probably decline in relative terms but grow slowly in absolute terms over the 1975-1980 period, producing a similar pattern in nonremittance factor earnings over the same period.

p"Nonaid transfers to households" comprises remittances from Jordanians permanently abroad (the distinction between those permanently and temporarily abroad is inherently arbitrary) and pensions to former employees of the Mandatory Palestine government. This is expected to grow at the same rate as remittances from Jordanians temporarily abroad.

Source: Central Bank of Jordan, *Fifth Annual Report 1968*, Amman, 1969. Because of year-to-year fluctuations, particularly in agricultural imports and exports, I have used the average of 1965 and 1966 for my base year.

and clothing and footwear were significantly higher in 1968 than in 1965/66. Thus my optimistic projection of a 10 percent average annual increase between 1966 and 1975 in exports of goods other than phosphates and unprocessed agricultural goods seems attainable. The rapid growth rate of 16 percent per year between 1975 and 1980 is in accord with my projections of rapid industrial development, which imply that about 10 percent of manufacturing output would be exported in 1980.

Rapid growth in industrial exports depends on a number of intangible and unpredictable elements. Jordanian entrepreneurs have experienced some success in exporting their manufactures, but in relative terms this progress has taken place from a very small base. The export capacity of Jordanian industry is as yet largely untested; indeed industry itself is at an early stage of development. Therefore, although there is some reason for optimism, based on the general temper of enterprise in the country, the degree of uncertainty attached to my projections is large. Most probably, Jordan's best potential market for industrial exports will be the oil countries of the Middle East. Scale limitations clearly inhibit Jordan from competing in mass-produced articles with Egypt or countries outside the Arab Middle East. Specialty products involving high levels of craftsmanship, enterpreneurship, or marketing skills present the best prospects. Jordan's production and export of batteries provides an example of such a product. I would not attempt to predict the products to be exported in the future—this is, after all, the the job the market rewards successful entrepreneurs so well for doing—but two possibilities may be mentioned. In terms of natural resources, Jordan is well endowed for the production of ceramics, and this industry may provide future exports. Also, with a peace settlement that returns the holy places held by Jordan before 1967, increased exports of souvenir handicraft products should be possible.

My projections of tourism earnings are the most speculative of all the estimates. It cannot be said that these are the most optimistic projections possible; indeed, they may be fairly conservative. A prewar study by the Battelle Memorial Institute estimated an increase in tourist arrivals at an average annual rate of 18 percent between 1966 and 1981.[49] Since some increase in average expenditure per tourist is likely, the corresponding growth of tourism earnings would be even faster.

Under the best of circumstances, tourism would be difficult to project. In Jordan's case additional uncertainties arise from the fact that different settlements will have different effects on the share of Holy Land tourism earnings

[49] J. W. Fay, J. W. Vigrass, D. N. Gross, G. H. Sewell, and John M. Duggan, *Report on Jordan Airports' Feasibility Study to the U.S. Department of State Agency for International Development* (AID), Battelle Memorial Institute, Columbus, Ohio, July 1967, p. V-26. For the period 1966–1981 the Battelle study made a pessimistic estimate of 13 percent per year growth and an optimistic estimate of 21 percent. Statistics of tourism arrivals and departures in Jordan are highly inaccurate, and estimates of expenditure per tourist are simply rough guesses.

accruing to Jordan. In the event of a mutually agreeable settlement there may be considerable potential earnings for Jordan from tourism by Israelis and from visitors to Israel who go on to visit Jordan. If we were to take an optimistic projection, more in line with the Battelle forecasts, say 10 percent average annual growth in tourism earnings from 1966 to 1975 and 20 percent from 1975 to 1980, tourism earnings in 1980 would be some $90 million higher than in my projections. Were this higher figure to be realized, it would be sufficient to reduce the projected foreign exchange gap to a level well below the savings-investment gap.

Tourist earnings may well be crucial if Jordan is to progress toward economic independence. I do not see any possibility that exports of minerals and manufactures and remittances from Jordanians abroad will come near to covering Jordan's undoubtedly large future import requirements.

My projections imply that, unless tourism turns in a spectacular performance, foreign exchange will be a greater constraint on Jordan's growth than domestic capital. This is the most probable development and follows a pattern common to most developing countries. However, there are enough uncertainties in the projections to warrant some doubt about this conclusion as well. In particular, if the projected rise in private savings rates does not occur, the large reduction in the share of defense expenditures in GNP does not materialize, and tourist earnings rise more rapidly than projected, the situation will be completely reversed, and savings will be limitational.

V. Problems and Policies

The Institutional Framework

Jordan maintains an essentially free market economy with few formal restrictions on private business activity, but it carries on a high level of public investment. For the two years 1965 and 1966, public investment averaged 43 percent of total gross domestic capital formation. Public investment was concentrated in the usual infrastructural areas: irrigation, roads, the development of the port of Aqaba, communications, and power. To promote industrial development the government purchased shares in a number of private companies engaged in such industrial activities as phosphate mining, cement production, tanning, and petroleum refining. Foreign investment has been encouraged, but remains negligible.

In the past the Jordan government's most important long-range economic decisions have generally involved investment decisions, both public (for example, the East Ghor Canal, expansion of Aqaba port, various road-building projects) and private (whether to license, subsidize, or buy shares in industrial enterprises). In the selection of projects a de facto planning function has been performed by various ministries, such as the Ministry of Public Works and the Ministry of Agriculture, and by national and international aid agencies, especially USAID. Decisions on government licensing and assisting of industrial ventures are centered in the Ministry of National Economy.[50] Most of the public invest-

---

[50] The economic roles of the ministries of Agriculture and National Economy are discussed in the sections on agriculture and industry, respectively.

ment projects of a developmental nature have been financed by foreign aid. Thus the pattern of public investment has in part been determined by the views and policies of aid agencies. In addition, the allocation of investment funds has been influenced by the initiative and skillfulness of the various ministries and agencies in preparing and presenting project proposals. Investment decisions have involved not so much decisions among competing investment proposals as seeking out acceptable investment proposals. At times potential aid donors have lacked acceptable projects to finance.

There has been little debate in Jordan over the broader sorts of economic policy issues, such as monetary, exchange rate, tariff, and tax policies, partly because these issues have not posed pressing problems. Foreign aid has helped Jordan to maintain sizable public expenditures and relatively low tax rates without generating inflation up to 1967. Tax revenues are dominated by receipts from customs duties, which are mainly levied for revenue purposes and are infrequently changed. Because Jordan's industry is so small, tariffs for purposes of protection are few and are generally decided ad hoc as part of the decision whether to license and aid the establishment of a particular firm.

Planning for economic development is nominally in the hands of the Jordan Development Board (JDB). The JDB has undergone a number or reorganizations since its inception in 1952 but has always been more an agency for administering foreign aid than a research, planning, or policymaking body. Its work has largely involved negotiation with aid-giving agencies and economic analysis of aid-financed projects, in which it sometimes duplicates the work of the agency providing the aid.

With the assistance of a large number of Ford Foundation advisors the JDB produced a five-year plan for 1962–1967 which was almost immediately superseded by a seven-year plan for 1964–1970.[51] The various ministries were, of course, intimately involved in the planning process as well. The seven-year plan includes a set of macro-economic projections, which do not appear to be the result of very extensive economic analysis. In the main, the plan is a collection of proposals for new projects, new governmental or quasi-governmental bodies, changes in government administration, and changes in certain economic policies. At this micro-economic level the quality of the plan appears quite high, especially in view of the limited statistical information available at the time and the very recent origin of planning in Jordan. In general, the plan avoided the common weakness for impressive but uneconomic projects.

For a few years a large amount of foreign and domestic talent was concentrated on the effort of plan preparation. After the departure of many of the foreign advisors, the JDB lost momentum. Some progress was being made, however, and at the time of the June 1967 War the JDB was probably fundamentally sound. Since the war the JDB, because of its long and close association with United States aid agencies, has suffered loss of prestige because of American

[51] Jordan Development Board, *Five Year Program for Economic Development 1962–1967*, rev. ed., Amman, 1961, and Jordan Development Board, *The Seven Year Program for Economic Development of Jordan 1964–1970.*

support for Israel. In addition, reduction in American aid since 1967 and the difficulty of planning under current conditions of uncertainty have further limited the activity and influence of the JDB, and many of its most competent people have left the Board. Economic decisions are now concentrated in the hands of an Economic Security Committee, established soon after the 1967 War and including the prime minister, the governor of the Central Bank, and the ministers of Finance and National Economy. In the event of a mutually acceptable peace settlement and the refocusing of the nation's energies on the problems of economic development, it will be necessary either to make many changes in the activities and personnel of the JDB or to establish a new body to evaluate policy issues and engage in long-term planning.

Aside from the Central Bank of Jordan, established in 1963, the main agency for short-term economic planning—potentially at least—is the Budget Department of the Ministry of Finance, established in 1962.[52] Nominally, it possesses extensive planning powers, but in practice its activities are largely limited to bookkeeping, with an emphasis on accountability. Its work is mainly that of budget preparation by a number of budget examiners, each responsible for a different ministry. Although considerable progress has been made in budget preparation and presentation, the budgeting process remains rather crude. Ministry appropriations are generally determined by negotiation at meetings between ministry representatives and Budget Department examiners. Generally, the ministry overstates its expected expenditures, anticipating that these figures will be reduced. In turn, the representatives of the Budget Department usually propose cuts in appropriations, based on subjective judgments, for very little supporting evidence is available to either side in the discussions. When differences occur in these negotiations, the final decision must be taken at higher levels, not rarely by the Council of Ministers. Even at high levels, however, relatively little supporting evidence is available or often even requested.[53]

[52] I distinguish between the JDB and the Budget Department of the Ministry of Finance as agencies concerned with long-term and short-term planning, respectively. This is only approximately true; there is another division of responsibility: the Budget Department concerns itself with activities financed from internal resources, whereas the JDB administers projects directly financed by aid, particularly those financed by USAID. To further complicate matters, aid from certain donors is administered by other bodies, such as the Ministry of Foreign Affairs. These various responsibilities increase the chances of duplication of efforts and make more difficult the detailed examination of alternatives.

[53] Compare Gordon V. Potter, *A Five Year Plan of Budget and Planning Improvement,* USAID/Jordan, December 1966, pp. 26–27: "Despite frequent admonition from different sources, the Council of Ministers continues to make decisions on budget, fiscal and economic proposals in an irresponsible way. The irresponsibility of these decisions arises almost wholly from either (1) not carefully examining and understanding the facts and alternative choices prepared by the interested Government agency or agencies, or (2) not demanding that all important proposals presented

Essentially, the operation of reviewing the budgets for the various ministries is a mechanical one. There is virtually no program or performance budgeting; at present the staff is probably not adequate to these tasks. The JDB, the Ministry of Finance, and the Audit Bureau prepare performance evaluation reports, but these are simply accounting and financial reports, rather than true evaluations. The emphasis on accountability has meant the multiplication of detailed rules for the transfer of allotted appropriations, which minimizes the opportunity for discretion by the ministries. The ministries have logically reacted by trying to include a great deal of slack in their expenditure requests, mainly in the form of large amounts for "development ordinary expenditures."[54] Further development of the budgeting process is clearly needed so that decisions may be based on reliable information, rather than guesswork and rules of thumb.[55]

Agriculture

From Tables 5-2 and 5-12 it is clear that Jordan's 7 percent per annum growth of agricultural value added is attributable mainly to rapid growth in the production of livestock, vegetables, and citrus fruit. Especially striking is the almost complete lack of growth in grains and legumes (mainly wheat and barley). In the 1950s wheat was by far the most important crop, constituting 34 percent of the value of agricultural output in 1954/55. Although wheat was still the single most important crop in 1965/66, its value had fallen to 27 percent of total value of agricultural output. Since there has been a modest decline in the acreage devoted to grains, the yield of grains has risen somewhat. On the whole, however, Jordan's development efforts have until recently rather neglected rainfed farming. Wheat and barley yields in Jordan, while fluctuating widely, are on average extremely low—partly because of the extension of cultivation onto marginal land and partly because modern methods have not yet been adopted in rainfed grain cultivation on the better land. At present grain cultivation makes very little use of fertilizers and chemical weed killers. Considerable improvement in seed qual-

---

to the Cabinet for decision be accompanied by a paper presenting all of the facts, listing alternative decisions, and the differing consequences of such alternatives."

[54] During 1965–1967 actual development expenditures averaged 51.9 percent of estimated. Compare United Nations Economic and Social Office in Beirut, *Meeting on Problems of Budget Classification and Management, 21–25 April 1968,* Part IV, "Planning and Budgeting in Jordan," Beirut, 11 April 1969, unpublished, Annex IV.

[55] The discussion of budgeting in Jordan is largely derived from Potter, *A Five Year Plan of Budget and Planning Improvement,* and three unpublished master's theses submitted to the American University of Beirut: Husayn Harrim, "Government Budgetary Process in Jordan," June 1968; Rima Faiq Halazun, "Fiscal Policy and Economic Development in Jordan," July 1968; and Wasfi Mahmoud Osman, "Major Problems of Government Budgeting and Planning: An Appraisal of Jordan's Experience (1948–1968)," September 1969.

Table 5-12
Annual Growth Rates of Value of Output
in Crops and Forestry[a]
(percent)

		1954/55-1965/66	1954/55-1959/60	1959/60-1965/66
1.	Grains and legumes	0	1	0
	2. Wheat	1.5	3	0.5
	3. Barley	−1	1	−3
	4. Others	−2	−5	1
5.	Vegetables	10	16.5	5
	6. Tomatoes	13	20	8
	7. Cucumbers, melons, and watermelons	6.5	14	1
	8. Others	11	16	5.5
9.	Fruits, vines, and olives	7	8	6
	10. Grapes	5.5	15	−0.5
	11. Olives	3	−4	7
	12. Citrus	45.5	50	42
	13. Other fruits	6	5	7
14.	Construction on farms (labor)	5	−20	27
15.	Tobacco	7	7	7
16.	Forest products	−7	−3	−9.5
17.	Total	5	6.5	4

[a]All growth rates are annual rates annually compounded and rounded to the nearest 0.5 percentage point.

Rows 1-13: The underlying data are smoothed estimates of value of output in constant 1964 prices. Agricultural prices of 1964 appeared to be the most representative of recent years. Where production figures included more than one category of crop, I used an unweighted arithmetic average of the prices of the different crops.

Where the regression was statistically significant, smoothing was done by means of a logarithmic regression of output against rainfall and time. I used a dummy variable to separate the time trends in the two arbitrarily chosen periods, 1953-1960 and 1960-1966. If the regression equation was not statistically significant, smoothing was by means of moving averages. Jordan Department of Statistics, *Statistical Yearbook*, various years.

Rows 14-16: 1954-1958 from Porter, *Economic Trends in Jordan 1954-1959*. 1959-1966 from *The National Accounts 1959-1967*. All underlying data in current prices.

ity is also possible.[56] Since so much room exists for the improvement of methods in cereal cultivation in Jordan, it is reasonable to anticipate the possibility of very large increases in yields per acre of wheat and barley.

The rapid increase in livestock output up to 1966 appears to be mainly an expansion of traditional activities starting from a small base. The chief exception is the rapid development of commercial poultry farming in the 1960s. Sheep and goats, which make up more than two-thirds of the value of meat production, are grazed on pastures and stubble, often by nomadic bedouins. As a result of the rapid expansion of livestock herds, Jordan was already suffering from destructive overgrazing by the time of the June War. The potential for further growth in livestock output along the lines of the prewar increase appear to be very limited. However, reversion of some marginal cultivated land to pasture and the addition of a leguminous fodder to the crop rotation system in areas of adequate rainfall will increase the fodder supply considerably. There also exists ample room for the introduction of modern livestock practices and improved breeds; weight of the animals at slaughter in Jordan is still quite low. Therefore, although expansion at the rapid pre-1967 level may be too much to expect, a quite respectable rate of growth—say 5 or 6 percent a year—should be attainable, but the nature of the expected future growth will be quite different from that of the prewar years.

The rapid growth in production of fruits and vegetables in the prewar years is attributable in large part to the East Ghor Canal. This project diverts water by gravity flow from the Yarmuk River into a 70-kilometer (43.5-mile) canal in the Jordan Valley, running parallel to the Jordan River on its east bank. The system also receives water from seven small perennial streams that flow westward toward the Jordan River. Construction of the main canal was begun in 1959 and completed in 1963. By 1966 all the lateral canals and primary drains had been completed, and the full 30,000 acres of the project area brought into irrigated cultivation.

A precise estimate of the contribution of the East Ghor Canal to Jordan's past and potential growth is impossible, but it appears that the increase in the value of annual crop output attributable to the canal between the 1959/60 and 1965/66 crop years was on the order of $7½ to 8 million.[57] This was about

[56] FAO Mediterranean Development Project, *Jordan Country Report,* United Nations Food and Agriculture Organization, Rome, 1967, pp. 59–61.

[57] Statistics of the value of crop output in the project area are contained in Abdul Wahhab Jamil Awwad, *Agricultural Production and Income in the East Ghor Irrigation Project: Pre-and Post-Canal,* USAID, Amman, August, 1967. This reports on sample surveys taken in the project area during the 1964/65 and 1965/66 crop years. I have made some rough adjustments for the low level of output in 1959/60 due to extremely low rainfall. No attempt has been made to adjust for price changes. No account has been taken here of changes in noncrop output, which is not likely to be significantly affected by the project and is relatively unimportant in the project area anyway.

half of the same period's increase in value of annual crop output for all Jordan, adjusted for fluctuations as a result of rainfall, or about one-fourth of the increase in the value of all agricultural output. The increase in annual agricultural value added between 1959/60 and 1965/66 in the East Ghor Canal area was about $6.0–$6.4 million, or about one-quarter of the total growth over the period in agricultural value added not attributable to changes in rainfall.[58] Thus the importance of the East Ghor Canal project in Jordan's agricultural growth between 1959/60 and 1965/66 has been large, but not completely dominating. It accounted for almost 2 percentage points of Jordan's 7 percent per annum rate of growth in agricultural value added.[59]

The investment cost of the East Ghor Canal and associated facilities is about $18 million, which does not include investments undertaken privately by individual farmers in the project area. The increase in value added in the project area of $6.0–$6.4 million implies an incremental capital-output ratio of 2.8–3.0. The apparently high level of this project's ICOR is misleading, for the full potential of the East Ghor Canal was by no means reached in 1966. Citrus trees planted but not bearing at full potential in that year were expected to add about $0.7 million to the value of annual output by 1970, and additional plantings of high-yield citrus trees were anticipated. Other improvements in cropping patterns and more double cropping were also anticipated. In addition, some 7 percent of available land was still uncultivated in 1966.[60] Even though 1965/66 was a poor rainfall year and 1964/65 a good one, the value of output in the project area increased by about 20 percent between 1964/65 and 1965/66. About half of the increase was due to cultivation of more acres, the rest to higher yield per acre. The value of annual production in the East Ghor Canal area in 1967, according to Awwad's estimate, could be doubled by 1970/71 over the 1965/66 figures.[61] This strikes me as rather optimistic: the original consultants' estimate of output per acre forecast a figure that was actually less than the one for 1965/66 in the project area. These estimates are of necessity approximate, but I think that an increase of 50 percent by 1970/71 over the 1965/66 total value of output would be a more reasonable forecast. This would imply an increase in annual

---

[58] No satisfactory information is available on intermediate costs in Jordan Valley agriculture. According to the 1966 input-output table, intermediate inputs into fruit and vegetable production were about 10 percent of the value of output. Since a higher proportion of input cost to output value is likely for the more intensively farmed East Ghor irrigation project area than for the country as a whole, I have arbitrarily used a figure of 20 percent in dividing gross output between intermediate costs and value added.

[59] Throughout this discussion I have been implicitly assuming that all the increase in value of crop output between 1959/60 and 1965/66 in the East Ghor project area was due to the canal project, which, although not exactly true, I believe to be adequately close to reality.

[60] Awwad, *Agricultural Production and Income,* pp. 36–37.

[61] *Ibid.,* p. 38.

value added of roughly \$3.5–\$4.0 million, reducing the ICOR for this project below 2.

Obviously, the June War and its aftermath have greatly changed this picture. Any target date for the achievement of the project's full potential must be moved forward to more than 5 years after the end of hostilities in the area. Probably, if peace is concluded in 1971 (my working assumption), the full potential of the canal can be reached by the end of the projection period, 1980. I cannot estimate the cost of repairing the damage to the canal and replanting the citrus trees that have been lost, but it should not be large in comparison with the original cost of the project.

Although the irrigation potential of the Jordan Valley is limited both by the number of irrigable acres and by the amount of water available, the East Ghor Canal does not exhaust the potential. In fact, the canal is only part of a more ambitious project to produce electricity and increase the land irrigated in the Jordan Valley: the Yarmuk project. The main features of the Yarmuk project are the following: (1) construction of two dams on the Yarmuk River and two power plants, providing water for irrigation and hydroelectric power; (2) raising the sides of the existing East Ghor Canal to accommodate a larger flow and construction of an extension running 40 kilometers southward to the Dead Sea; (3) construction of a 47-kilometer West Ghor Canal running parallel to the Jordan River on its west bank southward to the Dead Sea, together with a siphon across the Jordan River to connect the West Ghor Canal with a 60-kilometer canal to be constructed on the east bank parallel to the existing East Ghor Canal; (4) construction of seven dams to regulate the seasonal flow of seven perennial streams (side wadis) flowing into the Jordan Valley from the east; (5) construction of nine pumping stations to provide water to irrigable lands above the level of the two main canals; (6) land improvement and construction of lateral canals and flood protection and drainage facilities in the area to be irrigated by the foregoing projects.

In March 1967 work was completed on the construction of a dam to regulate the flow in the Wadi Ziqlab, one of the perennial East Bank streams. The completion of two other side wadi dams, in Wadi Kafrein and Wadi Shueib, was delayed by the June War and subsequent hostilities. By the beginning of 1969 both had been completed, although at costs above the original estimates. The project to raise the sides of the East Ghor Canal has also been completed. Construction is expected to commence in mid-1970 on the dam at Wadi Zarqa, the largest of the Jordan Valley side wadis. Construction began on one of the two Yarmuk River dams in May 1966 but was halted by the June War, which left Israel in control of the opposite bank of the Yarmuk. Construction has not been resumed and probably must await the conclusion of a settlement. No construction has begun on the West Ghor Canal or the extension of the East Ghor Canal, and none is expected until work on the Yarmuk dams is renewed. Of the major Jordan Valley irrigation projects, only construction of the remaining East Bank side wadi dams is likely to be undertaken under present conditions.

262

The total cost of the Yarmuk project, including the East Ghor Canal, was estimated in 1955 at $170 million, of which $117 million was allocated to irrigation facilities and $53 million to power generation. This dwarfs the East Ghor Canal project, which cost only about $18 million. The complete Yarmuk project was expected to irrigate a total of 127,000 acres in the Jordan Valley. About four-fifths of the acreage was to be irrigated by gravity flow, the remainder by pumping.[62] The increase in annual value added as a result of the complete project—after a period sufficient to allow it to reach full potential—would be on the order of $42 million.[63] This figure implies an ICOR for the irrigation part of the project of 2.8, somewhat above that of the East Ghor Canal alone. The higher capital-output ratio of the whole Yarmuk project compared with the East Ghor Canal is not hard to understand: not only does the part of the Yarmuk project still to be undertaken require expensive dams and pumping stations, but also the new land to be irrigated is at a greater distance from the water source than is the East Ghor Canal area.

Available water supplies are adequate to provide as much water per acre to the Yarmuk project area as is now supplied to the East Ghor Canal area. The water required would substantially absorb all of Jordan's water share under the "Johnston Plan" of the mid-1950s, the plan for unified development of the Jordan River waters that came closest to acceptance by both Arab and Israeli sides in the long history of proposal and counterproposal in regard to Jordan River development. Thus, outside of the Yarmuk project, few irrigation possibilities remain. The FAO Mediterranean Development Project suggested in 1967 that it would be possible by 1970 to irrigate about 14,400 additional acres by underground water projects and 16,500 acres from streams south of the Jordan Valley.[64] Together with the additonal acreage to be irrigated by the Yarmuk project, this implies the possibility of adding 128,000 irrigated acres to the area irrigated in 1966. The AID estimates in Table 5-13 suggest a potential irrigable acreage of 143,000. For the country as a whole in 1966 about 74,000 acres were fully irrigated and another 12,000 partially irrigated.[65] The irrigation possibili-

---

[62] The original detailed plan for the Yarmuk project was drawn up by two American engineering firms and presented in an eight-volume report: *Yarmuk-Jordan Valley Project,* Master Plan Report, Michael Baker, Jr. Inc., Rochester, Pa., and Harza Engineering Co., Chicago, Ill., 1955. See Awwad, *Agricultural Production and Income,* Chap. II, for a brief summary of the Yarmuk project and a more detailed presentation of the East Ghor project.

[63] I reach this figure by assuming per acre value of output at full potential of the Yarmuk project to be equal to 150 percent of the 1965/66 per acre value of output in the East Ghor project area. I again assume indirect costs to be 20 percent of the value of output. This gives $386 value added per acre. I also subtracted out a rough estimate for the pre-project value of production in the area.

[64] FAO, *Jordan Country Report,* p. 148.

[65] *Ibid.,* p. 55. These should be taken as orders of magnitude, as statistics on irrigated acreage are not especially reliable.

Table 5-13

Capital Costs of Alternative Irrigation Projects[a]

(1966 U.S. dollars)

Project	Total Annual Capital Charge (thousands)[b] (1)	Total Irrigated Acres (2)	Annual Capital Cost per Acre[c] (3)
East Ghor Canal	1,500	30,000	50
Ghor Safi (E. Bank)	200	2,500	80
Jordan River (both banks)	500	8,000	63
Wadi Wala (E. Bank)	1,050	7,000	150
Groundwater (E. Bank)	200	3,500	57
Groundwater (W. Bank)	200	3,000	67
Groundwater (E. Bank highlands)	2,200	31,000	71
Yarmuk River (E. Bank)	11,800	59,000	200
Wadi Mujib (E. Bank)	1,100	5,000	220
Zerka River (E. Bank)	2,200	9,000	244
Small wadis (E. Bank)	3,400	10,000	340
Local supplies (W. Bank)	1,700	5,000	340

[a]The data for the East Ghor Canal are actual figures. The remainder are cost estimates of potential projects, provided by IESA/Engineering Section of the Agency for International Development, Washington, D.C.

[b]Annual capital charges are based on water generated and supply and distribution costs, with opportunity cost of capital of 8 percent over 50 years for supply costs and 8 percent and 20 years life for distribution costs.

[c]Column 1 divided by Column 2.

ties suggested here will almost exhaust the irrigation potential in Jordan. The new irrigation projects will be somewhat more costly per acre irrigated than the East Ghor Canal was, as Table 5-13 shows.[66]

Taking into account that part of Yarmuk project potential output already realized by the East Ghor Canal project in 1966 and assuming an irrigation po-

[66] I have presented only capital costs per acre, since I lack satisfactory information on revenues and operating costs per acre. It is a reasonable first approximation that these will be equal in the different projects and therefore that the capital costs will be the sole differentiating factor. All the projects listed in Table 5-13 have been found to qualify for investment on cost-benefit criteria.

264

tential of about 35,000 acres outside the Yarmuk project, I estimate the potential increase in annual value added from the extension of irrigation (including an increase in the value of output from the East Ghor, which had not reached its full potential in 1966) to be roughly $48 million.[67] However, a considerable amount of time is required for the construction of the projects and for the full development of the project area. Thus, the full $48 million increase in annual value added cannot by any means be achieved by 1980. On the assumption of a peace settlement in 1971 and full resumption of construction activities shortly thereafter, the construction of the Yarmuk project can be completed toward the latter part of my projection period, but full potential cannot be reached before 1985.

As a rough guess, I project that $20 million of the $48 million potential can be achieved by 1980 and the remaining $28 million increase by 1985. This implies that the extension of irrigation can by itself produce about a 1½ percent per year increase in annual agricultural value added over the 1966–1980 period, mostly concentrated in the later years. This increase accounts for about a third of the growth in agricultural value added forecast for the 1966–1980 period. The $28 million remaining increase in value added from irrigation forecast for 1980–1985 is quite large for such a short period and represents a substantial contribution toward a rapid growth rate in the period. By itself it implies a 3.25 percent annual growth rate in agricultural value added over the 1980–1985 period. Thus a fast growth in agricultural value added of, say, 7 percent between 1980 and 1985 may be possible. This will contribute to a reduction of Jordan's large food and balance of payments deficits in the postprojection period. On the other hand, after 1985 Jordan can expect little contribution to agricultural growth from irrigation projects.

I will not attempt to review all the administrative and policy issues facing the Jordan government in the important field of agriculture. An excellent and thorough discussion of the agriculture of Jordan in the immediate prewar period is provided by the FAO Mediterranean Development Project report cited previously.

Effective agricultural development policies have been hampered in the past by serious inadequacies in information regarding the agricultural sector. Statistics on livestock production and crop output are subjective and highly unreliable. Only recently have efforts been initiated to collect crop production data on the basis of sampling methods; although these are not yet fully satisfactory, they are clearly a step in the right direction.

The development of more reliable agricultural statistics should go hand in hand with the development of the Agricultural Economics Division of the Ministry of Agriculture, which has only just been begun. When this division becomes more effective, it can provide a valuable service in indicating the areas where agricultural research is most needed.

[67] I continue to assume value added of $386 per irrigated acre, as in footnote 63. I arbitrarily reduce this by 10 percent for the areas outside the Yarmuk project to account for existing production in the areas to be irrigated.

Until the establishment of a dryland farming project in 1962, sponsored by the FAO and the United Kingdom, dryland farming was a seriously neglected aspect of agricultural research. At present, one of the areas most in need of intensified research would appear to be the livestock sector. Statistics on herd size, slaughter numbers, and slaughter weight are quite poor, and an effort should be made to improve them. Studies are needed to determine the economics of different kinds of livestock and fodder production and to develop policies toward the grazing of forest land and the range. Studies of existing Bedouin settlement projects and the possibilities for more such projects would also have some value.

Government agricultural activities in the past have been particularly concentrated in project areas, mostly connected with irrigation projects. In particular, the East Ghor Canal project has involved an intensive effort in many aspects of agricultural development. It is the one area in Jordan where there has been land reform. Conclusions drawn from developments in the East Ghor Canal area could provide valuable information for determining policies on future irrigation projects, particularly the Yarmuk project, of which it is the first step. I believe this concentration of resources has been wise. The undertaking of wider programs would have spread the limited administrative and technical resources too thin. In the immediate future this approach will probably be continued, as agricultural development efforts are concentrated in the Yarmuk project. But the necessary administrative and research institutions must continue to develop as well.

Industry

About one-third of Jordan's rapid growth of value added in manufacturing between 1959 and 1966 is attributable to the establishment of petroleum refining and the expansion of cement production—two industries that are frequently important in the early stages of industrialization. Obviously, future manufacturing growth will have to occur along a broader front.

If we compare the importance of various manufacturing sectors in Jordan in 1966 with what is to be expected, on the average, from a country of Jordan's level of population, per capita income, and level of industrialization, one sector —food and beverages—stands out as especially underdeveloped in relative terms. The share of food and beverages value added is less than half that predicted by regression equations derived from data for a large number of countries.[68] This is partly because of the small share of agriculture in the Jordan economy. In addition, there is less need for preserving and canning fruits

[68] Equations used are from United Nations Department of Economic and Social Affairs, *A Study of Industrial Growth*, 1963, p. 7. I used the levels of per capita income, population, and relative degree of industrialization prevailing in 1966. The predicted share of food, beverages, and tobacco in manufacturing value added was 49.3 percent, compared with an actual figure for 1966 of 24.3 percent. Since the cigarette industry is quite well developed in Jordan and even produces for· export, the disparity is presumably due to food and beverages alone.

266

and vegetables because of the availability of fresh produce from Jordan and nearby countries over much of the year. Nonetheless, the disparity is so large that these factors are unlikely to account for all of it. There would appear to be room for considerable expansion in the processing of food and beverages, particularly in vegetable and fruit canning.[69]

In evaluating the long-run industrial prospects for a reunited Jordan, it is clearly not possible to specify the outlook for each industry or activity, present and potential. Enumeration of the industries in which Jordan possesses an actual or potential advantage because of natural endowments very quickly exhausts the list: phosphates, handicrafts for tourists, cement, foodstuffs, hides and skins, ceramics, and a few others.

Possibly the most pressing question concerning Jordan's prospects for industrial development in the long run is: What constraints are imposed by the small size of the domestic market and the severely limited natural endowment? In attempting to answer this question, we can make use of the fact that Jordan and Israel are strikingly similar, particularly with respect to natural resources and size. Both have small populations (2.0 million for Jordan and 2.7 million for Israel in 1966), sparse mineral resources, and rather similar agricultural resources. Their locations are, of course, similar, with Israel having better access to the west. Both have had rapid population growth, large import surpluses, heavy defense burdens, and unusually large service sectors. In terms of per capita income Jordan has been perhaps two decades behind Israel, assuming prevailing prewar growth rates.

In view of these similarities I believe that the development of industry in Israel can throw some light on the possible future pattern of industrial development in Jordan. This is not meant to be an invidious comparison of Israeli and Jordanian industrialization. Nor do I imply that Jordan must slavishly follow the pattern of her neighbor.

The most likely near-term pattern of industrial development in Jordan is one based on import substitution, much as characterized Israel's past industrial growth and that of many less developed countries. There appear to be definite limits to the pattern and extent of import-substituting industrialization, however, particularly if the natural resource endowment and the size of the domestic market are specified. The example of Israel indicates how relatively important industry can become, given a particular natural resource endowment and size of domestic market. Since factors other than market size and resource availabilities are important in industrialization (for example, entrepreneurial and managerial talent, technological knowledge, an educated and disciplined labor force), this

---

[69] According to FAO, *Jordan Country Report*, p. 88: "Vegetable and fruit canning is still a small and ailing industry. . . . The size of operation is not economical and modernization and more aggresive management, particularly in the marketing field, would be required for its expansion. The potential for the expansion of this industry is quite substantial as production of fruits and vegetables grows and seasonal surpluses increase."

does not guarantee that similar industrial development will take place in Jordan, but indicates only that Jordan's market size and natural resource limitations do not prevent such development. My conclusions will have to be modified to the degree that Israel has overinvested in highly protected industries. Although this has happened to some extent, the phenomenon does not appear to be large enough to have a significant effect on the sort of broad macro-economic examination I am conducting.

Jordan's industry will presumably have to develop much as Israel's has: producing primarily for the home market on the basis of imported raw materials. By the end of World War II industry had reached a fairly high level of development in the part of Palestine that became Israel. Manufacturing and mining in Israel constituted 21.7 percent of GDP at factor cost in 1952 and 24.2 percent in 1965. The employment share rose from 23.6 percent in 1951 and 28.2 percent in 1964. The fastest growing sectors in the period 1951/52–1962/63 were mining, diamond polishing, rubber and plastics, and transport equipment.[70] Industrial sectors in which Israel is especially highly developed in relation to Jordan are textiles, diamond polishing, rubber and plastics, metals, machinery, and transport equipment.[71] The diamond polishing industry, as well as several others, reflects special skills in the Israeli population and undoubtedly would not be an advantageous industry for Jordan. However, the high level of development of some of the other sectors in Israel does suggest areas in which long-run growth may be especially rapid in Jordan.

Exports of industrial products have been quite important as a percentage of total merchandise exports, which were divided approximately as follows: agricultural products, 25 percent; diamonds, 30 percent; and other industrial products, 45 percent.[72] Yet direct industrial exports were only 10.4 percent of output in mining and manufacturing in 1958; another 4.1 percent of industrial output went indirectly into exports. The importance of exports to the industrial sector was rising rapidly, and a large part of subsequent industrial growth went into exports.[73] Many less developed countries have experienced considerable diffi-

[70] Nadev Halevi and Ruth Klinov-Malul, *The Economic Development of Israel*, Praeger Special Studies in International Economics and Development, 1968, pp. 83, 108, 150.

[71] Share in total manufacturing value added (percent):

	Israel, 1962/63	Jordan, 1966
Textiles	11.5	5.2
Rubber and plastics	3.7	.3
Metals	9.2	6.7
Machinery	8.2	1.5
Transport equipment	6.9	2.9

Source: for Israel, *ibid.*, p. 108, recalculated to omit the mining sector from the denominator; for Jordan, *The National Accounts 1959–1967*, p. 34.

[72] Halevi and Klinov, *The Economic Development of Israel*, p. 150.

[73] Michael Bruno, *Interdependence, Resource Use and Structural Change in Israel*, Jerusalem, 1962, pp. 66, 82, 123–124.

268

culty in the promotion of exports of manufactured products. Yet even if there had been no direct or indirect exports from the mining and manufacturing sector in Israel, this would only have reduced the 1958 share of manufacturing and mining in GDP from 22.1 to 19.0 percent, which is still almost twice that of Jordan in 1965–1966.

My projections for 1980 imply a share of manufacturing and mining value added in GDP of 13.7 percent. Although this represents a noteworthy rise over the 1966 ratio of 9.5 percent, it hardly seems overambitious in view of the Israeli performance or the normal ratios for countries at the general level of population and per capita GNP projected for Jordan. In fact, the Israeli experience suggests that rapid industrial growth is possible in the post-1980 period as well. On the other hand, my projection that roughly 10 percent of manufacturing output will be directly exported in 1980 is, in the light of Israeli experience, quite optimistic. This optimism should be taken as an assumption of the study, rather than as a probable outcome. At this early stage of Jordanian industrial development, I have reason neither for optimism nor for pessimism about the prospects for industrial exports.

Although industry is considered mainly a sphere for private enterprise, the Jordanian government undertakes a wide variety of promotional and regulatory activities and exercises a powerful influence in the industrial sector. The most important government bodies dealing with industry are the Ministry of National Economy and the Industrial Development Bank. In addition, the Ministry of Finance participates in decisions on tariff protection and the investment of government funds in private industry, and the Jordan Development Board arranges for industry feasibility studies and other industrial promotion.

A 1955 industrial promotion law allows approved industrial establishments exemption from or reduction of various taxes. It is apparently quite easy to qualify for this assistance, as a great many applications have been accepted.

Other forms of promotion of industry have also been important for large industries. The government, through the JDB, finances feasibility studies of an industry, usually at no charge to investors. Sometimes the government will organize and promote a group to undertake a particular activity. To assist some of the larger projects in their formative stages, the government has purchased shares in the firms involved.[74] It was intended that the government should sell its shares when an activity had established itself, but this has never yet been done,

---

[74] As of the end of 1966 the government had investments totaling $4.3 million in the potash and phosphate companies and $2.5 million in manufacturing firms (cement, oil refinery, vegetable oil, confectionery, tannery, woolen textiles, paper, and pharmaceuticals). Only in the phosphate mining company did the government have a majority of the shares. The government also has large investments in hotels and the national airlines. See FAO, *Jordan Country Report,* p. 39. Direction of the firms is in the hands of private managers. The government appoints its own representatives in proportion to its shareholdings and does not participate in the election of other representatives.

despite the obvious economic success of some of the industries in which the government owns shares. Recently, political uncertainty has been cited as the major obstacle to government divestment of shares in certain industries, but opposition by influential stockholders fearing a fall in the value of their shares has probably been a more effective obstacle.

Certain major industries—the petroleum refinery, the tannery, the cement company, and possibly some others—enjoy concessions guaranteeing them against all competition by means of prohibitions on imports and on the establishment of competing firms.[75] The government fixes the prices of such protected manufactures and generally levies a sizable excise tax on the product. The Ministry of National Economy licenses the establishment of new firms and sometimes prevents new firms from entering an industry in which a firm already is producing, although that firm may not have a concession guaranteeing it against competition, on the grounds that the market cannot support an additional firm.

Most frequently, firms are protected by tariffs, rather than quotas or outright prohibitions. The size of the tariff varies and is apparently determined ad hoc. It is sometimes so high as to be virtually prohibitive.

Because of its small size, Jordan will always confront the problem that certain industries that would be competitive in many other countries and could be left to the workings of the market will have to be regulated as natural monopolies.[76] Other industries, although not natural monopolies, will require assistance and, at least for a time, protection. It would appear on the basis of fragmentary information that there is considerable room for improvement in the means by which the Jordan government carries out these policies.

Decisions by the Ministry of National Economy are taken on an unsystematic basis, often with a minimum of hard information. Different industries may receive very different degrees of protection and assistance. This situation lends itself to political influence, especially since a decision to protect and assist an industry is in fact a decision to aid a particular investor or group of investors.

Corruption, in the sense of exchanging political favors for payment, is not unknown in Jordan but probably is no more serious there than elsewhere. Simple exchange of favors is a more serious problem. Jordan does not have a strong, independent civil service. Delegation of authority is uncommon, so that power tends to be concentrated in the Council of Ministers. Although ministries may change hands frequently, they rotate among a rather small circle of influential families, often possessing various business interests. Even the most scrupulous and energetic of ministers finds it difficult to resist the political presures for excessive government protection and assistance when he has very little information and no clear decision criteria with which to defend a negative position.

---

[75] These are long-term concessions—the tannery's for 40 years, the cement company's for 50.

[76] This may simply involve setting the tariff rate on competing imports. This is not precisely equivalent to the price fixing characteristic of public utility regulation, but the policy questions are quite similar in the two cases.

Aside from the possibilities for unjust enrichment, there is danger that because of the political influence on industrial promotion Jordan may develop an inefficient, uncompetitive industry capable of flourishing only behind heavy protection and government-enforced monopoly. To reduce this danger, a number of suggestions should at least be investigated. First, the use of quotas or outright prohibition of imports should be ended and tariffs substituted wherever possible. Second, the excessive granting of monopolies, either de jure in formal concessions or de facto by simply denying investment licenses to potential competitors, should be curtailed. And if monopoly concessions must be granted, it hardly seems necessary to grant them for such long periods. Third, it may be desirable to adopt a systematic approach to tariff protection, rather than to consider cases individually. There is much to be said for a policy of equal ad valorem rates on as wide a range of industrial goods as possible. The exact policy is less important than the establishment of some reasonable criterion not subject to political manipulation in each individual case.

The Jordan government makes credit available to industry and tourism by means of the Industrial Development Bank, established in 1965 as successor to the Industrial Development Fund. The Bank is a semiautonomous agency with both government and private participation in its capital. It generally makes quite large loans. With the resumption of industrial development it should widen its activities and attempt to expand into smaller loans, for which there is believed to be considerable unsatisfied demand.

Although labor unions exist in Jordan, they are not powerful since they virtually lack the right to strike. A labor law regulating hours of work and compensation for injury exists but applies only to firms of five or more employees, which firms constitute a large share of industrial value added and a much smaller share of the industrial labor force. However, the government has not been able to enforce strict compliance with the law.[77]

There are four industrial secondary schools run by the government, three UNRWA vocational training centers, and eight private vocational training centers in Jordan. These supply only a small fraction of the middle-level skilled labor force. A recent study concludes that, although secondary industrial schools are very expensive per student compared with general secondary schools, the graduates of industrial schools are only slightly, if at all, preferred by employers over general school graduates and that the job-specific parts of the training of industrial graduates are frequently unutilized when they are employed. Most job-specific training takes place within the employing establishment in Jordan. The study suggests that the educational system concentrate on providing generally educated and readily trainable, rather than specifically trained, graduates.[78]

[77] FAO, *Jordan Country Report,* pp. 38, 40.
[78] Najati Mohammed Amin al-Bukhari, *Issues in Occupational Education and Training: A Case Study in Jordan,* Stanford International Development Education Center, Stanford University, 1968.

Table 5-14

Growth Rates and Share in GNP of Savings, Investment, Foreign Aid, and Related Items[a]
(percent)

	Average Annual Growth Rate, 1959/60- 1965/66[b]	Share in GNP Average, 1959-62	Average, 1963-66
1. Gross national product	10.0	100.0	100.0
2. Private disposable income	9.0	86.5	85.2
3. Private consumption	8.5	79.5	77.5
4. Private savings	19.0	7.0	7.7
5. Government domestic revenue	13.0	13.5	14.7
6. Government consumption	6.0	22.9	20.7
7. Government defense expenditures	3.5	13.6	10.9
8. Government nondefense expenditures	10.5	9.3	9.8
9. Government dis-savings	−6.0	9.4	6.0
10. Gross domestic investment	10.5	14.4	14.6
11. Foreign aid	−1.0	16.9	12.7

[a]Underlying data, in current prices, are from *The National Accounts 1959-1967*. The definition of savings and foreign aid used here are identical to those used in Table 5-5. As in Table 5-5, current transfers to government from abroad are counted as foreign aid, but current transfers to households from abroad are not.

To be consistent with the concept of foreign aid used here, the concept of GNP in row 1 is not that of the national accounts. To GNP I have added "current transfers to households from abroad." In effect, I treat current transfers to households from abroad as if they were factor income from abroad. This approach does not affect the general character of the results, however, and it establishes a number of equalities. For each group of years the following equalities hold:

```
Row  Row  Row
 1 =  2  +  5
 2 =  3  +  4
 5 =  6  −  9
 6 =  7  +  8
10 =  4  −  9 + 11
```

Deviations from these equalities are attributable to rounding error and to certain minor inconsistencies in the data.

[b]All growth rates are annual rates annually compounded and rounded to the nearest half percentage point.

The Availability of Capital

As noted previously (Table 5-3), Jordan during the prewar years had been increasing the relative importance of domestic savings and reducing its relative dependence on foreign aid for the financing of domestic investment. Table 5-14

272

gives some idea of the various developments contributing to this result. Both an increase in private savings and a decrease in public dis-savings were important in the growth of domestic saving, but the latter made a somewhat larger contribution.

Private consumption fell from 79.5 percent of GNP for 1959–1962 to 77.5 percent for 1963–1966. Of this 2 percentage point decline, about 1.2 is due to a decrease in the share of private disposable income in GNP and 0.8 is attributable to a fall in the average share of private consumption in private disposable income. However, the decline in the share of private consumption should not obscure the fact that private consumption in current prices grew at an average annual rate of 8.5 percent over the 1959–1966 period. With 3 percent per annum population growth and possibly 1–2 percent inflation per year, this implies a rise in real per capita consumption of about 4 percent a year—a rapid rate of increase.

Gross private savings averaged 8.6 percent of private disposable income for the 1959–1966 period. There was a slight rise in the ratio from 8.1 percent for 1959–1962 to 9.0 percent for 1963–1966. However, the year-to-year variations are sufficiently large (the ratio ranges from 3.0 percent in 1959 to 13.6 percent in 1964) that I cannot place much confidence in observed trends in savings.

I have previously noted that in comparison with other countries private savings per capita in Jordan are low, given the level of private disposable income per capita. This may seem rather surprising, particularly since there are a number of reasons why savings should be relatively high in Jordan. The country's high GNP growth rate should produce a high personal saving rate, according to the permanent income or life-cycle theories of consumption. A relatively small proportion of GDP is paid as compensation to employees in Jordan. Since savings rates out of wage income can be expected to be lower than those out of property and entrepreneurial income, this should result in higher personal savings rates in Jordan.

One possible explanation of Jordan's relatively low savings lies in the unsettled political situation prevailing throughout the country's existence. We expect political uncertainty to affect private investment, rather than private saving, but in a less developed country the savings and investment decisions are much more closely linked than in a developed country such as the United States. Another possible explanation is that Jordan's liberal import system may not have stimulated private saving as much as a system in which foreign travel and many imports, particularly luxury goods, are sharply restricted.

A third possible cause of the apparently low private savings rate is the relatively high level of private investment in education in Jordan. Throughout the world national income account estimates of savings and investment include only savings for and investment in physical assets. Money spent on education is invariably counted as consumption, and earnings forgone by the student are not counted at all. Yet only a part of the resources devoted to education is in fact

273

consumption; the remaining part (of unknown, but doubtless not insignificant, size) is investment. If private investment is concentrated in education to a greater extent in one country than in another, its private savings as recorded in the national accounts will be unusually low, even if the true saving rate is normal. This appears to be the case for Jordan. For a less developed country, enrollment rates in Jordan are quite high. Furthermore, a relatively large share of Jordanian investment in education is financed privately, rather than by the government. Below the university level, UNRWA and private schools are relatively quite important.[79] At the university level most students have studied abroad at their own or their families' expense.

Because of the reasons just cited for the low private savings rate observed in the Jordanian statistics, I believe there is reason to expect a rise in the private savings rate as normally defined, but I do not expect the rise to proceed all the way to the level characteristic of the average less developed country. The conclusion of a durable peace, an assumption of this study, should increase investor confidence and, to the degree that saving is undertaken as part of the investment decision, private savings as well. Some increase in tariff barriers is likely to accompany import-substituting industrialization, and this may cause some increase in savings if people reduce expenditures on high-price protected consumption goods in favor of saving. Private investment in education is likely to remain high in comparison to other countries, but its relative importance in Jordan's economy will probably decline somewhat as government schools take over from private and especially UNRWA schools (assuming a settlement that ends the refugee problem in a reasonably short time) and as government expenditures on the newly established Jordan University rise. Because of the high enrollments already achieved, Jordan may not in the future be able to increase the average level of schooling as rapidly as the average less developed country, which starts from a lower base.

In view of the above considerations I have projected a rise in the ratio of gross private savings to gross private disposable income by 1980 that increases the Jordanian saving rate from about 60–65 to about 80–85 percent of normal. The savings rate is projected to rise from 8.6 percent in 1965/66 to 12.0 percent in 1980. Of these 3.4 percentage points about 0.5 percentage point is due to

[79] In the 1957–1958 academic year about 33 percent of students below the university level in Jordan were in private or UNRWA schools. By 1966–1967 this had fallen slightly to 31 percent: Jordan Ministry of Education, *Yearbook of Educational Statistics in the Hashemite Kingdom of Jordan for the Year 1966–1967*, Amman, pp. 34–35. Although UNRWA educational expenditure requires no private saving, the Jordanian national accounts include it as part of private disposable income and private consumption. If we consider education to be investment, UNRWA educational expenditures will cause the recorded ratio of private consumption to private disposable income to be higher than the "actual" (counting education as investment) ratio.

274

the rise in per capita disposable income, the remainder to reduction of the disparity between the Jordanian and average rates.[80]

Table 5-14 makes clear the important contribution made by reductions in defense expenditures to the prewar increase in the relative importance of domestically generated savings. The forecast of a substantial reduction in dependence on foreign aid by 1970, made in the seven-year plan for 1964–1970, was very much dependent on a relative reduction in the defense burden. The plan forecast no increase in the absolute level of defense expenditures over the 1963 level, implying a fall in the ratio of defense expenditures to GNP from 13.5 percent in 1963 to 8.2 percent in 1970. The projected reductions for the 1963–1966 period were achieved in relative (to GNP) terms, but not in absolute terms. Since the June War military expenditures have, of course, soared.

From these considerations it seems reasonable to conclude that only if Jordan achieves a substantial reduction in the relative burden of defense expenditures will it be able to attain independence of foreign aid as a source of capital while maintaining a reasonably high and sustained rate of growth. My projections in Table 5-10 imply a major decline in the relative importance of defense expenditures in GNP by 1980 to only 5 percent of GNP. That ratio I take to be normal for a country not in serious conflict with its neighbors.[81] (My assumption of full settlement with Israel in 1971 is critical to this result, of course.) In view of the large military buildup since 1967 this projection is a fairly optimistic one. If it is attained, the concomitant reduction in military employment may result in a serious rise in unemployment. The potential problem will have to be given serious consideration, but in view of the prewar performance of the Jordan economy it does not appear to be insoluble. Work on the construction of the Yarmuk project during the 1970s should absorb a relatively large amount of unskilled and semiskilled labor.

Although past defense expenditures have been quite large, they have not placed a real burden on the economy, since foreign aid inflows have permitted a reasonably high level of investment and a rapid growth rate. Per capita consumption grew rapidly during the prewar period. Nor does it seem likely that shortage of capital has reduced the investment rate, in view of substantial increases in Jordan's holdings of foreign assets. Much the greater part of foreign aid to Jordan has taken the form of grants or loans at generous terms, so that Jordan is not burdened with a large foreign debt or heavy debt-service charges. All these considerations carry over into the postwar period, in which sizable increases in defense expenditures have been more than matched by increased foreign aid from grants by oil-rich Arab countries.

[80] Arrived at by applying the 1966 and projected 1980 levels of per capita disposable income to the regression of Houthakker, mentioned in footnote 7.

[81] For a very small sample of less developed countries the average ratio of defense expenditures to GNP is about 3–5 percent. See Simon Kuznets, "Quantitative Aspects of the Economic Growth of Nations: VII. The Share and Structure of Consumption," *Economic Growth and Cultural Change,* Vol. X, No. 2, Part II (January 1962), p. 8.

The share of government nondefense expenditure in GNP is a little above average for Jordan's level of per capita income. We might expect government expenditure on education to be relatively high because of the high proportion of children in the population and the relatively high enrollment ratios, but this is not the case because UNRWA and private schools enroll a sizable portion of the school population. Government nondefense expenditure rose slightly faster than GNP over the 1959–1966 period, suggesting an income elasticity slightly greater than 1, a conclusion supported by evidence for other countries. My projections for 1975 and 1980 imply unitary income elasticity of government nondefense expenditures. This represents an optimistically low forecast, particularly in view of the possibility that government educational and health services may have to expand as UNRWA operations are reduced or eliminated after a settlement.

Government current domestic revenue was 15 percent of GNP for the 1959–1966 period, about average for a country of Jordan's per capita income. However, Jordan was an exceptionally open economy, with imports plus exports amounting to about 50 percent of GNP in the early 1960s. Among underdeveloped countries the governments of open economies are generally able to raise a higher share of GNP in taxes than are those of more closed economies, largely because of the administrative ease of taxing foreign trade. When the effect of the openness of Jordan's economy is taken into account, we find that the country's "tax effort" was markedly below average. Because of Jordan's relatively liberal import system and several other factors, the pattern of government revenue resembled that of a developing country with only average openness.[82]

This suggests the possibility of increased revenue from the taxation of international trade, and indeed increases in such taxation had much to do with the rise in government current domestic revenue from 14.5 percent of GNP in 1963/64 to 17.1 percent in 1965/66.[83] The most rapid growth of imports in the future is expected to be in intermediate and capital goods, which are generally either lightly taxed or exempted from customs taxes. Imports of nonagricultural consumer goods, on which customs taxes are highest, are projected (Table 5-10) to grow at a significantly slower rate than GNP. Without a rise in tax rates we would expect the share of customs revenues in GNP to fall slightly between 1966 and 1980. Some rise in customs tax rates is possible and—in view of large rate increases since 1967 and a likely policy of import-substituting indus-

[82] Comparisons with "average" or "normal" countries in this paragraph utilize the following studies: Kuznets, "Quantitative Aspects of the Economic Growth of Nations: VII"; Jorgen R. Lotz and Elliott R. Morss, "Measuring 'Tax Effort' of Developing Countries," *IMF Staff Papers*, Vol. XIV, No. 3 (November 1967); Harley H. Hinrichs, *A General Theory of Tax Structure Change During Economic Development,* Harvard University Law School, Cambridge, Mass., 1966.

[83] Of the increase in the ratio of 2.6 percentage points between 1963–1964 and 1965–1966, about 1.2 points were due to an increase in the rate of tariffs on imports. That rise is due to an across-the-board increase of 3 percent ad valorem on all goods subject to tax.

trialization—probable. However, the ease of smuggling from such low-tariff countries as Kuwait and Saudi Arabia imposes a practical limit to increases in tariff rates. Altogether, an increase of 1 or 2 percentage points in the ratio of customs revenue to GNP is the most that can be expected.[84] As for other indirect taxes, the institution of a value-added or sales tax, as proposed in the seven-year plan, and substantial increases in excise tax rates appear possible and together could contribute an additional 1 percent of GNP to government revenue.[85]

Direct taxation presents substantial possibilities for increasing government revenue. Direct taxes were equal to only 1.6 percent of GNP over the 1959–1966 period, a very low ratio when compared with an average figure for developing countries of about 5 percent.[86] The income tax provided less than 10 percent of government current domestic revenues. According to a study by Tukan, this low revenue level could be significantly raised by reforms in the income tax and agricultural land taxation and by reduction of income tax evasion. These changes could increase government revenue by approximately 1½ percent of GNP.[87]

Combining these figures in an optimistic forecast, I think it possible that a number of reasonable tax reforms and rate increases, combined with substantial reduction of tax evasion, could increase government revenue by about 3 percent of GNP. Since government current domestic revenue was roughly unit-elastic with respect to GNP under the prevailing system and rates, no increase in the share of government revenue in GNP could be expected from increases in GNP alone.[88] Thus an optimistic projection suggests that over a reasonably short pe-

[84] A not-insignificant share of Jordan's customs revenue is earmarked for particular uses, including airports, Jordan University, and a sports stadium. This practice merits reconsideration.

[85] The plan (p. 35) set 1967 as the date to begin a turnover or sales tax, but as of 1969 it was not in existence. Tukan suggested that substantial rises in excise taxes on cigarettes and wine could take place without raising prices of the goods above those in neighboring countries. Abdul R. S. Tukan, "The Implications of Achieving Fiscal Independence for Jordan," unpublished Ph.D. dissertation, Vanderbilt University, Nashville, Tenn., 1967, pp. 136–137.

[86] Averages from Kuznets, "Quantitative Aspects of the Economic Growth of Nations: VII," p. 8.

[87] Tukan, "The Implications of Achieving Fiscal Independence for Jordan," pp. 130–134. His proposed income tax changes are (1) elimination of the exemption of capital gains and dividends from personal income taxation, (2) an increase in the maximum marginal rate from 50 to 60 percent, and (3) elimination of the deduction of land and building tax liability from income tax liability. He estimates that the almost complete elimination of evasion could produce 1.6 percent of GNP. Complete elimination of evasion is simply impossible, but another 0.5 percent of GNP from better income tax administration certainly seems possible.

[88] Tukan ("The Implications of Achieving Fiscal Independence for Jordan," p. 101) projects government current domestic revenue from 1964 to 1970 on assumption of

riod (something on the order of 5 years, if all the suggested changes were implemented rapidly), government current domestic revenue could be increased to 20 percent of GNP. But for the June 1967 War, this rise might have been achieved within the time span of the 1964–1970 plan. In Table 5-10 I have projected this ratio to be achieved by 1980.

VI. Conclusion

The June 1967 War interrupted a period of sustained and remarkably rapid economic growth in Jordan. Although Jordan had received large amounts of aid per capita throughout the prewar period, these payments largely offset an unusually heavy defense burden and were not the sole cause of the rapid growth. Much of the growth was due to especially productive use of available resources, as indicated by the low level of the historical incremental capital-output ratio or the large "residual growth factor." On the quite pragmatic grounds that one does not bet against past success without good cause, I have projected the resumption of a rapid rate of growth in the event of a mutually acceptable peace settlement. However, the pattern of future development of the Jordanian economy will necessarily be different from what prevailed up to 1967. For this reason past performance is a less reliable guide to the future than would otherwise be the case. In particular, industry, which in the prewar years expanded from a small base mainly by seizing certain readily perceptible import substitution opportunities, will in the future require development of a wider range of more complex activities.

In the immediate prewar years economic growth and employment abroad were gradually reducing unemployment, but they do not appear to have eliminated it by early 1967. I have not attempted to distinguish the employment situation among the refugees of 1948/49 from that for the rest of the population, but there is no doubt that the refugees shared in the general growth of employment. On the other hand, it is not unlikely that rates of unemployment and underemployment were higher among the refugees than for the remainder of the population. Future economic growth can be expected to reduce overall employment only very slowly, if at all.

One major unexploited irrigation opportunity, the Yarmuk project, exists in Jordan. This could make a sizable contribution to growth in the agricultural sector over about a 10-year period. But Jordan will have to rely more and more on complex technological and economic changes for an increased yield of agricultural products. Even with fairly optimistic projections of future growth in agri-

---

the fulfillment of the 1964–1970 plan. The ratio of his projected revenue to GNP as projected in the plan remains constant over the period. For some revenue sources he is unable to separate out the effect of changes in rates in estimating the regressions from which the projections are made. The effect of this on the calculation of overall elasticity is unlikely to be large, however.

culture, most of the increase in agricultural output will be absorbed by higher domestic consumption. Jordan cannot expect to earn foreign exchange as a net exporter of foodstuffs. Agriculture will never be as important in Jordan as in most less developed countries; the natural resource base simply is not there.

Although not claiming much certainty for my projections, I have suggested that a shortage of foreign exchange is likely to be the most serious bottleneck to future long-term economic development. The importance and unpredictability of tourism earnings render this conclusion particularly uncertain. In relation to the size of its population and its economy, Jordan's endowment of resources for tourism is undoubtedly very great and had not been fully exploited up to June 1967. If the most optimistic yet plausible assumptions about the growth in tourist demand are realized, foreign exchange availability will not represent an effective constraint upon Jordan's future economic development. On the most pessimistic plausible assumptions, Jordan will be forced to rely upon large foreign aid payments for an indefinitely long period or to endure economic growth at a very slow pace.

CHAPTER 6

Economic Development of Iraq

Albert Y. Badre*

* I wish to express gratitude to John Murray of Economist Intelligence Unit, Ltd., who read the manuscript and offered very valuable suggestions. Of course, I am responsible for any errors of fact or judgment.

Iraq is oil-rich. So far, oil resources have been sufficient for the economy to maintain a reasonable rate of economic progress. Badre's essay is essentially a discussion of whether this situation can continue in the future. His conclusion is tempered.

Oil revenues will continue to keep the Iraqi balance of payments healthy and to provide resources needed for deepening the country's capital stock. What is at issue is whether these resources can be combined with effective policies to promote rapid and substantial expansion in both industry and agriculture. Badre finds the critical issue to lie in improving the quality of the labor force. The level of literacy is low, labor force skills are minimal, the population is young and growing rapidly. At the same time, the public sector is playing an increasingly important leading role, and the quality of its labor force has become of crucial significance.

One factor that is new, and basically hopeful, is the postwar commitment to development. As oil revenues decline relatively, this commitment must be made effective by raising savings rates and avoiding politically popular but economically unjustified public expenditures. Should the future bring a greater degree of political stability than has been seen in the past, these requirements may prove more tractable than they have to date.

Economic Development of Iraq

I. Perspectives

Iraq is a country of great potential with wide expanses of fertile land and, in its two great rivers, both irrigation and a valuable source of electric energy. Its well-developed petroleum industry has poured more than ID 1.5 billion (over $4 billion) into the public treasury from the commencement of production in 1931 to the late 1960s.[1] Its petroleum exports have not only provided it with a reliable source of development finance but have also assured it of a substantial and continuous flow of foreign exchange, thus sparing it the problems of inflation and balance of payments with which many a developing country has to contend. For almost two decades, the ruling governments have assumed responsibility for developing the resources of the country toward a rapid attainment of its economic potential. It is the purpose of the present study to show the past performance of the economy, particularly in the last two decades, to assess its future prospects, and to point out major problems that it may have to face in the realization of these prospects.

Viewed in long-term historic perspective, the prosperity of Iraq has depended largely on the abilities of its rulers to exploit the water flow from the Tigris-Euphrates system in such a way as to irrigate the alluvial soils of the valley and the plain. This is still a basic requirement for development. In recent years, however, the impetus for development and the performance of the economy have been strongly linked to petroleum. Apart from the post-World War II general awakening to the necessity of rapid economic development, which it shares with many a less developed country, Iraq has evolved a special sense of urgency attributable to the growth of its oil industry.

Development Planning

From the early 1930s, when oil revenue began to flow into the public coffer, there was a general realization that oil was a vanishing resource. At hardly any time was there an expectation of a continued flow of oil beyond half a century

---

[1] Zuhayr Mikdashi, *A Financial Analysis of Middle Eastern Oil Concessions, 1901–65,* Frederick A. Praeger, New York, 1966, pp. 106, 196; United Nations, *Yearbook of International Trade Statistics, 1966,* New York, 1968, p. 384.

into the future.[2] In consequence, the feeling developed that it was incumbent upon those in authority to prevent the wasteful dissipation of this windfall by promoting and implementing a development policy that would turn the current yield into a continuing future productive capacity in other economic activities. This has been the declared goal of all governments for over a third of a century and continues to be the basic guideline of development.

In the period before World War II, however, the use of the oil revenue did not attract as much public notice and hence did not give rise to as much dissension and controversy as it did in the postwar years. In those early years, of course, oil revenue was not of a magnitude to warrant much public notice. After the Iraq Petroleum Company (IPC) had been incorporated and had taken over an expanded concession of the earlier Turkish Oil Company in 1931,[3] the oil revenue accruing to the Iraqi government was only 400,000 dinars ($1.9 million). Since the first field of Iraqi oil, near Kirkuk in the north of the country, was land-locked, the expansion of production was strictly constrained by the development of transportation facilities. It was not until 1934 that the first pipeline to the Mediterranean was completed.[4] Before that, government oil revenue had mounted very slowly to 700,000 dinars ($2.8 million) for 1933. In 1935, with the terminals at Tripoli and Haifa in operation, oil revenue jumped up to ID 1.5 million ($6 million). No further substantial increase was encountered until

[2] Of course, estimates of existing reserves have been continuously stepped up, but so have rates of extraction, leaving the exhaustion date at a relatively invariant distance. At the end of 1968, the published proved reserves had gone up to 28 billion barrels, and annual production amounted to some 540 million barrels during the same year, indicating that the resource would still be exhausted in a little over 50 years, in the absence of new discoveries. (The 1968 figures were taken from *Oil and Gas Journal,* December 30, 1968, p. 102.)

[3] For the early history of oil concessions in Iraq see Benjamin Shwadran, *Middle East Oil and the Great Powers,* Frederick A. Praeger, New York, 1955, pp. 244–264; and Stephen H. Longrigg, *Oil in the Middle East,* 3rd ed., Oxford University Press, London, 1968, pp. 66–83.

[4] The first pipelines completed in 1934 were two 12-inch lines which ran together from Kirkuk about 150 miles west and then bifurcated, the northern line going through Syria and Lebanon to Tripoli, a total distance of 532 miles; and the southern line through the then Trans-Jordan and Palestine for a total length of 620 miles to Haifa, where the Iraq Petroleum Company established a refinery in 1939. After World War II the company started two other lines of 16-inch diameter. The southern line was stopped in Jordan when Haifa became a port of the state of Israel in 1948. The northern line was completed to Tripoli in 1951, carrying 6 million tons a year and thus tripling the capacity of the throughput. A little over a year later a single 30/32-inch line 555 miles long, with an annual capacity of 14 million tons, was completed to Banias in Syria. Two more 30/32-inch lines, running from Kirkuk to Tripoli and Banias, were completed in 1961, bringing total throughput capacity up to 48 million tons a year. (For a more detailed account of the pipelines see Longrigg, *Oil in the Middle East,* pp. 76–77, 179–182, 360–361.)

1950. In fact, the average annual oil revenue of the government for the first 19 years of IPC operations, 1931–1949, was only ID 1.76 million.[5] Royalty during this period was assessed as a specific tax on volume of production at the rate of 4 shillings a ton.[6]

The year 1951 marked a new era in Iraq, both in oil revenue and in development policy. Two events in the region led to a major alteration in the concessions of the IPC and its two subsidiaries, the Basra and Mosul oil companies. On December 30, 1950, the Saudi government agreed with Aramco on a 50 percent profit-sharing basis,[7] and in April 1951 the Iranian government nationalized its oil industry.[8] These events occurred while the Iraq government and IPC were locked in a dispute over the gold evaluation of the shilling. The Iraqi bargaining position was radically altered by these events, and the press and public opinion grew increasingly hostile to IPC. In August 1951 the government announced that it had reached an agreement with the company to share profits on a fifty-fifty basis.[9]

Government oil revenue had reached ID 3.1 million in 1949. It went up to ID 6.8 million in 1950, and then soared after the new agreement to ID 15.2 million in 1951 and ID 40.7 million in 1952. Except for a brief decline in 1956 and 1957 caused by the blocking of the pipeline in Syria as a result of the Suez conflict, the revenue continued to increase substantially, reaching a level of ID 141 million ($394 million) in 1966. In 1967, however, there was a decline in revenue to ID 131.7 million, owing to a pipeline dispute between the IPC and the

---

[5] Mikdashi, *A Financial Analysis of Middle Eastern Oil Concessions, 1901–65*, p. 100.

[6] The agreement reached in 1931 between the Iraq Petroleum Company and the Iraq government stipulated an annual rent of £200,000 (gold) and a royalty set at 4 shillings (gold) for a minimum production of 2 million tons a year for the first 20 years of the concession. (See Longrigg, *Oil in the Middle East*, p. 74.)

[7] Shwadran, *Middle East Oil and the Great Powers*, p. 106.

[8] *Ibid.*, p. 107.

[9] The agreement, which was ratified by the Iraq Parliament in February of 1952, provided an equal division of profits on crude production, calculated at seaboard value, between the government and the three companies. The government share was to be viewed as income tax. The government could choose to take part of its levy in kind, up to 12.5 percent of total crude produced for export. It could dispose of this share itself or resell it to the companies at the same valuation used for tax purposes. State income was not to drop below 25 percent of the seaboard value of the oil exports of the Iraq and Mosul Petroleum Companies, and 33 percent of the Basrah Petroleum Company. Subject to *force majeure,* the volume of production was to be maintained above a certain minimum; the MPC and IPC were to produce together a minimum of 22 million tons a year from 1954, and the BPC a minimum of 8 million tons from the end of 1955. The minimum revenue to be expected by the government from this agreement was £30 million in 1953 and 1954, and £50 million in 1955 and thereafter. (See Longrigg, *Oil in the Middle East,* p. 191.)

government of Syria and also to the Six-Day War. But in 1968 the revenue picked up again, reaching a new height of ID 203 million.[10]

As early as 1950, and in anticipation of increased oil revenues, the Iraq government established a Development Board which was to receive the total revenue from oil to be spent directly on development projects. Underlying this policy was the government desire to allay fears, increasingly voiced in the press, that this great windfall will be dissipated through useless expenditures by the various government departments and pilfered through political favoritism and misappropriation of funds. To give further assurance that the expenditure of oil revenue would be outside the political arena, the Board was to be composed of six nonpolitical members, including some foreign experts, appointed on the basis of technical and executive competence. In order that it have the required prestige and executive power, it was placed directly under the chairmanship of the Prime Minister, with the Minister of Finance as an ex officio member.[11]

The Development Board was charged with the threefold task of preparing a general plan for developing the resources of the country, undertaking the execution of projects, and turning over the completed projects to the ministries concerned for administration and maintenance. Under great pressure to start operation, it produced a hurried five-year plan for the period 1951/52–1955/56, anticipating a revenue of ID 951 million on the basis of royalties at the rate of 6 shillings (gold) per ton of crude oil, and estimating expenditures at ID 65.7 million, of which 70 percent was earmarked for water and transportation projects.[12]

The plan was enacted into law in 1951, but before implementation got underway it had to be revised because of new developments. The base of the government share altered from a specific tax on output to a 50 percent share in profit, considerably augmenting the expected revenue. Furthermore, sensing the need for a more adequate study of the economy, the government had requested the International Bank for Reconstruction and Development to survey the country's resources and make recommendations for a development program. The report of the Bank Mission was submitted early in 1952.[13] At about the same time, pressure from several government departments and various political groups led to an amendment of the law whereby the allocation to the Development Board was to be reduced to 70 percent of the oil revenue, leaving 30 percent to be disposed of through the general budget.[14]

---

[10] United Nations, *Yearbook of International Trade Statistics, 1966*, p. 384. Also, Central Bank of Iraq, Bulletin (in Arabic), October-December, 1967; and *World Petroleum Report*, Vol. XV (1969), p. 86.

[11] Government of Iraq, *Law No. 23 for 1950*.

[12] *Law No. 35 for 1951*.

[13] International Bank for Reconstruction and Development, *The Economic Development of Iraq*, The Johns Hopkins Press, Baltimore, 1952.

[14] *Law No. 25 for 1952*.

On the basis of these changes, and guided by the findings of the Bank Mission, the Development Board replaced the first five-year plan by a new six-year plan covering the period 1951/52–1956/57. This second plan was enacted into law in 1952 and provided for revenues of ID 168.7 million and expenditures of ID 155.4 million. The projected share for waterworks and transportation continued to figure very high, amounting to a full two-thirds of total expenditures.[15]

While the second six-year plan was being implemented, criticism of the administrative structure of the Development Board was intensifying. Several ministers were unhappy with the Board's bypassing the Council of Ministers and reporting directly to the Prime Minister, charging that such procedure would undermine the authority of the Council and would lead to duplication in the discharge of the executive function of the government. The outcome was the creation of a Ministry of Development in 1953, to be represented in the Council of Ministers by a Minister of Development and to undertake the execution of the projects approved by the Board. The Prime Minister continued to act as chairman of the Board with the Ministers of Development and Finance as ex officio members.[16]

With the modified structure of the development machinery, the development program was once more revised and a new five-year plan covering the period 1955/56–1959/60 was prepared and enacted into law in 1955. Once more, both revenues and expenditures were revised upward, the former projected at ID 215.7 million and the latter at ID 304 million. But almost a year later this plan was replaced by still another, based on a new projection of higher oil revenues and influenced by fresh studies of the economy conducted by a British expert. The fourth plan, which was enacted into law in 1956, covered the six-year period 1955/56–1960/61 and provided for an expenditure of ID 500 million and a revenue of ID 390 million.[17] This was the plan in force when the revolution occurred in 1958.

The new regime at once abolished the Development Board, which by that time had become the object of widespread criticism. The Ministry of Development was charged with the implementation of the existing plan, and a Ministerial Committee was set up for the purpose. The Committee decided to continue the implementation of certain projects already underway and to hold off on others until a new development machinery was established. The following year the Ministry of Development was replaced by a new Ministry of Planning and an Economic Planning Council composed of the ministers whose ministries are involved in the development program, and headed by the Prime Minister. Only 50 percent of the oil revenue was to be used for financing development.

Soon after the establishment of this new machinery, the Provisional Economic Plan was adopted on January 15, 1960, for the four-year period

[15] *Law No. 25 for 1952.*
[16] *Law No. 35 for 1953.*
[17] *Law No. 54 for 1956.*

1959/60–1962/63, with authorized expenditures of ID 393 million.[18] Two years later this plan was replaced by a more detailed five-year plan covering the period 1961/62–1965/66. Total budgeted expenditure in this new plan, known as the Detailed Economic Plan, was placed at ID 556.3 million. Income was estimated at ID 556.3 million, of which only ID 315.8 million was to come from oil revenues. Eastern bloc loans were to provide ID 77.3 million and profits of government departments and revenue from miscellaneous sources were to supply ID 30.8 million, leaving a gap of ID 142.4 million between budgeted expenditure and revenue.[19] As it turned out, however, allocations were enormously greater than actual disbursements even in the first full year of operation (1962/63), when only ID 59.3 million was spent against allocations of ID 180.2 million.

Just before the end of the fiscal year 1962/63, a new regime came into power. The new government abolished the plan, replacing it with a more realistic one-year program for 1963/64 and setting expenditures at ID 65.9 million (against the original allocation for that year of ID 125.1 million). Even then actual expenditure amounted only to ID 54.2 million while actual revenue reached ID 67.6 million. A further interim program was worked out for 1964/65 with estimated expenditures of ID 106.8 million. Here again actual expenditures fell considerably short of budget appropriations disbursements, amounting only to ID 75.3 million.[20] In 1965 a new plan was adopted to cover the 5 years from 1965/66 to 1969/70. Expenditures under this plan were budgeted at ID 561.2 million. This sum was to be provided by the government from Planning Board revenues, of which the sum of ID 390 million was to come from oil revenue, the projected total of which was ID 780 million for the relevant period.[21] The broad lines of a proposed plan to cover the period 1970/71–1974/75 were announced by the Minister of Planning in March 1969. Total expenditures were estimated at ID 973 million for the period. Of this amount, ID 490 million was to come from oil revenues; the balance was to be provided by Eastern bloc loans, state organizations, and the private sector. Particular emphasis was placed both on the revitalization of the agricultural sector, which is to receive 41 percent of total public investment, and on the industrial sector, to which is allotted 35 percent of the total budget.[22]

Development Policy

Throughout the development planning experience of Iraq, two years has been the average life span of a five-year plan. This has been primarily the result of a

[18] Republic of Iraq, *Provisional Economic Plan,* Baghdad, 1959.
[19] Republic of Iraq, *Detailed Economic Plan 1961/62–1965/66; Law No. 70 for 1961.*
[20] Central Bank of Iraq, *Annual Report for 1964* (in Arabic), Central Bank, Baghdad, 1965, p. 266 passim.
[21] *Republic of Iraq, Law No. 87 of 1965: The Five-Year Economic Plan, 1965–1969* (in Arabic), published in the Official Gazette No. 1135, July 1, 1965.
[22] *Etudes Mensuelles sur L'Economie et les Finances des Pays Arabes,* Vol. XII, No. 139 (July 1969).

combination of initial inexperience, technical incompetence, and political instability. The overriding objective of development policy thoughout two decades of
planning has been the expenditure of increasing oil revenues in ways designed to
expand the productive capacity of the country and thus render it less and less
dependent on oil revenues as they decline at some future point. Although there
has consistently been a consensus regarding this objective, sharp differences have
arisen regarding the means of attaining it.

The development venture of Iraq started in 1950 with rosy expectations.
Unlike many a less developed country, Iraq was in the specially favored position
of not having to squeeze domestic consumption too tightly to provide the needed
development capital, or to indulge in heavy foreign borrowing to provide the
needed foreign exchange. In the oil revenue, development planners were assured
of a steady flow of both funds and exchange. Furthermore, the country could be
spared the threat of inflation and balance of payments difficulties that are so
often attendant upon large development expenditures in the less developed countries.

Table 6-1 shows the balance of payments for 1963–1968. Oil exports during this period constituted on the average about 93 percent of the value of total
exports. Only about 44 percent of the foreign exchange generated from oil exports was used for repatriating the profits earned by the oil companies. The
remaining 56 percent, plus the foreign exchange generated by nonoil exports,
amounting together to some 60 percent of the total foreign exchange realized,
was available for meeting the import needs of the country. For the period
1963–1967, the total foreign exchange remaining at the disposal of the country,
after deducting the part used for repatriating oil profits, amounted to over ID
900 million. Of this sum only ID 5 million, or a little more than 0.5 percent, was
used to meet the current import needs of the oil companies. An additional ID 33
million, or 3.7 percent, was used by the oil companies during the same period
for capital movements representing direct investment or payment of debts. After
meeting all the needs of the oil companies, more than 56 percent of the total foreign exchange realized during the period, or some ID 874 million, was available
for the other needs of the economy. Of this sum, only ID 741 million, that is,
less than 85 percent, was used to finance imports of merchandise. As a consequence the country has consistently shown a surplus arising from current trans-
actions in goods and services. From 1963 to 1968, this surplus amounted to an
annual average of ID 24.1 million. Even after accounting for capital movements,
there remained an overall surplus averaging about ID 14 million a year for the
same 6-year period. This general surplus has resulted in a continuous increase of
more or less equivalent magnitude in the foreign assets of the central monetary
institutions.

The balance of payments trends from 1963 to 1968 have been typical of
the Iraqi foreign sector since oil began to yield substantial revenue to the government. As early as 1950 these revenues were anticipated with a high degree of
certainty, relieving the early planners of worries about sources of finance, availability of foreign exchange, and the internal stability of price level. It was felt that

Table 6-1
Statements of Balance of Payments, 1963-1968
(million ID)

	1963	1964	1965	1966	1967	1968
Goods and services	39.8	13.3	9.7	5.7	20.3	55.9
Exports	278.8	299.9	315.1	333.6	295.8	372.6
(oil-producing companies)	(259.9)	(282.0)	(294.0)	(307.1)	(272.0)	
Imports	−112.2	−145.4	−160.6	−176.0	−151.5	−144.3
(oil-producing companies)	(−1.6)	(−0.7)	(−0.9)	(−1.0)	(−0.8)	
Nonmonetary gold	−1.6	−0.8	−0.9	−0.8	−0.2	−0.7
Transport, freight, insurance	5.6	12.2	9.2	9.7	9.6	10.2
Travel	−9.3	−11.6	−10.2	−13.2	0.3	−12.4
Investment income	−108.2	−123.7	−129.6	−137.7	−122.6	−156.8
(oil-producing companies)	(−110.0)	(−126.1)	(−131.5)	(−139.9)	(−124.6)	
Government	−13.0	−16.8	−14.1	−6.8	−8.0	−9.9
Other services	−0.3	−0.5	−0.8	−3.1	−3.1	−2.8
Unrequited transfers	0.1	1.2	0.3	0.1	5.0	1.6

Table 6-1 (cont'd)

	1963	1964	1965	1966	1967	1968
Capital movements	17.6	−2.8	−15.7	26.7	6.8	14.4
Direct investments	−20.6	−14.0	−15.7	22.0	0.2	15.5
(oil-producing companies)	(−22.0)	(−14.9)	(−16.4)	(20.4)	(−0.1)	
Other private	−0.7	−1.0	−1.9	3.3	3.4	
Government	38.9	12.2	1.9	1.4	3.2	−1.1
Net errors and omissions	−20.8	−32.5	1.5	−8.6	−23.3	−31.3
Surplus or deficit (−)	36.7	−20.8	−4.2	23.9	8.8	40.6
Monetary system	−36.7	20.8	4.2	−23.9	−8.8	−40.6
Bank liabilities	−0.1	−0.1	−0.6	0.5	−0.7	0.4
Bank assets	−1.2	4.4	−0.6	3.0	1.2	−3.2
Central institution liabilities	0.8	0.3	0.5	4.4	5.7	−7.6
Central institution assets	−36.2	16.2	4.9	−31.8	−15.0	−30.2

Source: International Monetary Fund, *Balance of Payments Yearbook*, Vol. 20, June 1969, Iraq, pp. 1-5, for the years 1963-1967; and supplement of October 1969 for the year 1968.

the mere channeling of the whole of the oil revenue, or the major part of it, into capital expenditure under the direction of a technical group impervious to political currents would ensure the rapid, sound, and sustained development of the economy.

The next few years, however, brought much disillusionment and pressed home the reality that economic development cannot be insulated against social and political forces. Oil revenue, a sure and an increasing source of finance, was not entirely a blessing. It gave rise to exaggerated expectations among the people that could not be met and eventually turned a frustrated public against the government. Furthermore, easy access to finance led to a wasteful use of capital and generated a certain degree of complacency in the ranks of government regarding some basic and badly needed reforms in taxation, land tenure, and other spheres of the economy.

Most damaging to the original development policy and the government were, perhaps, the direction the development programs took and the unexpended surpluses. The first four development plans in force before the 1958 revolution were heavily loaded with irrigation and flood control projects, many of which were large and could not show quick results. Forty-six percent of the planned expenditures of the first plan were devoted to irrigation.[23] In the succeeding three plans the percentages were reduced to 34, 35, and 31, respectively, but dams and water storage remained the dominant class of expenditure.[24]

There is no denying, of course, the high priority that must be accorded to the harnessing of water resources in a country that is preponderantly agricultural and is dominated by the flow of two rivers. The flow volume of these rivers reaches a maximum in the spring when it is too late for the use of winter crops and too early for the summer crops. Very often the rivers flood and cause great damage to crops and property. Several studies of flood control and irrigation had been prepared before the oil revenues became a dominant source of financing development. Dams were projected for regulating a volume of some 70 billion cubic meters of water, two-thirds of which, or about 47 billion cubic meters, were included in two major projects, the Habbaniyyah on the Euphrates and the Wadi Tharthar on the Tigris. Plans for these projects were almost completed before the establishment of the first Development Board in 1950.[25]

Under great pressure to produce a plan without being given time to conduct more extensive studies, the Board heavily loaded its first plan with water projects, which had already received much study and were easier to implement by farming them out on competitive bids. To a large extent, the early plans were engineers' lists of projects rather than economic plans. These projects were too often conceived almost in isolation from the social and institutional changes that

---

[23] *Law No. 35 for 1951.*
[24] *Law No. 25 for 1962, Law No. 43 for 1955,* and *Law No. 54 for 1956.*
[25] Abbas Alnasrawi, *Financing Economic Development in Iraq*, Frederick A. Praeger, New York, 1967, p. 67.

should have accompanied them and even in isolation from such necessary secondary technical works as drainage, desalination, and irrigation networks. By 1958, the major projects of flood control and water storage had been completed, including the important Dokan and Derbendi Khan Dams on the Tigris tributaries. There is no doubt that as a result of these projects flood damage to crops and property was eliminated or at least greatly reduced. Furthermore, a large volume of water that had been wasted was now made available for use on summer crops.

It would be untrue to say that there were no other achievements. The basis for a national supply of power had been laid with the construction of three central power stations; the improvement of the road network had begun; government industrial plants and silos had been built; and the state had launched into the oil sector with the construction of refineries at Baghdad and elsewhere. But these achievements, far from earning popular gratitude for the government, seem only to have resulted in its further alienation from the public. For one thing, several years of large expenditures on water projects brought no visible evidence of progress in the cities, where political destinies are ultimately determined. Nor was progress clearly manifest in agriculture. Although the area brought under cultivation in the two major crops, wheat and barley, increased more or less steadily (from 2,288,000 hectares in 1953 to 2,690,000 hectares in 1958), the crops and the yield per hectare failed to show a consistent upward trend. Moreover, much of the secondary irrigation and drainage work in the form of canals and ditches lagged considerably behind the construction of dams and main arteries, thus slowing the process of reducing the dependence of agriculture on climatic conditions.[26]

[26] The continued dependence on climatic conditions is indicated below.

Cultivated Area and Yields of Wheat and Barley, 1950–1958

(area: 1,000 hectares; yield: 100 kg per hectare)

Year	Wheat		Barley	
	Area	Yield	Area	Yield
1950	950	5.5	1,000	8.0
1951	928	5.3	863	9.7
1952	968	5.0	882	7.4
1953	1,192	6.4	1,096	10.1
1954	1,390	8.3	1,122	11.0
1955	1,425	3.2	1,205	6.3
1956	1,314	5.9	1,171	9.1
1957	1,456	7.7	1,244	10.5
1958	1,533	4.9	1,157	8.2

Source: United Nations Food and Agriculture Organization, Production Yearbook, 1960, 1961, 1962.

Furthermore, lands that were being brought under irrigation were improving in value. Without bearing any costs, the landowners were reaping full benefits from public expenditures, but the bulk of the rural population did not have a direct share in these benefits. Nor did it appear likely that they would derive an appropriate indirect share through taxation and public expenditure, since the landlords, wielding great political power, could successfully resist the imposition of substantial taxes on land or agricultural yield. In the same manner redistribution of land for the purpose of a more equal spreading of the benefit seemed politically unlikely. Unable to meet this problem head on, the government attempted to outflank it by promulgating a policy of distributing government-owned land. But progress here was too slow, and the opening up of new settlements proved a much more complex operation than could be handled successfully and expeditiously by the existing administrative machinery.[27]

In the meantime, public discontent was further intensified by the accumulating surpluses within the development organization. Dominated by technicians whose main concern was with the legitimacy and effectiveness of expenditures, the Development Board was soon faced by a wide discrepancy between planned and actual expenditures. For the period 1951/52–1956/57, just 1 year before the revolution, the planned expenditures amounted to some ID 218 million ($610 million), whereas actual expenditures totaled only ID 121 million ($339 million) or about 55 percent of planned expenditures. At the same time the actual revenue of ID 220 stood a little above the estimated revenue of ID 210, but considerably above actual expenditures. The surplus resulting from the excess of actual revenue over actual expenditures for the 6-year period amounted almost to ID 100 million ($280 million), which is about 45 percent of total actual revenues.[28] During the year 1957/58, immediately preceding the revolution, with oil revenue continuing low as a consequence of the Suez crisis, the Development Board accounts registered a deficit for the first time, and the accumulated surplus was thus reduced. But even then, it remained about 31 percent of actual revenue over the whole 7-year period from 1951 to 1958. With little improvement in the economic and social conditions of the masses, the piling up in foreign banks of one-third of the development revenues became another source of popular dissatisfaction with the government and its development policy.

When the new authorities took over in 1958, they were fully conscious of the criticisms leveled at the policy of the previous regime. They immediately took a series of measures; some were destined to effect real alteration in policy, but others were merely political tactics aimed at winning popular favor. The main policy targets of the new regime seem to have been (1) elimination or reduction of the surplus, (2) development of agriculture, (3) expansion of manufacturing industry, and (4) promotion of the social welfare of the poorer sections of the population.

---

[27] See Doreen Warriner, *Land Reform in Principle and Practice,* Clarendon Press, Oxford, 1969, p. 91.
[28] Alnasrawi, *Financing Economic Development in Iraq,* p. 43 passim.

The excess of actual revenue over actual expenditures in the 7 years before the revolution amounted to 31 percent of actual revenue, whereas in the 7 years after, it was only 12 percent.[29] However, after the revolution only 50 percent of the oil revenue was being used for development as compared with 70 percent before. The reduction of the surplus cannot of course be construed as evidence of a better policy. Judgment here must be based on an evaluation of targets and attainment.

The five-year plan for 1961/62–1965/66 adopted in 1961 reflected the policy of the new regime well. Agriculture was to receive 20 percent of the expenditure budget, manufacturing 30 percent, and construction 20 percent; the rest was to go to transportation and communication.[30] The intention was to give much more serious attention to agriculture, manufacturing, and housing than these sectors had received from any previous government. Of the four main aspects of agricultural development—namely, water storage, irrigation and drainage, land tenure, and cultivation methods—the first was to receive minimum emphasis on the ground that much had already been spent on the building of dams for irrigation and flood control. Water storage was to receive only some 13 percent of the agriculture budget, mainly for completing projects near termination. The bulk of the expenditure, almost 60 percent of the total, was allocated to the construction of feeder canals and the undertaking of drainage projects designed to combat salinity, which is a major, age-old problem in Iraqi agriculture. Since the most important dams had already been built, this shift in policy seems to have been timely and sound.

The other major step undertaken by the new regime in the field of agriculture was the enactment of an agrarian reform law in 1958. The law had the triple objective of more equitable land distribution, rent control, and the establishment of minimum wages for agricultural workers.[31] With regard to land tenure, it stipulated that maximum personal holdings should be limited to 1,000 dunums (618 acres) of irrigated land or 2,000 dunums of rainfed land.[32] All landholdings in excess of these limits were to be confiscated and redistributed to individual holders in lots ranging between 30 and 60 dunums in irrigated land and double that amount in rainfed land. The expropriated owners were to be compensated in long-term interest-bearing bonds.[33] The whole operation was to be completed in 5 years. Total cultivable land is estimated at 48 million dunums, roughly half of which is under cultivation, and about half again left fallow each

---

[29] *Ibid.*, pp. 43 ff.

[30] *The Five Years Detailed Economic Plan 1961/62–1965/66, Law No. 70 of 1961.*

[31] *Agrarian Reform Law No. 30,* Baghdad, September 1958.

[32] The Iraqi dunum or "meshara" equals 0.25 hectare, unlike the metric dunum (0.1 hectare) used in some other Middle Eastern countries.

[33] *Agrarian Reform Law No. 30,* 1958. In 1963 the interest on the bonds was reduced from 3 to 2 percent, with half the landlords' compensation forcibly lent to the Agricultural Bank against bonds amortized over 20 years. The repayment burden on the purchasing peasants was also reduced in 1963 to half the value, the residue repayable over 40 years at 2 percent interest.

year.[34] The holdings subject to the reform law were estimated at 8.5 million dunums.[35] By September 1963, the end of the 5-year period, only 7.2 million dunums of the eligible land had been confiscated, and of this only 1.8 million dunums were redistributed to small owner-operators.[36] Technical shortcomings in preparing the land for settlement, administrative weaknesses, and deficiencies in credit and agricultural management contributed to the wide discrepancy between confiscation and distribution. The execution of the program was further hampered by the Kurdish rebellion.

The degree of success or failure of this major program of the revolutionary regime is difficult to assess. The impetus for agrarian reform and its main targets were dictated to a large extent by political motives.[37] It did reduce the political power of the large landowners and considerably weaken, if not eliminate, their resistance to change. From the standpoint of promoting a larger owner-operator class, it may have effected some improvements over the prerevolution program of distributing government-owned land by refraining from distribution to nonsettlers and by imposing a strict upper limit on the area of the distributed plots. On the other hand, the new policy could not be pronounced an economic success since it did not result in a larger agricultural product or higher productivity. In fact, before 1958 Iraq produced all the rice and wheat it consumed and exported barley. By 1963, however, the barley exports had ceased, and some 40 percent of the rice and wheat consumption had to be met by imports.[38] The decline in production was partly due to a long drought in the rainfed regions of the north, but it also resulted in good part from deficient implementation of the reform measures, which led to less than full use of the available land and less than proper upkeep of irrigation pumps.[39]

Government policy regarding the development of manufacturing industry varied in objective and in means of pursuit from period to period. Before World War II the government did not assume any major direct responsibility for the promotion of manufacturing industry. Its policy was confined mainly to granting

---

[34] El-Hadithy and El-Dujaili, "Problems of Implementation of Agrarian Reform in Iraq," in M. R. El-Ghonemy, ed., *Land Policy in the Near East,* United Nations Food and Agriculture Organization, Rome, 1967, p. 219.

[35] John L. Simmons, "Agricultural Development in Iraq," *The Middle East Journal,* Vol. 19, No. 2 (Spring 1965), p. 131.

[36] In 1965, the Minister of Agrarian Reform estimated that about 14.9 million dunums would eventually be subject to the reform. At that time, however, the area confiscated had not increased over the 1963 level by more than half a million dunums. Likewise, the redistributed area had increased by about half a million dunums.

[37] Rasool M. H. Hashimi and Alfred L. Edwards, "Land Reform in Iraq: Economic and Social Implications," *Land Economics,* Vol. XXXVII, No. 1 (February 1961), p. 75.

[38] Simmons, "Agricultural Development in Iraq," p. 131.

[39] Warriner, *Land Reform in Principle and Practice,* p. 95.

some tax privileges, including import duties, to certain categories of new factories and allowing them the free use of government land.[40] It also established the Agricultural Industrial Bank in 1936 to help in the financing of new manufacturing enterprises with authority to participate in their share capital.[41] Subsequently the Industrial and the Agricultural Bank became two separate institutions. However, the role played by the Industrial Bank in the promotion of industry was rather modest. Its loans, small in number and amount, were aimed chiefly at aiding industries processing domestic agricultural products and those producing building materials. It engaged also in a certain amount of equity participation. But very little was undertaken in the way of technical training, market research, or feasibility studies for the establishment of new industries.[42]

In the postwar period and before the revolution of 1958, industrial policy was on the whole very conservative, leaving to unaided private enterprise the main burden of developing the manufacturing sector. Foreign experts consulted by the Iraqi government during the 1950s were preponderantly against the promotion of government-owned industrial enterprise and discouraged measures for protecting or subsidizing industry.[43] They stressed agricultural development on the basis that it was more compatible with the comparative advantage of the Iraqi economy. This position was reflected in government development policy, where planned public expenditures on industry during the period 1951–1958 amounted to only 16 percent of total planned development expenditure. The proportion of actual expenditure on industrial development to total actual development expenditures was even lower, amounting to only 12 percent.[44] Nevertheless, the government did participate, through the Industrial Bank, in several industrial enterprises before the revolution. In addition, the state owned and operated a number of large nonindustrial enterprises such as banks, the railways, the airline, the Basrah port, and others.

The revolution brought about some change in government attitude toward public sponsorship of industrial growth. The rising dissatisfaction with the development policy of the previous regime, which had concentrated on water storage and flood control, became especially acute in urban centers. Several Iraqi economists were arguing for a more balanced growth with industry receiving a due share of public support. This, coupled with the fact that the major water works

[40] International Bank for Reconstruction and Development, *The Economic Development of Iraq*, p. 40.

[41] United Nations, *Industrial Development in the Arab Countries*, ID/CONF., I/R.B.P.16, New York, 1967, p. 63.

[42] Alnasrawi, *Financing Economic Development in Iraq*, p. 76.

[43] IBRD, *Economic Development of Iraq;* Lord Salter, *The Development of Iraq— A Plan for Action*, Iraq Development Board, 1955; Carl Iverson, *Monetary Policy in Iraq*, National Bank of Iraq, 1954; Arthur D. Little, Inc., *A Plan for Industrial Development in Iraq*, Cambridge, Mass., 1956.

[44] Calculated from the tables presented by Alnasrawi, *Financing Economic Development in Iraq*, pp. 44–51.

had been completed, brought about a readiness for a change in policy, even before the revolution. The resulting greater government concern with the growth of industry is reflected in the five-year plan for 1961/62–1965/66,[45] where planned expenditures for industry were increased to 20 percent of total expenditures, as compared with an average of 16 percent under the previous regime. The proportion of actual expenditures on industry was also higher than in the previous period. By the end of 1965 actual expenditures on the industrial sector amounted to 17 percent of total development expenditures, as compared with only 12 percent under the previous regime.[46] The stress on the development of industry continued in the 1965–1969 plan, and a substantial expansion in the industrial sector has been registered in the last few years.

The natural base for industrial development in Iraq consists of petroleum and sulphur. Until the Iraqis take in hand the full development of these two mineral resources and promote the multitude of chemical industries associated with them, industrialization will remain an anemic process. This ultimate objective has been recognized by the various governments that ruled the country. Movement toward its attainment, however, has been slow and often faltering, although it seems to have picked up momentum since 1964. With regard to petroleum there are two spheres of activity: the extraction, refining, and marketing of crude oil, gas, and refined products on the one hand, and the development of petrochemical industries on the other. The desire of the various Iraqi governments was to be active in both spheres. In 1961 a law was passed placing a ban on further exploration by the IPC group companies except within an area of some 730 square miles, which is virtually their present producing area.[47] The aim behind this law was to open the road for direct Iraqi participation in the extraction and marketing of crude.

It was not until 1964 that a national government company, the Iraq National Oil Company (INOC), was created with a capital of ID 25 million for the purpose of promoting national petroleum and petrochemical industries. It had a broad mandate to deal with every aspect connected with petroleum except refining and domestic marketing of the refined products, since these functions were already being performed by other government enterprises.[48] The company was reconstituted in 1967 and given the power of exploration over all the areas that had been removed from the IPC concession in 1961.[49] In November 1967, it entered into an agreement with a French group, Enterprise de Recherches et d'Activités Petrolières (ERAP), whereby the latter will act as a contractor to INOC in oil exploration in four different locations in the south, covering altogether some 10,800 square kilometers. Half the reserves discovered will be left

[45] *The Five Years Detailed Economic Plan 1961/62–1965/66, Law No. 70 of 1961.*
[46] See footnote 44.
[47] *Law No. 80 for 1961.*
[48] Central Bank of Iraq, *Annual Report 1964* (in Arabic), Central Bank, Baghdad, 1964, p. 23.
[49] *Law No. 97 for 1967,* Baghdad, August 1967.

for future direct exploitation by INOC; the other half will be developed by ERAP for 20 years on INOC's behalf for an agreed compensation payable in crude oil. The French group can also buy up to 30 percent of the production in accordance with an agreed upon price arrangement.[50] The first discovery by ERAP was made in 1969.

During 1968, a series of talks was conducted between INOC and several oil companies with the aim of putting the North Rumaila field into production. No agreement was reached, however, and in 1969 the government decided to develop the field directly through INOC.[51] For that purpose it concluded two agreements with the Soviet Union. The first agreement, signed in June, provided for the U.S.S.R. to supply petroleum machinery and geological equipment, together with the needed staff for installation, training, and initial maintenance. It also provided for the training of thirty Iraqi technicians. The second agreement, signed early in July, provided for a loan of $60 million for INOC to develop the North Rumaila field directly. The loan will be repaid in crude oil.[52] The importance of North Rumaila lies in the fact that it contains enormous reserves, estimated at a billion tons, of exceptionally good-quality oil. It is also close to the Persian Gulf and can connect with the deep-water port at Fao through an 80-mile pipeline. The first stage of the project will take 2½ years and will make possible the annual production of 5 million tons of crude; the needed pipeline will also be installed. The second stage will raise production to 18 million tons, which means a sales revenue of some $225 million a year at current prices.

In addition to the extraction, refining, and marketing of oil and natural gas, the government has a very suitable sphere in petrochemical industries for industrial expansion and for long-term economic growth. "Owing to its many-sided forward linkages, this industry, which proved to be among the most dynamic factors of postwar industrial growth in developed countries, can pave the way for the development of a broad range of manufacturing industries."[53] The techno-economic conditions of the petrochemical industry reflect a strong scale-variant. It is estimated that economies in capital investment may range from 20 to 45 percent with a large increase in the scale of output. Moreover, the production of any major petroleum chemical is likely to generate some by-products, which create a marketing problem for an isolated individual firm but may present less difficulty in this regard within the context of a wide range of products emanating from a fairly large complex. The capital, organization, and technical facilities required for the promotion of such a complex are clearly beyond the capabilities of private enterprise in Iraq at the present time. Government initiative and direction are indicated.

[50] *World Petroleum Report,* Mona Palmer Publishing Co., London, 1968, p. 81.
[51] *Ibid.,* 1969, p. 86.
[52] *Etudes Mensuelles sur L' Economie et les Finances des Pays Arabes,* July 1969.
[53] United Nations Economic and Social Office in Beirut, *Studies on Selected Development Problems in Various Countries in the Middle East,* United Nations, New York, 1967, p. 21.

The government has already taken some useful steps in this direction by promulgating a program that would put an end to the flaring of natural gas. The program included establishing a plant in Kirkuk (completed in 1968) for the extraction of sulphur from natural gas and using much of the sulphur in a fertilizer plant near Basra. The Kirkuk gas has a high ratio of hydrogen sulphide. After the extraction of the sulphur, the pure gas and a certain amount of liquid gas will be shipped through separate pipelines to Baghdad for generating thermic electricity and for use in industry.

The program provides further for the creation of a plastics enterprise. The main requirement for the success of the plastics industry is the availability of raw materials at low cost. The principal raw material is natural gas, which is both abundant and relatively inexpensive. Iraq imports a considerable amount of plastics both as finished and as semimanufactured products, the latter processed in local factories. It is estimated that consumption amounted to some 3,300 tons of plastics in 1965 and is on the increase to such an extent that by 1975 it will reach approximately 15,000 tons.[54] The projected enterprise will probably have a capacity for producing double this quantity, which gives rise to the problem of finding an external market partly in the region and partly beyond. The enterprise will have four units producing polyethylene, polyvinylchloride, ethylene, and chlorine and caustic soda.

Another important petrochemical project is a fertilizer plant at Basra, which utilizes the natural gas from the Rumaila field in the vicinity; there is already a pipeline carrying gas to the power station in Basra. The Rumaila gas, which is not sour like that of Kirkuk, can be used directly both as raw material and as fuel. The Basra plant will produce ammonia, urea, ammonium sulphide, and sulphuric acid. For the production of fertilizers the initial capacity of the plant is 120,000 tons of ammonium sulphate and 50,000 tons of urea per annum.[55] This plant should be in a very favorable position with respect to competitiveness because of low-cost natural gas, which is its basic raw material. It also has cheap, abundant labor, it is close to the harbor, and it can procure all the sulphur it needs domestically.

The marketing problem for the nitrogenous fertilizers is not as difficult as the one that may face the plastics industry. The use of fertilizers in Iraqi agriculture is expected to undergo vast expansion. From an average annual input of 12,000 metric tons for the period 1961–1963, it is expected to rise to 263,000 tons in 1985.[56] Since much emphasis is placed in Iraq on irrigated agriculture, it is felt that well over half the increase in fertilizer output should be in nitrog-

[54] United Nations, *Industrial Development in the Arab Countries,* New York, 1967, p. 43.
[55] *Ibid.,* p. 40.
[56] Food and Agricultural Organization, *Indicative World Plan for Agricultural Development, 1965–1985, Near East, Subregional Study,* No. 1, Vol. I (Provisional), Rome, 1966; p. 100.

enous fertilizers.[57] The bulk of the fertilizer output could be utilized domestically. Some of the rest will find a market within the region, and it may not be necessary to look for any wide markets outside the Middle East.

Although Iraq has had such plans for a long period, it has been very slow in implementing them, so that the other Persian Gulf countries have outstripped it. The marketing problem is going to be even more difficult since Kuwait, Iran, Saudi Arabia, and Qatar have all built or are building their own petrochemical and fertilizer plants. Nevertheless, Iraq seems to have taken a serious step at least toward developing its sulphur resources. On May 31, 1969, the government entered into an agreement whereby the Polish firm Centrozap, acting as contractor for the Iraq National Minerals Company, will extract sulphur from the deposits at Mishraq.[58] The project entails the establishment of a plant designed to produce some 250,000–300,000 tons of sulphur annually. This phase is to be completed by 1971. The second phase, which will be completed by 1975/76, will raise total annual production to a million tons.[59] The Mishraq reserves are estimated at several hundred million tons. If the recent trends of international demand for sulphur continue, Iraq will find very little difficulty in marketing pure sulphur and may open up a source of revenue as lucrative as petroleum.

In addition to petroleum and sulphur, considerable attention has been given to the promotion and expansion of other industries. In 1964 the government reorganized the department in charge of industry and passed laws nationalizing several industries, including cement, asbestos, and tobacco, thus preparing the way for more extensive government participation in the industrial sector.[60] In the next few years a number of sizable plants were established or are now under construction. These industries include electrical equipment, railway sleepers, glassworks, canning, cotton textiles, other clothing, antibiotics, and pharmaceuticals.[61]

With respect to the fourth objective of development policy, namely, the promotion of social welfare in the poorer sections of society, government policy since the revolution has been strongly influenced by a commitment to socialist principles. A declared objective of the 1965–1969 plan was that benefits from economic development should accrue largely to low-income groups and that the concentration of wealth in small sections of society should be reduced. The major components of social services—health, education, housing, and social welfare—had been looked after by various departments within the framework of the general budget, but they were not conceived as an integral part of the overall development program until after the revolution. It was in the five-year plan for 1961/62–1965/66 that housing appeared for the first time as part of the devel-

[57] United Nations, *Studies on Selected Development Problems*, p. 22.
[58] *Middle East Economic Digest,* August 8, 1969, p. 994.
[59] *Etudes Mensuelles sur L' Economie et les Finances des Pays Arabes,* July 1969.
[60] Central Bank of Iraq, *Annual Report, 1964* (in Arabic), p. 9.
[61] *Middle East Economic Digest,* p. 995.

opment program, and not until the 1965–1969 plan was a whole chapter devoted to social services.

The government has shown great diligence in applying preventive and curative medicine for combating disease and preventing its spread. Emphasis is placed on the construction of medical facilities, the training of medical personnel, and the involvement of medical authorities in development schemes likely to affect health, such as slaughterhouses, water systems, and various projects of community development. Likewise in education emphasis is placed on the provision of facilities and personnel to enforce compulsory education for boys and girls through the primary cycle, as well as on vocational training and technical education at the secondary level and on expanding the sciences at the university level.[62] There is little doubt that government concern with health and education increased immediately after the revolution; this is manifested by government expenditures in these two fields. Between 1957 and 1965, total government expenditures in all fields rose by 59 percent, whereas expenditures on health and education rose by the spectacular ratio of 278 percent. In other words, in 1957 health and education accounted for 7.5 percent of the public budget, and in 1965 they claimed 18 percent.[63]

In the field of housing, government policy after the revolution started by assuming direct responsibility but later shifted to a policy of assisting the private sector in undertaking this task. In the Detailed Economic Plan of 1961/62–1965/66, about 25 percent of the budget was allocated to construction. However, this included public buildings, houses for defense personnel, and military construction. Of the ID 140 million appearing in this chapter of the plan, only ID 14 million was allocated to what might be considered as popular housing.[64] Under direct government construction programs, some 2,800 units were constructed annually between 1958 and 1965, spread among various projects, including houses for army officers, for occupants of shanty towns in the big cities, and for residents of rural districts. At the same time, financial resources were made available to the Mortgage (Real Estate) Bank, which the government established in 1953 to extend loans to the private sector. Total housing construction amounted to 20,000–22,000 units a year.[65] The housing situation, however, remains serious because of rapid population growth and urban migration, with the further aggravation of rising expectations in housing standards as incomes increase. It is estimated that of the existing stock, some 500,000 must be considered substandard houses; of the 22,000 yearly additions, not more than 7,000 can be considered replacements.[66] Despite the magnitude of the problem, or perhaps because of it, the present government policy is to leave the

---

[62] United Nations, *Studies on Selected Development Problems*, pp. 48–51.
[63] United Nations, *Statistical Yearbook*, 1967.
[64] *Law No. 70 for 1961*, pp. 40–42.
[65] United Nations, *Studies on Selected Development Problems*, p. 52.
[66] *Ibid.*, p. 53.

responsibility mainly to the private sector, with government assistance provided in the form of distributing plots through cooperatives and extending loans through the Mortgage Bank.

The government also sponsors a varied program of social welfare to deal with such problems as destitution, dependency, delinquency, child welfare, malnutrition, and illiteracy. It also conducts centers for training women in home economics and child care and supports several community development projects, including the promotion of cooperatives.

Development Performance

The declared overall objective of development policy both before and after the revolution was the stimulation, through development expenditures, of the nonoil sections of the economy to proceed on a continuous rapid development path and thus reduce the heavy dependence of the economy on oil. Over the span of some 13 years, 1953–1965, development expenditures averaged a little over ID 45 million a year.[67] During those same years, the net national product at factor cost grew from ID 243.95 million in 1953 to ID 632.36 million in 1965, an average of ID 30 million a year.[68] These figures, however, include the mining and quarrying sector, which includes hardly anything other than oil extraction. Since development expenditures have little if any effect on the growth of the oil sector, they should be related to aggregate growth net of oil extraction. If the mining and quarrying sector is dropped, the net national product becomes ID 114.53 million for 1953 and ID 344.97 million for 1965, reflecting an annual growth of ID 18 million.[69] In other words, 1 dinar of growth in the net national product originating in the nonoil sectors of the economy has been associated with 2.6 dinars of development expenditures.

A comparison between the years before and after the revolution shows only a slight departure from this average, the ratio for the years 1953–1958 being 2.7, and that for 1959–1965 being 2.5. This slight dip may be a partial indication that some of the long-term investments undertaken in the 1950s had come into fruition and were not contributing to the expansion of the national product. These ratios, of course, do not constitute capital-output ratios since private capital formation is not included. They merely suggest that the nonoil segments of the economy, as judged by past performance, can command an expansion capable of recouping government development expenditures in an average of 2½ years. The responsiveness of these segments is further demonstrated by the fact that the gross domestic product at factor cost shows an annual growth rate of 8.18 percent between 1953 and 1965, but when the mining and quarrying sector is eliminated, annual growth rate rises to 8.96 percent.

[67] For the years 1953–1964, see Alnasrawi, *Financing Economic Development in Iraq*, p. 85; and for the year 1965 see Central Bank of Iraq, Bulletin No. III, July-September 1968, p. 29.

[68] United Nations, *Yearbook of National Accounts Statistics, 1967*, p. 313.

[69] *Ibid.*, p. 315.

The total development of the economy, therefore, has not been unsatisfactory. As can be seen in Table 6-2, gross national product at current factor cost rose from ID 265.32 million in 1953 to ID 698.22 million in 1965. This represents an annual growth rate of 8.4 percent. Even if allowance is made for statistical inaccuracy, the rate could not be much lower and would thus remain a very high rate over a 12-year period. Of course, the rate may be a little lower for the growth of the real product, but not much lower, since Iraq, following an open import policy, has not experienced significant price rises. In fact, at 1953 prices, GNP at factor cost amounts to ID 623.42 million and represents an annual rate of growth of 7.38 percent for the period 1953–1965.[70] Much of this growth in the national product is attributable, of course, to the continuously rising oil revenues, which grew from a level of ID 15 million in 1951 to ID 203 million in 1968,[71] ranging continuously between one-fourth and one-fifth of national income.

This total growth has not been spread quite equally among the various sectors of the economy. Table 6-2 presents the proportionate shares contributed in selected years to the gross domestic product by the various sectors of the economy. On the whole there has been some decline in the relative importance of the agricultural sector. What appears as a rise in that sector in 1957 is only a manifestation of the drastic decline in the mining and quarrying sector, following the decline in oil output and revenue in the wake of the Suez crisis. Practically all the other sectors during that year showed a similar relative increase. Manufacturing, however, has had a slight upward trend over the long range, and so has public administration in the 1960s as a result of increased proportions of the oil revenue being channeled into the general budget.

Iraq seems to have achieved its growth without much squeeze on consumption. In fact, private consumption expenditure at current market prices rose from ID 178.68 million in 1953 to ID 433.06 million in 1965. This represents an annual growth of 7.65 percent. In terms of 1953 prices the annual rise, though less, would still be very significant, amounting to 6.48 percent.[72] If the growth of population—from 5,620,000 in 1953 to 8,180,000 in 1965[73] is taken into consideration, per capita real consumption will have risen from ID 31.80 in 1953 to 46.44 in 1965, reflecting a growth rate of 3.2 percent per annum. During the 15-year period from 1950 to 1964, domestic savings are calculated at a cumulative figure of ID 2,310 million,[74] which amounts to about 37.5 percent

---

[70] The figures of current factor cost have been deflated by wholesale price indexes as published in *International Financial Statistics,* January 1962, p. 160; October 1964, p. 160; and July 1969, p. 166.

[71] See footnotes 1 and 10.

[72] The 1965 figure is deflated by the cost of living price index based on the figures appearing in *International Financial Statistics* (see footnote 70).

[73] United Nations, *Demographic Yearbook, 1966,* New York, 1967, p. 124.

[74] Calculations are based on the figures presented in United Nations, *Yearbook of National Account Statistics, 1966* and *1967.* Figures for the years 1950, 1951, and 1954 are extrapolated.

Table 6-2

Domestic Product by Industrial Origin at Current Factor Cost for Selected Years

	1953		1957		1961		1965	
	Million ID	Percentage of GDP	Million ID	Percentage of GDP	Million ID	Percentage of GDP	Million ID	Percentage of GDP
1. Agriculture, forestry, and fishing	71.50	22.3	111.57	25.9	116.98	19.0	172.08	20.8
2. Mining and quarrying	129.80	40.2	114.84	26.7	211.18	34.3	287.39	34.7
3. Manufacturing	19.74	6.1	36.25	8.4	59.51	9.7	73.77	8.9
4. Construction	11.27	3.5	27.68	6.4	23.88	3.9	18.50	2.2
5. Electricity, gas, and water	1.46	0.5	2.68	0.6	4.96	0.8	8.91	1.1
6. Transport, storage, communication	21.37	6.6	29.92	7.0	45.95	7.5	50.69	6.1
7. Wholesale and retail trade	17.85	5.5	29.67	6.9	36.58	6.0	47.81	5.8
8. Banking, insurance, and real estate	3.23	1.0	6.60	1.5	11.06	1.8	9.70	1.2
9. Ownership of dwellings	11.61	3.5	12.80	3.0	12.13	2.0	12.68	1.5
10. Public administration and defense	18.29	5.6	32.06	7.4	51.46	8.3	88.74	10.7
11. Services	16.83	5.2	26.99	6.2	41.37	6.7	57.44	7.0
12. Gross domestic product at factor cost	322.95	100.0	430.06	100.0	615.06	100.0	827.69	100.0
13. *Add* net factor income from abroad	−57.63		−46.40		−44.20		−129.47	
14. Gross national product at factor cost	265.32		383.66		520.86		698.22	
15. *Deduct* provisions for the consumption of fixed capital	21.37		30.94		36.62		65.87	
16. Net national product at factor cost (national income)	243.95		352.72		484.24		632.35	

Source: United Nations, *Yearbook of National Accounts Statistics, 1967,* New York, 1968, pp. 313, 315.

of the cumulative GNP. Of course, not all this saving was available for domestic investment, as a considerable portion of it, namely, ID 1,068 million, was net factor income owed to nonresidents, chiefly in the form of profits in the oil sector. Thus, national savings for the period amounted to ID 1,242 million, and with relatively very small leakage it was possible to have a gross domestic investment—including both fixed capital formation and increased stocks—of ID 1,203 million, equivalent to about 20 percent of GNP. The mean of the annual ratios of domestic investment to GNP over the period has been slightly higher, amounting to about 22 percent of GNP, with an average absolute deviation of slightly over 10 percent of the mean.

II. Prospects

In this section I examine the prospects of Iraqi development, casting an optimistic but realistic forward look at what the economy might become a decade hence, under favorable policies, and again what it might look like by the end of the century. Projecting into the future has necessarily required the examination of problems that will face future development and policies in the light of past activity.

In attempting to assess future prospects, my first concern is to make some informed guesses about the total performance of the economy in the past as measured by the magnitude and the rate of growth of the national product. Table 6-3 shows the growth of the domestic and national products at current and constant prices over the period 1953–1965. The figures reflect the fact that Iraq has experienced a continuous growth throughout the period with some minor interruptions. There was a slight decline in the gross domestic product at factor cost between 1956 and 1957, attributable mainly to the interruption in the oil flow across Syria as a result of the Suez crisis. From then on, domestic product has shown continuous increase. There was also some decline in gross national product at constant market prices and in national income between the years 1958 and 1959, and the years 1962 and 1963, attributable mainly to bad crops. The overall picture, however, is one of continuous growth at fairly high rates over the period 1953–1965, as can be seen from these figures:

Series	Annual Rate of Growth (percent)
Gross domestic product at current factor cost	8.15
Gross domestic product at constant factor cost	7.03
Gross national product at current market prices	8.25
Gross national product at constant market prices	7.22
Net national product at current factor cost or national income	8.26
Net national product at constant factor cost or national income	7.20

Table 6-3

The Product of Iraq, 1953-1965

(million ID)

	1953	1954[a]	1955	1956[b]	1957	1958	1959	1960	1961	1962	1963	1964	1965
1. Gross domestic product at current factor cost	322.95	376.57	386.76	428.90	430.06	484.70	509.62	565.36	615.06	658.42 675.67	688.69	782.02	827.69
2. Gross domestic product at factor costs of 1956 and 1962[c]	351.67	420.50	401.10	428.80	424.77	474.02	493.07	555.90	618.84	675.67	669.43	747.67	794.58
3. Gross national product at current market prices	286.94	333.16[e]	341.72	389.39	413.14	436.24	452.62	502.80	557.30	600.79 621.29	618.70	702.57	742.94
4. Gross national product at constant market prices (1956 prices)[d]	298.90	374.93[f]	367.44	389.39	397.25	469.08	443.79	474.34	549.81	603.19	578.22	632.95	687.91
5. Net national product at factor cost (national income) (current prices)	243.95	285.80	289.28	334.76	352.72	374.04	391.62	437.13	484.24	526.49 528.33	525.33	595.77	632.36
6. Net national product at factor cost (national income) (1956 prices)[d]	254.16	322.50	311.05	334.76	339.15	402.19	383.94	412.39	461.18	512.94	490.96	536.73	585.52

[a]Figures for 1954 are taken from, or based on, K. Haseeb, The National Income of Iraq 1953-1961, Oxford University Press, 1964, pp. 14-23.
[b]Figures for 1956 are taken from United Nations, Yearbook of National Accounts Statistics, 1966, pp. 279-280.
[c]The United Nations Statistical Office runs a new series starting with 1962. Constant figures are expressed in 1956 prices for the years 1953-1961 and in 1962 prices for the years 1962-1965. The figure for 1965 is estimated.
[d]Figures are deflated by a wholesale price index. (See footnote 70.)
[e]Indirect taxes are interpolated and added to Haseeb's gross national product at current factor cost.
[f]Indirect taxes are interpolated and added to Haseeb's gross national product at constant factor cost.
Source: United Nations, Yearbook of National Account Statistics, 1967, New York, 1968, pp. 313-315.

All current series have registered an annual growth rate of over 8 percent, and the growth rates for all constant series have exceeded 7 percent. An average of 7 percent growth in real output over 12 years is a considerable achievement, possible because of the continuous growth in the oil revenue accruing to the government and the continued use of large portions of it by the government for development purposes. The same high growth rates are shown when the oil sector is omitted. Gross domestic product without the mining and quarrying sector shows an annual growth of 8.95 percent when calculated at current factor costs and 7.06 percent when calculated at constant factor costs. The past performance of the economy would suggest that 7 percent might be adopted as the annual growth rate of real product for future projection. But I am inclined to believe that 7 percent is a fairly high rate to sustain for 30 years, especially as oil revenue is expected to become an increasingly smaller part of the continuously growing national income. For this reason I have favored the adoption of two rates of growth: 7 percent until 1980 and 6 percent from 1980 to the end of the century. Any higher rates seem out of reach, and even the rates predicated can be maintained only under a well-determined development policy.

On the basis of these rates the GNP at 1956 market prices would rise as indicated below:

	1965	1970	1980	2000
Gross national product (million ID)	687.9	965.0	1,898.0	6,087.0

By 1980 the GNP will have risen to more than 2.5 times its 1965 level, and between 1980 and the end of the century it will have tripled again.

Population has been increasing roughly at the rate of 2.5 percent a year.[75] On the basis of the experience of other developing countries, this rate can be expected to continue for some time into the future. With a rising income level, the spread of education, and already improved health standards, the gap between birth and death rates is expected to decline. I base my population projections on a growth rate of 2.5 percent until 1980 and 2 percent for the following decades. The population picture would then look like this:

	1965	1970	1980	2000
Population (thousands)	7,180	9,090	11,635	17,290

Using these population figures, I arrive at the following GNP per capita at 1956 prices:

[75] Calculations are based on figures presented in United Nations, *Demographic Yearbook, 1967,* New York, 1968.

	1965	1970	1980	2000
Gross national product per capita (ID)	96	106	163	352

On the assumption of some future decline in the relative magnitude of net indirect taxes and a more or less constant rate of capital consumption, the projected figures for total and per capita net national product will be as follows at 1956 prices:

	1965	1970	1980	2000
Net national product (million ID)	585.52	820	1,633	5,355
Net national product per capita (ID)	81	90	140	310

Although the total national income is expected to grow roughly at an annual rate of 7 percent between 1970 and 1980 and of 6 percent between 1980 and 2000, the national income per capita will grow at the rates of 4.5 and 4 percent, respectively, for the two periods. Such growth would place the Iraqi per capita income by the end of the century at a level roughly comparable to that of the poorer European countries (Spain, Greece, Ireland) today.

The real question is whether the economy can sustain the rates of growth that have been projected. As a first step toward an answer, we must first examine capital requirements. No studies are available of sectoral capital-output ratios for Iraq. Our analysis must, accordingly, be based on global capital-output ratios and on general expectations of change. For the period 1950–1964, gross investment, including fixed capital formation and change in stocks, amounted in the aggregate to 2.7 times the increment of the GNP. This ratio, however, was not uniform throughout the period. For the prerevolution years the ratio was about 2.5, but after the revolution it was considerably higher—about 3.0. As development proceeds, more capital-intensive projects will probably be launched, and the ratio of gross investment to the increment of GNP will eventually rise. On the other hand, past capital-output ratios may have been unduly high because of heavy investment in the agricultural infrastructure not associated with a corresponding increase in agricultural output owing to shortcomings elsewhere in the system. Capital-output ratios in the other sectors may have been lower than the global ratio, which included agriculture. Therefore, lower ratios may be possible in the short-run future as investment shifts away from agriculture or as agricultural output rises in response to past investments without corresponding increases in new capital formation. In the long run, however, I expect the global capital-output ratio to rise. As I have no way of predicting the extent of such rise, I am arbitrarily assuming that the postrevolution ratio of 3.0 will continue for a decade or so, and that the average for the following decades will be about 3.5.

If we adopt these ratios, it becomes clear that, in order to achieve the projected growth of 7 percent until 1980 and of 6 percent between 1980 and 2000, gross investment must continuously amount to 21 percent of GNP or some 24 percent of national income. This must be considered a high rate, which would be difficult to sustain for a third of a century. Fortunately, however, Iraq has been able to approach this rate without much squeeze on consumption. For the period 1953–1965, gross investment averaged about 19 percent of GNP. In the prerevolutionary part of the period, with a larger proportion of the oil revenue used for development purposes, the ratio was even higher, averaging a little more than 23 percent. After the revolution, however, with a larger portion of the oil revenue absorbed in public consumption, the ratio of gross investment to GNP dropped to an average of 15 percent.

In the light of this past performance it might appear relatively easy to squeeze a few extra percentage points to maintain a level of investment compatible with the projected rates of growth. A closer examination, however, would dampen any excessive optimism in this direction. It must be remembered that during this period of high investment rate oil revenue averaged about 19 percent of gross national product. It is not expected that oil revenue will grow in the future at the same rate as national product. If national product grows as projected above, oil revenue is not likely to constitute more than 13 percent of GNP by 1980, and will probably decline to some 5 percent by the end of the century. If the present policy of using only half the oil revenue for development purposes continues, 60–70 percent of gross national investment in the period 1970–1980, and 80–90 percent in the period 1980–2000 will have to be provided from sources other than oil revenue. The corresponding ratios for the years 1951–1958 and 1959–1964 were 30 and 50 percent, respectively.

To achieve this desired level of gross investment, consumption must inevitably be squeezed, at least in terms of its proportion to total product. The squeeze will have to be applied either to private or to public consumption or to both. This question cannot be separated from politics. The decision would depend to a considerable extent on the power of the rulers, the responsiveness of the people to government leadership, and the political and military situation in the region. However, after the revolution, expenditure on public consumption increased considerably both in relative and in absolute terms. The annual average for the 6 years before the revolution was ID 61 million, 17 percent of the gross national product. In the 6 years after the revolution, public consumption more than doubled, registering an annual average of more than ID 125 million, and amounting to 22 percent of gross national product. Expenditure on defense is a major component of public consumption, amounting in the period 1960–1965 to about 40 percent of total noncapital public expenditures. With political instability continuing in the region, it is unlikely that much saving can be made in this item. The next important component is social expenditures on education, health, and wel-

Table 6-4
National Investment[a]
(percentage of GNP)

	Annual Average, 1959-1964	1980	2000
Gross investment	17.3	21.0	21.0
Private investment	7.6	7.0	7.0
Public investment	9.7	14.0	14.0
From oil revenue	9.1	6.5	2.5
From tax revenue	0.6	7.5	11.5
Total oil revenue	18.2	13.0	5.0
Total tax revenue	7.5	14.5	18.5

[a]Calculations are based on figures taken from United Nations, *Statistical Yearbooks,* 1955-1967 and *Yearbook of National Account Statistics,* 1960-1967. Private investment for the period 1959-1964 is defined as the difference between gross investment (including increase in stocks) as shown in the national accounts and capital expenditures as shown in the budget accounts. It is assumed to remain at the same rate or slightly less for the coming 30 years. It is assumed further that half the oil revenue will continue to be used for development purposes and hence be considered as capital expenditure. The balance of the public investment is considered as coming from tax revenue. Finally, it is assumed that the portion of tax revenue used for current expenditures maintains the same ratio to gross national product, the increase being used fully for capital expenditures.

fare. Here, too, not much saving can be expected. The needed investment funds will have to be procured, therefore, by pressure on private consumption. Efforts in this direction should be more promising than in the area of public consumption, since the tax burden in Iraq has been comparatively light. For the period 1960–1965, total tax revenue was only about 8.5 percent of national income or 7.5 percent of gross national product. This is indeed a very low percentage when compared with countries in the same income range as Iraq. The extent to which the tax revenues would have to rise is shown in Table 6-4.

As the oil revenue becomes a smaller proportion of the GNP, an increasingly greater proportion of public investment will have to be financed from tax revenue. The share of tax revenue in financing public investment constituted a very low average of 0.6 percent of GNP for the period 1959–1964. By 1980, however, some 7.5 percent of national product has to be devoted to the financing of public investment, and by the year 2000 about 11.5 percent will be required. This would mean a considerable increase of tax levies to raise the tax revenue from 7.5 percent of gross national product (the average level prevailing in the period 1959–1964) to 14.5 percent in 1980 and 18.5 percent in 2000. This should not be beyond realistic achievement, as judged by comparison with some other countries who now enjoy the projected level of per capita income of Iraq in 1980 and 2000. Most of the increase will have to come through direct taxes. The income tax currently yields a revenue less than 1.5 percent of gross national product, and only about 20 percent of the total revenue. Private investment is expected to maintain the same ratio throughout. This belief is based on the consideration that Arab socialism as practiced in Iraq leaves trade, agriculture, and most small-scale industry in private hands and accepts mixed enterprise when capital and management are shared by the private and public sectors.

Labor statistics in Iraq are scanty and leave many gaps. The size of the labor force has not been determined with any degree of precision. The International Labour Organization estimated it as equivalent to 28.3 percent of total population in 1957.[76] This estimate appears to be somewhat low, particularly when compared with estimates for countries that fall broadly in the same income range as Iraq, such as Iran with 32 percent; Pakistan, 33.5; Indonesia, 34; Brazil, 33; and the Philippines, 37. But even if the estimate of 28.3 percent is correct, it should have risen since 1957, and it will continue to rise in the future with improvement in the status of women and an increasing life span among working people.

In view of these considerations, I have estimated the labor force to reach 31 percent of the population in 1970; 32 percent in 1980; and 36 percent in 2000. This implies an annual rate of growth of labor force of 2.83 percent between 1970 and 1980 and 2.61 percent between 1980 and 2000. With annual population growth projected at 2.5 percent in the first period and 2 percent in the second, these rates of growth in the labor force appear reasonable. In view of my projected rise in GNP, the above growth rates of the labor force would indicate that a 1 percent rise in the labor force is associated with 2.47 percent rise in GNP during the first period, and 2.3 percent during the second period. This again compares favorably with the figures for countries similar to Iraq. But to achieve the projected rise in GNP within the indicated dimensions of growth in the labor force, labor productivity has to rise at an annual rate of 4.05 percent in the first period and 3.31 percent in the second period. The first ratio seems a little too steep. But if one were to bring it down to a more acceptable rate like 3.3, and still maintain a 7 percent growth rate of aggregate output, the labor force would then have to grow at 3.5 percent or more, rather than at 2.8 percent, a year, which is again unrealistic.

Of course, it may be possible for employment to expand proportionately more than the labor force through a reduction in unemployment and underemployment. No figures are available to show the extent of current unemployment. I suspect, however, that no drastic reduction can be expected in unemployment during the coming decade. Another possibility is that productivity may increase

[76] International Labour Organization, *Yearbook of Labour Statistics, 1965*, Geneva, 1966, p. 24.

at a higher rate because of a possible shift of employment from agriculture to trade and industry. However, such a shift is likely to be dampened if economic policy for the next decade is to lay great stress on the development of the agricultural sector, as is proposed in this study. Under these circumstances, an annual growth rate in productivity of 4.05 percent would still seem too high. Iraq may very well be faced with the serious problem of having to raise its labor productivity at a faster pace than has seemed feasible in the experience of similar countries, increase its labor force by importing skilled labor from other Arab countries, or else accept a smaller growth in its national product than is compatible with its capital potential.

Obviously, my basic assumption in this connection is that the policy governing future development, whether it addresses itself to the volume or the quality of the labor force or both, will enable the economy to grow at the rates projected above. This growth will not be shared evenly by all sectors, nor will the pattern of national expenditures remain unaltered. If projecting the growth rates of the GNP is speculative, the breaking down of that total product into channels of expenditure and into industrial origins is even more uncertain. Yet despite the uncertainty and the unreliability of such projections, they do serve the useful purpose of affording a check on the aggregates and furnishing a clearer picture of the total economy with the interrelations of its major components, as well as more clearly revealing the basic assumptions underlying the projections. Accordingly, Table 6-5 presents my expectations regarding future national expenditures and origins of the national product, consistent with my global projections.

In conformity with the previous analysis, I have assumed that the share of total consumption will be somewhat reduced to enable the economy to undertake the needed investment. In the years 1959–1965, total consumption averaged about 80 percent of gross national product, and in 1965 it stood at 83 percent. The figures in Table 6-5 reflect a decline to 80 percent by 1970, and between 77 and 78 percent from 1980 on. The government component of total consumption, however, is slated to retain its share and perhaps even to rise slightly on the assumption that political and military conditions in the region do not permit a drastic reduction in defense expenditures. For the years 1959–1965, government consumption amounted to 24 percent of GNP. In 1965 it stood at 25 percent. Table 6-5 reflects the assumption that it will remain at this level till 1980 and perhaps rise slightly to 28 or 29 percent by 2000. The share of private consumption, however, will have to decline appreciably. In the period 1959–1965 it constituted 57 percent of GNP. In 1965 it was a little less than 58 percent. My figures show a decline to 55 percent in 1970, 53 percent in 1980, and 50 percent in 2000. The decline, of course, is only in proportion to total output and income. In absolute magnitude per capita private consumption would rise considerably—from ID 63 in 1970 to ID 188 in 2000.

In the foreign sector I assume a continued surplus of exports over imports of goods and services, still slightly above the continued negative net factor in-

Table 6-5

Projected National Expenditures in 1965 Market Prices[a]

(million ID)

	1965	1970	1980	2000
Private consumption	433.60	570	1,085	3,260
Government consumption	187.62	260	510	1,780
Gross domestic investment (including stocks)	110.65	200	430	1,375
Net exports of goods and services	138.50	180	260	425
Statistical discrepancy	2.57	. . .	. . .	. . .
Expenditure on gross domestic product	872.40	1,210	2,285	6,840
Net factor income from abroad	−129.46	−170	−240	−296
Expenditure on gross national product	742.94	1,040	2,045	6,544
Indirect taxes less subsidies	44.71	63	100	180
Capital consumption	65.87	92	180	580
Net national product at factor cost (national income)	632.36	885	1,765	5,784

[a]The 1965 figures are taken from United Nations, *Yearbook of National Account Statistics, 1967*, New York, 1968, p. 313. The figures for the gross and net national products in this table do not agree with the ones shown earlier because those were calculated at 1956 prices, whereas these are calculated at 1965 prices. Figures for 1970, 1980 and 2000 are the author's projections.

come from abroad. These calculations, of course, are based on continued foreign ownership of the oil companies with continued transfer of half the profits abroad. The net factor income from abroad represents more or less the transferred profits of the oil companies, which are presumably equal to the government oil revenue. Net factor income from abroad for the years 1970, 1980, and 2000 consequently is considered as equal to the projected oil revenue to the government but of opposite sign. Throughout the period 1959–1965, net exports of goods and services stood slightly above the absolute value of net factor income from abroad, the net excess in 1965 being ID 9 million. I have projected a comparable slight excess into the future, implying a continued growth in foreign reserves.

314

Capital consumption is assumed to maintain a more or less steady level of about 9 percent of GNP. Indirect taxes, however, although increasing in amount, are expected to decline in proportion to GNP as more direct taxes on income are levied by the government. Already there are indications that revenue from indirect taxes is growing at a lower rate than GNP. The average of the indirect taxes for the years 1959–1965 was 6.62 percent of GNP; but whereas GNP grew at the rate of 8.6 percent during that period, indirect taxes rose at the rate of only 7.6 percent a year. My figures show a decline in the ratio of indirect taxes to GNP such that they would be 6.1 percent in 1970, 4.8 percent in 1980, and 2.8 percent in 2000.

From the figures presented in Table 6-5 it can be seen that national savings, the significant measure of gross savings to compare with investment, are less than the so-called domestic savings because of the large oil profits accruing to nonresidents. Below are the projected domestic and national savings in 1965 prices. As oil profits become progressively a smaller proportion of GNP, the gap between domestic and national savings narrows. In 1965 national savings were only 48.6 percent of domestic savings, but according to the projections made here they would become 55.3, 65.2, and 83.6 percent in 1970, 1980, and 2000, respectively. Likewise, proportionately more of the national product is expected to be saved in the future than was the case in 1965 or earlier years. In 1965 gross national savings amounted to 16.5 percent of the national product, but the percentage is expected to become 20.2 in 1970 and between 22 and 23 thereafter. It will be remembered that investment was projected at 21 percent of GNP for 1980 and thereafter. The slight excess of gross national saving over gross investment is explained by leakage in the foreign sector, chiefly in the form of a building up of foreign reserves.

	1965	1970	1980	2000
Domestic savings (million ID)	251.71	380	690	1800
National savings (million ID)	122.25	210	450	1504
National savings as percentage of domestic saving	48.6	55.3	65.2	83.6
National savings as percentage of GNP	16.5	20.2	22.0	22.9
National savings as percentage of national income	19.3	23.7	25.5	26.0

Finally let us examine the breakdown by industrial origin of projected national product. My sectoral projections, based partly on past performance and partly on certain assumptions regarding future policy, are presented in Table 6-6.

Consistently with my conjectures regarding the declining importance of the oil revenue in the future, value added by the oil industry in the mining and

Table 6-6
Gross Domestic Product by Industrial Origin at 1965 Factor Cost
(million ID)

	1965		1970		1980		2000	
	Million ID	Percent	Million ID	Percent	Million ID	Percent	Million ID	Percent
Agriculture, forestry, and fishing	172.08	20.8	210	18.3	450	20.6	1,145	17.2
Mining and quarrying	287.38	34.7	380	33.1	580	26.5	1,425	21.4
Manufacturing	73.77	8.9	126	11.0	310	14.2	1,412	21.2
Construction and utilities	27.40	3.3	56	4.9	105	4.8	320	4.8
Ownership of dwellings	12.68	1.5	22	1.9	39	1.8	113	1.7
Public administration	88.74	10.7	106	9.2	212	9.7	673	10.1
Trade, transport, and finance	108.20	13.1	167	14.6	332	15.2	1,066	16.0
Other services	57.44	7.0	80	7.0	157	7.2	506	7.6
Gross domestic product at factor cost	827.69	100	1,147	100	2,185	100	6,660	100

Source: The 1965 figures are taken from United Nations, *Yearbook of National Account Statistics, 1967*, New York, 1968, p. 315. Figures for 1970, 1980, and 2000 are the author's projections.

quarrying sector is projected to increase at a lower rate than the growth rate of the total domestic product. Value added by oil is estimated at ID 360 million in 1970, ID 490 million in 1980, and ID 630 million in 2000. The balance of the sector account is made up, in the main, by expansion in the production of sulphur, which is expected to be yielding a greater value than oil wells before the end of the century.

In addition to these expectations regarding the future production of oil and sulphur, I have made two main policy assumptions. The first is that the government will concentrate in the immediate future on promoting production in the agricultural sector by treating the problem of salinity, by improving crops, and by applying better techniques. It is presumed that such policy will be successful. The outcome is reflected in Table 6-6 by a rise in the product originating in the agricultural sector from 18.3 percent in 1970 to 20.6 percent in 1980. In those 10 years the value of agricultural output is seen as doubling, rising at the annual rate of almost 8 percent. In the next 20 years the output should continue to rise, but at the lower rate of 4.8 percent annually. The product originating in this sector should decline accordingly in relative importance to about 17 percent of total product.

The second assumption concerns the manufacturing sector. I expect that the promotion of this sector will be the topmost economic concern of the government. With the start already made in the petrochemical field and the government contracts entered into with Eastern bloc countries, the value of the manufacturing product should rise from ID 126 million in 1970 to ID 310 million in 1980, an annual rate of growth of over 9.4 percent. In the following 20 years there should be an equally big push in this direction. With improvements in the skills of labor and in industrial management, and with the growth of an industrial institutional milieu, the growth of the manufacturing product for the next 20 years is expected to proceed at a fairly substantial rate, although possibly not quite so high as in the initial period, when the start was made from a low level of output. The figures in Table 6-6 reflect a rate of growth of 7.9 percent a year. The relative importance of the sector, however, grows considerably, with the value of the product originating in it rising from 14 percent in 1980 to 21 percent by the year 2000.

The rest of the sectors are not expected to alter much in relative importance. The government or public administration sector perhaps calls for a brief comment. Table 6-6 shows a slight but steady growth in the relative importance of this sector chiefly because of the projected growth in tax revenue discussed earlier, as well as the added revenue from sulphur. Although I expect oil revenue to rise very slowly, and at a declining rate, from ID 170 million in 1970 to ID 240 million in 1980 and ID 297 million in 2000, revenue from taxes and from the production of sulphur should increase at a rate compatible with the expanding responsibilities of the public sector. The annual average of the tax revenue for the years 1959–1964 amounted to 7.5 percent of GNP. The projected tax revenue is 9.4, 14.5, and 18.5 percent for the years 1970, 1980, and 2000, respectively.

III. Problems and Policy

In the foregoing exposition I attempted to gauge the economic potential of Iraq and to describe the past development policies within the framework of which development plans were formulated and implemented. It remains now to determine briefly the most salient problems likely to be associated with future development efforts and to examine future policies that might deal with these problems and move the country further toward the attainment of its great economic potential. In the somewhat speculative realm of future economic policy it is necessary to make some assumptions about political organization and social outlook. Assuming that Iraq will continue to follow an "Arab socialist" path, I believe that the government will be increasingly involved in major investment decisions and government enterprise and public employment will expand. Agrarian reform will also continue, entailing a redistribution of land ownership, a further reduction in the political influence of land and capital ownership, the continued existence of small capital private enterprise, and a deeper entrenchment in a social welfare approach to economic growth. On the basis of these assumptions, the future development of the country will be primarily a public and collective responsibility. The sources of financing such development will gradually rely more on tax revenue and revenue from public enterprise and relatively less on oil revenue, as I expect national income to grow at a faster rate than oil revenue. But I do expect oil revenue to continue growing and perhaps not to level off before the end of the century, regardless of whether production and marketing continue to be handled by a concessionary arrangement or become more fully a public enterprise. According to my projections, I expect oil exports and the expansion of other exports, particularly sulphur, to generate enough foreign exchange to enable the country to continue its development without undue pressure on the internal price level.

The continued drive of the Iraqi economy, under the above conditions, toward the attainment of the economic potentials outlined earlier requires successful solutions to (1) increasing agricultural productivity, (2) expanding the manufacturing sector, (3) strengthening fiscal capabilities, and (4) raising the efficiency of manpower and reducing unemployment.

Agriculture

Iraq has great agricultural potential. Its land and water resources, if utilized to a high degree of efficiency, could yield a much higher agricultural output and income and support a vast amount of employment.[77] In a recent study which ap-

[77] U.S. Department of Agriculture, *The Agricultural Economy of Iraq*, Washington, D.C., 1965, p. 71.

plied to Iraq the yield rates of physically comparable lands in countries having highly developed agriculture, it was shown that agricultural income, with present kinds of crops and prevailing prices, could be raised more than threefold.[78] In general, assessment of potential levels of productivity is a highly uncertain process, but there seems to be little doubt that the country's potential by far outstrips its present level of performance. This, of course, is no disparagement of the great efforts undertaken by various Iraqi governments to increase agricultural productivity and expand agricultural output.

As pointed out earlier, the country has come a long way in increasing the land area that can be brought under irrigation and in reducing the menace to crops, life, and property arising from the flooding of the rivers. Furthermore, Iraq has undertaken to reform the system of land ownership for the purpose of better distribution and more efficient use of land. Behind these and many other measures for improvement lay the conviction that the modernization and development of agriculture is basic to the overall development of the economy. Now perhaps more than ever before there is the realization that agriculture is a crucial sector in the total development of the country. In the first place, it is recognized that the growth of agricultural income has not kept pace with the average growth of total national product. This lag, it is believed, can be overcome, and the sector can be rendered capable of sustaining a higher rate of growth; likewise, fluctuations in agricultural income precipitated in the past by fluctuating climatic conditions can be reduced considerably through countervailing measures. Second, it is considered very important that food prices and the general price level be kept from rising unduly as the economy develops. In the past this has been feasible because of a relatively liberal import policy made possible through the large volume of foreign exchange yielded by oil exports. As the economy progresses, the share of oil income is likely to become proportionately less, and food and certain raw material imports must be substituted for by an expanding domestic agricultural production.

There is no doubt that government officials responsible for agricultural development and other enlightened citizens in the country are convinced that Iraqi governments have given serious attention and devoted considerable effort and funds to agricultural development. At the same time performance has fallen substantially short of projected or desired targets. There is no simple explanation for this discrepancy between effort and achievement. The rate of development of any sector is to a large extent bound to the entire social, political, and economic matrix. The success of a given development project depends quite often on the coordination of the efforts of several government departments other than the department directly responsible for the project. When coordination falters, good plans frequently sustain damaging delays in implementation and sometimes never come to full fruition. For instance, the redistribution of land fell consider-

[78] Hedayet Aminarsallah, "Iraqi Agriculture—Potential and Problems," unpublished thesis, Southern Illinois University, Carbondale, Ill.

ably behind schedule, not because the Ministry of Agrarian Reform responsible for the program was negligent, but because other organs of the government had to complete surveys, irrigation canals, selection of suitable farmers, construction of facilities, organization of education and health amenities, establishment of cooperatives, and a number of other functions. Practically each one of these functions fell behind schedule because of other constraints in the economy.

To take just one example, plans called for the establishment of 2,000 cooperatives between 1961 and 1965.[79] By the end of the period less than 100 were established. Cooperatives must be run by trained cooperative managers, and to obtain such a cadre the government established a Cooperative Institute for their training. By the end of 1964, not more than 60 managers had been graduated. Two years later the number of trained managers had reached 300, which is still far short of the 1,000 needed to cope with the number of cooperatives called for in the original plan, reckoning on one manager for every two societies.[80] Another condition for the success of cooperatives is the education of the farmer in the cooperative mode of life, so that the impetus for cooperatives will not be solely governmental but rather will derive from a desire by the farmer and an enthusiasm on his part for participation and support. Such education, like agricultural technical assistance, calls for an efficient extension service. But extension service requires trained personnel who are again in short supply.

The problems connected with the promotion of cooperatives are described here simply as an illustration of some of the obstacles encountered in the way of rapid progress. Similar obstacles are met at almost every aspect of agricultural development. The real bottlenecks in the end are the shortage of qualified personnel and the general inexperience of the community in modern development processes. Even when qualified persons are available, they are sometimes not placed where they can be useful because of political and other considerations, and more often their productiveness is seriously impeded by a general social atmosphere not conducive to diligent modernization and development. Failure tends usually to be attributed to deficient knowledge or ill-conceived policy. Although in certain instances better studies and improved plans would be useful, for the most part it is not the lack of these that accounts for limited success. There is hardly any effective policy measure to be recommended that has not already come to the attention of the government and been at some time or another the object of its concern. Over the years, a large number of foreign experts, hailing from East and West, have been invited to study agricultural and related problems and to advise the government on means of dealing with them. Many Iraqis have been trained at home and abroad to work in departments and institutions designed to contribute to agricultural development. Problems of credit, marketing, prices, seeds, fertilizers, pesticides, salinity and drainage, extension services, rural education, and a horde of others have been repeatedly studied by

---

[79] U.S. Department of Agriculture, *The Agricultural Economy of Iraq,* p. 58.
[80] Warriner, *Land Reform in Principle and Practice,* p. 97.

Iraqis and foreigners. Yet if achievement falls short of expectations, it is because the development process requires knowledge and competence that cannot be acquired except through systematic experience over a period of time which can hardly be abridged. There will be no attempt in this brief survey to map out in any detail a program of agricultural development capable of generating the output and income projected earlier in this study. Instead I stress my conviction that these levels of income and output cannot be attained without developing the agricultural sector with almost fierce endeavor.

What is needed above all is a decision to elevate the agricultural sector to a position of top priority for the coming decade. This would entail comprehensive planning, far-reaching change in institutions, devotion of a larger volume of human resources to agricultural development than has been the case in the past, and the earmarking of substantially greater financial resources for this purpose than seems to have been contemplated. The moving of the agricultural program to the focal point of national attention would imply the involvement of many more government departments than the Ministries of Agriculture and Agrarian Reform. Raising agricultural productivity would involve many indirect contributions, such as the construction of roads, schools, and hospitals; the development of industrial projects dependent on existing or prospective agricultural raw materials; improvement and modernization of techniques involving information services and scientific and research laboratories for innovations and maintenance; and, above all, the structuring and training of manpower to assume these developmental tasks in addition to the continuous training of those who will do the actual cultivation. In brief, what this amounts to is the firm establishment in the national consciousness of an agricultural decade, as it were, to ensure within this period a substantial rise in agricultural production and income.

Such strong emphasis on agriculture must not be construed as disparagement of industry. The tenet of this study is that Iraq can and must become an industrial nation by the turn of the century. The initial priority given to raising agricultural productivity is aimed primarily at bringing about a situation in which substantially greater agricultural product is generated by a comparatively smaller labor force. More labor can be liberated for industrial pursuit and industrial expansion without any severe handicap arising from shortage of food and raw materials and without placing undue strain on the internal price level and the balance of payments, as the oil revenue, though increasing, becomes a smaller proportion of a faster-growing national income.

Industry

Iraq is in a very favorable natural situation for the promotion of a manufacturing complex. Many an underdeveloped country is restrained in the adoption of advanced techniques in its industry because of shortages in foreign exchange needed for importing the machinery or hiring the foreign expertise that goes with the advanced techniques, or because of population pressure that militates against labor-saving devices. Iraq does not have to face such severe restrictions in promulgating an industrial development policy, being relatively free from balance of payments problems and population pressure.

Nevertheless, past performance, particularly before the revolution of 1958, did not reflect any vigorous effort toward the promotion of manufacturing industry. Some modest beginnings for the encouragement of domestic industry were undertaken by the royalist regime through tax laws and through the establishment and operation of the state-owned Industrial Bank.[81] The Bank, however, gave priority to enterprises that processed domestic agricultural products and produced building materials for local use. Technical training, which is perhaps the most crucial aspect in the promotion of the manufacturing sector in Iraq, was not integrated in industrial finance or coordinated with it. Moreover, the Bank neither undertook nor fostered market research and analysis, nor did it pursue a vigorous policy of promoting new products and new industries.

This early policy of feeble support to industrial development is explained partly by preoccupation with more pressing problems and partly by the weight of opinion of international experts consulted by the Iraqi government. In the early 1950s, a considerable number of foreign consultants were invited to study the problems of economic development in Iraq and to advise the government on policy. There seems to have been some kind of consensus among these experts that the promotion of manufacturing industry did not merit a high rank in the priority scale of economic development.[82] The reasoning underlying this conclusion was based mainly on the well-known principle of comparative advantage. Iraq, it was argued, possessed a comparative advantage in agriculture. Because of the growth in its population and world population, the future market for its agricultural products looked promising. In industry, on the other hand, it would have to compete with a greater handicap because of deficiencies in technical skills in the ranks of labor and management. Subsidizing or protecting industry would foster inefficiency, constitute a heavy burden on the consumer, and further increase the gap between industrial and agricultural incomes to the detriment of the latter.

These arguments seem to have influenced government outlook at the time, but somehow the government failed to understand that factor supplies can be substantially altered in the long run as a result of deliberate and direct intervention in the economy, and could thus lead to an altered cost structure and a different pattern of comparative advantages. Such transformation has its costs, and it is the task of the policymaker to weigh costs and benefits, not only at the present time but in the long run as well. Iraq's long-term development requires a drastic upgrading of its manpower. The buildup of a skilled labor force can be best attained within the folds of a growing industrial sector, as indeed is mani-

---

[81] Kathleen Langley, *The Industrialization of Iraq*, Harvard University Press, Cambridge, Mass., 1961, p. 137 passim.
[82] IBRD, *The Economic Development of Iraq*, p. 40; Iversen, *Monetary Policy in Iraq*, pp. 289–290; Lord Salter, *The Development of Iraq, A Plan for Action*, p. 71 passim; Arthur D. Little, *A Plan for Industrial Development in Iraq*, p. 3.

fested in the country's own experience with the Iraq Petroleum Company and the refinery at Daura.[83] It must also be recalled that labor productivity tends to be much higher in industry than in agriculture. For Iraq, the differential was estimated at one time to be sixfold.[84] Of course much of this improved productivity is attained at a high capital cost in shifting to the more capital-intensive processes of industrial production. But a good deal of it is also due to the upgrading of labor skills. Some subsidization or protection of industries may be necessary for a time. Such measures can be costly and may lead to some waste in capital, but in Iraq the supply of capital is elastic; the waste from a somewhat forced program of industrialization could be absorbed without resulting in long-term damage.

The development of the industrial sector will have the further advantage of expanding the domestic market for the country's agricultural products and absorbing displaced agricultural labor. The simultaneous development of both sectors is in conformity to the declared long-term policy before and after the revolution of the gradual decrease of reliance on oil revenue and the enabling of the economy to sustain a continuous growth even if the oil revenue should disappear or become a minor source of finance.

This target of a balanced growth became better understood and more strongly desired after the revolution. In the Detailed Economic Plan issued in 1961, about ID 167 million was earmarked as planned expenditure for industry.[85] This was 100 million dinars more than was devoted to industry in any of the previous development plans. The capital of the Industrial Bank was raised substantially, and several new branches of the Bank were opened in various cities. More assistance and protection were extended to domestic industry. Although such actions may reflect a greater awareness of the necessity of developing the industrial sector, and may be indicative of a more favorable disposition on the part of the government toward industry, they do not necessarily signify firmer commitment to a surer and faster development of industry. In fact, actual spending, despite the vast increase in planned expenditure, did not change during 1959–1965 much over what it was for 1952–1959. Industrialization is not effected by declaration of intentions or the making of budgetary provisions.

Some errors of policy have been committed at various times. For example, immediately after the 1958 revolution, the new government, in its enthusiasm for inducing new growth centers, scattered industrial projects around the country without proper consideration of the location of individual plants in relation to raw materials and markets, resulting in misallocation of resources that could have been avoided. Also some setback to private investment may have occurred as a consequence of the 1964 nationalization measures. But the major obstacles

[83] A. Y. Badre and S. Siksek, *Manpower and Oil in Arab Countries,* American University of Beirut, Beirut, 1960, p. 245.
[84] Langley, *The Industrialization of Iraq,* p. 5.
[85] *Law No. 70 for 1961, The Five Years Detailed Economic Plan for 1961/62 to 1965/66,* p. 11.

to industrialization in Iraq have been, all along, the scarcity of trained labor, the deficiency in entrepreneurial and managerial talent, and the narrowness of the market. The mitigation of these disabilities calls for much more than budget allocations. What is needed is an industrial leadership that will foster continuous search, experiment, and innovation; promote studies of products and markets; encourage pooling of resources; and organize and train labor. Given the political structure of the country, the paucity of the entrepreneurial talent, and the feebleness of the capital market, it is not likely that such leadership will be provided in abundance by the private sector. At least for major industrial undertakings requiring large capital and complex organization, the government must provide initiative and leadership. This does not preclude a certain amount of growth in private or mixed industry alongside a major growth in public industrial enterprise, particularly as private and mixed enterprise have a secure place within the ideology of Arab socialism followed by Iraq. But if the government is to promote industrial enterprise on a large scale, its administrative machinery must be restructured and modernized, not only in the departments dealing directly with the administration of industrial enterprise but also in several other departments involved with such matters—labor, housing, public hygiene, public transport, education, information.

The sphere in Iraq most suited for government industrial enterprise is perhaps that of petrochemicals. As was mentioned earlier, capitalization, technical, and marketing problems here are of such large scale as to lie, at present at least, beyond the capabilities of indigenous private enterprise. A possible alternative, of course, is to resort to private foreign companies under concessionary agreements or in partnership with the Iraqi government. This is unlikely, however, not only on nationalistic grounds but also because of conflict with the general domestic policy of entrusting major industrial undertakings to public enterprise. Nor is this alternative desirable from the standpoint of a long-run policy for the industrialization of the country. The assumption of full responsibility by Iraqis and the technical training of Iraqi personnel would probably proceed at a much faster pace if Iraq borrowed part of the required capital and sought foreign technical assistance on a contractual basis. This, in fact, is precisely the policy that guided the Iraqi government in its agreements with countries of the Eastern bloc, in 1969, for developing petroleum, sulphur, and petrochemicals.

The development of the petrochemical complex will not give direct employment to large numbers of people, because the industries concerned are manifestly capital intensive and require a comparatively high level of skills. The more salutary effect will probably lie in the hoped-for repercussion on the whole industrial sector as well as the entire economy. A growing petrochemical industry is capable of producing a wide range of chemical by-products, and an atmosphere of search, experiment, and technological adaptation is likely to grow around such industry. Such developments may trigger innovative activities on the part of private entrepreneurs to help expand the industrial sector into further fields of production. In fact, my assessment of economic prospects is based on the expectation of such expansion in the industrial sector, without which my projected figures for output and employment would have to be scaled down.

Manpower

The most difficult problems with which Iraq has to contend in planning its economic development are those relating to manpower. The growth of the volume and quality of human resources, including both labor and management, is perhaps the most crucial element in the process of development. In Iraq, as in any other country, the labor force is affected by population trends on one hand and by the evolution of social institutions on the other. From the mid-nineteenth century to the present, the Iraqi population has grown at rates varying from 1.3 to 2.4 percent a year. The current rate (and that on which the projections of the present study are based) is the higher figure, 2.4 percent.[86] A good deal of internal migration has also occurred over the years. There has been a marked decrease in the nomadic population, as nomads have settled in rural areas over the last 30 or 40 years. The urban population rose much more slowly, except in the last two decades as a result of rural migration into Baghdad and Basra.[87]

The most striking feature of the population structure in Iraq is that it is extremely young. This is attributed mainly to the combination of high mortality and high fertility rates,[88] which results in an unduly high ratio of dependent to active population and partly explains the low ratio of the labor force to total population. Iraq's problem is compounded further in that the level of skills in the labor force falls considerably short of that compatible with the country's capital possibilities. The level of literacy in Iraq is very low. Not more than one-sixth of the population can read and write,[89] and these persons are not spread evenly throughout the country. According to a study of a few years ago, about one-third of the literate males and almost one-half of the literate females lived in Baghdad,[90] leaving a very thin spread of literate people in the rest of the country. In addition, the population suffers from many diseases that reduce the productivity of its labor force. There is also a serious shortage of housing and other social amenities. In the big cities these shortages are made more complex by the large stream of migrants into shanty towns, where they live typically in small

---

[86] M. S. Hasan, "Growth and Structure of Iraq's Population, 1867–1947," *Bulletin of the Oxford University Institute of Statistics,* Vol. 20 (November 1958), pp. 349–350; also United Nations, *Demographic Yearbooks, 1956* to *1965.*

[87] George L. Harris, *Iraq: Its People, Its Society, Its Culture,* Human Resources Area Files, New Haven 1958, p. 34.

[88] Doris G. Adams, "Current Population Trends in Iraq," *Middle East Journal,* Vol. 10 (Spring 1956), p. 154.

[89] Joanne E. Holler, *Population Growth and Social Change in the Middle East,* George Washington University Press, Washington, D.C., 1964, p. 32.

[90] Hasan, "Growth and Structure of Iraq's Population, 1867–1947," p. 48.

mud or reed huts called *sarifas*. In the rural districts the problem is basically one of providing adequate accommodations for an increasing number of medical workers and other government officials who must live and work in those areas.

These problems of deficiencies in literacy, technical skills, health, housing, and social amenities have not eluded the various governments and the enlightened citizens of the country. Much has been done toward the solution of some of the more pressing manpower problems. For example, Iraq devotes a higher share of its national income to educational programs than most countries in the region. In 1965, it allocated 6 percent of its national income in the ordinary budget of the government for expenditure on education.[91] Government educational policy was cognizant of the gaps and imbalances in the system. It was realized that much greater effort should be exerted in promoting girls' education because of the wide gap between the school enrollment of boys and girls, and as a result girls have been enrolling in the past few years at a faster rate than boys. Emphasis is being placed on the development of vocational and technical education in secondary schools and on the expansion of university education, particularly in the sciences, which account currently for less than one-third of the students enrolled. In education, as in all other aspects of the manpower problem, the difficulty arises not so much from the lack of a properly conceived policy as from the gigantic dimensions of the problem. Despite all these efforts, illiteracy is still resistant to any drastic reduction because of the bottleneck in recruiting elementary school teachers. Although in recent years some centers of industrial training have been established, the level of vocational education and training is still far below that compatible with the desired industrial expansion. In the rural districts the educational program is still neither sufficiently widespread nor sufficiently relevant to rural conditions.

The same kind of problem is encountered in the fields of health, housing, and other social services. In one decade, between 1952 and 1962, government expenditure on health in the ordinary budget rose threefold. In one decade, reported malaria cases were reduced from 500,000 to 10,000, the number of physicians almost doubled, hospital beds likewise increased substantially, and scores of rural health centers were set up. Yet despite such progress the country still faces serious health problems attributable chiefly to shortages in medical personnel, particularly in the ranks of assistants, nurses, technicians, and other paramedical staff. It is estimated that nurses and assistant nurses together had become in 1965 only slightly more numerous than physicians.[92]

What is manifested in education and health is again encountered in housing and all other social services. The problems are fairly well known; the gaps and imbalances are identified with a good measure of clarity, government policy is often formulated with more or less proper emphasis, and programs emanating from such policies are often well conceived. Implementation, on the other hand,

[91] United Nations, *Studies on Selected Development Problems,* p. 48.
[92] *Ibid.,* p. 50.

326

not infrequently falters and falls short of designated targets. The main reason is invariably the shortage of qualified personnel to carry out the programs. The main target of the manpower program, namely, the development of higher levels of skills and efficiency, is not reached because of the very ills that the program sets out to treat. The situation may be further aggravated by a certain amount of improper allocation of human resources due to political and cultural reasons. Basically, however, it is the rapidly increasing magnitude of the demand for skills that reveals the shortage. Skills are increasing, but not as rapidly as the demand for them, a most difficult situation which can hardly be mitigated so long as capital possibilities continue to outstrip by a long distance the pace of labor.

The presence of widespread unemployment despite the rising demand for labor further aggravates the situation. The unemployment occurs primarily in the ranks of the unskilled. A high incidence is found among the dwellers of the *sarifas* who have drifted to Baghdad and Basra from rural areas in the south. Many reasons underlie this internal migration trend. It is not only expectation of better jobs and the promise of a more attractive city life that has lured the migrants there. Many other causes contributed: expropriation and oppression of tribesmen by tribal chiefs, political clashes among peasants, depressed conditions of small landholders, shortage of education and health facilities.[93] In 1963 the migrants to Baghdad formed almost one-seventh of the population of the city.[94] Many of them find jobs as policemen, soldiers, gardeners, guards, porters, janitors, and servants. Some provide only casual labor, some remain unemployed for long stretches, and some women augment the family income by selling dairy products.[95] Government training, housing, and health programs have in theory covered these groups as well, but progress has been slow for the reasons mentioned earlier.

IV. Conclusions

The major policy issue in the field of economic development facing Iraq in the immediate future is how to bring about a simultaneous, rapid, and substantial expansion in both agriculture and industry. The financing of a program of development in alignment with this policy, in respect to both domestic and foreign currencies, does not seem to constitute a major problem or precipitate a crucial bottleneck in the immediate future, so long as oil revenue continues to flow in substantial volume. No major problems are expected to arise either with domestic prices or with the external balance of payments. Eventually, of course, other sources of finance, particularly taxation and surplus returns on government enterprise, must supplement, and in time replace, oil revenue. With the sociopoliti-

[93] Fuad Baali, "Social Factors in Iraqi Rural-Urban Migration," *The American Journal of Economics and Sociology,* Vol. 25, No. 4 (October 1966), pp. 359–364.
[94] *Ibid.,* p. 362.
[95] *Ibid.,* p. 364.

cal outlook for economic development foreseen for Iraq—namely, that the government will continue to promote, own, and direct major enterprise—profits from government enterprise, including the development of sulphur mining, should become an increasingly important source for the financing of further development. Such profits alone, however, may not prove sufficient, and substantial increases in tax revenue, particularly taxes on income, may prove necessary.

The most difficult problem that faces the country is that of upgrading its manpower. The building up of the level of skills cannot move, even under the most favorable of conditions, as fast as the capital possibilities occasioned by the flow of oil revenue. The conditions, of course, are not always the most favorable. There are three major conditions that have to be ameliorated and brought under reasonable control before the upgrading of manpower can proceed even at a normal, to say nothing of an accelerated, pace. First, radical changes must occur in the public administration to move it toward greater technical competence and efficient execution. Second, a stronger and more all-pervading spirit of nationalism and patriotism must be developed in order to transcend the divisive loyalties to tribes, ethnic groups, and religious sects that continuously erode efforts to build for the common good. Finally, the country starves for political stability. The frequent, eruptive change of government makes any continuous long-term planning very difficult, militates against the building up of a public administration with cumulative experience and technology, and saps the energy of the public sector, which in Iraq constitutes the chief source of innovational activity and economic leadership.

CHAPTER 7

Economic Development of Syria

Bent Hansen

Knowledge of economic developments and conditions in Syria, particularly in recent years, is constrained by serious data gaps and other deficiencies of information. The resulting murkiness surrounding the past and present makes crystal-ball gazing even more of an art than is usually the case. Hansen, in the following essay, seeks to solve this problem by concentrating on the large issues, whose outlines, at least, seem reasonably clear. He confesses to uncertainty about the details. In general, he paints a picture of a somewhat simpler economy than those portrayed in the other essays in this book, but whether this simplicity is real or reflects the paucity of information is not clear.

Hansen finds agriculture to be the key to past economic performance in Syria. Substantial growth from 1946 to 1957 was based on a rapid extension of the cropped area, an extension that has since slowed down appreciably. Agricultural stagnation is due, then, to a classic case of Ricardian diminishing returns, observable in a steady decline in value added per cropped hectare. At the same time, the vagaries of weather have led to pronounced fluctuations in agricultural output and in national output as well. In regard to the future, past agricultural growth does not seem to be repeatable, and future progress will have to be sought in modernizing, rather than extending, agricultural production. The Euphrates Dam will help, but much more is needed. Hansen also finds the same problems in the public sector in Syria as he discribed in his paper on Egypt: increasing bureaucracy and economic controls but with questionable rationality. And in Syria the problem is aggravated by the shortage of skilled administrators.

On the plus side, the expected increase in petroleum exports should help maintain forward momentum at least through the mid-1970s. From then on the potential sources of growth appear to lie in technological improvement and increased efficiency. Such sources are real and important but not always easy to exploit. More than for any other country discussed in this book, there is a serious question about Syria's ability to sustain past rates of economic growth.

Economic Development of Syria

I. Introduction

Attempts to appraise the development possibilities of Syria meet with serious obstacles on the purely informational level, and any appraisal must contain so many uncertainities that it should be presented to the reader only with some caveats.

Statistical and other data are scanty, and those that do exist are rarely satisfactory. The country, for instance, has never had an agricultural census; the first population census was undertaken in 1960; and general cost of living indexes do not exist. The presentation of official data is usually deficient with respect to definitions, explanations of methods of estimation, and coverage of data. It is exceedingly difficult, therefore, to describe statistically what has actually taken place in the past and even what the approximate present position is. This study nevertheless attempts to give a picture of the past and present, but the reader should understand that at best it only tells us something about crude trends and orders of magnitude. Lack of factual information also throws its shadow on the projections of future growth possibilities, which are therefore discussed only in rather general terms.

In such circumstances, the opinions and views of well-informed, experienced people—technicians, government officials, experts in special fields—with inside information and a detailed, albeit unsystematic, knowledge of the economy and its modus operandi and problems would have been extremely valuable. Unfortunately, the political state of the country has made it increasingly difficult to obtain even this sort of information. Syria is today a totalitarian state, and the possibilities of communicating with knowledgeable Syrians are severely circumscribed. I visited Damascus in the summer of 1968 to discuss development problems with higher government officials, but the visit was completely abortive.

This study accordingly claims to be no more than an outside observer's description and analysis, based mainly on printed sources obtainable outside the country. This adds unnecessarily to the black areas on the map and increases the chance of misjudgments. Syriology is now a science almost comparable to Kremlinology. I hope, nevertheless, to give in broad outline a correct impression of what the Syrian economy is and may become.

The development prospects of Syria are not particularly bright, and they depend much on government and governmental efforts. Agriculture has ended

331

Table 7-1

Population and National Income,
1967 and 1980

Year	Population (millions) (1)	Net National Income at Constant 1963 Prices (million S£) (2)	Income Per Capita	
			S£ (3)	$ U.S.[c] (4)
1967	6[a]	3,742[b]	611	153
1980	8.8	7,516	854	214

[a]Economist Intelligence Unit, *Quarterly Economic Reviews, Syria, Lebanon, Cyprus,* Annual Supplement 1968, p. 3, official estimate. The United Nations estimate is slightly lower, namely, 3.45 million for 1966; see *United Nations Demographic Yearbook 1966,* New York, 1967.
[b]*Rapport 1967-1968 sur l'Economie Syrienne,* 1ère edition, Septembre 1968, Office Arabe de Presse et de Documentation, Damascus, p. A.99.
[c]Converted at 1 U.S. $ = 4 S£. The official rate is 3.82, but the market rate has been somewhat higher than 4.00.

up in a sort of cul de sac from which it can be rescued only by determined and imaginative efforts by the government. Syria is poorly endowed with raw materials, apart from the oil which during the next 5 years is expected to add significantly to the national income and to ease the balance of payments. But otherwise the country is now facing the problem of stimulating development and increasing production without being blessed by any spectacular natural advantage. Even under the most favorable external and internal political conditions, therefore, I find it difficult to imagine the country's growth rate exceeding 5–6 percent annually during the next decade. At a population increase of about 3 percent per year, the annual increase of income per capita should thus at best become 2-3 percent.

Working with an average of 5.5 percent increase of net national income and 3 percent population increase, I believe that the situation by 1980 should be as shown in Table 7-1.

II. Perspectives and Prospects

The Political and Economic Instability of Syria

Modern Syria's political and economic instability adds to the difficulties of interpreting and appraising Syrian development in the past. We become involved in intricate questions of both the influence of political environment on economic development and the relation between short-term disturbances and long-term growth.

Instability has predominated in politics ever since the country gained full independence in 1946. It has shown itself in a series of *coups d'état* and revolutions—minor and not so minor—often accompanied by constitutional changes. Quite apart from the impact of this political turbulence on current production and investment activities, it has probably done much to prevent efficient economic institutions from being established or developed. And at least since the mid-1950s, there has been so much uncertainty about the future of the ownership of means of production and the legal status of enterprise that the volume and patterns of private investment have been distorted. Until 1955, the Syrian economic system resembled that of present-day Lebanon, with the economic role of government limited to securing protection for developing private enterprise. Today, it has been transformed into a government-controlled mixed economy quite similar to the present Egyptian system but marked by uncertainty about the economy's future organization. And in between, the country experienced a decade of great confusion with respect to ownership and government controls.

With the elections of 1955, the Baath Party and the Communists became a real threat to the traditional capitalistic laissez-faire system of the country, and when the union with Egypt was established in 1958 the threat materialized. Land reforms, similar to those in Egypt, were instituted immediately, and President Nasser's nationalization decrees of July 1961, which brought big business in Egypt under state ownership, applied also to Syria (at that time the Northern Region of the United Arab Republic). When Syria broke the union a few months later, denationalization was immediately undertaken and the land reforms were, for all purposes and intents, discontinued. With the return of the Baath to power, big business was renationalized in 1964 and the land reforms reinstituted and sharpened. A new constitution—the sixth since independence—established a "peoples' democratic socialist republic" and declared all wealth and resources to belong to the people, and to be placed at the service of the people by the state—whatever that may mean. The constitution recognizes three different forms of ownership: state ownership, collective ownership to be exercised by the workers of individual enterprises, and private ownership, limited to small-scale business. Extensive further nationalizations were decreed in 1965.

Although the legal details may differ, from a practical point of view the situation is much the same as that in Egypt, with all big business (including most foreign trade) in the hands of the government, whereas agriculture, retail trade, small-scale industry and handicraft, housing, and the professions are privately run, although subject to various kinds of government control. The declared intention of the government is to go further in the direction of limiting private business. That the final establishment of Arab socialism in Syria has served to paralyze private initiative is clear. Indeed, this was the intention of the Baath. It is less clear to what extent the government has been able to replace private by government initiative.

Economic instability has shown itself primarily in strong fluctuations of national production and income and of the balance of payments, whereas prices

333

seem to have been relatively stable. The fluctuations of production and income seem to have had little to do with the political upheavals and uncertainties and the changes in ownership. They are related, above all, to changes in the annual rainfall, which give rise to strong crop fluctuations. Hitting agricultural production and income directly, the crop fluctuations have secondary effects on the rest of the economy—in particular, trade, transport, and industries processing agricultural products—and they give rise to sharp changes in the balance of current payments, which has alternated between small surpluses and very large deficits. The problem of crop fluctuations is one of the important challenges to future economic policies.

The Growth Rate in Retrospect

Little is known about the development of national wealth and income as Syria changed from a province in the decaying Ottoman Empire to a French mandate under the League of Nations in 1922 and finally to a fully independent country in 1946. Although the country was deeply impoverished under Turkish rule, increasing security and improved government control of Bedouin tribes had made themselves felt by the second half of the nineteenth century, and in this respect the country gained further through becoming a French mandate, although the French did little to develop the country economically.[1] Moreover, the general partition of the Middle East, the result of the *divide et impera* policies of France and Britain after World War I, and the French cession to Turkey at the outbreak of World War II of the economically valuable northwestern corner of Syria around the port of Alexandretta (now Iskanderun) and Antioch (Antaya) left the country rather dismembered and economically crippled. The new borders cut across the old road and rail lines so that the new nation tended to fall apart economically into three badly connected regions. The traditional transit trade to the northeast and southeast, which at one time was a source of great wealth for Syrian merchants, deteriorated rapidly as a consequence of the new artificial frontiers and growing nationalism in the area. Add to this the effects of the great depression of the 1930s and World War II, and it seems likely that at the end of the second World War Syria was no better off than before the first one.[2]

An economic upswing took place, however, after the country gained independence in 1946. To some extent this was a normal postwar recovery bolstered by reserves accumulated during the time of the war; but to some extent it was also a consequence of the protectionism that the new state could offer to indus-

[1] Norman N. Lewis, "The Frontier of Settlement in Syria, 1800–1950," *International Affairs,* Vol. XXXI, No. 1 (January 1955).

[2] Syria, of course, "gained" from the war, as did some other countries in the sense that substantial foreign claims were accumulated in connection with the improved export conditions and sales to the belligerent powers, and the severed import trade. Valuable though this gain was for postwar recovery and development, it was probably little more than "forced savings" out of inflation profits from a national income that may not have increased much in real terms.

try, and, finally, a response of agricultural prices. This upswing not only helped to improve the standard of living of the population but also fostered a myth about the Syrian economy and the Syrian entrepreneur, implying that if only the private sector were left to itself the "animal spirits" of Syrian entrepreneurship would automatically bring about a high rate of growth. The upswing did in fact slow down when from the mid-1950s economic policy changed toward more and more government control. But the growth rate would presumably in any case have tended to slow down; and compared with the period before 1956 increased government participation seemed a necessary condition for further development.

It is difficult to assess the performance of the Syrian economy even for the postwar years. The lack of reliable data is one problem. The heavy crop fluctuations unfortunately add to the difficulties. From 1953 to 1968, the period for which official estimates of the domestic product exist, the annual percentage change of NDP (at constant prices) varied between −15 percent (in 1953) and +27 percent (1962); for those years the changes in agricultural value added were −33 percent and +50 percent, respectively. With such violent variations a single year, more or less, in the period considered may make all the difference in

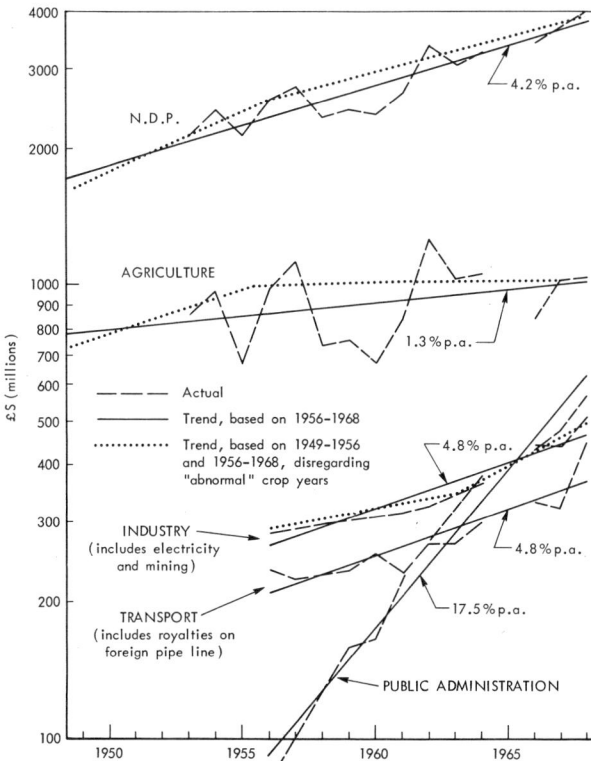

FIG. 7-1.   Syria: Net value added. NDP at constant 1963 prices.

335

the estimate of the average growth rate. Quite naturally, therefore, estimates of the average growth rate vary substantially.

Figure 7-1 brings together the most recent official estimates of total NDP from 1956 to 1968 at constant 1963 factor prices and some estimates for earlier years, together with four of the most interesting component parts of NDP—agriculture, industry (including electricity and extraction), transportation, and public administration. In addition to the actual annual data the figure also shows trends, and Table 7-2 gives data for the sectoral contributions to NDP in 1956 and 1968 and their average growth rates for this period.[3]

[3] Official national income data extend back only to 1953. For the year 1950 an estimate was made within the Ministry of Finance (see Muhammed Diab, "National Income Practices in Syria," in T. M. Khan, ed., *Middle Eastern Studies in Income and Wealth,* Bowes & Bowes, London, 1965, p. 132); for 1949, 1950, and 1953 a set of figures were presented by the International Bank for Reconstruction and Development (IBRD), *The Economic Development of Syria,* Washington, 1955, pp. 20–21. The IBRD estimates were used in Figure 7-1 (shown by dotted line); since the level of these estimates was substantially lower than the official estimates for 1953 onward, the IBRD estimates were increased in proportion to the official estimates for 1953. The agricultural value added for 1950 in Figure 7-1 (indicated by dotted line) is based on a series for gross crop production published by Edmund Y. Asfour, *Syria: Development and Monetary Policy,* Harvard Middle Eastern Monograph Series, Cambridge, Mass., 1959, p. 21.

Two official national income series have been published. The first is available for the years 1953–1966 and is at constant 1956 prices. It was subject to some revision at the end of the 1950s, but the revised figures seem only to have been carried back to 1956. Since the revision affected only two sectors (agriculture and transportation), which were revised upward by constant amounts for the years 1956–1960, I have revised the figures for 1953–1955 upward by the same amounts. The series at 1956 prices is published in the official *Statistical Abstracts,* Damascus, various issues, and the methods of estimation are described in Diab, "National Income Practices in Syria."

The second series covers the years 1956–1968 and is at constant 1963 prices. It has only recently been released [*Rapport 1967–1968,* pp. A. 98–99 and B. 83–84, for the years 1956–1964 and 1966 and 1967, and *Etude Mensuelle sur L'economie et Les Finances des Pays Arabes,* Vol. XII, No. 4 (April 1969), pp. 17–20, for the years 1967 and 1968]. Only a few comments about methods of estimation are presented in connection with the release, but the methods seem to be improved as compared with the old 1956 prices series. The old series is available at both factor cost and market prices, both net and gross; so far the new series is available only net and at factor cost. Neither series takes into account gains and losses from changes in the terms of trade, which for some years must have been substantial.

The two series are quite different, with respect to both sectoral distribution and growth rates. Since no detailed description of methods of estimation is available, an appraisal of the estimates is excluded. But they must be highly uncertain. Syrian primary data do not permit very reliable national income and production estimates.

Figure 7-1 confirms that national product has fluctuated strongly and that the fluctuations have originated mainly in agriculture. The growth of all the other sectors has been much more stable although there was a clear retardation of growth in some of them during the four years of severe drought and bad crops from 1958 to 1961.

The trends of income and production are difficult to ascertain. A mechanically fitted trend based on the years 1956–1968 (the unbroken straight lines in Figure 7-1) shows 4.2 percent annual growth of NDP, and the earlier years back to 1949 do not deviate significantly from this trend line, extrapolated backward. However, this mechanical way of looking at the trend is probably misleading. Production is highly dependent on crop fluctuations, and this factor requires

---

I have chosen to work on the new 1963 prices series, assuming it to be an improvement over the earlier ones. For agriculture, the official NDP estimate shows about the same development from 1953 to 1964 as the FAO index for total agricultural production; see FAO, *Monthly Statistics*. For later years the official estimates show a less favorable development than the FAO index. The annual fluctuations appear to be a little smaller in the FAO index, but the trend is about the same. For industry the UN production index shows a substantially faster rate of growth from 1956 to 1964 than does the official NDP estimate. This is quite natural, however, since the UN index tends to exclude small-scale industry and handicraft and concentrates on the "development commodities." Neither the FAO nor the UN index thus contradicts the official estimates. However, both the 1956 prices and the 1963 prices series exhibit peculiarities that warn against drawing far-reaching conclusions based on details. Commerce, for instance, not shown separately in Table 7-2, displays in the 1963 prices series a substantial fall over the period as a whole; this is not easy to understand. And the high growth rates in dwellings and public administration also deserve question marks. However, the fact that generally this new official series paints a less favorable picture of Syrian developments adds to its credibility.

Another series at constant 1963 prices has appeared in a UN publication, "Plan Formulation and Development Perspectives in Syria," United Nations Economic and Social Office in Beirut, ESOB/DEV/PLAN/MEET.2/6, 27 May 1968, provisional (hereafter cited as ESOB). With respect both to growth rates and to sector distribution it resembled the old series much more than the new one. Generally, the new 1963 prices series shows a slightly lower overall growth rate. Between sectors there are very substantial differences. The new series shows lower growth rates for agriculture and industry and a much higher growth rate for public administration. For the individual sectors the two series are unfortunately so different that it does matter which one is used.

In what follows I shall work mainly with the concept of net domestic product (NDP) at factor cost. The reason for this choice is that sectoral breakdowns are given on this basis and that the estimates at market prices, where at all available, seem to exaggerate the rate of growth through adding current indirect tax revenues minus subsidies to the fixed price estimates of GDP. Figures for net factor income from abroad are available for the years 1956–1968, but the amounts are in any case negligible. Incomes from royalties for foreign-owned oil pipelines are included as NDP in the transportation sector.

Table 7-2

Net Domestic Product, 1956-1968, Sectoral Distribution and Growth

| Sector | Net Domestic Product at Constant 1963 Factor Cost | | | | Average Annual Compound Rate of Growth,[a] 1956-1968 (percent) (5) |
| | 1956 | | 1968 | | |
	Million S£ (1)	Percent (2)	Million S£ (3)	Percent (4)	
Agriculture	981.0	38.4	1,046.5	25.9	1.3
Industry, incl. extraction and electricity	284.6	11.1	516.5	13.8	4.8
Construction	83.8	3.3	136.3	3.4	5.8
Transport	237.3	9.3	451.4	11.2	4.8
Commerce and finance	589.8	23.0	606.6	15.0	0.6
Dwellings	125.5	4.9	366.6	9.1	9.1
Public administration	79.7	3.1	568.6	14.1	17.5
Services	158.6	6.2	341.7	8.5	6.9
Total NDP	2,540.3	100.0	4,034.2	100.0	4.2
Total increase of NDP in 1967 over 1956			1493.9		
Of which: in commerce and finance, dwellings, public administration and services			929.9		

[a]This is the growth rate along the exponential, least-square trends shown in Figure 7-1.

Source: Rapport 1967-1968, pp. B. 83 and A. 99, and *Etude Mensuelle sur L'Economie et Les Finances des Pays Arabes.*

special attention. The years 1955, 1958–1961, 1965, and 1966 witnessed severe drought and/or bad weather conditions; 1957 and 1962, on the other hand, were particularly favorable crop years. If these clearly abnormal years are disregarded, it would then appear that the economy was growing by some 5–6 percent per year before 1956,[4] whereas from 1956 to 1967 it may only have grown

[4] This agrees with the estimate for that period of the IBRD, *The Economic Development of Syria,* p. 21.

by somewhat less than 4 percent per year. The exact figures are not very important, but to me, at least, it seems pretty clear that a marked decline in the growth rate took place around 1956. The years 1967 and 1968 may signify a somewhat higher growth rate related to the exploitation of the oil fields (see below).

The main cause of the decline of the general growth trend after 1956 is to be found in agriculture. Whereas agricultural production (value added) may have increased at an average rate of some 4–5 percent before 1956, after that year its average growth rate seem to have been as low as about 0.5 percent per year. This is brought out by Figure 7-1 if we base the trend for the first postwar decade, 1945–1956, on the years 1950, 1953, 1954, and 1956, and that for the following period, 1956–1968, on the years 1956, 1963, 1964, 1967, and 1968, these being relatively normal crop years. These trends are shown by the dotted lines in Figure 7-1. It is, of course, always difficult to say what exactly is a "normal" year, but a glance at the data given in Table 7-4 for the cropped area—which grew steadily by 5–6 percent per year until 1957, and from that year onward by about 1 percent per year only—makes it perfectly clear that there must have been a radical break (fall) in the agricultural growth trend around 1956/57.

After a decade of rapid growth, agriculture thus suddenly became almost stagnant. The very fast expansion of services nevertheless prevented the overall growth rate from falling from more than from 5–6 percent to about 4 percent.

The deceleration of the overall growth rate is remarkable also against the background of the development of fixed investments. Although information here is very shaky, in Table 7-3 an attempt is made to splice together existing bits of information to form a coherent picture. The table points to a slight increase of the investment ratio until around 1955/56. The ratio may have been about 13 percent of GNP at market prices in 1950, increasing to about 15 percent by 1956. During the period of the Union with Egypt, when Egyptian planners and administrators tried to push public fixed investments, the ratio rose to about 16 percent. During the private business-friendly interregnum of 1961–1964, the ratio rose a little further and reached about 18 percent in 1963. Thereafter it slipped back slightly, perhaps with some relationship to the nationalizations of 1964 and 1965, and not until 1967 did the investment ratio again creep up over the 18 percent reached in 1963. With all possible reservations for statistical shortcomings (see note to Table 7-3), it would thus seem that on the average the investment ratio was higher in the 1960s than earlier.

A slowdown of the growth rate has thus accompanied an increasing investment ratio. A partial explanation of this paradox is to be found in agricultural developments. The rapid growth of agricultural production before 1956 was based mainly on an expansion of the acreage and required relatively little capital input. Since then, however, investments in agriculture have given little return. Moreover, investment has been directed to an increasing degree toward infrastructure and other public investment where the immediate returns are relatively

Table 7-3

Gross Fixed Investments, 1950-1967[a]

| Year | Total Fixed Investments | | GDP at constant Market Prices (3) |
	Million S£ (1)	Of which: public, percent (2)	
1950	275	n.a.	(13)
1953	355	n.a.	(15)
1955	396	14.1	(16)
1956	426	18.5	14.9
1957	308	22.5	10.0
1958	402	26.3	15.1
1959	441	n.a.	16.0
1960	451	n.a.	16.3
1961	488	39.8	16.1
1962	654	26.6	17.3
1963	639	26.6	18.1
1964	612	26.2	16.3
1965	585	41.3 Plan	n.a.
1966	701	45.1 66-70:	(18)
1967	809	n.a. 69.7	(19)

[a] The series in column 1 for total fixed gross investment was spliced together from four different, overlapping series. For the period 1961-1967, estimates at constant 1963 prices are published in *Rapport 1967-1968*, p. B. 84. The same estimates have been reported to the United Nations; see *Yearbook of National Accounts Statistics*, 1967, New York, 1968. For the years 1956 and 1964, a set of estimates at constant 1963 prices have been published by the UN Economic and Social Office, see ESOB, p. 16. For the years 1961-1964 these estimates do not coincide exactly with those published in *Rapport 1967-1968*. Since the latter estimates seem to be the most recent, they were used for 1961-1967; for 1956-1960 the ESOB estimates were used. The year 1961 served for chaining the two series, it being assumed that the level of the 1961-1967 figures is correct.

For the years before 1961, estimates at constant 1956 prices have been reported in the United Nations *Yearbook of National Account Statistics*. Since these estimates seem to have been made earlier than the 1963 estimates discussed above, they were used only for the years 1953 and 1955, chained to the other series by the year 1956.

A fourth series covering the years 1950-1956 has been published by Asfour, *Syria: Development and Monetary Policy*, p. 73. Asfour's figures were communicated from the UN Bureau of Economic Affairs. This estimate has been used only for the year 1950 and was chained to the other series by the year 1953. Asfour's series may be at constant 1956 prices, but this is not clear from the source.

The GDP at constant market prices for the years 1956-1964 was obtained by adding to the series for NDP at constant 1963 factor cost the series for depreciation and indirect taxes

low. From Table 7-3, it seems that even before the takeover by the Baath in 1964 the share of public investment in total fixed investment was rising. On the other hand, the ratio of private investment to GNP may not have risen since around 1955/56, and has obviously fallen strongly during recent years after the nationalizations of big business in 1964 and 1965.

Syrian population statistics are poor. The first modern census was made in 1960, and the population registration statistics are not very reliable. Crude estimates of population growth vary from 2 to 3 percent per year.[5] Recent calculations of the Department of Statistics point to 2.7 percent as a minimum figure. It seems safe to assume that today the rate is closer to 3 percent than to 2. If this rate has actually prevailed during the whole postwar period, the growth rate of per capita income has fallen from a level of about 3 percent per year before 1956 to about 1 percent annually since then. If population growth has accelerated since World War II—and in most underdeveloped countries it has—the decline of the growth rate of per capita income has been even more pronounced. Since 1956 the average increase in per capita income must have been very small; and, as we shall see later, if defense is disregarded it has probably fallen.

Past developments give little clue to the future growth possibilities of Syria. Even assuming favorable political conditions and efficiency in government planning and implementation, we cannot point to the 5–6 percent growth of aggregate production actually obtained before 1956 and conclude that at least this much ought to be obtainable in the future. The decade of relatively high growth from 1946 to 1956 represented a stage in Syrian development that cannot be repeated. It was based on special circumstances and on the exploitation of natural advantages that are now exhausted. In order to ascertain future growth possibilities we must turn to the individual sectors and examine their potentialities.

Sectoral Developments

A glance at Table 7-2 immediately reveals the fundamental weaknesses in Syrian economic development. About two-thirds of the increase in value added from 1956 to 1968 took place in the four service sectors: commerce and finance, dwellings, public administration, and other services, which together increased annually by almost 6 percent between these 2 years. Public administration, though accounting for only 3 percent of value added in 1956, alone contributed about

[5] *Ibid.,* p. 4, and ESOB, p. 1.

---

minus subsidies related to the GDP series appearing in ESOB, p. 14. The figures in parentheses for the years 1950, 1953, 1955, and 1966, 1967 were obtained through extrapolating depreciation and indirect taxes etc.

The share of public investments for the years 1955-1966 were obtained from United Nations *Yearbook of National Account Statistics,* several issues. They are calculated on current price estimates. The plan figures for the second five-year plan were taken from *Second Five Year Plan, Basic Elements,* Office Arabe de Presse et de Documentation, Damascus, 1967.

Table 7-3 obviously cannot claim to be very reliable. It should be noticed that investments in inventories are not included in the investment estimates. Inventories have probably been falling at the end of the period.

one-third of the total increase in value added in the country. The three commodity-producing sectors and transportation together increased only by 3.2 percent per year. The contrast between the almost stagnating agricultural sector and the rather modest increase in industry (4.8 percent per year) on one side, and the almost incredible 17.5 percent annual increase in public administration on the other, highlights the flaws of Syrian development during the last decade.[6]

Moreover, the low growth rate is not unrelated to the relatively low growth rate of transportation. Syria is still in many respects a primitive country, and her infrastructure, badly damaged when the frontiers were drawn up, is entirely insufficient as a basis for development into a modern society. The transportation sector contributes no less than 10 percent of net production. But this reflects the dimensions of the transport problem rather than the adequacy of the transport system. Moreover, the sector includes royalties from foreign-owned oil pipelines, which account for about one-third of its net product. Actually or potentially important agricultural regions in the north and northeast portions of the country, including the Euphrates Valley, have been without railway or adequate road connections with the main economic and population centers around Damascus, Homs, and Aleppo, which themselves have been inadequately connected. Only recently has the government taken serious steps to overcome the inadequacy of the transport and communication system; once transport facilities are satisfactory, the prospects for a higher rate of growth in agriculture and for industrialization will be brighter.

Finally, we noticed the relatively high expansion of construction. This would be normal in a country with a well-balanced development program. However, in Syria, construction has largely been concentrated on residential buildings. Alongside the rapid expansion of construction we therefore find a relatively fast growth of net production in the dwellings sector.

While the general growth rate has been relatively modest, the sectoral developments have thus been lopsided and inadequate from the point of view of

---

[6] The estimates for value added in commerce and finance are odd. Commerce is estimated to have declined from S£543 million in 1956 to 488.8 million in 1968, while finance is estimated to have increased from S£46.8 million to 117.8 million. Neither estimate looks sensible. Since the decline in commerce took place between 1957 and 1958, it cannot be explained by nationalizations and shifts of activities (statistically) from the sector commerce to public administration. No nationalizations took place at that time, and if anything they would have affected finance much more than commerce. I see no other explanation than inadequate methods of estimation; but this, of course, throws some serious doubts on the estimates as a whole. The overall growth rate may for this reason be too low for the period 1956–1968. A reasonable, though crude, method of estimating the contribution of commerce is to assume that it changes in proportion to the commodity output from agriculture and industry. This would point toward an increase by about 2 percent per year of commerce, which in turn might increase the overall growth rate to 4.5 percent for 1956–1968. This, however, does not upset my main conclusions. There are other biases (pricing, for instance) that pull in the other direction.

growth. The subsequent Syrian governments have, naturally, been aware of this situation. Indeed, several foreign expert missions to Syria have called the attention of the government to the necessity for building up an adequate infrastructure; and plans for public investments in the 1950s, and later the first (1960–1965) and the second (1965–1970) five-year plans, have concentrated strongly on the infrastructure.[7] It is interesting to notice how few resources have actually been allocated in the plans to manufacturing industry as compared with allocations for electricity, fuel, and transport and communications. The second five-year plan (1966–1970) allocated only 8 percent of total investment expenditures to manufacturing industry and mining, compared with 12.4 percent to fuel and power and 18.0 percent to transport and communications.[8]

Agriculture

Syrian agriculture in the postwar period is almost a Ricardian textbook case of marginal returns decreasing with the extension of the margin of cultivation. This is the key to understanding the stagnation of agriculture.

Thanks to improved agricultural prices (and to some extent mechanization and greater security in remote areas) it became profitable during and after World War II to expand the cultivated area. Syrian agricultural developments in this respect closely resemble those of neighboring Turkey, where for similar reasons an expansion of acreage took place during the years of the Menderes regime. In Syria the cultivated area[9] expanded from about 2.3 million hectares in 1945 to a maximum of 7.1 million hectares in 1963 (see Table 7-4).

Only a minor part of the lands are irrigated with a stable water supply. In 1953 about 17 percent of the cropped area was irrigated. This percentage remained almost unchanged until 1967. The remaining lands depend on rainfall which is fairly adequate in the Fertile Crescent along the coastal plain and mountains and the mountainous Turkish frontier, but rapidly becomes more and more inadequate and unreliable as one moves to the south and east toward the arid Syrian Desert and beyond the Euphrates. The expansion of the cultivated area could therefore take place only through a process during which rainfed land with less dependable rainfall was brought under cultivation. Under such cir-

---

[7] Industrial Development in the Arab Countries, United Nations Symposium on Industrial Development in the Arab Countries, Kuwait, 1–10 March 1966, New York, 1967; "Plan Formulation and Development Perspectives in Syria," Meetings on Development Planning Problems and Policies, Beirut, 3–8 June 1968, United Nations Economic and Social Office in Beirut, 27 May 1968; Second Five Year Plan 1966–1970, Basic Elements.

[8] Second Five Year Plan 1966–1970, Basic Elements, p. 9.

[9] Syrian statistics work with three concepts: cultivable area, cultivated area, and cropped area. The cultivable area is the area that under favorable (not precisely specified) conditions could be cultivated. The cultivated area is under actual cultivation, although part of it during a particular year may be left fallow. The cropped area is the area actually under crops during a given year. It is not clear from the statistical sources how areas with more than one crop per year have been dealt with.

Table 7-4

Acreage, Production, and Yields in Agriculture, Prewar to 1967

Year	Culti-vated Area[a] (thousand hectares)	Cropped Area[b] (thousand hectares)		Cultivated Minus Cropped Area		Net Value Added at 1963 Prices[c] (million S£)	Net Value Added Per Hectare Cultivated Area (S£)	Net Value Added Per Hectare Cropped Area (S£)	Yields Per Hectare Cropped Area (metric tons)[d]			
		Total	Of which: Irrigated	Thousand Hectares	Percent of Cultivated Area				Wheat	Bar-ley	Cot-ton	To-bacco
Prewar	1,760	1,160	n.a.	600[d]	34.1				1.0	1.1	...	...
1945	2,290	1,510	n.a.	780	34.1				0.6	0.6	...	0.8
1950	3,090	2,050	n.a.	1,040	33.7	(770)	(249)	(376)	0.8	0.8	1.3	1.0
1945-50 avg.	n.a.	2,050	n.a.	n.a.	n.a.				0.8	0.8	1.1	0.8
1953	3,670	2,440	(400)	1,230	33.5	867	236	355	0.7	1.1	1.0	0.8
1957	4,950	(3,148)	...	(1,802)	36.4	1,118	226	355	0.9	0.9	1.1	0.9
1960	6,014	2,808	424	3,206	53.3	677	113	241	0.4	0.2	1.3	0.6
1963	7,091	3,218	475	3,873	54.6	1,038	146	310	0.8	1.0	1.4	0.5
1964	6,705	3,250	489	3,445	51.5	1,056	158	322	0.7	0.8	1.6	0.7
1965	6,341	3,347	522	2,994	47.2	...	...	...	0.9	1.0	1.7	0.7
1966	6,130	3,127	507	3,003	49.0	847	138	271	0.7	0.6	1.5	0.6
1967	6,095	3,338	538	2,757	45.3	1,039	170	311	0.9	0.9	1.4	0.5

Sources:

[a] 1957-1967, *Rapport 1967-1968*, p. B. 25. Prewar, 1945, 1950, and 1953, IBRD, *Economic Development of Syria.*, p. 19.

[b] 1960-1967, *Rapport 1967-1968*, pp. B. 27-8, 1957, M. Clawson, H.H. Landsberg, and L.T. Alexander, *The Agricultural Potential of the Middle East,* American Elsevier, New York, 1971. Appendix C-9-34. Prewar, 1945, 1950, and 1953, IBRD p. 19

[c] 1957-1967, *Rapport 1967-1968*, pp. B. 83 and A. 99. 1953. M. Diab, "National Income Practices in Syria," p. 132, adjusted for difference between the national income estimates in 1956 prices and the 1963 prices estimates. 1950, based on a series for agricultural gross production, Asfour, *Syria: Developmental Monetary Policy*, p. 21.

[d] 1946-1967, Clawson, Landsberg, and Alexander, *The Agricultural Potential of the Middle East,* Appendix Table C-9-35. Prewar and 1945, IBRD, *Economic Development of Syria*, p. 19.

cumstances the concept of "cultivable" land becomes rather tenuous, but official sources in 1963 considered about 9 million hectares out of the country's total area of 18.5 million hectares as "cultivable." The cultivated area thus increased from about 25 percent to almost 80 percent of the "cultivable" area during a period of 18 years, by itself certainly an extraordinary achievement, mainly on private initiative as a response to prices. However, since 1963 the cultivated area has again declined somewhat, and the cropped area has been almost stagnant since around 1957.

In terms of production the achievement was therefore much less impressive. The fact that less and less fertile land—mainly land with a lower average rainfall and larger annual variability of rainfall—was cultivated led to a fall of production per hectare of cultivated land. Although the heavy crop fluctuations blur the picture somewhat, the trend is clear. From 1950 to 1963 (both relatively normal years), when the cultivated area trebled, net value added per hectare of cultivated land fell to almost half, from S£249 to S£146. From 1963 to 1967, when the cultivated area again fell somewhat, value added per hectare recovered to S£170. This remarkable development in land productivity could take place only because marginal productivity was always much lower than average productivity per hectare. Net value added per hectare of cropped land fell also, although less markedly, from S£376 in 1950 to S£310 in 1963. Since then it has remained almost constant. To understand the different developments for cultivated and cropped land we must consider two factors: yield per cropped hectare, and percentage of cultivated land left fallow.

Since World War II there has been some progress in the methods of cultivation. Improved plant varieties have been introduced (in particular for cotton), the input of fertilizers and insecticides per hectare has increased, and some mechanization has taken place. Indeed, much of the expansion of the cultivated area has depended on mechanical methods because labor has turned out to be scarce in the regions (particularly in the hinterland along and beyond the Euphrates) where the expansion has taken place. All this, however, did not prevent the value added per cropped hectare from falling from 1950 to 1963 when the cropped area expanded. From Table 7-4, columns 9–12, it can be seen that the yields of wheat and barley, the two main cereals, have hardly increased since the late 1930s; there may have been a substantial rise in the yield of cotton compared with prewar years, but from 1950 cotton yield shows only slight improvement. Wheat, barley, and cotton account for about three-quarters of the total value of all crops. Since some minor crops show falling yields, it seems fair to say that during the postwar period yield per cropped hectare has, on balance, remained about constant, or at most has increased slightly, in spite of improved methods of production. In addition, however, there has probably been a fall in the output from husbandry, measured per cropped hectare; and inputs per hectare have increased. Value added per hectare of cropped area has thus been squeezed between constant crop yields, falling husbandry output, and increasing inputs.

Alongside the expansion of the cultivated area, an increasing share of the area has been left fallow each year. Both on rainfed and irrigated land Syrian farmers have (in spite of mechanization) followed a traditional Middle Eastern method of production by leaving land fallow every second or third year in order to restore fertility. Until the beginning of the 1950s about 34 percent of the cultivated area is believed to have been left fallow, but by 1963 fallow land had increased to 54 percent[10]—hence the greater fall of value added per cultivated hectare during this period. When the cultivated area again fell during the period 1963–1967, the percentage of fallow land also declined, to 45 percent.

This development of fallow land has made the cropped area develop quite differently from the cultivated area. The cropped area increased by 5–6 percent annually from 1945 to 1957; thereafter, the cropped area almost stagnated in spite of a continuous increase in the cultivated area. The 5–6 percent annual increase before 1957 was followed by an increase of less than 1 percent per year from 1957 to 1967. This is the basic reason for the change in the agricultural growth rate from rapid increase to stagnation.

With the existing outdated cultivation methods the percentage of fallow land is thus one of the ways in which the falling returns to land shows itself. It follows that, if the fallow-land problem can be tackled, returns per cultivated hectare can be improved accordingly.

Livestock suffered badly from the severe drought years 1958–1961. In addition, the extension of the margin of cultivation has had harmful consequences for animal husbandry, which in Syria is usually separated from cultivation and is largely in the hands of nomadic tribes.[11] Although these take advantage of fallow land, the increase of the cropped area has implied that the herds have been driven off to more and more meager pastures or rangeland, with detrimental effects on the animals. Moreover, with the herds turning increasingly to shrub and woodlands, deforestation and soil erosion have followed. This is by no means the least serious consequence of the extension of the cultivated area, and some of these results do not yet show up in value-added and national income estimates.

[10] A comment on the area statistics is needed here. Before 1956 they were based on unsystematic estimates by local officials. The constant percentage of fallow land (around one-third) was presumably an informed guess by those who made the estimates. In 1956 better and more systematic methods were introduced, and the since then the percentage of fallow land presumably reflects reality. Notice, however, that the conclusions of the text are borne out by Table 7-4, even if we disregard the years before 1956.

[11] The profits from the extension of the cultivated area seem to a considerable extent to have been reaped by tribal sheiks who had succeeded in registering common or public land as personal property and—thus alienated from their own tribes— shared cultivation with or rented the land to town people with capital and some technical know-how. See Lewis, "The Frontier of Settlement in Syria, 1800–1950," and Adnan Mahhouk, "Recent Agricultural Development and Bedouin Settlement in Syria," *The Middle East Journal,* Vol. 10, No. 1 (Winter 1956).

It seems likely that, in addition to the falling marginal and average productivity per hectare, the expansion of the rainfed cultivated area is responsible for a tendency to increased instability in agricultural production and thus in national income. It is the marginal rainfed lands that are particularly sensitive to fluctuations in the rainfall. Although lack of sufficiently long statistical series makes it difficult to establish this conclusion definitely, the developments since 1950 point in this direction.

It will immediately be understood from this brief survey of the development in the past 20 years that further growth of the agricultural sector cannot be expected to take place to any significant extent through expansion of the cultivated rainfed areas. There may even be certain advantages to a cutback in the cultivation of these lands, and the government has actually taken certain steps in this direction during recent years. Further progress has to be obtained instead through improved methods of cultivation on the rainfed areas already in use and through an extension of the irrigated areas.

Improvements in the methods of cultivating rainfed land should first concentrate on abandoning the traditional fallow-land system, thus increasing the cropped area. Through a suitable rotation between cereals and certain other crops (legumes, pulses, and animal fodder) not only can fallow land carry additional new crops, but the fertility of land may also be improved in such a way that the yields of cereals, and thus the production of cereals, increase simultaneously.[12] This will require, above all, strong educational efforts to teach the farmers new methods of cultivation and to convince them of the superiority of these methods over traditional ones. The agricultural cooperatives may here play an important role. But capital investments in tractors and other sources of power and in agricultural machinery will also be required, partly because labor is in short supply. In addition animal husbandry must be organized in an entirely different way and be based on fodder crops. It goes without saying that there is much to be obtained also by the introduction of better varieties of the crops already grown, as well as through more adequate use of fertilizers and other chemicals and better methods of storage.

Irrigation in Syria is dependent partly on water pumped up from wells and rivers, and partly on gravitational irrigation from rivers, springs, and small streams. Underground water is pumped up mainly around Hama and Aleppo, while most of the river pumps are to be found in the basin of the Euphrates and its tributaries. The total irrigated area (cropped) in 1967 was about 0.53 million hectares, perhaps double the prewar figure. Most of this increase was the outcome of private initiative, but the government was not inactive either. Even irrigated lands are to some extent left fallow, and the cropped irrigated area has

---

[12] FAO (Provisional), *Indicative World Plan for Agricultural Development, 1965–85, Near East,* Subregional Study No. 4, Vols. I and II, CCP/16, Rome, 3/67, January 1966, Vol. I, pp. 80 ff.

therefore regularly been somewhat smaller than the cultivated area.[13] Various sources agree that the total potentially irrigable area is about 0.9 million hectares.[14] Apart from a number of smaller projects the major part of the additional irrigation possibilities is in the basin of the Euphrates and its tributaries. This requires, however, the construction of quite a large storage dam on the Euphrates and an extensive network of canals, which, together with the necessary agricultural equipment, will entail high capital costs.

The Euphrates Dam, on which construction was started in April 1968, is a combined irrigation and hydroelectric power project. When it is completed the total irrigated area of the region should, according to the Ministry of Planning, be 0.53 million hectares.[15] This includes, however, areas already irrigated (by pumps), estimated by the FAO at 0.25 million hectares in 1965[16] and by another source reported to be 0.19 million hectares.[17] The addition to the irrigated area seems thus to become 0.28–0.35 million hectares, an increase of the country's total irrigated (cropped) area by some 50–60 percent, and of the country's total cropped area by about 10 percent. With its high yields and stable production it must make possible a very substantial addition to agricultural production. The expected output of electricity of the completed project is about 2.25 billion kilowatt-hours (the installed capacity is planned to be 0.8 million kilowatt-hours,[18] which implies a quadrupling of the present supply of electricity.

The dam will be built in two stages, of which the first one is planned to be ready in 1972. The installed capacity is then scheduled to be 0.3 million kilowatt-hours;[19] the irrigated area at that date is not known. The second stage is supposed to be finished around 1975, but so far contracts with the Soviet Union, which is supplying financial and technical aid, have been made only for the first stage.

For the complete project the Ministry of Planning has estimated the investment costs (including irrigation canals and drains) at S£2,228 million and the

---

[13] *Ibid.*, Vol. II, p. 102. The FAO estimates the total irrigated arable area as 500,000 hectares in 1962; of this, 350,000 hectares were cropped and the remainder left fallow. Entirely different figures for the cropped irrigated area are presented in the *Statistical Abstract*. We follow here as far as possible *Rapport 1967–1968*.

[14] IBRD, *The Economic Development of Syria*, p. 41, and FAO, *Indicative World Plan for Agricultural Development, 1965–85, Near East*, Vol. II, p. 168. The Ministry of Planning assumes that available water resources are sufficient for the irrigation of no less than 2.5 million hectares; see *Second Five Year Plan, Basic Elements*, p. 20.

[15] *Ibid.*, p. 21.

[16] FAO, *Indicative World Plan for Agricultural Development, 1965–85, Near East*, Vol. II, p. 168.

[17] Moshe Efrat, "Syria's Dam on the Euphrates," *New Outlook*, Vol. 10, No. 4 (88) (May 1967), p. 44.

[18] *Ibid.*, p. 45.

[19] *Ibid.*, p. 44.

annual revenue at S£685 million.[20] However, this cost figure does not include investments in the buildings, tractors, machinery, fertilizer, and so forth necessary for cultivating the irrigated areas. A cost estimate by the FAO of U.S. $750 million, or S£2,685 million, seems therefore both more comprehensive and more realistic.[21] The revenue figure is presumably gross, and the Ministry of Planning has given a lower figure of S£500 million as the annual national income from the project.[22] Thus, assuming a total cost of S£2,865, distributed equally over 8 years (from 1967 to 1975), and thereafter a constant annual net income of S£500 million, we find an internal rate of return of slightly above 10 percent on the completed project. Since the project may not be completed by 1975 and may cost more than expected, but that, on the other hand, some of the returns will begin to appear in 1972 when the first stage is finished, a 10 percent return does not seem unrealistic.[23] Also, since the foreign exchange part of the costs (for the first stage, at least) is financed by Soviet loans at a rate of interest of 2.5 percent per year and an amortization period of 12 years[24] (the same conditions as Egypt originally had on the Aswan High Dam loans), the returns to domestic capital exceed 10 percent by a considerable margin.

The project would thus appear to be economically sound and to justify the high priority accorded it in Syrian planning, though it cannot be expected to transform the Syrian economy to the extent envisioned by some of its most enthusiastic advocates. The project seems to be advancing according to schedule. A railway from Aleppo to the dam site has been constructed and began operating in 1968, and the construction work on the dam itself is in progress.

The future development of Syrian agriculture is thus bound to be radically different from that of the past. The rapid annual increase of net production by 4–5 percent during the 1940s and the first half of the 1950s was based largely on

[20] *Second Five Year Plan, Basic Elements,* p. 21.

[21] FAO, *Indicative World Plan for Agricultural Development, 1965–85, Near East,* Part II, p. 168.

[22] Efrat, "Syria's Dam on the Euphrates," p. 45. This implies that inputs brought from other sectors and depreciation amount to a little over one-quarter of the value of total output, which does not seem unreasonable.

[23] The only important snag in the cost-income calculations which I have been able to find (details have not been published) relates to the price of electricity. It would seem as if the income from the electricity has been calculated at the present high price of 0.077 S£ per kilowatt-hour while the future price is supposed to be only 0.013 S£; see Efrat, "Syria's Dam on the Euphrates," p. 45. At the lower price the annual income from the dam would fall to about S£400 million; this would still, however, imply an internal rate of return of 8.7 percent. It is something of a problem at which price of electricity the returns ought to be calculated, but it might be argued that a price of approximately $(0.077 + 0.015)/2 = 0.040$ should be used. This would in a crude way take into account the benefits of the consumers in having a larger supply at their disposal at a low price.

[24] Efrat, "Syria's Dam on the Euphrates," p. 440.

an extraordinary expansion of the cultivated rainfed area. This expansion possibility is, practically speaking, exhausted; indeed, it went too far and had to be reversed, with some decline as a result. Improved methods of cultivation and rotation, and increased irrigation, are the roads to be followed in the future. It therefore seems unlikely that price mechanisms will work in the effective way that they did in the past. Strong governmental efforts are now needed to educate farmers, reorganize animal husbandry, and make the necessary big capital investments, of which the Euphrates Dam project will be by far the most important. At the same time, farmers must be enabled to finance the improvements in the methods of cultivation; with the present institutional setup such credits will have to be provided by the government.

If these conditions are fulfilled, what is then the fastest growth rate that we can reasonably expect in Syrian agriculture? The Euphrates Dam alone seems to be able to push agricultural value added by about 2 percent per year between 1967 and 1980. The FAO[25] assumes that agricultural output can be brought to increase by about 3.3 percent from 1962 to 1975, and by 3.7 percent from 1975 to 1985. Value added should at the same time increase by 3.0 and 3.3 percent, respectively. The FAO estimates are admittedly on the conservative side.[26]

Taking everything into account, I consider it reasonable to believe that good, successful policies should be able to push the annual growth rate of agricultural output to at least 4 percent and of net value added to at least 3.5 percent. On the other hand, it is clear that, with the present institutional frameworks and the concrete problems to be solved, everything depends on powerful and successful government policies rather than on private capitalists' and farmers' initiative or responses to prices.

Industry

The only breakdown of value added in industry that I have been able to find is one from 1950. According to this (official) estimate, industry produced at that time about 10 percent of national income (against 13 percent in 1968; see Table 7-2), and the distribution of individual industries was as shown in Table 7-5. Industry was thus producing simple consumer goods almost exclusively. Apart from the textiles industry, where a number of relatively modern plants existed, most of this sector consisted of old-fashioned, small-scale handicraft, hardly worth the name "industry."

An official document has claimed, "No sooner was the country freed from colonialism, having gained complete independence at the cost of great sacrifices on the part of its people, than a great industrial renaissance took place in all fields, leading to the establishment of a modern mechanized industry."[27] This is,

---

[25] FAO, *Indicative World Plan for Agricultural Development, 1965–85, Near East.*
[26] This is explicitly pointed out by the FAO, *Indicative World Plan for Agricultural Development, 1965–85, Near East,* Vol. I, p. 77, note 3.
[27] *Industrial Development in the Arab Countries,* p. 116.

Table 7-5

Distribution of Value Added in Industry, 1950

Branch	Percent
Textiles	46
Food industries	28
Shoemaking	5
Carpentry and blacksmithing	5
Other industries	16
Total industry	100

Source: Diab, "National Income Practices in Syria," p. 132.

to put it mildly, a gross exaggeration. Although some industrial development did take place during the 1950s and 1960s, Syrian industry is still in its infancy, and by 1964 the structure of industry was much the same as in 1950. By 1964 textiles and food industries were still dominant, as measured by number of establishments, employment, and capital invested; and the average plant was still very small (see Table 7-6). It should be noticed also that what in Table 7-6 is called "engineering" industry bears little resemblance to industries of the same name in developed countries. Out of 558 "engineering" establishments in 1964, 49 were electrical power plants, mostly small ones, and a substantial part of the rest produced such things as plywood, cigarette paper, tiles, cut marble, and bamboo chairs. And of the 347 establishments in the "chemical" industry, more than half were producing soap and tanning hides, and 21 actually turned out to be laundries. It is characteristic also that there existed more than 1,000 grain milling establishments, mostly very small.[28]

Table 7-7 shows the development of some important products from 1945 to 1967. For a few, such as silk yarn and natural asphalt, production has declined. Food processing industries, such as vegetable and olive oil pressing, tobacco and tombac, and sugar, depend, of course, on the crops and have therefore tended to fluctuate irregularly. The most impressive progress up to 1964 was made in cotton textiles, cement, and electricity production.

The textiles industry in the modern sense—Syria has always been famous for brocades and other fine fabrics—started developing during World War II when the country was cut off from foreign supply. It was at this time that agri-

[28] *Ibid.,* pp. 127–128.

Table 7-6

Establishments, Employment, and Capital in Main Industries, 1953 and 1964

Economic Development of Syria

Industry	Number of Establishments		Number of Employees		Capital (million S£)	
	1953	1964	1953	1964	1953	1964
Textiles, incl. ginning	919	2,027	12,300	18,970	70	202
Engineering, incl. electrical	60	558	1,100	9,834	n.a.	73
Chemicals	160	347	4,950	7,403	38	117
Foodstuffs	567	1,412	6,600	12,615	46	84
Petroleum	0	1	0	700	0	65
Total	1,706	4,345	24,950	49,522	154	541

Sources: For 1953, Grunwald and Ronall, *Industrialization in the Middle East*, New York, 1960, p. 310. For 1964, *Industrial Development in the Arab Countries*, p. 127.

No definition of "main industries" is given in the sources. The coverage of the table is not known. The figures for 1953 and 1964 are not fully comparable; thus, for 1953 "engineering" covers only electrical power plants. No definition is available of the concept of "capital"; it is presumably a question of capital paid in by shareholders.

Table 7-7

Production of Important Industrial Commodities, 1945-1967

Commodity	1945	1956	1964	1967
Silk and cotton fabrics (tons)	n.a.	18,000	31,622	37,820
Cotton yarn (tons)	1,620	7,952	18,113	19,426
Silk yarn (tons)	n.a.	3,478	2,825	3,206
Oil, vegetable and olive (tons)	n.a.	22,670	52,363	39,456
Sugar (tons)	n.a.	50,391	78,341	71,314
Cement (tons)	46,000	326,000	635,000	688,000
Glass (tons)	n.a.	10,654	9,241	12,796
Soap (tons)	n.a.	11,146	26,550	13,917
Rubber shoes (thousand pairs)	. . .	789	3,081	2,225
Tobacco and tombac (tons)	1,529	3,123	4,470	4,114
Benzin (thousand tons)	. . .	. . .	159	n.a.
Crude oil, refined (tons)	. . .	. . .	1,014	n.a.
Natural asphalt (tons)	n.a.	43,031	10,354	n.a.
Electricity (million kilowatt-hours)	30	166	574	676

Sources: For 1945, Grunwald and Ronall, *Industrialization in the Middle East,* p. 311. For 1956 and 1964, *Industrial Development in the Arab Countries,* pp. 132-133. For 1967, *Rapport 1967-1968,* pp. 80, 88.

culture turned toward cotton cultivation on a large scale. But whereas the raw cotton turned out to be a good economic proposition in agriculture, the same cannot be said about the cotton textiles industry. When foreign competition made itself felt again at the end of the 1940s, the new industry proved unable to survive without protection and the government stepped in with tariffs and other measures. Even today, after 20 years of protection, there are grave doubts about the competitiveness of the Syrian cotton textiles industry.

Electricity has, so far, been produced mainly by a number of small thermal plants. The level of per capita consumption has expanded rapidly during the last two decades, but is still below that prevailing in Egypt, for instance. The supply of electricity is entirely insufficient as a basis for industrialization, and only recently have efforts been made to create a national grid. All this, however, will change when the Euphrates project is completed.

Except for textiles, modern industry has been established mainly in fields where a domestic raw material supply, combined with high transport costs for the finished product, offers the country a natural advantage, and where a domestic demand for the finished product existed in advance. This is a common and natural pattern of development. Since Syria is not very well endowed with mineral resources, the industries in question are therefore limited to cement, fertilizers, and oil. The cement industry was founded immediately after the war; several plants are now in operation and a small amount is exported. A nitrate fertilizer plant (based on oil) has recently started production, and a phosphate plant, based on domestic phosphate rock, is under construction. Oil was first struck in 1959, and a number of wells, all situated in the northeastern corner of the country, are now producing. A pipeline from the Syrian oilfields to the Mediterranean Sea was completed in 1968, and Syria is now a net exporter. The government expects that oil will make an annual contribution to national income by 1973 of about S£270 million,[29] corresponding to 60 percent of industrial value added, and 7.2 percent of NDP in 1967 (the last year before the oil boom). About two-thirds of the total output of crude oil, at a value of about S£225 million per year, will be available for export,[30] import savings may amount to about S £ 160 million. The existence of the old, foreign-owned pipelines over Syrian territory from the Iraqi oilfields around Mosul made the establishment of refineries an economic proposition even before Syria herself became a crude oil producer; a refinery was built in Homs in 1959 and is at present being expanded. However, all this amounts only to a handful of modern plants, which, so far, cannot be said to have changed the traditional character of industry in any essential way. It does seem clear, however, that the growth rate of industry (including extraction) speeded up somewhat after 1964 (see Figure 7-1), although it should not be overlooked that the severe drought years 1958–1967 kept down the growth rate until 1962. The high growth rate of industry for 1968 (16.4 percent) was due mainly to the expansion of crude oil production.

Until the beginning of the 1970s industrial development will presumably continue to be dominated by these "natural" industries. But this stage can be only a temporary one in the process of industrialization. The demand for both cement and fertilizer will, of course, continue to increase, but sooner or later other industries must take the lead; neither cement nor fertilizer production seems to have such cost advantages that the country could and should become a large-scale exporter of these products. This change in emphasis will have to take place in the 1970s, and from then on comparative advantages must be created. Before any more general industrialization can take place, the supply of electricity has to be expanded. It has already been pointed out, however, that the Eu-

---

[29] This figure includes the small amount of value added in the old refinery at Homs; see below.

[30] *Middle East Economic Survey,* Vol. XII, No. 13 (January 24, 1969).

phrates Dam should begin to deliver electricity in 1972, and around 1975 electricity production on a really large scale should be possible. So far the supply of electricity has been most inadequate and the costs have been relatively high, but from about 1975 sufficient cheap electricity should be available for a rapid expansion of manufacturing industry if this is otherwise feasible. Syrian socialists do not seem to have forgotten Lenin's words about electrification.

With the present institutional setup private entrepreneurs cannot be expected to take much initiative, nor does the Baath regime welcome their involvement. The initiative, as well as the choice, rests now basically with the government, and this fact is of some importance for judging future growth possibilities against the background of past experience. It is a question how much initiative toward a modern industrialization process could really be expected from private entrepreneurs. Their main achievement in industry has been gained in the textiles industry, and here they relied entirely on protection from the government. An acceleration of the industrial growth rate took place only after 1964. On the other hand, the choice of investment projects has so far been relatively simple and obvious—cement, oil, and fertilizers. There is little indication of what the government's choice will be when it really becomes a question of developing manufacturing industry on a large scale. This is the acid test of government planning and implementation. The list of investment projects for the period 1966–1970, however, looks remarkably down to earth and seems to have avoided the fancy projects that have led to so much waste in Egyptian planning.[31]

Under favorable conditions—which in particular would mean effective central planning and implementation, good working relations, and a sensible division of work between the public and private sectors and between domestic and foreign contractors—a relatively high industrial growth rate in the future can be visualized. The increase of oil production alone should correspond to about 3.8 percent annual growth of industrial value added between 1967 and 1980. And the electricity from the Euphrates Dam should create a basis for a further rapid development from 1975. An industrial growth rate of 8–9 percent between 1967 and 1980 does not seem impossible.

Most probably, the limitational factor in industrial growth will turn out to be technical personnel and management. If future expansion of manufacturing industry concentrates on simple, low-quality consumer goods and intermediary inputs, as will be suggested below, the problem of skilled laborers may not become so urgent. But technical personnel and management will in any case be needed. Syria does not at present have any abundant supply of technical cadres. It may be necessary therefore to employ foreigners in such positions, although under favorable political circumstances there may perhaps be a certain inflow from Egypt. Obviously this point is critical in the industrialization prospects of Syria.

[31] *Second Five Year Plan, Basic Elements,* p. 6.

355

Table 7-8
Employment and Unemployment, 1964

Sector	Persons Employed (thousands)	Persons Unemployed (thousands)	Unemployment (percent of labor force)
Agriculture and fishing	556	80	12
Industry	158	12	7
Construction	52	21	29
Transportation	39	5	11
Services	178	8	5
Miscellaneous	4	14	75
Total	1,121	144	12

Source: Industrial Development in the Arab Countries, p. 130. The table is based on sample surveys conducted by the Ministry of Planning and the Ministry of Social Affairs.

Construction

This sector performed relatively well between 1956 and 1968, with a growth rate of 5.8 percent, well above the average. In the past, construction was directed mainly toward residential building. There is a relation between the relatively high rates of growth in construction and the net domestic product of dwellings. Rightly or wrongly, the government plans put less emphasis on residential building. However, since the expansion of the infrastructure—in particular, the transportation network and the Euphrates Dam—has a high priority in the plans, the construction sector should be expected to expand faster than in the past.

This policy would also be rational from an employment point of view. There is a good deal of open unemployment in urban areas, and since construction permits highly labor-intensive methods, expansion of construction is one of the best ways of coping with this problem. Unemployment data are available for the years 1961–1964. Unemployment seems to have increased slightly over this period, but has probably fallen again since then.

Employment and unemployment in 1964 are shown in Table 7-8. The source from which this table is taken does not inform us about definitions, nor is it clear whether the figures are annual averages or refer to a particular date in the year. Moreover, the distribution of unemployment by sector cannot be very meaningful. Nevertheless, the table discloses a serious amount of open unemployment, concentrated in agriculture and construction. Unemployment in agriculture can perhaps be identified with rural unemployment, the rest with urban unemployment. The agricultural unemployment is presumably seasonal in the sense that there are peak seasons with a shortage of labor; it is known that during the agricultural peak seasons very high wages are paid to seasonal laborers.[32] The seasonal peaks in Syrian agriculture are short, however; and since, at least in areas with dry farming, mechanization has proved a profitable solution of the seasonal labor shortage problem, we are confronted with a problem of almost permanent open unemployment in agriculture. Some of the unemployment will disappear when the fallow land is put under cultivation, but otherwise the best immediate answer to this problem seems to be construction works synchronized with the agricultural peaks. Construction works, particularly when primitive techniques are used, have the advantage that they can be interrupted temporarily without significant loss.

Similar remarks apply to urban unemployment. The unemployed seem to crowd around the construction sector; presumably that means no more than that they are unskilled workers who can hope only for this kind of work. But whereas the agricultural unemployment calls for construction work in roads, canals, and so on, the urban unemployment points more toward residential construction, which in turn has consequences for investment planning. Laborers should not be shuffled around.

The unemployment situation, together with the need for infrastructure, points thus in the direction of a relatively vigorous expansion of construction, which in turn would call for a rapid expansion of the cement industry.

Transportation

We have already stressed the insufficiency of the Syrian system of transport and communication, and the fact that development has been "waiting" for the creation of an adequate transport system.

After independence the railway system consisted of three broken segments of railways that were connected only through Turkey and Lebanon and thus were of limited value to the country. Moreover, part of the system was narrow-gauged. The important ports of the area, Beirut, Tripoli, and Alexandretta, had been given to Lebanon and Turkey, and Syria was left with only the oil port Banias and the small, isolated, and badly equipped port of Latakia. The road system, finally, connected the Damascus region with the Aleppo-Homs region in only a most unsatisfactory way; road connections with the hinterland beyond the Euphrates (where most of the agricultural expansion of the 1950s took place) were virtually nonexistent.

Important steps have already been taken to fill the major gaps in the transport system, and by 1970 transportation should no longer be the most serious bottleneck in Syrian development. The road network between Damascus and the Aleppo-Homs region is being rounded out, and with the completion of the railroad connections between Latakia and the Euphrates region, and the pipeline

---

[32] Nadr Atasi, "Minimum Wage Fixing and the Wage Structure in Syria," *International Labour Review,* Vol. 98, No. 4 (October 1968), p. 339, note 1.

from the oilfields in the northeast to the new port of Tartus, the most urgent needs will have been satisfied.

Hereafter, it would seem, the transport and communications sector ought to be able to grow at a rate somewhat higher than the modest 4 percent experienced between 1956 and 1967. The very large increase in 1968 was due to increased oil transport through the pipelines; this factor will certainly keep the sector growing fast during the coming years. And, with the better transport system, the growth rates of other sectors should be able to rise as well. In short, the improvement of the transport system currently going on is one of the promising features of Syrian economic development.

Public Administration

There is little to be said in general about such sectors as trade, banking and insurance, and services, which presumably tend to follow the commodity-producing sectors rather passively. But we cannot finish this brief sectoral survey without a few words about the public sector.

The public sector in Syria has of course expanded much through the nationalization of large enterprises in all fields. Here we are concerned, however, with public administration (including defense) and its contribution to the national product. But even in this narrow sense the public administration sector showed a fabulous growth rate from 1956 to 1968. It is difficult to judge how much of the increase of the public sector's contribution to the national product was due to defense expenditures (salaries and wages in cash and kind paid to officers, soldiers, and employees). Information about actual expenditures on defense seems to be available only for the early 1950s. Since then, only budget estimates (appropriations) have been published, and actual expenditures may deviate substantially from budget estimates. Certainly, defense expenditures increased rapidly during the 1950s and 1960s. They may have been about 3 or 3.5 percent of GNP at current market prices in the years 1950–1952 and rose to about 9 percent in 1967 (the latest estimates for 1967 seem to have been made before the June War). Defense expenditures may have increased by about S£200 million from 1956 to 1964. Public consumption appears to have risen from 1956 to 1964 by S£400 million.[33] About half of the increase of public consumption seems thus to have been due to higher defense expenditures. This indicates that a considerable part of the increase in the public sector contribution to the national product may also be due to defense. Civil government employment is known to have grown by about 15 percent from the beginning of 1964 to 1966.[34] These items of information do not say very much, and I can conclude only that both civil and military expenditures contributed to the tremendous expansion of the public sector in the past.

The issue is of great importance, not only for appraising past growth rates but also for predicting future growth. Under favorable conditions the country

[33] ESOB.
[34] *Statistical Abstract,* various issues.

may not only avoid further expansion of its military machinery but should even be able to reduce it substantially. This will tend, of course, to slow down the growth rate of the public sector. There is little doubt, on the other hand, that the civil part of the public sector still needs to be expanded substantially if the government is to be able to fulfill its part of a well-balanced development program. The Syrian public sector (administration) is still relatively small, and many government services, such as health services and education, are badly in need of expansion. There is no point, on the other hand, in letting civil administration grow faster than competent personnel become available. Which of these conflicting factors will dominate is difficult to say. Clearly it is desirable, however, that the public sector contribution to the national product should not grow as fast as in the past, and there is much to be said in favor of limiting the public (administration) sector to its present relative size (at most), which will imply a growth rate not higher than the average in society.

The Future Rate of Growth

The discussion has given some, albeit incomplete, clues to the possible future growth rates of the national product. Independent estimates have been given for the commodity-producing sectors and transportation. The remaining sectors will be assumed to follow, at most, the general growth rate.

At a growth rate of 3.5 percent in agriculture, 8–9 percent in industry, substantially above 5.8 percent in construction, and somewhat above 4.8 percent in transport, an average growth rate of 5–6 percent emerges, which, by chance, happens to be the same as the economy seems to have experienced before 1956.[35] In spite of much higher growth rates in agriculture and industry as compared with the period 1956–1968, the overall growth rate should thus not show any spectacular increase. In per capita terms the increase is, nevertheless, significant. The 1 percent annual increase per capita from 1956 to 1968 implied a doubling of the per capita income in 70 years; a per capita growth rate of 2–3 percent means per capita doubling in 24–35 years. That makes quite a difference, after all. Moreover, it should be emphasized that growth in the past dec-

[35] Assuming, for instance, that the growth rates for construction and transport become 8 and 6 percent, respectively, we get the following average growth rate and sectoral distribution by 1980:

Sector	Value Added at Constant 1963 Prices, 1968 (million S£)	Annual Growth Rate (percent)	Value Added at Constant 1963 Prices, 1980 (million S£)
Agriculture	1,046	3.5	1,579
Industry	516	8.5	1,372
Construction	136	8	342
Transportation	451	6	907
Other services	1,883	5.7	3,715
Total NDP	4,034	5.7	7,915

ade was based mainly on an expansion of services, some of them (defense, in particular) of rather dubious value from a welfare point of view. The future growth pattern, sketched here, would be much more "real." If defense is disregarded, it may be the question of a change from something negative to 2–3 percent annual growth of income per capita.

III. Problems and Future Development

General Obstacles

In projecting a growth rate of the domestic product by 5–6 percent annually I have assumed that all conditions for growth are favorable. There are many reasons, therefore, why development could actually proceed at a lower speed.

The obstacles to growth are to some extent the same as those found in Egypt. All the problems related to Arab socialism, the growing government sector and the increasing bureaucracy, the organization and management of the nationalized industries, and the increasing general control of the economy, largely echo those in Egypt. With increasing government controls, improvement in the efficiency of government planning and implementation becomes more and more crucial. There is no need to repeat here what has already been said on this subject in my paper on Egypt.[36] It only needs to be added that, whereas Egypt has a relative abundance of competent administration, this may not be the case in Syria.

In Syria the problem is accentuated by the need for a radical change in the agricultural methods of cultivation; the farmers have to learn and be convinced of the superiority of a modern crop rotation system, and animal husbandry must be reorganized entirely. Food supply and, hence, the balance of payments depend crucially on these changes. If the government, be it socialist or nonsocialist, fails to transform agriculture, the general outlook for the Syrian economy will be rather gloomy in spite of the projected windfall from oil. More than ever, therefore, development also requires political stability, so strikingly absent in the past.

External Conditions

Peaceful conditions in the Middle East would be of importance for the economic development of Syria mainly through the implications for defense expenditures. The area occupied by Israeli forces is economically of little importance, and the number of refugees limited, though by no means negligible. The direct loss of production and income that would follow from a continued occupation would be small. But a reduction of the heavy defense expenditures to, say, about half their present size would certainly ease the economic situation. Manpower would be set free for more normal economic activities, and foreign exchange could be di-

[36] Bent Hansen, "Economic Development of Egypt," this volume, Chap. 2, Sec. IV, pp. 85–88.

verted from the purchase of military equipment to capital goods. The benefits to be derived are difficult to evaluate quantitatively, however.

The manpower released from defense would to some extent consist of skilled personnel (technicians and the like) who could immediately be absorbed in valuable production or civil administration. Unskilled personnel returning to urban areas might, on the other hand, only serve to increase the number of unemployed, unless the rate of growth and the composition and methods of production chosen sufficed to tackle both the already existing unemployment and the increase in the civilian labor force. In certain rural areas, returning soldiers might help to overcome labor shortages and thus contribute to production. But it is by no means self-evident that production would automatically increase in proportion to the reduction of the manpower at present called up to the armed forces.

The foreign exchange savings are equally difficult to gauge, since it is not known exactly to what extent military equipment received from the Communist countries has been and still has to be paid for. It is believed that in the past a substantial part of the equipment was given as grants. Should this be the case in the future too, the direct foreign exchange savings from a reduction of defense might be relatively modest.

Despite these reservations there can be no doubt that the armed forces are a very heavy burden on the Syrian economy in terms of both manpower and foreign exchange. They also contribute to the inflationary pressures in the country. The increase in domestic government expenditures does not seem to have been met by a sufficient rise in taxes and other current government revenues. This in turn hinders the expansion of normal, civil government activities, badly needed for promoting economic growth.

An additional, very subtle problem is whether the emergence of peaceful conditions will influence the amount of aid given by Communist countries to Syria. The military misfortunes of the Arab countries have certainly led to increased civil (in addition to military) aid from the Soviet Union. A radical change in the political scene, however, might have repercussions on the interest of the Communist countries in supplying aid for development purposes. Here we might also mention the problem of future trade patterns. With peaceful conditions Syria might find it possible and even preferable to switch her trade more toward the Western countries. It is always beneficial to have a greater choice, and the West has more to offer in the way of technology than does the East. In this respect also, Syria is in very much the same position as Egypt.

Financing Development

To judge from the very uncertain information about national expenditure that is available, the increase of fixed investments and public consumption from 1956 onward was mainly financed, in real terms, by keeping back private consumption.

In 1956 the share of fixed investment in GNP was about 15 percent at a balance of payments deficit of about 4 percent of GNP. Eighty-nine percent of GNP was thus available for private and public consumption (and inventory changes); in 1966 the balance of payments deficit was about 3 percent of GNP while fixed investments were running at a level of 18 percent, 85 percent of GNP thus being left for private and public consumption. Since the share of public consumption has increased, the share of private consumption must have fallen by at least 4 percentage units of GNP.

Reliable estimates of public consumption, geared to the most recent estimates of national product, do not exist,[37] but it is possible to form an opinion of the development of its share. Public consumption consists of wages and salaries paid to government employees, workers, and army personnel *plus* goods and services purchased by the government. In underdeveloped countries wages and salaries usually amount to about two-thirds of public consumption. Since the government's contribution (consisting of wages and salaries) to the national product increased from about 3 percent of GNP in 1956 to about 13 percent in 1966, the share of public consumption may have increased from about 5 to about 20 percent during the same period. On these assumptions the share of private consumption in GNP should have fallen from about 85 to 65 percent of GNP, which, by the way, implies a fall in private consumption per capita by more than 2 percent a year. For various reasons this crude estimate may exaggerate the decline in the share of private consumption,[38] But obviously it must have fallen strongly.

The question is, then, what will be required for financing future development? During the past decade a level of fixed investments of 16–18 percent of GNP was capable of producing annual growth above 4 percent. A growth rate in the future of 5–6 percent will require a higher level of investments. The fact that infrastructure, including dam building, irrigation and electricity, transportation, and communication, is bound to play a relatively big role some time ahead

---

[37] A series for public consumption at constant 1963 prices, estimated by the Ministry of Planning, is published in ESOB, p. 14. This estimate is completely out of line, however, with the most recent official estimates of the contribution of public administration to GNP, upon which the discussion here generally is based. Neither size nor rates of growth in the two estimates fit together. For a few years estimates at constant 1956 prices have been published by *International Financial Statistics*.

[38] Purchases of military equipment may easily lead to strong changes from year to year in the ratio between wages and salaries and other purchases. Purchases of military equipment have certainly played an important role during this period, but it is not known how equipment received as grants has been dealt with in the statistics. A further snag in the estimate in the text is the lack of inventory data. Inventory changes appear in the residual, private consumption, and part of the decline in the share of "private consumption" is most certainly due to a fall of inventories.

points to relatively high future investment requirements. If at the same time the balance of payments deficit has to be eliminated, some debt repayment may even have to take place, and the share of public consumption must be kept unchanged (with a fall in military and an increase in civil expenditures), a substantial further fall in private consumption is called for—in the worst case perhaps from 65 to less than 60 percent of GNP. This is a relatively low share of private consumption for a poor country, although at 5.5 percent growth of national income and 3 percent population growth it would still permit an increase of private consumption per capita by 1–2 percent annually between 1967 and 1980. A very energetic policy in terms of taxation and other measures for raising government current revenue and preventing private disposable income from increasing in proportion to national income will obviously be necessary. To the extent that foreign loans and grants in aid will be available, and the country deems it wise to accept them, the need for diminishing the share of private consumption will be smaller. But it seems entirely unlikely that loans and aid will continue to run at such levels that a decrease in the share of private consumption will be unnecessary. And, of course, foreign loans will at most postpone the time when the share of private consumption has to be reduced.

We shall not here try to set up concrete programs for increased taxation and government revenues. The Syrian revenue system could certainly be improved in several respects; in particular, agricultural taxation is badly in need of overhaul. We shall only stress that the tax and revenue programs have to be designed in such a way that they not only secure balance between total domestic demand and supply at the given balance of payments deficit or surplus, but also ensure that sufficient *exportable* commodities actually become available for covering import requirements. It does not solve the balance of payments problem to cut down domestic demand for commodities that cannot be sold abroad.

This problem is discussed in some detail in my paper on Egypt;[39] although orders of magnitude differ considerably, the problem and its solution are in principle the same for the two countries, and therefore no elaborate discussion is needed here.[40] The Syrian balance of payments has deteriorated over the last decade (see Table 7-9) but is less aggravated than that of Egypt and should presumably require smaller policy measures for its solution. Both the foreign debt and the current deficits have been (relatively) smaller, and the expected increase of foreign revenue from exports of Syrian oil should suffice not only to wipe out the current deficit but perhaps even to create a small surplus at the present level of imports. A reduction of defense expenditures should help further. The growth of national income, on the other hand, will imply increasing imports and require correspondingly increasing exports. Let it be added also that some of the present sources of foreign exchange—the royalties from foreign pipelines, emigrant re-

[39] Hansen, "Economic Development in Egypt," Section III.
[40] For a detailed discussion of export and input prospects related to Syrian official plans, see ESOB, pp. 14–25. The official plans are obviously entirely unrealistic.

Table 7-9

Balance of Payments, 1956 and 1966

	1956		1966	
	Million U.S.$	Million S£	Million U.S.$	Million S£
Exports	148	592	173	692
Imports	187	748	289	1156
Services and transfers, net	36	144	81	324
Balance of current payments	−3	−12	−35	−140
Foreign borrowing				
Private	−1	−4	2	8
Central government	5	20	1	4
Fall in exchange reserves, etc.	−1	−4	32	128
Foreign exchange reserve	63	252	30	120

Source: International Monetary Fund, *International Financial Statistics,* Washington, April 1963 and March 1969. Conversion from U.S.$ to S£ has been made at a rate of 1 U.S.$ = 7 S£.

mittances, and aid to the Palestine refugees—are highly dependent on political developments. Over and above the new oil exports, there will thus be a need for increasing exports and import substitution.

Agricultural development is quite crucial for solving the balance of payments problem. Provided that food consumption per capita is prevented from increasing,[41] the projected increase of agricultural output by some 4 percent per year should permit a reduction of food imports and a continuous increase of agricultural exports, which would cover part of the necessary import increase.

The remaining part of the problem would presumably have to be solved through import substitution by industry. In particular it seems important that a domestic production of inputs needed for the agricultural expansion be undertaken. There should also be great possibilities for import substitution with re-

[41] Constant food consumption per capita may be a feasible policy in the sense that the most basic nutritional requirements with respect to calories and protein are fulfilled already at the present level of per capita consumption; see FAO, *Indicative World Plan for Agricultural Development, 1965–85, Near East.*

spect to nonfood consumer demand. With per capita food consumption kept constant and total consumption per capita increasing by about 1.5 percent per year, a substantial increase of total nonfood consumption is bound to take place. It would be natural, moreover, to expect a socialist government to aim at greater equity in income distribution, along with the growth in income. To the extent that the government is successful in this respect the increased demand for non-food consumer goods will come from the lowest income brackets, and this means a demand for simple, unsophisticated, low-quality consumer goods. Demonstration effects and the need of living up to the Western Joneses are typical middle- and upper-class phenomena; the poor masses of people in underdeveloped countries have simpler demands. There are good reasons for believing that this is exactly the field of manufacturing industry in which underdeveloped countries may have an advantage and be competitive. Income equalization might thus give domestic industrialization a chance to embark upon production that both is competitive and implies import substitution.

IV. Conclusion

The period of relatively rapid growth that Syria experienced during the first decade after World War II cannot be duplicated. It was based on an extension of the cultivated and cropped area. Syria is now about to take another leap forward, this time based on the exploitation of oilfields. Valuable though this exploitation of course is, it will not by itself lead the country into a process of sustained growth. The oil boom will come to an end when maximum exploitation of the fields has been reached, just as the land boom came to an end when the extensive margin was reached around 1956/57. Political upheavals certainly played a role, but in any case the land boom was doomed to peter out without continuing into an industrialization process for the simple reason that the country did not then possess an infrastructure sufficiently developed for modern industry. In this respect the present oil boom is more promising. The infrastructure is now under development; the oil creates a basis for financing investments; and if the domestic and international political situation is assumed to be favorable, some important necessary conditions for industrialization should be fulfilled. But these are not sufficient conditions. In the longer run the food situation and thus the balance of payments require renewed progress in agriculture, and this will take place only if the government succeeds in radically transforming agricultural production methods.

Even in this event Syria is faced with the problem of obtaining technical cadres for industrialization. Everything seems to depend on whether they can be found, created, or otherwise acquired. For the sake of both agriculture and industry the Syrian government may have to look abroad for technical cadres; time seems too short to solve this problem on a purely domestic basis. It may not appeal strongly to nationalistic minds to have a significant number of foreign technicians in the country on a permanent basis to run current production in the new industries. Suspicion of foreign penetration might easily arise, and social problems related to the necessarily relatively high salary levels of the foreigners could become serious. However, if the choice is between industrialization based on foreign technical management and no industrialization at all, these inconveniences seem minor. And if it could be made clear to the Eastern and Western powers and the developed countries in general that neither governments nor private businesses will be allowed to take advantage of such technical aid and assistance for crippling the independence of the developing country, the whole problem would become a secondary one. It would be a great achievement if a settlement of the present conflict in the Middle East could create such an atmosphere of confidence.

Prospects and Problems of Economic Development of Saudi Arabia, Kuwait, and the Gulf Principalities

Edmund Y. Asfour

A single commodity dominates the economic landscape of the Arabian peninsula—oil. Far more than for any other country, even Iraq, oil explains the pattern of the peninsula's economic development and is the key to its prospects for the future.

Before the discovery of oil in the 1930s, the economy of the peninsula was confined essentially to pastoral livestock, fishing, and sea trade, with the few towns in the Hijaz heavily dependent on Moslem pilgrims. Oil meant rapid accumulation of wealth, a process that in Kuwait can only be termed spectacular. There the benefits have been spread relatively wide; a similar tendency is observable in Saudi Arabia only since 1960. Among the Gulf Principalities, Bahrein, Qatar, and Abu Dhabi have been the principle beneficiaries of oil discoveries and hence also of some degree of economic development.

Oil revenues will continue to be the predominant force shaping the development of the peninsula. As Asfour drily notes, the development problems of Kuwait, a state with one of the highest per capita incomes in the world and an annual level of gross savings almost half the size of GNP, "can be considered marginal." For Saudi Arabia and the oil-endowed Gulf states, the problems should not be too arduous either. On the assumption of no political interference in the growth of oil revenues, the peninsula's growth prospects have been projected as 6.5–10 percent per year. At these rates there should continue to be formed a savings surplus that may be invested abroad but may also be used to bolster the development programs of the oil-poor Arab states.

Prospects and Problems of Economic Development of Saudi Arabia, Kuwait, and the Gulf Principalities

I. Saudi Arabia

Background

Saudi Arabia was officially declared an independent kingdom within its present borders in September 1932. Its population, estimated at 4–6 million, occupies a vast area of 865,000 square miles (2.2 million square kilometers) or about three-quarters of the whole Arabian peninsula. Climatically, the subcontinent is an extension of the great African Sahara, from which it is physically separated by the Red Sea. Its aridity and extremely harsh climate allow little agriculture, except in the rainfed high mountains of the southwest and in small, scattered oases irrigated by underground water. With the exception of some coastal ports that engaged in fishing and sea trade, over the ages the area remained poor, isolated, and sparsely populated. Historically, its migrating herdsmen, the tribal Bedouins, moved with the seasons in search of grazing ground for their camels and sheep and occasionally settled in the more hospitable Fertile Crescent in the north. Sometimes the movement of population grew into relatively large waves, the most famous of which was the one that accompanied and followed the Arab conquests of the Middle East and North Africa in the seventh century. Until very recently, this historical picture changed little. The forbidding expanse and climate helped to maintain the country's local autonomy (except in a few coastal points) and to isolate it from foreign cultural and political influences.

Before the development of the oil industry in Saudi Arabia, that is, before World War II, the income of the bulk of the population fluctuated near the subsistence level. The economy was based essentially on pastoral activities, organized in an age-long tribal system, but small, settled farming communities existed in scattered desert oases and in the mountainous region in the southwest. The few towns that existed in Al Hijaz, such as Mecca, Medina, and Jedda, had rudimentary crafts and services but were dependent to an important extent on the tens or hundreds of thousands of Moslem pilgrims who annually converged from all over the world to visit the holy cities. Fees paid by the pilgrims constituted an important part of the small government revenue, and their expenditures on goods and services supported trade, transport, catering, and guiding activities. Although the income level of the pastoral-agricultural communities fluctuated considerably from year to year depending on the volume and distribution of rainfall and the seriousness of locust invasions and animal disease, the income level of the city dwellers varied with the importance of the pilgrimage season and with the income or subsidies that the government could eke out from other sources. The government budget in 1934, two years after the establishment of the kingdom, amounted to about 14 million riyals (about $4 million) only.

The poverty of Saudi Arabia before the discovery of oil can be attributed largely to the paucity of natural resources, particularly agricultural and grazing land. It can also be blamed on the serious shortage of investment capital and the virtual absence of communications between the small and scattered centers of production and the scattered town markets. Finally, the low level of skills and labor productivity in the crafts, agriculture, and services was also partly responsible.

Economic Growth and Structure

In the last 20 years or so the economic picture of Saudi Arabia has started to change perceptibly, after many centuries of a low living standard, a fixed pattern of production, and general economic stagnation. The period obviously coincides with the expansion of oil production and export[1] and with the substantial and increasing government expenditures made possible by the associated rise in its revenues from the oil industry (from $57 million in 1950 to $909 million in 1967).

The first half of this period (that is, the 1950s) was marked by the country's unbalanced efforts to raise itself above the low level of consumption it had previously suffered. Although the more pressing needs of large groups of the population, particularly in the growing cities, were somewhat relieved during that period, the spread of benefits was neither pervasive nor equally distributed. In the later part of the 1950s, the steady rise of government as well as private consumption expenditures, paralleled by a leveling off of oil revenue, led to an inflationary situation and to pressure on the balance of payments, and consequently to the adoption of a stabilization policy that involved a curb on some of the excesses.

[1] Oil was discovered in Saudi Arabia in 1937 and first exported by the Arabian-American Oil Company (ARAMCO) in 1944. It was not until 1950, however, that the rising volume of exports (about 200 million barrels) and the application of the principle of equal sharing of profits resulted in significant revenue for the government. In 1950, government oil revenue doubled in comparison with the previous year, reaching $57 million, and it doubled twice in the following 2 years, reaching $212 million in 1952. It took 10 more years and the added small revenue of two other companies, Getty Oil and Arabian Oil (Japanese), before oil revenue doubled again, reaching $410 million in 1962. By 1967, oil revenue reached $909 million, all but $50 million being paid by ARAMCO; and oil production exceeded 1 billion barrels. In April 1965, Saudi Arabia granted a concession, with participation option, to the French Auxilière du Régie Autonome des Pétroles (Auxrap) and in December 1967 to the Italian AGIP, a subsidiary of ENI, and also to a group of two American and one Pakistani companies.

EDMUND Y. ASFOUR

Since 1960, the substantial rise in oil revenue has contributed to the success of the stabilization policy and has enabled the government to embark on an active and expanding program to develop the economy outside the oil sector and particularly to develop the infrastructure. Budget allocations for expenditure on development projects rose from $24 million in 1960 to $570 million in 1969; although not all development allocations were spent, the rise in actual expenditure, both in absolute terms and as a proportion of total government expenditure, has been impressive. Actual development expenditures in 1968 are estimated at $350 million (or 29 percent of total government expenditure), compared with $200 million in 1967 and about $85 million in 1964.[2] The cumulative effect of such development expenditures, together with rising government consumption expenditure and rising private incomes, has been to infuse the economy with a certain degree of dynamism. These revolutionary economic changes have had profound effects on the social and political consciousness as well as the attitudes of ever-widening groups of the population, particularly in the cities, although it seems still early to forecast their direction or their force.

Tables 8-1 and 8-2 summarize the rate of growth of some of the major components of national product, national expenditure, oil revenue, and official reserves. The average annual rates of growth before and after 1960 can be summarized as follows:

	Annual Real Rates of Growth[3] (percent)		
	1954/55– 1960/61	1960/61– 1964/65	1964–1967
Gross national product	6	11	8
Gross fixed capital formation	3	15	17
Private consumption expenditure	8	10	7
Oil production	6	10	14
Oil revenue	2	14	20

Despite the fast progress in the last 20 years, the economy of Saudi Arabia remains today a "dual economy" with a very modern, highly capitalized oil enclave and a largely traditional sector. The oil sector accounts for almost all the exports of Saudi Arabia, and for nearly nine-tenths of the government's revenue and of the country's foreign exchange earnings.[4] Although the oil sector contrib-

[2] Saudi Arabian Monetary Agency, *Annual Report, 1387–88 AH,* pp. 1, 34, 90.
[3] National product data up to 1964–1965 are presumably at constant prices, while the new series, 1964–1967, is at current prices.
[4] Nonoil exports include small quantities of live animals, hides, and dates. Nonoil government revenue includes mainly customs revenue and miscellaneous fees. Nonoil earnings of foreign exchange include mainly the annual expenditures of pilgrims; in 1968 there were 375,000 pilgrims, who are estimated to have contributed $72 million (see SAMA, *Annual Report 1387–88 AH,* pp. 30, 93); dividends and interest on

Table 8-1

Rate of Growth of Major Components of National Product and Expenditure, and Official Reserves in Saudi Arabia[a], 1954/55-1964/65[a] and 1964-1969

(millions of Saudi riyals)[b]

| Year | | Gross National Product | Value Added in the Non-oil Sector | Gross Fixed Capital Formation | | Private Consumption Expenditure | Official Gold and Foreign Exchange Holdings[c] |
Hijri	Gregorian			Total	Nonoil Sector		
1374	8/54-8/55	2,535	1,452	487	261	1,338	n.a.
1375	8/55-8/56	3,016	1,853	671	383	1,624	n.a.
1376	8/56-7/57	3,269	2,162	904	594	1,819	n.a.
1377	7/57-7/58	3,442	2,267	734	437	1,993	98
1378	7/58-7/59	3,491	2,187	591	n.a.	2,007	464
1379	7/59-6/60	3,739	2,239	457	n.a.	2,127	778
1380	6/60-6/61	3,927	2,325	575	n.a.	2,165	976
1381	6/61-6/62	4,544	2,699	755	n.a.	2,317	n.a.
1382	6/62-5/63	4,847	2,797	681	n.a.	2,652	1,630
1383	5/63-5/64	5,022	2,668	865	n.a.	2,531	2,387
1384	5/64-4/65	6,068	3,107	1,094	n.a.	3,187	2,886
1964		7,333	4,618	n.a.	1,042	2,965	2,684
1965		8,308	5,090	n.a.	1,325	3,115	3,396
1966		9,070	5,651	n.a.	1,715	3,455	3,658
1967		9,891	6,226	n.a.	1,784	3,785	4,248
1968		n.a.	n.a.	n.a.	n.a.	n.a.	3,914
1969 Aug.		n.a.	n.a.	n.a.	n.a.	n.a.	3,810

[a]The figures for gross national product, value added in the nonoil sector, and private consumption expenditure represent 3-year averages, 2-year averages, and yearly figures for the periods 1374-79, 1380 and 1381-84, respectively.

[b]The rate of exchange was $1 = 3.75 Saudi riyals to the middle of 1379 AH and 4.50 Saudi riyals thereafter.

[c]Figures given for end of Hijri year up to 1384 AH by Saudi Arabian Monetary Agency, *Annual Report, 1386-87 AH*, and for the end of the calendar year for 1964-1969 by the IMF, *International Financial Statistics*, January 1970.

Source: 1374-1384 AH, United Nations, *Studies on Selected Development Problems in Various Countries of the Middle East 1968*, New York, 1968, p. 28. 1964 to 1967, data at current prices are from the Saudi Arabian Monetary Agency, *Annual Report*, 1387-88 AH. The two series are not comparable.

Table 8-2

Oil Production, Exports, Prices, and Revenues, Saudi Arabia, 1938-1967

Calendar Year	Crude Oil Production (million barrels)	Crude Oil Exports (million barrels)	Refined Oil Exports (million barrels)	Price per Barrel of Crude Exports ($)	Oil Revenues[a] (million $)
1938	0.5				
1939	4				3
1946	60				10
1950	200				57
1952	302				212
1954	351				277
1955	357	276	66	1.87	341
1956	367	288	64	1.87	290
1957	374	288	63	1.96	296
1958	385	307	53	2.06	297
1959	421	334	55	1.88	313
1960	481	373	72	1.78	334
1961	541	417	77	1.71	378
1962	600	463	78	1.70	410
1963	652	492	86	1.78	608
1964	694	527	92	1.82	523
1965	805	623	104	1.79	663
1966	950	760	105	1.78	790
1967	1024	822	112	1.78	909
1968	1114	893	138	1.82	926

[a]Including royalties, taxes, fees, and special payments and settlements.

Source: Saudi Arabian Monetary Agency, *Annual Report 1380 AH; 1387-88 AH.*

utes about half of total GNP, it employs only about 15,000 workers out of a total male population of working age estimated at 800,000.[5]

Table 8-3 indicates the occupational distribution of the labor force in 1967, although the data are only approximate, and brings out the predominance of the

Saudi investments and deposits abroad are also of some significance, but their value is not known.

[5] Assuming the population is 4 million and the population of working age about 40 percent, of whom half are men.

Table 8-3
Estimate of Occupational Distribution of Labor, 1967

Sector	Number	Percent
Agriculture	128,000	33.7
Oil industry	16,000	4.2
Other mining industry and crafts	24,000	6.3
Trade, finance, transport, and services	90,000	23.7
Construction	8,000	2.1
Government (armed forces excluded)	114,000	30.0
Total	380,000	100.0

Source: Derived from the results of the *Agricultural Surveys, 1380-1383 AH* and the *Survey of Establishments 1382/83* (the results of which are published in the *Statistical Yearbook* 1965 and 1967). The figures are adjusted upward by 10 percent to bring them up to 1967. Employment in government is based on allocations in the 1967 budget.

Recent official (provisional) estimates of GDP show the following distribution in 1967 among the various sectors (in percent):

Agriculture and livestock	7.7
Petroleum	52.5
Other mining	0.4
Manufacturing	1.9
Construction	4.1
Electricity, gas, water, and sanitary services	1.9
Transport, storage, and communications	6.9
Trade	7.1
Finance	0.4
Ownership of dwellings	3.8
Public administration and defense	8.5
Education, health, and other services	4.9
Total	100.0

government and agricultural sectors as sources of employment. The table also indicates the rather low participation rate of the labor force or, to put it differently, the high rate of unemployment or disguised unemployment. Less than half the male population of working age has been found to have known and regular employment. It should be also mentioned that over one-tenth of the employed persons are non-Saudis.

Prospects of Economic Growth

The prospects for the future economic development of Saudi Arabia will continue, as in recent years, to be very closely tied to the development of its oil in-

374

dustry and the efficiency and attitudes of its public administration in the economic field. The isolation of these two factors does not mean, of course, that the development of the nonoil sectors or the efforts of the private sector will have no influence on the shape and the rate of future growth. In fact, such activities as agriculture, transport, private construction, manufacturing, and nongovernment services represent a very substantial part of the economic activities in the country. However, the growth and progress of the latter activities will continue to depend on the initiative taken by the central government for their promotion and assistance, and government economic activities are dependent to a very large extent on revenue from oil. In other words, the nonoil and private sectors are still dependent sectors with little autonomous dynamism. In the past their rate of growth has tended to be slower than that of the oil and government sectors.

If it is assumed that no serious internal or external political upheaval will occur and that government revenue from oil will continue to increase in the 1970s as it did in the 1960s, it can be safely said that the prospects of continued economic development in Saudi Arabia in the 1970s appear both bright and assured. The rate of growth of national income should follow more or less closely the rate of growth of oil revenue. Whether the overall rate of growth exceeds or falls short of the growth rate for oil revenue will be largely determined by the growth of the sectors that do not depend directly on oil revenue, and this, in turn, will depend on the volume and pattern of domestic investment and on factors affecting the skills and productivity of indigenous or imported labor.

The rate of growth of oil revenue is a function of two factors: the volume of oil exports on the one hand, and the average revenue per barrel on the other. The volume of oil exports depends on several factors; the most important, assuming political stability in the world and in the Middle East, is European and Japanese demand, and the decision of the major oil producers of the Middle East as to the share, in total production, of each of the countries of the region in which they operate. If it is assumed that the current pattern will continue in the 1970s, the rate of growth of world demand, particularly that of Europe and Japan, will determine the rate of growth of Saudi Arabian production and export of oil.

Output and exports of crude oil in Saudi Arabia grew at 6 percent from 1955 to 1960 and at 11 percent from 1960 to 1967, compared with a rate of 9.2 percent for the Middle East as a whole over the entire period. Tentative projections of crude oil production derived from projection of world demand for energy indicate that the rate of Middle East export may be about 9 percent in the decade 1965–1975.[6] In view of the average rate of growth in the 1960s and the absence of any convincing reason why Saudi Arabia's share of Middle East oil exports should decline in the future, it is reasonable to assume that the rate of growth of Saudi Arabian oil exports should not fall below that of the Middle East as a whole, 9 percent per annum.

[6] United Nations, *Studies on Selected Development Problems*, p. 29.

375

Changes in average government revenue per barrel in the future are even more difficult to forecast with any degree of accuracy. Posted prices have been changed several times in the past, and various settlements were reached between the oil companies and the government involving back payments and changes in the basis of calculation of revenues. Nevertheless, the long-term trend in oil revenues showed a very high correlation with the long-term trend in oil production and exports. Such a direct relation between production exports and oil revenue can well be assumed to continue in the coming decade, notwithstanding various efforts and government participation in oil activities and despite the apparently improved terms that the government has been able to obtain from new concessionaires.

With about 9 percent annual rate of growth in oil revenue, the GNP of Saudi Arabia can be expected to increase at a rate not far behind.[7] A very high correlation has been found in the past between the rise in income as represented by GNP and the rise in oil revenue, just as a close correlation exists between the oil revenue of the government and the volume of production. The correlation between the first two variables in the period 1950/51–1960/61 was as high as 0.97, and between the last two during 1950/51–1961/62 as high as 0.98.[8]

Both the government and private persons have invested heavily in developing the infrastructure of the economy, as well as directly in agriculture and manufacturing. This has led to much higher income in nonoil sectors but not to an increase in the relative contribution of the private sector when compared with the oil and government sectors. This result, disappointing from the point of view of the policy that aims at greater diversification of the economy, may be explained by the exceptionally high rate of growth of oil exports and oil revenue. Although it is obviously not the intention of the Saudi Arabian government to reduce the rate of growth of oil revenue, diversification would require both raising the rate of investment in the other sectors and raising the productivity of labor through other means than capital investment at a higher rate than in the past. Although raising capital formation may be easily within the capacities of government budgets and private savings, a higher productivity level, both of capital and of labor, seems to be a more difficult goal at the present and for the foreseeable future.

Projection of Per Capita Income

The rate of per capita income growth is the difference between the rate of income growth and the rate of population growth. The size of the population of Saudi Arabia is not reliably known. However, the limited data available point to

[7] A new development plan adopted late in 1969 and covering the period from September 1969 to September 1976 aims at raising the GNP at an annual rate of 9.3 percent, developing human resources and national skills, and diversifying the sources of income.

[8] E. Y. Asfour, *Saudi Arabia: Long Term Agricultural Projections,* Beirut, 1965, p. 46.

a probable rate of growth of the indigenous population in the early 1960s of between 2.0 and 2.9 percent per annum. The population growth rate in the 1970s is likely to be higher because improving living standards and better medical services and disease prevention methods should bring the death rate down from the relatively high level of 2.4 percent per annum.[9] It should not be far off the mark, therefore, to assume that the net rate of increase of population will be about 3 percent per annum in the 1970s (such a rate would imply an increase of population from an assumed 4–6 million at present to 6–8 million by 1980).

The rate of growth of total income in the 1970s was estimated above to be of the order of 9 percent per annum. Average per capita income is thus likely to be of the order of 6 percent per annum. However, the growth trend of average per capita income, in the conditions of Saudi Arabia, may diverge quite considerably from that of per capita *private* income, and even more considerably from that of private per capita consumption expenditure. The first divergence is caused by oil revenue being channeled through government, which may decide either to save a varying part of its income, adding more (or less) to its gold and exchange reserves, or to spend more than its income, in which case the private income stream will flow slower (or faster) than oil revenue. Furthermore, the nature of government expenditures will considerably affect the size of private incomes. Government expenditures on imports (particularly for defense purposes, but also on equipment and on services of foreign contractors) and its expenditures abroad (particularly in grants in aid, including an annual $140 million to the United Arab Republic and Jordan) reduce the potential contribution of government expenditures to domestic private incomes. In view of the probable rising demand by government for foreign goods and services and the continued help to other countries, private per capita incomes may in fact grow at a lower rate than 6 percent per annum.

The second divergence, between average private incomes and average private consumption expenditures, is due to the distribution pattern of incomes, which has probably encouraged a high rate of saving and investment abroad on the part of the richer members of the community. The more equal the distribution of income becomes in the future, the smaller the rate of savings is likely to be and the narrower the gap between private incomes and private expenditures.

The Private Sector

In a "dual" economy such as that of Saudi Arabia, the rate of growth of the traditional sectors—those that do not depend directly on the oil industry—can be considered the significant measure of autonomous economic development. The modern oil sector was developed by nonindigenous skills and capital and remains very largely isolated from the rest of the economy. It depends for its rate of growth on external factors over which Saudi Arabia itself has limited influence.

[9] See E. Y. Asfour, *Saudi Arabia, Long Term Projections of Supplies of and Demand for Agricultural Products,* Beirut, 1965, particularly pp. 40, 41, 142–148.

Of course, the nonoil private sector could not have attained a high rate of growth in the past and will not attain one in the future if it is not stimulated by expenditures originating in the oil industry. The government spends the larger part of such revenue (together with other minor revenues) on services and development projects. But only a part of such expenditure is paid in the form of salaries and wages to Saudi nationals or for the purchase of local raw materials and other services; the other part is spent on imported goods and services or is invested or transferred abroad. It is evidently the first type of expenditure that influences the level of income of the private nonoil sectors in any one period. On the other hand, the rate of growth of this income is affected not only by the growth rate of the relevant type of government expenditure, but also by the new incomes created by the completed development projects and by new projects undertaken independently by the private sector.

The importance of the multiplier effects of such stimulating expenditures in the nonoil private sector depends, however, on its ability to create new production capacity through new investments, more employment, and the exploitation of new resources. This effect is weakened by leakages from the income stream and by payments for imports of consumer goods from abroad as well as by transfer of capital abroad. Because of the inability of the domestic economy to satisfy the rising domestic demand for consumer goods, the import leakage is large and growing. Similarly, not only are practically all investment goods imported from abroad, thus adding to the leakage of consumer goods import, but also the shortage of attractive investment opportunities at home, as well as of entrepreneurs to discover and exploit them, has added to the outflow of domestic savings abroad in search of better investment opportunities, thus further increasing leakage in the income flow. A higher rate of growth in the income of the nonoil private sector requires not so much the mobilization of financial resources as the creation and discovery of new investment opportunities at home, whether by indigenous or foreign entrepreneurs.

Besides investment and entrepreneurship, another factor that affects the level of output in the nonoil private sector and that, under the conditions of Saudi Arabia, is of particular importance is the level of technological skill of the workers and employees and their attitude toward work and its quality in modern establishments. Only in the last two decades or so were some Saudi Arabians introduced for the first time in history to modern technology and the discipline of modern office and factory work. If the oil companies themselves and the government are excluded, the few modern establishments that were set up will be found to have contributed only to a small extent to the spread of modern employment; the majority of such employment was taken by non-Saudis, very largely Arabs from the other countries of the Middle East. In this respect the successful experience of ARAMCO in employing and training Saudis in progressively more complex technical jobs is of interest. It indicates the primary importance of theoretical and technical training in improving the skills of workers and the importance and the limitations of financial incentive and employment security in securing efficient and disciplined workers. The government has allocated large funds and facilities to education and training at all levels, including technical and university training. Developments in mining (other than oil), manufacturing industry, and agriculture may indicate some of the problems and characteristics of the development process in Saudi Arabia and the continued dependence of the private sector on government.

Mining

Aside from oil production, transportation, and refining, certain areas seem to have a better chance of development than others. Mining, which had a short-lived development with the exploitation of gold mines at Mahd al Dhabab before 1954, has stagnated since. The prospects of future development would, however, seem quite promising in the 1970s. Several of the current intensive aeromagnetic, photogrammetric, geophysical, and geodetic surveys have prepared the ground for widespread exploration and proving, and selective exploitation should follow. So far, considerable medium-quality iron ore (40–50 percent oxide content) and some rich ore (64 percent oxide content) have been located, and a study has been undertaken for their exploitation. Several other minerals have also been reported.

Industry

Oil and, more particularly, large quantities of wasted gas have supplied the raw materials for several important manufacturing industries which are combined under the name "petrochemicals," in addition to oil refining. The narrowness of the local market and the substantial economies of scale which the petrochemical industry enjoys have directed development toward producing for the export markets, generally on the strength of a long-term purchase-guarantee arrangement. A urea plant (capacity, 1025 tons per day) has been practically completed at Damman, a fertilizer plant (capacity, 600 tons per day) is under construction there, and a sulphur extractive plant (capacity, 30–35 tons per day) is planned. An oil refinery (capacity, 12,000 barrels per day of crude) has been completed at Jedda, and another is planned in Riyadh (capacity, 15,000 barrels per day),

PETROMIN Projects in Saudi Arabia
Planned for Implementation by 1972

	Number of Projects	Approximate Cost (million riyals)
Oil and mineral exploration	9	680
Oil refinery or marketing	9	234
Fertilizer and petrochemicals	7	1,340
Iron and steel industries	7	206
Other industries	3	48
Total	35	2,508

379

as well as an oil-lube-blending plant in Jedda (capacity, 75,000 barrels per day). Outside the oil sector, modern industry includes a steel rolling mill in Jedda (capacity, 45,000 tons per year), cement plants, building materials, and light food manufacturing.

Agriculture

Traditional subsistence agriculture, largely represented by date growing and animal raising, suffers from a number of serious problems. Under the new economic conditions, these agricultural activities will at best maintain their level in the future and more probably will diminish as a source of employment and even of output. This expectation is based, in the case of date growing, on the fact that the domestic demand for dates tends to fall fast with the rise in income level of the consumer, particularly in that of the poor classes, who are the main consumers of this cheap food. On the other hand, world demand does not seem to rise significantly, and increasing Saudi exports will have to face stiff competition from the other main producers and exporters, such as Iraq. Furthermore, the available data indicate that the gross return at current prices of irrigated land under vegetables, alfalfa, or other fruits is higher than that under dates. In view of the very limited area of irrigated land this situation creates pressure for the conversion of date areas to other, more profitable uses.

Animal raising by roving Bedouins in search of pasture historically supported a large part of the Arabian peninsula. It now faces serious problems, despite the strong rise in the demand for meat and milk products, because of the long-term deterioration of the range and insufficient disease control. Also, the gradual settlement of Bedouins is encouraged by the government; and the attraction of well-paid employment with government, oil companies, or other private concerns tends to work against the expansion of this form of subsistence activity.

The prospects are improving, however, for the development of animal raising on settled farms, dairy farming, and growing fruits and vegetables because of the fast rise in demand for these products, now being met by increasing imports. The extent of this growth depends primarily on the expansion of the irrigated area. It is influenced also, of course, by the continued improvement in the methods of production, including the wider use of fertilizers, and by the establishment of efficient transport, credit, marketing, storage, and refrigeration facilities, and the supply of veterinary and extension services. Although the private sector should show initiative in improving the methods of production by undertaking small capital works and by participating in supplying some of the facilities referred to, the government will undertake the basic works leading to the expansion of the irrigated area through underground water exploration, water storage, and improvement of the road system. It has also taken a major part in supplying credit and in establishing marketing, storage, and refrigeration facilities.

The government is undertaking a comprehensive survey of the water resources of the kingdom, as well as an irrigation and drainage scheme for 20,000 hectares (about 15 percent of total irrigated land) in Al Ahsa in the east, a water storage and irrigation project covering 18,000 hectares in Wadi Jizan in the south, and a Bedouin settlement project based on the irrigation of about 3,000 hectares of desert land from underground water and the reclamation of about 2,000 hectares in Al Qatif. These projects should be completed by 1975 and may increase the irrigated area by about 30 percent. An agricultural bank was established, and studies are being undertaken in regard to marketing, storage, and feeder roads in agricultural areas.

However, when all available data are assessed, and unless new sources of abundant and cheap irrigation water are discovered and made available in the next 5 years, the gap between production and consumption of food is most likely to grow considerably rather than to be narrowed by 1980.

II. Kuwait

Background

Kuwait is a small, flat, desert country of about 6,200 square miles (16,000 square kilometers) on the northeastern coast of the Persian Gulf, between Iraq in the north and Saudi Arabia in the south. It shares with the latter the ownership and administration of a "Neutral Zone" of about 2,500 square miles (5,700 square kilometers) on the coast between the two countries. Kuwait's borders were fixed in 1922–1923, when Britain was both the mandatory power in Iraq and responsible for foreign affairs and the defense of the Sheikhdom of Kuwait under treaty. In June 1961, Kuwait was declared an independent state.

Like its two neighbors, Kuwait is rich in oil and gas resources, but, unlike them, it has no agricultural or other known mineral resources of value. Before World War II, Kuwait's subsistence economy depended on sea trade and fishing, particularly for pearls; drinking water was carried by boat from Iraq. The equal sharing by the government of the growing profits of the concessionary oil companies[10] since 1951 has dramatically raised oil revenues, which by 1968 totaled $8 billion and reached a peak of $890 million in 1966 (Table 8-4). The growing expenditures by government out of this revenue on construction works, welfare, and other services attracted immigrants, raising the total population

---

[10] Oil exploration was started during 1938–1942 by the Kuwait Oil Company (KOC), and oil was first exported in 1946. At present there are five concessionary companies in Kuwait and the Neutral Zone: The Kuwait Oil Company (British Petroleum, BP, and American Gulf, produces on the mainland); the American Independent Oil Company (AMINOIL, started production in 1954 in the Neutral Zone and islands); The Arabian Oil Company (Japanese and Kuwaiti, started production in 1961 offshore from the Neutral Zone); the Kuwait Shell Company Limited (British and Dutch, started exploration in 1962 offshore outside the 6 mile territorial water zone and in specific islands within it); the Kuwait National Petroleum Company (KNPC, Kuwaiti company, established in 1960, markets oil products locally and operates a refinery of its own; it also explores oil inland in partnership with Hispanoil through the Kuwaiti-Spanish Petroleum Company, KSPC).

Table 8-4

Oil Output, Export, and Revenues in Kuwait

Year	Crude Oil Production (million barrels)	Crude Oil Exports (million barrels)	Exports of Refined Products (million barrels)	Oil Revenues[a] (million)
1940	6			n.a.
1948	46			n.a.
1950	126			12
1952	273			57
1953	315			168
1954	350			194
1955	403			280
1956	406			292
1957	428			308
1958	524			357
1959	526			468[b]
1960	619	530	83	469
1961	633	541	91	470
1962	714	609	97	528
1963	765	653	97	557
1964	842	728	110	798
1965	861	442	110	817
1966	907	797	106	891
1967	912	806	98	818
1968	957	847	109	762

[a]Include settlement of claims on previous years.
[b]January 1959 to end of March 1960.

Source: Kuwait *Statistical Abstract, 1968* and other official sources; *Petroleum Press Service.*

from about 150,000 in 1949 to 200,000 in 1957, 500,000 in 1965, and possibly 700,000 at present, and transformed the poor subsistence economy with a per capita income of perhaps $50 in 1946 into a more diversified welfare economy enjoying one of the highest average per capita income levels in the world (estimated at about $3,200). However, diversification of output remains limited, the economy remains highly dependent on imports for the satisfaction of its consumption needs, and the level of economic activity remains strongly dependent on the level of government expenditures out of its revenue from oil.

Crude oil production (Table 8-4) increased continuously since 1946 but has risen rather unsteadily since 1956, reaching 130 million tons in 1968 or about 7 percent of total world production and 25 percent of Middle East output. Exports are largely directed toward Western Europe (particularly the United Kingdom and Italy) and the Far East (particularly Japan and Australia).

Refining is undertaken by the KOC refinery at Ahmadi (production, 13 million tons in 1968), by AMINOIL at Port Abdallah (production, 2 million tons in 1968), and by the KNPC refinery at Shuaiba (capacity, 4.7 million tons a year; production started in 1968 and reached two-thirds capacity by 1969). Thus in 1968 a total of about 17 million tons (120 million barrels) of crude oil was refined, representing 13 percent of total crude production of Kuwait. The proved oil reserves of Kuwait have been estimated at about one-third of the Middle East reserves and over one-fifth of world reserves. The government, in addition to its ownership in the KNPC (which owns 51 percent of KSPC), has participated with 10 percent of the capital of the Arabian Oil Company (Japan and Kuwait) and has an option to purchase up to 20 percent of the capital of the Kuwait Shell Company Limited.

The building up of Kuwait City, the capital, has been stimulated and accelerated by the extensive expenditures of the government on infrastructure, town planning, electricity and water supply, education, health, and other welfare services. In addition, a generous employment policy and considerable transfer of funds to the private sector in the form of compensation or purchase of land at inflated prices have stimulated private construction. As oil and natural gas offered the base for oil refining and the petrochemical industry, so the building and construction boom created the base for a small but growing manufacturing industry, and the growing population and rising incomes created the base for an expansion of the services sector. Agriculture, apart from fishing and some small-scale animal and poultry farming, is practically nonexistent. Mining activities are limited to oil extraction. Government expenditure out of its oil revenue remains a major support of employment in the country and the main determinant of the level of economic activity in the private sector. The autonomy of the private sector has increased, however, with the rise in the accumulated private financial assets and the increasing readiness of private entrepreneurs to invest part of their assets in business ventures in Kuwait was well as abroad.

In recent years, the rate of growth of GNP at current prices[11] has averaged almost 10 percent per annum (Table 8-5). Consumption grew at an average rate of 9 percent but represented only 57 percent of GNP in 1967/68.

[11] There is no price index in Kuwait. Prices of individual commodities show very moderate rise (perhaps 1 percent per annum) over the period 1964–1968.

Table 8-5

Components of GNP and Foreign Assets in Kuwait
(million KD)[a]

Year	Gross National Product	Gross Fixed Capital Formation		Consumption		Net Foreign Assets[b]	
		Private	Public	Private	Public	Banks	Government
1962/63	460	45	33	188	80	134	138
1963/64	500	47	45	192	89	176	180
1964/65	542	49	47	200	102	182	191
1965/66	565	70	43	198	105	254	264
1966/67	607	73	64	210	120	251	260
1967/68	734	95	68	280	135	298	315
1969 to September						288	327

[a]One Kuwaiti dinar = $2.8.
[b]End of calendar year.

Source: Kuwait, *Statistical Abstract, 1968,* except for 1967-68; IMF, *International Financial Statistics,* January 1970.

Capital formation, on the other hand, represented 22 percent of GNP, a ratio comparable to that in developed countries. The 21 percent excess of GNP over consumption *plus* capital formation is an approximate measure of the large net transfers by Kuwait of resources abroad.

The structure of the economy is also reflected in the employment pattern. Of a labor force of 180,000 in 1965, approximately 40 percent were employed by the government; 7 percent in manufacturing industry outside the oil sector; 16 percent in building and construction; and 30 percent in transport, trade, and other services. Only 1 percent were engaged in fishing and agriculture, and only 15,000 workers, or 8 percent of the total labor force, were employed in the oil sector (production, refining, transportation and distribution), which nevertheless contributed about 42 percent of the national income (over 60 percent of GDP) in that year. It is noticed that immigrant labor represented as much as 77 percent of the total labor force and that the proportion was 56 percent in government, 90 percent in the manufacturing sector, and 96 percent in the construction sector. The flow of immigrant labor has diminished considerably in recent years, and it is the policy of the government to reduce immigration further in order to bring the proportion of non-Kuwaitis to less than half the total population, compared with about 60 percent at present.

Planned Development

Two major policy goals, within the main goal of increasing income, which are embodied in the country's five-year development plan (1967/68–1971/72), are reducing Kuwait's heavy dependence on immigrants as a source of manpower and on oil exports as the main source of revenue. The means of achieving these goals include the further expansion of the infrastructure, the encouragement of industrial production, particularly for export, and the improvement of the country's labor productivity and skills through intensified school, vocational, and technical training and more intensive capital investment. Other objectives, not purely economic, include a more equal distribution of income and closer economic cooperation with the other Gulf states and with the rest of the Arab world.[12]

The expected rise in production (GDP) during the plan period was a modest 6.5 percent per annum, based on the assumption of an annual rate of growth of 5.9 percent in the export of oil production. The difference between the two rates implies a higher rate of growth in the nonoil sectors than in the oil sector. Although the government can influence the rate of growth of oil production and export through deliberate policy to only a small extent, it can accelerate the rate of growth of nonoil sectors (and it aims to do so) through various policy measures and in conjunction with the private sector. It is the manner in which and the extent to which the private and mixed enterprise sectors succeed in growing and diversifying their activities that can be considered the real measure of Kuwait's success in building a healthy and stable base for steady and long-term development in the future.

The task is not as easy as it may seem to analysts who consider capital to be the major factor determining the rate of growth. It is true that Kuwait has an abundance of capital in relation to exportable raw materials as well as in relation to available labor. In view of the major aims of Kuwait's development plan, however, there are two basic economic policy problems: first, how to find the best investment opportunities for the country's substantial savings; and, second, given the material and labor limitations, how best to explore and expand the opportunities for investment within the country through the use and adaptation of capital-intensive technologies and through raising the level of technological skill and encouraging entrepreneurial talent as far as possible.

Kuwait has already started to tread the dual road toward long-term economic stability with growth. There is no doubt that the cost of experimentation

[12] See "First Five Year Plan for Economic Development, 1967/68–1971/72" (revised, April 1967) (in Arabic); also United Nations, *Studies on Selected Development Problems*. The plan (envisioning a total expenditure of $1.46 billion) as been approved by the government but not by the National Assembly.

and learning will be high, but it will be paid. To an important extent, the limitation of waste and the final success of this economic venture will depend on the vitality and adaptability of the entrepreneurial class and on the willingness of the Kuwaiti citizens to acquire new skills and maintain achievement-oriented working habits.

Competition of foreign with domestic investment outlets for Kuwait's savings has obviously favored the former, particularly in view of the high rates of interest offered abroad in recent years. The interest situation may well shift in the coming decade, but such a change need not by itself result in the growth of the domestic share of total investment. Obvious investment opportunities in Kuwait are limited, and the total volume of savings is likely to continue to grow in the future. In addition, the returns from past investments abroad are likely to increase to a point where they will help to raise savings to a much higher rate than that of domestic investment. In 1964/65, for example, returns from public and private investments abroad were estimated at KD 43 million ($120 million), which represented as much as 45 percent of fixed capital formation, or about 18 percent of total gross national savings (and about 8 percent of national income during that year). National savings (KD 240 million in 1964/65) represent about 45 percent of GNP; this rate is expected to be maintained during the five-year plan. The practical impossibility of investing such a high proportion of GNP domestically year after year (capital formation in 1964/65 represented only 41 percent of gross national savings) points to the continued growth of investment abroad and, consequently, to the growth of income from foreign investments. Such income has now reached an estimated level of $250 million a year, or double the 1964/65 level. Foreign assets of the government are estimated at $900 million and those of commercial banks at $800 million (see Table 8-5). Private holding of foreign assets outside banks probably exceeds $1 billion.

Of course, political developments may upset these expectations. In the past, Kuwait has made substantial interest-free loans to Arab countries such as Iraq, Algeria, the United Arab Republic, and Jordan, in addition to low-interest loans advanced to these and other Arab countries by the government or by the Kuwait Fund for Arab Economic Development (KFAED). Government loans, mainly interest free, to Arab countries totaled more than KD 125 million ($350 million) by the end of 1968, and KFAED loans to seven Arab countries totaled KD 68.6 million ($192 million) by March 1969. Since the war of June 1967, Kuwait has agreed to pay £55 million ($132 million) a year to the United Arab Republic and Jordan, to help them cover their war losses, until the "effects of the aggression" are removed. These latter payments have resulted in reduction of the purchase of land by the government and to some extent may lower Kuwait's ability to invest at the rate prevailing before 1967, at least for a few years until the growth in oil revenue allows their absorption. Of course, political developments in the Middle East may stop these and similar payments, or halt their growth. This is an unmeasurable factor, which could considerably af-

386

fect the rate of growth of Kuwait's investments and hence of income in the coming decade.

Oil

There is little doubt that the main economic determinant of income growth in Kuwait in the coming decade will continue to be revenue from oil. Although possible changes in prices and profit-sharing arrangements between the government and the concessionary companies can influence the size of oil revenue, it is likely that, short of political upheavals in the area, these changes will be marginal. The volume of oil exports is therefore likely to remain the main determinant of changes in the size of oil revenue received by the government.

Kuwait's rate of growth of oil exports is not expected to be as high in the coming decade as in the previous 10 years or as for other major Middle East producers, despite the obvious cost advantages enjoyed by oil producers in Kuwait (cost per barrel is estimated at less than $0.06) and despite the recent opening of an island terminal 10 miles offshore, the only place in the world where giant tankers of more than 300,000 tons can be fully loaded. Apart from the closure of the Suez Canal, which may be only temporary, the main reasons behind this unoptimistic forecast include the relative advantages North African crude could enjoy in the West European market, as compared with Gulf crude, from the viewpoints of cost of transportation, lower sulphur content, and tied outlets; the low rate of growth of direct consumption by the two shareholders of KOC; and, significantly, Kuwait's diplomatic restraint until recently in pressing the concessionary companies for a larger share of Middle East exports, in view of the greater needs of its more populous neighbors.[13]

Recent official statements point to government intentions to press the major oil companies to raise its production by 6 percent per annum. The rate at which Kuwait's oil exports will grow in the future can only be guessed at; the range could well be between 6 and 9 percent per annum,[14] present indicators as well as the growth rate of recent years pointing toward the lower end of the range. The official revised five-year plan for Kuwait had in fact envisioned a rate of growth of 5.9 percent per annum in oil exports over the period 1966/67–1971/72,[15] which is equal to the actual rate of growth of production during 1962–1966.

If the annual rate of growth of oil production and of revenue is assumed to be 6 percent, the rate of growth of total income should be expected to be not far off. Depending on the assumptions adopted and the analytical model used, GNP may be expected to grow at an annual rate varying between 6.7 and 6.9

[13] See *The Times* (London), February 25, 1969, special report on Kuwait, p. II, "Foreign Competition Makes Its Mark."

[14] The annual rate of growth of Middle East oil exports has been tentatively projected for the years 1965–1975 at 9.1 percent. (See United Nations, *Studies on Selected Development Problems*, p. 29.)

[15] *Ibid.*, Table 1, 13.

percent.[16] If it is assumed, however, that all savings will be available for investment (that is, no transfers are made) and that satisfactory domestic investment opportunities can be found to absorb a rising proportion of these savings (and the labor and market requirements are assured), then the growth rate of GNP may rise to as much as 9.1 percent per annum.[17] However, these latter assumptions will be difficult to realize in the foreseeable future, given the past performance of the economy and the growing demand on Kuwait to aid other Arab countries.

A future rate of growth of GNP that moves more or less in line with that of oil production and continues from a per capita income base already one of the highest in the world is certainly a rare prospect. Political upheavals apart, the future problems of the economic development of Kuwait can be considered marginal. The main problems and policies are related to discovering or creating new domestic investment opportunities, forming the technical and working cadres to staff such projects, and improving the efficiency of government expenditures in terms of returns to such expenditures and in terms of shifting the emphasis toward expenditures that are expected to further the above aims. Of course, from the purely short-run point of view, it may be more profitable for Kuwait to live as a *rentier* state, investing its savings in foreign assets and living on the dividends and interest accruing on these assets. The policymakers, however, seem to place a high value on creating permanent employment opportunities within Kuwait, and on furthering Kuwaiti participation not only in the oil business, but also in other possible ventures where local raw materials and capital, or even local capital alone, can join with foreign enterprise to start new viable businesses. The foreign partners or associates may assure the foreign market or supply the raw materials and technical know-how, but preference seems to be given to projects located in Kuwait itself.

Although Kuwait-based enterprises seem to be generally the alternative to purely financial investments abroad, there are a few indications that Kuwaiti enterprises and capital may themselves move to exploit business opportunities abroad. Thus, apart from investment in real estate in neighboring Arab countries, individual Kuwaitis have sometimes participated in business enterprises and banks in these and other foreign countries. The operations of Gulf International are illustrative in this respect. Not only does this company own Gulf Fisheries, which operates in Kuwait, Iran, Saudi Arabia, Indonesia, Singapore, Madagascar, and Nigeria, but it also owns or has participated in a large textile factory, glass bottle factory, and pharmaceutical and cosmetic factories in Sudan, in an oil exploration firm in Somalia, in a match factory in Nigeria, and in food freezing and distribution in Lebanon. Total employment in these concerns is

---

[16] *Ibid.*, Table 1, p. 13, and Table 7, p. 20. In the first of these, calculations are based on a two-sector (oil and nonoil) growth model based on the Harrod-Domar production function; the second rate is that of the official revised five-year plan.
[17] *Ibid.*, Table 5, p. 17.

about 12,000, of whom only 20 percent work in Kuwait itself. In addition to purely private companies, two large mixed companies have been set up to invest in foreign enterprises, namely, the Kuwait Investment Company and the Kuwait Foreign Trading and Contracting Company.

In dealing with the prospects for the economic growth of Kuwait, it is inevitable that some words should be devoted to the distribution of this growing income among the small population. Already Kuwait can claim to be one of the most advanced among the welfare states. The state offers free education at all levels (including the university level, locally and abroad), free school meals for outside students, and full board and generous allowances for boarders; it also instituted compulsory elementary education in 1966/67. Health services are provided free, including hospitalization, surgery, and medicines to visitors as well as residents. The government has also built several thousand houses and will construct 15,000–20,000 air-conditioned houses over the next 3 years. It sells these houses to Kuwaitis with limited incomes ($350 per month or less), the cost to be paid over 40 years. Distilled water and electric power are sold to all residents at a subsidized price, the annual subsidy averaging about $115 per family.[18] In addition to all these free or subsidized services, the government transfers substantial funds to individual Kuwaitis by means of compensation for expropriated land or purchase of land at exceptionally generous prices. It has been estimated that as much as KD 600 million ($1.7 billion) has been transferred in this manner since the scheme started.[19] The budget allocation for this item was reduced, however, to KD 30 million in 1967/68 and KD 17 million in 1968/69. Finally, to encourage domestic enterprise the government participates generously in large business undertakings, and government-owned banks offer easy and cheap credit to prospective businessmen who intend to start or extend an industry or build houses. Despite the extensive redistribution of income among Kuwaiti nationals in the last two decades, however, there is still scope for raising the living standard of some of the poorest groups as well as for improving employment opportunities for a large part of the population of working age.

Industry

The growth of the industrial sector is considered by planning authorities in Kuwait as potentially a most important means of diversifying the structure of the economy by raising income outside the oil or government sectors. The virtual absence of cheap raw materials other than oil and natural gas, the abundance of capital, and the shortage of skilled and cheap labor have very largely determined the lines of recent industrial development and indicate the path it will probably follow in the coming decade. Capital-intensive industries based on oil and gas are being developed. Oil refining, to satisfy the local market, was an obvious selection. Petrochemical industries, based on natural gas, a large part of which is

[18] See "Revenues Pay for Welfare State," *The Times* (London), February 25, 1969.
[19] See "Machine for Spending Money," *The Times* (London), February 25, 1969.

flared off in the fields, were also natural candidates, despite the absence of a local market for their products. Thus one of the most technically elaborate and expensive refineries (with a capacity of 95,000 barrels per day or about 4.7 million tons per year) was completed at Shua'iba in 1968 at a cost of $150 million. This refinery, which is owned by the Kuwait National Oil Company, is in addition to the older KOC's 11 million ton refinery at Al Ahmadi and AMINOIL's million ton refinery at Port Abdallah. The three refineries together process about 13 percent of Kuwait's output of oil, and the cost of production of crude oil, at less than $0.06 per barrel, is probably the lowest in the world. If the problems related to marketing the refined products can be overcome in the coming decade, the prospects of considerably expanding refining capacity can be considered bright.

The petrochemical industry, based on natural gas, is represented at present by the Kuwait Chemical Fertilizers Company (KCFC), which is 60 percent owned by Kuwaiti mixed interests and 20 percent each by Gulf and British Petroleum. Its $34 million plant has a production capacity of 400 tons a day of ammonia and 400 tons a day of sulphur; from these, urea and ammonium sulphate can also be derived. Production started in 1966 for exports to India, Sudan, and Turkey. To assure an outlet for expanded production of ammonia the company participated with 40 percent of the capital of Mediterranean Fertilizers, which is building a plant in Turkey to produce nitrogenous fertilizers out of Kuwait ammonia and Turkish raw materials. To supply this plant in Turkey, the KCFC is building an 800 ton per day ammonia plant. To expand the production of urea by 1,400 tons per day, it is now building another 800 ton per day ammonium plant, both plants to cost about $67 million. Economies of scale are of particular importance in this industry, and the cost of production per unit in the larger plants could be reduced to about half that of the first smaller plant.

The use of natural gas as a source of energy (rather than as a raw material) in energy-oriented manufacturing industries has not been exploited in Kuwait. Neighboring Bahrein has embarked on an aluminum project.

Other smaller manufacturing industries have been established in Kuwait in answer to local demand created by the building and construction boom (such as sand, lime, brick, cement products, asbestos cement, marine paints, and spiral welded steel pipes), and some others are planned (wire nails, glues, electric cables, stone-cutting equipment). Licensed projects also include consumer-oriented industries—for example, plastic containers and tubes, dry cell batteries, clothes, woolen blankets, detergents, and aerosols.

Agriculture

The possibilities of developing the agricultural sector are very limited. Since 1953, domestic water needs have been met by distilling sea water in the largest sea water distillery in the world (in 1968 output reached 21 million gallons a day). Since 1962, additional water has become available in limited quantity from an artesian well discovered some 50 miles to the north of the city of Kuwait. Rainfall in Kuwait rarely totals 7 inches in one season and sometimes drops to only 1 or 2 inches.

Underground water is available in small quantities, particularly on the coast, but it has a high salt content. The high temperatures (rising to 130° F in the summer), the shortage and salinity of underground water, and the generally sandy and saline nature of the soil, which is deficient in nitrogen and phosphorus elements, render agricultural crop production highly uneconomical at present. A project is underway to irrigate some 5,000 hectares of forest with treated sewage water. Some poultry and dairy farming has started on the basis of imported feed and fodder, but its scale remains small. Fishing, particularly for shrimps, and processing are major local activities, employing about 4,000 persons, divided equally between traditional and modern industries. In addition to some 8,000 tons of shrimps caught annually by traditional dows, mainly for local consumption, a large fleet of about 110 modern trawlers and factory ships catches 12,000 tons annually in the Persian Gulf and supplies annual exports of 8,000 tons of frozen shrimps to the United States, Europe, and Japan. Plans are underway to double the size of the fleet in the near future, and the prospects of expanding the output and export of shrimps seem assured.

III. The Gulf Principalities

Background

The term "Gulf Principalities" is taken here to indicate the nine states and sheikdoms that formed "The Federation of Arab Emirates" on February 27, 1968. The Federation includes the two principalities of Bahrein and Qatar, and the seven sheikhdoms known as the Trucial States, which include Abu Dhabi, Dubai, Sharjah, Ajman, Umm Al Qaiwain, Ras Al Khaimah, and Fujairah. The Gulf Principalities lie on the northeastern coast of the Arabian peninsula and had a population of about 500,000 in 1968. Bahrein's population is about 205,000, Qatar's is probably 110,000, and the Trucial States have about 185,000 (of whom 50,000 are in Abu Dhabi, 60,000 in Dubai, 32,000 in Sharjah, 25,000 in Ras Al Khaimah, 10,000 in Fujairah, and 4,000 each in Ajman and Umm Al Qaiwain). Until recent years, when oil exports and increasing oil revenues started to flow in, the population of the Gulf Principalities lived at subsistence level from fishing, pearl diving, sea trading (particularly in Bahrein and Dubai), and limited agriculture (especially in Bahrein and Ras Al Khaimah).

Oil was discovered in Bahrein in 1932 and first exported in small quantities in 1934; production started in Qatar in 1949, and in Abu Dhabi in 1962. Offshore production in the waters of Dubai began in 1969. Oil production in 1968 is put at 3.8 million tons in Bahrein, 17 million tons in Qatar, and 26.6 million tons in Abu Dhabi. It is estimated that oil revenues in 1968 were about $30 million in Bahrein, $110 million in Qatar, and $180 million in Abu Dhabi. In past years oil revenues helped the governments of Bahrein and Qatar to build up the basic infrastructure of the economy and to develop health and education services and facilities. The Trucial States have recently started to follow the same path of development at an accelerated rate, particularly in Abu Dhabi, the largest of the seven states, where oil revenues are rising fast, and in Dubai City. In the other, poorer states, small development projects (roads, town development, house construction, water and electricity supply, economic and mineral surveys) have been jointly financed by the Trucial States Development Fund, to which the United Kingdom contributed, with an increasing share coming from Abu Dhabi (50 percent in 1966/67 and 90 percent in 1967/68). In addition, Kuwait has contributed in recent years to the establishment of schools and hospitals in the Trucial States and to the supply of teachers and doctors. Transfers from Abu Dhabi and Saudi Arabia have also financed roads joining the six sheikhdoms as well as other projects.

The problems of the economic development of the Gulf Principalities have much in common with those of Kuwait about 10 or 15 years ago. Although apparently less wealthy in oil revenues, they have similar natural resources and a similarly small population. Development is therefore likely to follow the pattern set by Kuwait in the last decade, although it may vary in some aspects and may not achieve the same speed.

The pattern of economic development that has so far emerged in the Gulf Principalities seems to support the above thesis. With the exception of Bahrein (which started its development at an early stage with the help of small oil royalties, a huge refinery, and active sea trade) the Gulf Principalities, led by Qatar and followed by Abu Dhabi and Dubai, have all embarked recently upon such projects as town planning, water and electricity supply, roads, school and hospital construction, airport construction, port construction or improvement, government building, and housing. All of them except Bahrein are also receiving a huge inflow of immigrant labor, largely of the same national composition as in Kuwait. As latecomers compared with other states in the area, these principalities may find themselves at a disadvantage insofar as the exploitation of similar resources, particularly natural gas, is concerned. However, the current political trend in the region seems to have a much stronger direct influence on the rate and pattern of economic growth in these small states than in Kuwait, with its expanded population and exceptional wealth from oil.

The economic development of the Gulf Principalities will be particularly influenced by the political framework that develops in the coming few years. At present, the Trucial States have special relations with and obligations to the United Kingdom in accordance with the provision of treaties signed by the sheikhs in 1833. Similarly, the Emir of Bahrein signed treaties with the United Kingdom in 1880 and 1882 and undertook certain further obligations in 1914. The Emir of Qatar also signed a treaty with the United Kingdom in 1916. These treaties generally entrust the defense of the principalities to the United Kingdom and provide for the control of their foreign political and financial affairs (including approval of oil concessions).

EDMUND Y. ASFOUR

The announcement by the United Kingdom on January 16, 1968, that it will complete the withdrawal of its forces from the Persian Gulf by the end of 1971 has created a new situation and has encouraged the Gulf Principalities to look for regional cooperation or federation. In February 1968, the sheikhs of the Seven Trucial States and the rulers of Bahrein and Qatar met in Dubai and declared the formation of the "Federation of the Arab Emirates." They created a Higher Council and set up a Provisional (executive) Council, as well as committees to draft the Federation's constitution and study the unification of the flag, the national anthem, the official gazette, the national currency, postal services, and so on. Several meetings of the Federation's Higher Council have taken place since, but the final form of the Federation has not yet been agreed upon.

Federation is important to the future economic development of the Gulf Principalities not only because of its political implications and possible contribution to security and political stability, but also because of the economic implication of a market for industries of an adequate size (for example, cement, asbestos, cement pipes, paint) and specialized services. It should also facilitate the coordination within the Federation, as well as with other Gulf states, of an industrial development policy for export-oriented petrochemical and fertilizer plants based on oil and gas resources.

Bahrein

The economy of Bahrein is more balanced and diversified than that of the other principalities. The main island of Bahrein enjoys a limited underground water supply in its northern part and is thus able to produce modest quantities of dates and vegetables. Agriculture, together with the traditional pearl industry and fishing, employed about 10 percent of the labor force of 31,000 in 1965. Sea trade is well developed, the port of Manama acting as a main center for shipping and entrepôt trade in the Persian Gulf. The airport of Muharraq Island, which is joined to Bahrein by a causeway, is also an important link in the chain of air stations joining Europe to India, the Far East, and Australia.

Crude oil, which was discovered as early as 1932, is a major but not the predominant support of the economy. Onshore reserves are limited, and the production of crude oil has risen slowly to reach 3 million tons in 1967. This, together with a refinery and a new offshore field shared with Saudi Arabia, has yielded a revenue of about $30 million to the government and employs about 5,000 workers or one-tenth of the labor force. Bahrein has, however, substantial dissociated natural gas resources. In addition, all the oil produced in Bahrein, as well as double the quantity imported from Saudi Arabia, is refined in a large refinery which was completed in 1952. Production in this refinery was about 11 million tons in 1967.

Industrial activity includes ship repairing; shrimp freezing; milling; and small food, beverage, carpentry, building materials, and repair workshops, which altogether employ perhaps 2,000 workers or about 4 percent of the labor force.

Bahrein, however, is attempting to strike out on a new path in its industrial development in its current project of setting up an aluminum smelter plant with a production capacity of 88,500 tons per annum at an expected cost of about $70 million. The project is financed to the extent of 27.5 percent by Bahrein and 72.5 percent by Swedish, British, and other firms. Full output valued at $90 million is expected to be reached in 1972. The raw material for the project (alumina) is to be imported from Australia and the output exported to Europe, natural gas being used to produce the required electric energy. The project is a means of utilizing and exporting natural gas, which is being wasted at present, as well as a source of employment for workers in the plant itself and in new aluminum-based industries that may be set up. The potential for establishing other export-oriented industries is being explored, but fertilizer and petrochemical industries have not been considered.

Its long trading tradition and early start on development, as well as the training programs of the oil companies, have helped Bahrein to achieve one of the highest levels of education and working skills in the Persian Gulf region. The level of health and municipal services is similarly high. Bahrein does not seem, therefore, to require as heavy an investment in basic infrastructure as the other principalities.

Unless new oil reserves are discovered in the offshore areas, Bahrein's economy should not be expected to markedly exceed the slow but steady rate of growth it has achieved in the past. Revenue from a small offshore field shared with Saudi Arabia since 1966 should help offset the effect of the withdrawal of British forces and a possible loss in the share of re-export trade. The rate of future development, particularly in the fields of trade and industry, depends strongly on wider economic cooperation with the other Gulf Principalities and states.

Qatar[20]

Qatar, an arid peninsula of about 4,000 square miles, lies south of Bahrein and has a common undefined border with Abu Dhabi and Saudi Arabia in the south. It is separated from the latter by a long gulf in the east. Onshore oil production started in 1949 and reached 9 million tons in 1967 but is leveling off and is expected to decline in the mid-1970s as depletion sets in. Offshore oil production started in 1965 and sharply increased in the following years, reaching 6 million tons in 1967. Oil revenue increased correspondingly, amounting to about $80 million in 1968.

In recent years Qatar has developed small-scale agriculture. It has also used its increasing revenues to develop its infrastructure and some light industries. An airport was completed in 1967, and construction of a deep-water harbor was started in the same year. The construction of roads, sewage stations, and com-

---

[20] Much of the information in this sector is based on a publication by the Qatar government entitled *Qatar 1968* (in Arabic), as well as on unpublished reports.

bined water desalinization and electricity power stations is underway. A cement plant with 100,000 tons capacity was completed in 1969. In addition, complete free education and health care, as well as subsidized water supply and electric power, are supplied to the population.

Qatar's fast economic growth, although apparently assured in the coming decade, nevertheless seems to face risks of slowing down in the 1970s. The country's proved oil reserves are the smallest in the Middle East after those of Bahrein, and its main onshore field at Dukhan is expected to yield lower production as depletion proceeds. Underground water, which supports 2,700 hectares of irrigated cultivation, is becoming more saline as pumping continues.

However, the rise in offshore production, which started in 1965, may make up for this slowdown. The government of Qatar, aware of the possible risks of future slowdown in the growth of oil production, has followed a diversification policy based on comprehensive feasibility studies. In addition to starting a $41 million nitrogenous chemical fertilizer project based on natural gas, which will be completed in 1972, it plans to expand the prawn and fish industry, encourage and assist the establishment of light industries (such as soft drinks, food processing, and textiles), set up a national oil refinery, and further exploit the large and now wasted national gas resources.

Abu Dhabi[21]

Although the largest principality in size (125,000 square miles), and probably the richest in oil and minerals, Abu Dhabi is very sparsely populated, with only 25,000–30,000 indigenous people. It has some underground water resources which are found largely in the Buraimi Oasis, to which Saudi Arabia has laid claim. It was only in 1962 that Abu Dhabi started to export oil from onshore and offshore discoveries, but the expansion in oil exports, oil revenues, and expenditures on development and welfare projects, particularly since 1966, has been remarkable. In 1968, production reached 30 million tons, oil revenues $150 million, and the population probably more than 50,000. Economic development and welfare projects include the establishment of a modern administration and legal system; planning of the towns of Abu Dhabi and Al Ain; and construction of a deep-water port (underway), a bridge joining Abu Dhabi to the mainland, 2,000 houses (completed), a road between Abu Dhabi and Al Ain in the Buraimi Oasis (completed), an airport (completed), a large gas-turbine electricity-generating and water desalinization plant (to be completed in 1970), a small refinery (completed), and water pipeline from Buraimi (completed).

In addition, a National Planning Council was set up in 1968, and an ambitious development plan was approved covering the period 1968–1972 and allocating expenditures of BD 296 million (about $622 million) over the period. In

[21] The information in this section is partly derived from a government publication entitled *Two Prosperous Years in the History of Abu Dhabi,* 1968 (in Arabic), as well as from unpublished reports.

the plan, the bulk of allocations are for the development of the basic infrastructure (including mostly the projects mentioned above), but substantial allocations
are also made for agricultural and industrial development, for welfare and housing projects, and, significantly, for the development projects of the other Trucial
States. The basic agricultural and industrial projects under study include an affor-
estation project, a controlled environment research project, a dairy factory, an
animal feed factory, a cement factory (capacity, 75,000 tons per annum), and
promotion of the fish and pearl industries, building materials industries, and petrochemicals.

The economic growth of Abu Dhabi at a very fast rate seems assured. The
problems facing it arise from supply bottlenecks, whether in the area of skilled
labor, the professions, construction materials, and even physical transportation
facilities. Better coordination and planning are needed to prevent excessive waste
or liquidity shortages such as appeared in 1969.

Dubai and Other Trucial States

The city of Dubai, with a population of 60,000, is the commercial center of the
Trucial States. It is also the seat of the Development Office of the Trucial States
Council and of the Kuwait Office, which runs an education and health program
in the Trucial States. Oil was discovered offshore in Dubai only in 1966, and exports started in 1969. An active trade and open economic policy have helped the
growth of Dubai without the benefit of oil revenues. In the other Trucial States
(Sharjah, Ajman, Umm Al Qaiwain, Ras Al Khaimah, and Fujairah) no oil discovery has been announced so far. With their extensive arid area (parts of
which lie on the coast of the Gulf of Oman, which opens on the Indian Ocean)
and a population of about 70,000, they are still in a predevelopment stage and
have depended on aid from the other Gulf Principalities and states for financing
a modest program for the improvement of health and education conditions; for
the supply of drinking water and electric power; and for the construction of essential roads, jetties, and wharves. Small-scale agriculture and fishing support the
bulk of the population.

Although the prospects of the future economic growth of Dubai seem
bright, those of the other Trucial States depend very strongly on the success of
the efforts to federate the Gulf Principalities in regard to the discovery of oil and
the exploitation of the rich fish resources in the Gulf of Oman.

IV. Conclusions

Saudi Arabia, Kuwait, and the Gulf Principalities, which together form the
northern and larger part of the Arabian peninsula, share more than a similar
physical environment and similar social and political structures. Their main and
by far most important source of wealth is crude oil, of which they claim almost
half the total proved world reserves. Other known natural resources include gas,
a few minerals of minor commercial value at present, and limited underground

water resources which can be used in agriculture. Oil provides the large bulk of government revenue and is the mainspring of economic growth. Gas is potentially of economic significance, but its use has been limited both as a feedstock for new petrochemical industries and as a source of electric energy.

Thus, although capital is abundant, there is clearly a relative scarcity of domestic investment opportunities based on available resources and able to supply the domestic market. There is also a serious shortage of skills, both administrative and technical. The result of this situation has been a tendency to invest in export-oriented industries and to import skilled manpower from the northern Arab countries, from the Persian Gulf region, and from Western countries. There is no reason to believe that this trend will be reversed in the coming decade, despite strong public efforts to support agriculture and locally oriented industries and to proceed as fast as practicable in educating and training nationals. At best, the growth of domestically based agriculture and industry may keep up with the overall rate of the economy, and the additional trained nationals may keep up with the rise in demand for skills. Although expansion of export-oriented petrochemical, oil refining, oil transportation, and other industries may absorb substantial capital investments, their growth hinges strongly on the resolution of the marketing problem.

The main determinants of economic growth in the region in the coming decade, political upheavals apart, will remain the oil revenues earned by the governments and the manner in which the governments spend them. On the assumption of no substantial change in the allocation pattern of oil revenues or in the average revenue per barrel, the growth rate of income will follow closely the rate of growth of oil production and exports. Projection of these rates may vary, depending on the source, between 6.5 and 10 percent per annum, and is likely to be nearer the low end of the range for Kuwait and the higher end for the Gulf Principalities and Saudi Arabia.

The pattern of allocation of oil revenues, which at present exceed $2 billion per annum, has witnessed evident changes in the last few years in the whole region. A substantial part will continue to be spent in raising the income level and the living and health standards of nationals, through direct transfers, subsidies, purchases of land, or employment at high salaries; however, increasing pressures have appeared in recent years to reduce the more unproductive and the more inequitable types of such transfers. On the other hand, development expenditures, particularly in Saudi Arabia and the Gulf Principalities, have accelerated in recent years; but, as in Kuwait, expenditure in infrastructure, which absorbs the bulk of development expenditures, will probably level off in a few years, or at least not rise at a faster rate than that of oil revenues, and relatively more will be spent on education, training, and employment-creating investments.

The high rate of increase in oil revenues in the last decade has enabled the region to raise its consumption level rapidly (at about 9 percent per annum in recent years in Kuwait, 10 percent per annum in Saudi Arabia, and probably a higher rate in the Gulf Principalities except Bahrein). It has also enabled the countries to allocate a substantial part, exceeding 20 percent of their GNP, to fixed capital formation. Nevertheless, a surplus in savings appeared which could not be invested domestically. This surplus (largest in Kuwait but quite substantial also in Saudi Arabia, Qatar, and Abu Dhabi) was transferred abroad in one form or another. The accumulation of official and private reserves of gold, foreign exchange, foreign securities, and other forms of assets (which probably exceed $3 billion in total) has absorbed the bulk of this surplus. A part, however, went to other Arab governments (including the poorer Trucial States) as grants and as loans for specific development projects, supplied particularly through the Kuwait Fund for Arab Economic Development. Since 1967, $280 million per year has been paid by Saudi Arabia and Kuwait to the United Arab Republic and Jordan in direct support, and other direct aid was extended by Abu Dhabi. The trend has thus been clearly toward allocation of a growing share of oil revenues to help less favored Arab countries.

Whether this trend will continue will depend largely on the political developments in the area. However, the growing development needs of the populous non-oil-producing Arab countries and the increasing surpluses of the sparsely populated Saudi Arabia, Kuwait, and Gulf Principalities point to the probable continuation of this trend in the coming decade, irrespective of the development of the war with Israel. It is possible, however, that such aid may become more institutionalized, linked more closely to specific development projects and to specific investment opportunities in which the governments and nationals of the region will jointly participate.

CHAPTER 9

Fertility Patterns and their Determinants in the Arab Middle East

T. Paul Schultz*

Assisted by Julie Da Vanzo

* I wish to thank for their generous assistance a few of the many persons who facilitated my research: Dr. Laila Hamamsy, Director of the Social Research Center, American University of Cairo; Dr. Malik El Nomrossy; Professor Matta Akrawi, Department of Education, American University of Beirut; Dr. A. A. El-Koussy, United Nations Economics and Social Office of Beirut; Dr. M. A. El Badry, Population Division, United Nations; and Professor Hanna Rizk, Director, Department of Middle East Studies, Baldwin Wallace College. Rand colleagues Charles Cooper, Alvin Harman, and Sidney Alexander read earlier drafts and contributed their valuable comments.

The following essay by Schultz sheds new light on population growth in the Middle East. In Appendix A, Schultz presents and evaluates much of the basic evidence on recent population trends in the area. By bringing together this material and presenting it clearly, Schultz makes a major contribution to our knowledge of what the facts are.

Schultz also attempts to sketch the economic consequences of rapid population growth. His brief discussion of this problem at least highlights its complexity. And by drawing attention to the distinction between long-run and transitional effects, he helps to place the population issue in far better perspective than it is usually seen.

The brevity of Schultz's discussion of the economic costs of population growth would be regrettable were it not that his major attention is focused on another problem of equal importance: explaining differences in fertility. Schultz presents a multivariate statistical analysis of factors affecting fertility in Egypt that is not only instructive in exploring the past and predicting the future but is also of considerable policy significance. Taking the number of children desired as the basic behavioral unknown, Schultz shows how this is explained by such factors as education, labor force participation of women and children, child mortality, income, occupation, religion, and residence. His conclusion, though tentative, is that development itself may serve strongly to influence the number of children wanted, and that, even with present knowledge of birth control, family size goals can be directly influenced by public policy. With better knowledge, public policy to influence family size goals could become a major factor in promoting the future development of the region.

Fertility Patterns
and their Determinants
in the Arab Middle East

I. Introduction

In the Arab Middle East, birth rates are high and death rates have only recently fallen to more moderate levels. Rapid population growth has become an impediment to the future development of the region. The social and economic consequences of this new world-wide phenomenon are only dimly understood today; without satisfactory data, the prospects for measuring or clarifying its precise consequences are not particularly good. Public policy must nevertheless cope with high fertility. It is my contention that reproductive behavior can be understood only in the context of a broader set of jointly determined choices that parents make over their lifetimes. Effective policy will ultimately depend on our understanding of the determinants of behavior in this sphere.

This section outlines the dimensions of demographic trends in the region (see also Appendix A) and their probable consequences. Section II sifts available demographic and economic data to cast light on the probable causes of high birth rates. The concluding section takes stock of current population policies in the region and suggests appropriate directions for new policy initiatives and further empirical research.

Demographic Trends

The population of the Arab Middle East is certainly growing very rapidly, but the lack of good statistics on population size and structure, and on the number of births and deaths, leaves the magnitude of demographic trends in doubt. Evidence on contemporary demographic trends in the Arab Middle East is restricted to the United Arab Republic, Jordan, and Iraq;[1] and even for these countries there remain gaps in the data that cannot be satisfactorily bridged.[2] Nevertheless, one can indirectly infer the pace of population growth in these countries and the levels of birth and death rates.

[1] Certain demographic features of Israel are also considered, but only for comparative purposes, since a separate study in this project deals with demographic developments in Israel.

[2] The best and most comprehensive discussion of demographic developments in the Arab Middle East is that of El Badry, 1965. The reader is urged to consult this source for a general and detailed overview of the subjects briefly investigated in Section II.

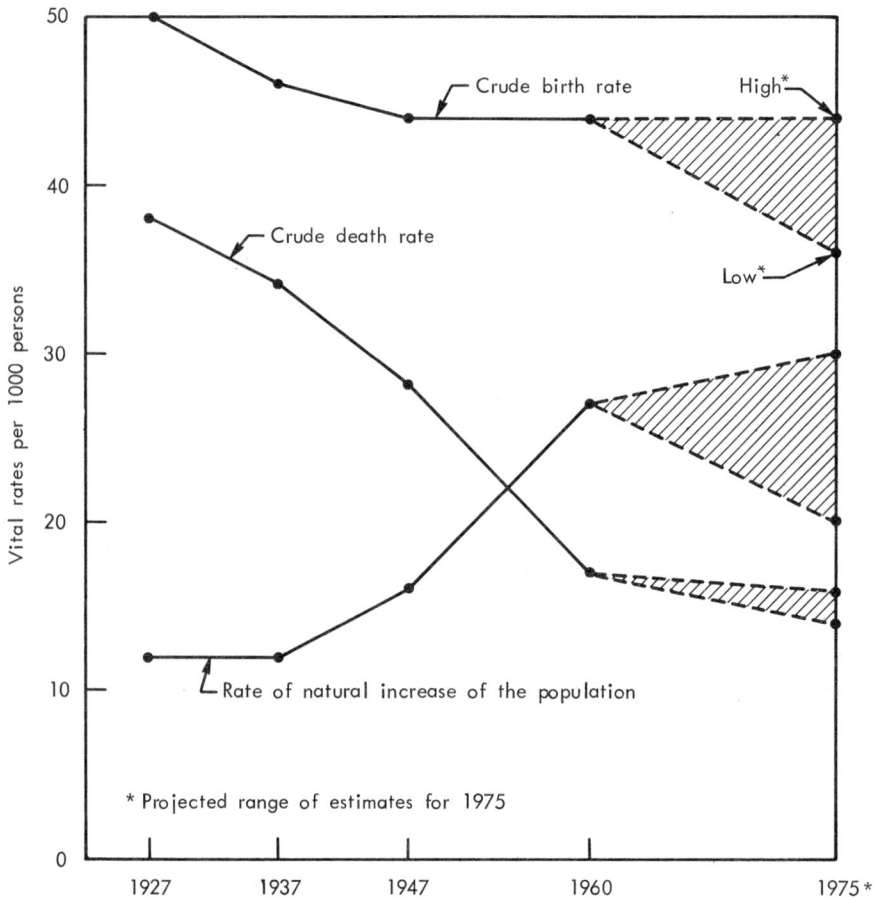

FIG. 9-1. Estimates of vital rates for the U.A.R. from 1927 to 1960 and projected range of estimates for 1975. Source: See statistical Appendix A.

For the United Arab Republic, most demographic evidence is consistent with a historic fall in crude death rates during the last several decades from 40 per thousand to about 16 per thousand by the mid-1960s. In this same period, crude birth rates may have declined from about 50 to 44 per thousand. As a consequence of these two demographic developments, the rate of population growth has risen sharply, from 1 to nearly 3 percent per year, as pictured in Figure 9-1. Future declines in the crude death rate are likely to be more moderate, as further improvements in health hinge increasingly on gradual improvements in nutrition, control of endemic diseases such as schistosomiasis, and increased personal incomes.[3] Consequently, unless fertility reverses its downward trend, the rate of population growth cannot continue to increase substantially. But for the rate of population growth to fall, on the other hand, the crude birth rate must begin to decline more rapidly than it has of late. From the 1960 census there is some evidence of declining birth rates among older women, and later age of marriage is becoming associated with a moderate reduction in fertility among the youngest women; but these two trends must grow stronger to precipitate an appreciable decline in the crude birth rate by 1975.

For Jordan and Iraq, reliance on single censuses in 1961 and 1957 respectively leaves great doubt about demographic trends and their recent change. Crude birth rates in both countries probably exceed those for Egypt, as do crude death rates. By the mid-1960s, the populations of Jordan and Iraq appeared to be growing at a rate of about 3 percent per year, somewhat faster than estimated for Egypt.

Without reliable contemporary information for Syria, it may be assumed that its population is subject to demographic trends similar to those estimated for Iraq and Jordan. Lebanon, on the other hand, may be experiencing somewhat lower birth, death, and population growth rates than her Arab neighbors, but again there is scant solid evidence for these judgments.

Israeli birth and death rates are about half those of the other Middle Eastern countries. Though these vital rates imply a more moderate rate of natural population increase of about 2 percent per year, immigration to Israel in the 1960s has sustained a rate of growth of population in excess of 3 percent per year. The wide variations in birth and death rates among ethnic groups in Israel is briefly explored later.

Estimates of population size and vital rates are summarized in Table 9-1 for all the countries of the region. As indicated above, however, many of the United Nations estimates should be regarded as official figures for which we have not found supporting empirical evidence.

Consequences of Demographic Trends

For analytic purposes, the implications of rapid population growth can be divided into two components: those which are associated with rapid population growth in the very long run, and those which arise in the short run when the rate of population growth changes. In general, a more rapid rate of population growth contributes to a somewhat younger composition of the population and a broader-based age pyramid. In the long run, the population of labor force age grows at the same rate as does the total population, creating a need to add more

[3] See Scrimshaw, 1966; and McDermott, 1966. One unfortunate side effect of the Aswan Dam development is that the extension of year-round irrigation into Upper Egypt is likely to expose this region to the debilitating effects of endemic schistosomiasis.

Table 9-1
Population Totals and Vital Rates for Middle Eastern Countries

	Most Recent Census		UN Estimate of Population in 1966	Estimate[a] of Annual Rate of Growth, 1958-1966 (percent)	Vital Rates: 1960-1966[a] (per thousand)		
	Year	Population			Birth Rate	Death Rate	Infant Mortality Rate
Middle East core area			51,064,000				
Egypt	1960	25,984,101	30,147,000	2.7[b]	44[b]	17[b]	119
Iraq	1957	6,339,960	8,338,000	3.0[b]	48-51[c]	17-20[d]	100-150[d]
Israel	1961	2,183,332	2,629,000	3.5	25	6	28
Jordan	1961	1,706,226	2,040,000	3.0[b]	48[b]	18[b]	(42)
Lebanon			2,460,000	2.6	38-42[e]	16-20[e]	(14)
Syria	1960	4,565,121	5,450,000	3.0	51[f]	21[d]	(31)
Arabian Peninsula			13,570,000				
Aden (colony)	1955	138,441	250,000	3.4	(38)	(8)	92
Bahrain	1959	143,135	193,000	4.1	n.a.	n.a.	n.a.
Kuwait	1965	467,339	491,000	10.5	52	(6)	(47)
Muscat and Oman			565,000	0.3	n.a.	n.a.	n.a.
Qatar			71,000	7.3	n.a.	n.a.	n.a.
Saudi Arabia			6,870,000	1.7	n.a.	n.a.	n.a.
Trucial Oman			130,000	5.3	n.a.	n.a.	n.a.
Yemen			5,000,000	1.6	n.a.	n.a.	n.a.
Nearby Islamic Countries			208,112,000				
Algeria	1960	9,745,480	12,150,000	2.0	48	28[d]	(70)
Iran	1956	18,954,704	25,500,000	2.8	48	25	n.a.
Libya	1964	1,564,369	1,677,000	3.7	37-40[g]	25-28[h]	n.a.
Morocco	1960	11,626,232	13,451,000	2.6	46	19	149
Pakistan	1961	93,831,982	105,044,000	2.1	43	15	n.a.
Sudan	1956	10,262,536	13,940,000	2.8	51-55[c]	23-27[d]	94[i]
Tunisia	1956	3,943,260	4,470,000	1.2	47	26	110
Turkey	1965	31,391,207	31,880,000	2.6	45-48[c]	19-22[d]	165

404

[a]Unless otherwise noted, rates are from United Nations, *Demographic Yearbook 1966*. Implausible figures are enclosed in parentheses. [b]My estimate: birth rates derived by applying quasi-stable-population techniques to census age distribution. See Appendix A. [c]1955-1960 estimate of Lee Jay Cho, "Estimated Refined Measures of Fertility for all Major Countries of the World," *Demography*, Vol. 1, No. 1 (1964). These estimates are consistent with those derived in Appendix A. [d]Death rate calculated residually by subtracting annual rate of growth (per 1,000) from birth rate. [e]My estimate: registered rates much lower. [f]For Damascus only. [g]For 1954, UN estimate derived by application of "reverse survival" method to 1954 census population. [h]For 1954, calculated residually on basis of 1.2 percent annual growth rate in 1954. [i]For 1956.

rapidly to the stocks of human and physical capital. To sustain an existing capital-labor ratio, a more rapidly growing labor force requires a higher savings rate.[4]

The development process, however, is more than a homogeneous process of factor augmentation. Development may be better analyzed as a process that draws an increasing share of the population into distinguishably different and more productive activities. These economic activities require more capital services and other modern inputs per worker than are used elsewhere in the economy; and because they are less routine, they typically require of the labor force more education and skills to cope with increasingly complex and changing modes of production. The rate at which labor is absorbed into this modern sector of the economy is restrained and the development process prolonged by rapid population growth, for many new jobs require that a greater share of output be saved and invested. In such a model of structural change in a dual economy, the savings constraint on development is exacerbated by rapid population growth.[5]

Even at this aggregate level, there are, of course, other distinguishable resource costs associated with rapid and accelerating population growth; for example, the hastened pace of urbanization that follows in the wake of population growth imposes heavy personal and social costs.[6] Nonetheless, the long-run bur-

[4] For example, if we conservatively assume that the marginal capital-output ratio is equal to the average ratio of, say, 3, then a net savings rate from output of 9 percent is required to accommodate a 3 percent annual growth in the labor force without deepening the capital stock or increasing per capita income. This stable state could be achieved with only a 6 percent savings rate if the labor force grew at 2 percent per year.

[5] R. R. Nelson, T. P. Schultz, and R. L. Slighton, *Structural Change in a Developing Economy: Colombia's Problems and Prospects,* Princeton University Press, Princeton, N.J., 1971.

[6] Associated with rapid population growth are the reinforcing processes of internal migration and urbanization, which in the Middle East appear to outpace industrialization and widen the gap between the modern and traditional sectors of the urban economy. The proportion of the Egyptian population residing in urban areas had risen to 38 percent by the 1960 census; in Jordan the doubling of Amman's population in less than a decade (1952–1961) accelerated the trend toward urbanization, with 47 percent of the population in urban areas by 1961; and in Iraq, according to preliminary 1965 census figures, the urban population represented 44 percent of the total population.

Sources: United Arab Republic—Rafael Salib et al., 1965, Table 4, p. 21; Jordan—United Nations, *Demographic Yearbook 1962,* p. 310; Iraq—Iraq, Republic of (no date—1967?), p. 305. Definitions differ among countries as to what constitutes urban areas, and thus these figures should not be regarded as precisely comparable over time or between countries. The lack of satisfactory data on migration precludes us from investigating the demographic and economic determinants and consequences of migration. A good discussion and analysis of the Jordanian census for evidence of internal migration may be found in Jordan, 1966, report 3.

405

den of population growth, from the economic viewpoint, is its constraining effect on the rate of structural transformation needed to raise labor productivity and personal income in the developing dual economy. There is also convincing evidence that, once the majority of the labor force is drawn into the modern sector, rapid population growth not only retards the advance in average income, but also increases the inequality of personal incomes in the society.

In the short run, changes in the rate of population growth can impose further burdens on the family and society. The nature and extent of these burdens depend on the source of the changes and their effect on the age structure of the population.

The reduction in death rates that initiated the increase in population growth rates after World War II affected infants and young children more than other age groups. Many parents now in their thirties and forties are supporting more children than their parents did at a similar age, not because of noticeably higher fertility or earlier marriage, but simply because more children have survived from the postwar generation than from earlier generations. There are fewer adults to work for each child that they must feed, clothe, shelter, train, and equip for adult employment and life. Parents are today less able than were their parents to spread the consumption demands of their offspring over their reproductive lifetimes. Although the initial costs of this child burden are carried by parents, in the 1970s this postwar generation will reach labor force age, and increasingly the society must contend with a youthful, rapidly growing labor force.

The effects of the acceleration in population growth in the Middle East are reflected in census age structures. The proportion of the Egyptian population less than 15 years of age was virtually constant from 1927 to 1947 at 38–39 percent, but rose to 43 percent in the 1960 census. In Jordan and Iraq this proportion has reached 45 percent, while in Israel the much lower birth rate contributed to the much lower proportion of children, namely 36 percent.[7] In Egypt, the drop in death rates from about 35 to 20 per thousand between 1940 and 1960 was responsible for this 10 percent increase in the proportion of the population under the age of 15, implying that there were approximately 15 percent fewer workers per dependent child in the United Arab Republic in 1960 than in 1947. This augmented dependency burden cannot continue to increase indefinitely.

A change in future fertility would have a clear short-run effect on the age structure. A 15 percent fall in birth rates would, within a decade or two, reduce the proportion of the population younger than 15 by a comparable 10–15 percent. A decline in fertility would, therefore, not only slow population growth but would also, in the short run, lead to a substantial reduction in the dependency burden.

The pattern of rapid population growth emerging in the Middle East is therefore likely to cause a sequence of events. First, because of the change in the age-specific structure of death rates, the postwar child population is growing

[7] See Appendix A tables.

more rapidly than the adult population. This creates a dependency burden, one that is largely borne by parents supporting additional surviving children, but is also transferred in part to the state, which provides educational, job-training, and child health services to this burgeoning population. During this initial phase of the "population explosion," the rate of growth of the adult population also increases, but the notable acceleration in the growth of the population of labor force age occurs about 20 years after the decline in mortality begins, when the large surviving cohort of those born in the postwar period enters the labor force. The dependency burden slows its ascent in this second phase, and adult population growth adds increasingly to the demands for physical savings and investment to employ the growing flow of new entrants into the labor force.

If a period of declining fertility follows, perhaps hastened by government subsidies for birth control and other inducements to have smaller families, a third phase may occur in which the dependency burden would promptly decline and, with a two-decade lag, growth of the labor force would diminish. Both of these developments would release resources from child consumption and savings for either current adult consumption or other investment activities.

Though it is not now possible to estimate the exact magnitude of the consumption cost incurred by the rising child dependency burden in the first phase and to compare it with the consumption cost due to the additional savings required to maintain employment and income levels incurred in the second phase, I hazard the judgment that the first outweighs the second. If I am correct, the net social costs of the demographic trends occurring today in the Middle East may be greater in the early transition phase than in the later phase. Moreover, when and if fertility falls substantially, the anticipated benefits to society may be substantial.

To recapitulate, the postwar decline in death rates creates a transitory burden of children for adult society to rear, train, and equip for modern employment. However, any reduction in fertility that follows will permit a comparable reduction in the dependency burden, with the associated social opportunities to educate and train the younger generation more adequately and to invest a sufficient amount to employ a larger proportion of it in modern high-productivity and high-wage sectors of the economy. From this aggregate perspective, the "population explosion" is in part a transitory burden for the current generation; and if the challenge that it poses to today's policymakers is met and fertility falls in the future, it may also represent an opportunity for future development.

II. Fertility Patterns and Determinants

Birth rates for Middle Eastern Arab populations are high, and development prospects in the region are likely to depend to a significant extent on their future decline. Influencing the number of children that parents have may, therefore, become one objective of a development strategy. But to design a policy to modify fertility requires an understanding of the actual determinants of fertility at the family level. This section investigates systematic patterns in reproductive behavior that permit us to infer the causal or conditioning factors responsible for differences in fertility among distinguishable groups.[8] Statistical analysis cannot generally establish causation; it can only confirm or contradict predicted associations.

Factors Affecting Birth Rates

Increasing attention has been given of late to fertility in less developed countries. The differences in fertility between developed and less developed countries have often been attributed to the practice of birth control in the former and its absence in the latter. The conspicuous variations in fertility within and among less developed countries, however, are difficult to understand unless "natural fertility" is affected by demographic, social, and economic factors operating through some means of birth control. One approach to understanding differences in fertility that is receiving increasing consideration is to begin with the preferences of parents for particular numbers of children and to seek the determinants of birth rates among the objective characteristics of the environment that could influence the parents' opportunities and goals. Empirical analyses of differential fertility in several other low-income areas of the world have found significant multivariate statistical associations between regional fertility and certain features of the environment that are throught likely to modify the number of births parents want: schooling, child labor, employment of women, and the incidence of child mortality.[9]

Schooling

School attendance for children imposes opportunity costs on parents; even if children do not work outside of the home, they provide help in the home by tending younger children and performing routine chores, and this help is reduced when they attend school. School attendance also adds, as a rule, to direct household outlays for better clothes, school materials, transportation, and support away from home. Overall, parents' decisions and opportunities to send their children to school increase child costs and may be strong determinants underlying a reduction in their family size goal. For a variety of quite different reasons the schooling of parents may also affect their family size goal.[10]

Child Labor

Expanded school facilities at the primary and secondary level provide a conflicting demand on the time of children and reduce child labor force participation. Parents must bear these opportunity costs of their children's schooling, and give

[8] Professor Hanna Rizk generously made available to the author his 1957 survey data, but delays in obtaining, decoding, and processing these data precluded their analysis in this study. They may be the basis for another report at some future date.
[9] Schultz, 1969b, 1969c, 1969d.
[10] Schultz, 1969c.

up some use of children's unpaid productive services in family employment. Improved opportunities for education may change the role of children in the family, undermine parents' desires for large families, and induce parents to invest in their children's education and acquisition of modern skills.

Employment of Women

A significant part of the costs of bearing and rearing children is the value of a mother's time devoted to these pursuits. When her most productive activities are easily combined with child rearing in the home, the opportunity cost of her time spent in caring for the children is small and a large family no great inconvenience. However, the household activities traditionally performed by women (weaving, processing family food, caring for livestock, and manufacturing handicrafts) tend to be displaced gradually in the development process by modern food processing, textiles, and manufacturing sectors, and depreciated in relative value by the growing commercial specialization in agricultural production itself. As development proceeds, the woman finds her most remunerative employment opportunities are increasingly outside of the home and even outside of the rural-agricultural sector of the economy.[11] These employment opportunities are difficult to combine with child rearing.

In this more specialized economic environment, therefore, a large family that limits a mother's labor force participation entails a substantial opportunity cost. This rising opportunity value of her time may induce more parents to accept a smaller family size goal. Though the opportunity value of a mother's time cannot often be measured directly, the frequency of women participating in the labor force may be a useful proxy for this crucial, but unobserved, wage variable. Therefore, in an environment where women can earn more income (per unit of time), there should be higher female participation rates and lower birth rates.

Child Mortality

It is reasonable to assume that parents frame their reproductive goals in terms of their preferences for a particular number of surviving children (or sons). Thus parents are likely to seek to regulate their fertility upon reaching or exceeding their traditionally desired family size; institutional change or foresight on the part of society or parents is not needed. Because childhood mortality is concentrated in the first years of life, many parents who are still fecund can decide to have an additional child when they lose one. This short-run replacement mechanism would become apparent at a community level only several decades after the onset of a decline in child death rates, when a substantial proportion of the fertile women in the population already had the number of surviving children they wanted and were seeking (with some degree of success) to avert further births.

Historical evidence suggests that for birth rates to fall the chances for child survival must first improve for an extended period. In this connection there are

[11] Hymer and Resnick, 1967.

two unanswered questions: how long a lag will separate the decline in death rates from the onset of the decline in birth rates, and (of particular relevance in the Middle East, where child mortality is still substantial) is there a threshold below which child death rates must fall to trigger the desired reduction in birth rates?

Contraception

The costs of birth control consist of acquiring and deciphering information about alternative contraceptive methods and accepting the outlays and inconvenience associated with using the method chosen. Traditional methods of birth control are less reliable and less convenient than modern ones.[12] When the range of alternatives is limited to traditional methods, large costs must be incurred to achieve a high degree of reliability, as in the extreme cases of continence and induced abortion. It may be very costly for the individual living in a "traditional" community to search independently for a more reliable and a more convenient (modern) method of contraception. For a society as a whole, however, informational costs are more modest per capita because of economies of scale in disseminating information. Once contraceptive supplies are understood and accessible, public subsidies may still be crucial for their rapid adoption.

Jointly Determined Decisions

Some of the factors enumerated above as probable determinants of fertility patterns may themselves be determined simultaneously with or subsequently by the number of births that parents want. For example, a woman's participation in the labor force may deter childbearing, but the decision to engage in labor force activity is probably reached at the same time as it is decided to postpone further children or not to have any. Thus, female participation and fertility should be treated as jointly determined within a system of household behavioral relations. The decision to participate in the labor force might be determined in part by desired fertility, in part by the opportunities a particular woman has to earn outside income, and in part by the attitudes of her peers toward the propriety of a woman working outside of her home. Since women's opportunity income is not generally an observed variable, the education of women may be the best predictor or proxy available for this factor.

Multivariate analysis may also seek a better understanding of the mechanism by which fertility is determined—either through timing of marriage or control of fertility within marriage. This dichotomy is an abstraction, for of course the two modes of fertility regulation may interact, but it is nevertheless a useful

[12] Though pregnancy rates differ among populations practicing similar methods of contraception, largely because of differences in motivation and understanding, the greater reliability of modern, as compared with traditional, methods of contraception is on the order of 10 to 1. See Southam, 1966, Table 3, p. 386.

one.[13] At the end of this section a simple simultaneous system of household behavioral relations is postulated and estimated from Egyptian census data for 1960. A relationship is assumed to exist between the prevalence of marriage and two exogenous factors: the educational attainment of women plus other unspecified regional characteristics and the jointly determined female activity rate. The prevalence of marriage is later treated as a jointly determined variable in the relationship accounting for fertility differences, as well as the exogenous agricultural composition of the population and the frequency of unpaid family workers in the labor force.[14] This formulation of a separate equation to account for the marital status of the population makes it possible to factor out whether the exogenous variables are associated with fertility principally through their association with different marriage patterns or whether they are associated directly with fertility differences after the marital status of the population has been taken into account.[15]

Some of the behavioral interactions discussed in this section are portrayed in Figure 9-2 and summarized here. Without external migration, population

[13] Illegitimacy appears to be uncommon in Moslem countries. In the United Arab Republic illegitimate births from 1952 to 1960 were only 0.1 percent of the total number of live births registered in the Health Bureau areas. Though this estimate may be biased downward, the observed proportion is very low. The only other country in the region for which illegitimacy data are reported in the United Nations, *Demographic Yearbook 1965* is Tunisia, which had 0.3 percent illegitimate registered live births.

[14] The prevalence of marriage among women and the level of surviving fertility, measured by the child-woman ratio, are assumed to be jointly determined by certain environmental variables described below. Symbolically it is assumed that more specifically

$$F = f(M, W, A, Z)$$

and

$$M = g(P, E, X)$$

where F, surviving fertility, is expressed as a function of the prevalence of marriage, M; the productive value of children, measured by the proportion of unpaid family workers in the region, W; and A, the dependence of the region on agricultural employment. The prevalence of marriage is in turn assumed to be a function of women's participation in the nonagricultural labor force, P, and women's completion of intermediate level of education E, which delays marriage and may open alternative roles to marriage and childbearing. The variables Z and X represent other determinants of marriage and fertility and are omitted from this simple formulation of these complex behavioral relationships.

[15] For example, if many differences in fertility were accounted for through variation in marriage prevalence and none through the exogenous variables, it might be concluded that the marital status of the population was the primary regulator of fertility. If marriage prevalence was not associated with fertility, while the exogenous variables accounted for much of the variation in fertility, then fertility regulation would appear to operate strongly within the marriage.

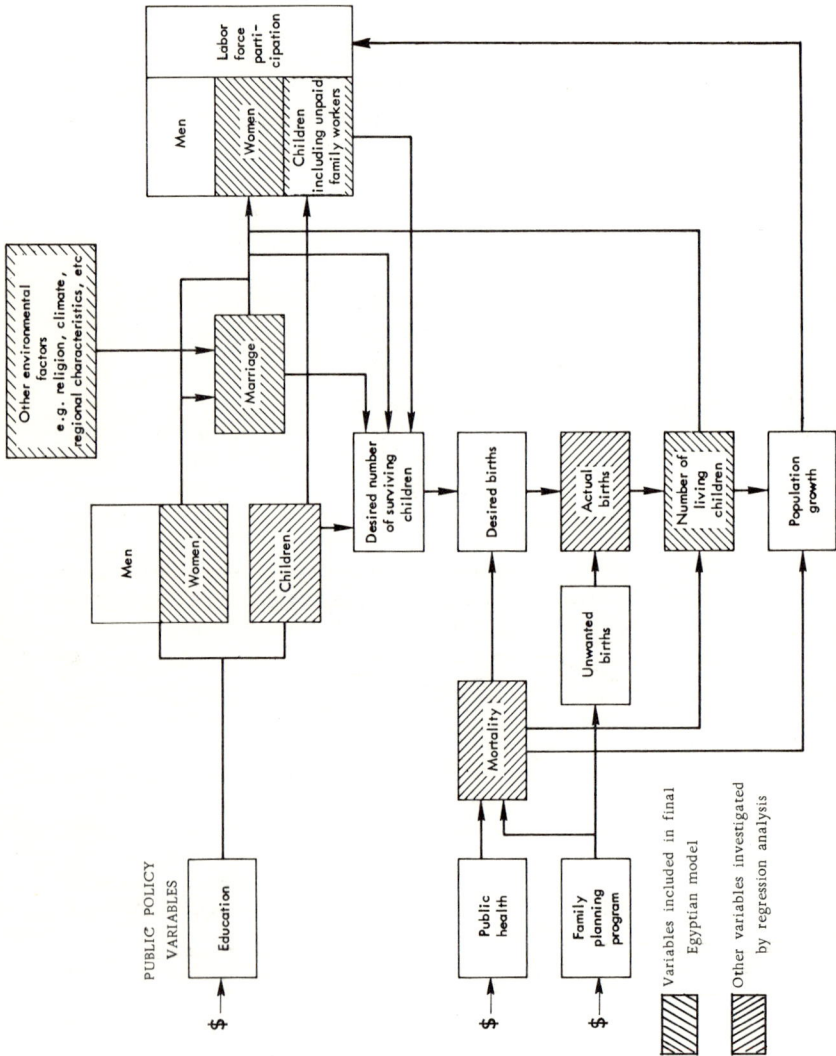

FIG. 9-2. Interrelations among demographic and economic aspects of the household and its environment.

growth is defined as the difference between births and deaths. Actual births are a lagged and imperfect reflection of the number of births that parents desire, which in turn is a complex function of the level of child mortality, the costs and rewards of rearing many versus few children in the society, women's opportunity income, and a variety of additional factors. The prevalence and timing of marriage, one such institutional factor, is itself influenced by the number of births parents want during their lifetime. Marriage rates may also be a function of whether women are economically active and able to support themselves and whether they have the opportunity to extend their education beyond puberty. Finally, women's participation in the labor force is related to desired fertility, her opportunity income (or its proxy, education), and other regional factors.

This system of household behavioral relations treats as exogenous the level of aggregate demand that determines employment; real wages and family income; and the influences of the public sector through education, health, and family planning activity in the community.

The exploration of this approach to understanding the determinants of fertility in the Middle East begins with a survey of the evidence of differential fertility by various classes or partitions of the population. These single-factor analyses of differential fertility, which are reported in the next subsection, appear to be consistent with the family planning hypothesis set forth above: birth rates are found to be directly associated with child death rates, and inversely associated with education and urban residence, when the lowest rural illiterate classes are excluded. The complete model elaborated here is investigated in the final subsection, using multivariate regression analysis. Though it is clear that the determination of fertility must be viewed as a multivariate process within a system of interrelated choices, the weakness of empirical materials for the Middle East deters us from immediately turning to this more indirect and complex interpretation of the available data without first considering the single-factor relationships.

Single-Factor Analyses of Fertility

Urban-Rural Differences

The 1960 census of the United Arab Republic distinguishes the number of children ever born to married women by the mother's educational attainment and either the duration of marriage or the mother's age. The level of cumulative fertility is greater than Cairo and Alexandria than for the rest of Egypt.[16] The age-specific birth rates (inferred from the census) show a similar pattern of higher birth rates for Cairo and Alexandria for women up to the age of 35. Women in the metropolitan areas exhibit somewhat lower age-specific birth rates after the age of 35.[17] This is consistent with the evidence noted earlier of small declines by 1960 in age-specific birth rates among older women.[18]

[16] See Table A-1.

[17] See Table A-2.

[18] See Appendix A for evidence. For further detail on urbanization and its correlates in the United Arab Republic, see Abu-Lughod, 1961, 1965a.

The higher fertility observed among the urban than among the rural population contradicts the traditional view that urbanization hastens the demographic transition to low birth rates. Moreover, when educational attainment is also distinguished in the U.A.R. census, as in Table 9-2, rural fertility levels appear only marginally to exceed urban fertility levels for all but illiterate classes, where urban fertility still exceeds rural by a significant margin.

The small and irregular magnitude of rural-urban fertility differences in the Arab Middle East is also evident in Jordan in 1961 (Table 9-3), in the Jordan West Bank and Gaza-Sinai region in 1967 (Table 9-4), and among Moslems from a Lebanese sample in 1959 (Table 9-5).[19] That urban-rural residence is not associated with substantial differences in reproductive behavior has been discussed in the case of Egypt,[20] but the pervasive character of this finding in the Middle East casts doubts on the assertion that urbanization will in itself contribute substantially to the resolution of the population growth problem in the region.

Child Mortality

An essential implication of my working hypothesis is that parents try to govern their reproductive behavior so as to obtain a particular number of *surviving children*. Parents who lose one or more of their offspring thus tend to have more live births than otherwise. Since most child deaths occur in the first years of life, the proportion of children surviving these early years is a good indication of the proportion that will reach maturity.

Unfortunately, without reliable death registrations, investigation of this postulated relationship between child deaths and subsequent births must be based on retrospective information collected by censuses and surveys.[21] The Jordanian census inquired of each married woman the number of children ever born and the number now living. This information is tabulated by urban-rural residence and age of mother as shown in Table 9-6. From these data we cannot separate the effects of the secularly declining death rate from the effects of the circumstance that the children of younger mothers had survived fewer years than had the children of older mothers. Nonetheless these data document the very high level of child mortality: 43 percent of the children born to mothers now 50 years

[19] In the Jordan West Bank population urban women tend to report slightly higher cumulative fertility than rural or refugee camp residents, at least until the age of 50. The absolute level of cumulative fertility of married women does differ systematically among these countries. For women between the ages of 40 and 49 the average number of children ever born in the United Arab Republic was 5.2 in 1947 and 5.7 in 1960; in Jordan 7.7 in 1960; in West Bank Jordan 8.5 in 1967; and in Gaza-Sinai 8.3 in 1967. One can reasonably assume that comparably high levels of fertility prevail in Syria, Iraq, and possibly rural Lebanon.

[20] Abu-Lughod, 1961, 1964, 1965a, 1965b.

[21] Retrospective data are not generally regarded as particularly reliable. See Mauldin, 1966.

414

Table 9-2

Number of Children Ever Born Per 100 Married Women for All Egypt
and for Urban and Rural Areas, by Educational Attainment of
Married Women in 1960[a]

Duration of Marriage (years)	Mother's Educational Attainment														
	Illiterate			Elementary			Primary			Secondary			College		
	All Egypt	Urban	Rural	All Egypt	Urban	Rural	All Egypt	Urban	Rural	All Egypt	Urban	Rural	All Egypt	Urban	Rural
Less than 5	58	65	59	53	50	54	47	44	49	29	27	30	22	20	22
5-9	256	286	260	232	219	235	204	191	213	126	120	133	95	96	98
10-19	480	537	488	435	412	442	382	358	400	237	226	250	177	180	185
20-29	661	738	671	599	567	608	526	492	552	327	310	344	246	248	254
30 and over	711	795	722	645	610	655	566	531	594	351	334	370	265	267	273
Average for all marriages	405	481	437	390	369	398	342	320	360	213	202	224	160	161	165

[a]Number of children ever born and number of married women by their educational attainment and duration of marriage are compiled from Table 55 in the General Tables of the *1960 Census for All Egypt* and the same table for individual governorates, published by U.A.R. Department of Statistics and Census, Government Press, Cairo, 1963 and 1962. Urban areas as used in this table comprise the Metropolitan Areas: Cairo, Alexandria, Canal, and Suez. Rural areas include other parts of Egypt but exclude the frontier areas.

Source: Abdel-Khalik M. Zikry, "Socio-Cultural Determinants of Human Fertility in Egypt, U.A.R.," unpublished Ph.D. dissertation, Syracuse University, 1963.

Table 9-3

Children Ever Born Per Woman, Jordan, 1961[a]

Age of Woman	Per Woman			Per Married Woman		
	Urban	Rural	Total	Urban	Rural	Total
13-14	n.a.	n.a.	n.a.	0.05	0.05	0.05
15-19	0.21	0.17	0.19	0.71	0.63	0.66
20-29	2.30	2.30	2.30	2.92	2.82	2.86
30-39	5.83	6.08	5.98	6.22	6.27	6.25
40-49	7.14	7.61	7.45	7.53	7.73	7.66
50+	6.52	7.08	6.90	6.89	7.22	7.11
Average	3.55	3.99	3.83	5.08	5.41	5.30

[a] n.a. = not available.

Source: Derived from The Hashemite Kingdom of Jordan, Department of Statistics, *First Census of Population and Housing, 18 November 1961,* Department of Statistics Press, Amman, 1965, Tables 2.4, 2.5, 4.5, 4.6, pp. 60-103, 308-311.

Table 9-4

Average Number of Children Ever Born, West Bank Jordan and Gaza, 1967

Age of Woman	Judea and Sumaria					Gaza Strip and North Sinai				
	Per Ever-Married Woman	Per Married Woman[a]				Per Ever-Married Woman	Per Married Woman[a]			
		All	Urban	Rural	Refugee Camp		All	Urban	Rural	Refugee Camp
15-19	1.00	1.00	1.00	0.90	1.30	1.10	1.00	1.20	1.10	0.90
20-29	3.34	3.39	3.49	3.31	3.44	3.22	3.22	3.11	3.05	3.38
30-39	6.51	6.61	6.71	6.55	7.02	6.27	6.37	6.11	6.14	6.47
40-49	8.36	8.52	8.61	8.48	8.85	8.05	8.31	8.31	8.42	8.31
50-60	7.92	8.39	8.34	8.43	8.12	8.14	8.50	8.80	8.75	5.92
Total	6.13	6.13	6.11	6.14	6.25	5.87	5.82	5.75	5.66	5.92

[a]Married at time of census.

Source: Derived from *Israeli Defense Forces Census of Population 1967*, Publication No. 3, *Demographic Characteristics of the Population in the Administered Areas*, Central Bureau of Statistics, Jerusalem, 1968, Tables 25 (p. 35) and 52 (p. 67).

Table 9-5

Fertility and Family Planning Practices among
a Sample of Married Women, Lebanon, 1959[a]

	Total Fertility Rate	Mean Age of Marriage	Percent of Those Married 10 or More Years	
			Ever Inducing Abortion	Ever Using Contraception
Urban-city				
Educated				
Moslem	5.56	19.0	31	83
Christian	3.44	21.1	26	86
Uneducated				
Moslem	7.35	17.9	13	60
Christian	4.14	21.2	20	56
Rural-villages				
Uneducated				
Moslem	7.43	17.2	2	2
Christian	8.16	18.1	0	16

[a]Sample of 909 couples, 613 in Beirut and 296 from two isolated villages.
Source: David Yaukey, "Some Immediate Determinants of Fertility Differences in Lebanon," *Marriage and Family Living,* February 1963, Tables 2, 4, 5, 6, pp. 29-33.

Table 9-6

Percent of Children Now Dead
By Age of Mother, Jordan, 1961

Age of Mother	Urban	Rural	Total
13-14[a]	20.0	33.3	28.6
15-19	12.0	17.1	14.9
20-29	17.0	21.3	19.6
30-39	22.3	26.9	25.2
40-49	30.2	32.0	31.4
50+	42.4	43.0	42.8
All	29.3	32.9	31.6

[a]Based on sample of less than 15, all other samples are greater than 100.
Source: Derived from *First Census of Population and Housing, 18 November 1961,* Table 4.5 (pp. 308-309) and Table 4.6 (pp. 309-311).

old or older had died, while only 25 percent of those born to women between the ages of 30 and 39 had died.[22] The incidence of child death was roughly comparable in rural and urban regions among older women, whose offspring experienced the mortality regime of earlier decades, but among the younger mothers, for whose offspring the contemporary pattern of mortality has prevailed, the urban incidence of child death is substantially less than the rural.

When we dispense with the rural-urban distinction and disaggregate these data on child death rates by the number of children to whom each woman has given birth, it is possible to distinguish, as in Table 9-7, between the "period effect" (the tendency for child mortality to be greater among the offspring of older women, who have also lived longer in earlier periods) and the "fertility effect" (the tendency for women who have lost a larger proportion of their children to have more births). Many forces may contribute to this second pattern, but it is clearly consistent with our postulated behavioral link between the loss of children and parents' subsequent desire for additional births.

For the population resident in Jordan's West Bank, the Gaza Strip, and Sinai in 1967, Table 9-8 shows the proportion of a mother's offspring who had died during the prior 5 years. In both populations more than one-fifth of the children died before reaching 5 years of age. These current data for a relatively progressive region reveal the still severe regime of child mortality prevalent in much of the Arab Middle East.

Within Israel birth rates vary greatly among religious and ethnic groups (Table 9-9). Jews born in Asia and Africa report a birth rate twice that of Jews from Europe and America and Jews born in Israel. Among non-Jews, Moslems report birth rates about twice those of Christians, with Druses in between. All non-Jewish groups are more fertile than Jews. Though these differences in birth rates cannot be associated precisely with differences in mortality rates, both crude birth rates and infant mortality rates were twice as high among non-Jews as among Jews in 1955 and again in 1966.

When the proportion of children now dead is tabulated against the number of children ever born, as in Tables 9-10 and 9-11, there is further confirmation that fertility and mortality are strongly associated within families as well as among ethnic and religious groups.[23]

The only case known to me of a more refined analysis of the influence of child mortality on fertility in the Middle East is a study by S. Hassan. Using a survey sample of Egyptian mothers between the ages of 45 and 49, Hassan

---

[22] Estimates of life tables for Jordan based on the 1961 census yield the child death rate in the first 5 years of life as 17 percent for 1959–1963: Jordan, 1966, Report 1, Table II, p. 19. This appears to be low when compared with the findings of the 1967 West Bank census shown in Table 9–8.

[23] This association, however, does not imply that high mortality necessarily causes high fertility. Rather there are likely to be other factors as well that are producing both high mortality and high fertility together—for example, low educational attainment, low social and economic status, and differential medical attention and health services.

Table 9-7

**Percentage of Children Now Dead by Number
Ever Born and Age of Mother, Jordan,[a] 1961**

Number of Children Ever Born	Mothers of All Ages	Age of Mother (years)					
		13-14	15-19	20-29	30-39	40-49	50 and Over
1	9	17	7	7	10	11	14
2	15	—[b]	17	12	15	18	28
3	19	—	24	15	16	24	33
4	22	—	33	18	19	22	42
5	26	—	33	22	21	27	39
6	28	—	51	25	22	28	40
7	30	—	38	29	24	29	41
8	33	—	25	32	26	31	42
9	35	—	—	35	28	30	43
10	38	—	90	39	45	33	31
11 or more	37	—	18	49	31	32	43
Total	31	17	14	19	27	30	41

[a]Any mother not reporting the number of her children living is excluded from the computations reported here.
[b]No observations available.

Source: First Census of Population and Housing, 18 November 1961, Table 4.3.

Table 9-8

Percentage of Children Now Dead Born During the Five Years Preceding the Census, West Bank Jordan and Gaza, 1967

Age of Mother	Judea and Sumaria				Gaza Strip and North Sinai			
	All Ever-Married Women	Non-refugees	Refugees	In Refugee Camps	All Ever-Married Women	Non-refugees	Refugees	In Refugee Camps
15-19	18.3	18.6	(2.5)[a]	(28.1)	21.7	(22.3)	22.3	(18.0)
20-29	18.0	18.3	15.5	18.1	20.9	21.7	20.5	20.1
30-39	20.6	20.7	18.9	19.7	21.6	22.7	19.9	20.8
40-49	24.7	25.3	23.8	23.1	23.9	26.4	24.0	22.0
50-60	43.1	43.3	(39.3)	(44.9)	41.2	45.5	(37.9)	39.5
Total	21.0	21.3	19.0	20.5	22.4	23.7	21.6	21.3

[a]Parentheses indicate that the number is subject to a high sampling error, for it is based on a sample of less than 450.

Source: Derived from *Demographic Characteristics of the Population in Administered Areas*, Table 27 (pp. 38-39) and Table 54 (p. 69).

421

Table 9-9
Vital Rates by Religion and Place of Birth, Israel, 1966
(per thousand)

Age-Specific Birth Rates: 1966	Jewish				Non-Jewish			
	Total	America and Europe	Asia and Africa	Israel	Total	Moslem	Christian	Druse
Up to 19	35.4	36.4	67.1	13.8	102.9	120.8	54.0	80.4
20-24	198.3	167.4	241.6	153.2	362.7	402.4	218.8	345.8
25-29	220.0	180.7	251.5	195.9	397.6	447.8	266.3	346.4
30-34	141.5	85.8	184.7	127.1	362.6	427.7	201.5	326.6
35-39	63.5	30.7	101.4	50.0	247.6	308.2	93.3	254.9
40-44	16.0	5.1	36.2	11.5	122.9	168.4	27.2	103.0
45 and over	4.1	0.6	10.6	3.5	45.7	62.5	7.9	26.3
Crude birth rate								
1955	27.2				46.0			
1966	22.4				49.5			
Infant mortality rate								
1955	32.4				62.5			
1966	21.7				41.8			

Sources: *Statistical Abstract of Israel 1968*, No. 19, Central Bureau of Statistics, Jerusalem, 1968, Tables C/25 and C/26, pp. 75-76; *Statistical Bulletin of Israel*, Vol. 19, No. 8 (August 1968), Central Bureau of Statistics, Jerusalem.

Table 9-10

Percentage of Children Deceased Before Age of 5 of Non-Jewish Women once Married, Israel, 1961

Religion	Total	Number of Children Ever Born per Woman								
		1	2	3	4	5	6	7	8	9 or More
Moslem	21.2	6.2	8.9	10.2	13.4	13.6	17.9	18.6	20.2	28.6
Christian	15.8	4.8	3.1	4.0	7.6	8.6	11.5	15.8	17.3	25.1
Druse	20.9	4.2	5.4	15.8	11.0	14.1	18.8	21.8	25.3	25.3
Non-Jewish Total	19.8	5.1	6.9	9.5	11.9	12.4	16.7	18.5	20.0	27.8

Source: Marriage and Fertility, Part II, Population and Housing Census 1961, Publication 32, Central Bureau of Statistics, Jerusalem, 1966, Table 35, p. 73.

423

Table 9-11

**Percentage of Children Born Abroad Deceased before Age of 5
of Jewish Mothers by Continent of Birth and Period of Immigration, Israel, 1961**

Continent of Birth and Period of Migration	Total	Number of Children Born Abroad per Woman				
		1	2	3	4-5	6 or More
Asia-Africa Immigrated:						
Up to 1947	28.8	20.4	27.6	25.0	22.7	33.1
After 1947	22.9	14.6	15.7	14.1	17.0	27.5
Average	23.5	15.1	16.7	14.9	16.7	27.8
Europe-America Immigrated:						
Up to 1947	11.6	8.1	6.9	9.0	11.8	7.9
After 1947	10.9	4.8	6.9	12.7	16.5	21.8
Average	11.2	5.4	6.9	12.1	15.5	15.2

Source: Marriage and Fertility, Part II, Population and Housing Census 1961, Table 24, p. 60.

shows that the loss of a child is associated with a mother having more births and desiring a larger number of surviving children than mothers who had not lost a child. These results were verified by his sample for mothers of five different educational attainment classes.[24] Most of the available evidence on the relationship between child mortality and subsequent fertility is indirect, and further inquiry into this important implication of the model is barred by the lack of appropriate reliable data.

Education and Occupation

The educational process may influence desired fertility by a number of channels.[25] Examining fertility in relationship to the educational status of the mother (or the schooling of her children) may help to identify an important source of differential reproductive behavior. Table 9-2, derived from the 1960 U.A.R. census, shows marriage duration-specific cumulative fertility rates for married women by five literacy-education classes. As anticipated, fertility is lower among better educated women. The fertility differences associated with education are somewhat greater among the urban population than among the rural, for illiterate women are reported to have more births in urban than in rural areas. For example, women with a secondary education had, on the average, 3.1 births in urban and 3.4 births in rural areas after 20–29 years of marriage. Illiterate women with the same years of marriage, on the other hand, reported 7.4 and 6.7 births, on average, in urban and rural areas of Egypt, respectively.

In addition to this marriage duration-specific difference in fertility, the more schooling a woman receives the later she tends to marry[26] and the fewer years she has left to bear children. But this evidence of differences in fertility associated with women's education needs to be modified somewhat. A sample survey conducted in 1957 found substantial differences in fertility associated with educational status among urban (Cairo and Alexandria) women, but not among rural women.[27] However, the absence of an education-fertility association in the rural areas may reflect the fact that there are few educated women in rural villages, and their unrepresentative character may be due to the selective rural-urban migration process. Rizk reports the lack of a difference in fertility between illiterate, literate, and elementary-primary schooled women in the rural areas. If the more educated women tend to leave the village for the urban environment more

[24] Hassan, 1966.

[25] Education may also be fostered by more fundamental changes in attitudes and environments, and these may be the more "fundamental" cause of the observed change in fertility.

[26] For example, in H. Rizk's 1959 sample survey the average age of marriage varied inversely with the education of the woman. For his most recent cohort the mean age of marriage for university-secondary graduates was 21.0, that for primary-elementary graduates 19.2, and that for illiterates 18.8 years: Rizk, 1963b, p. 71.

[27] Rizk, 1959, 1963b. For additional evidence on the urban population, see Abu-Lughod, 1961, 1965a.

often than other women, as they appear to from studies of migration elsewhere, those remaining in the rural area may well exhibit atypically higher fertility than those who migrate to the city.[28]

Evidence also confirms an unexpected pattern of low reported fertility among the least educated (agricultural) workers in Egypt. From the 1960 census El Badry has noted that in the nonurban (possibly poorer) governorates of Egypt fertility is not inversely associated with education, but rather there is a "unimodal" distribution with women who can "only read and write" reporting the highest fertility. Another reflection of this reversal in traditional fertility patterns is seen in the fact that farmers in the nonurban governorates exhibit the lowest fertility level among occupational groups distinguished.[29]

There are at least two possible explanations for this pattern of relatively low fertility among the very poor, illiterate agricultural workers. The first is nonbehavioral and attributes the lower fertility to the poor health and environmental conditions, which presumably contribute to greater pregnancy wastage, stillbirth, premature sterility, and possibly increased frequency of divorce and widowhood among this class. The second explanation is behavioral and postulates that at very low income levels many children constitute an unacceptable economic hardship for parents that they cannot recoup from the children's future earnings because of their lack of land or working capital.[30] Without evidence to distinguish between these two causal interpretations of the phenomenon, we should be cautious in concluding that economic and educational advance among this lowest stratum of rural Egypt will be associated with a reduction in their fertility. The converse may be true, even though the economic threshold beyond which fertility will fall in the more traditional manner may be low by usual standards.

No representative data on the association between a mother's fertility and her education are, to my knowledge, available for other Arab countries in the Middle East. The Yaukey sample for Lebanon (Table 9-5), however, reveals wide differences in fertility associated with educational and economic status among the urban (Beirut) subsample and particularly among Christians.[31]

Cumulative fertility rates are summarized for Israel in Table 9-12 by religion, place of birth, age, and education. Fertility tends to differ consistently with mother's education for all groups distinguished by religion or birthplace, though the differentials are somewhat smaller among the non-Jewish groups, particularly among the older generation.

In investigating the relationship between educational advance and fertility it is essential to distinguish between men's and women's levels of educational attainment. The extension of educational opportunities to women has come only lately and reflects other advances in the social status of women in Moslem com-

---

[28] For review of this literature see Nelson, 1968.
[29] El Badry, 1965, pp. 152–153.
[30] In economic terms, this association may reflect a positive income effect on the demand of parents for children. This relationship is also found in Jordan.
[31] Yaukey, 1961, 1963.

Table 9-12

Average Number of Children per Woman by Religion,
Place of Birth, Years of Study, and Age, Israel, 1961

Religion Place of Birth:	Druse			Christians			Moslems			Foreign-Born Jews						Israel-Born Jews					
Years of Study:	0	1-4	5+	0	1-4	5+	0	1-4	5+	0	1-4	5-8	9-10	11-12	13+	0	1-4	5-8	9-10	11-12	13+
Age																					
Up to 19	(0.8)	(0.6)	a	a	(0.5)	(0.6)	0.9	0.9	a	b	b	b	b	b	b	b	b	b	b	b	b
20-24	1.7	1.8	1.5	1.9	2.2	1.7	2.3	2.2	1.8	2.6	1.9	1.5	1.1	0.9	0.7	a	1.7	1.3	1.0	0.8	0.6
25-29	3.9	2.9	2.5	3.9	2.0	3.1	4.1	4.0	3.2	4.0	3.1	2.6	2.1	1.8	1.9	3.4	2.8	2.0	1.6	1.5	1.2
30-34	5.4	5.6	a	4.4	4.7	4.6	6.1	6.4	5.3	5.4	4.6	3.6	3.0	2.5	2.1	4.2	3.8	2.9	2.3	2.1	2.0
35-39	7.0	6.4	(6.7)	7.0	6.1	5.3	7.6	6.5	6.6	6.4	5.3	4.3	3.3	2.9	2.6	4.7	5.4	3.4	2.6	2.5	2.3
40-44	7.0	a	a	7.6	6.9	5.6	8.0	(5.0)	a	6.9	6.3	4.6	3.9	3.1	3.1	6.1	a	3.7	2.5	2.7	2.1
45-49	6.9	a	a	8.0	6.9	5.8	8.3	7.6	(4.3)	7.1	6.2	2.6	2.2	2.1	2.0	6.0	4.9	4.1	2.7	2.5	2.7
Total	4.6			4.9			5.3			3.0						2.9					

a Not represented in sample or not reported. b Not reported in table format. ( ) Small sample cell: sampling error large.

Source: *Marriage and Fertility, Part I, Population and Housing Census 1961,* Publication 26, Central Bureau of Statistics, Jerusalem, 1965, Table 11 (p. 32+) and Table 21 (p. 47).

munities that are likely to contribute to decreasing fertility. Table 9-13 shows the estimates of UNESCO education expert El-Koussy of primary and secondary education enrollment rates for both sexes in several of the Arab Middle Eastern countries. In primary male education Iraq has made very rapid progress, but girls have done much better in relation to boys in Lebanon, Jordan, and Egypt. At the secondary school level, Jordan has lately achieved notable progress in raising its enrollment rates, but Lebanon still has a greater proportion of its women enrolled in secondary schools than the other countries. Since 1957/58 the number of children of school age in the region grew rapidly because of the "population explosion." Consequently the reported increases in enrollment rates are remarkable in the face of the 3–3.5 percent annual increments in the number of children in need of schooling.[32]

Though observed progress is laudable, women still have far less access to and achievement in the educational process than men. This is undoubtedly a diminishing, but still valid, reflection of the inferior status of Moslem women, which has traditionally buttressed the very high fertility in these populations.

Multivariate Analysis of Fertility

The determination of desired reproductive patterns, as discussed earlier, is a complex process, and the interactions between desired fertility and other household decisions preclude analysis of the one behavioral relation by itself. Rather the propensity of women to engage in labor force activity and the prevalence of marriage among women should be interpreted as jointly determined components of a broader model of fertility determination. For only the United Arab Republic and Jordan can we investigate this more complete specification of the multivariate model.

The United Arab Republic

Since births and deaths are not reliably known in the Arab Middle East at the regional level, the only uniform regional sources of information are censuses. For the United Arab Republic the 1960 census is tabulated for 5 urban governorates, 4 rural areas, and separately for the rural and urban subpopulations of the remaining 16 governorates. A sample of 41 regional populations can accordingly be constructed, 20 rural and 21 urban. Because of substantial net migration flows between regions, the census age composition cannot be used to derive indirect estimates of birth and death rates. However, the age composition does provide an approximate basis for estimating a measure of "surviving fertility" as a proxy for the rate of natural increase of the regional population.

More precisely, the measures of surviving fertility are (1) the ratio of the number of children less than 5 years of age per thousand women of childbearing

---

[32] Public expenditures on education have been increasing rapidly in absolute terms or relative to total government expenditures. By 1965 the share of national income allocated to education had reached 3 percent in Jordan, Lebanon, and Syria and about 6 percent in Iraq: United Nations, 1967a, p. 60.

Table 9-13

School Enrollment as a Percentage of Age-Eligible Children[a]

	Primary School				Secondary School			
	1957-58/1958-59		1963-64/1964-65		1957-58/1958-59		1963-64/1964-65	
	M	F	M	F	M	F	M	F
Egypt	64.6	38.9	81.6	52.1	17.7	5.2	24.0	9.3
Jordan	87.2	53.1	96.9[b]	62.8[b]	33.8	9.1	43.4[b]	15.0[b]
Iraq	64.5	24.9	101.5	28.2	15.3	4.2	28.9	9.0
Lebanon	89.0	68.1	119.2	85.8	15.5	10.7	29.5	19.2
Libya	70.2	14.9	100.6	23.3	6.6	0.4	18.8	1.9
Palestine refugees	96.0	61.3	82.0	66.7	37.3	7.1	45.8	22.2
Sudan	29.9	9.7	39.3	18.2	4.1	0.9	6.0	1.3
Syria	70.6[c]	30.6	93.0	40.9	13.7	4.1	28.2	8.0
Tunisia	68.7	33.7	110.1	56.4	6.6	2.4	14.2	5.6

[a]Persons older or younger than "age-eligible" may be attending school. This is the reason why some figures are larger than 100 percent.
[b]1963-64 only.
[c]1957-58 only.

Source: A.A.H. El-Koussy, A Survey of Educational Progress in the Arab States, 1960-1965, UNESCO Conference of Arab Ministers of Education, Tripoli, Libya, March 5-10, 1966.

429

age (15–49); (2) the ratio of children aged 5–9 per thousand women of child-bearing age; and (3) the sum of these two ratios. If, as our evidence suggests, the levels of birth rates and child death rates are positively correlated across populations, other things equal, this synthetic measure of "surviving fertility" will vary less across regions than the actual birth rate the older the child population considered in the numerator. But it will correspond approximately with both the long-run size of surviving family in the region and the secular rate of natural increase of the population (population growth before migration or, alternatively, the birth rate minus the death rate).

The effect of the educational process is measured in two ways: school attendance of children and educational attainment of adults (women in particular). Since child and adult schooling are thought to add to the costs of rearing children in different ways, directly and indirectly, these two measures of schooling are included as separate variables in the model. When child schooling is not reported, it is assumed that the frequency of child participation in the labor force as an unpaid family worker is inversely related to child school attendance.

First, single equations are estimated for the two surviving fertility proxies with a variety of exogenous and endogenous factors thought likely to influence desired fertility. These exploratory results are summarized in Tables 9-14 and 9-15. The variables and units of observation are defined in Tables C-1 and C-2 of Appendix C. Several results are noteworthy. Where child labor force activity is common, surviving fertility is high; where agricultural activity is dominant, surviving fertility is low. Activity of women in the labor force is associated with relatively lower surviving fertility, but only for the ratio of children under 5 per thousand women of childbearing age is this association statistically strong. The educational attainment of women is associated with fertility, as we observed it to be from single-factor analyses. Although the proportion of illiterate women is negatively associated with surviving fertility and the proportion only literate is positively associated, actual years of schooling are associated with declining surviving fertility. Regional and rural-urban dummy variables are of little help in accounting for the remaining interregional variation in surviving fertility. Marriage rates are directly associated, of course, with regional fertility differences.

The more complete three-equation model developed earlier and schematically portrayed in Figure 9-2 is estimated by three-stage least squares (Tables 9-16 and 9-17).[33] The model is estimated using all three of the proxies for surviving fertility to confirm the stability of the associations.

All of the estimated coefficients of the structural equations are of reasonable sign, and all but one regional dummy variable are at least 2.7 times their asymptotic standard errors. Unanticipated structural equation estimates are clarified by interpreting the reduced-form equations (Tables 9-18 and 9-19), which

---

[33] Because the three-stage least-squares estimates of a correctly specified model are asymptotically more efficient than the otherwise similar two-stage estimates, only the three-stage estimates are reported and discussed here: Christ, 1966, p. 449.

summarize the combined direct and indirect associations of all the exogenous variables with each of the endogenous variables. Virtually all women in Egypt are married by middle age. Variation in the proportion currently married is thus, for the most part, a function of the timing or age of marriage and the prevalence of divorce and widowhood.[34] As might be expected, marriage rates are inversely associated with female labor force participation but directly associated with female intermediate education.[35] Though the direct effect of education on marriage rates is unexpected, the reduced-form equations indicate that there is a direct and indirect (via female activity rates) association of female education with reduced marriage rates, and hence higher education probably works to delay marriage.

Female activity in the nonagricultural labor force is powerfully, and directly, associated with female education and inversely associated with surviving fertility. Surviving fertility is directly associated with the prevalence of marriage and unpaid family workers, and inversely associated with the extent of agricultural activity in the region.

In regard to the structurally constrained reduced-form equations (Table 9-19), intermediate education appears to reduce surviving fertility and marriage prevalence rates for women and to increase their participation rates in the labor force. Where children are employed more frequently as unpaid family workers, surviving fertility and marriage rates are higher and female activity lower. Where agricultural activity engages a greater proportion of the labor force in the region, surviving fertility and marriage rates are lower and female activity may be somewhat higher. The North (Lower Egypt) has lower surviving fertility and marriage rates, and higher female participation rates. These relationships are generally consistent with my anticipations. Moreover, they confirm my judgment that it is important to advance beyond single-factor analyses of fertility toward analysis of persuasive multivariate representations of the several interactive choices of the household that have a strong bearing on desired reproductive behavior.

Though it is hazardous to assume that these estimates represent a reliable guide to future relationships among economic and demographic variables in Egypt, a few mean estimates of the responsiveness of the relationships is nevertheless useful for illustrative purposes. The differences in the apparent responsiveness of the child-woman ratios to various exogenous factors may be interpreted

[34] The rural areas, probably because of the more severe regime of mortality, report a larger proportion of the female population divorced or widowed than urban areas. This is confirmed between poorer and richer regions of Cairo as well. See Aref, 1964; and El Donoushary (no date). From Table 8, p. 34, of the Census of 1960, 14.4 percent of urban and 19.0 percent of rural adult (?) women are widowed. Age structure may also be a factor for this difference in marital status.

[35] One possible explanation of this direct structural relationship is that, though the educated women marry later, their marriages last longer, on the average, because their spouses are less likely to die and divorce is less common among the upper socioeconomic classes.

Table 9-14

Regressions on Child-Woman Ratio for Egypt, 1960

(dependent variable is children 0-4 per 1,000 women 15-49)

| Constant | Percent Active | Female Economic Activity | | | | Female Marriage |
		Percent Active in Nonagriculture	Percent Active in Manufacturing	Percent Active in Commerce	Percent Active in Services	Percent Ever Married
874.447	−10.239 (−1.62)					
863.889		−25.616 (−2.21)				
842.646		−28.631 (−2.45)				
886.517		−23.576 (−2.00)				
899.248			−49.854 (−2.04)			
889.250				−65.918 (−1.19)		
865.438					−24.379 (−1.36)	
880.793			−45.240 (−1.80)	−43.910 (−0.74)	−11.728 (−0.59)	
−121.892		−2.914 (−0.36)				+12.797 (7.31)
1292.579		−26.934 (−4.90)				
730.945		−24.675 (−4.42)				
877.097		−25.378 (−3.16)				
731.468			−38.513 (−1.63)	−17.377 (−0.30)	−23.901 (−2.66)	
−179.448			−51.274 (−1.01	+8.435 (0.24)	−4.816 (−0.78)	+12.255 (7.35)

Children 0-4 per 1,000 women 15-49

Mean of variable						
719.285	4.854	2.956	0.231	0.326	2.398	68.412

Standard deviation

68.673	2.287	2.280	0.359	0.211	2.098	3.970

[a]Percent of active population who are unpaid family workers.

Female Education				Child Activity	Regional Characteristics			
Percent Not Able to Read or Write	Percent Able to Read and Write	Percent with Intermediate Certificate	Percent with University Degree	Percent Unpaid Family Workers[a]	Percent Active Population in Agriculture	North-South Dummy (North=1)	Rural-Urban Dummy (Urban=1)	R^2
		−15.891 (−1.08)		+9.105 (2.86)	−4.546 (−4.32)			0.395
		+5.669 (0.28)		+7.767 (2.97)	−4.267 (−4.19)			0.428
		+9.894 (0.49)		+4.967 (1.50)	−3.244 (−2.56)	+31.345 (1.35)		0.456
		+6.064 (0.30)		+7.598 (2.90)	−4.503 (−4.30)		−31.778 (−0.99)	0.444
		−31.427 (−3.07)		+5.813 (2.31)	−4.187 (−4.06)			0.418
		−24.798 (−1.99)		+6.591 (2.49)	−4.291 (−4.02)			0.375
		+0.308 (0.01)		+7.612 (2.69)	−4.394 (−4.15)			0.383
		−10.443 (−0.39)		+6.933 (2.48)	−4.159 (−3.99)			0.443
		+1.056 (0.08)		+5.245 (3.08)	−2.298 (−3.27)			0.774
−7.560 (−2.83)				+6.105 (2.59)	−1.753 (−1.38)			0.531
	+7.482 (2.15)			+7.363 (3.07)	−2.962 (−2.65)			0.492
			+37.169 (0.47)	+7.711 (3.03)	−4.400 (−4.56)			0.431
	+7.250 (1.97)			+7.180 (2.91)	−2.877 (−2.50)			0.498
	+5.190 (2.23)			+5.001 (3.18)	−1.355 (−1.81)			0.810
66.550	11.804	2.014	0.117	14.560	45.323	0.512	0.512	
10.270	6.429	1.877	0.191	10.522	31.288	0.506	0.506	

Table 9-15

Regressions on Child-Woman Ratio for Egypt, 1960

(dependent variable is children 5-9 per 1,000 women 15-49)

Constant	Percent Active	Percent Active in Nonagriculture	Percent Active in Manufacturing	Percent Active in Commerce	Percent Active in Services	Percent Ever Married
			Female Economic Activity			Female Marriage
852.881	+4.351 (0.85)					
839.377		−3.923 (−0.40)				
813.150		−7.644 (−0.80)				
870.911		−1.080 (−0.11)				
842.982			+13.647 (0.67)			
836.362				−89.067 (−2.12)		
836.727					−6.114 (−0.42)	
841.107			+14.972 (0.75)	−98.714 (−2.08)	+5.657 (0.36)	
564.878		+2.399 (0.23)				+3.563 (1.58)
1221.384		−21.199 (−4.66)				
723.254		−17.905 (−3.55)				
790.331		−14.165 (−2.04)				
728.723			+22.077 (1.11)	−76.193 (−1.59)	−15.908 (−2.11)	
494.752			+28.046 (1.40)	−69.563 (−1.47)	−11.006 (−1.34)	+3.148 (1.43)
Children 5-9 per 1,000 women 15-49 Mean of variable 665.875	4.854	2.956	0.231	0.326	2.398	68.412
Standard deviation 64.281	2.287	2.280	0.359	0.211	2.098	3.970

[a]Percent of active population who are unpaid family workers.

434

Female Education				Child Activity	Regional Characteristics			
Percent Not Able to Read or Write	Percent Able to Read and Write	Percent with Intermediate Certificate	Percent with University Degree	Percent Unpaid Family Workers[a]	Percent Active Population in Agriculture	North-South Dummy (North=1)	Rural-Urban Dummy (Urban=1)	R^2
		−39.180 (−3.29)		+7.229 (2.81)	−5.173 (−6.07)			0.547
		−26.185 (−1.55)		+8.782 (4.01)	−5.230 (−6.11)			0.540
		−20.968 (−1.28)		+5.325 (1.97)	−3.967 (−3.86)	+38.700 (2.04)		0.589
		−25.634 (−1.56)		+8.546 (3.99)	−5.559 (−6.48)		−44.285 (−1.68)	0.575
		−32.391 (−3.82)		+8.590 (4.11)	−5.297 (−6.20)			0.544
		−21.431 (−2.26)		+9.234 (4.60)	−5.134 (−6.34)			0.590
		−23.786 (−1.12)		+8.910 (3.90)	−5.251 (−6.15)			0.541
		−28.300 (−1.34)		+9.028 (4.07)	−5.174 (−6.25)			0.599
		−27.469 (−1.66)		+8.080 (3.68)	−4.682 (−5.16)			0.571
−7.714 (−3.49)				+8.052 (4.12)	−2.135 (−2.03)			0.634
	+3.708 (1.18)			+9.459 (4.37)	−4.103 (−4.07)			0.528
			−40.328 (−0.59)	+9.9448 (4.29)	−4.753 (−5.70)			0.514
	+3.851 (1.24)			+10.029 (4.84)	−4.334 (−4.48)			0.596
	+3.322 (1.08)			+9.470 (4.55)	−3.943 (−3.98)			0.620
66.550	11.804	2.014	0.117	14.560	45.323	0.512	0.512	
10.270	6.429	1.877	0.191	10.522	31.288	0.506	0.506	

435

Table 9-16
Three-Stage Least-Squares Estimates of Final Four-Equation Egyptian Fertility Model[a]

Dependent Variable	Constant	Child-Woman Ratio (0-4)	Child-Woman Ratio (5-9)	Marriage	Female Activity	Agriculture	Unpaid Family Workers	Female Education	North-South Dummy
C/W (0-4)	−44.9 (.24)	+[b]	−[c]	11.5 (4.33)	—	−2.05 (−3.87)	4.72 (3.03)	—	—
C/W (5-9)	−8.79 (−.03)	—	+	10.3 (2.70)	—	−3.14 (−4.12)	7.74 (3.45)	—	—
Marriage rate	72.0 (58.1)	—	—	+	−6.32 (−5.33)	—	—	6.68 (4.91)	3.15 (2.32)
Female activity rate	7.00 (4.00)	−.0038 (−3.74)		−	+	—	—	1.13 (17.1)	.83 (3.17)
Mean of variable		719.3	665.9	68.41	2.956	45.32	14.56	2.014	0.512
Standard deviation of variable		67.8	63.5	3.92	2.252	30.90	10.39	1.854	0.500

[a]The number given in parentheses under each estimated coefficient is the value of the coefficient divided by its asymptotic standard error. For variable definitions see notes to Table C-1.
[b]+ Dependent variable in this equation.
[c]− Not included in this equation.

436

Table 9-17
Three-Stage Least-Squares Estimates of Final Three-Equation Egyptian Fertility Model

Dependent Variable	Contants	Child-Woman Ratio (0-9)	Marriage	Activity	Agriculture	Unpaid Family Workers	Female Education	North-South Dummy
C/W (0-9)	−53.2 (−.14)	+	21.8 (4.00)	−	−5.04 (−4.72)	11.9 (3.82)	−	−
Marriage rate	72.1 (56.4)	+	+	−6.56 (−4.84)	−	−	6.92 (4.49)	3.48 (2.46)
Female activity rate	6.37 (3.44)	−.0044 (−3.19)	−	+	−	−	1.14 (17.3)	.88 (3.15)
Mean of variable		1385	68.41	2.956	45.32	14.56	2.014	0.512
Standard deviation of variable		121	3.92	2.252	30.90	10.39	1.854	0.500

+ Dependent variable in this equation.

− Not included in this equation.

[a]The number given in parentheses under each estimated coefficient is the value of the coefficient divided by its asymptotic standard error. For variable definitions see Table C-1.

437

Table 9-18

Ordinary Least-Squares Reduced-Form Equations for Egyptian Fertility Model[a]

Endogenous Variable	Constant	Agriculture	Unpaid Family Workers	North-South Dummy	Female Education	R^2
			Exogenous Variables			
C/W (0-4)	884. (17.0)	-3.72 (-2.79)	4.11 (1.17)	20.4 (0.84)	-32.9 (-3.07)	0.363
C/W (5-9)	824. (20.9)	-4.09 (-4.05)	5.10 (1.91)	35.8 (1.93)	-32.4 (-3.99)	0.582
C/W (0-9)	1708. (21.6)	-7.81 (-3.84)	9.21 (1.71)	56.2 (1.51)	65.2 (-3.99)	0.537
Marriage rate	80.2 (25.3)	-.220 (-2.69)	.252 (1.17)	-1.81 (-1.21)	-2.28 (-3.48)	0.286
Female activity rate	-1.43 (-2.06)	.0165 (0.93)	.0299 (0.64)	.383 (1.17)	1.49 (10.4)	0.897

[a]Numbers given in parentheses under estimated coefficients are the *t*-statistics associated with those coefficients. For definitions of variables see Table C-1.

Table 9-19

Reduced-Form Equations for the Structurally Specified Model

Endogenous Variable	Constant	Exogenous Variables			
		Agriculture	Unpaid Family Workers	North-South Dummy	Female Education
Child (0-4)/woman ratio	379.0	-2.832	6.521	-33.29	-7.331
Marriage rate	36.86	-.06802	.1566	-2.895	-.6382
Female activity rate	5.560	.01076	-.02478	.9565	1.158
Child (0-9)/woman ratio	1925.	-13.59	32.09	-134.8	-32.83
Marriage rate	85.89	-.3924	.9264	-6.184	-1.506
Female activity rate	-2.103	.0598	-.1412	1.473	1.285

Source: Derived from Tables 9-16 and 9-17.

in part as a difference between short-run (5 year) and long-run (10 year) response. It seems unlikely that an abrupt 10 percent reduction in fertility could reduce the ratio of children 0–9 years old per woman of childbearing age by 10 percent in a decade, but such a reduction might follow in this interval for the ratio of younger children, 0–4, per woman of childbearing age. Consistently with this rough interpretation of the two sets of estimates, the response elasticities of women's reproductive and marital behavior to changes in the exogenous variables are greater for the longer-term than for the shorter-term child-woman ratio formulation of the model.

Change in the exogenous variables used in the model need not be slow, for today only a few women in Egypt have advanced to an intermediate education, and the number of unpaid family workers as a proportion of the labor force is already modest and is declining. For example, reasonable changes in these two exogenous variables over the next decade might be associated with 15 percent reduction in surviving fertility, which would approximately offset the acceleration in population growth since World War II. If the proportion of women with an intermediate certificate were to double in a decade from the 1960 national level of 2 percent to 4 percent, an associated reduction in surviving fertility of 2–5 percent might be anticipated in the short and the long run according to the model estimates, as marriage rates would fall by about the same amount, and female activity in nonagricultural activities would approximately double.[36]

A comparably drastic, but not unrealistic, fall in the proportion of unpaid family workers in the labor force from 15 to 7 percent might occur with the advance in intermediate education for women. The estimated model implies that this magnitude of change in the proportion of unpaid family workers would be associated with a decline in surviving fertility of between 7 and 9 percent and a 2–6 percent decline in marriage rates over the short and long run. However, it also seems likely that the proportion of the labor force employed in agriculture will continue to decline as development and industrialization progress in Egypt. If it is assumed that the agricultural share of the labor force falls from 45 to 40 percent, the model implies a rise in surviving fertility in the short and the long run of 2–5 percent, and a more modest 0.5–2 percent rise in the prevalence of marriage. Changes of this magnitude might be achieved, particularly for women, if education were given high priority in the next decade in Egypt.

The combined effects of all these changes might be associated with a substantial, 7–18 percent, reduction in surviving fertility, and with a 3–8 percent fall in the prevalence of marriage. These changes would occur if the nature and magnitude of the relationships implied by our analysis of cross-sectional data were stable over time and this represented a satisfactory basis for extrapolating behavior over time. However, many people would anticipate that feedback mecha-

---

[36] Enrollment of women in secondary school more than doubled in the United Arab Republic from 1953/54 to 1961/62: United States Bureau of Labor Statistics, 1965, p. 20.

nisms are still more important, and structural changes in the model would further accelerate the change in birth rates, dynamically reinforcing the estimated interactions between the economic and demographic areas of behavior.[37] Regrettably, much more research is needed to establish the quantitative dimensions of these dynamic interactions and to anticipate how model parameters may reasonably change over time.

Although these estimates are not sufficiently precise to project trends or forecast the future, they strongly suggest that changes underway and within reach, though only a partial solution to the population problem, can make a substantial contribution to economic and social advance through their alleviation of the current burdens of the "population explosion." Educational opportunities may be utilized to attract children out of the labor force and into the school system, appealing to parents to restrict their fertility to support fewer offspring through school. Also, as women gain improved access to schooling, their delay of marriage and increased propensity to engage in economic activity outside of the home may set the stage for further reductions in their desired and actual fertility.

If countries of the Middle East decide to reallocate their resources to slow population growth, much better data are needed to refine and probe more deeply the underlying behavioral relations postulated in this investigation: less aggregate, more carefully defined and collected economic and educational data; and direct observations on the actual frequencies of births and child deaths within families and communities. Only when these superior data are available and have been thoroughly analyzed will it be possible to conclude whether the statistical relationships found here among census aggregates for the United Arab Republic are valid indications of behavioral relations and represent a reliable base for the formulation of policy.

Jordan

For Jordan, similar, though not exactly comparable, 1961 census data were derived for a smaller sample of 21 urban and rural regions.[38] No satisfactory three-equation model was estimated from these data, and the various single-equation models yielded inconclusive and inconsistent results. (See Appendix D.)[39] Whether this lack of empirical confirmation for the model from Jorda-

---

[37] Obvious examples of this pattern of reinforcing change are Taiwan, Korea, Hong Kong, and Singapore, where birth rates have begun to fall while economic growth rates have accelerated, household savings increased, and education and health facilities expanded sharply.

[38] See Tables D–1 and D–2 for composition of the observations and the definitions of the variables. In addition to the tables included in the text, the additional regression and correlation findings are summarized in the other tables in Appendix D.

[39] First, economic activity of children is weakly associated inversely with surviving fertility, whereas child school attendance rates vacillate in their association with surviving fertility, depending on whether children aged 0–4 or 5–9 are used to define

nian census data is a result of the smaller sample, poorer data, more heterogeneous population, or simply the inadequacies of the model cannot be determined.[40]

III. Questions of Population Policy

The description and analysis of demographic trends in the Middle East suggest a non-Malthusian interpretation of the population problem. There are substantial differences in reproductive behavior across regions of these low-income countries and among individuals in low-income communities. The single-factor and multivariate relationships between fertility and the factors thought likely to modify desired fertility are consistent with the hypothesis that reproductive behavior is responsive to man's environment. This is an optimistic inference, in contrast to that drawn by Malthus. But it is not a basis for complacency.

Population policy is viewed as involving two fundamental elements: subsidizing the provision of birth control information, services, and supplies, and influencing family size goals. Until recently it could be argued that only a small proportion of the population of low-income countries understood the feasibility of limiting births or wanted to do so. But this study and others of patterns of fertility cast strong doubts on the assertion that few parents limit births. Moreover, KAP (knowledge, attitudes, and practices of contraception) surveys conducted in every region of the world have found parents in growing numbers expressing interest in modern methods of birth control, but as yet few of the less urban and less educated have obtained access to this information. Evidence from both historic and contemporary sources confirm that private diffusion of information on contraception is slow, even when apparently in great demand. What retards the private diffusion of birth control information? What can public action do to accelerate the process?

Though much remains to be learned about the dynamics of public information service campaigns in the birth control field, they nonetheless appear to have had on occasion a substantial impact on the extent and distribution of contraceptive practice and on the level of birth rate. But there is no reason why popula-

---

the child-woman ratio. Both results are contrary to our expectations. Second, there is a weak inverse association between female nonagricultural activity and surviving fertility, but no clear association is found between retrospective measures of child mortality and current surviving fertility. Third, many of the associations change signs when different age cohorts of women are observed and thus provide little confirmation (or strong reasons for rejection) of the working hypothesis.

[40] The UN-assisted evaluation and analysis of the Jordanian 1961 census is optimistic about the quality of the data, though some inconsistencies and weaknesses are observed. We were unable to find any obvious shortcomings or internal inconsistencies in the data from our processing and analysis of them. See Jordan, 1966, Vol. I.

tion policy must stop with spreading birth control information and promoting such practices. It is also possible to influence the birth rate by influencing the number of children that people want to have.

As the first family planning element of policy succeeds in providing parents with reliable means for regulating fertility, regardless of their socioeconomic class and educational advantage, the effectiveness of the second element of policy will be enhanced. Whatever configuration of development and public welfare programs is pursued, it has implications for how many children, on average, parents will want. Though few low-income countries today have the institutional capabilities to impose the "true" social costs of childbearing on parents through some scheme of tax transfer payments, they can now choose from among alternative development strategies the one that reinforces the socially preferred demographic trends.

It is tempting to believe that the public sector could effectively hasten the reduction in desired and actual fertility by selective policy measures. To this end, programs would promote child health, education, and interests within the family, and assist women to acquire and employ marketable skills in the paid labor force. But at the moment, the determinants of family decisionmaking and their bearing on reproductive behavior are not understood well enough to interpret them confidently. As working hypotheses, however, these inferences might help guide the more extensive micro-empirical research and multivariate analysis clearly needed in this field. At the moment, though, little is being done in the Middle East either to disseminate modern means of birth control or to discover how development policies should be structured to help more parents seek fewer children.

Among the countries of the Middle East only the government of the United Arab Republic has specifically responded to the population problem with a national family planning program. From a small-scale operation that expanded gradually from 24 clinics in 1958 to 38 in 1964, family planning activity has grown rapidly if unevenly since President Nasser's address to the National Assembly on March 26, 1964.[41] By May 1968, 2,632 rural and urban combined service centers were supplied with pills (oral steroids) and 470 provided for the insertions of intrauterine devices, allocating 3 afternoons a week to free family planning services.[42] By May 1968, domestic production of pills could have provided pregnancy protection for about 8 percent of Egyptian women of childbearing age, while another 2 percent may have been protected by intrauterine devices.[43]

Though an important start has been made toward reducing the number of unwanted births, the family planning program in the United Arab Republic has

[41] Husein, 1967, Table 1, p. 144.
[42] Gadalla, 1968, pp. 7–9.
[43] Substantially more than half of these women had obtained these modern means of birth control through the public family planning program: Gadalla, 1968, pp. 14–15.

also had its problems.[44] By relying only on the provision of services through health centers rather than mobilizing field workers to personally contact, inform, and motivate all members of the population, the program is likely to reach only the already motivated, educated, and upper social and economic groups.[45]

The second element of a population policy—influencing family size goals —has not, to my knowledge, received systematic attention in any country of the Arab Middle East. Obvious candidates for change are policies bearing on the status of women. Islamic and civil law are one in most countries of the Arab Middle East. In practice, however, the legal and religiously derived rights of women to inheritance and common property are often abrogated.[46] Because welfare schemes and institutions are widely adopted by low-income countries directly from industrialized high-income countries, such anachronisms as child allowances and maternity benefits are written into labor codes.[47] For example, the U.A.R. labor code shelters parents from the real costs of maternity and provides employers with strong incentives to avoid hiring women.[48] If the population policy is judged important, precisely the opposite goals should be stressed when the government intervenes in the labor market.

Extending primary and secondary schooling to rural and urban segments of the population, particularly women, should be viewed not only as a cultural advance and an economic investment, but also as a contribution to mitigating the population problem. Assigning greater priority to achieving universal basic education than to expanding further higher education might then appear a sound development strategy. At the minimum, the interactions between educational

[44] Aside from the lack of program leadership since the June 1967 War, many of these problems are common to other countries in the developing world: (1) The dropout rate is high for countraceptive acceptors. Three-fourths of the pill acceptors had stopped using the pill within 2 years, and the average duration of use after 2 years was only 11 months. (2) The price charged for pills (10 piasters or about 24 cents per monthly cycle), although low, still represents a constraint on their use by members of the lower economic classes. More subsidies and incentives are needed to give the program greater direction and flexibility. (3) The evaluation-research component of the program is weak, with the predictable result that it is impossible to determine the effectiveness of the program. A new design or reorientation of the program is not realistic until a firm progress report and evaluation are in hand.

[45] From survey data, students of the population problem conclude that only the upper classes of Egypt are now interested in adopting family planning methods and, therefore, the national program should be addressed to this group, allied with child and maternal health services that are equally in demand (Shawky, 1965; Rizk, 1963a). The field worker approach successfully employed in Taiwan and Korea has not to my knowledge been used or proposed in the U.A.R. program.

[46] Lee, no date, pp. 16–18; Schieffelin, 1967; Ayrout, 1963.

[47] United States Bureau of Labor Statistics, 1965.

[48] *Ibid.*

and population policies should be emphasized more frequently and explicitly in developmental planning.[49]

Finally, child and maternal health care could be expanded in conjunction with the provision of family planning services and supplies through the existing network of rural and urban combined service centers in the United Arab Republic and similar institutions elsewhere. Low-cost tetanus innoculations, nutritional supplements for pregnant women, and protein additives for young children could drastically cut death rates.[50] Such a program would require a new ordering of policy priorities and bold and resourceful leadership, as well as probably some outside financial assistance. But by its impact on child mortality and maternal health, it could establish the preconditions for increased demand for birth control in the 1970s, a subsequent fall in birth and population growth rates, and accelerated development prospects in the 1970s and 1980s.

[49] This point is made by El Koussy, 1966, p. 16, in reference to the research of A. M. Shafei. One can see signs of emphasis on primary education in the United Arab Republic, where the proportion of the educational budget allocated to primary education has increased from 39 percent in 1945 to 60 percent in 1964: El Koussy, 1967, p. 203.

[50] Scrimshaw, 1966; McDermott, 1966.

APPENDIX A

Estimating Population Trends

Indirect Estimates of Vital Trends

The United Arab Republic has perhaps the most satisfactory demographic statistical base in the Middle East, having inherited from the mid-nineteenth century a tradition of decennial censuses and an administrative structure for collecting vital statistics. Nonetheless, even for that half of the population for which local public health bureaus systematically collect vital statistics, the registrations of births and deaths are clearly incomplete, and the degree of underregistration varies from region to region and from year to year.[51]

Indirect evidence of natality and mortality must therefore be derived from analysis of the censuses. One indirect method, the "reverse survival" procedure, compares the number of persons surviving from one census to the next, deriving from this information the intervening period's regime of mortality and the approximate level of birth rates. This procedure requires at least two age distributions of the population that are not seriously distorted by misreporting or underreporting. Internal inconsistencies in the reported age structure, therefore, pose a problem for this type of analysis in the Middle East, as is evident in Figure 9A–1, where the sawtooth shape of the age distributions from 15 to 60 presumably reflects substantial misreporting. Moreover, only the United Arab Republic, among the Arab countries, has two recent censuses on which to apply the reverse survival procedure, and even for the U.A.R. the irregularities in the age distribution limit the usefulness of the exercise.[52]

Other methods for indirectly estimating vital rates rely on only one census but postulate additional information, sufficient to obtain estimates of the vital rates. Perhaps the best scheme, the "quasi-stable-population" method, is based on the regularities of the cumulative age distribution (Figure 9A–2) which correspond to synthetic quasi-stable-population age distributions for which the population parameters are known.

More precisely, in a closed population, not subject to substantial external migration, where birth rates are relatively stable and death rates have fallen in a specified fashion, the current rate of population growth, in conjunction with the age distribution of the population, implies a unique combination of birth and death rates. The quasi-stable-population method based on this relationship presumes further that the mortality experienced by the population under analysis conforms in shape but not necessarily in level with the age-sex specific mortality patterns reliably documented from the past experience of Europe, areas of

---

[51] For discussion of the inadequacies of vital statistics in the United Arab Republic, see Grais et al., 1956, pp. 160–161, 195; El Badry, 1955, pp. 289, 303; 1965, p. 144; see also Appendix B.

[52] El Badry, 1955, pp. 268–305; 1965, p. 142.

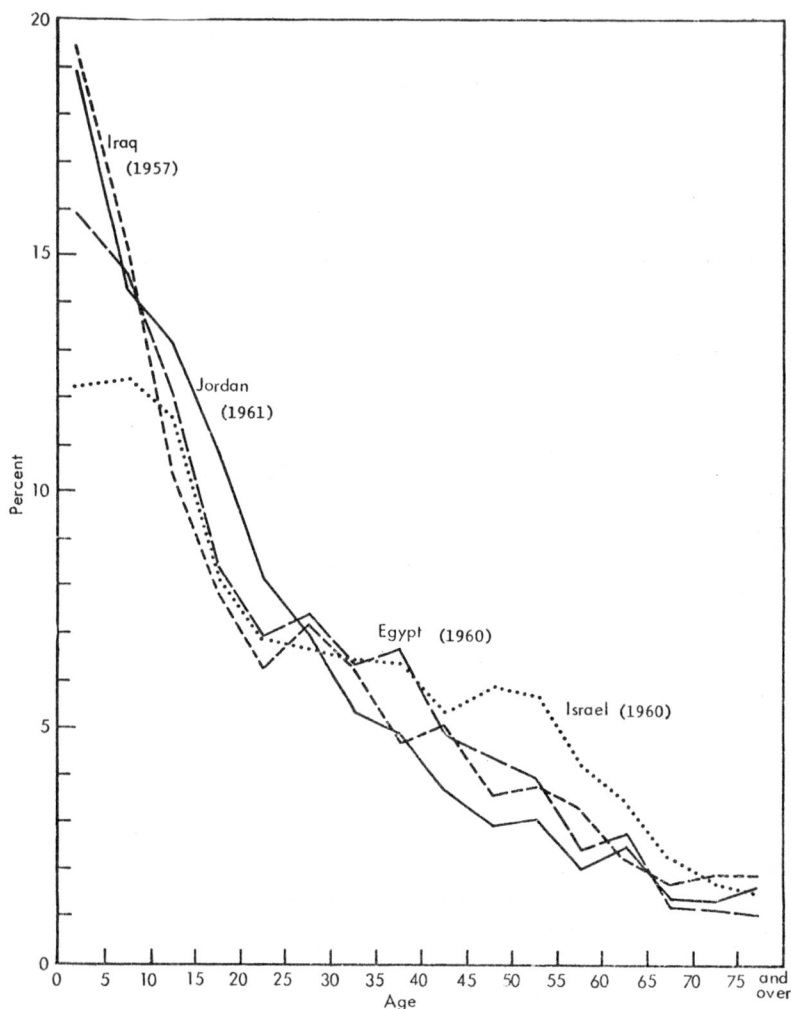

FIG. 9A-1. Age distribution (percent of population in five-year age interval)

European settlement, and Japan. A class of "West" life tables is used here to approximate the structure (not the level) of mortality in the Middle East.[53]

Another estimation technique relies on the multivariate relationship between several indirect but observed proxies for fertility and actual direct measures of fertility that are not known in the Middle East. The relationship has been estimated by linear regression techniques by Bogue and Palmore for a worldwide sample of countries with presumably reliable demographic information.

[53] Coale and Demeny, 1966; United Nations, 1967a.

448

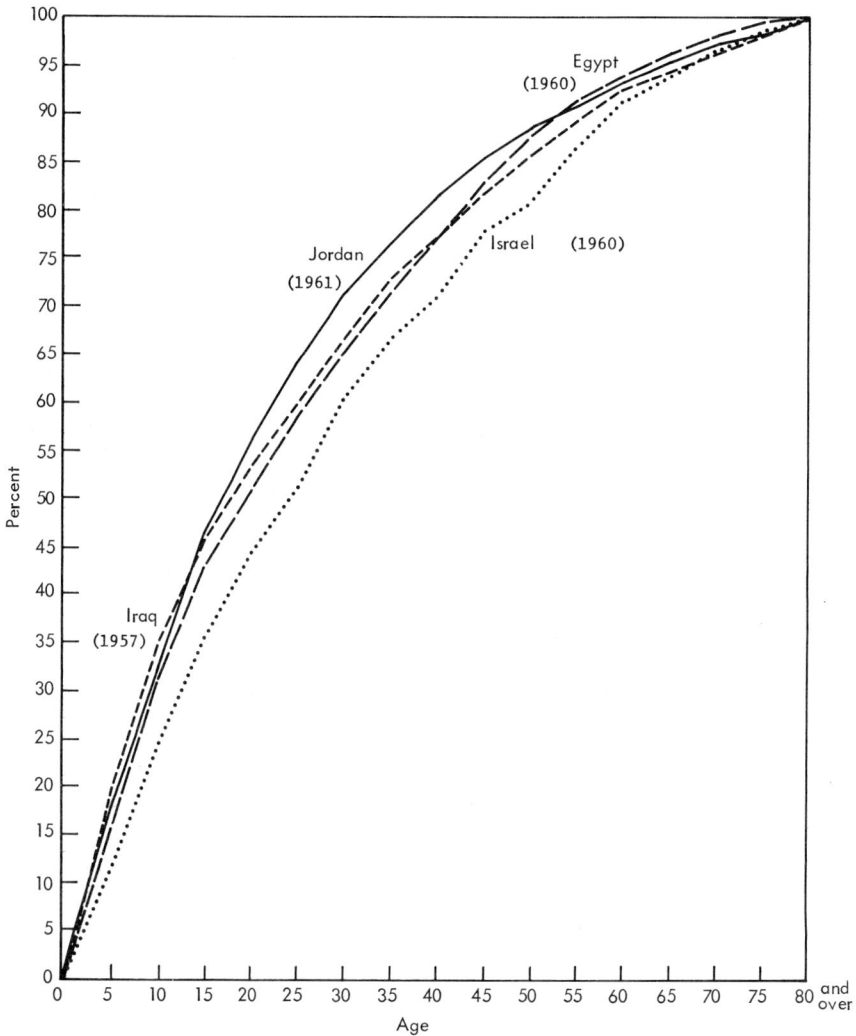

FIG. 9A-2. Cumulative age distribution (percentage of population younger than specified age).

These regression coefficients are then applied to estimate direct measures of fertility for the Middle East. Both the quasi-stable and the multivariate regression methods are used here.

The United Arab Republic

Two uncertainties weigh heavily in any interpretation of census materials for the United Arab Republic: (1) when did death rates begin to decline rapidly, and

449

(2) how much, if any, did the 1947 census overstate population size? Death rates appear to have begun to fall sharply in 1946, directly after World War II, as suggested by the demographic expert El Badry and others. The unadjusted census figures, in conjunction with the assumed 1946 decline in death rates, imply a first series of quasi-stable-method estimates for birth and death rates.[54] Consistently with El Badry's judgment concerning the timing of the decline in death rates, crude birth rates fell from 50 per thousand in the period immediately preceding the 1927 census to 43 per thousand in 1960. Crude death rates in the same period fell from 39 to 19 per thousand. The decline in birth rates for the entire period conceals a modest rise in the postwar period,[55] from a low of 39 per thousand in 1947.

Alternatively, if the death rate decline actually began somewhat earlier, in 1927, a second set of estimates by this procedure may be derived implying that the reduction in birth rates was more gradual and uniform. Birth rates then appear to have been about 41 per thousand in 1947 and 42 per thousand in 1960. This second set of assumptions implies that death rates were rather low, in the neighborhood of 17 per thousand, by 1960.[56]

All censuses, however, are not equally accurate enumerations of the population. El Badry has argued that, because the people thought the 1947 census was to serve as the basis for allocating rations, it exaggerates the population totals but does not distort the relative age and sex distribution.[57] Adopting his estimate of the magnitude of the 1947 census overcount (5.6 percent), I have computed a third series of quasi-stable-method estimates. This series is identical to those cited above for 1927 and 1937 but does not show a dip in birth rates around 1947. The crude birth rate is estimated according to these adjusted census materials as approximately constant between 1937 and 1947 at 46 per thousand, falling by 1960 to 44.[58]

If the decline in death rates began earlier than in 1946, say in 1927, the adjusted census series implies a fourth set of estimates that suggests birth rates fell to about 40 per thousand by 1960 and the death rate reached 11.4 per thousand.[59] Though the fourth set of assumptions implies implausibly low levels of death rates for 1960, other sources of information must be evaluated to determine which of the remaining three assumptions implies the most realistic description of demographic trends in the United Arab Republic. Did birth rates fall sharply during the 1940s and recover somewhat during the 1950s, or did birth rates continue to decline during the postwar period, though at a quite moderate pace?

[54] El Badry, 1955, 1965; Grais et al., 1956.
[55] See Table A–6 for these estimates, and for methodology see United Nations, 1967a, Chap. VI.
[56] Table A–6.
[57] El Badry, 1955, 1965.
[58] Estimates are presented in Table A–6; methodology is from United Nations, 1967.
[59] Table A–6.

450

Though a substantial fraction of U.A.R. births and deaths are not registered, vital registrations are relatively complete for Cairo and Alexandria, and analysis of birth registration series for all the health bureau areas yields some information as well about recent fertility trends. There is evidence that crude marriage rates rose during World War II, reaching a peak for the entire United Arab Republic in 1943 and in Cairo and Alexandria in 1944. There followed a modest rise in registered crude birth rates, in both the major cities and the countryside, that continued into the postwar years. Marzouk interprets this and other evidence as indicating that urban women were marrying earlier in this period and hastening their childbearing, but were not necessarily increasing the completed size of their families.[60]

Other evidence from country-wide health bureau registries confirms that an acceleration in births was associated with the rise in marriage rates during and immediately after the war. The proportion of first- through fourth-order births among all registered births rose sharply from 62 percent in 1940 to roughly 67 percent in 1944 and sustained that level until 1951, but thereafter fell secularly to 54 percent by 1961.[61] According to advocates of "numerator analysis," the proportion of lower-order births should inversely follow trends in general fertility with a lag of about 5 years.[62] The continuing decline in the proportion of lower-order births since 1951, therefore, suggests that either the registration system is disproportionately improving its coverage of higher-order (lower socio-economic classes?) births or higher-parity women are continuing to have high birth rates and total fertility rates were still very high in the mid-1950s.

From another point of view, birth registration data for the health bureau areas hints at a decline in fertility, most noticeable in Alexandria. When the total number of registered live births in these areas of relatively complete enumeration is divided by the estimated number of women of childbearing age (15–49), the general fertility rates thus derived show a tendency to fall during the later 1950s. From 1952 to 1960 general fertility declined 9 percent, and general marital fertility 8 percent. For Cairo and Alexandria, the general fertility rates declined 3 and 13 percent, respectively, and the general marital fertility rates fell by 3 and 17 percent.[63] Though vital registration coverage evidently deteriorated during the Suez crisis of 1957, there is little reason to suppose that these events exerted a downward bias on registration coverage in 1960. On the contrary, it seems probable that coverage increased from 1952 to 1960, thus concealing from our observation the full magnitude of the downward trend in fertility in the latter 1950s.

The 1947 and 1960 censuses provide additional comparative evidence on the number of children women have ever borne, by their age and duration of

[60] Table A–7; Marzouk, 1957.
[61] Table A–7.
[62] Ravenholt and Frederiksen, 1967.
[63] Table A–8. General discussions of vital registrations in Egypt suggest they have secularly improved: El Badry, 1965.

451

marriage (Tables A–1 and A–2). As Hansen and Marzouk have shown, these data confirm that women between the ages of 20 and 35 were giving birth at a more rapid rate during the 1950s than during the early 1940s. Only among women under 20 and over 35 was there a sign of a decline in age-specific fertility rates.[64]

If the high birth rates during and following the war are interpreted as a delayed response to the high wartime marriage rates, or as a transitory wave of catching-up of births postponed during the Depression, it remains a mystery why overall fertility rates have not declined more noticeably since 1950. Some indications from the late 1950s of declining age-specific birth rates among women over 35 and less than 20 years of age could be the first signs that the traditional pattern of transitional fertility decline is emerging in the United Arab Republic. Analyses in this study seek to identify the factors that appear to play an important role in facilitating this slow transitional change in reproductive behavior.

Returning to the three quasi-stable-population estimates of demographic trends in the United Arab Republic, the evidence assembled suggests that the 1947 census adjustments proposed by El Badry may be somewhat too large. Deflating the 1947 census totals by 3 rather than 5.6 percent yields a more reasonable set of demographic estimates. Under this assumption, with the death rate decline beginning in 1946, I estimate constant or perhaps only slightly declining crude birth rates for the period 1947–1960 in the vicinity of 44 per thousand, with death rates reaching 17 per thousand by 1960. (See Figure 9-1 for a historical summary for the United Arab Republic.

Another method for estimating vital rates, the multivariate regression model, postulates a systematic relationship between birth rates and a variety of indirect but observed evidence relating to (1) the age composition of the population, (2) its marital status, and (3) the level of infant mortality.[65] I estimate that Egyptian crude birth rates were between 42 and 48 per thousand in 1937, had fallen to 39 or 40 by 1947, and rose subsequently to between 41 and 44 by 1960.[66] These estimates parallel those obtained by the quasi-stable procedure, using unadjusted census figures for 1947. These findings confirm my judgment that El Badry's adjustment for the 1947 overcount may have been excessive, and that the more moderate adjustment proposed above is more consistent with all the evidence surveyed here.

Jordan

There has been only one census of population for Jordan, that of 1961.[67] To estimate vital rates from the relative age distribution of the population enumerated

[64] Hansen and Marzouk, 1965.
[65] Bogue and Palmore, 1964.
[66] Table A–9.
[67] Jordan, 1965, 1966. A copy of the 1952 census of housing could not be located, but it is assumed that this census did not yield population statistics in the form required here.

452

in a single census, using the quasi-stable method, two additional pieces of information are needed: (1) when did the recent decline in death rates begin, and (2) what was the rate of population growth in the decade preceding the census? It is reasonable to assume that the sharp decline in death rates began in Jordan, as in the United Arab Republic, shortly after World War II, in 1946. Regional experts have estimated the rate of population growth for Jordan during the 1950s as between 2.7 and 3.3 percent per year.[68] For these two extremes the implicit quasi-stable-population birth rates for the 1950s range from 49 to 53 and the death rates from 16.5 to 26 per thousand, respectively. A reasonable death rate of 18 per thousand implies a birth rate of 48 and a population growth rate of 3.0 percent per year.

From the multiple-variate regression procedure, the Jordanian crude birth rate is estimated as between 42 and 48 per thousand in 1961, somewhat lower than the quasi-stable-method estimate, but quite close considering the uncertainty surrounding my estimate of the infant mortality rate.[69] Since death rates have probably continued to decline in the 1960s, it is likely that Jordan has sustained a rate of population growth in excess of 3 percent since 1961.

Iraq

Only the aggregate totals of the 1957 Iraq census were published because of the irregularities in its collection.[70] The relative age distribution reported in these aggregates is consistent with an intrinsic birth rate of about 41 per thousand and a death rate between 14.5 and 10.9 per thousand depending on whether it is assumed that population growth was 2.7 or 3.0 percent per year in the early 1950s.[71] These quasi-stable-model estimates are not satisfactory, however, for they imply unreasonably low death rates and birth rates much lower than otherwise indicated.

When the multiple-variate procedure is applied to the Iraq data, the relatively large proportion of children in the total population contributes to much higher crude birth rate estimates, on the order of 44–55 per thousand.[72] If crude death rates during this period were about 25–30 per thousand, population would have grown at about 2.5 percent per year. The continued probable decline in death rates since the 1950s suggests that the population of Iraq is today growing at an annual rate of close to 3 percent per year.[73]

[68] El Badry, 1965; Jordan, 1966.
[69] Tables A–9 and A–11.
[70] El Badry, 1965; and for source of aggregates, Iraq, 1964.
[71] Table A–9.
[72] Table A–11.
[73] A preliminary report of a 1965 Iraqi general census reports a population of 8,261,527. If this recent enumeration is comparable to that obtained from the 1957 census, the average compounded rate of population growth during these 8 years was 3.4 percent per annum: Iraq, 1967 (?), p. 305.

Lebanon

For political reasons, Lebanon has not conducted a census since 1932.[74] Consequently, only informed guesses are available as to the demographic trends for this country. Although Lebanon encompasses great extremes in social and economic conditions, the country is, on the whole, relatively more developed than some of its neighbors.[75] Birth rates probably have already begun to decline and are possibly today in the range 38–44; death rates could be anywhere between 14 and 20 per thousand. These broad guesses suggest an overall natural rate of population growth of about 2.4 percent per year; but since firm evidence is not available, the United Nations estimate of 2.6 percent per year population growth is also plausible.

Israel

For the entire Israeli population the crude birth rate fell from about 35 in 1950 to approximately 25 per thousand in the early 1960s, whereas the crude death rate declined from about 7 to 6 per thousand in the same period.[76] As a result the natural rate of population growth for Israel diminished in this decade from about 2.8 to 1.9 percent, but because of substantial immigration the annual average compounded rate of population growth was 6.9 percent from 1949 to 1959 and 3.4 percent from 1959 to 1967.[77]

[74] El Badry, 1965.
[75] See, for example, the sample survey estimates of Khamis, 1957, of rural infant mortality rates between 200 and 350 deaths per thousand live births.
[76] See various issues of *Israel Statistical Abstract,* 1968; also Table 9-9.
[77] *Israel Statistical Abstract,* 1968.

Table A-1

United Arab Republic: Cumulative Fertility Rates —
Average Number of Children Born to Married Women by Age Group[a]

Age Group	Cairo and Alexandria		Other Parts of Egypt		All Egypt	
	1947	1960	1947	1960	1947	1960
Below 20	0.75	0.48	0.51	0.39	0.57	0.41
20-24	1.62	1.72	1.31	1.41	1.37	1.47
25-29	2.80	3.37	2.43	2.87	2.48	2.97
30-34	3.94	4.68	3.50	4.16	3.56	4.26
35-39	4.99	5.72	4.67	5.23	4.71	5.32
40-44	5.32	5.89	5.19	5.67	5.21	5.71
45-49	5.73	6.38	5.89	6.15	5.87	6.18
50 and over	5.80	6.08	5.94	6.06	5.89	6.16
Not stated	2.84	3.11	2.99	5.31	2.97	5.27
All age groups	3.69	4.35	3.82	4.14	3.80	4.17

[a]Excluding married women who did not state number of children born.
Source: Bent Hansen and Girgis A. Marzouk, *Development and Economic Policy in the U.A.R. (Egypt),* North-Holland Publishing Co., Amsterdam, 1965, p. 44.

Table A-2

United Arab Republic: Average Number of Children Born
to Married Women During Specific Age Limits[a]

Age Group	Cairo and Alexandria		Other Parts of Egypt		All Egypt	
	1947	1960	1947	1960	1947	1960
Below 20	0.75	0.48	0.51	0.39	0.57	0.41
20-24	0.87	1.24	0.80	1.02	0.80	1.06
25-29	1.18	1.65	1.12	1.46	1.11	1.50
30-34	1.14	1.31	1.07	1.29	1.08	1.29
35-39	1.05	1.04	1.17	1.07	1.15	1.06
40-44	0.33	0.17	0.52	0.44	0.50	0.39
45-49	0.41	0.49	0.70	0.48	0.66	0.47
50 and over	0.07	0.30	0.05	0.09	0.02	0.02

[a]Excluding married women who did not state number of children born.
Source: Bert Hansen and Girgis A. Marzouk, *Development and Economic Policy in the U.A.R. (Egypt),* p. 45

Table A-3

Age-Sex Distribution

(percentages of total population)

Age	Egypt, 1960		Jordan, 1961		Iraq, 1957		Israel, 1961	
	M	F	M	F	M	F	M	F
0-1	2.9	2.9	3.8	4.0	3.5	3.1	2.5	2.4
1-4	13.2	12.8	13.7	14.2	16.0	16.1	9.9	9.6
5-9	15.1	14.1	14.0	14.9	15.9	14.6	12.6	12.2
10-14	12.6	11.8	12.2	14.0	10.5	10.2	11.8	11.2
15-19	8.5	8.1	11.0	10.9	7.6	8.2	8.4	8.0
20-24	7.0	6.8	8.6	7.8	5.8	6.7	6.9	6.8
25-29	6.6	8.2	7.4	6.6	6.9	7.3	6.5	6.8
30-34	6.2	6.5	5.6	5.1	5.9	6.8	6.0	6.7
35-39	6.5	6.8	5.2	4.4	4.9	4.6	6.2	6.7
40-44	5.1	4.8	3.8	3.4	5.2	4.8	5.3	5.4
45-49	4.3	4.5	3.0	2.9	3.9	3.2	5.6	6.1
50-54	3.8	3.9	3.1	2.9	3.7	3.8	5.7	5.4
55-59	2.5	2.4	1.8	2.0	3.1	3.3	4.3	3.8
60-64	2.5	2.7	2.4	2.5	2.1	2.3	3.3	3.4
65-69	1.3	1.3	1.3	1.4	1.5	1.6	2.1	2.0
70-74	1.0	1.3	1.4	1.3 }	3.4	3.7	1.5	1.7
75+	0.9	1.1	1.7	1.7 }			1.4	1.7

Source: United Nations, *Demographic Yearbook 1963.*

T. PAUL SCHULTZ

Table A-4

Early Censuses of Egypt: Age-Sex Relative Distribution
(percentages of total population)

Age	1927		1937		1947	
	M	F	M	F	M	F
0-1 1-4	14.1	14.6	12.8	13.7	13.6	13.6
5-9	13.3	13.0	13.9	13.8	12.9	12.4
10-14	12.2	10.1	12.9	11.0	12.2	11.2
15-19	9.6	8.6	9.0	8.0	10.5	9.6
20-24	7.4	8.1	6.8	7.1	7.2	7.4
25-29	8.1	9.2	7.7	8.7	7.3	8.2
30-34 35-39	14.0	14.2	14.5	14.8	13.6	14.0
40-44 45-49	9.4	9.2	10.3	9.9	10.6	10.3
50-54 55-59	5.5	5.8	6.0	5.9	6.3	6.5
60-64 65-69	3.5	3.9	3.4	3.8	3.6	4.0
70-74 75+	2.6	3.2	2.4	3.1	2.0	2.5

Source: Annuaire Statistique, 1957 et 1958, Département de la Statistique et du Récensement, Cairo, United Arab Republic.

Table A-5

United Arab Republic: Population Totals and Rates of Growth, 1917-1960

Census Year	Males		Females	
	Population	Intercensal Rate of Growth[a]	Population	Intercensal Rate of Growth[a]
1960	13,068,012	0.02549	12,916,089	0.02303
1960[b]	13,068,012	0.02900	12,916,089	0.02816
1947	9,391,728	0.01647	9,575,039	0.01854
1947[b]	8,951,018	0.01164	8,955,585	0.01186
1937	7,966,675	0.01211	7,954,019	0.01108
1927	7,058,073	0.01026	7,119,791	0.01142
1917	6,369,517	n.a.	6,348,738	n.a.

[a]Rate of growth from previous census year.

[b]Using El Badry's adjustment of 1947 census totals (see text). All other population totals are census figures.

Source: Annuaire Statistique, 1957 et 1958, and *General Census of the United Arab Republic, 1960.*

457

Table A-6

United Arab Republic: Quasi-Stable-Model Estimates of Vital Rates

Males

	Using Census Data				Using Adjusted Data[a]			
	(A) Assuming Death Decline Began in 1946		(B) Assuming Death Decline Began in 1927		(C) Assuming Death Decline Began in 1946		(D) Assuming Death Decline Began in 1927	
Year	BR	DR	BR	DR	BR	DR	BR	DR
1960	44.50	19.01	42.80	17.31	46.50	17.50	41.00	12.00
1947	41.02	24.55	43.00	26.53	47.48	35.84	48.00	36.36
1937	45.13	33.02	45.00	32.89	45.13	33.02	45.00	32.89
1927	53.17	42.91	53.17	42.91	53.17	42.91	53.17	42.91

Females

	Using Census Data				Using Adjusted Data[a]			
	(A) Assuming Death Decline Began in 1946		(B) Assuming Death Decline Began in 1927		(C) Assuming Death Decline Began in 1946		(D) Assuming Death Decline Began in 1937	
Year	BR	DR	BR	DR	BR	DR	BR	DR
1960	41.70	18.67	41.00	17.97	41.70	13.54	38.85	10.69
1947	37.51	18.97	39.65	21.11	43.91	32.05	44.45	32.59
1937	46.82	35.74	46.82	35.74	46.82	35.74	46.82	35.74
1927	46.30	34.88	46.30	34.88	46.30	34.88	46.30	34.88

[a]Using El Badry's adjustment for over-reporting of 1947 census totals. (See text.)

BR = number of births per 1,000 population; DR = number of deaths per 1,000 population.

Table A-7

Parity Distribution of Births Registered in Health Bureau Areas, 1940-1961, in the United Arab Republic

(thousands)

Year	Total Number of Births (1)	Number of Births Parity Unknown (2)	Number of Birth of Order 1-4 (3)	Percent of 1st-4th Order Births of Total: (3)/(1) (4)	Crude Marriage Rate for Entire U.A.R. (5)
1940	236.9	1.5	146.3	61.8	11.8
1941	232.3	1.7	144.3	62.1	13.7
1942	243.7	1.8	153.9	63.2	15.1
1943	270.9	1.2	177.2	65.4	15.5
1944	298.7	1.5	199.1	66.7	15.4
1945	322.6	1.5	214.4	66.5	14.9
1946[a]	327.2	1.5	273.8	83.7[a]	15.2
1947	353.2	0.9	235.7	66.7	13.7
1948	362.2	0.9	237.2	65.5	14.0
1949	371.0	0.3	248.8	67.1	14.1
1950	405.9	0.3	274.4	67.6	13.4
1951	424.5	0.3	284.6	67.0	12.1
1952	441.0	0.2	286.0	64.9	10.8
1953	455.3	0.6	296.8	65.2	9.8
1954	473.7	1.2	302.6	63.9	9.7
1955	491.2	1.9	306.1	62.3	9.1
1956[a]	485.9	4.5	292.4	60.2	9.4
1957[a]	447.2	5.2	266.9	59.7	10.0
1958[a]	493.7	7.2	291.0	58.2	9.2
1959	521.3	17.6	292.8	56.2	9.1
1960	538.2	8.4	302.3	56.2	10.9
1961	576.5	6.3	313.3	54.3	8.6
1962					8.4
1963					9.8

[a]Implausibly high registration rate in 1946 and very low number of registered births from 1956 to 1958.
Source: United Nations, *Demographic Yearbook 1948/49, 1954, 1959, and 1965.*

Table A-8

Registered Birth Rates for Health Bureau Regions in the United Arab Republic, 1952-1960

Year and Region	Number of Live Births Registered (1)	Women Aged 15-49 (thousands)		Birth Rate per Thousand	
		All (2)	Married (3)	All Women (1)/(2) (4)	Married Women (1)/(3) (5)
1952					
Cairo	120,944	564.2	414.5	214	292
Alexandria	55,871	250.1	179.7	223	311
Total	441,152	2,026.4	1,506.5	218	293
1953 total	445,740	2,118.6	1,575.3	215	289
1954 total	474,183	2,204.7	1,639.7	215	289
1955 total	491,230	2,498.7	1,705.3	197	288
1956 total[a]	485,909	2,399.8	1,781.4	202	273
1957 total[a]	447,336	2,479.9	1,841.4	180	243
1958 total[a]	493,709	2,536.7	1,883.5	195	262
1959 total	521,349	2,618.7	1,944.5	199	268
1960					
Cairo	163,882	788.8	579.0	208	283
Alexandria	58,958	319.4	229.4	185	257
Total	538,187	2,704.5	2,008.4	199	268

[a]Implausibly low registered rates in 1956-1958.

Source: Vital Statistics, Vol. I, U.A.R. Statistics and Census Department, Cairo, various issues 1952-1960.

Table A-9

Jordan[a] and Iraq[a] : Quasi-Stable-Model Estimates of Vital Rates

Jordan 1961

	Assuming an Inter-censal Rate of Growth of 2.7%/year[b]		Assuming an Inter-censal Rate of Growth of 3.0%/year		Assuming an Inter-censal Rate of Growth of 3.3%/year[c]	
	BR	DR	BR	DR	BR	DR
Males	54.85	27.85	52.50	22.50	51.00	18.00
Females	51.85	24.85	49.70	19.70	48.00	15.00

Iraq 1957

	Assuming an Inter-censal Rate of Growth of 2.7%/year[c]		Assuming an Inter-censal Rate of Growth of 3.0%/year[b]	
	BR	DR	BR	DR
Males	41.05	14.05	40.30	10.30
Females	42.05	15.05	41.50	11.50

[a]All of these estimated vital rates have been adjusted for a mortality decline assumed to have begun in 1946. The annual rate of growth before 1946 has been assumed to be 2.0 per year.

[b]The annual rate of growth derived from census totals.

[c]El Badry's estimate of the annual rate of growth: M.A. El Badry, "Trends in the Components of Population Growth in the Arab Countries of the Middle East: A Survey of Present Information," *Demography*, Vol. 2 (1965).

461

Table A-10

Single-Factor Estimates of Crude Birth Rate, Using Bogue-Palmore Equations[a]

Dependent Variable	U.A.R., 1060	U.A.R., 1947	U.A.R., 1937	Jordan, 1961	Iraq, 1957
(1) Children 0-4 per 1,000 women 15-49	37.334	28.909	29.136	43.515	49.626
(2) Children 5-9 per 1,000 women 15-49	39.032	29.786	34.271	39.700	45.061
(3) Percent of population 0-4	37.494	31.541	30.543	43.018	46.532
(4) Percent of population 5-9	39.118	32.885	36.818	38.454	41.167
(5) Percent of population 0-14	38.887	33.211	34.630	41.962	41.377

[a]1. CBR = 0.1373 + 0.0529 (0-4 C/W)
2. CBR = −3.8590 + 0.0664 (5-9 C/W)
3. CBR = −4.2551 + 2.6263 (% pop. 0-4)
4. CBR = −8.6670 + 3.2723 (% pop. 5-9)
5. CBR = −11.7240 + 1.1835 (% pop. 0-14)

Source: Donald J. Bogue and James A. Palmore, "Some Empirical and Analytic Relations among Demographic Fertility Measures, with Regression Models for Fertility Estimation," *Demography*, Vol. 1, No. 1 (1964), Table 8, p. 235.

Table A-11
Multivariate Estimates of Crude Birth Rate, Using Bogue-Palmore Equations[a]

	U.A.R., 1960	U.A.R., 1947	U.A.R., 1937	Jordan, 1961	Iraq, 1957
Child-woman ratio (0-4)[b]	703	544	574	820	936
Child-woman ratio (5-9)[b]	646	507	574	656	737
Percent of population 0-4	15.9	13.6	13.2	18.0	19.3
Percent of population 5-9[b]	14.6	12.7	13.9	14.4	15.2
Infant mortality rate	130[c]	162[c]	199[c]	120[d]	130[c]
Median age at marriage[f]	20	19	18	19	19
Index of fertility-age composition[g]	1.018	1.002	1.037	1.037	1.038
Percent of women 45-49 ever married[h]	98.6	99.0	98.9	97.2	97.0
Estimate of crude birth rate					
Using child-woman ratio 0-4	43.5	40.1	44.6	48.4	54.7
Using child-woman ratio 5-9	43.8	39.9	48.4	44.6	50.1
Using percent population 0-4	42.1	40.0	42.1	46.6	50.5
Using percent population 5-9	41.2	39.0	45.8	41.3	44.2

[a]Using equations given in Table 10, p. 328, of Bogue and Palmore, "Some Empirical and Analytic Relations among Demographic Fertility Measures,"

[b]Derived from census age distributions.

[c]Average of figures given by El Badry, "Trends in The Components of Population Growth in the Arab Countries," for registered rates in urban and rural health bureau areas, Table 5, p. 147.

[d]From estimated life table for Jordan 1959/63, Table II, p. 19, in Analysis of the Population Statistics of Jordan, Vol. I, Department of Statistics

[e]My estimate.

[f]My estimates. Dudley Kirk (Factors Affecting Moslem Natality, Vol. II, United Nations, New York, 1967, p. 151) believes that "age at marriage is low," for women in Moslem countries; in the countries having statistical information the great majority of women are reported as married before age 20. . . . There is evidence that the age at marriage has been rising in the more progressive Moslem countries."

[g]See Bogue and Palmore, "Some Empirical and Analytic Relations among Demographic Fertility Measures," pp. 325-326, for an explanation of the determination of this index.

[h]Derived for data (age distribution by marital status) in the United Nations, Demographic Yearbook, for various years.

[i]Percent of women 40-49 ever married.

APPENDIX B

Investigation of Infant and General Mortality Statistics for the United Arab Republic[78]

Infant mortality rates in the United Arab Republic are among the highest in the world. In 1960 the rates reported in health bureau areas averaged 118 infant deaths per thousand live births in Lower (Northern) Egypt and 161 in Upper (Southern) Egypt. A working hypothesis regarding the factors influencing infant mortality is presented in this Appendix and tested with contemporary empirical materials for the United Arab Republic. The level of infant mortality is interpreted as a function of (1) infant care at birth, (2) general health and sanitation conditions, (3) social and economic characteristics of the population, and (4) geographic location.

Births are registered according to whether a physician, nurse, or midwife was in attendance. These professional attendants are assumed to be qualified to cope with complications at birth that might result in the death of the child. The presence at birth of a medical or paramedical person is also likely to increase the probability that the birth will be registered, particularly if the infant does not survive. This might bias downward the single-equation-estimated effects of medical attention.

General health conditions are summarized by three further factors: the general death rate for persons 1 year and older, the per capita supply of hospital beds, and the per capita supply of potable water in the region.

Some measures are also needed of the economic standard of living, adequacy of housing, and other aspects of the environment that may be associated with better health. Infant mortality is thus expected to be positively associated with the availability of television (the arbitrary choice of a luxury commodity) and the number of persons per household (inadequacy of housing), and postively associated with illiteracy (low social and economic status). Finally, a regional dummy is considered to test the hypothesis that some factors (for example, climate or endemic diseases) that could not be specified or observed might nevertheless lead to regional differences in infant mortality. The regional dummy has the value of one for Upper Egypt and zero for Lower Egypt.

The variables are defined in Table B-1. The infant birth attendance and noninfant death rates apply to the health bureau localities, which contain approximately one-half of the Egyptian population. The registration of vital events is thought to be more nearly complete in these areas, although seriously deficient elsewhere.[79] The other data used in the regression analysis refer to the governorate populations, requiring us to assume that the vital rates for the health bureau areas are those of the entire governorates.

[78] Appendix B summarizes the findings of a study by J. DaVanzo, made in 1968.
[79] El Badry, 1965, p. 146.

464

Table B-1

Variables Used in Infant Mortality Regressions

Infant mortality[a]	Number of infant deaths (from birth to age 1) per 1,000 live births
Care at birth	
Nurse or midwife[a] (paramedical)	Percentage of live births attended by a nurse or midwife
Physician or hospital[a] (medical)	Percentage of live births attended by a physician or hospital
Health and sanitation conditions	
Noninfant death rate	Number of deaths of persons over 1 year of age per 1,000 persons over 1 year of age
Scarcity of hospital facilities	Number of persons per hospital bed
Potable water	Average annual per capita consumption of potable water
Socioeconomic factors	
Household size	Number of persons per household
Television sets	Number of television sets per household
Illiteracy	Percentage of population who can neither read nor write
Geographic regions	
North-south dummy	A dummy variable whose value is 0 for Northern (Lower) Egypt and 1 for Southern (Upper) Egypt

[a]Data refer to health bureau areas only.

The regression results are shown in Table B-2. The infant mortality rate is negatively associated with the two attendance rates (nurse/midwife or physician/hospital) and positively related to the noninfant death rate. The measure of per capita potable water is negatively associated with infant mortality rates but reduces the explanatory importance of the other variables. Hospital facilities are not significantly associated with infant mortality rates.

The average household size is strongly associated with infant mortality rates, but with a negative sign that is contrary to expectation. It seems doubtful

Table B-2

Regressions on Infant Mortality Rates in Egypt

(dependent variable is infant death rate)

	Constant	Care at Birth		Health and Sanitation Conditions			Socioeconomic Factors			Geographic Location:	R^2	Sample Size
		Nurse or Midwife	Physician or Hospital	Noninfant Death Rate	Hospital Facilities	Potable Water	Household Size	Television Sets	Illiteracy	North-South Dummy		
(1)	128.626	−1.312 (−2.22)	−0.566 (−1.05)	+5.793 (3.15)							0.4729	20[a]
(2)	129.937	−1.308 (−2.14)	−0.573 (−1.03)	+5.935 (2.95)	−0.004 (−0.21)						0.4744	20
(3)	125.243	−0.309 (−0.42)	−0.396 (−0.52)	+4.653 (1.74)		−2.887 (−2.60)					0.6437	15[b]
(4)	404.397	−0.806 (−2.44)	−0.459 (−1.56)	+2.431 (2.15)			−50.125 (−6.28)				0.8546	20
(5)	126.446	−1.444 (−2.50)	−0.637 (−1.22)	+6.273 (3.47)				+673.187 (1.46)			0.5383	20
(6)	149.428	−1.274 (−2.13)	−0.627 (−1.14)	+6.668 (3.12)					−0.430 (−0.82)		0.4956	20
(7)	64.135	−0.469 (−0.94)	+0.581 (1.01)	+2.377 (1.26)						−40.656 (4.94)	0.8246	16[c]

[a]Twenty governorates.

[b]Excludes urban governorates of Cairo, Alexandria, Canal, Suez, and Damietta. (Potable water data not available for these governorates.)

[c]Excludes urban governorates of Cairo, Alexandria, Canal, and Suez.

Table B-3

Regressions of Registered Fertility Rates on a Measure of Death Incidence among Children across Regions of the United Arab Republic

Year	Dependent Variable	Constant	Coefficient of Child Death Incidence[a]	R^2 [a]	n [b]
1960	G[b]	386.732	−125.917 (−2.20)	0.2115	20
	L[c]	564.808	−204.437 (−2.99)	0.3316	20
1958	G	314.954	−85.025 (−1.49)	0.1103	20
	L	413.299	−109.701 (−1.80)	0.1527	20
1955	G	148.714	+34.774 (0.51)	0.0145	20
	L	204.912	+39.332 (0.43)	0.0106	
1955-1960 (pooled)	G	195.897	+0.655 (0.03)	0.000	118[d]
	L	282.504	−15.143 (0.66)	0.0037	118[d]

[a] R^2 = coefficient of determination; n = sample size.

[b] n = sample size.

[c] Child death incidence = reciprocal of the survival rate of children 0-5, lagged 2 years.

[d] G = general fertility rate, that is, the number of live births per 100 women aged 15-49.

[e] L = Legitimate fertility rate, that is, the number of legitimate live births per 100 married women aged 15-49.

[f] Two 1957 observations have been eliminated because values were implausibly low.

Source: Vital Statistics, Vol. I, various years (1953-1960), Statistics and Census Department, Cairo, United Arab Republic.

whether this variable reflects the inadequacy of housing or the lower social and economic status of large families. The availability of television and the illiteracy variables are not associated with infant mortality rates.

Finally, the dummy variable for the distinction between Upper and Lower Egypt accounted for much of the variation in infant mortality rates but reduced the role of the more specific variables. In general, this exercise in multivariate analysis of Egyptian death rates was not satisfactory, and it is believed that regional variation in the completeness of registration precluded much further progress in this direction.

Another exploratory investigation was undertaken to test the value of regional health bureau vital registrations. The family planning hypothesis postulates that parents have a target family size and that they compensate for child losses by trying to have further births. To test this implication of the working hypothesis, birth rates for 20 governorates were regressed on the reciprocal of the survival rate for children from birth to age 4 years, as estimated from the health bureau death registrations 2 years earlier.[80] A general fertility rate and a legitimate fertility rate are considered as dependent variables in the regressions reported in Table B-3. The first six regressions are cross-sectional samples for individual years, and in the last two regressions cross sections are pooled from 1955 to 1960, excluding data for Suez and Damietta in 1957, when registrations were virtually nil (because of the Suez crisis). The results are not encouraging, and the wide fluctuations in registered fertility rates from year to year within most of the governorates discouraged any efforts to examine these data more extensively.

[80] The lag of 2 years between the child death rate and the subsequent birth rate is derived from reproduction and biological lags observed from the analysis of similar (but more reliable) data for Puerto Rico and Taiwan: Schultz, 1969c.

APPENDIX C
Investigation of Child-Woman Ratios in the United Arab Republic

Table C-1
Variables Used in Regressions

Fertility	
C/W 0-4[a]	Number of children 0-4 per 1,000 women in the childbearing ages (15-49)
C/W 5-9[a]	Number of children 5-9 per 1,000 women 15-49
C/W 0-9[a]	Sum of the first two fertility variables
Female economic activity	
Active	Percent of females 6 years of age or over economically active
Nonagriculture[a]	Percent of females 6 years of age and over economically active in manufacturing, commerce, or services
Manufacturing	Percent of females 6 years of age or over economically active in manufacturing
Commerce	Percent of females 6 years of age and over economically active in commerce
Services	Percent of females 6 years of age and over economically active in services
Female marriage	
Marriage[a,b]	Percent of women 16 years or older who are currently married
Female education	
Illiterate	Percent of females 5 years and over not able to read or write
Literate	Percent of females 5 years and over able to read and write
Intermediate certificate[a]	Percent of females 5 years and over with an intermediate certificate
University degree	Percent of females 5 years and over with a university degree
Child activity	
Unpaid family workers[a]	Percent of all economically active persons aged 6 and over enumerated as "unpaid family workers"
Regional characteristics	
Agriculture[a]	Percent of all economically active persons aged 6 and over employed in agriculture, forestry, hunting, or fishing
North-south dummy	A dummy variable whose value is 1 for all governorates in Lower (Northern) Egypt and 0 for all governorates in Upper (Southern) Egypt
Rural-urban dummy	A dummy variable whose value is 1 for all urban regions and 0 for all rural regions

[a] Variables appearing in three-equation Egyptian fertility model (Tables 9-16 to 9-18).

[b] Age of population base is not defined in census, but total population allocated to marital status classes corresponds approximately with male population 18 years and over and female population 16 years and over: *General Tables of the Egyptian Census of 1960,* Table 8, p. 33.

Table C-2

Administrative Units Used in Regression Analysis
of the United Arab Republic

Code Number	Name	Urban-Rural Classification
1	Cairo	(Urban)
2	Alexandria	(Urban)
3	Port Said	(Urban)
4	Ismalia	(Urban)
5	Suez	(Urban)
6	Damietta	Urban subpopulation
7	Damietta	Rural subpopulation
8	Dakahlia	Urban subpopulation
9	Dakahlia	Rural subpopulation
10	Sharkia	Urban subpopulation
11	Sharkia	Rural subpopulation
12	Kalyubia	Urban subpopulation
13	Kalyubia	Rural subpopulation
14	Kafr-el-Sheikh	Urban subpopulation
15	Kafr-el-Sheikh	Rural subpopulation
16	Gharbia	Urban subpopulation
17	Gharbia	Rural subpopulation
18	Menoufia	Urban subpopulation
19	Menoufia	Rural subpopulation
20	Behera	Urban subpopulation
21	Behera	Rural subpopulation
22	Giza	Urban subpopulation
23	Giza	Rural subpopulation
24	Beni-Suef	Urban subpopulation
25	Beni-Suef	Rural subpopulation
26	Fayoum	Urban subpopulation
27	Fayoum	Rural subpopulation
28	Minya	Urban subpopulation
29	Minya	Rural subpopulation
30	Assyiut	Urban subpopulation
31	Assyiut	Rural subpopulation
32	Soubag	Urban subpopulation
33	Soubag	Rural subpopulation
34	Kena	Urban subpopulation
35	Kena	Rural subpopulation
36	Asswan	Urban subpopulation
37	Asswan	Rural subpopulation
38	Red Sea	(Rural)
39	El-Wade Ed-Gedid (Southern Desert)	(Rural)
40	Matrouh (Western Desert)	(Rural)
41	Sinai	(Rural)

Table C-3

1960 Census Data for U.A.R. Regional Model[a]

Regional Code	Child-Woman Ratios		Marriage Rate	Nonagri-cultural Female Activity Rate	Agri-culture	Unpaid Family Worker	North-South Dummy	Female Inter-mediate Education
	(0-4)	(5-9)						
1	687.7	638.6	66.59	7.867	1.440	1.406	1.0	6.202
2	676.0	667.8	64.13	6.573	4.789	2.027	1.0	4.473
3	693.4	701.3	65.78	4.966	6.508	2.114	1.0	4.027
4	841.0	770.8	72.99	1.956	44.783	15.300	1.0	1.567
5	862.4	768.7	74.95	2.363	10.380	2.737	1.0	2.733
6	745.1	699.5	67.52	4.735	13.848	6.276	1.0	3.719
7	790.9	730.4	69.51	2.775	68.292	20.166	1.0	0.897
8	726.1	705.2	65.28	6.183	17.251	7.468	1.0	4.601
9	776.4	714.6	68.92	1.298	78.924	27.559	1.0	0.378
10	784.4	716.4	68.70	4.945	20.641	9.191	1.0	3.700
11	747.6	664.5	70.15	0.985	81.780	30.058	1.0	0.274
12	794.2	693.1	74.00	3.122	15.995	5.323	1.0	2.355
13	756.8	652.2	72.52	1.101	71.508	25.386	1.0	0.382
14	715.3	703.3	65.81	3.947	36.416	15.678	1.0	1.653
15	684.3	688.9	64.10	1.340	86.153	36.382	1.0	0.153
16	731.1	712.6	66.87	6.620	10.487	5.615	1.0	4.125
17	699.5	667.6	65.35	1.445	76.921	27.497	1.0	0.289
18	723.0	683.3	67.60	4.697	29.554	12.540	1.0	3.421
19	716.1	648.1	68.78	1.098	77.399	26.788	1.0	0.448
20	727.5	735.6	65.72	4.523	22.771	9.765	1.0	2.394
21	658.0	664.0	64.23	0.913	84.810	33.750	1.0	0.163
22	674.1	614.3	67.11	9.363	5.445	2.339	0.0	6.888
23	729.0	614.3	71.70	1.244	65.303	21.928	0.0	0.272
24	644.7	600.4	64.86	4.456	32.059	7.360	0.0	3.724
25	594.9	521.1	63.41	0.755	84.538	21.151	0.0	0.141
26	705.4	614.8	66.66	5.803	27.431	8.363	0.0	3.705
27	672.3	579.3	67.41	2.955	81.572	25.056	0.0	0.181
28	684.0	612.4	66.36	4.790	21.749	4.512	0.0	3.636
29	626.7	548.1	67.48	1.020	85.401	18.730	0.0	0.135
30	722.8	646.8	65.90	3.444	31.570	6.210	0.0	3.835
31	707.6	625.0	68.71	0.677	85.809	21.059	0.0	0.107
32	723.8	639.3	67.65	2.598	29.634	7.281	0.0	2.159
33	687.6	613.0	66.80	0.477	86.601	26.836	0.0	0.048
34	679.9	622.5	67.30	2.147	24.517	5.785	0.0	2.348
35	695.5	592.3	69.88	0.430	82.152	22.342	0.0	0.085
36	697.8	633.4	71.54	1.598	23.741	3.221	0.0	2.009
37	634.0	595.2	65.70	0.251	71.513	19.800	0.0	0.084
38	923.4	843.4	81.16	2.084	2.834	0.545	0.0	2.794
39	803.3	672.8	79.76	0.424	73.946	28.521	0.0	0.154
40	564.1	741.7	63.99	1.910	70.523	20.286	0.0	0.193
41	781.0	742.1	71.86	1.301	11.275	2.591	0.0	2.117

[a]Regional code is explained in Table C-2, and variables are defined in Table C-1.

Table C-4

Regression on Child-Women Ratio for Egypt, 1960

(dependent variable is children 0-4 per 1,000 women 15-49)

| Constant | Female Economic Activity | | | | | Female Marriage |
	Percent Active	Percent Active in Nonagriculture	Percent Active in Manufacturing	Percent Active in Commerce	Percent Active in Services	Percent Ever Married
870.901	−12.983 (−2.38)					
868.232		−23.323 (−2.98)				
843.388		−25.299 (−3.20)				
888.452		−21.386 (−2.65)				
938.819			−63.937 (−2.54)			
886.540				−91.318 (−1.67)		
855.607					−25.636 (−2.38)	
895.939			−48.498 (−1.82)	−40.550 (−0.69)	−14.157 (−1.11)	
−129.196		−3.166 (−0.56)				+12.808 (7.33)
1140.202		−26.490 (−4.70)				
665.504		−22.517 (−4.16)				
867.512		−25.147 (−3.46)				
666.239			−29.436 (−1.23)	−47.189 (−0.86)	−19.084 (−2.26)	
−170.579			−11.761 (−0.75)	−12.413 (−0.34)	−1.692 (−0.28)	+11.978 (6.91)
Children 0-4 per 1,000 women 15-49						
Mean of variable 719.285	4.854	2.956	0.231	0.326	2.398	68.412
Standard deviation 68.673	2.287	2.280	0.359	0.211	2.098	3.970

| Population's Education | | | | Child Activity | Regional Characteristics | | | |
Percent Not Able to Read or Write	Percent Able to Read and Write	Percent with Intermediate Certificate	Percent with University Degree	Percent Unpaid Family Workers	Percent Active Population in Agriculture	North-South Dummy	Rural-Urban Dummy	R^2
		−6.840 (−0.69)		+9.884 (3.22)	−4.522 (−4.01)			0.383
		+1.089 (0.10)		+7.625 (2.98)	−4.312 (−4.00)			0.427
		+3.317 (0.31)		+4.818 (1.45)	−3.278 (−2.47)	+30.702 (1.31)		0.454
		+1.721 (0.16)		+7.460 (2.91)	−4.527 (−4.11)		−31.894 (−0.99)	0.443
		−22.955 (−2.77)		+5.701 (2.22)	−4.308 (−3.89)			0.395
		−12.511 (−1.29)		+6.717 (2.47)	−4.078 (−3.51)			0.338
		+2.243 (0.18)		+7.684 (2.86)	−4.319 (−3.86)			0.383
		−6.604 (−0.50)		+7.049 (2.65)	−4.286 (−3.90)			0.445
		+1.635 (0.24)		+5.256 (3.16)	−2.240 (−3.02)			0.774
−6.104 (−2.43)				+5.720 (2.31)	−1.961 (−1.47)			0.508
	+7.463 (2.48)			+6.507 (2.72)	−2.654 (−2.36)			0.511
			+14.401 (0.54)	+7.754 (3.04)	−4.311 (−4.47)			0.432
	+7.286 (2.28)			+6.460 (2.63)	−2.547 (−2.17)			0.515
	+3.969 (1.86)			+4.685 (2.90)	−1.424 (−1.83)			0.802
55.210	19.545	4.029	0.595	14.560	45.324	0.512	0.512	
10.879	6.26	2.742	0.642	10.522	31.288	0.506	0.506	

Table C-5

Regressions on Child-Woman Ratio for Egypt, 1960

(dependent variable is children 5-9 per 1,000 women 15-49)

Constant	Female Economic Activity					Female Marriage
	Percent Active	Percent Active in Nonagriculture	Percent Active in Manufacturing	Percent Active in Commerce	Percent Active in Services	Percent Ever Married
886.748	−0.276 (−0.06)					
873.198		−9.295 (−1.43)				
842.441		−11.742 (−1.85)				
900.084		−6.720 (−1.02)				
888.049			−1.099 (−0.05)			
868.915				−96.980 (−2.41)		
864.649					−12.081 (−1.40)	
855.522			+10.428 (0.49)	−89.163 (−1.89)	−4.88 (−0.48)	
613.458		−4.046 (−0.55)				+3.335 (1.49)
950.091		−19.138 (−3.76)				
728.938		−16.886 (−3.36)				
797.683		−15.574 (−2.47)				
686.942			+27.406 (1.35)	−92.284 (−1.98)	−13.365 (−1.87)	
489.765			+31.571 (1.55)	−89.089 (−1.81)	−9.267 (−1.19)	+2.822 (1.26)
Children 5-9 per 1,000 women 15-49						
Mean of variable 665.875	4.854	2.956	0.231	0.326	3.398	68.412
Standard deviation 64.281	2.287	2.280	0.359	0.211	2.098	3.970

| Population's Education | | | | Child Activity | Regional Characteristics | | | |
Percent Not Able to Read or Write	Percent Able to Read and Write	Percent with Intermediate Certificate	Percent with University Degree	Percent Unpaid Family Workers	Percent Active Population in Agriculture	North-South Dummy (North=1)	Rural-Urban Dummy (Urban=1)	R^2
		−23.881 (−2.91)		+8.569 (3.39)	−5.473 (−5.91)			0.524
		−15.741 (−1.77)		+9.148 (4.30)	−5.507 (−6.15)			0.549
		−12.983 (−1.51)		+5.673 (2.13)	−4.228 (−3.96)	+38.008 (2.02)		0.596
		−14.901 (−1.72)		+8.928 (4.28)	−5.793 (−6.48)		−42.901 (−1.71)	0.580
		−24.211 (−3.52)		+8.481 (3.97)	−5.468 (−5.94)			0.524
		−16.168 (−2.26)		+9.285 (4.63)	−5.327 (−6.22)			0.590
		−13.622 (−1.36)		+9.296 (4.31)	−5.518 (−6.15)			0.548
		−12.097 (−1.15)		+9.591 (4.51)	−5.34 (−6.07)			0.594
		−15.599 (−1.79)		+8.531 (4.00)	−4.968 (−5.22)			0.576
−3.575 (−1.58)				+8.475 (3.78)	−3.390 (1.20)			0.541
	+2.332 (0.83)			+9.234 (4.16)	−4.262 (−4.07)			0.519
			−8.545 (−0.37)	+9.480 (4.28)	−4.83 (−5.76)			0.511
	+4.131 (1.53)			+9.616 (4.63)	−4.103 (−4.15)			0.605
	+3.349 (1.22)			+9.197 (4.41)	−3.839 (−3.83)			0.623
55.210	19.545	4.029	0.595	14.560	45.324	0.512	0.512	
10.879	6.26	2.742	0.642	10.522	31.288	0.506	0.506	

Table C-6

**Correlation Matrix for Variables Used in Regressions
on Egyptian Child-Woman Ratios**

	Fertility		Female Economic Activity				
	C/W 0-4	C/W 5-9	Percent Active	Percent Active in Nonagri-culture	Percent Active in Manu-facturing	Percent Active in Commerce	Percent Active in Services
Fertility: C/W 5-9	0.709						
Female economic activity							
Active	−0.195	0.064					
Nonagriculture	−0.042	0.105	0.606				
Manufacturing	−0.318	0.001	0.163	0.178			
Commerce	−0.151	−0.159	0.557	0.713	0.044		
Services	0.025	0.130	0.575	0.985	0.018	0.666	
Female marriage	0.808	0.428	−0.527	−0.299	−0.262	−0.345	−0.246
Female education							
Illiterate	−0.383	−0.490	−0.256	−0.775	0.059	−0.347	−0.818
Literate	0.371	0.414	0.204	0.738	−0.096	0.351	0.783
Intermediate certificate	0.107	0.175	0.410	0.926	−0.038	0.562	0.956
University degree	−0.020	0.019	0.500	0.817	0.018	0.436	0.841
Child activity:							
Unpaid family workers	−0.208	−0.236	0.030	−0.666	0.053	−0.309	−0.702
Regional characteristics							
Agriculture	−0.321	−0.404	−0.136	−0.750	0.072	−0.381	−0.789
North-south dummy	0.311	0.495	0.507	0.247	−0.060	0.293	0.249
Rural-urban dummy (1 = urban)	0.098	0.152	0.217	0.750	−0.075	0.516	0.776

T. PAUL SCHULTZ

Female Marriage	Female Education				Child Activity	Regional Characteristics	
Percent Ever Married	Percent Not Able to Read or Write	Percent Able to Read and Write	Percent With Intermediate Certificate	Percent With University Degree	Percent Unpaid Family Workers	Percent Active Population in Agriculture	North-South Dummy (1 = North)
−0.121							
0.106	−0.981						
−0.128	−0.899	0.866					
−0.098	−0.655	0.574	0.823				
−0.086	0.871	−0.867	−0.833	−0.563			
−0.107	0.951	−0.929	−0.890	−0.613	0.944		
−0.088	−0.254	0.246	0.149	0.047	0.081	0.507	
−0.165	−0.759	0.770	0.815	0.501	−0.776	0.217	0.219

APPENDIX D
Investigation of Child-Woman Ratios in Jordan

Table D-1
Variables Used in Regressions

Fertility	
C/W 0-4	Number of children 0-4 per 1,000 women 15-49
C/W 5-9	Number of children 5-9 per 1,000 women 15-49
CEB/W 15-19	Number of children ever born per woman 15-19
CEB/W 20-29	Number of children ever born per woman 20-29
CEB/W 30-39	Number of children ever born per woman 30-39
CEB/W 40-49	Number of children ever born per woman 40-49
CEB/W $\geqslant$ 50	Number of children ever born per woman aged 50 or older
Death incidence among children (age-specific)	Death incidence among children ever born to women in a specific cohort (e.g., 15-49 when used with C/W 0-4 or C/W 5-9, 15-19 when used with CEB/W 15-19); the variable is defined as the reciprocal of the traction of surviving children ever born to these women
Female economic activity (age-specific)	
Nonagriculture	Percent of females in a given cohort economically active in nonagricultural activities (It has been assumed that the percent of economically active women in nonagriculture is the same for all cohorts in a region; i.e., for each cohort in a region, the age-specific female activity rate has been multiplied by the percent of all economically active women in the region who are employed in nonagricultural activities.)
Children's economic activity	
Child activity	Percent of children 5-14 who are economically active
Unpaid family workers	Percent of total economically active who are unpaid family workers
Female education (age-specific)	Percent of females in a given cohort who have completed 6 years of elementary education
Children's education	Percent of children 5-14 in school
Marriage (age-specific)	Percent of women in a given cohort who have been married
Religion (Christian)	Percent of total population who are Christians[a]

[a]The census gives only the number of Christians for towns with more than 5 percent Christians. Six of the towns used here have fewer than 5 percent Christians. The towns of Maan, Nablus, Tulkarm, and Aqaba have been assumed to have 2.5 percent Christians. It has been assumed that all the Christians living in Hebron District live in the capital city of Hebron (which is then 0.44 percent Christian). Aljun District is 4.1 percent Christian; since the Christians are more likely to live in urban areas, it has been assumed that Irbid Town (in Aljun District) is 4.5 percent Christian.

Table D-2
Jordanian Administrative Units Used in Regression Analyses[a]

Code Number	Name	Districts Contain the Following Towns (code no.) Which Were Removed to Create Rural Districts
1	Amman District	9, 17
2	Balqa District	10
3	Ajlun District	11
4	Karak District	12
5	Ma'a District	13, 21
6	Hebron District[b]	14
7	Jerusalem District[b]	15, 18, 19
8	Nablus District[b]	16, 20
9	Amman City	
10	Salt Town	
11	Irbid Town	
12	Karak Town	
13	Ma'an Town	
14	Hebron Town	
15	Jerusalem Town	
16	Nablus Town	
17	Zarqa Town	
18	Bethlehem, Beit Jala, and Beit Shaur Towns	
19	Ramallah and Biro Towns	
20	Tulkarm Town	
21	Aquaba Town	

[a]Total sample consists of 21 regions, 8 "rural" and 13 "urban."
[b]West Bank districts.

Table D-3

Fertility of Jordanian Women Aged 15-49

(dependent variable is children 0-4 per 1,000 women 15-49)

	Constant	Death Incidence among Children Born to These Women	Females 15-49			Children				Socioeconomic Population Characteristics			R^2
			Economic Activity in Nonagriculture	Education	Marriage	Unpaid Family Workers	Economic Activity	School	Agriculture	Urban	No Toilet	Christian	
	355.309	+233.426 (0.81)	-0.123 (-1.22)			+0.156 (0.03)		+3.682 (1.29)					0.1736
	604.853	+172.229 (0.55)	-13.747 (-1.33)				-3.206 (-0.10)	+1.503 (0.41)	-1.301 (-0.96)				0.2222
	564.940	+140.521 (0.45)	-15.914 (-1.53)				-2.122 (-0.07)	+1.515 (0.46)		+90.05 (1.25)			0.2517
	695.452	+200.988 (0.68)	-12.451 (-1.26)				-0.592 (-0.19)	-0.504 (-0.12)			-1.975 (-1.41)		0.2708
	145.863	+192.714 + (0.70)	+7.570 (0.58)	-10.265 (-2.18)			+39.394 (1.21)	+8.296 (2.57)					0.3727
	55.807	-540.023 (-3.82)	-1.958 (0.35)	-2.478 (-1.13)	+16.422 (8.77)		+0.977 (0.07)	+6.258 (4.24)				-1.714 (-1.55)	0.9097
Children 0-4 per 1,000 women 15-49													
Mean of variable	808.018	1.366	5.008	16.389	73.263	5.965	2.319	52.781	27.041	0.619	30.043	8.725	
Standard deviation	87.685	0.088	3.419	12.375	7.261	5.866	0.830	14.540	28.822	0.498	32.720	10.818	

480

Table D-4

Fertility of Jordanian Women Aged 15-49

(dependent variable is children 5-9 per 1,000 women 15-49)

| | | Females 15-49 | | | Children | | | | Socioeconomic Population Characteristics | | | |
Constant	Death Incidence among Children Born to These Women	Economic Activity in Nonagriculture	Education	Marriage	Unpaid Family Workers	Economic Activity	School	Agriculture	Urban	No Toilet	Christian	R²
763.453	+131.858 (0.70)	+9.433 (1.43)			-1.132 (-0.33)		-6.018 (-3.23)					0.6189
1326.468	-41.884 (-0.24)	+9.408 (1.64)				-35.227 (-1.99)	-9.916 (-4.86)	-1.623 (-2.15)				0.7394
1235.893	-64.003 (-0.37)	+7.291 (1.27)				-32.967 (-1.95)	-9.515 (-5.27)		+97.077 (2.44)			0.7559
1254.997	+15.333 (0.09)	+11.024 (1.85)				-34.015 (-1.84)	-10.261 (-4.20)					0.7168
1017.621	+56.842 (0.29)	+7.172 (0.79)	+1.975 (0.60)			-34.140 (-1.50)	-7.919 (-3.49)			-1.473 (-1.75)		0.6669
1046.196	-319.606 (-1.62)	+6.237 (0.79)	+6.310 (2.06)	+7.860 (3.01)		-58.260 (-2.78)	-9.514 (-4.62)				-1.885 (-1.22)	0.8106
Children 5-9 per 1,000 women 15-49												
Mean of variable 666.415	1.366	5.088	16.389	73.263	5.965	2.319	52.781	27.041	0.619	30.043	8.725	
Standard deviation 84.563	0.088	3.419	12.375	7.261	5.866	0.830	14.540	28.822	0.498	32.720	10.818	

Table D-5

Fertility of Jordanian Women Aged 15-19

(dependent variable is children ever born per woman 15-19)

Constant	Females 15-19				Children				Socioeconomic Population Characteristics			R^2
	Death Incidence among Children Born to These Women	Economic Activity in Nonagriculture	Education	Marriage	Unpaid Family Workers	Economic Activity	School	Agriculture	Urban	No Toilet	Christian	
0.5433	−0.1957 (−0.41)	+0.0039 (0.43)			−0.0031 (−0.76)		−0.0023 (−0.97)					0.0763
0.4918	−0.0799 (−0.17)	+0.0009 (0.10)				+0.0001 (0.01)	−0.0032 (−1.18)	−0.0016 (−1.62)				0.1857
0.2602	−0.0086 (−0.02)	−0.0017 (−0.16)				+0.0036 (0.17)	−0.0022 (−0.82)		+0.0831 (1.40)			0.1544
0.2531	+0.1731 (.34)	−0.0014 (−0.15)				+0.0010 (0.05)	−0.0038 (−1.37)			−0.0022 (−1.80)		0.2139
0.4139	−0.3321 (−0.83)	+0.0116 (1.33)	−0.0044 (−2.47)			+0.0299 (1.35)	+0.0035 (1.10)					0.3210
−0.0984	−0.1029 (−0.75)	+0.0024 (0.71)	−0.0019 (−2.80)	+0.0064 (10.33)		+0.0211 (2.73)	+0.0042 (3.67)				−0.0002 (−0.33)	0.9336
Children ever born per woman 15-19												
Mean of variable 0.189	1.173	3.981	30.185	29.584	5.965	2.319	52.781	27.041	0.619	30.043	8.725	
Standard deviation 0.061	0.060	2.491	19.580	9.406	5.866	0.830	14.540	28.822	0.498	32.720	10.818	

Table D-6

Fertility of Jordanian Women Aged 20-29

(dependent variable is children ever born per woman 20-29)

Constant	Females 20-29			Children					Socioeconomic Population Characteristics			R²
	Death Incidence among Children Born to These Women	Economic Activity in Nonagriculture	Education	Marriage	Unpaid Family Workers	Economic Activity	School	Agriculture	Urban	No Toilet	Christian	
-2.259	+3.120 (3.05)	-0.040 (-2.08)			-0.002 (-0.20)		+0.017 (2.30)					0.5504
-2.131	+3.074 (2.82)	-0.046 (-2.26)				+0.029 (0.40)	+0.016 (1.66)	-0.002 (-0.76)				.5739
-1.963	+2.867 (2.72)	-0.053 (-2.59)				+0.031 (0.45)	+0.014 (1.68)		+0.234 (1.41)			.6093
-1.777	+3.137 (3.11)	-0.044 (-2.31)				+0.018 (0.26)	+0.009 (0.93)			-0.005 (-1.55)		.6186
-2.695	+3.282 (2.98)	-0.046 (-1.77)	+0.001 (0.13)			+0.036 (0.48)	+0.019 (2.31)					.5581
-0.476	-0.256 (-0.27)	-0.016 (-0.90)	+0.015 (2.25)	+0.036 (5.30)		-0.043 (-0.85)	+0.004 (0.64)				-0.009 (-2.02)	.8603
Children ever born per woman 20-29 Mean of variable 2.267	1.250	5.801	16.610	79.737	5.965	2.319	52.781	27.041	0.619	30.043	8.725	
Standard deviation 0.274	0.071	4.234	12.347	9.015	5.866	0.830	14.540	28.822	0.498	32.720	10.818	

483

Table D-7

Fertility of Jordanian Women Aged 30-39

(dependent variable is children ever born per woman 30-39)

Constant	Females 30-39				Children				Socioeconomic Population Characteristics			R^2
	Death Incidence among Children Born to These Women	Economic Activity in Nonagriculture	Education	Marriage	Unpaid Family Workers	Economic Activity	School	Agriculture	Urban	No Toilet	Christian	
3.778	+0.365 (0.29)	−0.139 (−2.70)			+0.030 (1.22)		+0.035 (2.72)					0.3893
2.931	+0.732 (0.53)	−0.123 (−2.39)				−0.009 (−0.06)	+0.040 (2.27)	+0.009 (1.37)				0.4141
4.272	+0.453 (0.32)	−0.120 (−2.23)				−0.039 (−0.27)	+0.031 (1.87)		−0.286 (−0.81)			0.3682
4.193	+0.262 (0.19)	−0.128 (−2.36)				−0.038 (−0.26)	+0.032 (1.52)					0.3559
4.574	−0.380 (−0.33)	−0.067 (−1.32)	−0.048 (−2.63)			+0.139 (0.97)	+0.041 (3.29)			+0.004 (0.60)		0.5484
2.796	−1.651 (−1.23)	−0.008 (−0.13)	−0.015 (−0.60)	+0.047 (0.90)		−0.039 (−0.22)	+0.025 (1.66)				−0.025 (−1.64)	0.6349
Children ever born per woman 30-39												
Mean of variable 5.847	1.356	3.358	9.617	94.778	5.965	2.319	52.781	27.041	0.619	30.043	8.725	
Standard deviation 0.470	0.100	2.635	9.365	3.659	5.866	0.830	14.540	28.822	0.498	32.720	10.818	

Table D-8

Fertility of Jordanian Women Aged 40-49

(dependent variable is children ever born per woman 40-49)

Constant	Females 40-49			Marriage	Children				Socioeconomic Population Characteristics			R^2
	Death Incidence among Children Born to These Women	Economic Activity in Nonagriculture	Education		Unpaid Family Workers	Economic Activity	School	Agriculture	Urban	No Toilet	Christian	
6.265	−0.251 (−0.39)	−0.271 (−3.62)			+0.031 (1.07)		+0.039 (2.82)					0.4927
6.289	−0.192 (−0.26)	−0.251 (−3.03)				−0.026 (−0.14)	+0.037 (2.00)	+0.006 (0.77)				0.4802
7.053	−0.285 (−0.39)	−0.259 (−3.11)				−0.042 (−0.23)	+0.031 (1.79)		−0.172 (−0.40)			0.4652
7.034	−0.335 (−0.46)	−0.264 (−3.19)				−0.045 (−0.24)	+0.031 (1.34)			+0.002 (0.20)		0.4611
5.663	−0.058 (−0.10)	−0.019 (−0.18)	−0.115 (−3.10)			+0.136 (0.86)	+0.041 (3.56)					0.6710
3.814	−0.206 (−0.28)	+0.009 (0.08)	−0.064 (−1.03)	+0.028 (0.32)		−0.032 (−0.18)	+0.033 (2.93)				−0.027 (−1.83)	0.7493
Children ever born per woman 40-49 Mean of variable 7.332	1.516	2.863	5.618	96.481	5.965	2.319	52.781	27.041	0.619	30.043	8.725	
Standard deviation 0.633	0.190	2.147	6.097	3.414	5.866	0.830	14.540	28.822	0.498	32.720	10.818	

Table D-9

Fertility of Jordanian Women Aged 50 and Older

(dependent variable is children ever born per woman 50 or older)

Constant	Females 50 and Older				Children				Socioeconomic Population Characteristics			R²
	Death Incidence among Children Born to These Women	Economic Activity in Nonagriculture	Education	Marriage	Unpaid Family Workers	Economic Activity	School	Agriculture	Urban	No Toilet	Christian	
6.278	+0.495 (1.20)	−0.356 (−4.44)			−0.007 (−0.27)		+0.006 (0.56)					0.6433
7.116	+0.365 (0.79)	−0.361 (−4.30)				−0.090 (−0.60)	+0.000 (0.00)	−0.004 (−0.52)				0.6534
7.092	+0.324 (0.72)	−0.364 (−4.49)				−0.098 (−0.67)	−0.003 (−0.26)		+0.340 (0.98)			0.6683
7.949	+0.335 (0.77)	−0.359 (−4.53)				−0.111 (−0.76)	−0.011 (−0.64)			−0.008 (−1.17)		0.6765
5.625	+0.461 (1.26)	−0.051 (−0.39)	−0.187 (−2.70)			+0.125 (0.88)	+0.010 (1.23)					0.7628
11.175	+0.535 (1.43)	−0.012 (−0.11)	−0.196 (−2.12)	−0.057 (−0.85)		+0.105 (0.72)	+0.011 (1.41)				−0.029 (−2.47)	0.8396

Children ever born per woman 50 or older
Mean of variable 6.858
Standard deviation 0.644

	Death Incidence	Economic Activity in Nonagriculture	Education	Marriage	Unpaid Family Workers	Economic Activity	School	Agriculture	Urban	No Toilet
Mean of variable	1.826	1.718	1.917	96.570	5.695	2.319	52.781	27.041	0.619	30.043
Standard deviation	0.237	1.558	2.872	3.842	5.866	0.830	14.540	28.822	0.498	32.720

Table D-10

Correlation Matrixes for Logarithmic Variables Used in Regressions on Fertility of Jordanian Women[a]

	Fertility			Females (age 15-49)			Children (age 5-14)		
	Number of Children 0-4 per 1,000 Women 15-49	Number of Children 5-9 per 1,000 Women 15-49	Reciprocal of the Proportion Died among Children Ever Born to These Women[b]	Percent Economically Active in Nonagriculture	Percent with Elementary Education	Percent Ever Married	Percent Unpaid Family Workers	Percent Economically Active[c]	Percent in School
Females 15-49									
Children 5-9 per 1,000 women	0.179								
Child death incidence	0.183	0.450							
Nonagricultural activity	0.170	-0.614	-0.589						
Education	0.149	-0.700	-0.637	0.934					
Marriage	0.564	0.698	0.746	-0.599	-0.646				
Children									
Unpaid family workers	-0.216	0.488	0.333	-0.609	-0.758	0.322			
Economic activity	-0.134	0.250	-0.029	-0.328	-0.322	0.208	0.398		
School	0.265	-0.751	-0.523	0.908	0.934	-0.574	-0.685	-0.489	
Religion Christian[d]	-0.191	-0.309	-0.449	0.468	0.541	-0.406	-0.574	-0.186	0.369

[a] All variables are expressed as logarithms to the base 10.
[b] If parents desire a surviving number of children, this goal, multiplied by the reciprocal of the child death rate, yields the number of births required to achieve, on average, the parents' goal. The child death variable constructed here should, under these conditions, enter linearly in the parents' reproductive behavioral equation estimated in logarithmic form.
[c] Percent of economically active population who are enumerated as unpaid family workers.
[d] Percent of total population who are Christians.

487

Table D-11
Correlation Matrixes for Variables Used in Regressions on Fertility of Jordanian Women[a]

	Females 15-19					Children		
	Children Ever Born per Woman 15-19	Reciprocal the Proportion Died among Children Ever Born to These Women[b]	Percent Economically Active in Nonagriculture	Percent with Elementary Education	Percent Ever Married	Percent Unpaid Family Workers	Percent Economically Active[c]	Percent in School
Females 15-19								
Child death incidence	0.033							
Nonagricultural activity	0.104	-0.683						
Education	-0.036	-0.862	0.894					
Marriage	0.812	0.421	-0.328	-0.517				
Children								
Unpaid family workers	-0.154	0.753	-0.628	-0.734	0.170			
Economic activity	0.131	0.327	-0.328	-0.363	0.253	0.398		
School	0.015	-0.817	0.875	-0.485	-0.485	-0.685	-0.487	
Religion								
Christian[d]	-0.260	-0.479	0.471	0.481	-0.338	-0.574	-0.186	0.369

[a]See Table D-10.

Table D-12
Correlation Matrixes for Variables Used in Regressions on Fertility of Jordanian Women[a]

	Females 20-29					Children		
	Children Ever Born per Woman 20-29	Reciprocal of the Proportion Died among Children Ever Born to These Women[b]	Percent Economically Active in Nonagriculture	Percent with Elementary Education	Percent Ever Married	Percent Unpaid Family Workers	Percent Economically Active[c]	Percent in School
Females 20-29								
Child death incidence	0.583							
Nonagricultural activity	−0.280	−0.739						
Education	−0.190	−0.793	0.872					
Marriage	0.806	0.815	−0.611	−0.616				
Children								
Unpaid family workers	0.080	0.532	−0.626	−0.745	0.304			
Economic activity	−0.045	0.191	−0.355	−0.369	0.154	0.398		
School	−0.125	−0.718	0.896	0.917	0.531	−0.685	−0.487	
Religion:								
Christian[d]	−0.383	−0.553	0.466	0.563	−0.377	−0.574	−0.186	0.369

[a]See Table D-10.

489

Table D-13
Correlation Matrixes for Variables Used in Regressions on Fertility of Jordanian Women[a]

	Females 30-39					Children		
	Children Ever Born per Woman 30-39	Reciprocal of the Proportion Died among Children Ever Born to These Women[b]	Percent Economically Active in Nonagriculture	Percent with Elementary Education	Percent Ever Married	Percent Unpaid Family Workers	Percent Economically Active[c]	Percent in School
Females 30-39								
Child death incidence	0.025							
Nonagricultural activity	0.060	−0.665						
Education	0.208	−0.632	0.878					
Marriage	0.228	0.739	−0.728	−0.609				
Children								
Unpaid family workers	−0.052	0.348	−0.527	−0.698	0.382			
Economic activity	−0.228	0.098	−0.296	−0.311	0.174	0.398		
School	0.338	−0.595	0.870	0.945	−0.602	−0.685	−0.487	
Religion								
Christian[d]	−0.372	−0.507	0.423	0.509	−0.513	−0.574	−0.186	0.369

[a]See Table D-10.

490

Table D-14

Correlation Matrixes for Variables Used in Regressions on Fertility of Jordanian Women[a]

	Females 40-49					Children		
	Children Ever Born per Woman 40-49	Reciprocal of the Proportion Died among Children Ever Born to These Women[b]	Percent Economically Active in Nonagriculture	Percent with Elementary Education	Percent Ever Married	Percent Unpaid Family Workers	Percent Economically Active[c]	Percent in School
Females 40-49								
Child death incidence	0.183							
Nonagricultural activity	0.039	−0.187						
Education	−0.121	−0.192	0.869					
Marriage	0.516	0.462	−0.408	−0.613				
Children								
Unpaid family workers	0.079	−0.100	−0.429	−0.723	0.372			
Economic activity	−0.262	−0.297	−0.210	−0.243	0.134	0.398		
School	0.173	−0.081	0.846	0.899	−0.531	−0.685	−0.487	
Religion								
Christian[d]	−0.523	−0.135	0.321	0.576	−0.507	−0.574	−0.186	0.369

[a] See Table D-10.

Table D-15
Correlation Matrixes for Variables Used in Regressions on Fertility of Jordanian Women[a]

	Children Ever Born per Woman 50 or over	Reciprocal of the Proportion Died among Children Ever Born to These Women[b]	Percent Economically Active in Nonagriculture	Percent with Elementary Education	Percent Ever Married	Percent Unpaid Family Workers	Percent Economically Active[c]	Percent in School
		Females 50 or Over				Children		
Females 50 or over								
Child death incidence	0.272							
Nonagricultural activity	−0.577	−0.081						
Education	−0.611	−0.210	0.902					
Marriage	0.844	0.303	0.658	0.655				
Children								
Unpaid family workers	0.297	−0.085	−0.718	−0.708	0.325			
Economic activity	−0.010	−0.303	−0.390	−0.168	0.140	0.398		
School	−0.318	−0.096	0.894	0.856	−0.441	−0.685	−0.487	
Religion								
Christian[d]	−0.560	−0.165	−0.515	0.582	−0.475	−0.574	−0.186	0.369

[a]See Table D-10.

492

Bibliography

Abdel-Aty, S. H., 1961, "Life-Table Functions for Egypt Based on Model Life-Tables and Quasi-Stable Population Theory," *Milbank Memorial Fund Quarterly,* Vol. 39, No. 2 (April), pp. 350–377.

Abu-Lughod, Janet, 1961, "Migrant Adjustment to City Life: The Egyptian Case," *American Journal of Sociology,* Vol. 67, No. 1 (July).

——, 1964, "Urban-Rural Differences as a Function of the Demographic Transition: Egyptian Data and an Analytical Model," *American Journal of Sociology,* Vol. 69, No. 5 (March), pp. 476–490.

——, 1965a, "Urbanization in Egypt: Present State and Future Prospect," *Economic Development and Cultural Change,* Vol. 23 (April), pp. 313–343.

——, 1965b, "The Emergence of Differential Fertility in Urban Egypt," *Milbank Memorial Fund Quarterly,* Vol. 43, No. 2 (April), pp. 235–253.

Aref, Marzouk Abdel Rahim, 1964, "Fertility of Married Women in Cairo," North African Demographic Centre, Cairo, November.

Ayrout, Henry Habib, S. J. (trans. J. A. Williams), 1963, *The Egyptian Peasant,* Beacon Press, Boston.

Baer, Gabriel, 1966, *Population and Society in the Arab East,* Frederick A. Praeger, New York.

Ben-Porath, Yoram, 1966, *The Arab Labor Force in Israel,* Maurice Falk Institute for Economic Research in Israel, Jerusalem, October.

Bogue, Donald J., and James A. Palmore, 1964, "Some Empirical and Analytic Relations Among Demographic Fertility Measures, with Regression Models for Fertility Estimation," *Demography,* Vol. 1, No. 1, pp. 316–338.

Cho, Lee Jay, 1964, "Estimated Refined Measures of Fertility for All Major Countries of the World," *Demography,* Vol. 1, No. 1, pp. 359–374.

Christ, Carl F., 1966, *Econometric Models and Methods,* John Wiley, New York.

Cleland, W. Wendell, 1944, "A Population Plan for Egypt," *Milbank Memorial Fund Quarterly,* Vol. 22, No. 4 (October), pp. 409–423.

——, 1936, *The Population Problem in Egypt,* Science Press Printing Co., Lancaster, Pa.

Coale, Ansley J., 1956, "The Effect of Declines in Mortality on Age Distribution," in *Trends and Differentials in Mortality,* Milbank Memorial Fund, New York.

—— and Edgar M. Hoover, 1958, *Population Growth and Economic Development in Low-Income Countries,* Princeton University Press, Princeton, N.J.

—— and Paul Demeny, 1966, *Regional Model Life Tables and Stable Populations,* Princeton University Press, Princeton, N.J.

Da Vanzo, Julie, 1968, "An Analysis of Infant Mortality in Egypt," unpublished paper, March.

Demeny, Paul, 1968, "The Demography of the Sudan: An Analysis of the 1955/56 Census," in William Brass et al., *The Demography of Tropical Africa,* Princeton University Press, Princeton, N.J.

Denison, Edward F., 1967, *Why Growth Rates Differ,* Brookings Institution, Washington, D.C.

El Badry, M. A., 1955, "Some Demographic Measurements for Egypt Based on the Stability of Census Age Distributions," *Milbank Memorial Fund Quarterly,* Vol. 33, No. 3 (July), pp. 268–305.

——, 1956, "Some Aspects of Fertility in Egypt," *Milbank Memorial Fund Quarterly,* Vol. 34 (January), pp. 22–43.

——, 1965, "Trends in the Components of Population Growth in the Arab Countries of the Middle East: A Survey of Present Information," *Demography,* Vol. 2, pp. 140–186.

——— and Hanna Rizk, 1967, "Regional Fertility Differences Among Socio-Economic Groups in the United Arab Republic," *World Population Conference, 1965,* Belgrade, 30 August–10 September, United Nations, New York, Vol. II, pp. 137–141.

El Daly, El Sayed Abdel Hamid, 1953, "The Birth Rate and Fertility Trends in Egypt," *L'Egypte Contemporaine,* Tome 274, October, pp. 1–12.

El-Darwish, M., and H. El-S. Azmi, 1934, "A Note on the Population of Egypt," *Population* (London), February, pp. 43–56.

El Donoushary, R. A. (no date), "Some Factors Affecting Fertility of Women in the United Arab Republic," North African Demographic Centre, Cairo.

El Henawi, N. H. (no date), "Preparation of Abridged Life Tables for the U.A.R. and the Governorate of Alexandria," North African Demographic Centre, Cairo.

Eliot, Johan W. (no date), "Urban-Rural and Berber-Arab Differential in Desired Numbers of Male Children and Related Factors in Algeria," Center for Population Planning, University of Michigan.

El-Koussy, A. A. H., 1966, *A Survey of Educational Progress in the Arab States, 1960–1965,* Regional Centre for the Advanced Training for Educational Personnel in the Arab States, Beirut. Prepared for UNESCO Conference of Arab Ministers of Education, Tripoli, Libya, March 5–10.

——, 1967, "Recent Development in Education in the Arab Middle East," *International Education Review,* pp. 198–211.

——, 1968, *Trends of Educational Research in the Arab World,* Regional Centre for Educational Planning and Administration in the Arab States, Beirut, March 19.

Elmolla, Mohamed (no date), "Induced Abortion as Means of Fertility Control in Family Planning," North African Demographic Centre, Cairo.

Enke, Stephen, 1960, "The Economics of Government Payments to Limit Population," *Economic Development and Cultural Change,* Vol. 8, No. 4 (July).

——, 1966, "The Economic Aspects of Slowing Population Growth," *Economic Journal,* Vol. 74, No. 301 (March).

Fisher, W. B., 1950, *The Middle East,* E. P. Dutton and Co., New York.

Gadalla, Saad, 1968, "Population Problems and Family Planning Programs in Egypt," paper presented at the VIIIth International Congress of Anthropological and Ethnological Sciences, Tokyo, Japan, September 3–10.

Grais, Munir, Deward E. Waggoner, and Parker Malden, 1956, "The Role of Mortality in Recent Population Trends in Egypt," *Journal of the Egyptian Public Health Association,* Vol. 31, Nos. 4 and 5.

Grunwald, Kurt, and Joachim O. Ronall, 1960, *Industrialization in the Middle East,* Council for Middle Eastern Affairs Press, New York.

Hamza, Muzhtar, et al., 1967, *Research Report on Employment Problems in Rural Areas, U.A.R. Report F on Impact of Social and Educational Policy,* United Arab Republic Institute of National Planning.

Hansen, Bent, 1965, "The Distributive Shares in Egyptian Agriculture, 1897–1961," Memo. No. 583, United Arab Republic, Institute of National Planning, Cairo, June.

——, 1966, "Marginal Productivity Wage Theory and Subsistence Theory in Egyptian Agriculture," *Journal of Development Studies,* Vol. II, No. 4 (July), pp. 367–399.

——, 1968, "The Distributive Shares in Egyptian Agriculture, 1897–1961," *International Economic Review,* Vol. 9, No. 2 (June), pp. 175–194.

—— and Girgis A. Marzouk, 1965, *Development and Economic Policy in the U.A.R. (Egypt),* North-Holland Publishing Co., Amsterdam.

Harbison, Fred, and Ibrahim Abdul-Qadir, 1958, *Human Resources for Egyptian Enterprise,* McGraw-Hill, New York.

Hassan, S., 1966, "Influence of Child Mortality on Fertility," paper presented at annual meeting of the Population Association of America, New York City, April.

Heer, David, 1968, "Economic Development and the Fertility Transition," *Daedalus,* Spring.

Holler, Joanne E., 1964, *Population Growth and Social Change in the Middle East,* Population Research Project, The George Washington University, Washington, D.C.

Husein, Hasan M., 1954, "Contributions to Demography Through Census Enquiries," in *Proceedings of the World Population Conference, 1954,* pp. 11–21.

——, 1963, "Demographic, Economic, and Social Factors in Fertility in U.A.R.," *Journal of Family Welfare* (Bombay), Vol. 9, No. 3 (March), pp. 40–45.

——, 1967, "Evaluation of Progress of Fertility Control in the United Arab Republic," *World Population Conference, 1965, Belgrade,* Vol. 2, pp. 142–144.

Hymer, S., and S. Resnick, 1967, "Responsiveness of Agrarian Economies and the Importance of 'Z' Goods," *Economic Growth Center Discussion Paper* No. 25, Yale University, October 1.

Institute of Statistical Studies and Research, Proceedings, Vol. 1, 1966, *Preliminary Study of Techniques for Constructions of Models For Demographic Change,* Cairo University Press, Cairo.

——, 1967, Vol. 2, *Analysis of Physical and Health Measurements of School Population* (age 6–18 years), Cairo University Press, Cairo.

International Bank for Reconstruction and Development, 1952, *The Economic Development of Iraq,* Johns Hopkins Press, Baltimore.

——, 1955, *The Economic Development of Syria,* Johns Hopkins Press, Baltimore.

——, 1957, *The Economic Development of Jordan,* Johns Hopkins Press, Baltimore.

——, 1965. *The Economic Development of Kuwait,* Johns Hopkins Press, Baltimore.

International Labor Office, 1961, "Employment of Women in Israel," *Industry and Labour* (Geneva), Vol. 26, No. 4 (15 August), pp. 146–148.

Iraq, 1964, *Statistical Abstract, 1963,* Government Press.

Iraq, Republic of (no date—1967?), Director of Technical Section, Directorate General of Civil Status Registration, *A Special Number Covering Field Operations of General Census of 1965,* Vol. 6, No. 34–35–36.

Israel, State of, Central Bureau of Statistics, 1965–66, *Marriage and Fertility,* Parts I and II, *Population and Housing Census 1961,* Publications No. 26 and 32, Jerusalem.

——, 1968, *Statistical Abstract of Israel, 1968,* No. 19, Central Bureau of Statistics, Jerusalem.

Issawi, Charles, 1963, *Egypt in Revolution, An Economic Analysis,* Oxford University Press, London.

Jordan, The Hashemite Kingdom of, 1965, Department of Statistics, *First Census of Population and Housing, 18 November 1961,* Vols. 1–4, Department of Statistics Press, Amman.

——, 1966, *Analysis of the Population Statistics of Jordan,* Vol. I, Department of Statistics Press, Amman.

Jorgenson, Dale W., 1965, "Subsistence, Agriculture and Economic Growth," *Working Paper* No. 66, Institute of Business and Economic Research, University of California, Berkeley, April.

Jurkat, Ernest, 1944, "Prospects for Population Growth in the Near East," *Milbank Memorial Fund Quarterly,* Vol. 22, No. 3 (July), pp. 300–317.

Kardouche, George K., 1966, *The U.A.R. in Development: A Study in Expansionary Finance,* Frederick A. Praeger, New York.

Khamis, Salem H., 1957, "A Report on a Pilot Infant Mortality Survey of Rural Lebanon," *Thirteenth Session of the International Statistics Institute.*

Kindleberger, C. P., 1967, *Europe's Postwar Growth: The Role of Labor Supply,* Harvard University Press, Cambridge, Mass.

Kirk, Dudley, 1967, *Factors Affecting Moslem Natality,* World Population Conference 1965, Belgrade, 30 August–10 September, United Nations, New York, Vol. II, pp. 149–154.

—— and Dorothy Nortman, 1967, "Population Policies in Developing Countries," *Economic Development and Cultural Change*, Vol. 15, No. 2, Part 1 (January), pp. 129–142.

Kiser, Clyde V., 1944, "The Demographic Position of Egypt," *Milbank Memorial Fund Quarterly*, Vol. 22, No. 4 (October), pp. 383–408.

Lapham, Robert J., 1968, "Family Planning Attitudes and Knowledge Among Married Women in Central Morocco," paper contributed to the February 1968 Annual Meeting of the Population Association of America.

Lee, Luke T. (no date), *Law and Population: A Preliminary Study of the Relation Between Population Problems and Law,* prepared for the Population Council by The Rule by Law Research Center, Duke University, Durham, N.C.

Leff, Nathaniel H., 1967, "Population Growth and Savings Potential," preliminary report to the Office of Program Coordination, Agency for International Development, Washington, D.C.

McDermott, Walsh, 1964, "The Role of Biomedical Research in International Development," *The Journal of Medical Education*, Vol. 39, No. 7 (July), pp. 655–669.

——, 1966, "Modern Medicine and the Demographic/Disease Pattern of Overly Traditional Societies: A Technological Misfit," paper presented at the Institute on International Medical Education of the Association of American Medical Colleges, Washington, D.C.

Marzouk, G. A., 1957, "Fertility of the Urban and Rural Population in Egypt," *L'Egypte Contemporaine*, Vol. 48, No. 287 (January), pp. 27–34.

Mauldin, W. Parker, 1966, "Estimating Rates of Population Growth," in B. Berelson, ed., *Family Planning and Population Programs,* University of Chicago Press, Chicago, pp. 635–654.

Mead, Donald C., 1967, *Growth and Structural Change in the Egyptian Economy,* Richard D. Irwin, Homewood, Ill.

Myrdal, Gunnar, 1968, *Asian Drama,* Pantheon, New York.

Nasrat, M. Mohiey El-Din, *Research Report on Employment Problems in Rural Areas U.A.R.,* Institute of National Planning, August.

National Bank of Egypt, 1963, "Population and Manpower," *Economic Bulletin* (Cairo), Vol. 16, Nos. 1–2, pp. 5–16.

Nelson, Joan M., 1968, "Migrants, Urban Poverty and Instability in New Nations: Critique of a Myth," Center for International Affairs, Harvard University, draft.

Nelson, R. R., Merton Peck, and Edward Kalachek, 1967, *Technology, Economic Growth, and Public Policy,* Brookings Institution, Washington, D.C.

Nelson, R. R., R. L. Slighton, and T. P. Schultz, 1971, *Structural Change in a Developing Economy,* Princeton University Press, Princeton, N.J.

Notestein, Frank W., 1944, "Problems of Policy in Relation to Areas of Heavy Population Pressure," *Milbank Memorial Fund Quarterly*, Vol. 22, No. 4 (October), pp. 424–444.

O'Brien, Patrick, 1966, *The Revolution of Egypt's Economic System,* Oxford University Press, London.

Ohlin, Goran, 1967, *Population Control and Economic Development,* Development Centre, Organization for Economic Co-operation and Development, Paris.

Ravenholt, R. T., and Harald Frederiksen, 1967, "Numerator Analysis of Fertility Patterns," paper presented at the A.I.D. African Population Conference, Kampala, Uganda, August 19–22.

Rizk, Hanna, 1959, "Fertility Patterns in Selected Areas in Egypt," unpublished Ph.D. dissertation, Princeton University, Princeton, N. J.

——, 1963a, "Population Growth and Its Effect on Economic and Social Goals in the United Arab Republic," *Population Review* (Madras), Vol. 7, No. 1 (January), pp. 51–56.

——, 1963b, "Social and Psychological Factors Affecting Fertility in the United Arab Republic," *Marriage and Family Living,* Vol. 25, No. 1 (February) pp. 69–73.

Ruprecht, Theodore K., 1961, "The Demographic Factor in Egyptian Economic Development," unpublished Ph.D. dissertation, University of California, Berkeley, Calif.

Sabagh, Georges, and Christopher Scott, 1968, "A Comparison of Different Survey Techniques for Obtaining Vital Data in a Developing Country," University of California at Los Angeles, unpublished.

Salib, Rafael, et al., 1965, *Research Report on Employment Problems in Rural U.A.R.,* Report A, *Impact of Population Trends in U.A.R. on Rural Employment,* U.A.R Institute of National Planning, Cairo.

Schieffelin, Olivia, ed., 1967, *Muslim Attitudes Toward Family Planning,* Demographic Division, The Population Council, Inc., New York.

Schultz, T. Paul, 1969a, *Population Growth and Internal Migration in Colombia,* RM–5765–AID, The Rand Corporation, Santa Monica, Calif., March.

——, 1969b, "The Effectiveness of Family Planning in Taiwan: A Proposal for a New Evaluation Methodology," P–4069, The Rand Corporation, Santa Monica, Calif., April.

——, 1969c, "Population Growth: Investigation of a Hypothesis," P–4056, The Rand Corporation, Santa Monica, Calif., April.

——, 1969d, "An Economic Model of Family Planning and Fertility," *Journal of Political Economy,* Vol. 77, No. 2 (March/April), pp. 153–180.

Scrimshaw, Nevin, 1966, "Pre-School Child Malnutrition: Primary Deterrent to Human Progress," *An International Conference on Prevention of Malnutrition in the Pre-School Child,* Washington, D.C., December 7–11, 1964, National Academy of Sciences, Publication 1282, Washington, D.C.

Seklani, M. M., 1962, "Population Active et Structures Economiques de L'Egypte," *Population* (Paris), Vol. 17, No. 3 (July-September), pp. 465–490.

498

Shafei, Abdel Moreim N., 1960, "The Current Labour Force Sample Survey in Egypt (U.A.R.)," *International Labour Review* (Geneva), Vol. 82, No. 5 (November), pp. 432–449.

——, ed., 1968, *Egyptian Population and Family Planning Review,* Vol. I, No. 1, The Egyptian Society for Population Research and Institute for Statistical Studies and Research, Cairo University Press, Cairo, May.

Shanawany, Haifa, 1967, "Family Planning: An Equilibrium Response to Demographic Conditions in the United Arab Republic (Egypt)," unpublished doctoral thesis, Cornell University, Ithaca, N.Y., University Microfilms, Ann Arbor, Mich.

——, 1968, "Overall Aspects of the Population Problem in the United Arab Republic (Egypt)," July, article prepared for the *Middle-East–North African Review.*

Shawky, Karnal El Din, 1965, "Births and Birth Control in the United Arab Republic: A Study in the Assessment of Attitudes," *Journal of the Egyptian Public Health Association,* Vol. 40, No. 3.

Shorter, Frederic C., 1968, "Information on Fertility, Mortality and · Population Growth in Turkey," *Population Index,* Vol. 34, No. 1 (January-March), pp. 3–21.

Simon, Julian L., 1968, "A Huge Marketing Task—Birth Control," *Journal of Marketing Research,* Vol. 5 (February), pp. 21–27.

Southam, Anna L., 1966, "Contraceptive Methods: Use, Safety and Effectiveness," in B. Berelson, ed., *Family Planning and Population Programs,* University of Chicago Press, Chicago.

Stolnitz, George J., 1956, "Comparison Between Some Recent Mortality Trends in Underdeveloped Areas and Historical Trends in the West," in *Trends and Differentials in Mortality,* Milbank Memorial Fund, New York.

Sutter, J., 1969, "The Action of Birth Limitation on Genetic Composition of Populations" in R. Freedman et al., ed., *Fertility and Family Planning: A World View,* University of Michigan Press, Ann Arbor, Mich.

Symposium on Family Planning, 1963, *Journal of the Egyptian Medical Association,* Special Number.

United Arab Republic (no date), *Population Census of Egypt, 1947,* General Tables, Government Press, Cairo.

——, Statistics and Census Department, *Vital Statistics,* Vol. I, 1952 through 1960.

——, 1964, *1960 Census of All Egypt,* Cairo.

United Nations, 1964, Department of Economic and Social Affairs, *Provisional Report on World Population Prospects as Assessed in 1963,* New York.

——, 1966, Economic Commission for Africa, "Demographic Projections for North African Countries," Sub-Regional Meeting on Economic Cooperation in North Africa, Tangier, 20–27 June 1966 (United Nations Economic and Social Council).

——, 1967a, Department of Economic and Social Affairs, *Population Studies* No. 42, Manual IV: *Methods of Estimating Basic Demographic Measures from Incomplete Data,* ST/SOA/Series A/42, New York.

——, 1967b, *Studies on Selected Development Problems in Various Countries in the Middle East,* United Nations Economic and Social Office in Beirut, New York.

——, 1968, Educational, Scientific, and Cultural Organization Regional Centre, *Regional Seminar of Technical Assistance on Investments in Education in the Arab States: Expenditures, Cost and Financing of Education in the Arab States,* Study prepared by Regional Centre for Educational Planning and Administration in the Arab States, Beirut, 16–24 September, Paris, 30th July 1968, 68/OEA/43/300/32–7115.

United States Bureau of Labor Statistics, 1965, *Labor Law and Practice in the U.A.R.,* BLS Report No. 275.

Weir, John M., 1952, "An Evaluation of Health and Sanitation in Egyptian Villages," *Journal of the Egyptian Public Health Association,* Vol. 27, No. 3, pp. 55–122.

Wheeler, D. K., 1966, "Educational Problems in Arab Countries," *International Review of Education,* Vol. 12, No. 3, pp. 300–315.

Yaukey, David, 1961, *Fertility Differences in a Modernizing Country: A Survey of Lebanese Couples,* Princeton University Press, Princeton, N. J.

——, 1963, "Some Immediate Determinants of Fertility Differences in Lebanon," *Marriage and Family Living,* Vol. 25, No. 1 (February), pp. 27–34.

Zaidan, Farouk Georges, 1967, "Benefits and Costs of Population Control with Special Reference to the U.A.R. (Egypt)," unpublished Ph.D. dissertation, Harvard University, Cambridge, Mass.

Zikry, Abdel-Khalik M., 1963, "Socio-Cultural Determinants of Human Fertility in Egypt, U.A.R.," unpublished Ph.D. dissertation, Syracuse University, Syracuse, N.Y., University Microfilms, Inc., Ann Arbor, Mich.

——, 1964, "Urbanization and Its Effects on the Levels of Fertility of U.A.R. Women," *L'Egypte Contemporaine,* No. 316, October, pp. 27–42.

CHAPTER 10

Fertility in Israel,
an Economist's Interpretation:
Differentials and Trends, 1950-1970

Yoram Ben-Porath*

* In this paper I have drawn on my current research at the Maurice Falk Institute for Economic Research
in Israel. In the preparation of the manuscript I benefited
greatly from the cooperation of the Central Bureau of Statistics, particularly the staff of the Demographic Department
and the Labor Section. Professor Haim Barkai of the Maurice
Falk Institute, Jerusalem, kindly made available to me his
unpublished data on the kibbutzim in Israel. Research assistance was provided by Miss Lea Kfir, Mr. Aharon Bartal,
and Mr. Avner Halevy. Miss Susanne Freund edited the manuscript, and her comments contributed as much to the substance as to the form of the paper.

An earlier version of this paper was read by Dr. Alvin
Harman and Dr. T. Paul Schultz of The Rand Corporation,
Professor Judah Matras and Professor Helmut Muhsam of
the Hebrew University, Professor Simon Kuznets, and Professor T. W. Schultz. Their comments (and doubts) helped
me to weed out some of the errors and clarify some obscure
passages. The responsibility for any remaining deficiencies
rests with me.

Ben-Porath explores for Israel, as Schultz does for the Arab Middle East, the evidence in support of the basic hypothesis that the number of children families have depends on how many they want. To some, analyzing family desires for children in terms of price and income effects may seem too mechanistic to be believable. The answer to this is that it works: such a model can explain a large number of the differences in family size. The problem is partly one of language; using the metaphors of the marketplace seems somehow wrong and even offensive. In fact, the terminology is simply a convenient shorthand for describing complex social processes, not accounting decisions.

One of the interesting aspects of Ben-Porath's paper is that it shows how powerful an influence on population growth social and economic variables are even in a country where public policy encourages rather than limits population growth. Without detailed knowledge of the influences on desired family size, public programs will be constrained to limited effectiveness. Two other pieces of evidence in Ben-Porath's essay merit comment: the absence of a negative education effect on fertility in kibbutzim, and the existence of a positive income effect for the Arab population. Both of these pieces of evidence confirm that there is no simple sociological explanation for fertility and that what is at work is better understood in the relatively more complex model of income and price effects that Ben-Porath applies. A positive income effect does not mean that, as incomes rise, fertility will increase. It means only that, if incomes rise and nothing else changes, families may decide to "spend" more of their income on additional children. In the real world, rising incomes are usually associated with many other effects; and changes in fertility reflect the influence of all of these, not just the income variable.

Fertility in Israel,
an Economist's Interpretation:
Differentials and Trends, 1950-1970

I. Main Trends in Fertility and Associated Variables

Introduction

The population of Israel is composed of two groups, Jews and non-Jews (mostly Arabs) of distinct socioeconomic, cultural, and demographic characteristics. At the end of 1968 the Jewish population was 2,435,000, and the non-Jewish population was about 406,000, of whom 69,000 lived in Jerusalem. (In the subsequent analysis I refer mostly to the non-Jewish population excluding those in East Jerusalem.)

The main source of growth of the Jewish population has been immigration. Over 1948–1968 the Jewish population grew at an average annual rate of 6.8 percent, to which net migration contributed almost two-thirds (Table 10-1). Immigration was uneven; the largest influx was the "mass immigration" of 1948–1951, when the Jewish population more than doubled. In terms of countries of origin and the revelant correlates, these immigrants differed drastically from the pre-1948 population; and there were also differences among the various waves of immigration during the period under review.

The high proportion of foreign-born means that a large part of the country's Jewish population has spent a significant portion of its formative and child-bearing years under economic and other conditions totally different from those prevailing in Israel. The passage from one set of conditions to another and the subsequent adjustment process necessitate a more dynamic view of the past than would otherwise be called for and make it more difficult to identify stable relationships that may be useful for predicting the future. Also, of course, some of the relationships among various demographic characteristics present in a stable population cannot be assumed. Within the Jewish population the classification by continent of birth and length of residence is the least that can be done to control for these special conditions. Variations in the demographic characteristics within each continent-of-birth group suggest that this may not be adequate. Within the non-Jewish population it is necessary to distinguish among Moslems, Christians, and Druse.

On the economic scene, it should be noted that the Israeli economy has experienced a relatively high rate of growth—over 1950–1965, total real GNP rose at an annual rate of 11.4 percent and per capita GNP at 6.3 percent. (The years

Table 10-1

Sources of Increase of Population, 1948-1968

(thousands)

	Population at Beginning of Period	Natural Increase	Migration Balance	Total Increase	Population at End of Period	Annual Rate of Increase (percent)	Migration as Percent of Total Increase
Jews							
1948-68	649.6	673.6	1,111.6	1,785.2	2,434.8	6.6	62.3
1948-51	649.6	88.4	666.4	754.8	1,404.4	23.7	88.3
1952-54	1,404.4	101.4	20.2	121.6	1,526.0	2.8	16.6
1955-57	1,526.0	100.7	136.1	236.8	1,762.8	4.9	57.5
1958-64	1,762.8	235.7	240.7	476.4	2,239.2	3.9	50.5
1965-67	2,239.2	108.9	35.5	144.4	2,383.6	2.1	24.6
1967-68	2,344.9	72.9	17.0	89.9	2,434.8	1.9	18.9
Non-Jews							
1950-68[a]	160.0	174.8	-1.0	246.3	406.3	4.0	0.0
1950-51	160.0	11.4	2.0	13.4	173.4	4.1	14.9
1952-54	173.4	18.2	0.2	18.4	191.8	3.4	1.1
1955-57	191.8	21.2	0.2	21.4	213.2	3.5	0.9
1958-64	213.2	70.1	-0.8	69.1	286.4	4.6	-1.2
1965-67	286.4	38.6	-0.5	38.1	324.3[b]	4.4	-1.3
1967-68[a]	312.5	27.6	-2.4	25.2	406.3	4.0	-9.5

[a]Non-Jewish population of East Jerusalem included.
[b]Non-Jewish population of East Jerusalem excluded.

Source: Central Bureau of Statistics, *Statistical Abstract of Israel 1969*, No. 20, p. 21, Table B/2.

1965–1967 were a period of depression and no growth, but it appears that by 1968 the economy was back to its "normal" pace.)

Major Demographic Characteristics

Several major demographic characteristics emerge from Table 10-2. The Jewish population constitutes more than 85 percent of the total. By comparison, the non-Jewish population is younger and has much higher fertility; these differences are reflected by the birth rate, family size, and total fertility[1] (see columns 4–6.).

There is no difference to speak of in the crude death rate, but the non-Jewish population has a lower life expectancy at birth and a higher infant mortality (column 8). Jews from Europe-America (EA) have lower fertility than those from Asia-Africa (AA), with the Israel-born closer to the former; the mortality of EA Jews is only slightly lower.

The AA group becomes more similar to the EA group with greater length of residence; among the Israel-born, those of AA parentage have lower fertility than their parents. The convergence is mostly toward the lower fertility levels (data not shown).

The non-Jewish population, as mentioned earlier, consists of Arabs (Moslem and Christian), Druse, and a few non-Arab Christians. Of the total, about three-quarters are Moslems, less than one-fifth are Christians, and the rest are Druse. As Table 10-2 shows, there are sharp differences between the Moslems and the Christians. The total fertility of Christians is less than half that of Moslems, and a little less than that of AA Jews; Christians marry later than Moslems and slightly later than Jews (data not shown), and their age structure is closer to the Jewish than the Moslem age structure; the infant mortality of Christians is lower than that in the Moslem population. The total fertility and infant mortality of the Druse are high, but fertility is somewhat lower than among the Moslems; age at marriage is lower for the Druse than for any other population group.

Trends Over Time

Some of the major demographic series are presented in Table 10-3 and Figure 10-1. The total fertility of the Jewish population declined by 0.6 of a child from 1951 to 1968, or by 15 percent of the initial level.[2] The birth rate declined by 9.9 births per thousand. Over the period, the AA group experienced the greatest decline in total fertility, by 2 children, or almost one-third of the initial level. The total fertility of the EA and the Israel-born declined by about one-fifth of the initial level.

The years 1951–1966 can be divided into three equal periods. In the first of these, fertility declined steeply in all three origin groups (most steeply in the Is-

[1] Total fertility represents the average number of children a woman is expected to bear during her lifetime; it is calculated by single years from the unweighted sum of *current* age-specific birth rate. No allowance is made for the incidence of mortality.
[2] I leave the 1950 figure out of this discussion because it is markedly out of the long-term trend.

505

Table 10-2

Some Demographic Characteristics, 1968

	Population By Group (1)	Population By Subgroup (2)	Median Age, 1967 (3)	Average Family Size[a] (4)	Fertility Birth Rate[b] (5)	Fertility Total Fertility[c] (6)	Mortality Death Rate[b] (7)	Mortality Infant Mortality[d] (8)	Average Age of Single Brides, 1967 (9)
Total population	100.0		23.2	3.8	25.5		6.8	24.8	
Jews									
Total	85.7	100.0	24.7	3.6	22.8	3.4	6.9	20.3	22.6
Israel born	37.7	44.0	11.4	3.3		2.9			23.3
Asia-Africa born	23.3	27.2	32.5	4.7		4.3			21.9
Veterans[e]			48.6	4.4					
New immigrants				4.7					
1948-54			34.9			4.1			21.1
1955-60			28.3			4.5			21.6
1961+			21.6			5.1			23.4
Europe-America born	24.7	28.8	49.1	2.9		2.6			22.3
Veterans[e]			55.1	2.9					
New immigrants				2.9					
1948-54			46.7			2.6			21.4
1955-60			42.3			2.5			23.0
1961+			41.3			3.1			24.1
Non-Jews									
Total	14.3	100.0	14.8	5.8	45.1	7.7	6.1	42.4	
Moslems	10.6	74.1	13.6		49.5	8.9	6.2	43.0	
Christians	2.5	17.5	20.2		29.2	4.1	6.1	35.2	
Druse and others	1.2	8.4	15.4		43.1	7.6	5.4	46.1	

[a]Including single persons. [b]Per thousand population. [c]See note a in Table 10-3. [d]Per thousand live births. [e]Immigrated before 1948.

Source: Abstract 1968, No. 19; Abstract 1969, No. 20; and unpublished data of the Central Bureau of Statistics.

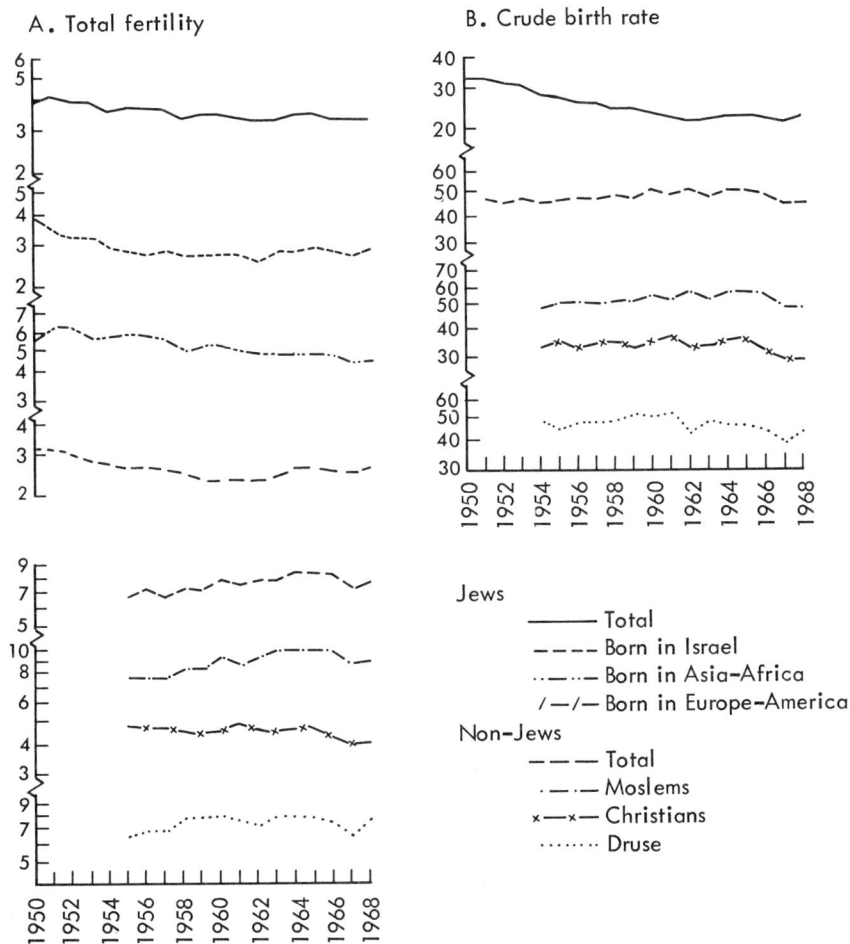

FIG. 10-1. Fertility trends: 1950–1968 (semi-log scale). Source: Table 10-2.

rael-born group). In the second period AA fertility declined faster (absolutely and relatively) than before, and the decline continued—much more slowly—in the third period. The fertility of EA declined in the second period (rather less than in the first) and in the third period rose to return to the 1956 level. The same is true of the Israel-born, although here the fluctuation was so small that in practice the rate can be considered stable over the 10 years. The net effect is that there was no change in total fertility of the whole Jewish population over 1961–1966. A depression in 1966/67 caused a dip in the fertility of all groups.

Table 10-3

Fertility Indicators: 1950-1968

a. Total Fertility[a]

	Jews				Non-Jews			
	Total (1)	Israel (2)	Asia-Africa (3)	Europe-America (4)	Total (5)	Moslems (6)	Christians (7)	Druse (8)
1. Annual data								
1950	3.9	3.9	5.6	3.2	..	..	..	..
1951	4.0	3.6	6.3	3.2	..	..	..	..
1952	4.0	3.3	6.2	3.0	..	..	..	..
1953	3.9	3.2	5.6	2.8	..	..	..	..
1954	3.6	2.9	5.7	2.7	..	..	..	..
1955	3.6	2.8	5.7	2.6	6.9	7.7	4.8	6.5
1956	3.7	2.8	5.6	2.6	7.3	7.6	4.7	6.9
1957	3.6	2.8	5.4	2.6	6.9	..	..	..
1958	3.4	2.7	4.9	2.5	7.3	8.3	4.5	7.7
1959	3.5	2.7	5.2	2.3	7.4	..	..	..
1960	3.5	2.8	5.1	2.4	8.0	9.3	4.6	7.9
1961	3.4	2.7	4.8	2.3	7.6	8.6	4.9	7.5
1962	3.3	2.5	4.6	2.3	7.9	9.3	4.6	7.2
1963	3.4	2.5	4.6	2.4	7.8	9.8	4.6	7.8
1964	3.4	2.8	4.6	2.6	8.4	9.9	4.7	7.8
1965	3.5	2.9	4.6	2.6	8.4	9.9	4.7	7.7
1966	3.4	2.8	4.5	2.5	8.2	9.7	4.3	7.4
1967	3.2	2.7	4.2	2.4	7.4	8.6	4.0	6.5
1968	3.4	2.9	4.3	2.6	7.7	8.9	4.1	7.6
2. Absolute change over period								
1951-56	−0.3	−0.8	−0.7	−0.6	..	..	..	..
1956-61	−0.3	−0.1	−0.8	−0.3	+0.3	+1.0	+0.2	+0.6
1961-66	0.0	+0.1	−0.3	+0.2	+0.6	+1.1	−0.3	−0.1
1951-68	−0.6	−0.7	−2.0	−0.6	..	..	..	..

[a] Average number of children a woman is expected to bear during her lifetime, calculated by single years from the unweighted sum of *current* age-specific birth rates.

Table 10-3 (cont'd)
Fertility Indicators: 1950-1968
b. Birth Rate[b]

| | Jews (1) | Total (2) | Non-Jews | | |
			Moslems (3)	Christians (4)	Druse (5)
1. Annual data					
1950	33.0	...	...	...	...
1951	32.7	46.5	...	...	...
1952	31.6	45.6	...	...	...
1953	30.2	48.4	...	...	...
1954	27.4	45.1	48.8	33.6	48.0
1955	27.2	46.0	50.0	34.8	44.5
1956	26.7	47.1	51.7	33.8	47.1
1957	26.0	46.7	50.6	34.5	47.1
1958	24.1	48.0	51.1	34.6	49.3
1959	24.3	47.4	51.6	33.6	51.0
1960	23.9	50.3	55.2	35.8	50.0
1961	22.5	49.3	53.1	36.6	51.7
1962	21.8	50.6	57.3	33.7	43.0
1963	22.0	48.8	53.5	33.7	49.3
1964	22.4	51.4	56.6	34.7	47.8
1965	22.6	50.7	55.5	34.5	47.1
1966	22.4	49.5	55.0	31.8	44.1
1967	21.5	44.9	49.6	29.3	39.9
1968	22.8	45.1	49.5	29.2	43.1
2. Absolute change over period					
1951-56	− 6.0	+ 0.6	...	...	...
1956-61	− 4.2	+ 2.2	+ 1.4	+ 2.8	+ 4.6
1961-66	− 0.1	+ 0.3	+ 2.4	− 2.1	− 4.6
1951-68	− 9.9	+ 2.9	...	...	...

[b]Live births per thousand population.
Source: Central Bureau of Statistics, *Abstract 1968*, pp. 54-55, Tables C/2-C/3; *Abstract 1969*, pp. 58-60, Tables C/2-C/4; *Vital Statistics 1965-1966*, Special Series No. 258, Jerusalem, 1969, Table 58 (p. 86), Table 60 (p. 87); and unpublished data of the Central Bureau of Statistics.

It should be noted that the foreign-born group was not static but was constantly reinforced by new immigrants; the movement of the fertility indicator, therefore, reflects both the changing behavior of the population and its changing composition. This apparently provides the explanation for the path of the AA fertility rates in the early period when this group grew tremendously in size: the high initial fertility of the newcomers counteracted the decline in fertility of the veteran groups. Compositional changes by parents' origin occurred also among the Israel-born.

The age pattern of the fertility decline suggests a possible tendency to curtail the childbearing period at both ends. Comparison between the mean age-specific rates for 1965/66 and 1955/56 shows that the relative decline was very high among women over 35 (especially those from EA) and below 20 (and, in the AA group, even at 20–24), reflecting both a curtailment of early marriage and a declining proportion of immigrants who married early abroad. There was some increase in the 25–29 age group among the EA and the Israel-born.

The general tendency toward a decline in fertility observed in the Jewish population was not replicated in the non-Jewish population. The crude birth rate was lower at the beginning of the period, and the total fertility also increased. Data for the subgroups of the non-Jewish population are not available for the first five-year period. In the second period, 1956–1961, all three groups showed increased fertility. In the third, the fertility of Moslems continued to rise, but the other two groups showed a decline. The recent similarity between the fertility time trends of Jews and non-Jews resulting from the 1965–1968 business cycle should be noted.

II. The Role of Education

Education in the Fertility Model

The following discussion does not present any rigorous testing of closely formulated hypotheses; rather, it is an economic analysis of fertility.[3] The main hypothesis is that the number of children that families have depends largely on their own desires. In turn, the number of children desired depends on a family's resources and on the price, in terms of other objectives, of raising children.

[3] My approach follows in broad terms the ideas presented by Gary S. Becker in "An Economic Analysis of Fertility," *Demographic and Economic Change in Developed Countries,* National Bureau of Economic Research, Universities–National Bureau Conference Series No. 11, Princeton University Press, Princeton, N.J., 1960, and in his "A Theory of the Allocation of Time," *Economic Journal,* Vol. LXXV (September 1965), pp. 413–517; and by Richard A. Easterlin, *Population, Labor Force, and Long Swings in Economic Growth: The American Experience,* National Bureau of Economic Research, General Series No. 86, Columbia University Press, New York, 1968. I also benefited from Easterlin's "Towards a Socio-Economic Theory of Fertility: A Survey of Recent Research on Economic Factors in American Fertility" (mimeo.). The approach is similar to that adopted by T. Paul Schultz in his analysis of fertility in other Middle Eastern countries in this volume.

This statement must be qualified: constraining the actual number of children to the desired number is costly, directly in terms of utility or in terms of resources. Variations in fertility control (over time or cross-sectionally) can thus result either from variations in these costs or from variations in the benefits of control. Also important, though perhaps less so, are considerations on the other side. The desired number of (live) children may not be achieved because sickness or other hardship intervenes or because some of the children die. In areas where mortality, particularly of infants, is high, a given desired family size requires more births than where mortality is low. High mortality therefore raises the cost of achieving a given number of children but will not necessarily reduce the actual number, because uncertainty may lead to some "overshooting," depending on the risk preference of the population. When death rates, particularly of infants, go down, the actual number of children may exceed the desired number because of a lag in the adjustment of expectations.

Aside from the purely demographic variables, education seems to be the factor whose relation to fertility is most widely studied and richly documented. Data on income and other relevant variables are scarce. Therefore, the fertility model is presented from the start in terms of the role of education.

To clarify the role played by the various education variables I shall briefly survey how education enters the fertility model, either because it is directly relevant or because it is a good proxy for something on which direct evidence is not available. One limitation of the discussion that follows is that I consider education as exogenously given.

Income

To view the number of children in terms of household decisions some permanent income concept is needed. Decisions about family size have long-term implications and presumably depend on the most permanent aspects of income prospects. Years of schooling is probably an acceptable, though imperfect, proxy for human wealth. When earnings predicted on the basis of education deviate from measured earnings, very often the reason is that measured earnings deviate from the relevant income concept and not that the education measure is inadequate.

When the unit being analyzed is the family, the household's earning capacity is affected by the education of both husband and wife. Children are regarded as normal goods if (other things being equal) families desire more children the greater their resources.

The Cost of Children

In the economic analysis of fertility one has to take into account the fact that children, or the enjoyable services that their presence entails, are, at least partly, a home-produced good. In other words, parents take part in raising their children, together with other inputs purchased or received from the outside. The cost of a child or the cost function relating costs to the number of children depends on the "technology" and the prices of the inputs. With respect to the home-provided inputs the prices are the value of the marginal product of these inputs in the best alternative use, at home or outside the home. The most important home-provided input is usually the time of the mother. To the extent that women who differ in their productivity in the labor market do not differ, or differ less, in their productivity in raising children, the cost of children will be higher for women with higher market productivity.

Ample evidence concerning the relation between years of school or other measures of educational attainment and hourly earnings suggests a strong relationship between education and market productivity. There are reasons to suppose that education raises productivity within the home, including child rearing. If the effect of schooling is neutral between home and market, the cost of children is not higher for families with more educated women. I shall assume, however, that in fact education is not neutral and that the cost of children is higher for more educated women.

The preceding discussion referred to the cost of children as a function of their number. In fact more or fewer resources can be spent on a given number of children, resulting in children who are better or worse educated, fed, or clad. If parents actually enjoy better educated, fed, and clad children, then the utility function and the cost function interact.[4] If those who spend more on a child get more, that is, enjoy him more, then the higher expenditure does not really mean that the cost is higher. Although economists generally try to avoid making statements about differentials in tastes, perhaps it would be acceptable to argue that the utility implications of the objective characteristics of children depend on the parents' own characteristics or history (for example, more educated parents "need" more educated sons).

Education may, however, affect not only the preference with respect to quality/quantity, but also the relative costs. More educated parents forgo more per hour spent with their children and, as suggested, may not be significantly more productive on the quantity dimension. They may, though, be more productive in terms of quality; that is, an hour spent with their children produces higher-quality children. Their contribution to quality can be regarded as complementary to the other child-oriented activities. If so, even with equal tastes the more educated may choose more quality and less quantity.

Family Planning

Actual fertility and family size are determined partly by the degree of success parents have in achieving their desired family size. Family planning involves certain costs that must be weighed against the cost of deviating from the desired family size. The willingness to take the risk of "unwanted children" increases with the cost of birth control and decreases with the marginal cost of children. Education affects both of these elements. New birth control devices reduce the pecuniary or psychic cost of birth control or increase efficacy. Education facilitates access to new techniques, reducing the cost of information and thereby the

[4] See the exchange between Becker and Duesenberry following Becker's article in *Demographic and Economic Change in Developed Countries.*

512

cost of family planning. However, the benefits of birth control should not be neglected: given the costs of family planning, the demand for it depends on the steepness of the loss function. The loss from an "unwanted child" is the difference between the marginal cost of children and the money-weighted marginal utility of children. With identical utility functions, the higher the cost of children, the greater the marginal loss and the greater the rewards of birth control. To the extent that the cost of children rises with the parents' education, the tendency to plan increases with education.

I have listed both economic and noneconomic aspects of the relationship between education and fertility. The arguments that rely on systematic differences in tastes belong in the second group. It is also useful to distinguish between statements on dynamic and static relationships. Most of the arguments here are in static terms, though dynamic considerations were brought into the discussion of birth control. If there is a once-and-for-all improvement in the availability of birth control techniques (perhaps through confrontation with a new social environment), and if the better educated have an advantage in terms of the cost of information, we would expect the better educated to be the first to adopt the new technique and to practice family planning. These differences in the practice of family planning are likely to narrow as the new technique is diffused and the cost of getting the information declines.

The Evidence

Husband's Education

Table 10-4 presents the number of children ever born to women aged 35–39 by the wife's and husband's educational attainment. Figure 10-2a plots the relationship between number of children born and husband's education, with wife's education held constant. The better educated the husband, the higher, according to the preceding discussion, the family's permanent income will be. The price of children associated with wife's education is thus held constant; and to the extent that other components of the price of children are independent of husband's education, we would expect the income effect to show up here.

Figure 10-2a shows in some cases a weak U-shaped relationship between number of children and husband's education and in most cases no relationship at all. The two variables are almost completely independent for EA couples, whereas the AA group shows steeper negative slopes. If we accept education as a proxy for permanent income, the income elasticity of the number of children is low enough to be swamped by price elements that are correlated with husband's education even when wife's education is held constant.

Wife's Education

In Figure 10-2b husband's education is held constant and wife's education is allowed to vary. Here, the better educated the wife, the higher will be the family's full income on the one hand, and the price of children on the other. For most groups a negative relationship between the number of children and wife's educa-

Table 10-4

Number of Children per Jewish Woman Aged 25-39, by Origin and by Education of Husband and Wife, 1961[a]

Years of Schooling Wife → ↓ Husband	0	1-8	9-12	13+
Israel born				
0	...	...	...	
1-8	...	3.8	2.4[c]	
9-12	...	3.1	2.5	2.4
13+		(3.3)[b]	2.5	2.3
Asia-Africa born				
0	6.3	5.2	...	
1-8	6.0	4.6	3.6[c]	
9-12	5.8	3.9	3.1	...
13+		4.5[b]	3.1	(2.0)
Europe-America born				
0	...	(2.5)	...	
1-8	(4.3)	2.2	2.0[c]	
9-12	...	2.2	2.1	1.8
13+		2.4[b]	2.1	1.9

[a]Husband and wife in first marriage only. Origin is by wife's country of birth.
[b]Includes 0 year of schooling of wife.
[c]Includes 13+ years of schooling for wife.

Source: Central Bureau of Statistics, *Families in Israel,* Part I, Census Publication No. 36, Jerusalem, 1968, p. 100, Table 45.

tion is observed. The fact that wife's education has a clear-cut negative effect on the number of children, compared with the ambivalence of the effect of husband's education, reflects the stronger price implications of a wife's education.[5]

If wife's education is treated as the key variable in the explanation of fertility differentials, it is important to see what extent the large differences between the major population groups are explained. Table 10-5 presents data on the number of children ever born to Jewish women aged 35–39 by origin and

[5] Some support for the view that education affects fertility chiefly through the time-allocation mechanism can be deduced from a recent survey: Ziona Peled, *Problems and Attitudes in Family Planning,* Israel Institute of Applied Social Research, Jerusalem, March 1969 (Hebrew mimeo.).

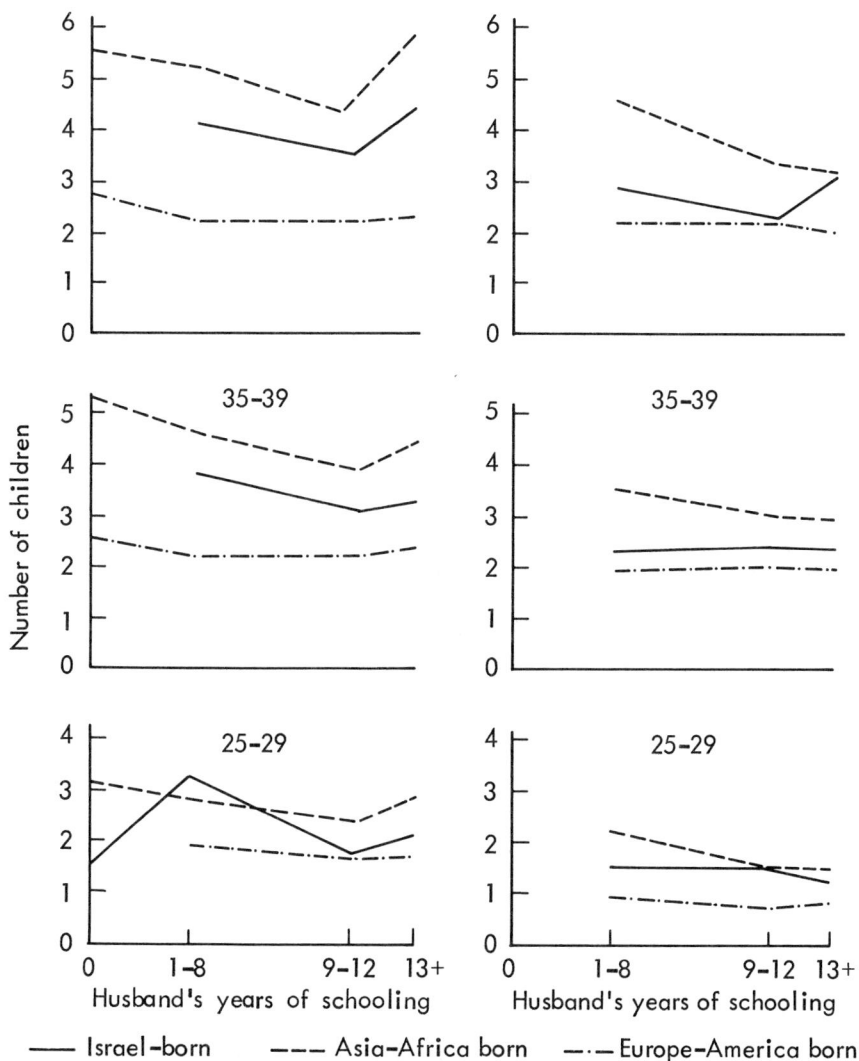

I. Wife's schooling 1-8 years and age: 45-49

II. Wife's schooling 9-12 years and age: 45-49

35-39

35-39

25-29

25-29

Husband's years of schooling

Husband's years of schooling

——— Israel-born   ——— Asia-Africa born   —·— Europe-America born

FIG. 10-2a. Number of children per Jewish woman (husband present), by wife's education, age, and origin, and by husband's education: 1961. Source: See caption of Fig. 10-2b.

515

I. Husband's schooling 1–8 years
and wife's age: 45–49

II. Husband's schooling 9–12 years
and wife's age: 45–49

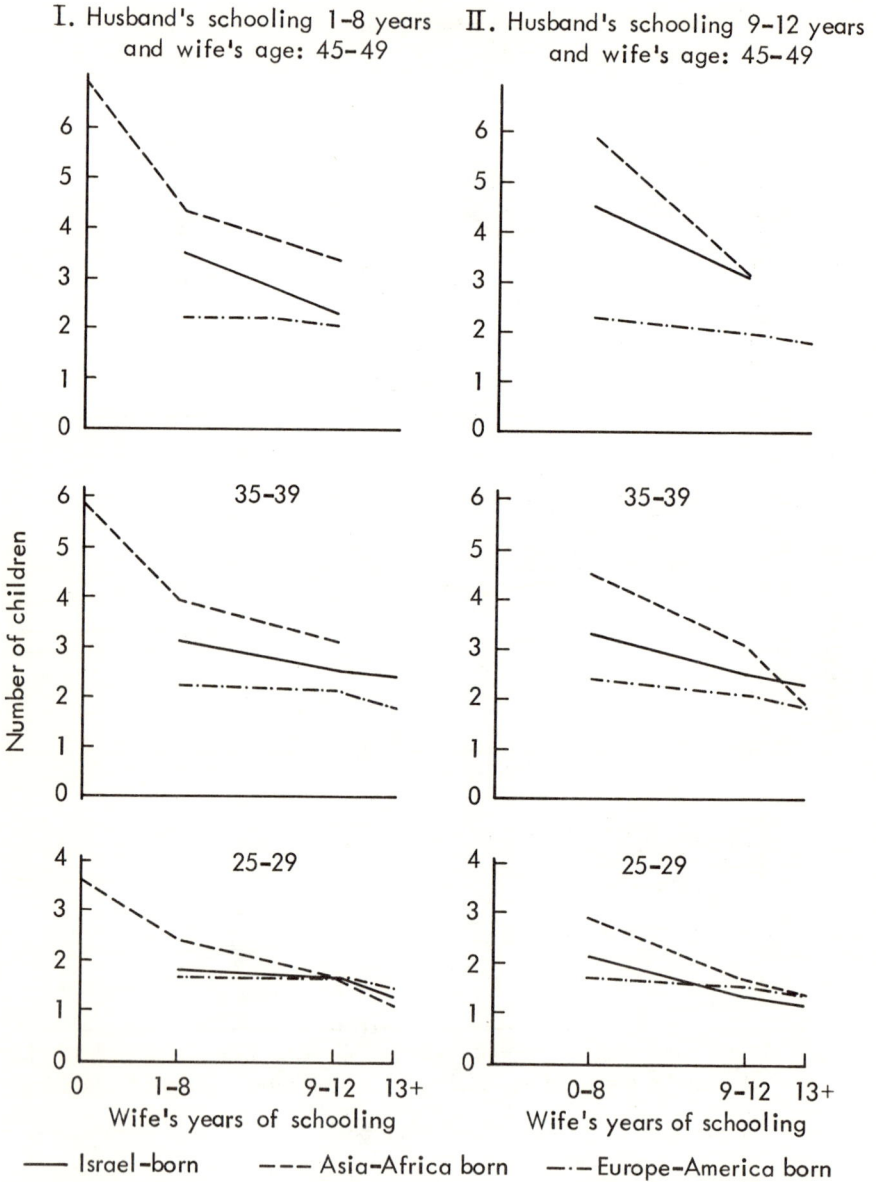

Number of children

35–39

35–39

25–29

25–29

0   1–8   9–12   13+
Wife's years of schooling

0–8   9–12   13+
Wife's years of schooling

——— Israel-born   – – – Asia–Africa born   –·–Europe–America born

FIG. 10-2b. Number of children per Jewish woman (husband present), by wife's education, age and origin, and by husband's education: 1961. Source: Central Bureau of Statistics, *Families in Israel—Part 1,* Census Publication No. 36, Jerusalem, 1968, Table 45.

Table 10-5

Standardized Number of Children per Woman Aged 35-39, by Continent of Birth and Period of Immigration (Jews), and by Religion, 1961

	Average Number of Children Unadjusted	Adjustment by Israel-born Education			Adjustment by Non-Jewish Education		
		Adjusted Number of Children[a]	Difference from Israel-born[b]		Adjusted Number of Children[a]	Difference from Non-Jewish Population[c]	
			Unadjusted	Adjusted		Unadjusted	Adjusted
	(1)	(2)	(3)	(4)	(5)	(6)	(7)
Sum of absolute differentials[d]			5.0	2.5		19.2	12.2
Jews							
Israel born	3.0	3.0	0	0	4.4	−3.9	−2.5
Asia-Africa born	5.2	3.7	2.2	0.7	5.8	−1.7	−1.1
Veterans[e]	4.2	3.2	1.2	0.2	5.2	−2.7	−1.7
Immigrated 1948+	5.3	3.8	2.3	0.8	5.9	−1.6	−1.0
Europe-America born	2.2	2.2	−0.8	−0.8	3.6	−4.7	−3.3
Veterans[e]	2.4	2.4	−0.6	0.6	4.0	−4.5	−2.9
Immigrated 1948+	2.1	2.1	−0.9	−0.9	3.5	−4.8	−3.4
Non-Jews	6.9				6.9	0	0
Moslems	7.7				7.3	0.8	0.4
Christians	6.0				6.6	−0.9	−0.3
Druse	6.9				6.9	0.0	0.0

[a]Jews (column 2): Education-specific number of children per woman aged 35-39 in each population group (from source 1, Tables 11 and 21), weighted by the years-of-schooling distribution of Israel-born women aged 35-39 (from source 2, Tables 28 and 29). Non-Jews (column 5): As for Jews, that is, actual figures weighted by average non-Jewish distribution (from source 2, Tables 32 and 33). [b]Absolute difference between the number of children of stated group and the number of children of Israel-born children; adjustment by education of wife. [c]Absolute difference between the number of children of stated group and the number of children of non-Jewish population, adjustment by education of wife. [d]Sum of absolute differentials excluding the Asia-Africa and Europe-America average lines. [e]Immigrated before 1948. *Source:* 1. Central Bureau of Statistics, *Marriage and Fertility,* Part I, Census Publication No. 26, Jerusalem, 1965: 2. Central Bureau of Statistics, *Languages, Literacy, and Educational Attainment,* Part I, Census Publication No. 15, Jerusalem, 1963.

length of residence. When we apply the years-of-schooling distribution of the Israel-born to each set of the education-specific fertility measure, the difference between Israel-born and AA women is significantly reduced, but the difference between Israel-born and EA women is not affected. Altogether, the sum of absolute deviations from the standard group is reduced by half.[6]

In the same table, I compare the religious groups in the non-Jewish population with each other and with the Jewish population. When the standard years-of-schooling distribution is that of non-Jewish women, the difference between Moslems and Christians is reduced from 1.7 to 0.7 children, and the difference between Moslems and Druse is reduced from 0.8 to 0.4. The differences between non-Jews and the origin groups in the Jewish population are reduced by about one-third.[7]

Let us now turn to the association between wife's education and fertility within the origin groups. Figure 10-2 shows that the effect of education is strongest in the AA group and is very weak in the EA group, with the Israel-born in the middle. The more detailed Table 10-6, which shows the difference in number of children between women with 5–8 and with 11–12 years of schooling, indicates that within each origin group length of residence in the country tends to reduce the effect of education. Among the Israel-born the pattern observed above is sustained when we classify women by parents' origin.

In interpreting these findings, it is useful to observe the age pattern of the education effect (Figure 10-3). When women in the different postfertility age groups (45 +) are compared, what we observe is mainly due to the difference among cohorts: as we move to more recent cohorts, there is an unmistakable decline in the effect of education except in the very early period.

The findings suggest that a static economic interpretation of the relationship between wife's education and fertility will not suffice. The differences by origin in the education effect, its age pattern in the EA group, and the effects of length of stay in Israel suggest that a dynamic process is involved. The level of fertility can be visualized as a function of both the individual and the general level of education. When the general level of education is low, the economic and social differences between the educated and the uneducated tend to be sharp in general and are associated with reduced fertility among the educated. As the general level of education rises, there is some tendency for the economic differentials between education groups to narrow, and there may be greater diffusion and perhaps even a larger demonstration effect on the lower education groups, resulting

---

[6] The importance of women's education in the explanation of fertility differentials by origin, particularly among women with more than primary education, has been noted by H. V. Muhsam, "Some Fertility Differentials among Jewish Women in Israel," presented at the Fifth World Congress of Jewish Studies, Jerusalem, August 1969.

[7] Note that the standardization procedure is based on wife's education without holding husband's education constant. Although the two variables are positively correlated, the preceding discussion of the net effect of husband's education suggests that the bias involved is of little importance.

Table 10-6

Differences in Average Number of Children Between Jewish Women with
11-12 and 5-8 Years of Schooling, by Age and Continent of Birth: 1961

		Israel Born				Asia-Africa Born			Europe-America Born		
		Father Born in				Immigrated			Immigrated	
	Total	Total	Israel	Asia-Africa	Europe-America	Total	Before 1948	1948+	Total	Before 1948	1948+
	(1)	(2)	(3)	(4)	(5)	(6)	(7)	(8)	(9)	(10)	(11)
20-24	0.6	0.5	0.7	0.2	0.4	0.5	0.4	0.5	0.4	0.7	0.4
25-29	0.7	0.5	0.7	0.6	0.3	0.8	0.8	0.8	0.3	0.3	0.4
30-34	0.7	0.8	1.0	1.0	0.3	1.1	0.6	1.2	0.2	0.3	0.3
35-39	0.6	0.9	1.3	1.1	0.2	1.4	0.8	1.4	0.2	0.2	0.3
40-44	0.6	1.0	0.6	...	0.7	1.5	1.0	1.7	0.2	0.2	0.4
45-49	0.6	0.6	0.6	1.5	...	1.8	1.9	1.5	0.1	0.1	0.4
50-54	0.6	1.4	...	...	...	2.4	...	2.3	0.1	0.2	0.3
55-59	0.8	1.5	...	...	...	1.9	...	1.8	0.4	0.3	0.6
60-64	1.2	1.1	...	...	...	1.9	...	2.5	0.9	0.9	0.9
65+	0.8	0.7	...	...	...	0.5	...	0.3	1.0	1.3	0.8

Source: Central Bureau of Statistics, *Marriage and Fertility*, pp. 32-34, Table 11.

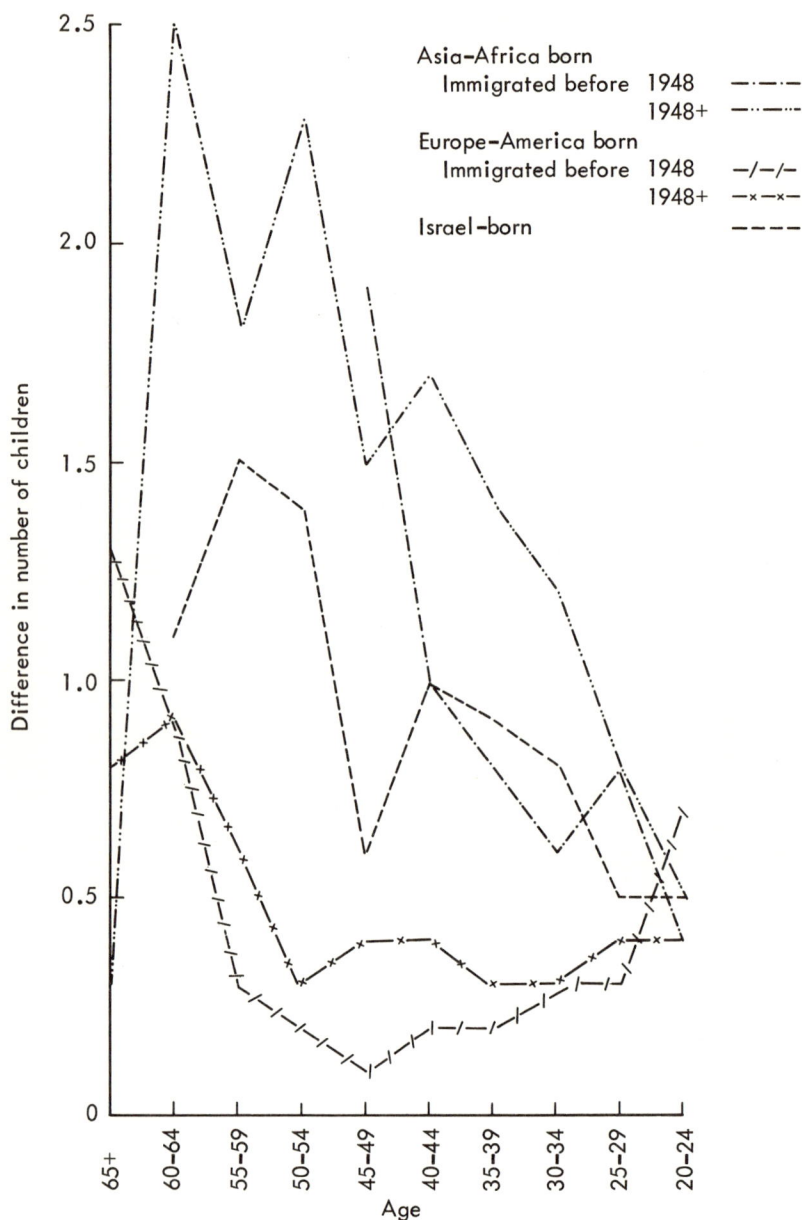

Fig. 10-3. Difference in average number of children between Jewish women with 11–12 and 5–8 years of schooling, by woman's age and origin. Source: Table 10-6.

from the higher share of the educated, leading the former to reduce fertility also. The EA women with completed fertility (in 1961) belonged to cohorts with high general levels of education, whereas the AA women had a very low level of education, leading to very high (but declining) differentials of fertility by education. The cross-sectional relationship between number of children and schooling reflects, in the case of the AA group, the fact that the more educated are at any point in time closer to where they will be in the long run than the uneducated. In the case of EA women, whose levels of education have been high and slowly changing for a considerable time, the cross section reflects more or less a steady-state situation.

Employment and Education

Fertility and women's employment are often linked as being affected one by the other. I prefer to say that in the long run both are affected by (among other things) the earning capacity of the wife. How strong is the link between these two dependent variables, and what is the quantitative trade-off involved?

The labor force participation rate of Jewish women is presented in Table 10-7, and their employment rate in Table 10-8. It can be seen from these tables that (1) education affects employment (participation) very strongly in all origin groups, and seems to be the main explanatory variable for the large intergroup differences in employment; (2) within each of the categories of origin and years of schooling there is a tendency for labor force participation to decline as the number of children increases, the exception being that the effect of number of children is small and inconsistent in size for women with no schooling; and (3) in a comparison of the origin groups, the effect of the number of children on labor force participation increases quite steeply with education in the AA group, tends to increase among the Israel-born, and declines in the EA group. The highest observed effect is for AA women with 13 + years of schooling, indicating greater ability or willingness on the part of EA women to substitute other forms of child rearing for their own time; this is consistent with the finding in regard to the effect of education on the number of children in the EA group.

These figures, if combined with data on the full-time earnings of women, can provide a rough estimate of the forgone-earnings element in the cost of children. The conclusion that emerges from these calculations is that the forgone-earnings element in the cost of the marginal child rises with education among Israel-born and AA women, but remains fairly constant among EA women with some schooling.

An attempt to attack the problem from another direction and to treat it in a life cycle context is summarized in Table 10-9. The calculations are based on the assumption that it is the age of the youngest child rather than the number of children that is relevant for participation in the labor force. The table indicates that a woman with one child forgoes, depending on the level of her schooling, between one-tenth and one-quarter of her earnings (but no more than one-tenth

Table 10-7

Labor Force Participation Rate of Jewish Women, by Number of
Children Aged 0-17, Continent of Birth, and Years of Schooling, 1968[a]

Number of Children	Years of Schooling					Differences	
	Total	0	1-8	9-12	13+	9-12 *less* 1-8	13+ *less* 9-12
	(1)	(2)	(3)	(4)	(5)	(6)	(7)
Total population	25.5	12.3	19.0	32.7	61.9	13.7	29.2
0	24.7	8.9	19.5	37.1	58.5	17.6	21.4
1	34.8	17.1	25.9	36.7	69.1	10.8	32.4
2	28.1	20.4	19.8	26.9	61.5	7.1	34.6
3	19.7	16.5	12.9	22.9	58.0	10.0	35.1
4+	13.5	14.2	10.8	11.7	52.3	0.9	40.6
Israel born	35.8	11.7	16.2	33.2	65.7	17.0	32.5
0	41.7	14.3	18.0	48.4	78.1	30.4	29.7
1	42.5	19.3	22.2	36.1	69.9	13.9	33.8
2	30.4	. . .	20.1	26.5	60.6	6.4	34.1
3	24.5	22.6	9.7	24.5	53.2	14.8	28.7
4+	10.1	. . .	4.0	18.7	43.2	14.7	24.5
Asia-Africa born	16.7	13.0	15.6	27.4	55.1	11.8	27.7
0	16.0	9.5	21.9	44.0	72.7	22.1	28.7
1	25.5	17.0	22.7	33.1	63.5	10.4	30.4
2	18.5	20.8	13.1	24.7	39.1	11.6	14.4
3	15.1	16.4	13.5	16.1	36.5	2.6	20.4
4+	13.4	14.4	11.6	10.8	10.0	−0.8	−0.8
Europe-America born	29.8	6.6	21.7	34.2	60.1	12.5	25.9
0	26.6	5.5	19.1	35.1	53.2	16.0	18.1
1	38.3	12.9	29.4	39.0	69.9	9.6	30.9
2	32.3	19.2	26.0	28.2	67.3	2.2	39.1
3	27.7	14.6	13.7	29.0	68.7	15.3	39.7
4+	18.4	21.8	11.2	9.9	46.6	−1.3	36.7
Difference between women with 3 children and 1 child							
Total	−15.1	−0.6	−13.0	−13.8	−11.1		
Israel born	−18.0	+3.3	−12.5	−11.6	−16.7		
Asia-Africa born	−10.4	−0.6	−9.2	−17.0	−27.0		
Europe-America born	−10.6	+1.7	−15.7	−10.0	−1.2		

[a]Married, divorced, and widowed.

Source: Central Bureau of Statistics, unpublished data.

of her potential earnings). The marginal loss from a second child, however, is
very slight.[8]

[8] A finding of the family planning survey mentioned above (Peled, *Problems and
Attitudes in Family Planning*, p. 30) is interesting in this connection. Respondents
were asked which of several possible spheres of assistance to large families was the
most important; only 3 percent chose "assistance to working mothers," compared with
28 percent for "employment," and 18 percent each for "education" and "housing."

Table 10-8

Employment Rates of Jewish Women, by Number of Children
Aged 0-17, Continent of Birth, and Years of Schooling, 1968[a]

		Years of Schooling				Differences	
Number of Children	Total	0	1-8	9-12	13+	9-12 less 1-8	13+ less 9-12
	(1)	(2)	(3)	(4)	(5)	(6)	(7)
Total population	17.8	8.3	13.4	24.3	38.4	10.9	14.1
0	18.0	6.0	14.3	28.5	38.4	14.2	9.9
1	24.2	11.3	18.4	27.1	43.1	8.7	16.0
2	18.6	13.9	13.6	18.4	36.5	4.8	18.1
3	12.9	10.7	7.9	17.8	33.4	9.9	15.6
4+	8.8	9.5	7.2	7.6	24.1	0.4	16.5
Israel born	22.7	8.2	9.6	23.9	37.6	14.3	13.7
0	28.1	8.9	12.3	36.4	45.3	24.1	8.9
1	27.1	19.3	13.8	25.7	41.0	11.9	15.3
2	21.2	. . .	10.8	18.0	33.6	7.2	15.6
3	15.9	22.6	4.5	19.4	30.8	14.9	11.4
4+	5.0	. . .	4.0	14.2	15.3	10.2	1.1
Asia-Africa born	11.7	8.8	11.0	22.2	33.2	11.2	11.0
0	11.8	6.5	15.7	36.3	49.0	20.6	12.7
1	16.8	11.6	14.9	22.8	31.9	7.9	9.1
2	12.9	14.1	9.8	16.7	23.9	6.9	7.2
3	9.9	10.4	8.4	13.4	17.8	5.0	4.4
4+	8.8	11.3	7.8	6.0	33.5	−1.8	27.5
Europe-America born	21.4	4.3	15.7	25.5	39.5	9.8	14.0
0	19.6	3.4	3.0	26.8	36.1	23.8	9.3
1	27.2	5.7	20.9	28.9	45.8	8.0	16.9
2	22.1	14.8	18.0	19.5	43.1	1.5	23.6
3	18.5	14.6	9.5	21.3	40.0	11.8	18.7
4+	12.5	21.8	8.0	8.4	27.2	0.4	18.8
Difference between women with 3 children and 1 child							
Total	−11.3	−0.6	−10.5	−9.3	−9.7		
Israel born	−11.2	+3.3	−9.3	−6.3	−10.2		
Asia-Africa born	−6.9	−1.2	−6.5	−9.4	−14.1		
Europe-America born	−8.7	+8.9	−11.4	−7.6	−5.8		

[a]Fully employed plus half of partly employed *divided by* number of women in group.

Source: Central Bureau of Statistics, unpublished data.

Table 10-9

Effect of Children on Lifetime (17-54)
Employment Rates of Jewish Women, by Years of Schooling[a]

(percentages)

	0	1-4	5-8	9-10	11-12	13+
A. Employment rates of women at age 17-54, by number of children ever born						
0	10.6	17.9	23.5	32.9	38.7	49.4
1	9.4	15.9	17.4	24.9	30.7	44.5
2	9.0	14.9	16.8	24.2	29.7	43.6
B. Absolute difference between women with[b]						
0 and 1 child	−1.1	−2.0	−6.1	−8.0	−8.0	−4.9
1 and 2 children	−0.4	−1.0	−0.6	−0.7	−1.0	−0.9
C. Relative difference between women with						
0 and 1 child	−10.7	−11.2	−26.0	−24.3	−20.4	−9.7
1 and 2 children	−4.2	−6.7	−4.6	−2.8	−3.2	−2.0

[a]The basic information in this table was derived from another table giving the labor force characteristics of Jewish women by years of schooling, age, and age of youngest child present. This was translated into employment rates or proportion of time worked.

In order to arrive at the proportion of lifetime (17-54) employment forgone by women who will have altogether a specified (1, 2) number of children, the following calculations were made. From birth order and age-specific birth rates (for 1960) the probability that a woman will give birth to a first (and to a second) child at a given age was calculated. It was assumed that an only child and a first child have the same age pattern of mother at birth, and likewise that the second child in a family with only two children and all second children have the same age pattern of mother at birth. From these data the distribution of each age group of mothers by the age of their youngest child was calculated for mothers who will eventually have one child and those who will eventually have two children. These were used in conjunction with the employment rates computed to get the figures shown in this table.

It is assumed that the timing of a given child is independent of education.

[b]Percentage points.

Source: Central Bureau of Statistics, *Families in Israel,* Part I, Table 70; and unpublished Central Bureau of Statistics data.

Table 10-10

School Attendance and Labor Force Participation
Rates, by Population Group

(percentages)[a]

		Jews[b]			
	Total	Israel Born	Asia-Africa Born	Europe-America Born	Non-Jews
A. Age 14-17					
Pupils in post-primary education (1968/69)					
Both sexes	56.3	71.5	41.1	75.5	19.5
Men	51.8	66.5	36.9	71.2	25.4
Labor force participation (1968)					
Both sexes	27.6	28.0	34.1	18.8	32.2
Men	29.6	33.2	36.9	19.5	49.5
B. Age 18+					
Students in institutions of higher learning (1968/69)					
Both sexes	7.8	11.7	2.0	14.1	...

[a]Percentage of population in each cell.
[b]Origin by father's country of birth.

Source: Abstract 1969, No. 20, pp. 560, 563, 571, and 42 for school attendance; p. 253
(and unpublished Central Bureau of Statistics data) for labor force participation.

Education and Employment of Children

The net economic burden of children is affected by the careers that they follow.
The main population groups differ in their post-primary school attendance and
their labor force participation. Table 10-10 shows the proportion of youths aged
14–17 in post-primary school. The school attendance rate of children of AA parents is a little more than half that of children of EA parents; the rate for non-
Jews is less than half the AA rate. The differentials are much greater in higher
education. There is surprisingly little difference between the labor force participation rates of the Israel-born men and the AA men, indicating in conjunction
with the difference in school attendance that a significant proportion of the latter
are neither in school nor in the labor force. The participation rate of non-Jewish

525

Table 10-11

Rates of Labor Force Participation at Age 14-17 by Continent of Birth and Years of Schooling of Family Head, 1961[a]

(both sexes)

	0	1-8	9-12	13+	9-12 less 1-8
Jews					
Total	34.5	24.7	14.9	10.8	−9.8
Israel born	30.0	28.6	17.5	10.4	−11.1
Asia-Africa born	30.4	31.5	23.8	18.8	−7.7
Europe-America born	19.7	12.5	9.5	7.2	−3.0
Non-Jews					
Total	36.8	27.5	17.1	. . .	−10.4
Moslems	39.3	28.4	19.5	. . .	−8.9
Christians	23.2	23.2	15.5	. . .	−7.7
Druse	27.9	32.2	. . .	. . .	. . .

[a]Families with one child aged 14-17.

Source: Central Bureau of Statistics, *Families in Israel,* Table 74.

men is much higher. In spite of the lower school attendance, the rate for both sexes is not high because the reported participation of girls is extremely low. The data for both sexes are relevant for the expected earnings of children, since the sex of children cannot be controlled by parents. Thus, expected earnings from children are rather similar in the Israel-born, AA, and non-Jewish groups, but are for all three significantly higher than for the EA group. This conclusion, of course, takes into account only what children earn while still at home and not transfers from children to parents at a later stage. If such transfers were taken into account, the gaps between the groups would increase.

Within each group there is a negative association between head of family's education and child's labor force participation (Table 10-11). The effect of parents' education on child's participation rate is weakest in the EA group. This result is again consistent with the weak effect of education on number of children in this group.

Family Planning

Family planning is a complex topic, and I shall only cite some findings from the available studies that are of particular relevance here. The principal sources are the studies of Bachi and Matras and their associates,[9] based on in-depth interviewing of mothers in maternity wards, and on the findings of the Israel Institute of Applied Social Research (IIASR) cited earlier.[10]

1. In the IIASR study, 60 percent of those interviewed reported that all or some of their children were planned. This finding appears to be higher than the not entirely comparable finding of the Bachi-Matras study made about 10 years earlier.

2. The attitude toward and the practice of family planning vary, on the whole, by origin and education on the lines noted above in connection with family size; in addition, planning is negatively associated with age and degree of religious observance.

3. The association between planning and education is very strong at low education levels; that is, the difference between those with some schooling and those with none is very marked. Differentials between those with even incomplete primary education and those with more, however, are relatively small.

4. The relationship between family planning (practice and attitude) and education is stronger for the AA group than for the others.

5. The negative association between education and number of children planned or desired is present also among those who practice family planning.

The observed association with schooling is not only or even mainly a reflection of the accessibility of birth control devices. However, it is not clear how one can distinguish, within the nonplanning group, between those who want a large number of children and those who have a large number of children because they do not plan.

A Cross-sectional Community Analysis

In this section are some preliminary results of a cross-sectional analysis of communities, based mostly on data from the 1961 Census of Population. The analysis of schooling of women and men, labor force participation rate of women and is based on ordinary least-squares multiple regression: the dependent variable is a birth rate standardized for women's age structure (see notes to Table 10-12). The independent variables are all community averages and include median years

[9] Roberto Bachi and Judah Matras, "Contraception and Induced Abortions Among Jewish Maternity Cases in Israel," *Milbank Memorial Fund Quarterly*, Vol. XL, No. 2 (April 1962), pp. 207–229; Judah Matras and Chana Auerbach, "On Rationalization of Family Formation in Israel," *Milbank Memorial Fund Quarterly*, Vol. XL, No. 4 (October 1962), pp. 453–480; R. Bachi, R. Toaff, J. Matras, and D. Ayalon, *Natality and Contraception Among Women of Tel Aviv-Jaffa*, Hebrew University, Jerusalem, 1961 (in Hebrew).

[10] Peled, *Problems and Attitudes in Family Planning*.

Table 10-12

Multiple Regression of Communities in Israel by Type, 1961

(dependent variable: difference between age adjusted and actual birth rate)

(beneath each regression coefficient is the ratio of the coefficient to its standard error or its *t*-statistic)

	Mean of Dependent Variable	Constant	Median Years of Schooling Men (1)	Median Years of Schooling Women (2)	Labor Force Participation Men (3)	Labor Force Participation Women (4)	Less than 5 Years in Present Place of Residence (5)	Percent of Population Immigrated from Asia-Africa 1948+ (6)	Israel Born (7)	Percent Employed in Agriculture (8)	R^2
Jewish towns[c]	4.765										
b		-19.340	-0.434	-1.630	0.033	-0.010	0.274	0.317	0.403		0.823
t		(1.679)	(0.315)	(2.196)	(0.504)	(0.072)	(7.291)	(3.804)	(3.813)		
b		-19.138		-1.786			0.269	0.326	0.389		0.822
t		(2.651)		(3.609)			(8.039)	(4.403)	(3.964)		
Moshavim, pre-1948[d] (112)	2.963										
b		22.095	-0.164	-1.421	0.010	0.046	-0.008	0.093	-0.245		0.368
t		(2.797)	(0.196)	(2.313)	(0.159)	(1.145)	(0.176)	(1.143)	(4.796)		
b		22.694		-1.393			0.004	0.083	-0.246		0.357
t		(4.528)		(3.062)			(0.086)	(1.051)	(4.853)		
Moshavim, 1948+[d] (259)	14.820										
b		12.107	-1.007	-2.282	0.216	-0.057	0.067	0.062	0.016		0.529
t		(2.062)	(2.420)	(6.018)	(3.800)	(1.675)	(2.636)	(1.398)	(0.311)		
b		22.270		-2.752			0.077	0.060	0.025		0.487
t		(6.086)		(8.838)			(2.944)	(1.343)	(0.496)		
Non-Jewish communities[e] (133)	29.651										
b		6.686	0.603	-2.997	0.200	-0.014		0.251	0.201	-0.153	0.264
t		(0.595)	(0.898)	(2.683)	(1.860)	(0.175)		(3.303)	(2.162)	(2.578)	
b		-1.969		-3.218				0.243	0.218	-0.208	0.230
t		(0.281)		(3.118)				(3.214)	(2.379)	(3.942)	

Kibbutzim (180)	−1.321								
b		−20.592	0.459	1.316	0.110	−0.155	0.171	−0.212	−0.051	0.194
t		(1.795)	(0.724)	(1.521)	(1.437)	(2.440)	(4.854)	(0.782)	(0.224)

[a]The dependent variable is the difference (per thousand population) between (a) number of births (average 1961/62) of the community (town, village, etc.) and (b) the number of births predicted on the basis of women's ages.

The predicted number of births was calculated by multiplying the number of Jewish women aged 15-44 (5 and 10 year intervals) by the age-specific birth rates of Jewish women.

[b]The number of observations is given in parentheses in the stub.

[c]Includes Jewish population of mixed towns.

[d]Cooperative rural settlements (all Jewish). The date refers to foundation of settlement.

[e]Includes non-Jewish urban population.

Sources: Actual births by community, unpublished Central Bureau of Statistics data. Independent variables, Central Bureau of Statistics, *The Settlements of Israel,* Part II, Table 1, and *The Settlements of Israel,* Part III, Table 2 (for columns 5-7): *The Settlement of Israel,* Part IV, Tables 13 and 14 (for columns 1-4 and column 8).

of schooling of men and women, labor force participation rate of women and men, percentage employed in agriculture, size of community, and origin and religious composition of the population.

The analysis was carried out separately for towns, *moshavim,* [11] kibbutzim, and Arab communities (mostly villages). Some of the main results (some of them are presented in Table 9-12) can be summarized as follows.

1. Except in the kibbutzim, there is a significant negative net association of women's education with birth rate, with a coefficient implying that there are 1.5–3.0 fewer births annually per thousand population for each additional year of schooling of women (in terms of the median).

2. The association between men's level of schooling and birth rate is not statistically significant, and the absolute size of the coefficient is small.

3. There is a negative but generally not statistically significant association of women's labor force participation rate with the birth rate.

4. Men's labor force participation is positively but on the whole significantly associated with birth rate in all but the Arab communities, where the coefficient is negative. The interpretation of these relationships must await the specification of a more complete model.

5. The percentage employed in agriculture is negatively associated with birth rate in Arab villages. The share of employment in agriculture is likely to be negatively associated with income in Arab villages.

6. Size of community has no effect (not shown).

7. Length of stay in Israel has a strong negative effect.

The analysis of kibbutzim gives two interesting results:

8. Wife's education is not negatively associated with the birth rate; in fact, a positive correlation is observed.

9. There is a net *positive* and significant association between the birth rate and per capita land. The association between the birth rate and preliminary estimates of per capita disposable income and per capita consumption is positive but not significant statistically.[12]

The difference between men and women in the performance of the education variable (seen also in the aggregate data) tends to support the view that wife's education represents a price effect. This conclusion is greatly strengthened by the quite different performance of the education variables in kibbutzim. In most kibbutzim child care is centrally organized, but differentials in alternative uses of time by education are smaller than elsewhere. In particular, there is no connection between parents' consumption levels and education, so that the argu-

---

[11] Cooperative villages. "New" *moshavim* were established from 1948 on, and "old" were established before 1948.

[12] Data kindly supplied by H. Barkai of the Falk Institute, Jerusalem. The income and consumption series are being revised currently and will be reanalyzed with the fertility series.

ment for viewing education as a proxy for the price of children does not hold here.

The tentative indications of a positive income effect should also be noted.

III. Interpretation of the Time Trends

The major time trends mentioned at the beginning of this paper were a mono-tonic decline in fertility of the AA group, and a decline in the 1950s with some increase in the 1960s (distributed by the 1966/67 recession) for the Israel-born and the EA groups. Among non-Jews the fertility of Moslems increased, though it dipped in the mid-1960s; among the Christians a decline started in the early 1960s.

In the preceding discussion evidence from the cross-sectional fertility differ-entials was advanced in support of the hypothesis emphasizing the role of wom-en's education in fertility. How far does this single variable contribute to the explanation of the time trends? In Table 10-13 I make a tentative attempt to pro-vide an answer. Birth rates were calculated (from 1966 data) for women aged 20–34, by level of education and origin; these rates were applied to estimates (from the 1961 census) of the educational distribution of women aged 20–34 in 1951, 1956, and 1961. The birth rates of AA women declined throughout the period, so that the number of births "predicted" from the 1966 rate (without ad-justment for education) is a gross underestimate of the number of births in the earlier years. Standardization for women's education works in the right direc-tion: since the educational level of AA women has improved continuously, the standardization reduces the gap between actual and predicted births in 1951 and 1956 and closes it in 1961. For the other two groups, the prediction falls short of actual births only in 1951 and the gap is reduced by standardization. In 1956 and 1961, when the birth rates of the two groups were lower than in 1966, the prediction gives an overestimate which is increased by standardization.

The extent to which wife's education can account for variation over time depends on the rate at which the level changes and on how strongly education affects fertility. The cross-sectional results suggest that the effect of education on fertility is negatively associated with *level* of education: that is, in population groups with a high educational level, by-education fertility differentials tend to be small.

Although AA-born women in the main childbearing ages have the lowest initial level of education, the *rate of improvement* in education has been fastest for this group. This can be seen from the 1961 educational age profiles shown in Figure 10-4. For the other groups, the level of education (measured by median years of schooling) has risen only slowly (although there has been a continuous decline in the percentage of those with only 0 4 years of schooling) Also, given the low educational level of AA women and the corresponding large fertility dif-ferentials by education, a given change in the level of education affects fertility more than it would in the other groups. Eventually, as the educational level of the AA group improves, differentials narrow through the accelerated decline in the fertility of the less educated. Therefore, I believe that the education variable by itself is more fertility depressing for AA women than for others (and more so than can be accounted for by the fixed end-of-period coefficients standardization attempted in Table 10-13).

The cross-sectional evidence also suggests that the length of stay in Israel affects fertility. The 1961 census shows that the smaller number of children per woman who immigrated before 1948 cannot be explained by differences in education. Moreover, the figures for total fertility (which are based on the flow of births in Israel) and not only the total stock of children—partly brought from abroad—are higher for new immigrants. Total fertility declines over time as the period of immigration is held constant (Table 10-14). Average length of stay of the foreign-born also increases over time because mass immigration was concentrated in the period 1948–1951: AA women aged 40–44 who immigrated after

Table 10-13

Effect of Women's Education on Number of Births,
1951, 1956, and 1961

	Absolute Figures			Percent Difference	
	Actual (1)	Predicted by Origin[a] (2)	Predicted by Origin and Education[b] (3)	[(2)−(1)]/(1) (4)	(3)−(1)]/(1) (5)
1951					
Total	43,249	31,433	34,829	−27.3	−19.5
Israel born	4,799	3,600	3,961	−25.0	−17.5
Asia-Africa born	18,501	11,887	14,224	−35.7	−23.1
Europe-America born	19,771	15,946	16,644	−19.3	−15.8
1956					
Total	43,411	41,739	44,102	− 3.8	+ 1.6
Israel born	5,885	6,203	6,664	+ 5.4	+13.2
Asia-Africa born	24,424	19,333	22,564	−20.8	− 7.6
Europe-America born	12,973	14,281	14,874	+10.1	+14.6
1961					
Total	43,691	42,174	45,628	− 3.4	+ 4.4
Israel born	8,530	8,688	9,033	+ 1.8	+ 5.9
Asia-Africa born	25,956	22,965	25,727	−11.5	− 0.9
Europe-America born	9,205	10,521	10,868	+14.3	+18.1

[a]1966 births by origin divided by women aged 20-34 by origin. These birth rates were applied to the estimated population in the earlier years based on source 2, Table 19; source 3, Tables 28 and 29; and source 4.

[b]Distribution by years of schooling was estimated for women aged 20-34 in each of the years estimated (from source 3). Births by education and origin of mother (unpublished Central Bureau of Statistics data), divided by the number of women in each education category derived from estimate of the 1966 Labor Force Survey.

Source:
1. Central Bureau of Statistics, *Vital Statistics 1965-1966*, p. 92, Table 66.
2. M. Sicron and B. Gil, *Jewish Population by Sex, Age and Country of Birth (1931-1954)*, Central Bureau of Statistics, Special Series No. 37, Jerusalem, 1955, Table 19.
3. Central Bureau of Statistics, *Languages, Literacy and Educational Attainment*, Tables 28 and 29.
4. *Abstract 1957/58*, No. 9.

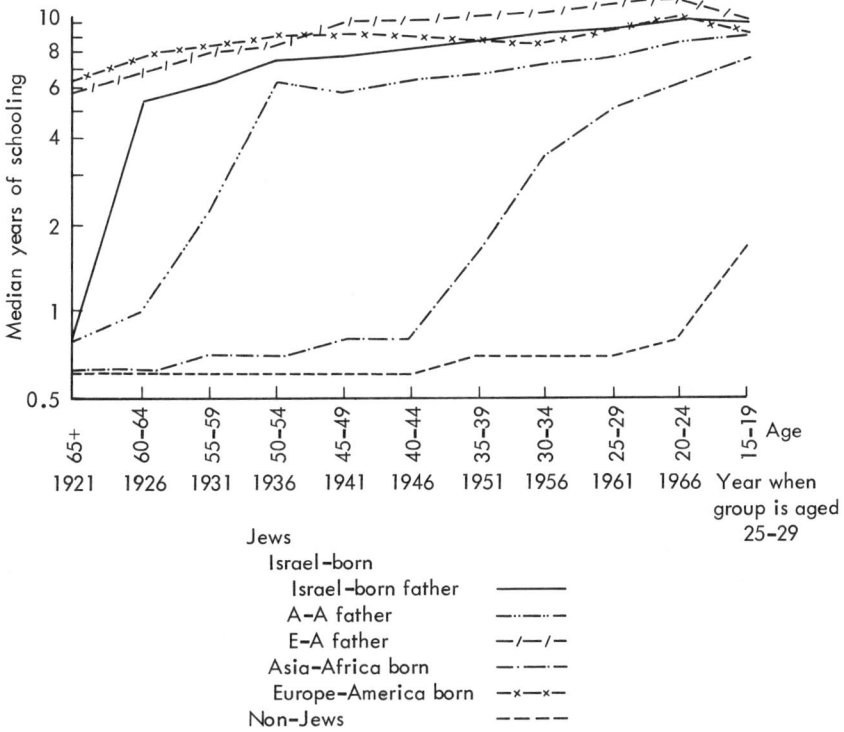

FIG. 10-4a. Age profiles of women's education, by population group: 1961. Median years of schooling (semi-log scale). Source: Central Bureau of Statistics, *Languages, Literacy and Educational Attainment—Part 1,* Census Publication No. 15, Jerusalem, 1963, Tables 28 to 34.

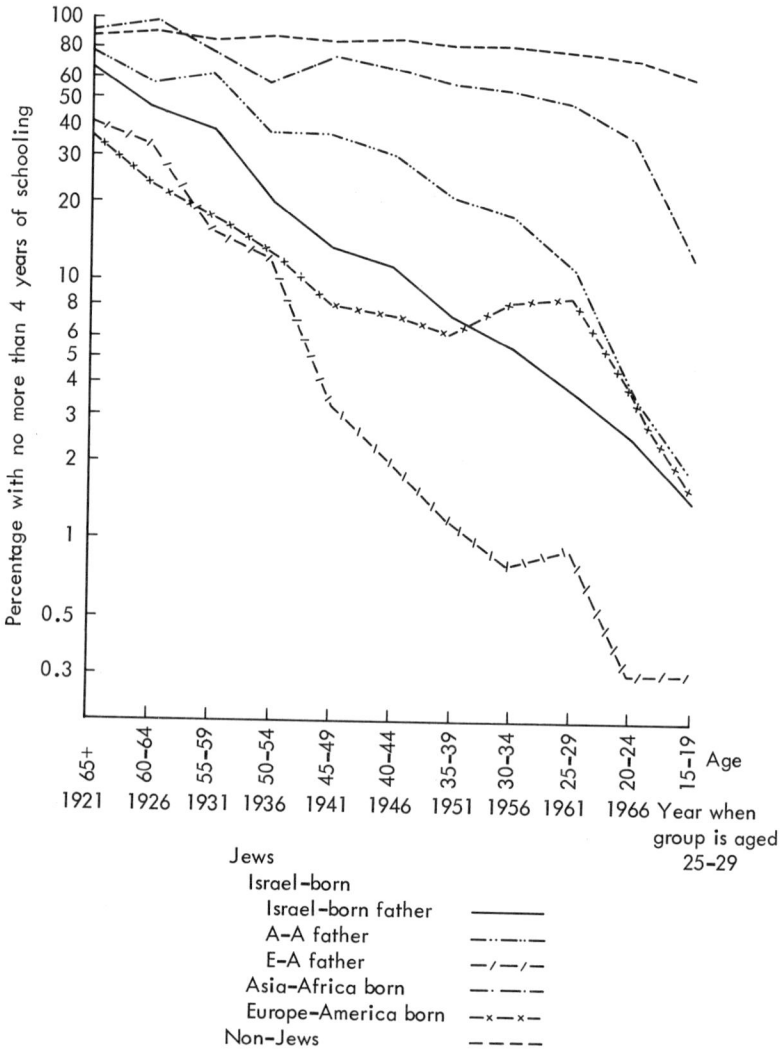

Fig. 10-4b. Age profiles of women's education, by population group: 1961. Percentage with no more than 4 years of schooling (semi-log scale).

1948 had, on the average, been in Israel 9 years by 1961 and 12 years by 1966. Only in the very first years of the State was there a decrease in average length of stay in Israel (and an increase in fertility) in this group. There was a similar decline in average length of stay among post-1948 EA immigrants, but the decline was smaller for the whole EA group because of the existence of a sizable pre-1948 population.

534

Table 10-14

Predicted Number of Children of Women Aged 40-44 in Selected Years[a]

	Actual 1961 (1)	1966[b] (2)	1971[b] (3)	1976[b] (4)	(I) 1981[b] (5)	(II) 1981[c] (6)	Change from 1961 to 1981 (I) (7)	Change from 1961 to 1981 (II) (8)
Jews	3.3	3.2	3.6	3.9	3.7	2.9	+0.4	−0.4
Israel born								
Father Israel born	3.4	3.2	3.0	2.9	2.7	2.5	−0.7	−0.9
Asia-Africa born	3.6	3.5	3.3	3.2	3.0	2.6	−0.6	−1.0
Europe-America born	4.2	4.2	4.1	4.0	3.7	2.8	−0.5	−1.4
Europe-America born	2.6	2.5	2.4	2.4	2.3	2.3	−0.3	−0.3
Asia-Africa born Veterans[d]	5.2	4.9	4.5	4.3	3.8	2.9	−1.4	−2.3
Immigrated 1948+	6.2	6.0	5.9	5.7	5.3	3.3	−0.9	−2.9
Europe-America born Veterans[d]	2.4	2.4	2.4	2.3	2.3	2.4	−0.1	0.0
Immigrated 1948+	2.0	2.0	2.0	2.0	2.0	2.6	00.0	0.6
Non-Jews	7.3	7.1	7.1	7.1	6.7	6.1	−0.6	−1.2

[a]Based on 1961 structure.

[b]Computed as follows: actual number of children per woman in each origin/years-of-schooling cell, multiplied by the schooling distribution of the cohorts due to reach age 40-44 in the specified years.

[c]The alternative 1981 prediction is based on the following assumptions: (1) by 1981 all Jews will have the education-specific number of children of children of Israel-born whose father comes from Europe-America; (2) by 1981 all non-Jews will have the education-specific number of children of new immigrants from Asia-Africa.

[d]Immigrated before 1948.

Source: Central Bureau of Statistics, Marriage and Fertility, Tables 11 and 21; Languages, Literacy, and Educational Attainment, Tables 28, 29, 32, and 33.

535

The effect of the length of stay in Israel on fertility is complex, and I do not feel qualified to analyze it here. In all the discussion I have abstracted from marriage habits, time, and location, which are crucial in this context; and there are significant differences between couples married in Israel and those married abroad. Apparently a learning process is involved. In the case of the AA group not only the learning of birth control techniques and the adjustment of the desired number of children to new levels of the determining variables are involved, but also changes in preferences or tastes.[13] The economist as such is not in a position to elaborate on changing tastes except to note that (partial) residential[14] and school integration, universal military service, and a reduction in endogamy are some of the channels through which consumption aspirations and tastes with respect to the number of children have operated on successive waves of AA immigrants. Of course, these forces also operate through some of the variables mentioned before, such as the increase in the amount of children's schooling, the decline in infant mortality, and the adjustment of expectations about child survival.

What explains the fertility movement of the EA and Israel-born groups? The initial decline of the early 1950s was only partly a result of an increase in the level of education. One additional possibility is that this decline was really a return to a normal long-term level of fertility following the rather extended postwar baby boom.[15] The very high fertility of the early 1950s might also have been due to postponement of births during the 1948/49 war. As regards the Israel-born, the composition by father's country of birth changed: the proportion of women of childbearing age with EA parents grew over the 1950s, and this is the Israel-born subgroup with the lowest fertility. There may also have been a decline in the proportion of Jews who are religiously observant and have high fertility.

What does seem to require explanation is the slight increase in fertility in the first half of the 1960s. As suggested by Table 10-13, an increase in the level of education should by itself have caused some *reduction* in fertility between 1961 and 1966 (using the education-specific 1966 rates, we get a higher number of births than expected on the basis of origin alone). Thus, some counteracting variables must have been at work. One such variable could be the group's internal composition. In fact, new EA immigrants seem to have had somewhat higher

[13] Matras and Auerbach, "On Rationalization of Family Formation in Israel," suggest that there may also be a reduction in the number of people for whom family size is not in any sense a matter for decision.
[14] There is much less integration in rural areas because many *moshavim* were established by groups of homogeneous origin. The effect of this in birth control practices is noted in Bachi and Matras, "Contraception and Induced Abortions Among Jewish Maternity Cases in Israel."
[15] See Roberto Bachi, "Trends of Population and Labour Force in Israel," *The Challenge of Development,* Eliezer Kaplan School of Economics and Social Sciences, The Hebrew University, Jerusalem, 1958, pp. 41–80.

fertility than those entering Israel before 1948, but some increase in fertility occurred in the 1960s even within the latter group. As far as the Israel-born are concerned, there was almost no change in the composition (by father's country of birth) of this group of childbearing women.

One possibility, suggested with some hesitation, is the operation of a positive income effect. In a regression analysis of the short-term variation in fertility among the origin groups, there was statistically significant procyclical conformity.[16] This was particularly marked in the last few years. An economic recession from late 1965 to early 1967 produced a "depression" in the fertility indicators of all groups in the population. In regard to the early 1960s, the figures may reflect the operation of a direct income effect only partly offset by the depressing effect of rising education. This, however, could reflect mostly sensitivity of the timing of birth.

I rely on some kind of income effect when discussing the differences in trend between non-Jews and Jews, particularly the AA group. If in Figure 10-4 we regard the age profile as a time series, the level of education of non-Jewish women has been low and almost unchanging for a long time, and a spurt in the level of education of Arab women of childbearing age occurs only now—20 years after it occurred among Jewish AA-born women and 40 years after it occurred among the Israel-born of AA parentage. Thus, there has up to now been no reason to expect any significant reduction in fertility among non-Jewish women stemming from improvement in their education.

On the other hand, the Arab population has experienced a rapid increase in income during the period reviewed (except in 1965–1967), an increase largely dependent on the gradual penetration of Arab labor into the Jewish labor market.[17] It seems that there has been a positive income effect without the commonly observed associated characteristics making their appearance. Improvement in women's education is only one of these.

The Arab population lives mostly in Arab settlements. All rural Arabs reside in exclusively Arab villages, and only some urban Arabs live in mixed Jewish-Arab cities, and even then mostly in distinct neighborhoods (so that the school system is in effect segregated). Most contacts between the two groups have been through the labor market, but even here they seem to have remained mainly functional. Thus, it could perhaps be said that the majority of Arabs have been screened from much of the demonstration effect of the high and rising Jewish consumption levels and that therefore some of the income increase may

---

[16] Some degree of cyclical conformity among the Jewish population of Palestine before 1948 was noted by R. Bachi, "Demographic Development in Israel," *Economic Quarterly* (in Hebrew), Vol. II, No. 8 (June 1955), pp. 379–392. P. Schwinger has found cyclical conformity in the post-1948 period in his "The Business Cycle and Fertility," The Leon Recanati Graduate School for Business Administration, Tel Aviv University, May 1969 (Hebrew mimeo.).

[17] See Yoram Ben-Porath, *The Arab Labor Force in Israel,* Falk Institute, Jerusalem, 1966.

well have been allocated to having more children. This is in contrast to the AA-born Jews, whose integration into the general economy and society has gone much deeper and for whom rising income has been coupled with rising aspirations in consumption, education, and mode of living. In short, the veterancy or learning effect that operated forcefully on the Jewish immigrants who came from Arab countries has been operating on only a small fraction of the Arab population of Israel.

IV. Outlook

The prediction of future fertility trends requires us to make judgments about possible changes within each population group and predictions of the future relative sizes of the various groups. It is reasonable to expect a continued rise in the educational level of the Jewish population, more steeply for AA than for EA women. The education effect is thus likely to persist in both groups, but much less in EA than in AA. Table 10-14 presents the number of children of women due to reach age 40–44 in the specified years, predicted on the basis of the 1961 census; the prediction takes into account only the changes in educational composition. Column 6 gives the lower limit for the number of children, based on the assumption that the education-specific standard of the Israel-born with EA fathers is adopted by all other Jewish groups.

In regard to income prospects, a continuation of long-term growth can be expected, although in the next few years balance-of-payments problems are likely to force some reduction in the rate of growth. However, the early 1970s will be marked by a disproportionately large entry of young people into the labor force. In 1968, there were about 141,000 persons aged 25–29 and about 223,000 aged 20–24; the 20–24 group was 17.7 percent of the 20–64 population in 1968, compared with 12.6 percent in 1961. This large jump in labor force entrants is a result of the mass immigration that followed the establishment of Israel in 1948 (see Table 10-1). The relative position of the young in the labor market may be somewhat weakened.[18] With higher immigration forecast than in the 1960s, rates of labor force entry are likely to be higher than they have ever been except in the first years of the State. All in all, once fertility has completely recovered from the depression of 1966/67, there is no ground for relying on a positive income effect.

As for the non-Jewish population, the following points seem relevant. The effect of rising education is only now beginning to be felt. Of the Arab women now *entering* their childbearing period, more than half had 5 or more years of school and the proportion is increasing: in the second half of the 1960s less than one-third of the women in the main childbearing period had 5 or more years of schooling and only one-eighth in the early 1950s. The two alternative predictions

[18] The importance of this consideration in the fertility context of the United States was suggested by Easterlin, *Population, Labor Force, and Long Swings in Economic Growth*.

of the expected number of children of Arab women aged 40–44 in 1981 in Table 10-14 are still very high.

It is reasonable to predict that incomes of the non-Jewish population will grow more slowly than in the past, when they increased to a large extent because an increasing proportion of non-Jews entered the general labor market. A severe setback accompanied the 1966/67 depression, followed by recovery. However, the population of the territories occupied by Israel in June 1967 constitutes a new factor in the labor market. Although the entry of these persons into the Is-raeli labor market has been controlled, the number of Arabs from the occupied territories working in Israel today is probably as much as two-thirds of the num-ber of Israeli Arabs employed outside their own settlements. The prospects are for a sizable increase, and this factor will surely depress the rise in real wages and income of Israeli Arabs. Thus, there are, on the whole, grounds for predict-ing some decline in the fertility of the non-Jewish population (a decline which up to now has been clearly observed only among the Christians).

One should note that the single most important goal of population policy in Israel is to increase the country's Jewish population through immigration or births ("internal immigration"). The government has therefore done nothing to curb the fertility of the high-fertility groups (Jews *and* non-Jews alike), and there is no likelihood of its adopting any fertility-control policy in the foreseea-ble future. Relief of the economic hardship suffered by large families[19] is visual-ized in terms of public assistance in the form of transfers or services. What the policymakers are concerned with is how to *increase* the birth rate and in particu-lar how to induce Jewish families whose goal is two children to have three or four.[20]

The changing group weights in the population must be taken into account, as well as the considerations specific to each group. Thus, the total number of children of women aged 40–44 is expected to rise, in spite of a decline over time within each group, because the proportion of AA women aged 40–44 will be larger in the future than it was in 1961 (on the basis of the population present in 1961 and also in 1968).

Within the Israel-born group there will be a large increase in the proportion of women with AA-born parents. In Table 10-14 the predicted number of child-ren of Israel-born women aged 40–44 is 2.7 in 1981. If subsequent cohorts have the same level of education in each origin group as those who will be 40–44 in 1981, and if the 1961 education-specific number of children is used, then the av-erage number of children of Israel-born women aged 40–44 will rise from 2.7 in 1981 to 2.8 in 1991 and 3.1 in 1996. This view is, however, incomplete because it does not take account of the size and structure of immigration, which is likely to be biased toward Europe and America, as compared with the existing stock of population.

---

[19] Recently documented in A. Nizan, "A Study of Living Conditions of Multichild Families," National Insurance Institute, Jerusalem, 1969 (Hebrew mimeo.).

[20] See *Report of the Committee on Problems of Fertility,* April 1966, Jerusalem (He-brew mimeo.).

CHAPTER 11

Factors Affecting Adoption of New Agricultural Techniques in Lebanese Agriculture*

Fawzi M. Al-Haz and Salah M. Yacoub

* Approved for publication as Journal No. 287 by the Faculty of Agricultural Sciences of the American University of Beirut.

Empirical investigations of the diffusion of new technology in agriculture in the Middle East are very scarce. This chapter by Al-Haj and Yacoub of the American University of Beirut reports on two such studies in Lebanon and assesses their implications for development. The authors are careful not to use their data too ambitiously to try to prove some particular theory of development or to support a particular set of policies. What they do show convincingly is that sweeping generalizations about traditional agriculture, the factors influencing its modernization, or the policies that are desirable are likely to be more satisfactory on paper than in practice. Even in a single country, differences between communities and individuals are large enough to warrant special handling if government programs are to be effective. One of the most interesting of their findings is the selectivity of farmers in adopting new techniques. Improved techniques may resemble each other to the planner or the local official; but to the farmer, for whom change is risky as well as rewarding, differences in cost, complexity, and certainty will make one kind of change very different from another. Finally, the reliance of farmers on neighbors and friends for information and advice about new techniques indicates how important it is to design government programs carefully if they are to be effective. Finding the local innovators and concentrating on them may be far more efficient than attempting to change everybody at once.

Having read Al-Haj and Yacoub, an economist will probably think to himself that all this work is unnecessary—left to its own devices, the market will find, stimulate, and reward the local innovators. But the important kernel of truth in that thought must be digested carefully. Al-Haj and Yacoub are talking about communities in which there are important gaps in the market—monopoly, ignorance, and inappropriate public policies—as well as about accelerating nonmarginal changes when market solutions may be deemed too slow. Perhaps the right conclusion is that better information cannot hurt and may be indispensable.

Factors Affecting Adoption of New Agricultural Techniques in Lebanese Agriculture*

I. Introduction

In the past two decades, research dealing with the adoption of agricultural technology has contributed to our understanding of the problems in the human communication process in relation to the adoption of farm ideas and practices. Such research has provided information from which conclusions and generalizations about the communication process may be drawn. In general, farmers do not tend to adopt a farm practice or idea as soon as they hear about it, even if the practice has been tested by agricultural research experts and the results clearly indicate its usefulness. There is also a variation in the rate at which different farmers adopt a farm practice. The responses of farmers have been correlated with a variety of social, psychological, and economic factors such as income, education, size of farm, age, and participation in organizations.

Agricultural development is a planned process that uses any type of action or communication designed to affect the institutions, techniques, environment, and minds of rural people in such a manner as to raise their standard of living and improve their way of life.[1] Agricultural development, therefore, involves changes in the productivity of farmers, which is possible when they learn and adopt improved methods of cultivation. Adoption of the improved methods is greatly influenced by certain sociological and economic factors, and a knowledge of the factors that contribute to the acceptance or rejection of the new practices can be useful in removing the obstacles in the way of agricultural development. The rapid technological development of U.S. farming was largely a result of the diffusion and acceptance of new ideas and practices.[2]

In addition to the contributions that adoption research can make to agricultural development, we believe that the findings of diffusion studies will continue to be highly useful in developing greater understanding of educational and change processes, in allocating resources more efficiently, and in providing a sound basis for the evaluation of educational programs in various Middle East-

---

[1] U. A. Aziz, "Scope for National and International Action: The Interdependent Development of Agriculture and Other Industries," Tenth International Conference of Agricultural Economists, Mysore, India, 1958.

[2] Everett M. Rogers, *Social Change in Rural Society*, Appleton-Century-Crofts, New York, 1960, p. 398.

ern countries. Such research studies can also help commercial firms, extension workers, and other adult educators to upgrade the quality of their educational programs and services for farmers. Furthermore, through their contributions to educational programs, these research findings can help to cut the time lag in the acceptance of new ideas. This, in turn, can help to make agriculture a more efficient enterprise.

The investigation of the phenomenon of adoption has been limited largely to the United States. Thus far, more than five hundred studies on the adoption of innovations have been conducted, but none of these was done in any of the Arab Middle Eastern countries. We have recently begun to direct some research activities to this area.[3]

The objective of the study is to show that both traditional agriculture and technical change have many dimensions: degree of subsistence farming, scale, remoteness, crop mix, and others. The rate at which improved technology is diffused will depend on how policies and operational practices interact with this complex setting. The underlying assumption is that traditional farmers are rational and will change their agricultural techniques when proper inducements are present.

II. Methodology

Nine villages in the Extension Pilot Project area around the Agricultural Research and Education Center (AREC) of the American University of Beirut (AUB), Beka'a, Lebanon were selected in Al-Haj's study on the basis of the intensity of contacts that took place during 1959–1965 between the extension advisor and wheat growers in the area.[4] In Hammad's study, another nine villages in the Abey area, where olive growing constituted the greatest part of agriculture, were selected for the survey.[5] The latter study represents a relatively more progressive area than does the former one.

The data were collected by interviews with a sample of 137 wheat growers and 160 olive growers selected at random from the list of wheat and olive grow-

[3] Fawzi M. Al-Haj, "Evaluation of Selected Programs and Teaching Methods of the AREC Extension Pilot Project, 1957–1966," Faculty of Agricultural Sciences, American University of Beirut, Publication No. 31, April 1968; Ola J. Hammad, "Relative Effectiveness of Various Extension Methods and Programs in Abey Area of Mount Lebanon," unpublished M.S. thesis, Faculty of Agricultural Sciences, American University of Beirut, September 1968; Salah M. Yacoub, "Factors and Sources of Information Related to the Growing of Sunflower as a Replacement of Hasheesh in the Northern Beka'a, Lebanon," Faculty of Agricultural Sciences, American University of Beirut (forthcoming).

[4] The villages covered were Beit Chama, Hazzine, Housh Barada, Housh el-Nabi, Housh el-Rafika, Kafr Dabash, Lower Sarein, Majdaloun, and Talia.

[5] These include Aynab, Ayn Enoub, Baysoor, Bennay, Bshamoun, Dakkoun, Faskin, Rimhala, and Shwayfat.

ers by the extension agents of the two areas. The data were then coded, punched into IBM cards, and analyzed through the facilities of the AUB Computer Center.

III. Factors Influencing Differences in the Rate of Adoption of New Technology

Differences in the rate of adoption of seven recommended wheat practices and four olive practices are shown in Tables 11-1 and 11-2. The responses showed

Table 11-1
Rate of Adoption of
Seven Recommended Practices on Wheat
(137 farmers)

Recommended Practice	No.	Percent
Seed treatments for smuts	126	92
Seed preparation	42	31
Rate of fertilization	30	22
Time of fertilization	22	16
Improved varieties	20	15
Crop rotation	17	12
Planting by drilling	0	0

Table 11-2
Rate of Adoption of
Recommended Practices on Olives
(160 farmers)

Recommended Practice	No.	Percent
Proper rate of fertilizer	119	74
Proper time of fertilization	87	54
Proper pruning	131	82
Pest control	39	24
Treatment of olive fruit fly	39	24
Treatment of olive leaf spot	3	2

definite technical change among wheat and olive growers, but the degree of change was different for different practices. For example, planting by drilling of wheat seeds and olive leaf spot control were, for all practical purposes, not adopted by growers. In contrast, nearly all wheat grower respondents (92.0 percent) and a little over four-fifths (82.0 percent) of the olive growers interviewed adopted the practices of seed treatments for smuts and the proper pruning of olive trees, respectively. About one-third of the wheat growers used proper techniques in seedbed preparation. The practices pertaining to fertilization, selected varieties, and crop rotation were adopted by over one-fifth of the wheat growers, but not necessarily by the same farmers in each case. Three-fourths of the olive growers used the proper rate and combination of fertilizer, and over one-half applied it at the proper time. Only one-fourth of the olive growers interviewed protected their trees against commonly encountered pests.

The speed with which adoption takes place is influenced by many cultural, economic, educational, and social factors, some of which will be discussed later. One of the two areas under study represents a traditional community in transition, where agricultural work is largely performed according to old inherited practices, and the other represents a somewhat more progressive community. With the exception of the planting of wheat by drilling and the olive leaf spot control practices, farmers in the two study areas were receptive rather than resistant to technical change when requisites necessary for implementation were made available. Wheat and olive growers in the two areas would probably adopt planting by drilling and pest control, especially the treatment of olive leaf spot, if the necessary equipment, technical know-how, and money were provided to them. The fact that some wheat- and olive-related practices were accepted to a greater extent among the two groups of growers than were others was mainly due to the reduced cost, simplicity, and feasibility of such practices. This point will be discussed later in greater detail when the reasons for not adopting each individual practice are analyzed.

Research on diffusion, as a whole, has revealed important information about the way in which change takes place and the influences that operate in relation thereto. A multiplicity of social, cultural, personal, and situational factors will have some bearing on the rate of adoption of new technology.[6] In this section, an attempt is made to investigate the influence that community, individual, and situational differences may exert on the rate of adoption. In addition, the influence of the nature of practices on the rates of their adoption will be discussed.

The Community Differences

The areas under study represent two of the most commonly prevailing types of rural communities in Lebanon. The AREC area is typical of the plain sector of agricultural settlement. It is characterized by subsistence farming; agricultural work is largely performed according to inherited practices. People in these com-

[6] H. F. Lionberger, *Adoption of New Ideas and Practices,* The Iowa State University Press, Ames, 1960.

munities have experienced a very limited amount of technical and social change. On the contrary, the people of the Abey area, being in close proximity to Beirut, are in direct and extensive contact with the outside world and with new innovations. Thus, they are relatively modernized and progressive. The majority of the people in this area are part-time farmers depending on nonagricultural sources of employment for most of their income. This area is typical of the Mount Lebanon region and other rural communities near the large cities of Lebanon.

Though basic data related to community differences were not collected to allow for precise measures of their relative influence, it was assumed that farmers in the Abey area would show a higher rate of adoption than the Beqa'a farmers. The analysis in Tables 11-1 and 11-2 tends to support this assumption; in general, the percentage of various practices adopted was consistently higher among the olive growers of the Abey area.

The study also included an analysis of possible relationships between certain demographic and situational factors and the adoption patterns of certain recommended practices. Frequencies and percentages were used to describe the nature and direction of relationships. Because of the small sample size and the fact that the observed frequencies were too low in many cells of the tables, the use of chi-square analysis would have some serious limitations. However, the interdependence between several variables implies that there is an inherent multivariate model underlying the results. This was not accounted for in the original plan for analysis of the raw data.

Differences Among Respondents

Age

Age can be regarded as an important factor in influencing the adoption of improved farm practices. Van den Ban found that progressive farmers tend to be young.[7] Considerable support was found for the hypothesis that age is a deterrent to the adoption of new ways. Elderly farmers were found to be less inclined to adopt a change in farm practices than younger ones.[8]

The data from the wheat study also show that the rate of adoption is inversely related to the age of the respondents. The younger age group (35 years or less) treated their seeds for smuts before planting and applied the proper formula for fertilization. In contrast, all those who did not use chemical fertilizer

[7] A. W. Van den Ban, "Some Characteristics of Progressive Farmers in the Netherlands," *Rural Sociology*, Vol. 22 (1957), p. 205.

[8] J. H. Copp et al., "The Function of Information Sources in the Farm Practice Adoption Process," *Rural Sociology*, Vol. 23 (June 1958), pp. 146–157; H. F. Lionberger, "Information-Seeking Habits and Characteristics of Farm Operators," Missouri Agricultural Experiment Station, Research Bulletin No. 581, pp. 7–8; E. A. Wilkening, "Communication and Acceptance of Recommended Farm Practices Among Dairy Farmers of Northern Victoria," *Rural Sociology*, Vol. 27 (June 1962), p. 164; Lowell Brander and Bryant Kearl, "Evaluation for Congruence as a Factor in Adoption Rate of Innovations," *Rural Sociology*, Vol. 29 (September 1964), p. 296.

Table 11-3

Age in relation to the Adoption of
Seed Treatment Practice on Wheat

Age (years)	Seeds treated by Farmer		Already Treated		Untreated	
	No.	Per-cent	No.	Per-cent	No.	Per-cent
35 or less	20	20	5	19	...	...
36-45	20	20	12	46	6	55
46-55	26	26	1	4	2	18
56 or more	34	34	8	31	3	27
Total	100	100	26	100	11	100

Table 11-4

Age in Relation to the Adoption of the
Rate of Fertilization Practice on Wheat

Age (years)	Recommended Formula		Nitrogen Only		No Fertilizers	
	No.	Per-cent	No.	Per-cent	No.	Per-cent
35 or less	5	17	18	22	...	...
36-45	12	40	19	23	...	...
46-55	5	17	20	24	2	17
56 or more	8	26	26	31	10	83
Total	30	100	83	100	12	100

were in the upper age groups (46 years of age or more) (Tables 11-3 and 11-4).

On the other hand, age among the sample population of the olive study seemed to have no bearing upon the farmers' adoption of any of the practices studied.

Level of Education

It was assumed in the two studies under review that the rate of adoption of new practices is conditioned by the level of education. Farmers having more education were expected to be more receptive to technical change. Higher than grade school education is almost always associated with high adoption rates to a greater degree than is lesser education.[9]

Among the Lebanese wheat growers interviewed, it was found that all farmers with secondary education adopted the seed treatment practice whereas all those who did not treat their seeds had acquired only some elementary education or no education whatever. In relation to the rate of fertilization practice, over three-fourths of the wheat growers adopting it had elementary or secondary education. In contrast, three-fourths of the nonadopters were illiterate. Level of education was also significantly related to the time of fertilization practice on wheat. All farmers adopting it were found to have completed their elementary or secondary school education (Tables 11-5 through 11-7).

Educational level was also an important factor in influencing olive growers to accept improved practices. Tables 11-8 and 11-9 show a relationship between the level of education of the respondent and the adoption of the proper fertilization practice in terms of rate and time of application. The two tables indicate an increase in the number of respondents with elementary and secondary education who used these two recommended olive practices. Farmers with elementary education showed the highest adoption of the rate of fertilization practice, while those with secondary education fertilized more at the right time. Moreover, education was also related to the pruning or pest control practices on olive trees. The differences in percentages favored the farmers who had completed elementary and secondary education over the illiterate ones (Tables 11-10 and 11-11).

In conclusion, there is evidence that education tends to make a difference in the acceptance of new agricultural techniques by Lebanese farmers. Generally, the more education the farmers have the greater is the likelihood that they will adopt approved practices. The implications of these findings to an extension agent would be to precede his teaching efforts with a proper identification of the various educational groups among his clientele, and to adjust his teaching-learning activities and methods to the different levels for effective results.

Experience in Farming

The assumption that farmers with many years of experience develop some well-established ways of doing their field work and, therefore, tend to resist or even reject change more than newly established farmers was examined for both the wheat and the olive growers interviewed. From the analysis of the data, the results pertaining to the effect of farming experience on the adoption of new wheat and olive practices can be summarized as follows. There was an inverse relationship between the wheat farmers' experience and their adoption of the rate of fertilization practice. Almost all wheat farmers who did not use fertilizer had over

[9] Copp et al. "The Function of Information Sources in the Farm Practice Adoption Process," pp. 146–157; Lionberger, "Information-Seeking Habits and Characteristics of Farm Operators," p. 9; and C. P. Marsh and A. L. Coleman, "The Relationship of Farmer Characteristics to the Adoption of Recommended Farm Practices," *Rural Sociology,* Vol. 20 (December 1955), pp. 289–296.

Table 11-5

Level of Education in Relation to the
Adoption of the Seed Treatment Practice on Wheat

Level of Education	Seeds Treated by Farmer		Already Treated		Untreated	
	No.	Per-cent	No.	Per-cent	No.	Per-cent
Second education	5	5	5	19	. . .	. . .
Elementary education	53	53	18	69	9	82
Read and write	7	7	. . .	. . .	. . .	. . .
Illiterate	35	35	3	12	2	18
Total	100	100	26	100	11	100

Table 11-6

Level of Education in Relation to the
Adoption of the Rate of Fertilization Practice on Wheat

Level of Education	Recommended Formula		Nitrogen Only		No Fertilizers	
	No.	Per-cent	No.	Per-cent	No.	Per-cent
Secondary education	8	27	2	2	. . .	. . .
Elementary education	16	53	49	59	3	25
Read and write	1	3	6	7	. . .	. . .
Illiterate	5	17	26	32	9	75
Total	30	100	83	100	12	100

Table 11-7

Level of Education in Relation to the
Time of Fertilization Practice on Wheat

Level of Education	Recommended Time		Phosphorus at Sowing, Nitrogen in Spring		Nitrogen in Spring only	
	No.	Per-cent	No.	Per-cent	No.	Per-cent
Secondary education	1	11	2	15	2	3
Elementary education	8	89	9	70	47	59
Read and write	. . .	. . .	. . .	. . .	6	8
Illiterate	. . .	. . .	2	15	25	30
Total	9	100	13	100	80	100

Table 11-8
Level of Education in Relation to the
Adoption of the Rate of Fertilization Practice on Olives

Level of Education	No Fertilizers		Pure Ammonium Sulfate or Animal Manure Alone		Recommended and Accepted Formula			
					Mixed by Farmers		Commercial Ready Mix	
	No.	Per-cent	No.	Per-cent	No.	Per-cent	No.	Per-cent
Illiterate	1	20	7	20	9	12	6	14
Elementary education	1	20	25	71	41	55	28	63
Secondary education or above	3	60	3	9	25	33	10	23
Total	5	100	35	100	75	100	44	100

Table 11-9
Level of Education in Relation to the
Adoption of the Time of Fertilization Practice on Olives

Level of Education	Recommended and Accepted Time					
	All in Feb.		All in Nov. and Dec.		Nov., Dec., and Some Later in Feb.	
	No.	Per-cent	No.	Per-cent	No.	Per-cent
Illiterate	11	16	8	15	3	9
Elementary education	48	72	32	59	13	41
Secondary education or above	8	12	14	26	16	50
Total	67	100	54	100	32	100

Table 11-10

Level of Education in Relation to the Adoption of the Pruning Practice on Olives

Level of Education	No Pruning		Very Heavy Pruning		Recommended Method	
	No.	Per-cent	No.	Per-cent	No.	Per-cent
Illiterate	4	26	1	8	18	14
Elementary education	6	37	11	84	78	59
Secondary education or above	6	37	1	8	35	27
Total	16	100	13	100	131	100

Table 11-11

Level of Education in Relation to the Pest Control Practice on Olives

	Recommended and Accepted Practices						
	Regularly		Sometimes		When Needed Only		Never
Level of Education	No.	Per-cent	No.	Per-cent	No.	Per-cent	No.	Per-cent
Illiterate	2	13	1	11	3	20	17	14
Elementary education	9	60	5	56	8	53	73	60
Secondary education or above	4	27	3	33	4	27	31	26
Total	15	100	9	100	15	100	121	100

Table 11-12

Experience in Farming in Relation to the
Adoption of the Rate of Fertilization Practice on Wheat

Experience in Farming (years)	Recommended Formula		Nitrogen Only		No Fertilizers	
	No.	Per-cent	No.	Per-cent	No.	Per-cent
10 or less	4	13	9	11	. . .	. . .
11-20	13	43	25	30	. . .	. . .
21-30	8	27	13	15	4	33
31-40	3	10	22	27	4	33
41 or more	2	7	14	17	4	33
Total	20	100	83	100	12	99

Table 11-13

Experience in Farming in Relation to the
Adoption of the Rate of Fertilization Practice on Olives

Experience in Farming (years)	No Fertilizers		Pure Ammonium Sulfate or Animal Manure Alone		Recommended and Accepted Formula			
					Mixed by Farmers		Commercial Ready Mix	
	No.	Per-cent	No.	Per-cent	No.	Per-cent	No.	Per-cent
10 or less	2	40	5	14	16	21	12	27
11-20	1	20	11	32	19	26	13	30
21-30	0	0	7	20	16	21	5	11
31-40	2	40	5	14	12	16	6	14
41 or more	0	0	7	20	12	16	8	18
Total	5	100	35	100	75	100	44	100

20 years of experience in farming. In contrast, over one-half of the users of the recommended fertilizer formula had less than 20 years of experience (Table 11-12). In the case of olive growers, experience in farming seemed also to be inversely related to the adoption of the recommended fertilizer formula. In other words, the less experienced farmers were more likely to accept the recommended rate of fertilization and vice versa (Table 11-13). Experience in farming seemed to have no clear effect, however, on the adoption of any of the remaining wheat and olive practices studied.

These observations seem to confirm the trend implied in the assumption. Experience in farming could be associated with age of the farmers, since usually older farmers tend to have more experience and to be less inclined to change their traditional practices. The implication of these findings to the extension agent would be to select and use appropriate extension teaching methods which would appeal to various groups of farmers with different degrees of experience. Farmers with many years of experience can be persuaded to adopt improved practices through the use of convincing methods with local and tangible proof of their values, such as the result and demonstration method, whereby the farmer can observe step by step how a given practice is done in his own village situation and can see for himself its merits over the local practices.

Differences in Farmers' Circumstances

Size of Farm

Size of farm was significantly related to early adoption of the recommended practices.[10] Nonadopters generally operated fewer acres than adopters did. Therefore, it was assumed in the two studies under review that owners of large

[10] J. H. Copp, "Personal and Social Factors Associated with the Adoption of Recommended Farm Practices Among Cattlemen," Kansas State College Agricultural Experiment Station, Technical Bulletin No. 83, September 1956, p. 2; M. C. Wilson and G. Gallup, "Extension Teaching Methods and Other Factors That Influence Adoption of Agricultural and Home Economics Practices," Federal Extension Service, U.S. Department of Agriculture Circular No. 495, August 1955; Brander and Kearl, "Evaluation for Congruence as a Factor in Adoption Rate of Innovations," p. 296.

Table 11-14

Size of Farm in Relation to the Adoption of the Seed Treatment Practice on Wheat

Size of Farm (dunums)	Seeds Treated by Farmer		Already Treated		Untreated	
	No.	Per cent	No.	Per cent	No.	Per cent
Less than 30	8	8	1	4	1	9
30-89	38	38	3	12	3	27
90-149	17	17	3	12	4	37
150-219	16	16	8	31	2	18
220 or more	21	21	11	41	1	9
Total	100	100	26	100	11	100

Table 11-15

Size of Farm in Relation to the
Adoption of the Rate of Fertilization Practice on Wheat

Size of farm (dunums)	Recommended Formula		Nitrogen Only		No Fertilizers	
	No.	Per-cent	No.	Per-cent	No.	Per-cent
Less than 30	. . .	. . .	6	7	4	24
30-89	6	20	30	36	6	41
80-149	4	13	13	16	2	35
150-219	8	27	15	18	. . .	. . .
220 or more	12	40	19	23	. . .	. . .
Total	30	100	83	100	12	100

Table 11-16

Size of Farm in Relation to the
Adoption of the Time of Fertilization Practice on Wheat

Size of Farm (dunums)	Recommended Time		Phosphorus at Sowing, Nitrogen in Spring		Nitrogen in Spring Only	
	No.	Per-cent	No.	Per-cent	No.	Per-cent
Less than 30	. . .	. . .	1	8	6	8
30-89	2	22	5	38	29	36
90-149	2	22	2	15	13	16
150-219	. . .	. . .	4	31	14	18
220 or more	5	56	1	8	18	22
Total	9	100	13	100	80	100

farms would be more receptive to adopting the recommended practices than owners of small farms.

Data presented in Tables 11-14 through 11-16 show a relationship between size of farm and the adoption of the seed treatment practice for wheat, with the greatest proportion of adoption being exercised by farmers owning 30–89 dunums. In addition, over one-half of the wheat growers who adopted the rate and

555

Table 11-17

Size of Farm in Relation to the
Adoption of the Time of Fertilization Practice

			Recommended and Accepted Time			
	All in Feb.		All in Nov. and Dec.		Nov., Dec., and Some Later in Feb.	
Size of Farm (dunums)	No.	Per-cent	No.	Per-cent	No.	Per-cent
10 or less	14	21	13	24	3	9
11-20	24	36	16	30	11	34
21-40	18	27	16	30	4	13
41 or more	11	16	9	16	14	44
Total	67	100	54	100	32	100

time of fertilization practices owned large farms, whereas none of the small farm owners adopted the recommended formula for fertilization at the right time.

For olive growers, size of farm seemed to be related to one practice only, namely, applying fertilizer at the right time. The direction of this relationship is seen in Table 11-17. Of the large farm operators 44.0 percent applied fertilizers at the right time, compared with only 9.0 percent of the small farm operators. These findings therefore support the assumption that operators of larger farms are generally more receptive to improved methods of agriculture.

Proportion of Income from Agriculture

Slocum assumed that "every one who lives on a farm has some interest in agriculture. A person whose major occupational role is that of a full-time farmer has a much more vital interest in prices for agricultural products and other aspects of agricultural policy than one who earns most of his living from a nonfarm job."[11] This assumption could also apply to interest in adopting technical innovations. Thus it was assumed that the rate at which farmers adopt recommended practices on wheat and olives is positively related to the proportion of the income these farmers earn from agriculture.

The major findings, in relation to this assumption, can be summarized as follows. Over two-thirds of the wheat growers who adopted the seed treatment practice depended on agricultural pursuits for over 75.0 percent of their income. Only one-tenth of the adopters derived less than one-fourth of their income from agriculture. There is a relationship, therefore, between the proportion of income

[11] Walter L. Slocum, *Agricultural Sociology,* Harper and Brothers, New York, 1962, pp. 36–37.

derived from agriculture and adoption of the seed treatment practice on wheat (Table 11-18).

The analysis pertaining to the rate and time of fertilization practices on wheat yielded results similar to those for seed treatment, with over two-thirds of the adopters being fully dependent on agriculture for their livelihood. In contrast, two-thirds of the nonadopters of the proper fertilization formula obtained only one-fourth of their income from agricultural sources. The direction of relationship, as shown by the percentage distribution, between proportion of income from agriculture and acceptance of each of the fertilization practices, rate and time, was as expected (Tables 11-19 and 11-20).

In the case of olive growers, no relationship was found between income derived from farming and readiness to adopt improved techniques, for any of the four practices under investigation.

In conclusion, full-time wheat farmers earning most of their income from agricultural pursuits were more concerned with the technical improvement of their cultural operations and more receptive to change in practices than part-time wheat farmers who depended mainly on nonfarm sources of income for their livelihood. The olive grower study failed to support such findings. The area from which the sample of olive growers was drawn was characterized by part-time farming, and a little over one-half of the population interviewed depended mainly on their income from nonagricultural jobs. A variable that could be suggested here as having some bearing on the adoption of recommended practices is the total income, irrespective of its source, particularly for practices that involve some capital. Reasons other than financial could also be attributed, and therefore further investigations are needed to identify them.

Land Tenure

The hypothesis was that owner-operators would tend to be more receptive to change than tenants (both cash renters and sharecroppers). This trend was

Table 11-18

Proportion of Income from Agriculture in Relation to the Adoption of the Seed Treatment Practice on Wheat

Proportion of Income from Agriculture (percent)	Seeds Treated by Farmer		Already Treated		Untreated	
	No.	Per-cent	No.	Per-cent	No.	Per-cent
25 or less	7	7	1	4	5	45
26-50	10	10	2	8	1	10
51-75	15	15	1	4	. . .	. . .
76-100	68	68	22	84	5	45
Total	100	100	26	100	11	100

Table 11-19

Proportion of Income from Agriculture in Relation to the Adoption of the Rate of Fertilization Practice on Wheat

Proportion of Income from Agriculture (percent)	Recommended Formula		Nitrogen Only		No Fertilizers	
	No.	Per-cent	No.	Per-cent	No.	Per-cent
25 or less	. . .	. . .	6	7	7	66
26-50	5	17	5	6	3	25
51-75	2	7	12	14	2	9
76-100	23	76	60	73	. . .	. . .
Total	30	100	83	100	12	100

Table 11-20

Proportion of Income from Agriculture in Relation to the Adoption of the Time of Fertilization Practice

Proportion of Income from Agriculture (percent)	Recommended Time		Phosphorus at Sowing, Nitrogen in Spring		Nitrogen in Spring Only	
	No.	Per-cent	No.	Per-cent	No.	Per-cent
25 or less	. . .	. . .	1	8	6	8
26-50	2	22	2	15	5	6
51-75	1	11	1	8	12	15
76-100	6	67	9	69	57	71
Total	9	100	13	100	80	100

observed, however, only in the case of adoption of pest control practice on olives (Table 11-21). A practice of this type, which requires money, equipment, and technical knowledge, needs the authority and possibly the financial support of the landowner. The relationship between land tenure and pest control practice, though, must be interpreted with caution since the number of tenants in the sample of olive growers was very small, 6.0 percent.

Table 11-21

Land Tenure in Relation to the
Adoption of the Pest Control Practice on Olives

Land Tenure	Recommended and Accepted Practices							
	Regularly		Sometimes		When Needed Only		Never	
	No.	Per-cent	No.	Per-cent	No.	Per-cent	No.	Per-cent
Owner-operator	12	80	9	100	15	100	115	95
Tenant	3	20	0	0	0	0	6	5
Total	15	100	9	100	15	100	121	100

Land tenure was not related to the adoption of any of the other olive and wheat practices studied. Wilson and Gallup reported similar findings; they concluded that whether the farmer owns or rents his farm seems to have little bearing upon the use of extension information.[12]

Differences in Improved Practices

The recommended agricultural practices were the result of research findings at AREC, the reports of the extension service, and the opinions of subject matter specialists in the Ministry of Agriculture. Included were simple and complicated practices as well as cheap and costly ones. For example, seed treatment for smuts is easy to learn by farmers and involves little cost, whereas planting by drilling and controlling pests on olives are complicated and require some capital for implementation. The results of several years of trials and demonstrations on these practices showed definite effects in increasing yields and improving quality. To illustrate, the application of the recommended rate of fertilizers at the recommended time can increase the yield of wheat and olives by 60–80 percent. If this is supplemented by the other recommended practices, the yield can be further multiplied. The economic values of these practices were explained to farmers by the extension agents through various teaching methods.

The preceding analysis revealed that the use of improved varieties of wheat, the recommended crop rotations, and pest control (particularly for the olive fruit fly) was not widespread and that neither planting by drilling nor olive leaf spot control was adopted by any of the respondent wheat and olive growers. Why were these practices not adopted, while others, such as seed treatment and pruning, received wide acceptance? Data presented in Tables 11-22 and 11-23 indicate that the explanation is related to differences in the recommended practices themselves.

[12] Wilson and Gallup, "Extension Teaching Methods and Other Factors That Influence Adoption of Agricultural and Home Economics Practices," p. 24.

If seeds can be bought already treated or if they can be easily treated by farmers, the technical complexities are not overwhelming. In contrast, crop rotation requires more sophisticated knowledge and management experience and was often rejected.

Tables 11-22 and 11-23 show that nearly three-fourths of the respondents in the wheat study were informed of the improved varieties of wheat and that over one-half of the olive growers were informed about fertilization practices. These farmers were not convinced, however, that the new varieties were superior to local ones or that the returns from them would be high enough. The high rate of possible dropout regarding wheat and olive fertilization may be due to a relatively large proportion of respondents (see Tables 11-26 and 11-27) following their own personal experience or the instructions of fertilizer dealers, family members, neighbors, and friends in fertilizing their crops. The personal experience of farmers in the two study areas is not always brought up to date in terms of new technological developments, and fertilizer dealers may have motives different from or contradictory to those of farmers. For both reasons, it is quite possible that the farmers did not adopt the most economical practices for fertilization. In addition, many of the farmers who used the proper rate of fertilizer applied it at the wrong time. Therefore, the return from the additional cost of fertilizers was negative or at least insignificant; this experience, in turn, contributed to the farmers' reluctance to continue to use the new fertilization practices. Also, most of the land is dry-farmed, and in dry years chemical fertilizer gives little if any benefit.

Over three-fourths of the respondents who did not follow the practice of wheat planting by drilling and one-half of the respondents who did not follow pest control practice on olives gave lack of facilities such as seeds, pesticides, machines, and sprayers as their main reason for not adopting or discontinuing these practices. When the same wheat farmers were asked whether they would use the drilling practice if the machine were made available at a reasonable cost (either through renting or purchasing), 80.0 percent responded in the affirmative.

IV. Diffusion of Technical Improvement

The diffusion of improved practices among farmers is carried out through various teaching methods and other media. The data obtained from the two studies revealed that the wheat growers made fewer contacts with the extension staff for the purpose of acquiring information about farming than the olive growers. When respondents in the two studies were asked to indicate whether or not they had had any previous contacts with either the AREC or the government extension agents in their respective areas, only 27.0 percent of the wheat growers interviewed responded positively to this question, as compared with 78.0 percent of the olive growers. The difference may be due to the fact that the AREC extension agent in the wheat-growing area was devoting less time per week to farm visits than the government agent in the olive-growing area.

560

Table 11-22

Reasons for Nonadoption or Discontinuance of
Selected Recommended Wheat Practices

| | Recommended Practices | | | |
| | Improved Varieties | | Planting by Drilling | |
Reasons for Nonadoption or Discontinuance	No.	Per-cent	No.	Per-cent
Lack of information about the practices	13	14	4	3
Informed but not convinced	64	70	24	18
Informed and convinced, but seeds or machine not available or too expensive	15	16	108	79
Total	92	100	136	100

Table 11-23

Reasons for Nonadoption or Discontinuance of the
Recommended Olive Practices

| | Recommended Practice | | | | | |
| | Fertilization | | Pruning | | Pest Control | |
Reasons for Nonadoption or Discontinuance	No.	Per-cent	No.	Per-cent	No.	Per-cent
Lack of information	19	24	7	24	19	16
Informed but not convinced	42	51	7	24	11	9
No facilities	7	9	5	17	62	50
Too expensive	9	11	4	14	13	11
Have animal manure	4	5	. . .	. . .	. . .	. . .
Carelessness	. . .	. . .	3	10	13	11
No markets	. . .	. . .	3	10	4	3
Total	81	100	29	100	122	100

When respondents were asked to name the most important source of information for acquiring knowledge about farming, 72.0 percent of the wheat growers interviewed mentioned their own personal experience, whereas 53.0 percent of the olive growers considered the government extension agent to be their most important source of information (Table 11-24). When wheat growers were asked the same question, but in relation to individual practices, their most important source changed to "neighbors and friends" and personal experience was perceived by the majority as being the least important source of information. The inconsistency in the wheat growers' responses may be due to their traditional attachment and feeling of pride toward their ways of doing farm work. Such an attitude is usually considered unfavorable for effecting technological changes in traditional societies.

The AREC extension agent was considered an important source of information by 27.0 percent of the wheat growers, while personal experience was mentioned as important by only 23.0 percent of the olive growers. Of the latter group 14 percent felt that family, friends, and neighbors were an important source of information for them.

It was found that the contacts wheat and olive growers had with extension personnel were largely limited to office calls, farmers' group meetings, farm and home visits, demonstrations, and extension publications. In general, "office calls," including visits to the office or telephone calls, were found to be the media most frequently used by wheat growers seeking information about farming. Over one-third of this group had made office calls to AREC personnel, particularly the extension agent. In contrast, among olive growers "office calls" were found to rank among the least used media. Only 2.0 percent of the group indicated that they learned about agricultural practices related to olive growing through office calls. Instead, farm and home visits were considered by the majority (74.0 percent) of the olive growers interviewed to be the most important method through which information was sought. This method, on the contrary, was ranked third by the wheat growers in terms of its importance for gaining information (Table 11-25). Farmers' meetings were found to be the second most effective method used by extension agents to establish contacts with both wheat and olive growers. Demonstrations were found to be more important to wheat growers than to olive growers in providing new agricultural information related to these two crops, and more wheat growers than olive growers learned about agricultural practices through the use of demonstrations. The reason for this difference may be that extension agents were somewhat reluctant to demonstrate on olive trees because the nature of the tree itself makes the results of such demonstrations not highly visible and not easily comparable with the results of the previous practices followed by olive growers. The time element may have been another important factor that discouraged extension agents from demonstrating on olive trees. Olive growers have to wait much longer than wheat growers before they can really see the results of demonstrations conducted on olive trees.

562

Table 11-24

Respondents Classified by Intensity of
Contacts with Various Sources of Information

Source of Information	Wheat Growers		Olive Growers		Total	
	No.	Per cent	No.	Per- cent	No.	Per- cent
AREC[a] or government[b] extension agent	38	17	92	58	130	44
Respondent's own experience	97	72	38	23	135	45
Family, friends, and neighbors	0	0	22	14	22	7
AREC or government subject matter specialist	2	1	3	2	5	2
Merchants and dealers	0	0	3	2	3	1
Other sources	0	0	2	1	2	1
Total	137	100	160	100	297	100

[a]Applies to wheat growers.   [b]Applies to olive growers.

Table 11-25

Respondents Classified by
Extension Teaching Methods Used

Extension Teaching Methods	Wheat Growers		Olive Growers		Total	
	No.	Per- cent	No.	Per- cent	No.	Per- cent
Office calls	19	34	2	2	21	11
Farmers' group meetings	15	27	25	20	40	22
Farm and home visits	12	21	94	74	106	59
Demonstrations	10	18	4	3	14	8
Publications	0	0	1	1	1	. . .
Total	56	100	126	100	182	100

Table 11-26

Most Important Sources of Information
Used by Adopters of Selected
Recommended Practices of Wheat

Source of Information	Seed Treatment		Rate and Time of Fertilization		Improved Varieties	
	No.	Per-cent	No.	Per-cent	No.	Per-cent
Neighbors and friends	66	52	63	51	15	35
AREC extension agent	24	19	9	8	10	23
Government officials	22	17	2	2	9	22
Government extension agent	12	10	5	4	6	14
Seed or fertilizer dealers	2	2	20	16	1	2
Personal experience	0	0	24	19	2	4
Total	126	100	123	100	43	100

Technical information related to the eleven recommended wheat and olive practices was disseminated to a significant extent by neighbors and friends, as well as by both the AREC and government extension agents, among wheat and olive growers in the two areas. Farmer adopters were asked to indicate the sources from which they acquired the necessary technical information before adopting it. The responses pertaining to three wheat practices showing relatively high rates of acceptance and to five olive practices are summarized in Tables 11-26 and 11-27.

"Neighbors and friends" was the most frequently cited source of information for the three wheat practices, namely, seed treatments, rate and time of fertilization, and improved varieties. The same source was also the one most often cited by olive growers for rate of fertilization, time of application, and pruning practices. Over one-half of the wheat farmers adopting seed treatment and fertilization practices and one-third of those adopting improved wheat varieties obtained the needed information from friends and neighbors. This source is referred to in extension terms as the "indirect influence," defined as the ability of extension or any other out-of-school educational agency to reach the masses of farmers and to spread technical change through their own influential lay leaders.

These findings have significant implications for extension personnel. They suggest that more stress should be placed on the degree to which farmers obtain information from neighbors and friends and use it in making their own decisions. Also, a contrast between experimental results and field results can be drawn, using the hypothesis that information on the latter comes more from

Table 11-27

Most Important Sources of Information Used
by Adopters of Recommended Practices on Olives

Source of Information	Rate of Fertilizer		Time of Application		Pruning		Treatment of Olive Leaf Spot		Treatment of Olive Fruit Fly	
	No.	Per-cent	No.	Per-cent	No.	Per-cent	No.	Per-cent	No.	Per-cent
Family and friends	43	37	47	43	104	76	0	0	4	11
Government extension agent	40	33	36	32	30	22	3	100	25	68
Fertilizer agent	34	28	24	22	0	0	0	0	3	8
Subject matter specialist	0	0	2	2	2	2	0	0	3	8
Dealers and merchants	1	1	0	0	0	0	0	0	0	0
Other	1	1	1	1	0	0	0	0	2	5
Total	119	100	110	100	137	100	3	100	37	100

friends and neighbors than from the extension agents. This might suggest two major implications to extension:

1. Extension agents should attempt to influence the field results diffused by neighbors and friends in order to improve the quality and productivity of the practices utilized.

2. Two different strategies of extension work can be suggested: attempting to diffuse improved practices generally, and concentrating on a few leading farmers and expecting favorable results to seep outward to others.

The AREC extension agent was the second most frequently cited source of information for adopting the practices of seed treatment and improved varieties of wheat. About one-fourth of the adopters in each case received the necessary technical information from the AREC extension agent. The government extension agent in the olive-growing area was also the second most important source of information for adopting rate of fertilizer, time of application, and pruning practices for olives. He was the first and most important source of information for treatment of olive leaf spot and fruit fly practices. All farmers who treated the olive leaf spot and a little over two-thirds of those who treated olive fruit fly received their information about these practices from the government extension agent. These findings indicate the farmers' growing interest in and appreciation of the extension programs in their areas.

The seed and fertilizer dealers were considered to be a relatively important source for information pertaining to fertilization of wheat and olive trees but not for other practices. Nearly one-fifth of the wheat growers and about one-fourth of the olive growers adopting fertilization practices obtained information from such sources. Fertilizer dealers and their representatives maintain frequent contact with the masses of farmers.

V. Conclusion

Even in a single country such as Lebanon the concept of "traditional agriculture" is highly suspect. The problem of diffusing improved technology, however, is complex and has many dimensions. Farmers' acceptance of improved practices is a function of individual differences; differences in communities and economic circumstances; differences in simplicity, profitability, and compatibility of the practices being introduced; input requirements; and sources of information. Improving technology is a complex process, not a simple one, and good intentions and even the willingness to provide resources are no substitute for relevant social and economic information as a basis for an effective policy. However, the findings of this study support the hypothesis that traditional farmers are rational and will change their agricultural practices when proper inducements are present.

CHAPTER 12

Adaptive Modernization: the Case for Lebanon

Samir Khalaf*

* Department of Sociology and Anthropology,
American University of Beirut

Khalaf's essay provides some needed sociological leavening for this book. By discussing what modernization means, and does not mean, he helps to show that economic development is different from economic growth. He also shows that the performance criteria frequently used to assess a country's development efforts are unduly narrow and mechanistic.

Khalaf examines three important Lebanese institutions—the family firm, the family association, and the labor union—and shows that each has a significant role to play in mediating the demands of economic development with those of social and individual stability. This mediation is important not just because it eases tensions but also because it makes possible continuing change. Along the way Khalaf also provides a picture of a society and an economy that is somewhat richer than economists are wont to present. Family associations, in particular, exemplify the institutional idiosyncrasies of developing countries that are seldom noted in standard scholarly analyses of development.

One implication of Khalaf's paper that he himself does not bring out is that the political management of the development process is extraordinarily demanding. The political leadership required to steer between stagnancy and disruption and to accommodate the interests and behavior of a wide range of existing social institutions is great indeed. Such leadership is as much a condition for successful development as is enlightened economic policy. Khalaf's paper gently induces the reader to such insights without ever assaulting him frontally. To some degree, Khalaf is guilty of sly sociological subversion of economists and policymakers alike.

Adaptive Modernization:
the Case for Lebanon

I. Introduction: Tradition and Modernity

The comparative study of modernization, despite the impressive list of recent theoretical and empirical studies, remains conceptually cloudy and obscure. This is not surprising, given the complexity and diversity of this process. All modernizing societies, as David Apter puts it, are in a process of becoming. Becoming what is the puzzle.[1] Although the passing of traditional society seems inevitable, the shape or form of the new emerging order is not yet clear. Certain underlying features of modern Lebanese society, however, may still be identified in an effort to shed some light on the nature of the process of modernization in Lebanon.

Despite the conceptual ambiguities of "modernization," the term is nevertheless convenient and heuristically significant since it implies transformations in the total fabric of society and draws attention to both the disruptive and the reintegrating forces of a society in motion. Whatever form modernization takes (and it has appeared in many guises and occurred under many auspices), analysts seem to agree that its unique feature is the thoroughgoing and continuing transformation it generates within the social system as a whole. The revolution of modernization, Manfred Halpern asserts, "involves the transformation of all systems by which man organizes his society—the political, social, economic, intellectual, religious, and psychological systems."[2]

For analytical clarity and for purposes of understanding the nature and character of this process in Lebanon, it is assumed that modernization generally involves three underlying elements:

1. The willingness to innovate and the capacity of the society to adopt new ideas.
2. The capacity to cope with the discontinuities and tensions inherent in a developing and changing society.
3. A concern for identity and the mechanisms that guarantee national consciousness and social integration.

[1] David Apter, *The Politics of Modernization,* The University of Chicago Press, Chicago, 1965, p. xi.
[2] Manfred Halpern, "Toward Further Modernization of the Study of New Nations," *World Politics,* Vol. XVII, No. 1 (October 1964), p. 173.

Adaptive Modernization: The Case for Lebanon

Modernization raises the question of which are the appropriate agencies capable of generating change and of absorbing and mediating tensions without threatening national identity. It is often assumed that modernization requires only the expansion of production and communication, the broadening of loyalties from family, village, and community to nation, the secularization of public life, the rationalization of political authority, the promotion of functionally specific organizations, and the substitution of ascriptive criteria for achievement.[3] All these attributes are necessary but not sufficient. Of equal importance is the capacity of the system to incorporate traditional social groupings and agencies that can help to absorb some of the imbalances and maintain some measure of political consciousness and national identity.

Modernization, then, should not be taken to mean the erosion of traditional loyalties and groupings, or a process of "disengagement from traditions."[4] It is doubtful whether a pluralistic society such as that of Lebanon could ever sustain substantial change and development if such transformations were seriously to dilute the rooted traditional interests and loyalties. Likewise, modernization can never involve the emergence of exclusively rational and secular agencies.

At the expense of some oversimplification, this paper will argue that the basic problem of modernization in Lebanon has been and will continue to be one of assimilation: how to assimilate some of the rational instruments of a modern nation-state into the fabric of a pluralistic society that is still sustained by traditional allegiances and particularistic loyalties. The former are necessary for development, the latter for national consciousness and identity. Both, however, are necessary for sustaining modernization.

Insofar as modernization is a disruptive process, the effectiveness of a modernizing agency should not be measured solely in terms of its capacity to absorb and generate change. Of equal importance is its capacity to cope with tensions and discontinuities. In Lebanon, agencies such as family firms, kinship associations, confessional bureaucracy,[5] parochial voluntary associations, company unions, and the political za'im[6] have all been effective in reconciling universal standards with particular interests, and in adapting rational elements to the traditional sentiments rooted in society. These adaptive instruments of modernization have proved to be effective. This should not be considered unusual or surprising,

[3] See Samuel P. Huntington, "The Political Modernization of Traditional Societies," *Daedalus,* Summer 1966, p. 766.
[4] See Claude E. Welch, "The Comparative Study of Political Modernization," in C. E. Welch, ed., *Political Modernization,* Wadsworth Publishing Co., Belmont, Calif., 1967, pp. 8–14.
[5] A bureaucracy in which administrative offices are allotted in proportion to the sectarian or confessional representation in society.
[6] The political *za'im* is often a traditional political leader of a tightly knit local community. He sustains his political power and influence by dispensing favors and protecting the interests of his clients. For further details, see Samir Khalaf, "Primordial Ties and Politics," *Middle Eastern Studies,* Vol. 4, No. 3 (April 1968), pp. 253–259.

since the pluralistic character of Lebanese society mitigates against violent and militant transformation, and in favor of the absorption and alleviation of some of the tensions and problems caused by modernization. "The more pluralistic in structure (and hence dispersed in power) a traditional political system, the less violent the process of political modernization and the more democratic the resulting modern political system."[7] This absorptive and tension-reducing capacity of the pluralistic structure of Lebanese society is not limited to the political process but has also been instrumental in helping to maintain the relatively low incidence of social disorganization and deviant behavior in the society.[8]

The interaction between tradition and modernity in Lebanon can be interpreted within still another perspective, one that has been the subject of controversy and scholarly debate. One view held by many social scientists is that the existence of certain modern values and attitudes is a precondition for modernization.[9] Accordingly, it is often implied that kinship loyalty, family particularism, attitudes of fatalism, and confessional and communal loyalties are all impediments to modernization. Other social scientists take issue with this view and draw attention to the institutional blockages to modernization. They suggest that the appropriate attitudes and behavior will follow once the institutional structure provides the necessary opportunities and incentives for participating in modern institutions. Albert Hirschman cites interesting experimental evidence from the study of cognitive dissonance in support of the proposition that, in the event of a conflict between people's behavior and their values, it is usually the values that change.[10] But if value changes are more inclined to follow than to precede behavioral changes, they cannot then be a precondition for modernization. It is on this assumption that many economists, notably Staley, Spengler, Millikan, Rosenstein-Rodan, and Wharton, focus on the institutional blockages to development.[11]

The intention of this paper is to provide further support to this point of view in the case of Lebanon. On at least two counts, the history of modernization in Lebanon provides evidence in support of these propositions. First, the so-called traditional agencies and groupings have been instrumental in generating change and absorbing imbalances. Second, an appreciable measure of gradual

[7] Huntington, "The Political Modernization of Traditional Societies," p. 785.

[8] For further details see Samir Khalaf, "Basic Social Trends in Lebanon," *Cultural Resources in Lebanon,* Librairie du Liban, Beirut, 1969, pp. 147–159.

[9] David C. McClelland, "Business Drive and National Achievement," *Harvard Business Review,* Vol. XL (July-August 1962), pp. 99–112. For a succinct treatment of his central argument, see also "The Impulse to Modernization," in Myron Weiner, ed., *Modernization: The Dynamics of Growth,* Voice of America Forum Lectures, 1966, pp. 29–40.

[10] Albert Hirschman, "Obstacles to Development: A Classification and a Quasi-Vanishing Act," *Economic Development and Cultural Change,* Vol. 14 (July 1965), pp. 385–393.

[11] For further details, see Weiner, *Modernization: The Dynamics of Growth,* pp. 5–14.

and adaptive modernization has taken place without eroding the traditional values that thus far have been effective in providing psychic reinforcement and a sense of national identity.

II. Instruments of Adaptive Modernization

In a broad sense, Lebanon can follow one of three possible alternatives or courses of modernization:

1. In line with many newly emerging nations, it could adopt a coercive and disciplined model whereby the state becomes the exclusive agency of political socialization and modernization. Such an unmediated approach to modernization has been not only badly battered by academic critics but also faulted by events. Suffice it to note here that, given the pluralistic structure of Lebanese society, along with the pervasive traditions of laissez-faire and individualism, such an approach cannot possibly gain any widespread appeal.

2. Lebanon could opt for a more liberal and secular approach wherein change is mediated through predominantly rational agencies of modernization, and political allegiance and loyalty are sustained by the civic instruments of a nation-state. This approach too, at this juncture of Lebanon's social and political development, is not likely to be successful.

3. The third, and perhaps most realistic and effective, alternative is in the particularistic or adaptive path for modernity and development. This approach does not exclude the possibility of mobilizing traditional groupings in the process of modernization. It is an adaptive course in two senses: first, because it attempts to mediate change through agencies that need not be exclusively rational or secular; second, because it tries to reconcile some of the universal and rational principles with the indigenous cultural traditions.

The Lebanese tendency to justify change within traditional contexts should not be dismissed as solely a conservative gesture to glorify the sacred traditions of the past. Putting new wine in old bottles, to borrow a trite metaphor, can help to avoid conflict and promote the acceptance of new ideas. Furthermore, because an agency is traditional in form or structure does not imply that it must espouse traditional values, or that it must devote itself exclusively to perpetuating sacred values or preserving traditional lore and skills. Conversely, creating a seemingly modern institution, or increasing exposure to modern values and practices, is no guarantee that modern values will be widely adopted.

There is a tendency among analysts to exaggerate the differences and discontinuities between so-called modern and traditional societies. The change from traditional to modern qualities, it is often argued, means "someone must give up ways of thinking and feeling that go back decades, sometimes centuries; and to abandon these ways often seems to be abandoning principle itself."[12] It is also

[12] Alex Inkeles, "The Modernization of Man," in Myron Weiner, ed., *Modernization: The Dynamics of Growth*, p. 152.

asserted that one of the marks of the contemporary man is that "he will no longer live enmeshed in a network of primary kin ties, . . . but rather will be drawn into a much more impersonal and bureaucratic milieu."[13]

This essay argues that we cannot begin to understand the modernization of Lebanon unless we abandon the idea that it is an inevitable movement from one polar end of the scheme to the other. All such dichotomous analyses—from Henry Maine's distinction between "status" and "contract" to Parson's pattern variables—leave highly ambiguous the nature and characteristics of transitional societies. They also fail to recognize that traditional patterns always exist and are of functional significance even in the most advanced societies.

Modernization should not be thought of in terms of a quantitative decline in traditional patterns and a rise in modern ones. We must consider instead what blend of traditional and modern patterns is most effective in meeting the three requirements of modernization outlined above. The evidence presented in this paper suggests that there are several instances in which Lebanese traditions have had a reinforcing rather than a retarding effect on development and modernization. The patrimonial manager, the political za'im, the confessional bureaucrat, the company union, and the parochial voluntary association are all, in fact, devices for reconciling the universal with the particular, the rational with the traditional. They have all been effective in helping to achieve the appropriate blend for sustaining change without breakdowns and discontinuities.

The "family firm," in this sense, becomes a kind of compromise between the corporate enterprise and the domestic putting-out system, and the patrimonial manager a crossbreed of the rational impersonal administrator and the paternalistic employer. The "political za'im," in much the same way, becomes the mediating link between communal and local allegiances and the impersonal central bureaucracy. The "company union," too, is a halfway arrangement between craft guilds and national labor federations. Finally, "family associations" are also a crossbreed of informal tribal groups and formal voluntary associations, combining the wisdom of kinship elders and rational administration.

The choice of the specific agencies to be examined is not arbitrary. All three display features typical of other institutions in Lebanon. The intention is to demonstrate how traditional agencies—in this case family firms and family associations—have undergone considerable secularization and have served as effective instruments of modernization. The one rational agency analyzed—the labor union—was chosen to demonstrate how it has retained traditional features. In all three, however, traditional and rational elements interplay and reinforce each other.

Family Firms

The extended kinship system and its associated attitudes have been widely decried by students of economic development. In particular, development problems

[13] *Ibid.,* p. 153.

are attributed to the prevalence in developing countries of the family firm or family-dominated enterprises. The so-called patrimonial manager[14] is often depicted as a person with an almost built-in disposition for nepotism and paternalism, and as a security-minded conservative who resists change and retains vast authority in his own hands. In short, it is argued that family firms are incompatible with the logic of industrialization and development. The contrary point of view will be advanced here. Family firms in Lebanon have been effective organizations in coping with urgent industrial problems and have exerted a supportive influence on industrial development. They have been effective also as palliative agents in absorbing some of the disruptions and imbalances involved in industrialization and have continued to play this role without betraying industrialization as a rational and secular process.

In Lebanon, the industrialization process is relatively limited in comparison with other developing societies. The process is nonetheless painful, because it has entailed a considerable degree of disruption and change in social institutions. Traditional forms of social organization not only have served as tension-reducing and integrative mechanisms but also have been functionally significant as innovative agents; and, indeed, the most successful and viable industrial organizations in Lebanon are not impersonal corporations but paternalistic family firms in the strict meaning of the term. In the absence of other agencies and a more consistent policy of government control, and in the context of the pervasive traditions of familism and kinship obligations, family firms have played an important role in the development process in helping to reconcile some of the secure and tested traditions of the past with the rational and secular requirements of a contemporary society.

Case studies of ten family firms provide support for the foregoing observations.[15] Ghandour, Jabre, Badarou, Boutros, Ouseily, Kortas, and a score of others are the leading firms in their respective industries. Apart from being the largest firms, in terms of both size and capital invested, the family firms surveyed represented the most important industries in Lebanon, including food processing, textiles, tanning, leather articles, wooden and metal furniture, soap, paints and polishes, metal works, and water pumps. In order to assess the practices and attitudes of patrimonial managers with respect to the operation of their organizations, the survey explored the histories of the firms, ideologies of top management, organizational structure, delegation of authority, personnel policies, and performance of managerial functions such as planning, organiza-

[14] The term is used here as defined by Harbison and Myers: "Patrimonial management is business management in which ownership, major policy-making positions, and a significant proportion of other jobs in the hierarchy are held by members of an extended family." Frederick Harbison and Charles A. Myers, *Management in the Industrial World: An International Analysis,* McGraw-Hill, New York, 1959, p. 69.
[15] See Samir Khalaf and Emilie Shwayri, "Family Firms and Industrial Development: The Lebanese Case," *Economic Development and Cultural Change,* Vol. 15, No. 1 (October 1966), pp. 59–69.

tion, staffing, directing, and controlling.[16] My observations here will be confined to an effort at absolving family firms—at least those still functioning in Lebanon —of four of the charges often leveled against them.

Nepotism

Among the most frequent charges made against family firms is nepotism. The extended family's control of an enterprise, it is argued, enables less competent members of the family to hold managerial positions for which their training and ability would not otherwise qualify them. Kinship ties, rather than competence and training, are alleged to constitute the principal avenue to key managerial positions. In short, it is maintained that family firms in general fail to conform to two vital requirements of industrialization as a rational process, namely, functional specificity and universalistic criteria.[17]

So much has been written about industrial and organizational inefficiency and its inextricable association with family favoritism that one is led to believe there must be a special "cult" in Lebanon that condones inefficiency and sustains its growth. The argument usually runs as follows. Since family loyalty is deeply rooted in the Arab world, and since the "subordination of the individual to his family and his participation in larger social groupings on a family basis"[18] is still a predominant characteristic of the culture, this naturally has had an appreciable effect on industrial life. Economically speaking, the extended family is often regarded as the basic social unit. And since the average business unit is relatively small, industry is often regarded as a purely family affair. The argument goes on to point out that this narrow conception of business as a family affair has led many employers to "view their firms in much the same way as they view their private house and estate. . . . The firm is the source of the family income and prestige, to be managed, inherited, or sold in the interests of the family alone."[19] Moreover, the focal position that the family occupies in Lebanese culture and its unshaken internal loyalty are also seen to be reflected in the lack of any broader sense of social responsibility among many industrialists.[20]

Plausible as these charges may appear, I found no evidence to warrant their support. True, the administration of the ten enterprises under study is entirely in the hands of the patrimonial group, and no employee possesses decisionmaking power in the strict meaning of the term. But to hold this as prima-facie evidence

[16] For a detailed presentation of the study and its results, see Emilie Shwayri, "Family Firms as a Factor in Lebanon's Industrial Growth," M.A. dissertation, American University of Beirut, June 1964.

[17] See Marion J. Levy, Jr., *The Structure of Society,* Princeton University Press, Princeton, N.J., 1952, p. 431.

[18] Raphael Patai, "The Middle East as a Culture Area," *The Middle East Journal,* Vol. 6, No. 1 (Winter 1952), p. 20.

[19] Arthur E. Mills, "Economic Change in Lebanon," *Middle East Economic Papers,* Economic Research Institute, American University of Beirut, 1956, p. 80.

[20] *Ibid.,* p. 80.

of nepotism, and to associate this nepotism with inefficiency, is an entirely different matter.

First, there is a critical shortage in Lebanon of people with professional and managerial skills who can occupy positions of authority without ownership. In fact, the organizational elite and the supervisory talent required for industrialization are virtually nonexistent. Such a shortage, particularly at the levels of middle management, has had far-reaching consequences on the country's capacity for disciplined and rational growth. Under such conditions, and in view of their training and experience, patrimonial managers should not be blamed for drawing upon their own resources for the needed talent and skills. Furthermore, they still harbor the conviction—and perhaps rightly so—that "ownership creates a sense of responsibility." To them, such assertions are not trite platitudes to disguise their nepotistic inclinations. Rather, they reflect a genuine belief, sustained by long experience, that their competent employees, who are also relatives and thus sparked by a sense of kinship loyalty, seem to have a higher degree of involvement in the affairs of the enterprise.

Second, another derivative of familism is the predisposition to believe that the environment is hostile, that people outside one's family or group are generally antagonistic. The cultural persistence of this value orientation in Lebanon has made the outsider a suspect and has, among other things, intensified rivalries and factions at all levels of the social structure. Under such circumstances, it is little wonder that patrimonial managers are inclined to avoid placing "outsiders" in key positions. In itself, this preference for kin, then, should not be feared or decried. Indeed, it would be foolhardy to do so, particularly when the relatives happen to possess the needed skills and experience.

Finally, Lebanese family firms have not as yet reached such a size as to make the employment of outsiders in managerial positions a major issue. Typically, the members of the patrimonial group are adequate in number to share among themselves the responsibilities of managing the firm. Furthermore, they recognize that the process of dividing responsibilities among themselves cannot continue indefinitely and that, as the firm expands, outsiders must be hired to fill important managerial positions.

In sum, nepotism as such need not always conflict with rational and universalistic principles. In societies "where trained skills are scarce and the sons of the wealthy have much of the training, nepotism may be relatively costless."[21] In Lebanon it has been not only relatively costless, but also functional. At Lebanon's present stage of industrialization, the family has proved to be a source not only of talent and service, but of initial capital for investment as well. Hagen might well have been referring to Lebanon when he noted, "Where one can neither trust a stranger or an acquaintance as a business associate, nor persuade him to lend one money, then the extended family may be a necessary source of

[21] George B. Baldwin, *Industrial Growth in South India,* as quoted by Harbison and Myers, *Management in the Industrial World,* p. 70.

capital and a necessary bond between business associates. Its abolition would not modernize the society; in the circumstances it would merely paralyze large-scale relationship."[22]

Centralization of Authority

The patrimonial manager is often depicted as an autocratic despot who monopolizes and jealously guards authority and the prerogative to make decisions. He also tends to think of his authority in terms of personal power, it is argued, rather than as a function inherent in an office. In general, the profile of the patrimonial manager depicts an uncompromising person who delegates too little, concerns himself too much with operational detail, and has little time left for effective and creative management. As a consequence, "this type of management is likely to be defensive, enervated, and static. It breathes only at the top, and when the top disappears, the organization either collapses or must be completely rebuilt."[23]

Lebanese industrialists in general subscribe to some of these practices and attitudes. So long as authoritarianism and the presupposition of hostility remain persistent cultural themes, it is natural to expect all managers—patrimonial, salaried, or otherwise—to be inimical to delegation of authority.[24] Family firms are not to be singularly blamed for generating attitudes or condoning practices that are deeply rooted in the culture. That such authoritarianism is not something inherent in, or peculiar to, family firms is also suggested by a preliminary comparison of the ten firms under study with a broader sample of Lebanese industrialists. It is true that neither group is markedly predisposed to delegation of authority, but the heads of the firms in the patrimonial group at least delegated some of their managerial responsibilities or shared them with other family members. Authority in the Lebanese family firms does not appear to be exclusively concentrated in the hands of a single individual, but is shared by the members of the patrimonial group, which may involve at times anywhere between five and ten persons. Far from being uncompromising in his insistence on undivided authority, like perhaps Unternehmer,[25] the Lebanese patrimonial manager at least favors the horizontal sharing of authority at the top. In this sense he displays a curious blend of highly centralized authoritarianism and "democratic-participative" management. In one respect, major authority is concentrated at the top,

[22] Everett E. Hagen, "The Process of Economic Development," *Economic Development and Cultural Change,* Vol. 5, No. 1 (April 1957), p. 198.

[23] Clark Kerr et al., *Industrialism and Industrial Man,* Harvard University Press, Cambridge, Mass., 1960, p. 147.

[24] For a detailed analysis of the degree of consultation and delegation of authority among a sample of Lebanese industrialists, see Samir Khalaf, "Managerial Ideology and Industrial Conflict in Lebanon," Ph.D. dissertation, Princeton University, 1963, pp. 159–167.

[25] See Heinz Hartmann, *Authority and Organization in German Management,* Princeton University Press, Princeton, N.J., 1959, p. 60.

and even the most routine decisions are pushed up from below because subordinates are reluctant to assume responsibility. In another respect, there is likely to be rather wide participation in decisionmaking. Top executives (members of the patrimonial group) seldom take individual responsibility. They act only after thorough discussion and examination of alternatives by the group. Under such conditions centralized authority cannot be said to be "suffocating."

It should also be noted that, even in the absence of vertical delegation of authority, subordinates are encouraged to express their opinions on matters where their knowledge and experience may be appropriately put to use. Moreover, contrary to what is frequently charged, Lebanese patrimonial managers appear to utilize the services of the foreman as a link between managers and workers.

In addition, the Lebanese patrimonial manager does not believe that he is born to rule his enterprise and that his authority is based upon a kind of natural law or "calling," in the Weberian sense of the term. Rather, he justifies the legitimacy of his authority primarily on the basis of his functions in the organization, and to a lesser extent by virtue of his ownership or property rights. Firmly believing that property creates a sense of responsibility, he may still sustain some skepticism regarding the earnestness and motivation of salaried employees. But such attitudes have not been uncommon in the early stages of industrialization of even the most developed economies, and there is no reason to believe that they should act as serious deterrents to industrial growth in Lebanon.

Finally, the charge that centralization of authority hinders the growth of an enterprise must also be qualified. The Lebanese patrimonial manager is more than eager to expand his business, provided market conditions are favorable. In fact, such expansion has taken place. In all ten family firms surveyed, the number of employees has been increasing sharply. From an average of 46 employees at founding, firms have grown to an average of 244 employees.

Paternalism

The persistence of relatively small, tightly controlled enterprises and the survival of paternalism in employer-employee relationships has also been taken as an obstacle in the face of industrial development. To some extent, "the employer's attitude to his workers is one of superiority, a legacy of the feudal system which still persists, in spirit if not in form, in most Arab countries, including parts of Lebanon."[26] Such paternalism is alleged to have restricted mobility and incentives and furthered the growth of apathy, timidity, and lack of venturesomeness among subordinates. It is further argued that, by obligating workers to reciprocate management's paternal responsibility, industrialists can easily manipulate the docile and faithful workers for their own ends. Finally, this reciprocal obligation has also been held responsible for retarding the growth of an aggressive labor movement.

These features have indeed been, in some form or other, a liability to the

[26] Mills, "Economic Change in Lebanon," p. 10.

industrial system in Lebanon. What is in question is the charge that family firms should bear the guilt for generating such impediments to progress. The timidity of the work force and the weakness of the labor movement, for example, reflect some underlying socioeconomic conditions (such as the persistent surplus in the labor supply) that have no bearing on the nature of patrimonial management. The paternalism of the employer may in fact be a reaction to, and not a cause of, such conditions.

Indeed, the Lebanese industrialist sparked by a spirit of paternalism, for whatever motive, appears to be offering his workers certain welfare benefits and social services that other agencies in society have so far failed to provide. With a minimum of government intervention, a weak and ineffective labor movement, and the absence of collective bargaining and other means of labor negotiation, the paternalistic employer is one of the few remaining agents who can provide some of the benefits that the worker fails to obtain elsewhere. In addition to such material benefits, paternalism "often serves to smooth the major dislocations which an industrial way of life forces on the newly recruited worker."[27] In serving this function, the paternalistic employer provides a large measure of psychic reinforcements and social support.

He also appears to be an effective shock absorber and tension-reducing agent. His success in this role is evident, if nowhere else, in the relatively low incidence of industrial unrest and labor protest in family firms. It is significant to note that none of the ten family firms under study considers itself in the category of "conflict-prone" industries I have surveyed elsewhere. Judged by their record of labor disputes and grievances brought before the Conciliation Board, family firms are relatively more "conflict-free" than the average industrial establishment in Lebanon.[28] Rather than being resented as an intruder who meddles with the private lives of his employees, the paternalistic employer in Lebanon still plays the role of the benevolent provider.

Paternalism, in its Lebanese form, is not entirely dysfunctional. It has not violated the workers' sense of justice and equality in competitive opportunity, nor has it betrayed some of the rational and universalistic principles of evaluating talent. Instead, it has offered some of the needed social and welfare benefits and has served to soften the impact of the major dislocations associated with industrialization.

Conservatism

The patrimonial manager is often seen as a conservative, motivated by a desire to assure a regular income and protect the family's status and prestige. He is depicted as a "care-taker rather than as a risk-taker."[29] Because of excessive pru-

---

[27] Kerr, *Industrialism and Industrial Man,* p. 150.

[28] For further details see Khalaf, "Managerial Ideology and Industrial Conflict in Lebanon" pp. 203–207.

[29] Frederick Harbison and Eugene Burgess, "Modern Management in Western Europe," *The American Journal of Sociology,* Vol. IX, No. 1 (July 1954), p. 19.

dence and concern with security, the patrimonial manager is constantly "playing it safe" and is haunted by the risks of "sticking his own neck out." The cumulative effect of such attitudes, among other things, is to create rigid and timid enterprises drained of any of the dynamic and venturesome attributes required for industrial take-off and sustained growth.

From the evidence supplied by case studies, an entirely different impression emerges. When asked, for example, what they conceive their major function to be, the respondents rated such things as "following up the developments in the West" and "studying market conditions" as the most important. "We must not only keep ourselves informed about the machines already existing in Europe and the techniques being used," said one of the respondents, "but we must also be aware of the new technical advances." These are hardly timid responses. Furthermore, the Lebanese patrimonial manager, far from learning the business by sitting at a desk and listening to what his father says, gets his training by traveling abroad. All ten respondents have traveled extensively within and outside the Arab world.

In general the patrimonial group displays a remarkable facility and readiness to emulate the new and experiment with novel ideas. Indeed, in all fields but marketing, Lebanese family enterprises seem to be animated by the same propensity for adaptive innovation that played an important part in Japan's economic transformation from an agrarian to an industrial society. True, they evince some timidity in facing the market, but such an attitude is far from being peculiar to patrimonial managers. Writing about Lebanese entrepreneurs, Yusif Sayigh observes, "It is indeed puzzling that a group of men that seem so active in trying to innovate in their production and organization should declare themselves largely unaggressive in their sales policies and practices."[30] A nonaggressive approach to marketing, however, need not necessarily be regarded as a symptom of conservatism and resigned attitude but should be recognized as being, at least in part, a consequence of the limited size of the internal market.

Kinship Associations

The kinship association in Lebanon is another, perhaps unique, institution that supports the hypothesis that extended kinship relations need not be inconsistent with urban and industrial requirements. Efforts to coalesce the family by creating formal kinship associations are not merely nostalgic and irrational gestures, but also a functional response to real needs. In Lebanon, one's society begins and ends with his family. Despite the emergence of other secular and specialized functional groups, kinship relationships and family norms remain the most important mechanisms of social control. The family is still the major security device in Lebanese society. Were the family in Lebanon to decline in social importance, the consequences could be quite damaging as people lost the emotional supports and restraints the family now provides. It is perhaps reasonable to infer

[30] Yusif Sayigh, *Entrepreneurs of Lebanon,* Harvard University Press, Cambridge, Mass., 1962, p. 87.

that the incidence of suicide, alcoholism, drug addiction, and other mental and psychological disturbances is still relatively low in Lebanon in part because of the persistence of family solidarity. All preliminary evidence thus far available indicates that family disorganization or the breakdown of primary group ties is a crucial variable in accounting for prostitution, juvenile delinquency, vagrancy, and other symptoms of personal and social disorganization. In short, family disintegration is a predisposing and not merely an incidental factor in social disorganization.[31]

It is neither surprising nor irrational for the Lebanese to be protective and defensive toward the family. Typical perhaps of most kinship cultures, the Lebanese is eager to enjoy some of the liberal and material rewards of urbanization, but he is equally eager to ward off some of its unsettling consequences. He is understandably touchy about his kinship ties, because he is moved by little else. Although other nonkinship loyalties are beginning to attract the allegiance of the more secular segments of the society, most such ties—particularly those of party, class, or profession—are still relatively slender and tenuous. The so-called crisis of identity in Lebanon is, to a large measure, the crisis of the family.

Because of this pervasive familism in Lebanon, the scope and range of family activities often extend beyond the functions usually associated with kinship systems. Family associations are not simply an expression of kinship sentiments; they also discharge certain social and integrative functions that in other societies are handled by nonkinship organizations. The incidence and trend displayed by family associations, along with their structure and functions, show that they should be viewed as a major response to the dissociative forces inherent in urbanization and secularism.

Trend and Pattern of Family Associations[32]

It is often suggested that extended families, tribal clans, and other such communal groups come to assume certain social functions by default, and that the absence of welfare agencies and other voluntary specialized associations accounts for the survival of such corporate kin groups.[33] The survival of such groups is then viewed as a relic of primitive societies and tribal communities. In much the same vein it is also asserted that the emergence of special-purpose groups and voluntary agencies will ultimately undermine the significance of corporate kin groups as agencies of social organization and social control in society.[34]

[31] For the impact of family disorganization on prostitution, see Samir Khalaf, *Prostitution in a Changing Society,* Khayats, Beirut, 1965, pp. 45–50.

[32] For a more detailed analysis see Samir Khalaf, "Urbanism and Family Associations in Lebanon," a paper read at the Round Table on Law and Social and Economic Development, Civil Service Board, Republic of Lebanon, December 7–15, 1968.

[33] Norman W. Bell and E. F. Vogel, "Toward a Framework for Functional Analysis of Family Behavior," in N. Bell and E. Vogel, eds., *A Modern Introduction to the Family,* rev. ed., The Free Press, New York, 1968, p. 8.

[34] William J. Goode, *World Revolution and Family Patterns,* Free Press, New York, 1963, p. 369.

Neither of these observations has been borne out by our preliminary findings. It is true that the process of modernization in Lebanon has been marked, as elsewhere, by the emergence of a variety of voluntary associations and welfare agencies. The proliferation of such agencies has not made corporate kin groups obsolete, however, nor have the increasing efforts of governmental and nongovernmental agencies in social welfare and community development been accompanied by a decline in the incidence of family associations. In both absolute numbers and their rate of annual increase, family associations exceed those of all other active voluntary associations in the country.

The first striking feature of Table 12-1 is the steady and continuous increase in the growth rate of family associations. From an average of less than one family association per year being formed between 1860 and 1919, the annual rate has risen gradually to 18.5 in the last decade. Contrary to what is often remarked, this growth suggests that corporate kin groupings are not being undermined and swept away by industrialization.[35]

The genesis of family associations in Lebanon dates back to the 1860s, when widespread turmoil and civil strife were major threats to family security and status.[36] In the absence of other voluntary agencies, the major portion of welfare and benevolent activities at the time was assumed by kinship and religious organizations. All of the 18 welfare agencies in existence during the second half of the nineteenth century were, without exception, sponsored by religious organizations.[37] An equal number of family associations was also in existence during the same period.

As shown in Table 12-1, there is a slight preponderance of urban over rural family associations.[38] Although urban family associations have maintained an almost stable and uniform rate of growth with signs of decreasing incidence during the 1960s, rural associations have demonstrated a consistent and gradual increase with a sharper rise occurring during the 1960s. This may perhaps be taken as an evidence of the encroachment of secular and urban features into rural communities, and the decline in the sense of kinship that normally accompanies such tendencies.

It is of interest to note that the incidence and the trend in welfare associations display almost identical patterns. As shown in Table 12-2, the rural-urban

---

[35] Manning Nash, "Kinship and Voluntary Associations," in W. E. Moore and A. Feldman, *Labor Commitment and Social Change in Developing Areas,* Social Science Research Council, New York, 1960, pp. 313–325.

[36] Unfortunately, the early entries in the Ministries of the Interior and Social Affairs were not adequately recorded. Consequently, the specific identity of some of the earlier associations could not be identified in any precise fashion.

[37] See Ministry of Planning, Lebanese Republic, *Social Welfare in Lebanon,* Beirut, 1965.

[38] For purposes of classification, Beirut and its suburbs, along with the Zahle, Tripoli, Saida, and Sour, are considered urban. The urban-rural category refers to associations that indicated they have branches or meet in Beirut in winter but move to their respective villages in the summer.

Table 12-1

Trends in Family Associations: Urban-Rural Variations

(percent in parentheses)

Type of Association	1860-1919	1920-29	1930-39	1940-49	1950-59	1960-68	Date Unknown	Total
Urban	23 (43.4)	25 (53.2)	21 (53.8)	38 (52.8)	53 (56.4)	82 (49.4)	4 (66.7)	246 (51.6)
Rural	24 (45.3)	14 (29.8)	14 (35.9)	27 (37.5)	41 (43.6)	79 (47.6)	2 (33.3)	201 (42.1)
Urban-rural	6 (11.3)	8 (17.0)	4 (10.2)	7 (9.7)	0 0	5 (3.0)	0 0	30 (6.3)
Total	53 (100.0)	47 (100.0)	39 (99.9)	72 (100.0)	94 (100.0)	166 (100.0)	6 (100.0)	477 (100.0)
Average per year	0.9	4.7	3.9	7.2	9.4	18.5		

Table 12-2

Trend in Welfare Associations: Urban-Rural Variations

(percent in parentheses)

Type of Association	1860-1919	1920-29	1930-39	1940-49	1950-59	1960-64	Date Unknown	Total
Urban	28 (59.6)	18 (50.0)	25 (50.0)	36 (56.2)	50 (42.0)	35 (42.6)	5 (62.5)	197 (48.7)
Rural	16 (34.1)	12 (34.3)	20 (40.0)	23 (35.9)	62 (52.1)	44 (53.6)	3 (37.5)	180 (44.4)
Urban-rural[a]	3 (6.3)	5 (14.2)	5 (10.0)	5 (7.8)	7 (5.8)	3 (03.6)	0 0	28 (6.9)
Total	47 (100.0)	35 (99.9)	50 (100.0)	64 (99.9)	119 (99.9)	82 (99.8)	8 (100.0)	405 (100.0)
Average per year	0.8	3.5	5.0	6.4	11.9	16.4		

[a]Established in Beirut with branches in rural regions. Data based on the *Directory of Social Welfare Agencies*, prepared by the Ministry of Planning, Lebanese Republic, Beirut, 1965.

Table 12-3
Trend in Family Associations: Religious Variations
(percent in parentheses)

Religious Group	1930-39	1940-49	1950-59	1960-69	Total
Christians	28 (71.8)	32 (44.4)	35 (40.2)	51 (31.3)	146 (40.4)
Sunni	6 (15.4)	29 (40.3)	22 (25.3)	17 (10.4)	74 (20.5)
Shi'a	5 (12.8)	3 (4.2)	23 (26.4)	77 (47.2)	108 (29.9)
Druse	0 0	8 (11.1)	7 (8.0)	18 (11.0)	33 (9.1)
Total	39 (100.0)	72 (100.0)	87 (100.0)	163 (100.0)	361 (100.0)

distribution and rate of annual increase of all nongovernmental welfare agencies do not depart significantly from those manifested by family associations. The fact that both have been increasing at the same rate suggests that family associations continue to satisfy certain needs that cannot be adequately fulfilled by other means.

The religious distribution is equally instructive. It is apparent from Table 12-3 that the major religious groups have been active in organizing family associations at different periods. In intensity of organization, the Christian community reached its peak during the 1930s. More than 71 percent of all family associations formed during that period belonged to Christians, compared with 15.4 percent for Sunnis and 12.8 percent for Shi'ites. Since then, however, Christian family associations have gradually and consistently declined; they now constitute less than one-third of all family associations formed during the past 8 years. Sunni Moslem associations, on the other hand, were relatively few during the 1930s, witnessed a sharp increase during the 1940s (from 15.4 to 40.3 percent), and have been sharply declining since. Shi'ites reached their peak organization only during the 1960s. Although Shi'ite family associations made up only 4 percent of those organized during the 1940s, they now constitute 47.2 percent.

These major religious communities followed generally the same order in undergoing the process of absorbing some of the secular tendencies inherent in modernization. In this sense family associations can be viewed as both symptoms of and reactions to social change. Having undergone the process of modernization relatively earlier than the other groups, it was by and large the urban Christian population that had to face the brunt of social change first.

During and after World War II, the Sunni Moslems began to undergo similar experiences; hence a greater proportion of such families established their associations during that period. The last decade or so, when there has been a heavy flow of Shi'ite rural migrants into urban areas, has witnessed similar tendencies among Shi'ites.

SAMIR KHALAF

It is of interest to note that the number of family associations among the Druse is still relatively low. This should not be taken to mean that the Druse remain untouched by the demands of secularization. Rather, as a community they are comparatively more cohesive and clannish, and their communal structure is sustained by stronger affinities. It is perhaps for this reason too that the incidence of social and personal disorganization among the Druse is still relatively low.[39]

Structural Features

Like any other formal organization in Lebanon, a family association is not legitimate unless it has been licensed by the government. All such licensed associations, the year and place of their establishment, the names of elected officers, and a brief statement of their objectives are recorded. From 1860, which marks the genesis of the first such association, until November 1968, the records show a total of 477 such associations. By comparison there are 405 nongovernmental welfare agencies, 127 labor unions, 85 employer associations, and not more than 12 recognized political parties and parliamentary blocs.

Some of these family associations are very large. The president of the Atallah association, at the general assembly meeting in Zahle in August 1968, claimed a membership of 15,000. Very few single associations in Lebanon—political, industrial, or otherwise—can boast of similar numbers. These family associations in no sense exhaust the scope and activities of kinship groups. A large measure of benevolent welfare and cooperative activities are no doubt discharged by family members outside the formal boundaries of organized associations.

The fact that family associations are particularistic does not imply that they are based exclusively on traditional and nonrational criteria. In most of their organizational features and operational procedures they subscribe to formal and impersonal expectations. The qualifications for membership and for holding office, duties of officers, frequency of general meetings, solicitation of funds, and nature of sanctions are all clearly stipulated in written bylaws. True, insofar as membership is restricted to descendants of the same lineage, the association cannot be thought to possess an "open" structure and therefore fails to satisfy one of the basic requirements of a modern agency. Yet admission to membership is no guarantee that one will retain his membership. There are uniform norms and expectations to which a member must subscribe if he is to maintain his position within the corporate group. Strict sanctions are imposed to ensure conformity. Penalities for disapproved conduct, ranging all the way from warnings to discharge and public censure, are frequently meted out to ward off deviant behavior which may otherwise taint or defame the family's reputation and honor.

As in any other formal association, payment of dues, no matter how nominal, is a prerequisite for membership. Fees vary from 3 to 25 L£ annually. In

[39] I am conducting an empirical survey on criminal activity in Lebanon. All preliminary evidence so far supports this observation.

cases of proven financial need, this requirement is often waived. All associations, however, stipulate the payment of a fee before one attains eligibility for membership. Income from membership fees is the main source of revenue. Other funds are solicited through charitable donations and recreational activities, during which lotteries and other such inducements encourage contributions. In some instances, the government regards family associations like any other welfare or voluntary agency and accordingly contributes to the financial support of the active ones. Among some Moslem associations, contributions in the form of *Zakat,* particularly during the holy month of Ramadan, also form a significant source of financial support. In the event that an association is disbanded, its capital or financial assets are frequently bequeathed to religious and charitable institutions.

In their administrative structure, too, family associations do not diverge much from the features that characterize other formal and rational associations. The bylaws call for a general assembly of all members which meets at least once a year to elect an Executive Committee. The size of the committee and its duration in office vary from one association to another. The number of executive officers ranges from 4 to 25, and tenure in office varies from a minimum of 6 months to a maximum of 5 years. On the whole, the Executive Committee meets rather regularly, an average of once a month. Special *ad hoc* committees may be appointed from time to time to resolve some pending familial problems. Expert advice is often sought from outside the ranks of the kinship group, but under no circumstances are such advisors admitted to membership. The Executive Committee may also appoint an honorary president, who in many an instance is an elderly or a religious figure. As in most other appointments, special consideration is given to age and religiosity, both of which add weight and prestige to the position. A member, for example, regardless of his special skills and competence, cannot be eligible for election before the age of 30. In cases of a tie between two contestants, priority is given to the elder.

In short, in their organizational structure and operational procedures, family associations combine elements of informal tribal groups and formal bureaucracies. By so doing, they combine the wisdom of kinship elders with the virtues of rational administration.

Functional Significance

The need to coalesce the family seems to correspond with secularization and movement into urban areas. As has been suggested earlier, family associations are quite effective in providing some measure of economic, social, and psychological support to those in the throes of transition. Even when voluntary associations are available, recent migrants may find it comparatively difficult to establish new personal contacts with institutional and nonkinship agencies. Consequently family associations serve an important protective function for recent migrants—a form of social insurance and an effective means for smoothing the adaptation to urban life.

Empirical evidence provides support for the assertions just made. In terms

Table 12-4
Objectives of Family Associations:
Rural-Urban Variations

Objective	Rural	Urban	Rural-Urban	Total
Solidarity	65 (48.9)	117 (65.4)	3 (50.0)	185 (58.0)
Benevolent	88 (66.2)	94 (52.5)	1 (16.7)	183 (57.4)
Educational	62 (46.6)	84 (46.9)	5 (83.3)	151 (47.3)
Social	42 (31.6)	63 (35.2)	4 (66.7)	109 (34.2)
Economic	25 (18.8)	38 (21.2)	5 (83.3)	68 (21.3)
Cooperative	14 (10.5)	15 (8.4)	0 0	29 (9.1)
Health	9 (6.8)	17 (9.5)	0 0	26 (8.2)
Moral-religious	8 (6.0)	7 (3.9)	0 0	15 (4.7)
Mediation	2 (1.5)	7 (3.9)	0 0	9 (2.8)
Recreational	2 (1.5)	2 (1.1)	0 0	4 (1.2)
Total N[a]	133	179	6	319

[a] Totals add up to more than 100 percent because of multiple response. An association may state an interest in more than one objective.

of the professed objectives, as stated in their formal bylaws, family associations expect to provide an extensive and varied range of services. Table 12-4 provides a general summary of these objectives and explores the question of whether variations are likely to occur within rural and urban communities.

The overriding concern of family associations in Lebanon is maintaining family solidarity. Fifty-eight percent of all associations mentioned this concern as one of their prime objectives. In some respects all the other collective activities of family associations—ceremonial, ritualistic, or otherwise—are in fact occasions to demonstrate and reinforce family solidarity. Apart from the conventional welfare and benevolent activities, there are countless occasions on which such kinship sentiments are expressed: weddings, funerals, feasts, extended bereavement over deceased members of the family, the show of concern and sympathy during hard times, sickness, and other crises, and the continued allegiance that some families pledge to traditional political leaders all serve to strengthen family solidarity and reinforce family values. There are also other manifestations, perhaps of a more symbolic nature, such as the preservation of family property, the restoration of old houses, the concern for ancestral homes or family home-

587

steads, the drawing up of family trees and genealogies, and the manner in which family folklore is remembered—all these are cherished symbols of family unity.

Closely associated with kinship solidarity is the concern for benevolence, which manifests itself in a wide range of activities and interests designed to assist the needy and the poor. Solidarity, after all, not only motivates members to abide by the norms and expectations of the group, as Durkheim has shown, but is equally important in dealing with individual and group problems. The concern for benevolence, or at least the way it has been formally manifested, takes one of two forms: an expression of general concern for charity and adoption of welfare projects, or more specific efforts such as the support of orphans, assisting in the costs of funerals, and extending assistance to poor brides by providing trousseaux. As shown in Table 12-4, rural associations express more concern for welfare and charitable activities, and perhaps realistically so, than urban associations.

The desire to raise the educational and cultural status of the family is also important. Forty-three percent of family associations included this as one of their objectives. The interest in education has also been expressed in two ways: a general concern ranging from "reviving the spirit of learning" and "preparation of an enlightened and responsible youth" to organizing literacy campaigns and rendering elementary education mandatory, and more specific efforts such as establishing libraries, reading rooms, cultural clubs, and scholarships for needy and gifted students.

The social and economic objectives follow the same pattern. There is first a general interest in uplifting the social and economic standards of the family through the adoption of "development projects," a concern for the well-being and comfort of the family, as manifested through campaigns for fighting unemployment. Quite often, though, this interest assumes more specific efforts such as job hunting and extending credit in times of need.

Two of the other objectives, mediation and the concern for moral and spiritual values, are areas in which the actual activities and accomplishments of the family may well exceed their professed objectives. Even without the reinforcement of kinship associations, family bickering and private problems are still resolved in large measure outside the impersonal and rational proceedings of a legal court. Family mediation not only avoids the costly and complicated court system, but also serves as an effective mechanism for resolving conflict without public embarrassment.

The concern for "piety and righteousness" and efforts to "enhance the spiritual and moral awareness of the family" and to protect "family virtue and morality" are set as precepts for moral conduct. Family honor and the care that is often taken not to blemish or taint the family's name or integrity are, after all, expressions of this value.

In Lebanon, family associations provide services and functions that are akin, if not identical, to the three major tasks of any welfare institution—income maintenance, deviance prevention, and social participation. Apart from the conventional welfare and benevolent functions, family associations assist individuals in the quest for opportunity and employment. They are also a vehicle for family solidarity and the advancement of the social, economic, and political interests of the family as a social group.

Insofar as family associations have been able to reconcile universal with particular expectations and rational principles with traditional sentiments, they are effective in achieving the blend necessary for sustaining change in a pluralistic and transitional society. Furthermore, the survival of corporate kin groups sheds some light on the nature and character of urban social groups that are likely to persist within developing societies. The city is usually viewed as a place where individuals live for the most part under conditions of anonymity and indirect social control, and where social contact is temporary, segmental, and generally impersonal. Accordingly, urbanites, it is often asserted, "hang together by the slenderest threads."[40] The Lebanese evidence suggests that such assertions cannot be accepted without important qualifications.

Although there is undoubtedly a large measure of truth in the portrayals of Wirth, Tonnies, Maine, Durkheim, and Simmel, they have nevertheless described the rural and urban worlds as extreme poles of life. This description hardly fits the outstanding features of urban development in Lebanon, where formal professional associations and political parties are still sustained by nonrational and personal considerations, and, conversely, traditional associations are not devoid of rational and impersonal elements.

The Company Union

In developing economies labor unions are often small, company-level organizations. The small-scale single-plant union is a natural form of organization in countries where feudal and paternalistic traditions still survive and where the employer and the workplace are sources of allegiance and loyalty. In India, for example, there are reportedly 4,000–5,000 such plant-wide or firm-wide unions, embracing all the employees irrespective of occupational group. Many of these small groups have maintained their independence from national centers or federations but tend, according to one source, to be subjected to rapid disintegration.[41] This fragmentation of the union movement into small, one-plant groups is also apparent in other areas of Asia and in Africa.[42] In Japan, too, the most vital level of postwar unionism has been "the individual enterprise or plant. Around this 'familial' unit have been concentrated the bulk of the workers' loyalties, the major share of basic union functions, and a large measure of autonomous power."[43]

[40] E. Gordon Ericksen, *Urban Behavior,* The Macmillan Co., New York, 1954, p. 304.
[41] Bruce H. Millen, *The Political Role of Labor in Developing Countries,* The Brookings Institution, Washington, D.C., 1963, p. 21.
[42] See E. Daya, "Freedom of Association and Industrial Relations in Asian Countries: I," *International Labour Review,* Vol. LXXI, No. 4 (April 1955), pp. 364–393.
[43] Robert A. Scalapino, "Japan," in Walter Galenson, ed., *Labor and Economic Development,* John Wiley, New York, 1959, p. 132.

The weaknesses of single-plant or single-firm unions are well known. To begin with, most such unions lack the resources to carry on an effective system of collective bargaining. Second, by virtue of their dependence on the employer for benefits and security, leaders of these house unions are more inclined to become company dominated. Third, insofar as the unions are company based, leaders may not be as enthusiastic about extending the scope of organization into a broader occupational base. Fourth, this excessive fragmentation has often led to the emergence of undifferentiated and amorphous general labor federations. Finally, such loosely organized structures lend themselves to political manipulation and may become unresponsive to some of the specific demands and interests of labor.

The Lebanese labor movement has also been characterized by house unions, but such unions do not display the weaknesses exhibited elsewhere. Compared with those organized on a craft or industrial basis, house unions in Lebanon are the largest, most stable and cohesive, and relatively the most effective bargaining agents. The proliferation of house unions, apparently a recent phenomenon, has not resulted in the dilution of craft or industrial consciousness. Nor has it led to the emergence of large "blanket" unions and national centers, which tend to organize all workers regardless of craft or occupational distinctions. Finally, and perhaps most important, the labor movement has remained relatively nonpolitical in character.

Lebanon is one of the few countries in the Middle East with a comparatively well-developed labor movement. From its inception (and there are evidences of organized labor groups in existence at the turn of the century) the movement has been predominantly businesslike and reformist in character. It has been generally oriented toward the improvement of wages and working conditions within the framework of the existing economic and political system. Contrary to the experience in other developing societies, the union movement in Lebanon has not been much of an agency for national and political change.

Numerically, trade union membership is estimated around 50,000, distributed among 125 licensed unions. This constitutes roughly 7 percent of the economically active population and 15 percent of the potential nonagricultural labor force. As shown in Table 12-5, almost 43,000 (about 85 percent) of union members are in nine federations. The Confederation of Lebanese Labor (CLL), which was established in 1962, unites four of the oldest and most established federations in the country, encompassing a total of 67 unions with a membership of nearly 28,000. All the other independent federations, with the exception of Petroleum Employees and Workers, which was licensed in 1964, have just come into existence and have not had much impact on the organizational structure of the movement as a whole.

In terms of both their historical development and their present organizational structure, Lebanese labor unions do not appear to use any consistent principle as a criterion for recruiting membership. The classic Western jurisdictional debate over the rival principles of union membership has not been a major fea-

Table 12-5

Labor Federations in Lebanon

Name	Year of Establishment	Membership	Number of Unions	International Affiliation
Confederation of Lebanese Labor (CLL)	1962	28,000	67	None
League of Trade Unions of Workers and Employees in Lebanon (JAMI'AT)	1946	6,000	21	ICFTU
United Unions of Employees and Workers (UUEW)	1952	16,200	21	ICFTU
Federation of Unions and Workers and Employees of North Lebanon (FUNL)	1954	3,700	14	ICATU
Federation of Independent Trade Unions (FITU)	1953	2,250	11	ICATU
Federation of Petroleum Employees and Workers (FPW)	1964	2,100	12	IFPW
Federation of Autonomous Office Unions (FAOU)	1967	4,900	3	None
Federation of Autonomous and Private Offices (FAPU)	1967	3,500	5	None
Federation of Labor Unions in South Lebanon (FUSL)	1967	1,200	11	ICATU
National Federation of Labor Unions (NFLU)	1967	2,800	7	WFTU/ICATU
Unaffiliated unions		7,405	20	None
Total		50,000	125	

Source: Based on the directory of labor organizations prepared by the Office of Labor Attache, American Embassy, Beirut, 1967.

Table 12-6

Trend in Craft and Industrial Unions

	1900-1910	1911-19	1920s	1930s	1940s	1950s	1960s	Total
Craft	0	0	2	6	7	21	10	46
Industry	0	1	1	2	11	18	12	45
Company union	1	0	0	1	7	10	15	34
Total	1	1	3	9	25	49	37	125

Table 12-7

Union Organization: Craft vs. Industry

	Number of Unions	Percent	Member-ship	Percent	Average Size (hundreds)
Craft	46	36.8	11,265	23.3	244
Industry	45	36.0	18,555	38.1	412
Company union	34	27.2	18,655	38.6	548
Total	125	100.0	48,475	100.0	387.8

Source: Data for both tables are based on the directory of labor organization prepared by the Office of Labor Attache, American Embassy, Beirut, 1967.

ture of Lebanon's labor history. Neither the internal structure of local unions nor the regional or national federations espouse any particular principle along craft or industrial lines.[44] As shown in Tables 12-6 and 12-7, the Lebanese movement had its origin first among specific crafts, which have continued— though lately at a declining rate—to maintain a slight edge over other forms of organization.

Perhaps as a reflection of the continuing survival of the old-style guilds, which remained active in some trades, it was among cooks, barbers, drivers, and

[44] For purposes of analysis "craft unions" have been assumed here to include not only such obvious examples as carpenters, barbers, and tailors, but also craft-oriented organizations (drivers, stablemen) and semiprofessional groups (teachers, pharmacists' assistants). "Industrial unions" include unions of employees and workers employed in more than one establishment, such as airline companies, bank and hotel employees, textile and construction workers, and all other such employees of industrial and commercial establishment unions, that is, workers and employees of a specific firm or institution.

Table 12-8
Twelve Largest Unions in Lebanon

Name of Union	Number of Members
Textile Workers' Union	3,500
Regie (Tobacco) Employees and Workers	2,600
Middle East Airlines Employees and Workers	2,500
Hotel Establishments Employees and Workers	2,440
Bank Employees	2,100
Railway Employees and Workers	1,300
Teachers Union	1,200
Office of Common Transportation Employees and Workers	1,100
American University of Beirut Employees and Workers	1,000
Lebanon Office of Electricity Employees and Workers	1,000
Port Company Employees and Workers	1,000
Shekka Cement Employees and Workers	1,000

carpenters that the urge for organization began. This slant in the direction of craft organizations persisted until the outbreak of World War II. To be more specific, eight of the fourteen unions in existence before the war were craft oriented. With the appearance of white-collar unionism during and after the war, enterprise and industrial organizations emerged as alternative structures, as indicated by the growth of unions among bank employees, clerks, teachers, technicians, and airline and oil company employees. Though unions are almost equally divided between craft and industry, industrial organizations attract significantly more members. Roughly 38 percent of organized workers are affiliated with industrial unions, compared with 23 percent in craft-oriented unions.

Apart from the persistence of craft unionism, another distinctive structural feature of the labor movement in Lebanon is the recent prominence of the house or single-plant union as an organization form. Though house unions constitute no more than 27 percent of the country's unions, they comprise more than 38 percent of its workers. As might be expected, they are also the largest unions. As shown in Table 12-8, of the twelve largest unions in Lebanon, eight are single-plant unions such as Tobacco, Middle East Airlines, Railway, Office of Common Transportation, Shekka Cement Companies, American University, Office of

Electricity, and Port Company, most of which are either public or of special governmental concern.

This preponderance of small craft-oriented unions on the one hand and single-plant unions on the other should not be too surprising. It is not, as often assumed, a mere reflection of the relative infancy of the trade union movement in Lebanon. Nor is it simply an expression of the petty rivalries and personal feuds of labor leaders squabbling to build their own tight little empires. As has been suggested earlier, this tendency reflects some of the traditional loyalties and sentiments rooted in the culture. There is an inevitable association between the persistence of such loyalties and the structure of union organization. Although for nearly 60 years now Lebanese workers have had some experience with collective action and rational organizations, their ties and sentiments have not been completely dissociated from those of kinship, fealty, and other communal attachments. Furthermore, since the more impersonal and rationalized system of management has not as yet taken any effective root in the industrial system, the paternalistic and very often benevolent employer remains a potent and meaningful object of loyalty to the workers.

The tendency of unions to splinter into small fragments organized mostly at the company level may also be a reflection of the nature and scope of collective bargaining. Since there is very little industry-wide collective bargaining, and since most issues and grievances are resolved at the company or enterprise level, it is not unusual for a worker to manifest a closer identity with his employer or place of employment than with his industry or profession. Besides, the internal organization of the labor movement is such that it lends little support to generalized occupational loyalties beyond the employer or the workplace. To begin with, the internal structure of union organization does not reach the local level. In fact, the local as a level of organization is almost absent in Lebanon. Only 8 of a sample of 83 unions indicated that they had any type of organization below the national level.[45] Of the 63 unions that represent workers in more than one workplace, only 44 reported that they have a union representative of the nature of a steward in each of these workplaces.

Relationships between member unions and their federations follow a similar fragmented pattern. No national federation speaks for more than a small fraction of the industrial labor force or, indeed, for more than a small portion of union members. As shown earlier, the nearly 50,000 union members—estimated to be no more than 20 percent of the entire industrial labor force—are distributed among 9 federations, averaging around 4,800 members in each. The organizational structure of these federations does not subscribe to any structural principle of either craft or industrial organization. Furthermore, 20 unions, encompassing 7,500 members, remain unaffiliated with any national or regional center. It is exceedingly difficult under such conditions to establish strong, well-financed, well-supported national federations.

[45] See Samir Khalaf, "Lebanese Labor Unions: Some Comparative Structural Features," *Middle East Economic Papers* (1968), pp. 111–138.

In this respect, too, the structure of Lebanese unions appears to diverge from the pattern often observed in some emerging countries. The scattered "house unions" and the excessively small craft-oriented unions have not been compelled legally or politically to amalgamate into general structures. Nor has there been any trend, as is perhaps the case in some African states, toward highly centralized federations to which the affiliates are responsible. Member unions, whether affiliated or not, enjoy a great deal of autonomy. All of the unions surveyed, with the exception of three or four, considered the union to be the center of policy planning and execution with regard to wages, strikes, working conditions, and grievances. As one union president stated it, "the decisions of the union may or may not be approved by the federation." The advice of the federation is nevertheless sought on such matters as assistance in dealing with the government, transmitting the point of view of labor to the public, mediation with other unions, and rendering legal aid. Only eleven unions mentioned the help of the federation in setting union jurisdiction or in organizing new members. Still fewer reported that the federation provides educational and financial help and on occasion office space and meeting rooms to those who need them.

Beyond these subsidiary services, labor federations have not succeeded so far in creating a class or craft consciousness among the labor force or in strengthening the sense of commitment to the norms and practices inherent in the industrial system. Neither have they diluted the traditional and nonindustrial ties of the workers. The industrial worker and the white-collar employee have not developed the occupational class consciousness necessary for the emergence of general industry-wide labor organizations. So long as loyalties to place of work and employer supersede those to class and craft, workers and employees will continue to prefer the single-plant unit to the distant and more impersonal entity of the national or general labor federation. Company unions are perhaps the most natural and realistic form of labor organization at this stage of industrialization in Lebanon. They continue to enjoy an appreciable measure of independence and autonomy, and have so far been relatively more successful than other types in integrating workers and employees and in reducing the incidence of industrial unrest.

More than any other form of labor organization, company unions have been responsible for allaying some of the side effects of class consciousness and status differentiation between manual and nonmanual workers which threaten the solidarity of labor. Mixed and company unions are logical and convenient devices for recruiting sizable membership and, consequently, enhancing the solidarity and bargaining strength of labor. But more important, by bringing workers and employees together and providing them with the opportunities and incentives to participate equally within the same organization, they may ultimately soften the impact of status differentiation and class antagonism. Some 43 percent of union members in Lebanon belong to mixed unions of workers and employees.[46] This reflects the predominance of the enterprise or house union.

[46] *Ibid.*

With a few exceptions, all the house unions are in fact joint unions of workers and employees. Expectedly, they are also the largest unions. The average size of mixed unions is more than twice that of either workers' or employees' unions. In fact, of the 12 largest unions, those with a membership of 1,000 or more, 9 are mixed, and 8 of these are company unions (see Table 12-8).

The survival of autonomous single-plant unions has, in some respects, averted the development of politically oriented and amorphous general unions, a feature that has plagued unionism in many developing areas. Leadership, and the movement as a whole, have been more of the "bread and butter" variety and less of an instrument for national and political change. Unlike unions in other developing societies, the labor movement in Lebanon did not participate in the national struggle for independence. It has not attracted politically oriented leaders from outside the ranks of labor. Neither have there been any alliances between parties and unions. In the event of civil and political crises, union leaders have opted for a neutral and restrained role.

To say that the Lebanese labor movement is nonpolitical in character is not to say that union actions do not have any political ramifications. In this sense, it is doubtful whether there can ever be a nonpolitical labor movement. Certainly there have been instances in the history of the Lebanese labor movement when union behavior was motivated more by political than by economic or welfare aims. The wave of strikes that swept the country during the summer of 1966 was one instance in which industrial unrest was in part encouraged by a few political leaders to embarrass the government in office and thereby hasten its downfall. But in general the labor movement in Lebanon has been basically oriented toward better wages and improved working conditions.

The Lebanese labor movement, in general, is neither an agency of protest nor an instrument of transformation in the true meaning of the term. It is more akin to a mutual aid society or a social welfare organization, and it could not have had much success in any other role. Industrialization has not as yet diluted kinship and other traditional loyalties. So long as these ties persist (and they are not likely to disappear overnight), the Lebanese industrial worker will not develop any strong commitments to general unions as a rational association. Craft unions are becoming gradually obsolete, and the general "blanket" unions are too broad to be of any real value to workers. Company unions have therefore emerged as effective agencies for helping workers to cope with their problems. They make it possible to provide some measure of industry-wide bargaining without destroying workers' loyalties associated with craft, occupation, or place of employment.

III. Concluding Observations

This study has challenged the popular view that traditional values are impediments to modernization. It also questions the widespread assumption that the emergence of rational instruments of modernization presupposes the prior existence of modern values. Instead, historical and empirical evidence suggests that the so-called traditional agencies have been functional in generating change and absorbing imbalances within society. Similarly, the study has argued that an appreciable measure of gradual and adaptive modernization has taken place in Lebanon without eroding traditional values, particularly those that have been effective so far in maintaining psychic reinforcement and group identity.

In short, the synthesis between modernity and tradition is basic to the process of modernization in Lebanon. In this sense the study departs from the conception that often depicts modernization as the "breakdown of tradition"[47] or as a process of "disengagement from traditionalism."[48] It is doubtful whether traditional values will disappear in Lebanon under the impact of increased mobility, urbanization, and literacy. Notwithstanding the intensive and transforming character of modernization, modern values are not likely to supplant traditional sentiments, particularly where loyalties are rooted in early childhood socialization and shaped by the same force. It is doubtful, for example, whether political modernization in Lebanon has involved a dramatic shift in the locus of political authority. Kinship, communal, and religious authorities have not been supplanted by secular and rational authority.

It is true that the persistence of such traditional ties may actually temper, perhaps even delay, the development of political modernization in the true meaning of the term. Some would view such a possibility with alarm. It is still considerably less alarming, however, than the consequences of imposing some of the civic instruments of a nation-state on an unreceptive society, one that is still sustained by ties of fealty, kinship, and parochial loyalties. The premature introduction of rational and secular ideas may be as much of an impediment to modernization as the excessively long retention of traditional practices and beliefs.

In no sense should this argument be taken as a defense in favor of the preservation of the status quo. Neither is it being implied that the various instruments of a nation-state—political parties, civil bureaucracy, the military, a national school system, the mass media, and other such modernizing agencies—are of doubtful importance as integrative mechanisms or in generating a sense of national identity. What is being questioned is the exclusive reliance on such agencies at the expense of eroding traditional loyalties, particularly when the whole fabric of society is still sustained by these attachments.

Apart from the pluralistic character of Lebanese society, the average Lebanese still seeks and finds his self-image in his close identification with family, sect, and community. To erode or undermine these is to erode his main source of identity, and to undermine his will and creative resources. It is because of the persistence of such ties and their critical importance as a source of personal identity and social cohesion that care must be taken lest they be destroyed in the

[47] Joseph La Palombara, "Distribution and Development," in Myron Weiner, ed., *Modernization: The Dynamics of Growth*, p. 237.
[48] Samuel Huntington, "Political Modernization: America vs. Europe," *World Politics*, Vol. XVIII, No. 3 (April 1966), p. 378.

effort to create a larger sense of national entity. So far, at least, they have been preserved in Lebanon.

The inference that might be drawn from all this, at the risk of some generalization, is that there is more than just one brand of modernity. The Western notion of development, with the high premium it places on rational, secular, and universal criteria, is likely to remain ineffective unless these criteria are mediated through a meaningful cultural context. In whatever manner modernization is defined, it ultimately involves moving people to acquire new roles. They are more likely to be moved if the new patterns of behavior and their supportive values are expressed in some meaningful and pertinent cultural context. The instruments of adaptive modernization surveyed here appear to be particularly effective in bringing about such reconciliation of the new and the old.

Author Index

Page numbers set in *italics* designate those pages on which the complete literature citation is given.

Numbers in parentheses designate the footnote numbers where information is given.

599

600

601

Subject Index

Entries followed by *n* indicate that information is given in a footnote.

603

607

608

612

615

618

619

620